The Archaeology of Measurement: Comprehending Heaven, Earth and Time in Ancient Societies

The construction of formal measurement systems underlies the development of science and technology, economy and new ways of understanding and explaining the world. Human societies have developed such systems in different ways in different places and at different times, and recent archaeological investigations highlight the importance of these activities for fundamental aspects of human life. The construction of measurement systems constituted new means of recognising and engaging with the material world, and their implications, and the motivations behind them, also extend beyond the material world. Measurement systems have provided the structure for addressing key concerns of cosmological belief systems, as well as the means for articulating relationships between the human form, human action and the world – and new understanding of relationships between events in the terrestrial world and beyond.

The Archaeology of Measurement explores the archaeological evidence for the development of measuring activities in numerous ancient societies, as well as the implications of these discoveries for an understanding of their worlds and beliefs. Featuring contributions from a cast of internationally renowned scholars, it analyzes the relationships between measurement, economy, architecture, symbolism, time, cosmology, ritual and religion among prehistoric and early historic societies throughout the world.

Iain Morley is a Fellow and Tutor in Archaeology and Anthropology at Keble College, Oxford, and until 2009 was a Fellow of the McDonald Institute for Archaeological Research and Research Fellow of Darwin College, Cambridge. A scholar of Palaeolithic archaeology and the evolution of human cognition, he is also coeditor, with Colin Renfrew, of *Becoming Human: Innovation in Prehistoric Material and Spiritual Culture* and *Image and Imagination: A Global Prehistory of Figurative Representation*.

Colin Renfrew (Lord Renfrew of Kaimsthorn) is Emeritus Disney Professor of Archaeology at Cambridge University, where he is a Senior Fellow of the McDonald Institute for Archaeological Research. He is author of many influential books on archaeology and prehistory, including, with Paul Bahn, *Archaeology: Theories, Methods and Practice*, which is one of the standard textbooks on the subject.

The Archaeology of Measurement

Comprehending Heaven, Earth and Time in Ancient Societies

Edited by

Iain Morley
Keble College, Oxford

Colin Renfrew
The McDonald Institute for Archaeological Research

CAMBRIDGE UNIVERSITY PRESS
Cambridge, New York, Melbourne, Madrid, Cape Town, Singapore,
São Paulo, Delhi, Dubai, Tokyo

Cambridge University Press
32 Avenue of the Americas, New York, NY 10013-2473, USA

www.cambridge.org
Information on this title: www.cambridge.org/9780521135887

First published 2010

Printed in the United States of America

A catalog record for this publication is available from the British Library.

Library of Congress Cataloging in Publication data

ISBN 978-0-521-11990-0 Hardback
ISBN 978-0-521-13588-7 Paperback

Contents

List of figures and tables   *page* vii

List of contributors   xiii

Acknowledgements   xv

    Introduction: Measure: Towards the construction
of our world 1
Colin Renfrew and Iain Morley

**SECTION I. NUMBER: COUNTING, MATHEMATICS
AND MEASURE**   5

  1 Conceptualising quantification before settlement: Activities
and issues underlying the conception and use of measurement 7
Iain Morley

  2 Measurement in navigation: Conceiving distance and
time in the Neolithic 19
Helen Farr

  3 The token system of the ancient Near East: Its role
in counting, writing, the economy and cognition 27
Denise Schmandt-Besserat

  4 Grasping the concept of number: How did the sapient
mind move beyond approximation? 35
Lambros Malafouris

  5 Numerical cognition and the development of 'zero'
in Mesoamerica 43
John Justeson

  6 Recording measure(ment)s in the Inka khipu 54
Gary Urton

SECTION II. MATERIALISING THE ECONOMY   69

  7 Measuring by weight in the Late Bronze Age Aegean:
The people behind the measuring tools 71
Anna Michailidou

8 The concept of weighing during the Bronze Age
   in the Aegean, the Near East and Europe 88
   Lorenz Rahmstorf

9 Measuring the Harappan world: Insights into the
   Indus order and cosmology 106
   J. Mark Kenoyer

SECTION III. DIMENSIONS AND BELIEF   123

10 Architectural measurements in the Indus cities:
    The case study of Mohenjo-Daro. 125
    Michael Jansen

11 Teotihuacan city layout as a cosmogram: Preliminary
    results of the 2007 Measurement Unit Study. 130
    Saburo Sugiyama

12 Aztec dimensions of holiness. 150
    John E. Clark

13 Establishing direction in early Egyptian burials and
    monumental architecture: Measurement and the spatial
    link with the 'other'. 170
    Kate Spence

SECTION IV. CALENDAR AND COSMOLOGY   181

14 The measurement of time and distance in the heavens
    above Mesopotamia, with brief reference made to other
    ancient astral sciences 183
    David Brown

15 Evolution of the calendar in Shang China 195
    Mark Edward Lewis

16 The measure of time in Mesoamerica: From Teotihuacan
    to the Maya. 203
    Anthony F. Aveni

17 Measuring time, sacred space, and social place
    in the Inca Empire. 216
    Charles Stanish

18 Measuring time in the European Neolithic? The function
    and meaning of Central European circular enclosures 229
    Peter F. Biehl

SECTION V. THE SPIRITUALITY OF MEASURE   245

19 The roots of spirituality and the limits of human mensuration. . . 247
    F. LeRon Shults

20 Worldview, measurement and 'the roots of spirituality'. 250
    Jeremy S. Begbie

Index   257

List of figures and tables

FIGURES

1.1	Types of measurement	*page* 7
1.2	Concepts of measurement related to the group	8
1.3	Concepts of measurement associated with resources and commodities	9
1.4	Properties of features of the world that may be variously subject to measurement concepts	10
1.5	Concepts of measurement that may be associated with navigation	12
1.6	Concepts of measurement that give rise to, and arise from, awareness of time and cycles	14
2.1	Adriatic islands	21
2.2	Likely routes taking into account prevailing winds, currents and location of islands	22
2.3	Accounting for lateral drift	23
3.1	Pictographic tablet from Godin Tepe, Iran, ca. 3100 BC	27
3.2	Correspondence between cuneiform signs, pictographs and tokens	28
3.3	Plain tokens from Tepe Gawra, Iraq, ca. 5000 BC	29
3.4	Complex tokens from Uruk, Iraq, ca. 3300 BC	29
3.5	Ovoid tokens standing for jars of oil, from Girsu, Iraq, ca. 3300 BC	29
3.6	Envelope from Habuba Kabira, ca. 3300 BC, with ovoid impressed markings	30
3.7	Impressed tablet showing three wedges = three small measures of grain and two circular signs = two larger measures of grain, from Godin Tepe, Iran, ca. 3100 BC	30
3.8	Mesopotamian grain measure	30
4.1	Line bisection effect	36
4.2	How did the sapient mind move beyond approximation?	38
4.3	Three stages in the developmental trajectory of the Near Eastern concept of number	39
6.1	Khipu structures	55
6.2	Inka decimal administration	58
6.3	Khipu with colour banding	60
6.4	Khipu with colour seriation	61
6.5	Khipu with untied knots	61
6.6	A pair of matching khipus	62

6.7   The Puruchuco accounting hierarchy   65
7.1   Ox-hide ingot of copper carried by Cretan messenger depicted
      in an Egyptian tomb painting of the Eighteenth Dynasty   71
7.2   The melon-shaped stone weight from Aghia Photia, Crete,
      with incised Linear A inscription   72
7.3   Lead discoid-shaped balance weights from the settlement
      of Akrotiri on the island of Thera   72
7.4   Linear B tablet KN Oa 730 and the sign for the balance
      in Linear A script   73
7.5   A stone balance weight from Akrotiri on Thera   74
7.6   Linear B tablet KN Sc 245+5064 displaying the ideogram
      for chariot, followed by one digit   74
7.7   Linear B tablet KN F(2) 852+8071 featuring the numeral sign
      for 10,000 immediately preceded by the ideogram for grain   74
7.8   Linear B tablet KN Og 7504+7844 recording one
      talent of ivory   75
7.9   Linear B tablets KN Np (2) 860 and Np (2) 861 displaying
      the ideogram for saffron, followed by metrograms for weight
      and numerals   75
7.10 Linear B tablet KN F(2) 853+5947+6035 recording
      quantities of grain and olives measured in units of capacity
      for dry commodities   76
7.11 Linear B tablet KN K 700 displaying the account for
      1,800 stirrup-jars in two entries of 900 each   76
7.12 Linear B tablet KN Lc (1) 527+7143+7331 with entries for
      textiles, followed by the unit of wool in quantities required
      for these qualities of cloth   78
7.13 The four houses of Complex Delta at Akrotiri, upper floor level   78
7.14 Lead weight from Mochlos with incised Linear A inscription   80
8.1   Spool-shaped balance weights from Tiryns with markings   89
8.2   Spool-shaped balance weights and a 'macehead' from
      EBA II Tarsus   92
8.3   Haematite balance weights from EBA I (?) and EB III Tarsus   93
8.4   Applying the Kendall formula on spool-shaped balance
      weights from the EBA Aegean   94
8.5   Distribution of balance weights of the Aegean (spool-shaped),
      the Near Eastern (sphendonoid haematite and other types
      of weights) and the Harappan types (cubic and other shapes) in
      the third millennium BC   96
8.6   Distribution of quadruple spirals, etched cornelian
      beads, lapis lazuli and flat beads in the third millennium BC   97
8.7   Balance weights from Steinfurth, Hesse, in Germany (Bz D)
      with application of the Kendall formula   99
9.1   Major traditions of prehistoric South Asia   106
9.2   Early Food Producing and Regionalization Era sites   108
9.3   Integration Era, Harappa Phase sites   109
9.4   Ravi Phase pottery   110
9.5   Ravi and Kot Diji Phase spindle whorls   111
9.6   Ravi and Kot Diji Phase steatite beads   112
9.7   Steatite microbeads: Ravi and Harappan Phase   113
9.8   Ravi Phase mud bricks   113
9.9   Cubical stone weight and seal impression: Kot Diji Period   114
9.10 Cubical stone weights: Harappan Period   115
9.11 Harappan bricks   117
9.12 Harappan well bricks   118

9.13 Harappa: Reconstruction of city walls and gateway,
       Mound E and ET   119
10.1 Map of Mohenjo-Daro with different tourist paths and
       the excavated areas   125
11.1 Aerial view of the Teotihuacan central zone, viewed from
       the south   131
11.2 The main façade of the Feathered Serpent Pyramid   135
11.3 General plan of the city's central zone with possible
       measured distances in TMU   136
11.4 3D map of the Sun Pyramid   137
11.5 Plan of the Sun Pyramid complex with the Avenue of
       the Dead   139
11.6 Plan of the Moon Pyramid with the locations of seven
       overlapping construction stages and measurements in TMU   140
11.7 Plan of the Moon Plaza complex with measurements in TMU   142
11.8 Plan of the Citadel complex with measurements in TMU   143
11.9 General plan of the Teotihuacan city layout in AD 200–250   144
11.10 Reconstruction plan of the Teotihuacan city layout around
       AD 350   145
12.1 Aztec units of measure and their body referents   150
12.2 Symbols of Aztec units of measure   151
12.3 The Oztoticpac palace and its dimensions   152
12.4 The Oztoticpac palace adjusted to scale   153
12.5 The general proportions of the Oztoticpac palace   154
12.6 The Oztoticpac palace in *yollotli* units   155
12.7 Tropical year counts (366) of the Oztoticpac palace
       in *yollotli* units   156
12.8 Jupiter counts (399) of the Oztoticpac palace in
       yollotli units   157
12.9 Possible astronomical divisions of the Oztoticpac palace   158
12.10 Drawing of the Sacred Precinct at Tenochtitlan showing
       the central position of the main pyramid and its twin
       temples to Tlaloc and Huitzilopochtli   159
12.11 The Sacred Precinct of Tenochtitlan and various of its
       dimensions in Aztec units of linear measure   161
12.12 The Sacred Precinct of Tenochtitlan as organized by
       Venus counts (584)   162
12.13 The Sacred Precinct of Tenochtitlan showing solar
       counts (365) centered on the Templo Mayor   163
12.14 Distances based on the 260 ritual count at the Templo Mayor   164
12.15 Spacing of buildings at the Templo Mayor based on 360 counts   165
16.1 Footprints in a cosmogram from the Madrid Codex showing
       time's 260-day journey via feet about the periphery of the
       sacred space of the gods   203
16.2 Copan (Honduras), Stela D, dating from the Classic Maya
       Period (eighth century AD), depicting the gods of number
       carrying their own bundles of time   204
16.3 A part of the user's preface to the Eclipse Table in the
       Dresden Codex showing a column of 13 13s hastily squeezed in   206
16.4 Maya almanac concerning the burdens of particular
       periods of time, shown being carried by a goddess
       who personified the earth   207
16.5 An almanac in the Dresden Codex in which time's pathway
       zigzags its way down the page   207
16.6 An almanac in the Madrid Codex related to deer hunting   208

16.7 Scene from a Mixtec codex showing a figure situated in a temple doorway looking toward the horizon over one of a number of putative crossed-stick sighting devices 208

16.8 Uxmal, the Governor's House, an oddly oriented Maya temple likely arranged to summon the resurrected ancestor lord Venus/Kukulcan 209

16.9 Pecked cross carved in the floor of Str. A-V, Uaxactun 210

16.10 Histograms showing distribution of a) tallies on segments of pecked cross petroglyphs and b) total tallies for all pecked cross petroglyphs in Mesoamerica 211

17.1 South America 216

17.2 Western South America 216

17.3 The Lake Titicaca Basin 219

17.4 Aerial view of the Island of the Sun 220

17.5 The Island of the Sun 220

17.6 The upper Inca road on the Island of the Sun 221

17.7 View of the sacred area on the Island of the Sun, distance view from the southeast 221

17.8 View of the sacred area on the Island of the Sun, closeup view from the southeast 222

17.9 The sacred area from the Tikani ridge 222

17.10 The Titikala or Sacred Rock, northeast side 223

17.11 The Titikala or Sacred Rock, southeast side 223

17.12 La Raya de los Incas, the wall separating the sacred area from the rest of the island 224

17.13 Sight line in the structure known as the Mama Ojila 224

17.14 The sight line of the winter (June) solstice from the Titikala to the Tikani towers 225

17.15 A view from the Mama Ojila to the road that descends from the La Raya de los Incas and site 019 225

17.16 Schematic view of the sight line and other features in the sanctuary area 226

18.1 Distribution of Neolithic enclosed sites 229

18.2 Distribution of the Middle Neolithic stroke-ornamented pottery culture (*Stichbandkeramik*) in Central Europe 230

18.3 Distribution of Middle Neolithic enclosed sites in Central Europe 231

18.4 Aerial photograph of the Goseck enclosure after removing the topsoil 232

18.5 Reconstructed enclosure in Goseck at its original location 232

18.6 Goseck excavation plan 233

18.7 Goseck excavation plan with disposition patterns 233

18.8 Diagram of the multi-scalar approach to cult places 234

18.9 The Middle Neolithic enclosure in Meisternthal, Bavaria, Germany: a) geophysics, b) map with other enclosures, c) winter solstice, d) summer solstice, e) midsummer sunrise 236

18.10 The construction of the Goseck circular enclosure using perfect circles for comparison 237

18.11 Diagram of the Goseck enclosure indicating astronomical features 237

18.12 Bearing at the southeast entrance gate during the sunrise on the winter solstice (ca. 4900 BC) 237

18.13 Bearing at the southeast entrance with azimuth angles, showing entries in the palisades directly connected with the entrances in the circular enclosure 238

18.14 Sunrise and sunset during the summer solstice (ca. 4900 BC) 238

18.15 Timeline of the winter solstice (40–20 days before)
in relation to the profile of the horizon in Goseck 239
18.16 Closeup of the southeast entrance of the reconstructed enclosure
in Goseck at its original location (from outside and inside) 239

TABLES

5.1 Container terms as numeral bases in Mesoamerican languages 46
5.2 Epi-Olmec phrase represented by the sequence 7 16 3 2 13 48
5.3 Transcription of long count dates on Takalik Abaj Stela 5 49
5.4 Expressions for multiples of 100,000 in the Tecpatán Soke
Vocabulario of 1733 51
6.1 Khipu record of summation, subdivision, and proportional values 57
6.2 Khipu with all decimal values 59
6.3 Khipu with two divisions of 100 59
6.4 Close match of khipus from Puruchuco 63
8.1 The conversion of units (talent, mina and basic units) in
LBA Syria according to N. Parise (1984) 90
8.2 The 21 marked or inscribed balance weights of the third
millennium from seven sites in the Aegean, Syria and
Mesopotamia published to date 91
8.3 Multiples and common denominators of basic units 95
8.4 The convergence of the basic units used between the eastern
Mediterranean and the Indus valley 101
8.5 Some multiples and common denominators of basic
units: 7.83 (= 10), 9.4 (= 12), 11.75 (= 15) and 13.71 (= 17.5) 102
9.1 Indus tradition chronology: Harappa and early Mehrgarh 107
9.2 Early Harappan spindle whorls 111
9.3 Indus cubical weights from Harappa and Mohenjo-daro 115
11.1 Comparative data on the size of paired platforms
in the Moon Plaza 137
11.2 Deviation from two north-south axes of the Avenue
of the Dead to the midpoint of central structures or
to the midpoint of paired platforms at the Moon Plaza 138
12.1 Aztec linear measures and their metric values 151
12.2 Dimensions of Nezahualcoyotl's Palace in different
Aztec measures 152
12.3 Dimensions of the different stages of the Templo
Mayor in meters 159
12.4 Dimensions of the Templo Mayor in *yollotli* (0.8359 m) 160
16.1 Seasonal intervals at Teotihuacan and Uaxactun 212

List of contributors

ANTHONY F. AVENI is the Russell Colgate Distinguished Professor of Astronomy, Anthropology and Native American Studies at Colgate University. Two of his most recent books are *Empires of Time* and *Stairways to the Stars: Skywatching in Three Great Ancient Cultures*.

JEREMY S. BEGBIE is Associate Principal of Ridley Hall, Cambridge, and Honorary Professor of Theology at the University of Saint Andrews. A lecturer in a variety of departments at Ridley Hall and the University of Cambridge, he is the author of *Theology, Music and Time*.

PETER F. BIEHL is Assistant Professor in the Department of Anthropology and Associate Director of the Institute for European and Mediterranean Archaeology at the State University of New York at Buffalo. He has published widely on the meanings and functions of Neolithic circular enclosures, including (with F. Bertemes and H. Meller) *Neolithic Circular Enclosures in Europe*.

DAVID BROWN is a German Research Foundation Fellow in the Department of Idology at the Free University of Berlin. He has previously been a British Academy Research Fellow in Oxford and Alexander von Humboldt Fellow in Berlin. He is the author of *Mesopotamian Planetary Astronomy-Astrology*.

JOHN E. CLARK is Professor of Anthropology at Brigham Young University and Director of the New World Archaeological Foundation of Brigham Young University based in Chiapas, Mexico. He has published numerous articles on Mesoamerica including "The Birth of Mesoamerican Metaphysics: Sedentism, Engagement, and Moral Superiority" in *Rethinking Materiality: The Engagement of Mind with the Material World*.

HELEN FARR is a Fellow of the McDonald Institute for Archaeological Research. She has contributed articles to a number of books including (with John Robb) "Substances in Motion: Neolithic Mediterranean 'Trade'" in *The Archaeology of Mediterranean Prehistory*.

MICHAEL JANSEN is Professor at RWTH Aachen University of Technology and a senior member of the UNESCO International Technical Committee for Mohenjo-Daro.

JOHN JUSTESON is Professor in Anthropology at the State University of New York at Albany. Most recently, with Terrence Kaufman, he has produced a decipherment of a major portion of the Late Preclassic epi-Olmec hieroglyphs.

J. MARK KENOYER is Professor of Anthropology at the University of Wisconsin, Madison. His publications focus on South Asia and include *The Ancient South Asian World*.

MARK EDWARD LEWIS is Kwoh-Ting Li Professor of Chinese Culture at Stanford University. He is the author of *The Construction of Space in Early China*.

LAMBROS MALAFOURIS is the Balzan Fellow in Cognitive Archaeology at the McDonald Institute for Archaeological Research at Cambridge University. His recent publications include *Philosophical Transactions of the Royal Society B 363*, which he coedited.

ANNA MICHAILIDOU is the Research Director for the Center for Greek and Roman Antiquity of the National Hellenic Research Foundation. She is the author of numerous articles and the editor of *Manufacture and Measurement: Counting, Measuring and Recording Craft Items in Early Aegean Societies*.

IAIN MORLEY is a Fellow and Tutor in Archaeology and Anthropology at Keble College, Oxford, and until 2009 was a Fellow of the McDonald Institute for Archaeological Research at Cambridge University. He has written articles for numerous journals and books, including (with Colin Renfrew) *Image and Imagination: A Global Prehistory of Figurative Representation*.

LORENZ RAHMSTORF is Assistant Professor and Research Assistant in the Department of Pre- and Protohistory at the University of Mainz.

COLIN RENFREW is a Senior Fellow of the McDonald Institute for Archaeological Research and Emeritus Professor of Archaeology at Cambridge University. He has authored and edited numerous archaeological publications and books, including (with Iain Morley) *Becoming Human: Innovation in Prehistoric Material and Spiritual Culture*.

DENISE SCHMANDT-BESSERAT is Emeritus Professor of Art and Middle Eastern Studies at the University of Texas at Austin. Her work on the origin of writing and mathematics was published in *How Writing Came About*, which was listed in *American Scientist* as one of the 100 books that shaped science in the 20th century.

F. LERON SHULTS is Professor of Theology and Philosophy at the University of Agder in Kristiansand, Norway. He has published a number of books, including most recently *The Evolution of Rationality* and *Christology and Science*, as well as numerous articles and book chapters on a variety of interdisciplinary themes.

KATE SPENCE is Lecturer in the Archaeology of Ancient Egypt at the University of Cambridge. She was a British Academy Post-Doctoral Fellow and a McDonald Institute Research Fellow in Cognitive Archaeology. She has published numerous articles and book chapters on aspects of Egyptian architecture.

CHARLES STANISH is Director of the Cotsen Institute of Archaeology and Professor of Anthropology at the University of California, Los Angeles. A Fellow of the American Academy, he has published several books including *Ancient Titicaca: The Evolution of Southern Peru and Northern Bolivia*.

SABURO SUGIYAMA is Professor at the Graduate School of International Cultural Studies, Aichi Prefectural University. His involvement with excavations at Teotihuacan in Mexico led him to publish *Human Sacrifice, Militarism, and Rulership: Materialization of State Ideology at the Feathered Serpent Pyramid, Teotihuacan*.

GARY URTON is Dumbarton Oaks Professor of Pre-Columbian Studies in the Department of Anthropology at Harvard University. He is the author of numerous articles and books on Inka civilization and Andean and Quechua cultures and societies, including *Signs of the Inka Khipu*.

Acknowledgements

The editors would like to thank the following people and organisations for their valuable contributions to making this volume possible:

The John Templeton Foundation, which funded the 'Roots of Spirituality' project, of which this volume is a product, and the 'Measuring the World and Beyond' symposium, which was the initial forum for these papers. Dr. Paul Wason at the JTF has consistently provided valuable advice and support throughout the project.

The Director, Fellows and staff of the McDonald Institute for Archaeological Research, Cambridge, which hosted the project and the symposium; the conference's smooth running was greatly facilitated by the voluntary assistance of Pamela de Condappa and Sarah Ralph.

The late Dr. D. M. McDonald, whose interest in early metrology partly motivated his generous foundation of the Institute, and whose own writings on the subject formed the first of the monographs that it produced.

The Syndics of Cambridge University Press and our editor, Beatrice Rehl, for publishing this book; our production editor, Janis Bolster, and copy editor, Susan Thornton, for their excellent work; Dora Kemp, for preparing the index; and the two anonymous readers employed by Cambridge, who gave valuable feedback on the original manuscript.

Although regrettably unable to contribute themselves, Eleanor Robson, Sir Geoffrey Lloyd, Joyce Marcus, Michael Smith, Lothar Von Falkenhausen and Barry Kemp all made valuable suggestions of potential contributors to the symposium and volume, as did many of the contributors themselves.

The Archaeology of Measurement: Comprehending Heaven,
Earth and Time in Ancient Societies

INTRODUCTION

Measure: Towards the construction of our world

Colin Renfrew and Iain Morley

It was a profoundly significant step when, in the remote past, a human being, in undertaking an act of measurement, formulated the notion of measure. For to measure – whether in the dimensionality of weight, or of distance or of time – is to develop a new kind of material engagement with the world that is at once practical and conceptual. It is an act of cognition – a cognitive act. Such an act has philosophical implications, for measurement allows us to transcend the limitations of the here and the now. It involves observation, and it facilitates construction. It encapsulates the seeds of mathematics and of science. It makes possible architecture and design. It is the basis for systematic observation and prediction. It leads on towards astronomy and cosmology. It is the basis for any complex economic system. It is one of the foundations of all urban civilisations.

This volume, arising from the Roots of Spirituality project conducted at the McDonald Institute for Archaeological Research, sets out to explore the new and creative relationships with the world implied by the first deliberate development of measurement and of systems of measure in the early days of the human story.

The theme was chosen as a means of investigating, at a global level, some fundamental issues in the origins of human cognition in the early days of the different trajectories of cultural development. These issues bear upon the very process of becoming fully human in an increasingly complex world.

The dawn of human cognition

How does one define what it is to be human? What special qualities distinguish the human species from other animals? And how does one set about tracing the origins of those special qualities back through time to the origins of humankind? Or, reversing the process of inquiry, how can one detect the first emergence of those special qualities in the material record that has come down to us from prehistoric and from historic times?

These are questions that must occur to anyone who contemplates the human story in a wide perspective. At once it is clear that these are not easy questions to answer. For among the first responses must be the observation that communication by means of a fully developed language is a feature of all human societies and of none other – even though students of animal behaviour can show that members of other species do communicate in an impressive variety of ways. If we could trace the origins of language from the earliest times, we would certainly be outlining the development of one important element of what constitutes the human condition.

Yet, in reality, language was not directly recorded until the inception of writing, just over 5,000 years ago. That is a relatively recent period. It does not take us far enough back in the human story, which extends back over at least 150,000 years. So we have to look for evidence that will take us further. That inescapably leads us to the field of prehistoric archaeology. For prehistory deals with the human past before written records are available, and archaeology deals with the investigation and reconstruction of the past on the basis of its material remains.

The archaeologist can ask the big questions – when did language develop, when did self-consciousness emerge, what were the first coherent belief systems, when were religion and ritual first practised, when did the first artists create painting and sculpture, when did the first musicians play? But to answer them with more than mere speculation requires evidence of some kind. And there one must turn primarily to prehistoric archaeology. For it is there that some evidence for and some understanding of the early development of human cognition must originate.

Prehistoric archaeology has its limitations. It is dependent primarily upon the archaeological record – upon the material remains of past cultures and civilisations, where the archaeologist can hope to excavate, and so to find evidence of human activity from the period that is of interest. There may be other sources of relevant information; molecular genetics is certainly one. But in general the procedure must be to dig: to excavate in order to recover those material remains and to make some sense of the archaeological record that emerges.

The task is made much easier, however, by the existence already of a broad outline for the basic narrative of the human story. In *On the Origin of Species*, Charles Darwin (1859) set out a framework that later scholars

1

including anthropologists have been able to flesh out. The human species is descended from ancestors, in effect apes, who lived in Africa several millions of years ago. We can now say that it was in Africa between 200,000 and 150,000 years ago that our species, *Homo sapiens*, emerged. And expansions out of Africa by members of that species, from around 60,000 years ago, led to the peopling of the world. The first sedentary societies, where communities formed permanent settlements and began to practise farming, were founded some 10,000 years ago. The first cities, with their more sophisticated way of life, emerged nearly 6,000 years ago, and in some cases their development was accompanied by the inception of writing.

It is among the material remains of these early activities that evidence relevant to the big questions about the development of humankind, and of the special attributes of humankind, is to be found. And it is the task of contemporary archaeology to explore the cognitive and spiritual dimensions of these developments as well as the purely practical ones.

The roots of spirituality

In shaping a project, generously funded by the John Templeton Foundation, to seek to define and explore the origins of some of these specifically human qualities, it was first necessary to develop a strategy. The intention was certainly to take a global approach, recognising that by 15,000 BC humans had settled on all the world's continents (except Antarctica). On each, societies followed different trajectories of development. But in the early millennia after the out-of-Africa dispersals, those communities were not in long-distance communication with each other. In some respects they developed independently. So the development in many of them of such specifically human features as art and architecture, as a worldview that in most cases involved the practice of a religion, and of a range of analogous developments including the custom of burial, is a matter of enormous interest. To find a name for such a project was not easy. 'The Roots of Spirituality' was selected as sufficiently vague to cover many areas of interest, yet sufficiently specific to indicate the focus of our concerns.

A first international symposium, devoted to early beginnings in the Palaeolithic period, before 10,000 BC, was held in 2004. The resulting volume, *Becoming Human: Innovations in Prehistoric Material and Spiritual Culture* (Renfrew and Morley 2009), addresses some of the issues touched on earlier. One theme of central interest to the project is the emergence of religious thought,

reflected in the construction of temples or other buildings for the purposes of cult practice. But existing studies in archaeological theory and practice (e.g., Renfrew 1985) have shown how difficult it is to infer the practice of religion from the material remains, unless there are accompanying written records or at least a rich figurative iconography. It is the case that human representations – small sculptures, some of them perhaps regarded as idols – make their appearance in the archaeological record on most continents much earlier than do temple complexes or shrines that can confidently be identified as serving a religious function. So for the first focus of study of the project we decided to examine the inceptions of human representation, on a global basis. Such representations are not necessarily a feature of all religious rituals, yet in favourable cases they may give an indication that religious rituals were possibly being practised, and certainly may provide insights into their makers' views of humans, nonhumans, the natural and the supernatural. The result of this global study of the inception of figurative representation, *Image and Imagination: A Global Prehistory of Figurative Representation* (Renfrew and Morley 2007), is now available. And while it does not set out to resolve the problems of identifying early religious practices in each area under review, it certainly presents much of the evidence on which such an analysis must be based.

For a further component of our project we selected what is perhaps a less obvious element in the development of human cognition: measure.

Measure and early symbolic relationships

In the development of human cognition, the emergence of symbolic thought is highly significant. Words, of course, are in one sense symbols. The spoken word 'bird' evokes (for a speaker of our language) an image, and if the word is appropriate for several bird species, it implies that a category ('bird') has already been formulated. This degree of abstraction is presumably a feature of all human communities, since all have a spoken language.

To understand the word 'bird' implies some knowledge and experience of the world: you have to have seen a bird to know one. Any notion of measure implies experience of the world in a more involved way. It involves also some notion of equivalence. For to measure some feature of the world means to compare it with some other feature of the world. It implies the formulation of an aspect or quality in respect of which things may be compared: a scale. One obvious example is the notion of 'weight'. If one is to have some measure of heaviness, one needs to have a sense or vision of two things balancing, being equal in terms of that dimension of measure. The most obvious instance is the balance arm, where a metrical object (which we refer to as a 'weight') is balanced at the end of one arm of the scales against the object being measured, placed symmetrically at the end of the opposite arm. The metrical object, if the scales do indeed balance, can be used to represent the specific quantity in terms of the aspect being measured of the object under study. That is the quality (and the quantity) that we call the 'weight' of the object under study. And we measure it with standard objects that are frequently also termed 'weights'.

The use of units of measure can be recognised, in favourable cases, quite early in the archaeological record. They document the construction of symbolic relationships, of the kind just described. Indeed these are among the earliest symbolic relationships that we can recognise. Yet they do not appear as early as the figurative representations discussed in *Image and Imagination*. These are among the earliest cases where we document the functioning of symbols archaeologically. Yet the significance of these new symbolic relationships, implicit in the practice of measure, is vast.

When we review the broad span of human existence, in a broad evolutionary sense, it is possible to speak of two phases of development (Renfrew 2007, 97): the speciation phase and the tectonic phase. The speciation phase represents that considerable span of time, from several million years ago down to 150,000 or 100,000 years ago, when our hominin ancestors were already using stone tools (in the so-called Lower and Middle Palaeolithic periods), but when our own species *Homo sapiens* had not yet fully emerged. With the out-of-Africa dispersals of that new species, some 60,000 years ago, and in particular with the emergence of sedentism, some 10,000 years ago, it is possible to speak of a tectonic phase (i.e. a constructive phase – the name is taken from the Ancient Greek word *tecton* for a constructor, a carpenter). With the development of permanent dwellings and indeed of settled village communities, a new, more constructive span of human existence began, with the development of buildings, property rights and ownership, and of course the origins of agriculture. It is around, or shortly after, this time in most trajectories of development that direct indications of the practice of measure can be observed.

To formulate a notion of measure, and then to formulate a unit of measure in order to quantify, is a very large conceptual step. That observation holds whether we are speaking of the measurement of length or volume or weight or time or of other features such as pitch or temperature. It represents a degree of abstraction that many will have considered radical. Such a step could at once be highly practical: it was constructive, in the literal sense. In the field of architecture, if you want rectangular rooms you must be able to measure walls of equal length. The notion of planning may well lead to the construction of a model or a plan using the concept of deliberate scale, involving the definition of the specific ratio by which the model must be scaled up to match the intended reality. Measure is a fundamental component of the constructive or tectonic arts.

Considering the use of standard units of weight allows one to define the relative values of commodities – that a unit of bronze may be 'worth' (regarded as equivalent to) 100 units of wheat. These abstractions enable individuals and societies to reach out in a systematic way, and to give effective structure to their world.

These abstractions do more than that. In some cases they offer a suggestion, a hint of order in the world. Yet these indications of order in the natural world are difficult to observe and record until we ourselves have developed some concepts of order and of measure. The successive cycles of the Maya calendar, for instance, offer a picture of time flowing steadily forward through a series of eras. Such ideas must first have been stimulated by the practice of measuring time. And they lead on to offer the possibility also that human affairs can be ordered in such a way as to fall into step with the harmonious structure that may have been detected.

Measurement also allows speculation about dimensions on a larger scale than those encountered daily. The measurement of time, in particular, involving astronomical observation and systematic contemplation of the cosmos, often became involved with formulations conceiving of the universe and of the spiritual or religious forces postulated as motivating it. From the stones of Stonehenge to the alignments and calendars of Mesoamerica, measurement stands at the dawn of cosmology. The term 'cosmology' is used here not just in the sense of explanation of the celestial, but in the sense of the conception of the universe – the set of beliefs about the world, material and immaterial, and the rules through which interaction with it can occur. Cosmology represents one of the serious attempts by human communities to reach an understanding of their place in the world.

The study of early measure can thus, in favourable cases, bring us close to very early speculations by a range of societies about their place in the world. Such speculation is, of course, an important part of what is intended by the term 'spirituality'.

The forms and underlying principles of the belief systems of different societies have, of course, formed the focus of much anthropological research over the last century or so (see, for example, Lévy-Bruhl 1935; Evans-Pritchard 1965; Horton 1993). 'Belief systems' can naturally be concerned with all aspects of the world, terrestrial, celestial, natural and supernatural, often without the same distinctions made between those categories as we might make. The relationships between religion and state have formed the stock trade of studies of ancient 'civilisations' (and their influence on worldview formed the particular focus of Frankfort et al.'s 1942 monograph); rarely, however, have the relationships between spirituality and measurement activities within those systems been thematically explored, in studies of either recent-contemporary or past societies.

The archaeology of early quantification and cosmology

It is our intention that this volume explore how the various aspects and implications of measuring activities discussed previously were developed in a broad selection of past cultures from around the world, and to allow comparison of how different or how consistent were the local developments. This book considers, on a cross-cultural basis, the origins and early development of counting and of measurement in a number of different areas of the world and periods of time, using the available archaeological evidence. It grows out of a symposium that took place at the McDonald Institute for Archaeological Research, Cambridge, from 13 to 17 September 2006. In inviting contributions the intention was to achieve coverage of as wide a range as possible of expertise, method, period and place; areas covered include Europe, Mesoamerica, South America, India, China and the Near East, and periods encompassed range from the Palaeolithic through to early history in the different parts of the world. The papers were each read by every contributor in advance, discussed communally at the symposium, and subsequently revised for this volume by the authors in light of the discussions.

The volume is organised into five sections dealing with different aspects of measurement and cosmology, grouped by linking themes rather than by geography or period: I. Number: Counting, Mathematics, and Measure; II. Materialising the Economy; III. Dimensions and Belief; IV. Calendar and Cosmology; and V. The Spirituality of Measure. Each of these sections features an editorial introduction and, in the case of section 5, some concluding remarks.

It should be noted that there would have been other possible ways of arranging the contributions to this volume, and many of the chapters contain considerations relevant to more than one of the sections. The inclusion of a given chapter in a particular section should not be taken to indicate an absence of content related to other sections in the book; it is indicative of what we have identified as a prominent theme.

REFERENCES

Darwin C., 1859. *On the Origin of Species by Means of Natural Selection.* London, John Murray.

Evans-Pritchard, E. E., 1965. *Theories of Primitive Religion.* Oxford, Oxford University Press.

Frankfort, H., H. A. Frankfort, J. A. Wilson, T. Jacobsen and W. A. Irwin, 1942. *The Intellectual Adventure of Ancient Man: An Essay on Speculative Thought in the Ancient Near East.* Chicago, University of Chicago Press.

Horton, R., 1993. *Patterns of Thought in Africa and the West: Essays on Magic, Religion and Science.* Cambridge, Cambridge University Press.

Lévy-Bruhl, L., 1935/1973. *Primitives and the Supernatural.* Translated by L. A. Clare. New York, Haskell House Publishers.

Renfrew C., 1985. *The Archaeology of Cult: The Sanctuary at Phylakopi.* London, British School at Athens.

Renfrew, C. and I. Morley, 2007. *Image and Imagination: A Global Prehistory of Figurative Representation.* Cambridge, McDonald Institute.

Number: Counting, Mathematics and measure

The volume opens with a section that deals with the conceptualisation of number and measurement, how systems of thought and recording impacted upon the capabilities for measurement activities and numerosity in different parts of the world.

Direct archaeological evidence for measurement activities is the focus of the vast majority of the contributions to this book; however, it begins with a consideration of the extent to which measurement capabilities of various kinds are inherent requirements for other activities for which we have archaeological evidence – activities that do not themselves provide *direct* evidence of measurement. Amongst prehistoric hunter-gatherer populations there is no unambiguous direct evidence of numeracy of the kinds discussed in the other contributions to this volume, but many of the activities they carried out would have required various kinds of relative and absolute reckoning, including time, distance and division. This first chapter seeks to deconstruct measuring activities into key types, to identify the significant differences and interdependencies between them. It does so in the context of some of the types of reckoning and measurement that would have been required for activities that we know were essential parts of hunter-gatherer life and discusses how these should be conceived. The principal focus of the latter part of this first chapter is the identification of time, cycles and causal relationships, and how these impact on ritual practice and belief systems.

Helen Farr's chapter explores in detail the measuring activities and capabilities requisite for one particular such activity that we know was an important part of prehistoric behaviour: marine navigation. Much archaeological evidence, especially from the trade of obsidian, which in the Mediterranean area, as in the Pacific, is sourced primarily from islands, indicates that extended marine voyages were made by prehistoric peoples. These would have required a considerable set of skills including conception of distance, its relation to time, vectors, and relations between celestial cyclical and terrestrial spatial measurements. Farr explores the implications of archaeological, environmental and ethnographic evidence for the nature of such skills and their relation to early measurement and cosmology.

Denise Schmandt-Besserat gives a concise overview of her theory of the stages of development of representation of number in the Near East and how this relates to the development of complexity in counting, conceptualisation of quantity, abstraction of reality and the development of writing. She outlines how the earliest accounting systems are associated with contexts corresponding to advent of agriculture and exhibit the practice of *concrete counting*, in which specific shapes/representations stand for specific commodities and are replicated to stand for different quantities. There is a transition from *objects* representing commodities, to *markings* representing commodities and separate markings representing quantities. According to her thesis it is this step that allows the emergence of a concept of abstract number – the process of externalising and abstracting quantities and commodities allowed for the manipulation of these concepts in new ways, being able to record objects that were not present, that were owed, or yet to be produced, for example.

Turning to the other side of the world and another, quite different type of numerical recording, Gary Urton focuses in his contribution upon the recording and measuring system used by the pre-Columbian Inka of Peru, the khipu knotted string. These heirarchically organised sequences of knot markers constituted a complex information-storage system, including a decimal accumulative (and possibly double-bookkeeping) accounting system. Not all of the dimensions of their meaning have yet been deciphered, but Urton's work has been pivotal in interpreting their numerical content in the context of Inka archaeology and economy. Much has been learnt from the khipu regarding native South American accounting and numeracy, which developed quite independently of that in the Near East and, by extension, Europe.

The khipu could be used for accounting Inka measures, for accounting land, commodities, and the work-time contributed by provinces in the form of labour-tax, but were also used for recording relative values such as 'species' types of livestock, colours of livestock, and their quality. The system of their use was widespread, spanning the whole empire, and with a very large number of specialists involved in the process. In addition to situating interpretations of individual khipu records in their economic and social context, Urton goes on to propose how such a system was likely to have functioned on the large scale.

John Justeson starts with an overview of number terms in different languages, and how the cognition of number can relate to the way in which it is linguistically expressed. He goes on to discuss the presence – and absence – of a linguistic concept of zero in different traditions, evidence that suggests that zero is not an innate element of human numerical cognition, but appears to have been 'added on' to some traditions of numeracy.

He suggests that the significant correlations between cultures in the way that humans talk about number are suggestive of their emergence from a shared numerical cognition. Basic number terms, which exist in all cultures, correspond with those quantities that are cognisable in a single glance – one, two, three. Furthermore there is a strong relationship between the body and numerical cognition, and concepts of numbers as metaphors with other objects/containers/collections. However, the development of numerical systems more complex than these, including a concept of zero, seems to be related specifically to cultural practices and the interpersonal interactions they define. Zero cannot be conceived in basic number terms, or in terms of the body or objects and containers, and it seems that it has to arise in the context of specialised notational systems. Justeson goes on to explore the emergence of a concept of zero, and its numerical representation with a sign, in the development of ritual calendrical and counting systems in Mesoamerica.

Continuing the exploration of cognition of number, Lambros Malafouris's chapter discusses the mechanism and timing of the shift from approximating and subitizing capacities (the ability to discriminate between the numerical values of small sets of objects), which are exhibited by infants and other primates, to the ability to manipulate exact numerocities and deal with abstract number. Taking an innovative approach, Malafouris examines findings from neuroscience relating to the location of numerical cognition functions in the brain, and their relatedness to other functions such as spatial cognition and language. He then goes on to relate these to the archaeological record of the Near East, as discussed by Schmandt-Besserat, proposing a scenario for the emergence of numerocity in this context as a consequence of the interaction between material culture and cognition.

Conceptualising quantification before settlement: Activities and issues underlying the conception and use of measurement

Iain Morley

Introduction

This chapter discusses a number of different aspects of measurement relevant to past societies, and the archaeological record. First, it explores some of the concepts underlying different types of measurement, the differences between them, and the implications of those differences for how measurement might be, and has been, conceived. Different types and concepts of measurement are labelled with specific terms, and the relationships between them considered. Whilst it is hoped that the concepts discussed and terms used might be useful in wider considerations of measurement, the chapter is written keeping in mind the nature and implications of the types of measurement activity that are likely to have been important in the context of hunter-gatherer subsistence, especially concepts of time, cycles and distance. In particular, this chapter seeks to highlight the fact that a great many of the activities that were carried out by past societies would have involved quantification in some form. In order to explore fully the use of measurement of the world and beyond in past societies we must explore the implications of the activities for which we do have archaeological evidence, in addition to looking for direct evidence of quantification.

The final sections of the chapter in particular relate some of these conceptualisations – especially of time and cycles of events – to supernatural and spiritual systems of belief for their explanation, and ritual systems of practice for their mediation.

Early measurement – circumstances and types

Direct archaeological evidence for measurement amongst prehistoric hunter-gatherer populations is sparse, or perhaps sparsely identified. Apart from notational systems such as are proposed by the analyses of Marshack (1964; 1972; 1991) and others (see D'Errico 1991, and Bednarik 1991, for a consideration and replies), there is little direct evidence to suggest systems of reckoning such as addition (as opposed to 'accumulation'), division, assessment of weight, and so forth. However, measurements of a variety of forms must have underpinned many activities that we do know about, and an exploration of these activities illustrates that we would be wrong to dismiss any past societies as 'nonmeasuring' or even innumerate, on the basis of a lack of direct evidence for 'conventional' measurements such as weights, currency or architectural dimensions, for example.

Amongst most, if not all, societies there is a variety of aspects of daily life that involve the use of concepts of measurement. These can be thought of as falling into five main areas, or foci, for measurement: (1) the group itself, (2) resources/commodities, (3) natural and created features of the world, (4) navigation, and (5) time (see Figure 1.1). There are overlaps between aspects of at least some of these categories, as will be seen (for example, concepts of distance and time), but there are elements that are particular to each category, and these will be considered in turn. A particular emphasis will be placed on their manifestation within a hunting-gathering context.

(1) The group itself

There are several ways in which aspects of an understanding of the group might rely on quantifiable or relative assessment, from fundamental characteristics such as the number of people in the group or subgroups, to concepts such as relatedness, hierarchy, contribution and age (see Figure 1.2).

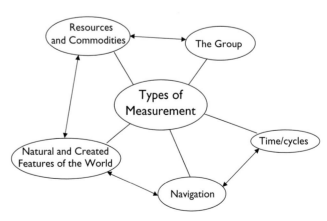

Figure 1.1. Types of measurement. There are practical relationships between all types; arrows indicate conceptual and methodological overlaps.

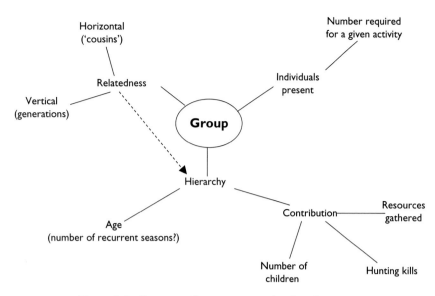

Figure 1.2. Concepts of measurement related to the group.

In what ways does an awareness of the total collective of people in a group, or in a household, or of households in a group, relate to quantification? People may be capable of reckoning (recognising) the presence of all persons in a group, or absence of some, through the recognition of the presence or absence of individuals, without ever needing to explicitly 'head-count' – rather, undertaking 'head recognition'. Nevertheless one might expect beliefs to be held regarding an optimal number of individuals to take part in a hunting or foraging foray, such as the number of individuals required to bring down a particular animal, or in line with expectations regarding the potential yield of the environment at that time or location (in itself a quantification). It could be argued that all that might be in place is a concept of 'the more people the better', but this would not be adequate when the group is required to divide its labour resources between more than one task at a time, which would undoubtedly be the case much of the time. Unless individual members of the group always fulfilled the same task roles, with no redistribution of labour according to requirements – which could be true for some, but not all of the time – such considerations, whilst not necessarily requiring numerical quantification, would rely on a finely honed sense of optimal labour input versus potential yield – that is, relative values.

In addition to values associated with the group and subgroups there are other aspects of the group the assessment of which might be considered to require quantification of a sort. Vertical and horizontal relationships within a group might be quantified – if not numerically, then in relative terms. For example, in a vertical direction, the number of generations alive: your grandfather, your mother, yourself and your daughter. This is a numerical concept but is not likely to require the use of greater reckoning than can be provided by the digits of one hand. In a horizontal direction, degree of relatedness may be considered important – cousins, second cousins and so forth. Whilst this seems on the surface to be numerical – it can be quantified in a similar way to generations in that it is possible to identify 'number of points removal' from one person to another – in practice it could equally be a far vaguer attribution of level of 'connectedness' between one individual and another.

Any kind of hierarchy requires some conception of relative seniority. This relative measure may rely, for its reinforcement, on comparatively nebulous concepts such as relatedness, but it might also be predicated on attributes such as age (e.g. number of cycles of seasons an individual has been alive), number of children, or tally of hunting kills, for example, all of which are judged on the basis of quantity.

Concepts such as an individual's contribution to the group's well-being (or survival) tie in with considerations of the value of resources and commodities. This contribution may be easily quantifiable, in discrete units, such as number of animals caught or number of tubers gathered, or may be reckoned in more subjective terms. These ideas are explored further in the next section.

(2) Resources and commodities

The size of the group (and any subgroups) would be relevant to not only planning and executing foraging and hunting activities, but the division of the resources consequently gathered. Even (or, perhaps, especially) within in a system whereby all resources gathered were considered to be communal and people helped themselves, there would be an enormous potential for abuse of the system and a concomitantly strong sense of what would be considered 'fair' and what would be considered 'unfair', or greedy, in terms of peoples' allocations. Where such a communal system does not exist, the sharing of resources frequently relates to finely honed responses to perceived need of individuals or collection of individuals within the group (for a discussion of the complexities of forms of sharing see, for example, Ingold 1999), a process that requires not just summation, but division and sharing. The process of dividing and sharing resources involves dealing with quantities of whole objects, division of whole objects into parts, as well as, possibly, creating collections of smaller collections (which involves conceiving of collective units of units and multiples of multiples).

Quantification of resources and commodities can be said to involve '*fundamental*' quantification, in the sense of the reckoning of whole objects (e.g. 1 reindeer, 20 shells), and '*attributive*' quantification (measurement of attributes of the object such as mass, length etc.). A commodity may also be said to have 'relative' value, which is its value relative to other commodities/resources; this may be fixed or variable (e.g. in a barter system). Variable relative value would be influenced by factors including 'survival value' (physical need) and 'social value' (quality). Quality might be determined socially by considerations such as time or labour required, longevity or contribution to the group and may or may not be officially sanctioned (see Figure 1.3).

There are clearly many potential overlaps between survival value and social value, of the order typically manifest in any debate about the relative importance of 'culture' and 'biology'. It could be argued that survival value is a factor in determining social value, and, conversely, that 'survival' involves both physical and social well-being. Social value might constitute a determining factor in the true survival value of an object, with socially created 'needs' that directly impact on membership of the community, and thus survival. These are more akin to physical needs than the concept of 'quality' intended here.

Conceptions of the value of one thing in relation to another (*relative* value) would be necessary for a barter system of trade. We know that in the Upper Palaeolithic commodities were transported or exchanged over very great distances (e.g. Gamble 1999). Would a barter system have been necessary for such long-distance transport? This is one likely mechanism, but it is important to consider other ways in which such exchange can be conceptualised. Rather than a set of beliefs about equivalent *commodity* values, the exchange could also occur through reciprocal gift giving. In this case there would be some perception of relative values of gifts or actions, but the emphasis could lie with the action of the exchange itself (reciprocation) rather than the objects exchanged. The exchange of one *thing* for another might be entirely meaningless; gift giving may not be seen as a *swap* of objects (with the objects thus having a directly comparable value) but as the giving of a gift, followed by the reciprocation of that action; it is the exchange of *actions* rather than *objects*.

Returning to direct exchange of objects, there are several aspects of the conception of such a system that require further consideration. If one conceives that 1 reindeer is fair exchange for 20 pierced shells, and one also knows that 3 foxes is fair exchange for 1 reindeer, does it automatically follow that 3 foxes is fair exchange for 20 pierced shells? Such rationalising relies both on the ability to conceive of this three-way relationship of commodities, and on practical predicates – the idea that someone with foxes needs shells may be laughable, whilst the idea that someone with reindeer needs shells and that someone with foxes needs reindeer may be well established. It is here that the 'social' and 'survival' values

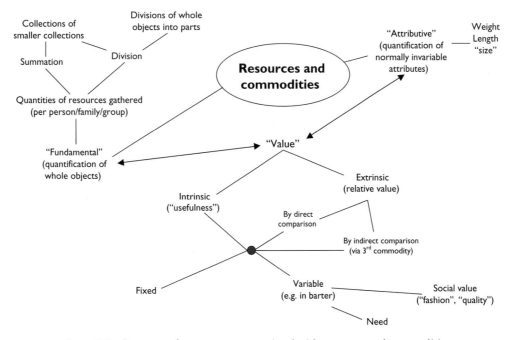

Figure 1.3. Concepts of measurement associated with resources and commodities.

discussed earlier come into play. Further, there is no point in thinking of 3 foxes as being worth 20 pierced shells if there is no prospect whatever of encountering someone with 20 pierced shells at the time when one has 3 foxes.

At the risk of seeming to impose a modern economic construct, in practical terms the three-way relationship of equivalence of value effectively relies on the presence of a 'market', where multiple commodities are available at once, or a situation (and the ability) via which one can envisage such a market as a longer-term prospect (i.e., a market spread over time rather than space – not all of the commodities and potential exchange partners being available at the same place and time, but all being available within a year, for example). This latter case relies on the ability to conceive of long-term needs, not just of yourself (which Upper Palaeolithic populations certainly possessed) but also of others with whom you hope to trade. It also requires the individual mental capability, the social constructs and the environmental circumstances that allow or even encourage deferment of short-term gain/need for potential long-term prospects of recompense.

(3) Natural and created features of the world

Properties of an object that are not dependent upon or affected by anything outside the object can be considered 'absolute' or 'attributive' properties of the object[1] (e.g., mass, volume). Properties of an object that are only attributable to it by virtue of its relation to other things can be considered 'relative' properties of the

object, such as orientation, location (nearer, farther, left of, right of) (see Figure 1.4). The reckoning of 'relative' properties of objects, in this sense, has an important role in navigation; this activity is discussed in its own right in section (4).

Whilst the properties themselves can be 'attributive' or 'relative', quantification of those properties is always relative, in the sense that attributes of an object can only be reckoned in terms of something else. For example, the length of a given object can be considered to be either one whole unit of itself long, or, alternatively, some multiple (or fraction) of some other unit long. The former could be considered to be an absolute measure of that object but is of absolutely no use for telling you anything about the object, and the latter would be a relative measure, whatever the unit. We can only usefully consider any property of anything in relation to that property of something else.[2]

So, whilst the *attribute* of the object may be absolute – in the sense that it exists independently of other objects – there is no such thing as an absolute unit of measurement *of* that attribute. Measurement of 'absolute' properties of anything has to be in terms of something else, namely, (multiples of) an agreed standard unit. In this sense we only *ever* measure things in relative terms – there is no such thing as 'absolute' *measurement*.[3]

The units by which a property is measured may be part of a conventionalised system whereby the numerical units are agreed and standardised (perhaps arbitrarily, or relative to another object). Such relative standardisations may be derived from naturally occurring and

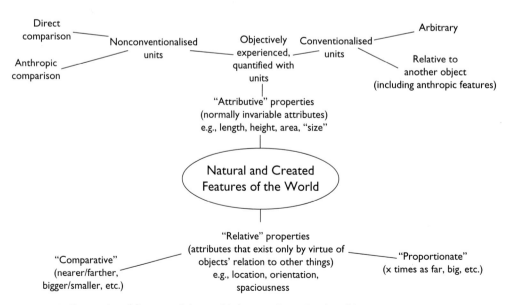

Figure 1.4. Properties of features of the world that may be variously subject to measurement concepts. Note that this represents *properties* of natural and created features of the world, not techniques for quantification. For example, 'attributive properties' may be quantified using relative (comparative) measures, and 'relative properties' may be quantified in comparison to attributes of other objects.

fairly consistent anthropic attributes, such as the length of the forearm, the thumb, a stride, the amount a person can carry, and so forth (see also Justeson, Urton, Michailidou, Clark, Jansen, this volume). It is worth bearing in mind that this could lead to an equifinality in measuring systems; a general human tendency towards utilising anthropic attributes to derive units may lead to systems of measurement that appear to be derived from a common ancestor, when in fact they are derived from a common rationale independently generated.

It is worth noting here the cognitive difference between the relative measurement that recognises merely difference and that which recognises proportionate difference. These might be termed 'comparative' relative measurement (e.g. bigger/smaller) and 'proportional' relative measurement (e.g. 1.75 times as big), respectively. Proportional relative measurement would seem unlikely to be an essential capability in traditional subsistence and economic contexts, whilst comparative relative measurement would have many applications. The notion of the emergence of proportional measurement is discussed a little further later.

Another distinction that might be made when discussing measurement in the context of semimobile traditional subsistence societies is that between the concepts of 'area' and 'space'. *Area*, in the mathematical sense of length multiplied by width, might come to be of particular importance when allocating shares of land for cultivation purposes, or habitation purposes, in a settled society. It is unlikely to be of any great importance to seminomadic societies, for whom a judgement of personal (and at the group level, collective) *space* would be more significant. An amount of *space* may be of a precise size, clearly delineated, but a numerical value of the size of that space (its area) is not necessary; it is judged on a sensory rather than numerical basis.

Several important questions remain to be answered. To conceive of the value of one thing in relation to another thing is one skill; to be able to conceive of the relative value of two things by reference to a third commodity of *conventional* value involves another layer of understanding. When does an agreed (arbitrary) standard unit become agreed and standardised? What is required socially? What is required cognitively? Is the cognitive requirement the same as is required for the agreed arbitrary symbolism of language and symbolic representation? Or is it more akin to 'orders of intentionality' involved in understanding relations between humans?

(4) Navigation

Successful navigation of the world requires an ability to reckon and remember relative positions of 'objects'

(natural and anthropogenic features of the environment – people, groups, resources, geological and ecological features). An important aspect of this skill, particularly when dealing with objects that are out of sight, is determining and communicating the distance between them. I have attempted to represent the relationships discussed in the following section in Figure 1.5. In a traditional context, with the exception of the placement of objects in the immediate vicinity, 'absolute' measures of distance (i.e. standardised divisions of the length of ground, air or water between one object and another) would be essentially meaningless. The very value of the standard units of distance is that they exist independently of other factors, but like currency, they have value that is only realised by their conversion into something else. The only practical conception of distance is of the time taken to traverse it. Our understandings of distance and of time are intimately related (cf. Brown, Aveni, this volume); the very terminology of *length* and *spans* of time – in Romance and Germanic languages at least – betrays the equation of the two concepts in our minds, as do phrases such as 'the distant past'. Even today, in our age of varied and rapid transport, we readily convert distances into time, in speech and in thought:

"How far is it to the restaurant?" "Oh, it is only about 10 minutes from here."

"We live about 20 minutes along the river, by bike".

"It's about three and a half hours to Oxford, by bus".

Even if the stated distance is in standard units such as miles or kilometres, we convert it according to our mode of transport and the prevailing ecology – in the sense of terrain and weather. The role of the ecology in determining the time-distance is mediated by the transport used. If we are told that the town is three miles away, we must transform that information into time before it has any value to us; this will be dictated by our transport and whether the distance is by road or 'as the crow flies'. If by road and we are on foot, the town is an hour away; if we are in a horse and cart, it is half an hour away; if we are on a bike, it is 20 minutes away; in a car, probably 5 minutes. Alternatively, if it is three miles away over the moors this may be two hours away by foot, one hour by horse, and an infinite way away by motor vehicle, the terrain being impassable to vehicles. All of the preceding examples have assumed an individual of average fitness, but other factors that are important considerations are the fitness and age of the person undertaking the journey, and the energy, or 'effort', required to undertake the journey. This, of course, is also mediated to an extent by transport available.

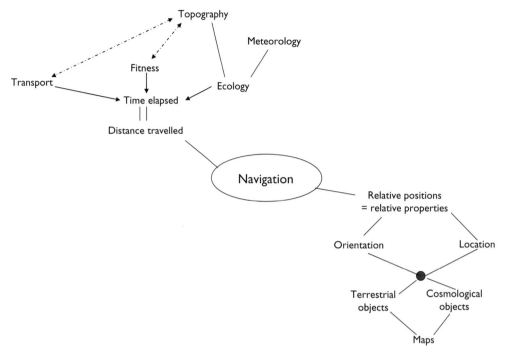

Figure 1.5. Concepts of measurement that may be associated with navigation. Solid arrows signify influence; dashed signify relevance.

Of course, the mediating role of transport is a very recent phenomenon, with the vast majority of the population in most parts of the world travelling largely by foot until the 20th century. Interestingly there is a unit of measure that, by design or by chance, actually unites distance and time – the league. A league has historically and geographically a somewhat variable value in terms of 'absolute' measures but usually equates to about three English miles and thus equates to the distance of one hour's walk. However, even the unit of time of 'an hour' is a recent phenomenon. An hour is an arbitrary unit and, in archaeological terms, a recent division of the day.

So we must now ask, If distance can only usefully be quoted and understood in terms of time taken to traverse it, what units of time might be available to be quoted? The shortest naturally occurring divisions of time are days/nights. These in turn can be divided into parts by using the position of the Sun (or other celestial bodies at night) as markers, most easily into periods before and after the Sun is overhead. This then provides us with the following means of quoting distance:

"It's a day away"

"It's half a day/a morning/an afternoon away"

"It'll take you less than half a day/a morning/an afternoon to get there"

"You could get there and back again in a day"

"You could get there and back again in half a day/a morning/an afternoon"

"You could get there in less than a day, but you couldn't get back again before nightfall"

… and then multiples of these units. The next naturally occurring unit is provided by the cycle of the Moon, allowing the potential to describe distances in terms of the passage of proportions of the cycle of the Moon. The implications of divisions of time, cycles and their relationship with cosmology are explored further later.

The principal context in which distance would have been relevant to Palaeolithic hunter-gatherers would have been distance from settlement to resources (and between resources). This includes static resources such as lithics, water and plant foods, but also mobile resources – animals. When large migrating herds of particular animals, such as reindeer, horses or mammoth, provided a major food and materials resource it would have been extremely beneficial to be able to estimate, and express, the length of time it would take a hunting party to access them, and factored into this would need to be not only the time taken for the group to reach the animals, but the movement of the animals themselves. In terms of the movement of the people themselves there is currently no widely accepted evidence that people travelled by any means other than by foot, so the principal factors affecting perceived distance between two 'objects' would be the prevailing ecology – terrain and weather – and the fitness and age of the individual(s) undertaking to travel the distance.

One way in which societies can seek to record and explain the distances between 'objects' is via the use of maps. From the ethnographic examples of hunter-gatherer/forager societies that they review Zubrow and Daly (1998) conclude that mapmaking is in fact relatively rare, and many hunter-gatherer/forager societies do not make maps. They are more prevalent, and when they exist, more detailed, amongst peoples who live in areas where the topography is minimal, those with greater uncertainty in their subsistence pattern, and where the area covered on a daily basis is larger. In the latter case, of course, transport can have a part to play, such that those societies that make use of animals or boats more frequently require maps as a result of the larger range covered. The majority of known prehistoric and archaeological maps have a local focus, with variable levels of detail, generally decreasing from centre (local) to periphery. Zubrow and Daly (1998) suggest that since most prehistoric maps focus so much on the local they are not likely to have been of use as way finders, as the territory depicted would be familiar anyway, but perhaps as mnemonic devices for purposes of explaining activity within particular areas, or as illustrations of territory to nonlocal persons.

Terrestrial objects' positions can be illustrated relative to each other in this way but can also, of course, be reckoned relative to nonterrestrial – cosmological – features, and cardinal directions. Interestingly, in many of the societies reviewed by Zubrow and Daly (1998), mapmaking is a religious or ideological activity, not secular, and information relating to cosmology and relationships between the local area and the heavens is included in the maps too. This is perhaps not surprising, because as noted, successful navigation of the world relies on an ability to reckon and remember relative positions of 'objects', and included in this category are not only the aforementioned natural and anthropogenic features of the world, but also features of the heavens. Most commonly, hunter-gatherer societies do not make reference to true cardinal points (geographical north, south, east, west) for orientation purposes. According to Brown (1983, cited in Fowler and Turner 1999) there are four main ways in which the 127 societies that he sampled determine cardinal directions:

a. by reference to the movement of celestial bodies, especially the Sun
b. by reference to atmospheric features (e.g. winds)
c. by reference to the process of movement itself (e.g. upwards, downwards, towards, away from)
d. by reference to fixed geographical features

Which of these systems of reckoning the world has the potential to be most useful will depend to a great extent upon the nature of subsistence activities undertaken, and the nature of the ecology and geography. Zubrow and Daly (1998) note that many island societies, for example, use the directions 'inland' and 'outward' rather than fixed cardinal directions. The relationship between cosmological features and spiritual and ideological considerations is explored further later.

(5) Time

The identification of cycles and time

The identification of fixed durations derived from – and measured by – cycles must constitute the earliest examples of units of time. These are not arbitrary measures that exist by convention (though it may be a matter of cultural convention to acknowledge their existence or importance), in contrast to 'abstract', conventionalised measurement of units of time such as clocks (which artificially subdivide a natural fixed cycle). These latter might be considered to be more equivalent to units of weight or monetary value, whose value (and, indeed, existence) is determined only by convention.

Natural (including celestial) phenomena have the potential to be used as cues in reckoning of cycles, and reckoning of fixed units of time (cycles do not necessarily represent fixed units of time, though the latter may be derived from the former). Some potential implications of the identification of terrestrial and celestial cues for time reckoning are represented in Figure 1.6.

A regular recurrent sequence of events need not have the same duration each time that it occurs (the same events in the same order need not total the same duration each time). On the other hand, the overall cycle might have the same duration each time, but the component subdivisions do not – for example, the (solar) year (fixed duration) versus the four seasons (variable both within and between years). But the only way of knowing which of these longer-term phenomena are of fixed duration and which are variable is by reference to some standard whose duration is known; the only suitable naturally occurring unit of time available would be days. It is only relative to days that the solar year (and constituent solar events – solstices and equinoxes) and lunar cycles can be demonstrated to be of fixed duration. Not even the fixed-duration lunar cycles can be used relative to the year, as they do not align with the solar events.

In fact, although days and nights exist as natural discrete units, in terms of the durations of the periods of light and dark, even the 730 subdivisions of the year into days and nights are variable – although the total number

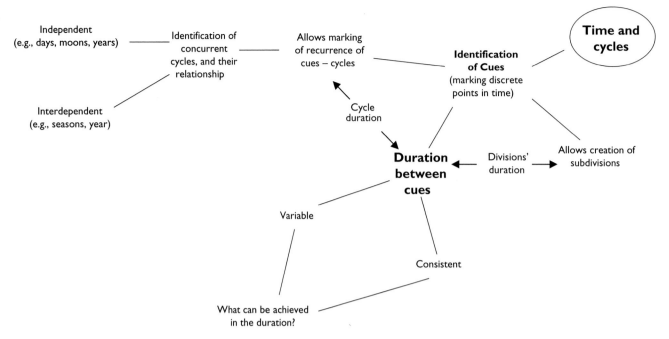

Figure 1.6. Concepts of measurement that give rise to, and arise from, awareness of time and cycles.

of units is always the same (365.25). How could one *know* that the time between the Sun's highest point on one day and the next is the same throughout the year,[4] in spite of the variation in the length of the day and the night? It is difficult to think of anything likely to be encountered in the natural world that would provide the opportunity to measure the duration of the day and night directly, with the exception of regularly dripping water. But to count such drips for a day would involve having in place a system of numeracy allowing an individual to count into at least double figures, and probably triple figures. It is possible that an individual might attempt to count the number of beats of his or her heart between sunrise and sunset, but this would require a system of numeracy running into the tens of thousands, which seems exceedingly unlikely. To recognise the existence, and timing, of equinoxes requires a precise level of knowledge of the duration of day and night, however. So by the time that we see equinoxes being identified, we should certainly attribute to the population concerned a detailed knowledge of the durations of day and night.

Although the smallest 'naturally occurring' unit of time is the day/night, it is worth remembering that there are other naturally occurring and consistent cues (at particular times of the year, at least) that have the potential to be used as markers of particular times (and thus subdivisions) of the day, for example, the time when crickets start to sing, the time when the snails come out, and so on.

Once there is an awareness of sequence of events and of recurrence of events (together constituting an

awareness of cyclicality), recurrent cues (such as leaves turning brown in autumn, the migration of birds, the appearance of buds in spring) can act as signals of the imminence of events. An awareness of sequence of events, and of recurrence of sequences of events, thus allows for expectations about the future to be held.[5] Once the capacity is in place to identify them, there are thus many cyclical patterns in nature of considerable significance in relation to subsistence and survival. In what ways might a preoccupation with cycles of natural events affect people's perception of their own lives, and expectations about change and recurrence? If people observe that the world is apparently full of recurrent cycles, it is only a small step to believe that all events are part of cycles, and that at the largest scale, time is cyclical; certainly such ideas feature prominently in many belief systems (e.g., the Mayan: Aveni, Sugiyama, this volume; Mesopotamian: Brown, this volume). To what extent might such ideas also inform an understanding of daily life? Even if some small daily activities, actions and interactions are novel, most are replications of the preceding day's (and the same probably applies when conceived of at an annual level). In a traditional subsistence lifestyle, actions would be repetitive from day to day, with variation between seasons, which would in turn be repeated on an annual basis; any variation and variety would be provided largely by human interaction and variation in natural phenomena (such as the weather). In certain geographical locations even these natural phenomena might be as cyclical on a seasonal basis as other aspects of life. So it may be that there would be typically much in a traditional subsistence context to enforce an idea of cyclicality to human life, and very little to reinforce any idea of free will and agency. In fact, when human actions *do not* result in the same effects as previously, this could be seen as a profound disjuncture, a sign that what was done was done wrongly, or of displeasure on the part of the powers influencing such outcomes (see also Brown, this volume). Expectation of change may well be a very recent phenomenon; there is more to suggest that a default expectation of continuity would be most reasonable – which in fact is variation with repetition, or cycles.

Whilst discussing the subject of reckoning the passage of time by natural cycles, it is perhaps time to return to the issue of the ability to conceive of *proportional relative* measurement, and the reckoning of fractions. Is it possible that observations of phases of the Moon could constitute an early incidence of the use of fractions? The decline and renewal of the Moon could be seen either as 'growing' and 'shrinking' or in terms of fractions of a whole. Likewise, seasons can be viewed as fractions of a year: is it possible to conceive of a year as a sum of four seasons without also conceiving of a season as one-fourth part of a year? (Equally, is it possible to conceive of the year as a sum of 13 months (or as a sequence of 13 moons) without also conceiving of each of those moons as one-thirteenth of the year?). This leads to the observation that when dealing with time, multiple sums/components are possible to conceive simultaneously: a year can be the sum of four seasons, the sum of 13 months, and the sum of 365 days, all at the same time. These very different divisions are not mutually exclusive.

Finally, is there a difference between conceiving of a thing (season) that is one-fourth of another thing (year) and conceiving of a quarter, which is one-fourth division of a single whole? That is, is it conceptually different to divide a horse into four different parts (head, neck, body, legs) and to divide a liver into four pieces? In the former case, the component parts are different from each other, and from their sum, but in the latter case the quarters are the same as each other and their sum. Both activities must surely have taken place throughout prehistory; the question is of whether each leads to a different understanding of parts of wholes, and the extent to which such understanding can be considered to be a cognisance of fractions.

Cycles, cause-and-effect relationships and the spiritual

As discussed earlier, an awareness of sequences of events and of recurrence of cues allows for expectations about the future to be held. Such expectations are also tempered by beliefs about causal relationships between these events, and the ability to influence them. We seem to have a profound awareness of cause-and-effect relationships in sequences of events, including chains of human actions, intentions and models based on experience, and it seems that there are rather blurry boundaries between our comprehension of sequences of events, and of cause-and-effect relations between them. As Barber and Barber (2004, 249) put it, we have a tendency to rationalise events on the basis of *post hoc ergo propter hoc – after* this, therefore *because* of this, that is, retrospective attribution of a cause-and-effect relationship to two events that are temporally close. By extension we have an ability, and tendency, to extend such models of cause and effect to a belief that certain behaviours should always cause certain outcomes, and sometimes by extension, that certain outcomes *depend* upon certain behaviours. A desire to influence such cause-and-effect sequences underlies much of ritual activity, although this may be (mis)applied to sequences of events with no cause-and-effect chain linking them. Such behaviours may be relatively straightforward, such as a particular gesture or action (what we tend to call superstitious behaviours, such as wearing a particular pair of socks for exams), or may be (or become) highly complicated and stereotyped sequences of actions (what we tend to call formal rituals).

The practice of such behaviours would appear to fulfil important roles, not just at the social level, but at the individual level too. The awareness that humans have of sequences of cause and effect, and of our potential for agency in the world, is a double-edged sword. With it comes the realisation that there are many phenomena in the world that have a direct impact on our survival, over which we evidently have no direct physical causal control, such as the weather, or the movement of wild animals, for example. A sense of powerlessness and lack of control over key elements of life is a prime factor in the incidence of anxiety and depression, and such a state of mind frequently leads to loss of appetite, withdrawal, disinclination to procreate and sleeplessness in both humans and other mammals (e.g., Gleitman 1995), detriments to fundamental elements of survival behaviour. Belief in the ability to influence the natural world through particular stereotyped behaviours diminishes this sense of powerlessness and the corresponding potential for frustrated inactivity or, at worst, debilitating depression.

The awareness of – or at least tendency to see – causal relationships between sequences of events can apply in the case of purely terrestrial events but can also provide an apparently powerful link between terrestrial and celestial events. Because certain terrestrial events occur at certain times of the year, and certain cosmological events occur at certain times of the year, it is a small step to believe that there is a causal relationship between the two. At the very least, the precursor can be used as a predictor for the subsequent other change. Because the movement of the celestial bodies and the progress of the seasons (and all else that entails – animal migrations, etc.) are both actually caused by the same thing, namely, the Earth's movements in space (rotation and orbit around the Sun), there can easily appear to be causal relationships between these phenomena[6] – when in fact they do have a relationship, but from a shared cause, rather than a causal relationship between them. Forming such a belief in a causal relationship between the celestial and terrestrial events is a particularly easy step to make given that certain terrestrial natural phenomena *are* directly influenced by celestial objects – for example, the Sun causes some flowers to open and snow to melt; the Moon causes tides and is related to menstrual cycles – of at least some of which phenomena peoples subsisting in a sensitive relationship with their environment would be well aware.

Throughout the world various foraging societies have observed cyclical patterns in the night sky. The astronomical knowledge of traditional societies is not something that has always been investigated (or reported, at least), but Fowler and Turner (1999) review a selection. It seems that observation of the cyclical movements of astronomical bodies (Sun, Moon, stars, including planets) occurs in several traditional foraging societies, and that this knowledge is integrated into other cyclical activities and phenomena that are experienced – ecological, subsistence, ritual/ceremonial and social. This integration of the celestial cycles can be through interpretation of them as having a powerful causational relationship, or as markers for existing events.

The appearance and disappearance of particular constellations have been used by different groups to mark the passage of time, or to mark the appropriate moment at which to carry out a particular activity (Fowler and Turner 1999). Indeed, according to Fowler and Turner (1999) the hunter-gatherers whom they review appear not to have used planetary movements as a cue for the orientation of any buildings, only for calendrical purposes, although it is possible that much rock art was orientated towards celestial events. The progress of the cycles of celestial bodies is often followed with reference to particular terrestrial features, which naturally leads to the sense of movement of the heavenly bodies in relation to a fixed Earth. Ecological conditions do have a bearing upon how significant such observations are likely to be – largely because they can determine the extent to which

such phenomena can be observed. For example, living in deep forest, in which views of the sky are rarely unobstructed, it is much more difficult to make observations of long-term movements of the stars – as is evidenced by the Malaysian Batek, who live in deep forest (Endicott 1979, cited in Fowler and Turner 1999). Of course, a group living in an environment that experiences heavy cloud cover frequently during a particular season will experience a perhaps strikingly punctuated progress of the stars on the occasions when they are clearly visible. The same would be true of a population that spent certain periods of the year under dense forest cover and other periods in open ground.

Most hunter-gatherer societies use the cycle of the Moon as a marker for durations of fixed length (the 29.5 day cycle being extremely regular) (Fowler and Turner 1999). In addition to providing a fixed duration period, lunar cycles are tied in with terrestrial events such as women's menstrual cycles, thus linking a cosmological phenomenon to a terrestrial/biological one that is of great significance, relating as it does to fertility and reproduction, as well as the various social and ritual activities attendant upon female fertility.

There is also an explicit association between celestial bodies and spiritual beings amongst most hunter-gatherer societies, with the Sun and the Moon both being considered as spiritual beings (Fowler and Turner 1999). Humans have an ability and, in fact, a tendency to extend anthropomorphic properties to objects, environmental features and phenomena (see, for example, Guthrie 1993, Hinde 1999; Lévy-Bruhl 1935 discusses a wide selection of examples in his early review of anthropological case studies),[7] which then provide a basis on which to interact with these entities. This is derived from profound awareness of theory of mind and individual intentionality, extremely important and characteristically human abilities for managing complex social worlds, which provide a powerful and largely effective framework for understanding the world at large. The explanation of the movements of celestial bodies in a narrative form (involving anthropomorphic and natural, familiar mechanisms and motivations) lends itself towards a conception of such beings as 'spiritual' or, at least, supernatural. Whilst the patterns of movement are explained in terms of the familiar (see, for example, Fowler and Turner 1999, Gibbon 1964, 1972), there are aspects of their movements that are clearly at odds with the terrestrial, natural behaviour that provides the models for the explanation; thus these aspects are considered to be supernatural, and the entities themselves supernatural/spiritual (Boyer 2001).

As Fowler and Turner put it, "The strong spiritual essence attributed to celestial beings has provided both charter and explanation for seasonal recurrences" (1999, 422–23) and, one might suggest, for the social and ritual activities that are related to these seasonal cycles. In addition to the culturally determined and spiritual aspects of religions, the preceding cognitive foundations (a tendency towards anthropomorphisation, and to the attribution of cause-and-effect relationships to sequences of events) are prerequisites for the ability to pursue religious and spiritual thought. Such behaviours are widely occurring, if not universal, features of religious beliefs around the world (e.g., Tylor 1871, Boyer 1996). The point where measurement truly meets with the spiritual is where it becomes involved with the relationships between the cosmological and terrestrial, where the natural and supernatural meet in explanations of the world.

Conclusions

It has been the aim of this chapter to explore the nature of measuring and quantification under different circumstances, specifically, various activities that are most likely to have formed parts of the lives of traditional societies. Part of the intention has been to make some steps towards recognising conceptual differences between different types of activity that we would subsume under the heading 'measurement'. Whilst largely a thought exercise, it is hoped that these initial explorations might form foundations for further investigations relating these different types of activity to cognitive capabilities of higher primates and modern humans, as well as for further exploration of the extent to which different types of measurement rely upon each other, or build upon shared cognitive foundations. Certainly much can be added, beyond the space constraints of this chapter, regarding the activities of other recent and historical traditional societies.

Another objective has been to use the consideration of the nature and types of measurement activity to formulate a definition of measurement that can be applied to all such activities. The following might fit the bill:

Assessment of a property of (an) object(s) or of the world in relation to that property of another object, which may constitute a conventionalised division of that property.

Such assessment may be unitary and thus numerical or may be relative (e.g., bigger, smaller, heavier, nearer, farther, north of here). Time can only be measured in terms of the movement of things, usually in terms of numbers of, or divisions of, repeated cycles of movement.

If measurement of the passage of time is considered in terms of distance of movement relative to apparently static objects/features then the preceding definition can encompass that too.

A further aim of this chapter has been to highlight the fact that there are many measuring activities that must have been essential parts of the activities that we know past societies carried out, but that do not in themselves involve measuring-dedicated material culture. Many, if not all, of the cognitive and conceptual foundations for the activities that we see later in prehistory (as discussed in other chapters in this volume) must have been in place in Upper Palaeolithic humans, and many must have been exercised. Furthermore, there are direct connections between the reckoning of relative positions of objects, the passage of time, the awareness of cyclical patterns of events and explanations of the world in terms of seeking to have, or to identify, agency in cause-and-effect relationships in sequences of events. Such activities form an important element of ritual activities and spiritual thought.

NOTES

1. Relating to its attributes; they nevertheless require relative *measurement* for their quantification; see following paragraph.
2. It might be argued that properties cannot be said to exist at all unless they are quantified; in a somewhat analogous way to the question as to whether a falling tree makes a sound if there is no one to hear it, what is the length of something, without a means to state its length? For the sake of sparing a rehearsal of well-explored philosophical arguments, we will consider here that objects have properties that exist, even if they cannot be described without relative quantification.
3. Although, because the *units* are standardised (including such commodities as are used as 'gold standards') and are independent of the object or property of that object being measured, these could be considered to have an 'absolute' value, *because* of their role as an independent comparator.
4. In terms of human experience, at least – in reality 24 hours ± up to 50 seconds.
5. As Confucius would say, "Study the past if you would divine the future".
6. As a hypothetical example: "the reindeer migrate when Orion occupies *that* position in the sky'", or even "Orion the hunter causes the reindeer to migrate when he stands *there*".
7. The tendency towards anthropomorphism as an explanatory mechanism for natural phenomena, and thus an ingredient of conceptions of deities, was observed by Andrew Lang in the late 19th century and neatly summarised by Evans-Pritchard (1965): "This response [seeking a logical cause] to a stimulus from without, combined with a tendency towards personification, gives [humans] this idea of a divine person, a supreme being" (p. 103).

REFERENCES

Barber, E. W. and P. T. Barber, 2004. *When They Severed Earth from Sky: How the Human Mind Shapes Myth.* Princeton University Press, Princeton, NJ.

Bednarik, R., 1991. Comment on F. d'Errico: Microscopic and statistical criteria for the identification of prehistoric systems of notation. *Rock Art Research* **8**:2, 89–91.

Bloch, M., 1998. *How We Think They Think: Anthropological Approaches to Cognition, Memory, and Literacy.* Westview Press, Boulder, CO.

Boyer, P., 1996. What makes anthropomorphism natural: Intuitive ontology and cultural representation. *Journal of the Anthropological Institute* 2, 83–97.

Boyer, P., 2001. *Religion Explained: The Human Instincts That Fashion Gods, Spirits and Ancestors.* William Heinemann, London.

Brown, C. H., 1983. Where do cardinal direction terms come from? *Anthropological Linguistics* 25, 121–61.

D'Errico, F., 1991. Microscopic and statistical criteria for the identification of prehistoric systems of notation. *Rock Art Research* **8**:2, 83–89; 91–93.

Endicott, K., 1979. *Batak Negrito Religion: The World-View and Rituals of a Hunting and Gathering People of Peninsula Malaysia.* Clarendon Press, Oxford.

Evans-Pritchard, E. E., 1965. *Theories of Primitive Religion.* Clarendon Press, Oxford.

Fowler, C. S. and N. J. Turner, 1999. Ecological/cosmological knowledge and land management among hunter-gatherers. In *The Cambridge Encyclopedia of Hunters and Gatherers,* eds. R. B. Lee and R. Daly. Cambridge University Press, Cambridge, 419–25.

Gamble, C., 1999. *The Palaeolithic Societies of Europe.* Cambridge University Press, Cambridge.

Gibbon, W., 1964. Asiatic parallels in North American star lore: Ursa Major. *Journal of American Folklore* 77, 236–50.

Gibbon, W., 1972. Asiatic parallels in North American star lore: Milky Way, Pleiades, Orion. *Journal of American Folklore* 85, 236–47.

Gleitman, H., 1995. Psychology. 4th ed. W. W. Norton, London.

Guthrie, S., 1993. *Faces in the Clouds: A New Theory of Religion.* Oxford University Press, Oxford.

Hinde, R. A., 1999. *Why Gods Persist: A Scientific Approach to Religion.* Routledge, London.

Ingold, T., 1999. On the social relations of the hunter-gatherer band. In *The Cambridge Encyclopedia of Hunters and Gatherers,* eds. R. B. Lee and R. Daly. Cambridge University Press, Cambridge.

Lee, R. B. and R. Daly, 1999. *The Cambridge Encyclopedia of Hunters and Gatherers.* Cambridge University Press, Cambridge.

Lévy-Bruhl, L., 1935/1973. *Primitives and the Supernatural.* Translated by L. A. Clare. Haskell House Publishers, New York.

Marshack, A., 1964. Lunar notation on Upper Paleolithic remains. *Science* **184**, 28–46.

Marshack, A., 1972. Upper Paleolithic notation and symbol. *Science* **178**, 817–28

Marshack, A., 1991. The Tai plaque and calendrical notation in the Upper Palaeolithic. *Cambridge Archaeological Journal* **1**, 25–61.

Renfrew, C. and C. Scarre, 1998. *Cognition and Material Culture: The Archaeology of Symbolic Storage.* McDonald Institute, Cambridge.

Tylor, E. B., 1871. *Primitive Culture: Researches into the Development of Mythology, Philosophy, Religion, Art, and Custom.* John Murray, London.

Williamson, R. A and C. R. Farrer, 1992. *Earth and Sky: Visions of the Cosmos in Native American Folklore.* University of New Mexico Press, Albuquerque.

Zubrow, E. B. W. and P. T. Daly, 1998. Symbolic behaviour: The origin of a spatial perspective. In *Cognition and Material Culture: The Archaeology of Symbolic Storage,* eds. C. Renfrew and C. Scarre. McDonald Institute, Cambridge, 157–74.

2

Measurement in navigation: Conceiving distance and time in the Neolithic

Helen Farr

The conception and use of measurements are inherent within certain prehistoric activities. This chapter analyses the skills and knowledge needed for seafaring in the Neolithic and questions how distance and time may have been conceived and measured in relation to the land and seascape. Our modern notions of measurement dictate the development of science, technology and religion, which in turn guide our comprehension of the world. For example, the question as to *who we are* has been reduced to *what we are* and the quest to identify the smallest particles that can currently be measured. That of *where we are* becomes the study of the universe and the largest conceivable measurements. This in turn connects to concepts of time, the speed of light, the creation of time and of course, the end of it. These lines of thought lead us to cosmology and world-view. Whilst we are still striving to think about these things let alone understand them, how do we begin to investigate how people in prehistory constructed measurement to understand their world?

One place to start is with the physical archaeological correlates for measuring practices: written records and measuring devices, for example, weights or calendars (as discussed in other chapters in this volume). Yet, in earlier prehistoric periods and in contexts where these are not preserved, we can still detect the early incidence and understanding of quantification or measurement through consideration of the knowledge and skills that underpin various activities. This chapter provides an example of this 'embedded' quantitative knowledge from the Neolithic period in the central Mediterranean. It is possible to deduce Neolithic mensuration, and to a certain extent, conceptual understanding of distance, space and time, through an analysis of Neolithic boat construction, seafaring and navigation.

Neolithic seafaring in the central Mediterranean

As no Neolithic seafaring vessels have been found in this region, the evidence for seafaring in the central Mediterranean comes from the maritime circulation of raw materials, principally obsidian, a type of volcanic glass.

Obsidian is thought to have been valued in prehistory for its sharp knapped edge and aesthetic qualities (Shackley 1998; Whitten and Brooks 1972; Williams-Thorpe 1995). As such, it was an important raw material in the Neolithic and was widely circulated around the Mediterranean. There are only four volcanic sources of obsidian in the central Mediterranean and these are all located on islands: Lipari, Pantelleria, Palmarola and Monte Arci on Sardinia. Even accounting for sea levels ca. 20 meters lower than the present day, due to the depth and the steeply shelving nature of the Mediterranean basin in this region these would all have been islands in the Neolithic (Lambeck 1996; Morhange et al. 2001; Pirazzoli 1991; Pirazzoli 1998). This means that Neolithic trade in this material would have necessarily involved seafaring. Thus, obsidian circulation in the central Mediterranean was a maritime phenomenon (Robb and Farr 2005).

Maritime prehistory is a rapidly growing area of research, embracing discussions on early human dispersals, trade and exchange, insularity and colonization studies. In the Mediterranean most of this work has focused on the Early Bronze Age onwards because of the evidence of organized long-distance maritime trade and the presence of wonderfully preserved wrecks (for example, Broodbank's exemplary work on early seafaring in the Mediterranean) (Broodbank 2000).

The importance of seafaring in prehistoric trade and exchange has been highlighted (Ammerman 1985; Castagnino Berlinghieri 2003) but there has been very little research undertaken into the circulation of obsidian as a maritime activity. Equally the *process* of Neolithic seafaring itself has been overlooked (Broodbank 1999; Broodbank 2000; Farr 2001; Johnstone 1980). Whilst seafaring is acknowledged as a mechanism for trade, as an activity it lies outside the sphere of settlement-specific landscapes that are the normal centre of terrestrial research. Equally, maritime archaeologists in the past have tended to focus research upon technology – boat construction and shipwrecks – or methodology, underwater excavation and conservation. As such the process of seafaring and the light it can shed on social organization (Helms 1988), cognition, early quantification and prehistoric spatial and temporal understanding have been missed.

The evidence for Neolithic seafaring in the central Mediterranean is derived from the circulation of obsidian from the Aeolian island of Lipari from ca. 6500 to 3500 BC. As indicated, no Neolithic seafaring vessels are known to be preserved in this region. The earliest known Italian boats are log boats found at the submerged Neolithic site of La Marmotta on Lake Bracciano (Farr 2001; Fugazzola Delpino 2002; Fugazzola Delpino et al. 1993; Fugazzola Delpino 1995). It is most likely that on the coast similarly simple vessels such as reed or log boats would have been used. It would be unfounded to hypothesize anything more complex during the Neolithic; there is, as yet, no convincing evidence for sailing anywhere in this period, with the first evidence for a sailed boat dating to ca. 3100 BC. Sailed vessels are still believed to have developed in the specific context of the River Nile, where the wind blows upstream, enabling vessels to float down the river and then to be blown back upstream (Johnstone 1980). It is likely, therefore, that Neolithic boats would have been paddled, and this assumption has direct consequences for the interpretation of long-distance maritime trade and exchange, as evidenced by the appearance of Pantellerian obsidian on the Italian mainland and Sicilian or Liparian obsidian on Malta. Additionally, knowledge of the energy and time it would take to propel a paddled vessel, even over what seem today to be short water crossings, would have been considerable.

Knowledge of the type of vessels that were used in the Neolithic and an understanding of the general capacity of these boats, combined with ethnographic research and detailed analysis of prehistoric vessels in other areas, enable seafaring to be studied as a sociotechnical process (Blue et al. 1997; McGrail 1987; Ushijima 2000). As such, questions about specific journeys, social organization, skill, knowledge and temporality can be addressed and this can begin to shed light on Neolithic mensuration.

Measuring seaworthiness

Whilst it is not the purpose of this chapter to discuss boat building technology in detail, it is worth mentioning that boat construction reveals a level of planning and design and an understanding of the concept of seaworthiness in even the most simple boats. Successful boat building may have been developed from experience, trial and error, but at some point in prehistory this was formalized, allowing open boats to undertake significant open water crossings regularly.

Building a boat, even a simple log boat, involves considerable planning. For example, choosing and felling a tree are best undertaken in winter when the wood contains less sap. It can then be hollowed and shaped more easily. The size of the selected tree trunk determines the size of the boat, its carrying capacity and the sea conditions in which it can be used. In a recent experiment by experienced boat builders at the Center for Maritime Archaeology at Roskilde the process of building a prehistoric log boat took six weeks. They discovered that for a log boat to have adequate stability the hull and sides had to be shaped and hollowed out to an equal thickness. This was important as it gave the boat necessary strength and flexibility. To judge hull thickness during shaping and hollowing, small holes were drilled so the thickness of the wood could be gauged in different positions around the boat. These were then caulked.

In addition to measuring the thickness of wood, an understanding of weight and weight distribution on small prehistoric vessels would have been vital. In the Neolithic, boats were used to carry people, raw materials, food, water and animals, and to do this successfully an understanding and quantification of weight and stability would have been necessary. It is not inconceivable that in some contexts the difference in buoyancy between fresh and salt water was even observed.

The practice of seafaring

Materials or artefacts that have been transported through trade and exchange around the landscape provide us with evidence for prehistoric travel. However, these materials may have reached their final destinations via a number of different processes, such as direct procurement or down-the-line exchange. Thus the transport of these items may have included any number of short increments of travel over any length of time (Renfrew 1975). This problem of equifinality means that it is difficult to understand how far people were actually travelling and to what extent long-distance exchange was reflective of long-distance travel. On land, archaeologically speaking, it is rarely possible to glimpse people or goods 'in motion', yet an analysis of seafaring enables a finer-grained resolution in which it is possible to identify specific journeys or voyages[1] that were undertaken in one feat (Robb and Farr 2005; Farr 2006). Consequently it is possible on occasion to deduce the minimal length of journey that would have been undertaken by any individual or group from the minimal distance from the mainland to an island, for example, from Sicily to Malta, or across the Adriatic. From this we can infer specific knowledge regarding spatial awareness, familiarity with the landscape and the ability to navigate, as well as social organization, including factors such as the duration and time seafarers spent away from village life. The study of these journeys provides a time scale for given activities, and this temporal depth can help us deduce how people thought about time and distance in the Neolithic.

Case study: Crossing the Adriatic

One journey that is evidenced by the presence of Liparian obsidian on coastal and island sites is that between Italy and the Balkans in the Neolithic (Forenbaher and Kaiser 1997; Forenbaher et al. 1992). People were travelling across the Adriatic in both directions and there are marked similarities between the southeastern Italian Neolithic and Balkan Neolithic, as discussed by Robin Skeates, amongst others (Skeates 1992). It has also been argued that the initial spread of the Neolithic may have followed this maritime route across the Adriatic into Italy, as evidenced by the initial spread of impressed wares (Price 2000).

A suggested crossing can be outlined in relation to the shortest distance, currents and winds and the presence of islands necessary for rest stops. It is known that comparable routes must actually have been used, as these islands – Tremitis, Palagruža and the Dalmatian islands – feature Neolithic sites with Liparian obsidian, showing not only that there was Neolithic activity in this region but also that these islands were within the obsidian exchange network (see Figures 2.1 and 2.2).

The distance of this entire crossing is approximately 100 nautical miles (NM) direct (185.2 km), although winds and currents would have affected the actual route. A crossing of this length would have necessitated

stopping at islands wherever possible; however, at a speed of around 2 knots (nautical miles per hour) (3.7 km/hour), a generous estimate for prehistoric vessels (based on Tzalas 1995), it would have taken anywhere between 24 and 60 hours, and possibly more, to have reached the mid-Adriatic island of Palagruža (Farr 2006).

The identification of prevailing wind directions in the Neolithic, drawn from Murray (1987), shows that prehistoric winds were similar to those of today. Whilst changes in coastal morphology due to rising sea levels, erosion, sedimentation and tectonic activity mean that the *local* coastal currents may have differed in the past, there has been no significant bathymetric change, so the direction and strength of prevailing major currents would have been similar to those today. This environmental information combined with a basic knowledge of the capabilities of Neolithic boats allows us to identify probable routes, and when this is combined with the archaeological evidence, the argument for these routes is strengthened.

When examining the number of hours it would have taken to cross the Adriatic in good conditions, the importance of islands such as Palagruža within the Neolithic world becomes clear. To be able to stop and rest at the mid-Adriatic island would have been a necessity; additionally, the island had a flint source that was utilized in the Neolithic (Bass 1998; Kaiser and Forenbaher 1999). Palagruža is today sometimes visible from the mainland but only in good conditions; even in the Neolithic, when it is thought that visibility would have been better because of lower levels of pollution, the island would not always have been visible from land. Without the ability to orient oneself whilst out of sight of land, and the ability to keep track of elapsed time and direction, this small island could not have been reached. Knowledge of the island's existence and the ability to navigate to it would have been of great value to seafarers crossing the Adriatic in the Neolithic and they would have relied on these geographical and temporal orientation skills.

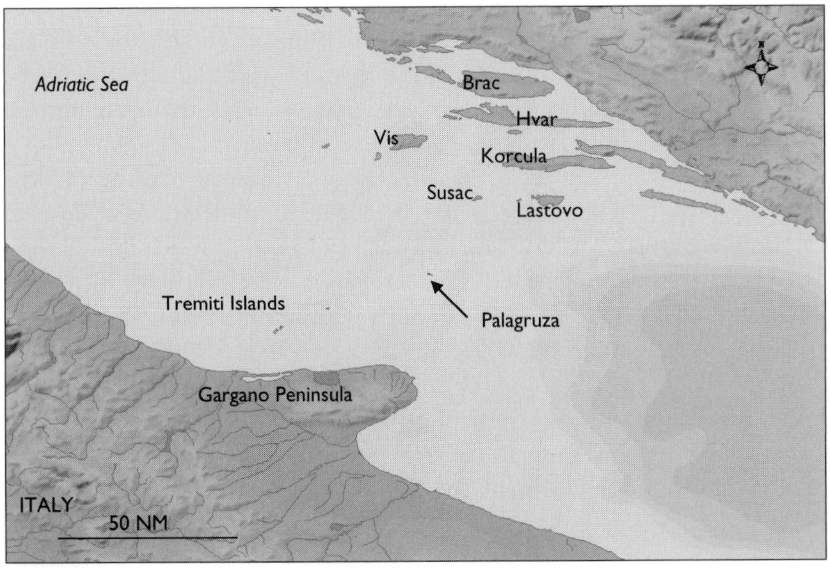

So we can say that the construction of boats in the Neolithic would have involved an understanding of measurement in terms of boat size, weight, displacement and thickness of hull. These are all critical measurements for building boats that would be able to cross 100 NM (185.2 km) of open water. The crossing itself would then have necessitated a conceptual understanding of space and distance, an understanding

Figure 2.1. Adriatic islands.

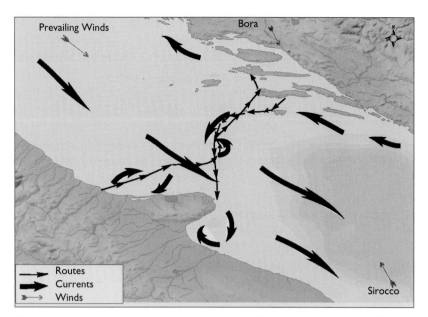

Figure 2.2. Likely routes taking into account prevailing winds, currents and location of islands.

of seasonality, affecting prevailing winds and currents, speed and directionality.

Understanding distance and orientation

Seafaring has been described as a specialist occupation; even in its simplest form it is a skill that requires knowledge on a number of different levels. What may be referred to as 'world' knowledge involves spatial and temporal awareness and a perception of one's place within a land and seascape. 'Local' knowledge, on the other hand, involves navigational lore, local weather and current conditions and knowledge of the location of resources and other social groups (Farr 2006).

Knowledge of the land and seascape would have been vital especially when traversing open water or when visibility was bad. Bourdieu (1980) used the concept of practical mastery theory to describe familiarity with practical space, which is subjective, as opposed to Cartesian space, which is objective (such as a map or a chart). With the practical mastery of space, knowledge could be passed between people and maintained through subjective oral traditions and collective memories. Mental maps of a sequence of memorized images or a chain of events could be recollected. Gell (1985), however, argues that this would be insufficient, as in order to be oriented to an external coordinate it is necessary to create a logical form of spatial knowledge, so that perceptual information and images can be matched with recalled spatial knowledge. In the case of navigation this includes knowledge of landscape and

seascape (which would include currents, prevailing winds and wave formations), lunar cycles, star courses and navigational lore to enable speed, drift and heading to be reckoned. These do not represent accurate reflections of position in terms of distance, but relative position with respect to recognizable conditions and locales. In the case of a prehistoric trans-Adriatic crossing, the notion of distance may not have been a unitary concept but tied to the idea of time passing and local knowledge of the sea.

Understanding elapsed time and celestial cycles

The question as to when to make an open water crossing in the Neolithic must have taken account of general prevailing weather conditions, but also seasonality, tides and currents.

Whilst the Mediterranean is not strongly tidal, there are tides and local currents that considerably affect small boats travelling at low speeds. The gravitational pull of the Sun and Moon causes the vertical rise and fall of the sea that constitute tides. As well as rising and falling twice daily, tides follow monthly and seasonal cycles governed by the Moon. When the Sun and Moon are in line with the Earth their combined gravitational pull creates very high and very low waters known as spring tides; these occur every 14 days at the time of the full and new moon. Spring tides also create stronger tidal streams, manifest as horizontal currents. The rest of the month when the Sun and Moon are at right angles to the Earth and the Moon is in the first and third quarters, neap tides occur. Neap tides are more moderate and are associated with weaker tidal streams.

Initially the effect of tide may seem to be of little relevance in the Mediterranean. In the Strait of Messina, however, the tidal stream can run at 6 knots during spring tides. This stretch of water between Sicily and Italy would have to have been negotiated for obsidian to reach the Adriatic in the Neolithic, which suggests that seafarers understood the cyclical rhythms of the tides and could calculate when to make a voyage. Neolithic seafaring in other parts of Europe such as the Orkney Isles, which have even stronger tides, would certainly have placed a great premium on such knowledge.

It is conceivable that people living on the coast, regularly taking to the water in small open boats, would be attuned to the rhythms of the daily and monthly cycles of tides and their effect on both land and sea. It is also likely that the relationship between the Moon and the sea and their cyclicality would be perceived. A general understanding of the tides, and thus lunar time, would have been necessary to at least a basic extent for the planning of prehistoric voyages.

Whilst at sea, perhaps the most important question after where you are *going* is where you *are* at the present time, and this relies on spatial awareness, local knowledge and navigational lore. Pilotage skills (when in coastal waters and in sight of land) and navigational knowledge (when in open water out of sight of land) would have been necessary. In addition to knowledge of the coastal landscape and island recognition, knowing where you are relies on a local knowledge of seascape and the cues that this provides: knowledge of prevailing wind directions and strength in certain locations, of sea state and water colour, reflecting depth and direction of current (tidal stream), wave height, wave length and direction, and cloud configurations, together with a host of other natural and environmental phenomena.

However, in calculating position by dead reckoning without the use of a chart, one must also be able to track the amount of time that has elapsed. As well as the spatial awareness required, temporal awareness is something that can be critical, and knowledge of Sun or star tracks helps the calculation of elapsed time (Irwin 1992; Kirch 2000). In addition to this, before one can calculate heading (i.e., in which direction to travel), lateral drift, a fairly invisible force when travelling in open waters at slow speeds, must be considered and compensated for (Figure 2.3).

Figure 2.3. Accounting for lateral drift. If the direct route (dot-and-dash arrow) were followed toward the island, the vessel would drift south along the route depicted by the dashed arrow. To reach the island successfully, drift would have to be compensated for and the route depicted by the dotted arrow followed.

Ethnographic accounts

Certain ethnographic case studies may help us to conceptualise different ways in which distance and time may have been conceived by seafaring populations without modern equipment. The Pacific has a long history of seafaring and open water navigation, and there is a wide collection of ethnographic accounts of nonliterate societies from which to draw.

The first evidence for seafaring is derived from the Flores Island hominids that appear to have evolved from *Homo erectus*. As Flores has always been separate from the Indonesian archipelago these hominids must have crossed a stretch of water to the island around 100,000 years ago. The first evidence for modern human seafaring comes from the dispersal of humans to Sahul (Pleistocene Australia-New Guinea) around 60,000 years ago and from New Guinea to Australia around 40,000 years ago. Subsequent island colonization included Japan and the Philippines (ca. 30,000 BP), Near Oceania (3,000 BP) and Far Oceania (2,000 BP) (Irwin 1992). According to Irwin's research on island colonization, the first exploration of the Pacific was navigationally systematic (Irwin 1989). This means that at an early date people were travelling upwind on outward explorations to ensure an easy return to the home island. This necessitated specific navigational knowledge. In his work, Turnbull has argued that this navigation involved neither writing nor mathematics but relied upon a profound understanding of the world (1991:3). Whilst it impossible to state that the navigation skills and practices that have been recorded in recent history are identical to those used in prehistory, it is certainly true that they can inform us of navigational techniques that are possible in nonliterate seafaring societies.

One basic navigational tool utilised across the Pacific to maintain heading and orientation is the star compass (Finney et al. 1986:43). The star compass is a conceptual compass envisaged upon the continuous circle of the horizon. To maintain heading and navigate whilst at sea known locales are marked by the rising and setting of key stars throughout the year. To do this the rising and setting of these stars and their relation to locales on or over the horizon need to be learnt by rote. It can take many years of formal tuition to learn this information.

In Micronesia, the knowledge of the stars was integrated with the skill of dead reckoning to form the Etak or Hatag system (Turnbull 1991:21). This system enabled the seafarers to calculate how far they had travelled, the effects of drift, wind and speed. Within this system, to maintain a sense of orientation, the canoe is perceived to be stationary whilst the land and seascape move around it over the duration of the voyage. When it is believed that the currents are creating lateral drift, or the boat is being blown off course, the canoe is then perceived as moving against the stationary sea or landscape (Turnbull 1991:23). This illustrates how a conception of space and orientation within the world that is very different from our own can underlie very successful navigation through a seascape.

Amongst the Marshall Islanders this dynamic spatial organisation of knowledge is combined with physical maps that correspond to local knowledge and environmental cues. The map is constructed from sticks, with ribs from coconut leaves used to illustrate predominant wind directions, currents and where these change; cowry shells are used to mark safe landing spots (Grant McCall personal communication 2005).

These examples illustrate the importance of both local and universal knowledge. This includes calendrical knowledge of time: the cyclicality of stars and how and when they rise and set throughout the year. This is combined with an understanding and measurement of elapsed time – the duration of trips and of distance travelled – which is necessary for dead reckoning, and the Etak and Hatag systems.

In terms of how ethnographic examples can inform our view of prehistoric seafaring, it becomes clear that the knowledge needed for navigation includes a perception and understanding of time as well as space and distance. This can be perceived in terms of tracking elapsed time, and cyclicality in terms of star courses and tides.

In nonliterate cultures with oral traditions it is important that this knowledge is maintained and transmitted accurately. This is achieved through narratives and metaphor, encoding knowledge in song, ritual, mnemonics and formal group learning (Gladwin 1970). For example, on Puluwat Atoll in the Caroline Islands, poetry was used to help understand and remember star courses. Learning was both informal and formal, each supporting and reiterating the other, and the training of a master navigator could take over 20 years (Gladwin 1970:126).

Such knowledge and its accurate transmission are sustained by tradition. Navigation on these islands is not achieved via an isolated body of knowledge but intrinsically attached to social organisation and economics. The maintenance of knowledge depends upon the maintenance of a society that values it. The young must remain on the islands and listen to their elders, learn the traditional stories and songs and practice the skills. In the past the Pacific Islanders depended on the connectivity between the islands, economically, socially and politically, and as such the master navigators became leaders with high social status (Gladwin 1970). Today, the

social, economic and political organisation of life on the islands is changing and islanders are less dependent on traditional navigation. As such these skills are being lost alongside traditional value systems.

There are, of course, many differences between ocean voyaging in the Pacific and seafaring in the Mediterranean. The distances between islands in the Pacific is much greater and the cloud coverage less because of the lack of nearby land, but the prevailing winds and sea swells are more constant. The majority of these voyages were undertaken in sailing canoes. In the prehistoric Mediterranean, where vessels were paddled across shorter stretches of open water with multidirectional local currents and circulating winds, the knowledge base would have had to have been different, yet it would not necessarily have been simpler. To navigate across 100 NM (185.2 km) of open water, out of sight of land, would have necessitated equivalent skills of navigation, orientation and training in the Neolithic to those required today.

Dynamic seascapes: Distance and time

So to return to the specifics of the prehistoric Adriatic, crossing from the Gargano peninsula to Palagruža and on to Croatia, and vice versa, prehistoric people must have had a good knowledge of the local environment and understanding of navigation. On making such a crossing one must take water current and prevailing wind direction and strength into account. An average current of 1 knot (1.852 km/hour) can be expected. This travels northwest up the Dalmatian coast and southeast down the center of the Adriatic and down the Italian coast, with variations around the Gargano peninsula and island of Palagruža (Figure 2.2). To a modern vessel traveling at 5 knots (9.26 km/hour) or more, this has only a slight effect; however, this is quite a considerable force if acting upon a vessel travelling at just shy of 2 knots (3.7 km/hour), which is the speed estimated for prehistoric vessels on the basis of Tzalas's trial of a papyrella (Tzalas 1995) and Broodbank's calculations for log boats (Broodbank 2000). When your vessel is travelling sideways at between half and the same speed as it is travelling forwards, a basic understanding of vectors and relative speed would have been necessary if any planned destination were ever to be reached. Lateral drift becomes obvious when in sight of land and must be compensated for; paddling directly towards an island in a straight line would result in a vessel's drifting off course. In the case of Palagruža the next landfall would be a considerable distance farther on – if at all (Figure 2.3).

An additional set of risk factors that must be compensated for are of bad weather or storms blowing up once out to sea. If the weather changed some hours into a journey there would be no chance of returning to shore. The Sirocco regularly blows in the summer months with strong hot winds, whilst the Bora can blow from the northeast with fierce cold winds funneling down the Adriatic at speeds of up to 60 knots. Both these winds produce bad weather and can last for several days at a time. For a small paddled vessel the risks of being blown off course or being swamped by large swells and choppy water would have been considerable.

Even without extreme conditions, when travelling by boat one is constantly subject to forces affecting motion in a number of directions simultaneously, in contrast to land travel. The boat is constantly drifting with the current and being pushed by the wind; therefore, unless these are both in the direction in which one wishes to travel, it is not possible to stop and rest. On land, it is possible for a journey to be broken into any number of increments, and, therefore, archaeologically, the temporality of the journey is difficult to decipher. Crossing open water, however, the temporality of the journey is clear. The journey has its own impetus. Seafaring is an immediate and dynamic activity, and success would have been reliant on the crew's working together in close co-operation, sharing skills and knowledge, as well as the risk. The sociality of seafaring as process, therefore, would lead to the creation of relationships and identity amongst Neolithic seafarers; it is possible that this led to, or at least contributed to, the particular value that was placed upon certain raw materials that were transported by sea, including obsidian.

Conclusions

Through an analysis of early seafaring we can identify key abilities that must have been possessed by Neolithic populations directly related to quantification and an understanding of their world. They clearly had the ability to conceptualize and plan journeys temporally and spatially, and to reach specific locales successfully, even when out of sight of land, using core navigational skills.

A temporal awareness may be gauged on a number of different levels, from the perception of elapsed time, perceived through star and Sun positions, to an awareness of the tides and currents, from the daily ebb and flow to the monthly highs and lows. This in turn may have been understood to relate to lunar cycles, a connection that would have enabled forward planning. Equally, an appreciation of drift and the ability to judge position with dead reckoning are predicated upon an understanding of the relationship between time and distance in the active maritime environment, perhaps including a notion of speed.

Within the maritime landscape the perception and experience of time and space are interlinked as the seascape has its own dynamic temporality. The manner in which Neolithic seafarers conceived of and engaged with this dynamic relationship may have influenced their understanding of distance and time in other spheres of activity. In terms of how prehistoric people used this information to form an understanding of the world in general, perhaps we can argue that it reveals an awareness of the connectivity of abstract measures with universal cycles and cosmology. These connections and rhythms and the risks inherent in seafaring have habitually led to the construction of associated beliefs and rituals; accounts of journeys by boat have often been used as metaphors for life or the beginning or end of time. Perhaps then it is possible to begin to see how these belief systems became necessary as a means of ordering and defining knowledge of the world.

ACKNOWLEDGEMENTS

I would like to thank the Arts and Humanities Research Council (AHRC) for supporting my research. Furthermore, I would like to thank Dr. John Robb, Dr. Jonathan Adams, Dr. Fraser Sturt and the Centre for Maritime Archaeology at Roskilde, Denmark, for providing such inspiration.

NOTE

1. Traditionally the term 'journey' should be reserved for travel across land, whilst 'voyage' refers to maritime travel. However, the term 'voyage' holds many modern connotations that are unnecessary in this discussion.

REFERENCES

Ammerman, A. J. 1985. *The Acconia Survey: Neolithic Settlement and the Obsidian Trade.* Occasional Publication no. 10. London: Institute of Archaeology.

Bass, B. 1998. Early Neolithic Offshore Accounts: Remote Islands, Maritime Exploitations, and the Trans-Adriatic Cultural Network. *Journal of Mediterranean Archaeology* **11**:165–190.

Blue, L., E. Kentley, S. McGrail, and U. Mishra. 1997. The Patia Fishing Boat of Orissa: A Case Study in Ethnoarchaeology. *South Asian Studies* **13**:189–207.

Bourdieu, P. 1980. *The Logic of Practice.* Stanford, California: Stanford University Press.

Broodbank, C. 1999. Colonization and Configuration in the Insular Neolithic of the Aegean, in *Neolithic Society in Greece, Sheffield Studies in Aegean Archaeology.* Edited by P. Halstead. Sheffield: Sheffield Academic Press.

Broodbank, C. 2000. *An Island Archaeology of the Early Cyclades.* Cambridge: Cambridge University Press.

Castagnino Berlinghieri, E. F. 2003. The Aeolian Islands: Crossroads of Mediterranean Maritime Routes. A Survey on Their Maritime Archaeology and Topography from the Prehistoric to the Roman Periods. Vol. 1181. *BAR International Series 1181.* Oxford: Archaeopress.

Farr, R. H. 2001. *Cutting through Water: An Analysis of Neolithic Obsidian from Bova Marina, Calabria.* MA Dissertation, University of Southampton.

Farr, R. H. 2006. Seafaring as social action. *Journal of Maritime Archaeology* 1:85–89.

Finney, B. R., B. J. Kilonsky, S. Somsen, and E. D. Stroup. 1986. Relearning a Vanishing Art. *Journal of the Polynesian Society* 95:41–90.

Forenbaher, S., and T. Kaiser 1997. Palagruža: Jadrnanski Moreplovci I Njihova Kamena Industjia na Prijelazu iz Bakrenog u Broncano doba. *Opuscola Archaeologica* 21:15–28.

Forenbaher, S., et al. 1992. *A Preliminary Report of the Adriatic Islands Project (Contact, Commerce and Colonization 6000BC–600AD).* Vjesnik Arheoloskog Muzeja u Zagreba 86.

Fugazzola Delpino, M. A. 2002. "La Marmotta," in *Le Ceramiche impresse nel Neolitico antico. Italia e Mediterraneo., Studi di Paletnologia, Collana del Bulletino di Paletnologia Italiana.* Edited by M. A. Fugazzola Delpino, A. Pessina, V. Tiné, 374–395. Roma: Istituto poligrafico e Zecca dello Stato.

Fugazzola Delpino, M. A., G. D'Eugenio, and A. Pessina. 1993. "La Marmotta" (Anguillara Sabazia, RM): Scavi 1989 – un abitato perilacustre di età Neolitica. *Bullettino di Paletnologia Italiana* 84:181–342.

Fugazzola Delpino, M. A., and M. Mineo 1995. La piroga Neolitica del Lago di Bracciano, La Marmotta 1. *Bullettino di Paletnologia Italiano (Rome)* 86:197–266.

Gell, A. 1985. Cognitive Maps of Time and Tide. *Man (N.S)* 20:271–286.

Gladwin, T. 1970. *East Is a Big Bird: Navigation and Logic on Puluwat Atoll.* Cambridge, Massachusetts: Harvard University Press.

Helms, M. W. 1988. *Ulysses' Sail: An Ethnographic Odyssey of Power, Knowledge and Geographical Distance.* Princeton, New Jersey: Princeton University Press.

Irwin, G. 1989. Against, across and down the Wind: A Case for the Systematic Exploration of the Remote Pacific Islands. *Journal of the Polynesian Society* 98:167–206.

Irwin, G. J. 1992. *The Prehistoric Exploration and Colonization of the Pacific,* 1st edition. Cambridge: Cambridge University Press.

Johnstone, P. 1980. *The Sea Craft of Prehistory.* London: Routledge and Kegan Paul.

Kaiser, T., and S. Forenbaher. 1999. Adriatic Sailors and Stone Knappers: Palagruža in the 3rd Millenium BC. *Antiquity* 73:313–24.

Kirch, P. V. 2000. *On the Road of the Winds.* Berkeley: University of California Press.

Lambeck, K. 1996. Sea-Level Change and Shore-Line Evolution in Aegean Greece since Upper Palaeolithic Time. *Antiquity* 70:588–611.

McGrail, S. 1987. *Ancient Boats in North West Europe: The Archaeology of Water Transport to AD 1500.* London: Longman.

Morhange, C., J. Laborel, and A. Hesnard. 2001. Changes of Relative Sea-Level during the Past 5000 Years in the Ancient Harbour of Marseilles, Southern France. *Palaeogeography, Palaeoclimatology, Palaeoecology* 166:319–329.

Murray, W. M. 1987. Do Modern Winds Equal Ancient Winds? *Mediterranean Historical Review* 2:139–167.

Pirazzoli, P. A. 1991. *A World Atlas of Holocene Sea-Level Changes. Oceanography Series:* Vol. 58. Amsterdam: Elsevier.

Pirazzoli, P. A. 1998. *Sea-Level Changes: The Last 20,000 Years.* John Wiley & Sons.

Price, T. D. 2000. Editor. *Europe's First Farmers.* Cambridge: Cambridge University Press.

Renfrew, C. 1975. Trade as Action at a Distance: Questions of Integration and Communication, in *Ancient Civilisation and Trade.* Edited by J. A. Sabloff and C. Lamberg-Karlovsky, 3–59. Albuquerque: University of New Mexico Press.

Robb, J., and R. H. Farr. 2005. Substances in Motion: Neolithic Mediterranean "Trade", in *The Archaeology of Mediterranean Prehistory.* Edited by E. Blake and A. B. Knapp, 24–46. Malden, Massachusetts: Blackwell.

Shackley, M. S. 1998. Editor. *Archaeological Obsidian Studies, Method and Theory.* Vol. 3. *Advances in Archaeological and Museum Sciences.* New York: Plenum Press.

Skeates, R. 1992. Neolithic Exchange in Central and Southern Italy, in *Trade and Exchange in Prehistoric Europe – Proceedings of a Conference Held at the University of Bristol, April 1992.* Edited by C. Scarre and F. Healy. Oxbow Books in association with the Prehistoric Society and Société Préhistorique Française.

Turnbull, D. 1991. *Mapping the World in the Mind: An Investigation of the Unwritten Knowledge of the Micronesian Navigators.* Geelong: Deakin University Press.

Tzalas, H. 1995. On The Obsidian Trail: With a Papyrus Craft in the Cyclades, in *Tropis III. 3rd International Symposium on Ship Construction in Antiquity.* Vol. 3. Edited by H. Tzalas, 441–471. Athens.

Ushijima, I. 2000. Editor. *Bisayan Knowledge Movement and Identity: Visayas Maritime Anthropological Studies.* Third World Studies Centre. University of the Philippines.

Whitten, D. G. A., and J. R. V. Brooks. 1972. *The Penguin Dictionary of Geology.* Penguin Books.

Williams-Thorpe, O. 1995. Review Article: Obsidian in the Mediterranean and the Near East: A Provenancing Success Story. *Archaeometry* 37:217–248.

3

The token system of the ancient Near East: Its role in counting, writing, the economy and cognition

Denise Schmandt-Besserat

Figure 3.1. Pictographic tablet from Godin Tepe, Iran, ca. 3100 BC. The account features 33 units of oil. (Courtesy Cuyler Young, Jr.)

This chapter deals with a system of counters – clay tokens – used for over 4,000 years in the prehistoric Near East (7500–3100 BC). Relying on a database of some 8,000 tokens from Turkey, Syria, Jordan, Israel, Iraq and Iran (Schmandt-Besserat 1992, I & II), I discuss the evolution of the token system, the method of counting it implies and how it led to writing and abstract numbers (Butterworth 1999, 29–32; Rogers 2005, 81–84). Lastly, in the light of the token system, I address the relation of counting and measurements to the economy and to cognition.

Tokens and pictographic writing

Before starting my discussion I explain how the Mesopotamian pictographic and cuneiform scripts are critical to understanding the token system (Schmandt-Besserat 1996).

During the first 500 years following its invention about 3200 BC, writing in Mesopotamia was used exclusively for accounting (Cooper 2004, 72). The tablets served a city state administration scrupulously to record entries and expenditures of goods in the temple and palace. The first Mesopotamian script featured two kinds of signs: impressed signs stood for numerals and signs traced with a stylus represented the goods accounted (Figure 3.1). As is explained later, both of these types of signs, impressed and traced, were images or 'pictographs' of small counters, that is, tokens previously used for record keeping. Some of the pictographs can be understood by matching them to the cuneiform signs that derived from them. The pictographs therefore constitute a 'Rosetta Stone' to decipher the age-old token system. For example, the third millennium cuneiform sign for 'oil' can be traced backwards to the fourth millennium

pictograph in the shape of an ovoid with a line at the largest diameter. In turn the pictograph can be matched to earlier ovoid tokens with a line around the maximal diameter (Figure 3.2).

Plain tokens

Tokens appeared in the Fertile Crescent about 7500 BC. They are about 1 or 2 cm across, modeled in clay in different shapes, among them cones, spheres, cylinders, disks, tetrahedrons and ovoids (Figure 3.3). At sites such as Mureybet in Syria, the earliest tokens belong to the archaeological layer marking the beginning of agriculture (Mureybet III), showing that counting and accounting first began when survival depended upon cultivating and hoarding staple goods such as barley (Cauvin 1978, 73–74 and 43). By the seventh and until the end of the fourth millennium BC, the token system was used in a vast region of the Near East including present-day Turkey, Syria, Jordan, Israel, Iraq and Iran. During these 4,000 years the tokens showed no change in manufacture, material, shape and size. Among the more frequently used shapes were small and large cones as well as small and large spheres standing for four different units of barley, cylinders representing animals of the flocks and small and large tetrahedrons standing for labour.

Complex tokens

In the middle of the fourth millennium BC, coinciding with cities, state formation, and the development of workshops, the token system grew more complex. The number of shapes of tokens multiplied to include parabolae, rectangles, triangles and some in the form of miniature vessels, tools and furniture (Figure 3.4). Also,

Token	Pictograph	Neo-Sumerian/ Old Babylonian	Neo-Assyrian	Neo-Babylonian	English
					Sheep
					Cattle
					Dog
					Metal
					Oil
					Garment
					Bracelet
					Perfume

Figure 3.2. Correspondence between cuneiform signs, pictographs and tokens. (Courtesy *Archaeology* **32** [4] 22.)

markings in the form of incised lines proliferated on the face of the counters, bringing the number of token subtypes to over 300. Whereas the earlier plain tokens dealt mostly with products of the farm, such as barley and domesticated animals, the complex Early Bronze Age tokens were concerned with finished products such as bread, oil, honey or perfume; imports such as metal; and manufactured goods such as textiles and garments.

Tokens and counting

The different token shapes used to count various specific commodities bring to mind 'concrete counting', an

archaic technique of counting that was still prevalent in the early third millennium BC in Mesopotamia and is still practiced today in various parts of the world (Diakonoff 1983, 88). Concrete counting is characterized by different sets of number words – numerations – to count different items. Sets of words of our own vocabulary, such as 'twin, triplet, quadruplet' or 'solo, duo, trio, quartet' referring to children of a common birth and groupings of musicians, may help explain the concept of concrete counting. Namely, a word like 'solo' fuses together two concepts, 'one' and 'musician', without any possibility of separating them. The same was true for tokens. For example, one ovoid token (Figure 3.5) stood for 'one jar

Figure 3.3. Plain tokens from Tepe Gawra, Iraq, ca. 5000 BC. (Courtesy Denise Schmandt-Besserat.)

Figure 3.5. Ovoid tokens standing for jars of oil, from Girsu, Iraq, ca. 3300 BC. (Courtesy Musée du Louvre, Département des Antiquités Orientales.)

was expressed in one-to-one correspondence. Three jars of oil were represented by three ovoid tokens – literally 'one jar of oil', 'one jar of oil', 'one jar of oil'. The token system illustrates therefore a technique of counting fundamentally different from ours. There were no tokens to express 'one', 'two' and 'three', independently of what was being counted. But instead, as is typical of concrete counting, each token type counted exclusively a specific category of items: ovoids could count only jars of oil and jars of oil could only be counted with ovoids.

The envelopes

About 3500 BC, at the time of state formation, envelopes in the shape of round, hollow balls of clay were invented to store tokens in archives. The clay envelopes were a convenient way to keep together groups of tokens representing a transaction. The envelopes were particularly well suited to the Near Eastern administration because they provided a clay surface where seals could be applied. Indeed, each of the 150 envelopes recovered from Turkey, Syria, Jordan, Iraq and Iran bears the imprints of between one and four different seals that, according to Enrica Fiandra (1979, 36–38), may have represented various levels of the Mesopotamian bureaucracy.

The envelopes prompted a turning point in data processing when accountants pressed the tokens onto the surface of the envelopes to make their shape and number visible from outside after the envelope was sealed. The three-dimensional tokens were reduced to two-dimensional markings – the first signs of writing. Envelopes, such as that of Habuba Kabira (Figure 3.6), showing on the outside the impressions of the seven ovoid tokens (= seven jars of oil) which were found still inside when it was excavated, are precious in providing evidence that complex tokens were still handled in one-to-one correspondence in 3200 BC. The seven ovoid markings pressed on the outside of the envelope shared therefore the same value as that of the seven ovoid tokens inside. Consequently, it may be concluded that concrete counting was still practiced at the time of the invention of writing.

It is interesting to note that from the beginning, the markings on the envelopes were laid out according to a

Figure 3.4. Complex tokens from Uruk, Iraq, ca. 3300 BC. (Courtesy Vorderasiatische Museum, Berlin.)

of oil' without the possibility of splitting up the notion of number 'one' with the notion of the object counted, 'jar of oil'. Because these two types of information could not be abstracted from each other, numerosity

Figure 3.7. Impressed tablet showing three wedges = three small measures of grain and two circular signs = two larger measures of grain, from Godin Tepe, Iran, ca. 3100 BC. (Courtesy Cuyler Young, Jr.)

Figure 3.6. Envelope from Habuba Kabira, ca. 3300 BC, with ovoid impressed markings. (Courtesy Museum für Vor- und Fruegeschichte, Berlin.)

Figure 3.8. Mesopotamian grain measure (Schmandt-Besserat 1992, 151).

standardized format. They were set in straight lines, each line featuring only one kind of sign repeated as many times as needed. For example, a line of circular signs is followed by a line of wedges. The lines of signs were arranged in hierarchical order. Namely, the signs representing the largest units of merchandise were placed on the uppermost line, followed by lines representing lesser units in descending order. It is noteworthy that this strict format was to govern the order and direction of the signs of writing for centuries to come.

The archaic impressed tablets

The envelopes had a relatively short duration of use because, once writing was established, the tokens inside the envelopes were no longer useful. Within three centuries, therefore, the envelopes were replaced by solid balls of clay bearing the impressed markings of tokens. These were the first Mesopotamian impressed tablets.

The accounts presented on the some 250 known Syrian, Mesopotamian and Elamite impressed texts were identical to those on envelopes, showing the continuity between the two types of artifacts (Figure 3.7) (Nissen, Damerow and Englund 1993, 127–128). The signs on the tablets, like the markings on the envelopes, pictured tokens and continued to exclusively feature units of goods. Among the most frequent markings (Figure 3.8), a wedge, standing for a cone token, represented one small unit of barley (probably equivalent to a Mesopotamian *ban* and a modern litre); a circular marking, standing for a sphere token, represented one medium unit of barley (equivalent to the Mesopotamian *bariga*, or a modern

bushel); a long wedge standing for a cylinder token represented one domesticated animal. The number of units of goods was still shown in one-to-one correspondence: one wedge = one small unit of barley; two wedges = two small units of barley. Consequently, it can be safely assumed that, by the time of the impressed tablets, the system of counting was still concrete.

The pictographic tablets

Several thousand of the so-called pictographic tablets, dated to about 3100 BC, were excavated in Uruk, Iraq, as well as a small number of sites including Godin Tepe, Iran. The sketched pictographs initiated a new technique of writing that departed from the impressing token; namely, the images of tokens were traced on the tablet with a stylus. The pictographic tablets, however, signified far more than just representing tokens more clearly. The fact that pictographs, such as that standing for 'jar of oil', were never repeated in one-to-one correspondence signals a radical change in counting. The sign for 'jar of oil' was preceded by numerals – signs for 1, 10 and 60 (Figure 3.1) The numerals were indicated by the former signs for measures of barley carrying a new abstract meaning:

- The impressed wedge stood for '1'.
- '10' was an impressed circular marking.
- '60' was a large wedge.

Abstract numbers

Pictography thus marks the extraordinary event when the concept of number was abstracted from that of the item counted. As a result, writing and counting could evolve in separate ways, generating two parallel and complementary sign systems. It was also momentous in overcoming one-to-one correspondence, which had governed counting during the entire token era. This meant a great economy of signs: 33 jars of oil were expressed by seven signs (3 x 10 + 3 x 1 + 'oil') – instead of 33 signs (Figures 3.1 and 3.5)

Of course, the process of abstraction of numbers spun by pictography was to take many steps and many centuries to be fully realized (Justus 1999a). It is clear that, at the pictographic stage, the commodity counted still determined the arithmetic value of numerical signs. For example, when animals were being counted the circular sign signified '10' whereas it was to be read '6' when it referred to measures of grain. Also the relation between measuring units varied with the kind of entities dealt with. For example, the units of grain (*ban, bariga* etc.) followed a sequence of factors: 5, 6, 10, 3 (Figure 3.8), compared to 6, 3, 10, and 6 for the units of area measures (*ikus, eshe*3, *bur* etc.). Moreover, one-to-one correspondence was still clinging on in order to express the number of units and of 10s: 33 jars of oil were expressed by three 10s (three circular signs) and three units (three wedges) (Figure 3.1)

Counting and writing

In the light of the evolution of counting, the origin of writing can be viewed as a by-product of the abstraction of numbers. Namely, the split between the notion of numerosity and that of the item being counted created the necessity for two systems of recording. From this point on, numerals and counted items were recorded by different types of signs: numerals were impressed whereas the signs identifying the counted items were traced. Far more importantly, the two types of signs evolved separately: numerals, like the tokens, remained logographic and continued to be used in one-to-one correspondence. In contrast, writing severed all ties with the tokens by emulating language. New pictographic phonetic signs were created about 3000 BC and by 2700 BC the cuneiform writing emulated the syntax of speech. Writing was no longer confined to accounting real goods. Only then was it able to be applied to topics dealing with intangibles as well as tangibles, concerning the world and beyond.

What is critical is that it is archaeology, rather than philology, that provides us with the means of tracing the origins of writing. Some philologists have taken the view that such a focus on material culture is not warranted, but the evidence for "tokenism", as Michalowski (1993) puts it, is substantial. First, the quantity of data itself is considerable: thousands of tokens, 200 envelopes and 240 impressed tablets. Second, the evidence for the evolution from tokens to writing leaves no gap: each transitional phase is copiously illustrated. Namely, the plain tokens continue through the phase of complex tokens; there are as many as 19 marked envelopes; and the impressed markings go on with no discontinuity through the pictographic stage. Other criticism, based on the small number of complex tokens of particular subtypes (Zimansky 1993, 516), misses the important point that exactly the same types and subtypes have been excavated in such distant sites as Uruk and Girsu in Mesopotamia, Susa and Chogha Mish in Elam and Habuba Kabira and Jebel Aruda in Syria. Whether each site yields 1 token or 100 tokens of each subtype reveals the same significant information: all these fourth millennium city states were administered using the same token system that immediately preceded and led to writing. Such a conclusion is recognized by the vast majority of fourth millennium experts including, to name only a few, Algaze (1993, 15, 39); Englund (2004, 119–122); Frangipane, Ferioli, Fiandra (2007, 22 and 114); Friberg (2007, 282); and Liverani (2006, 54–55)

Tokens and the economy

The prehistoric and protohistoric Near East practiced a redistribution economy that could not have functioned without counting and accounting. Tokens and tablets were necessary to keep track of entries and expenditures in the community warehouses. Vice versa, counting and accounting evolved in order to serve an ever more complex management of the communal goods.

The third millennium cuneiform economic tablets of Girsu make it clear that a major part of the Mesopotamian redistribution economy consisted of 'gifts to the gods'. These offerings in kind, featuring grain, animals, dairy products, fish, jewelry, textile, tools and so on, were supplied by the community on a monthly basis on the occasion of religious festivals (Rosengarten 1960, 251–301). The Girsu tablets also make it clear that the 'gifts to the gods' were strictly regulated. High officials were expected to give one yearling a month, fishermen were required to deliver a given number of baskets of fish and so forth. In other words, in our own vocabulary, the 'gifts to the gods' were taxes.

Proceeding backwards in time, the fourth millennium archaic pictographic tablets functioned in addition as the receipts of temple offerings, which were also strictly regulated. The festival of 'Princely Inanna' at Uruk called for offerings of quantities of dairy products, bread and wool, whereas that of 'Evening Inanna', in a different season, required delivering domesticated animals and tools (Szarzynska 1997, 115–140). Again, the efficient system of pooling together the economic surplus of the society could not have functioned without keeping track of those who had delivered the required dues and those who had not.

Contrary to a common assumption, there is no evidence that tokens or pictographic tablets were ever used in trade. Because early trade was based on barter it required no counting or measurements. The first economic tablet relating to commerce is dated to the Akkadian period in the middle of the third millennium BC. On the other hand, the complex tokens of the fourth millennium BC excavated in the precinct of Inanna at Uruk dealt with the same types of merchandise, in the same quantities as those featured on the pictographic tablets. Consequently, they can safely be considered to have been used to keep a record of temple offerings. In fact, the complex tokens, mostly standing for manufactured goods, may be viewed as marking the period when crafts and workshops started being taxed on their production.

The original function of the token system has to be left to theory. However, because its role, and that of the following pictographic tablets, was consistently and exclusively administrative, it is likely that from the start, tokens were the backbone of the incipient Near Eastern economy of redistribution. The tokens made it possible for the headmen of agricultural communities to control the pooling of communal goods and their redistribution.

In turn the redistribution economy dominated counting and accounting and thereby determined the evolution of the administrative devices. Only a few token shapes were necessary when the required offerings were limited to agricultural products. The forms of tokens multiplied when taxes were levied on industrial products. Finally, concrete counting was supplanted by abstract counting when the large amounts of goods dealt with by a city state administration could no longer be handled by tokens in one-to-one correspondence.

Measurements

It is likely that, in the ancient Near East, measurements were also tied to the levy of 'the gifts to the gods'. Standard measurements were increasingly necessary to regulate and enforce the delivery of specific quantities of goods by an ever larger and diverse community.

The evolution of weight and measures may include the following stages:

1. Casual daily life items such as our present-day 'mug' or 'carafe'.
2. The standardization of these units: the size of containers becomes uniform; the king's foot becomes the standard unit of length for a community.
3. The different units of a same commodity become multiples of one another: a large basket = 10 small baskets, a foot = 12 inches.

The Near Eastern tokens 7500–3500 BC seem to correspond to the first stage, when measures consisted of casual daily life containers. Nothing in the archaeological record suggests that containers such as pottery jars and flasks were standardized.

The beveled-rim bowls common from Syria to Iran during the Uruk period, 3500–3000 BC, may provide the first evidence for the standardization of units of capacity. The crude pottery vessels, thought to serve for the daily distribution of food rations to male and female temple/palace dependents, were molded in two main sizes, which, according to T. W. Beale (1978, 291–292), were each of consistent capacity.

The calibration of units as multiples of one another did not take place before 3100–3000 BC. This is evidenced by a tablet from Jebel Aruda, Syria, ca. 3200 BC, showing 3 large impressed wedges followed by 22 circular signs (= 3 large measures of barley + 22 medium measures of barley). The tablet shows that each type of unit was still counted separately. In other words, the third millennium relation 1 large wedge = 6 circular signs was not yet established (Justus 2004, 24; 1999b, 226; Englund 1998, 118).

One should not forget that the standardization of weights and measures occurred very slowly in the Near East. In the first millennium BC Mesopotamian cities such as Babylon and Assur still had their own 'cubit' to measure length. One of King Darius's greatest achievements was to give some uniformity to the weights and measures within the Persian Empire.

Tokens and cognition

The greatest significance of the token system was probably its impact on human cognition. Tokens were symbols of goods. They introduced new ways of handling merchandise in abstraction. Accounting with tokens abstracted the data from context. Furthermore, the manipulation of tokens using patterning, such as columns and lines, helped to abstract data such as entries and expenditures, the relative value of products and finally the abstraction of numbers.

With ovoid tokens, jars of oil could be counted in abstraction. It did not matter whether the quantities of oil were already produced or planned for the future, their location in storage or in transit, whether they were owned or owed.

With the use of patterning or the presentation of data in particular configuration the many variables of a large budget could be easily abstracted. The tokens of multiple shapes could be arranged in columns abstracting the types of merchandise, entries, expenditures, surplus or debts, donors or recipients.

The tokens also provided strategies by which to abstract the relative value of merchandize. Tokens of the same kind could be organized in lines. These lines could be organized hierachically with the larger units above the lesser ones (presaging the layout of markings on the envelopes and tablets).

Because they were small objects, easy to manipulate, tokens facilitated counting. They made it easy to add, subtract, multiply and divide by manually moving and removing counters. In turn, the visualization of two tokens added to two tokens, and three tokens to three tokens, and so on, no doubt contributed to the conceptualization of abstract numbers (Justus 1999b, 56, 64; Hoyrup 1994, 70).

Conclusion

In much the same way that geological and archaeological evidence disproves the notion that the world was created in a week, it also gives the lie to the notion that writing was created in a day (*contra* Michalowski 1993, 998). It took millions of years to shape the world, and writing emerged from an evolution of over four millennia, starting when the Near Eastern redistribution economy gave rise to a system of counting, and accounting, to control the production of real goods. These tokens, created in an oral world when information was exchanged face to face, by word of mouth, revolutionized data communication by being extra-somatic. The tokens made it possible to visualize and manipulate numerosity, and as a result, they were instrumental in the evolution from concrete to abstract counting and were responsible for the evolution of record keeping from three-dimensional counters to writing.

REFERENCES

Algaze, G., 1993. *The Uruk World System*. Chicago: University of Chicago Press.

Beale, T. W., 1978. Beveled Rim Bowls and Their Implications for Change and Economic Organization in the Later Fourth Millennium B.C. *Journal of Near Eastern Studies* **37** (4) 289–313.

Butterworth, B., 1999. *The Mathematical Brain*. Oxford: Macmillan.

Cauvin, J., 1978. *Les Premiers Villages de Syrie-Palestine du IXeme au VIIeme Millenaire avant J.C.* Lyon: Maison de l'Orient.

Cooper, J. S., 2004. Babylonian Beginnings: The Origin of the Cuneiform Writing System in Comparative Perspective, in *The First Writing*, ed. S. D. Houston. Cambridge: Cambridge University Press, 71–99.

Diakonoff, I. M., 1983. Some Reflexions on Numerals in Sumerian towards a History of Mathematical Speculations. *Journal of the American Oriental Society* **103** (1) 78–98.

Englund, R. K., 1998. Texts from the Late Uruk Period, in *Mesopotamian Spaeturuk-Zeit und Fruedynastische Zeit*, eds. Josef Bauer, Robert K. Englund and Manfred Krebernik (Orbis Biblicus et Orientalis, 160/1). Freiburg Schweiz: Universitaetsverlag, 15–217.

Englund, R. K. 2004. The State of Decipherment of Proto-Elamite, in *The First Writing*, ed. Stephen D. Houston. Cambridge: Cambridge University Press, 100–149.

Fiandra, E., 1979. The Connection between Clay Sealings and Tablets in the Administration, in *South Asian Archaeology 1979*, ed. H. Hartel. Berlin: Dietrich Reimer Verlag, 29–43.

Frangipane, M., Ferioli, P., Fiandra, E., et al., 2007. *Arslantepe Cretulae: An Early Centralized Administrative System before Writing*. Roma: Universita di Roma La Sapienza, Edizione CIRAAS.

Friberg, J., 2007. *A Remarkable Collection of Babylonian Texts*. New York: Springer.

Goody J., 1977. *The Domestication of the Savage Mind*. Cambridge: Cambridge University Press.

Hoyrup J., 1994. *In Measure, Number, and Weight*. Albany: State University of New York Press.

Justus, C., 1999a. Pre-decimal Structures in Counting and Metrology, in *Numeral Types and Changes Worldwide*, ed. Jaranda Gvozdanovic. Berlin: Mouton de Gruyter, 55–79.

Justus, C., 1999b. Can a Counting System Be an Index of Linguistic Relationship? *Journal of Indo-European Studies*, Monograph **33**, 219–240.

Justus, C., 2004. On Language and the Rise of a Base for Counting. *General Linguistics* **42**, 17–43.

Liverani, M., 2006. *Uruk, the First City*. London: Equinox.

Michalowski, P., 1993. Tokenism. *American Anthropologist* **95** (4) 996–999.

Nissen, H. J., Damerow, P., and Englund, R. K., 1993. *Archaic Bookkeeping*. Chicago: University of Chicago Press.

Olson, D. R., 1980. Introduction, in *The Social Foundation of Language and Thought*, ed. D. R. Olson. New York: W. W. Norton.

Rogers, H., 2005. *Writing Systems: A Linguistic Approach.* London: Blackwell.

Rosengarten, Y., 1960. *Le Concept sumerien de consummation dans la vie economique et religieuse.* Paris: Editions E. de Boccard.

Schmandt-Besserat, D., 1992. *Before Writing. Vol. I, From Counting to Cuneiform.* Austin: University of Texas Press.

Schmandt-Besserat, D., 1992. *Before Writing. Vol. II, A Catalogue of Near Eastern Tokens.* Austin: University of Texas Press.

Schmandt-Besserat, D., 1996. *How Writing Came About.* Austin: University of Texas Press.

Szarzynska, K., 1997. *Sumerica* (Philologia Orientalis). Warszawa: Wydawnictwo Akademickie, Dialog.

Zimansky, P., 1993. Book review of *Before Writing. Journal of Field Archaeology* **20** (4) 513–517.

4

Grasping the concept of number: How did the sapient mind move beyond approximation?

Lambros Malafouris

Introduction

When and how did humans begin to count? Where does arithmetic come from? Are humans innately endowed with arithmetical abilities or is human numerical cognition a strictly cultural achievement? To a large extent the answers to the preceding questions depend upon how precisely we define human numerical cognition and arithmetical abilities.

If by numerical cognition we refer to the property of *approximation* – that is, the capacity for a basic appreciation of changes in quantity and a simple number sense (oneness, twoness, and threeness) – then several lines of evidence in contemporary cognitive neurosciences clearly support the view that this can be considered to be an evolved, innate biological competence shared by human infants and other animals. For example, a number of studies show that both preverbal infants and animals are able to detect numerocities, discriminating between small sets of objects or sequences of sounds both within, but also beyond, the so-called subitizing range (up to three or four objects) (Antell & Keating 1983; Wynn 1996; Davis & Pérusse 1988; Brannon & Terrace 1998; 2000; 2002; Biro & Matsuzawa 2001) – provided that in the latter case the comparison ratios are large enough (i.e., infants were able to discriminate 8 from 16, but not 8 from 12 items) (Xu & Spelke 2000; Lipton & Spelke 2003). More characteristic might be the finding that infants as young as five months old (Wynn 1992), but also untrained rhesus monkeys, seem to have additive and subtractive expectations when they observe or choose between arrays containing small number of objects.

However, if by arithmetic abilities we are referring to the possession of a concept of number – that is, the ability to manipulate large *exact numerocities* beyond the subitizing range of three or four mentioned – then matters appear to be far more complicated. I should clarify that numerocity (or cardinality) refers to the size of a set. The ability to understand exact numerocities means that you can answer the questions 'How many?' and 'How much?', which presupposes/involves also an awareness that each numerocity N has a unique successor N + 1 (see Nieder 2005; Gelman & Butterworth 2005, 6).

Although most people today take the notion of abstract number for granted, we should not forget the mental leap required to go from counting specific things (concrete counting) to the abstract concept of number as a representation of quantity. In fact, this mental leap is of the type that distinguishes the capabilities of the human mind from those of other species. Although, as mentioned, we share a common numerical basis with many other animals, none of them seems capable of making that mental leap even after years of training in a controlled environment (e.g., see Biro & Matsuzawa 2001).

So how did the sapient mind make that leap forward, overcoming the limits of approximate numerical thinking? My aim in this chapter is to attempt to formulate the outline of a possible research framework for dealing with this question by integrating recent findings in archaeology, anthropology and cognitive neuroscience. After reviewing the recent neuroscientific data my purpose in this chapter is to explore what might be the role of material culture in the emergence of numerocity and more specifically in the ontogenetic and phylogenetic passage from approximate to exact arithmetic.

The neuroscience of numerocity

Over the last decade considerable progress has been made in our understanding of human numerical competence and its functional neurophysiological architecture. The neuroscience of 'exact' arithmetic does not seem to offer much in relation to our purposes here. Most of the studies in that field are based on adult subjects – well equipped with an elaborate vocabulary of number words – who as expected display significant activity in the speech-related areas of the left frontal lobe when engaged in exact numerical tasks. Since our principal concern in this chapter is with what happens when such an explicit vocabulary of number words does not exist, I shall be focusing on the neuroscience of 'approximate' arithmetic.

In this area, a number of neuroimaging studies during number processing tasks reveal a clear cerebral substrate in the form of a set of neuronal networks primarily located in the parietal lobe and in particular in a small subregion in the depths of the horizontal segment of the intraparietal sulcus (HIPS). This brain region presents consistent activation patterns when subjects discriminate numerocities in estimation and approximation tasks and can be differentiated from the brain area more active in exact calculation tasks, that is, the left angular gyrus (e.g., Dehaene et al. 1998; 1999; 2003). For example, a recent functional magnetic resonance imaging (fMRI) study by Eger et al. (2003) showed that both spoken and written numerals (e.g., comparing the activation of an arabic digit to a similar looking letter, or the activation elicited by listening to the word 'two' in comparison to the word 'red') specifically activate the human intraparietal sulcus. Further evidence for the close relation between numerical cognition and HIPS can also been found in the case of people with lesions to the parietal cortex, who present severe impairments in calculation while remaining very capable in the other cognitive domains (e.g., Dehaene & Cohen 1995; 1997; Lee 2000). Moreover, neuroimaging studies of children suffering from developmental dyscalculia have revealed intraparietal lesions associated with early (prenatal or perinatal) injuries (Isaacs et al. 2001; Levy et al. 1999).

In summary, neuroimaging and lesion studies indicate that our approximate number sense appears to be language-independent, relying primarily on visuospatial neuronal networks of the left and right parietal lobes.

Having discussed the neural substrates of our basic numerical abilities there are two further fundamental issues in the neuroscience of numerical cognition that deserve our attention. The first concerns the link between number and space. The second concerns the role of language in numerical thinking.

Number and space

The close interaction between number and space permeates the most elementary aspects of human numerical thinking, such as the notion of measurement. Again recent findings in cognitive neuroscience seem to support the view, obvious in the archaeological and historical record, that number and space are inextricably linked. The neuronal basis of this link is now starting to be understood in the form of neuronal networks of interactions clearly observable in the parietal cortex (Hubbard et al. 2005).

A simple demonstration of the neurological connection between number and space that might underpin the evolution of the various cultural developments of measurement and spatial representations can be seen in the

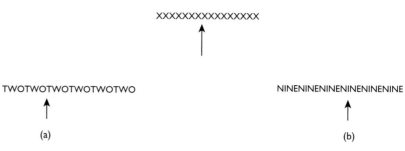

Figure 4.1. Line bisection effect.

so-called spatial numeric association response code effect (SNARC effect, Dehaene 1997). The SNARC effect refers to the recurrent finding that "subjects respond more quickly to larger numbers if the response is on the right side of space, and to the left for smaller numbers" (Hubbard et al. 2005, 436). In addition to the difference in response times there is strong evidence that numbers can automatically bias attention to the left or the right as the following line bisection experiment can be seen to demonstrate (Figure 4.1): Although participants can, on average, accurately indicate the midpoint of a line composed of 'x's, when asked to do the same task in a line composed (a) of either the digit 2 or the word 'two' and (b) of the digit 9 or the word 'nine', they consistently deviate, in the first case (a) to the left, and in the second case (b) to the right (e.g., Calabria & Rossetti 2005).

Another simple demonstration of automatic numerical-spatial interactions can be seen in the study of Zorzi et al. (2002), who found that neglect patients (people who cannot attend to anything on either their left or right side) were unable to perform a number bisection task accurately. More specifically, when asked to indicate the numerical middle of two arabic numerals (such as 11–19), they tended to make right-shifted errors (e.g., they chose 17).

We should also mention in this connection that the classic 'numerical-distance effect' (Moyer & Landauer 1967) – that is, the phenomenon found in animals and humans in number comparisons tasks, that the discrimination between two numbers is easier with increasing numerical distance between them (e.g., subjects respond faster and make fewer errors when asked to discriminate between two and eight than they do when they discriminate between, for instance, seven and eight) – can also be interpreted as indicating the intimate cognitive links between number and space (e.g., Hubbard et al. 2005; Nieder 2005, 185).

In summary, the preceding studies support the hypothesis of numerical-spatial interactions in the form of neuronal networks of interactions clearly observable in the parietal cortex (Hubbard et al. 2005) and thus the argument for a fundamental connection between number and space. What is important to clarify here is that although the association between number and space is automatic, the direction of the effect – small numbers left, large numbers right – is certainly related to and might even be determined by cultural factors and conventions such as the orientation of one's reading and writing system. For example, although a number of studies have confirmed the existence of a spatialised mental number line with a left-to-right orientation in the case of English monoliterates (with smaller magnitudes associated with the left side of space and larger magnitudes associated with the right side of space), recent studies with groups of Arabic monoliterates who use only the right-left writing system indicate a reverse SNARC effect (that is, the mental number had a right-to-left directionality) (see Zebian 2005).

As such, what is important to keep in mind for our purposes in this chapter is that besides the increasing evidence for an intimate neurological link between numeric and spatial processes, there seems to be an additional and especially notable finding that those neurological links may be directly modified by engaging cultural artifacts. The broader implications of this latter premise for our understanding of the relation between cognition and material culture and in particular for the crucial role that materiality may have played at the origin of numerical cognition will be discussed later. For the present I want to turn to the second major issue in the neuroscience of numerocity, which pertains, of course, to the relation between number and language.

Number and language

What precisely is the role of language in the origin of numerical concepts? (For a recent review see Gelman & Gallistel 2004.) There are two major hypotheses currently entertained by most researchers working in this field.

The first hypothesis derives from the strong form of the classical Whorfian thesis, namely, that language determines thought and thus arithmetic thinking. More simply, the argument is that counting words are necessary for developing concepts for numbers larger than three or four. The implication of such a view would be that children growing up in cultures where there are few, or no, counting words will not develop 'true' or 'exact' understanding of the concept of number. For most proponents of this strong view this is precisely what happens in the case of two carefully studied Amazonian tribes. In the cultures of Pirahã (Gordon 2004) and Mundurukú (Pica et al. 2004), which lack exact number words, the ability to reason about exact numerocities is restricted to very small numbers.

Suggestive as the preceding studies might seem for an intimate relation between language and numerocity, current neuroscientific research indicates a rather more complicated picture and points to a possible alternative interpretation. For instance, as Gelman and Butterworth (2005, 7) observe, with the possible exemption of the left angular gyrus, the crucial brain systems involved in numerical processing, as already discussed, are in the parietal lobe, which in the geographic scale of the human cerebral map means 'some distance from any classic language areas'. However, more important seems to be the finding that lesions in brain areas that can cause impairment to exact calculation are not necessarily followed by language disorder, and vice versa. For example, there are many case studies of adult brain-lesioned or autistic patients in whom language dysfunction did not abolish exact arithmetic suggesting that complex calculation may be performed without words (Pica et al. 2004 citing Butterworth 1999). Characteristic in this connection is the neuroimaging study by Pesenti et al. (2000), which has found "that activity in Broca's area is depressed relative to rest during numerical tasks, suggesting that numerical and linguistic processing are even in opposition" (Gelman & Butterworth 2005, 7).

The preceding observations have led to the view that although the possession of an elaborate number vocabulary may be helpful in learning to count and in advancing arithmetic abilities and their ontogenetic realization, such a vocabulary is not *necessary* for the development and possession of true numerical concepts. In other words, "it would be surprising if there were no effects of language on numerical cognition, but it is one thing to hold that language facilitates the use of numerical concepts and another that it provides their causal underpinning" (Gelman & Butterworth 2005, 9).

But how might such a view explain the case of tribes like the Mundurukú? One very simple answer might be that the observed deficits in the numerical capacities of tribes like the Pirahã and Mundurukú may derive from the fact that "numbers are not culturally important and receive little attention in everyday life" (Gelman & Butterworth 2005, 9). Another possibility, more interesting for our own concerns in this chapter, may be the one suggested by Pica et al. (2004, 503), that is, that the crucial element in the case of Mundurukú may not be lack of number names but the lack of a 'counting routine'. A good anthropological example of such a possible counting routine can be found in the classic work of Ifrah (1985, 11–14). The example refers to the 19th-century Torres Islanders and the elaborate technique that they used for keeping track of time, which can be seen to incorporate a mixture of 'visual counting' and 'tallying'.

More specifically, visual counting in this case was more of an embodied sensorimotor association of quantity with the movements of touching various parts of the body in a fixed order. In this case the absence of abstract number was substituted with a complex enactive bodily system in which a certain date like 'the tenth day of the second moon' can be expressed as 'Moon, right elbow; day, left shoulder'. In order to remember that date, "the chief of the tribe uses some sort of durable colouring substance to mark his own right elbow and left shoulder; he may, for example, draw a line on his left shoulder to indicate the day of the ceremony, and a circle on his right elbow for the 'rank' of the corresponding moon" (ibid., 12–13). This complex bodily system also incorporates a 'tallying technique' also described by Ifrah. However, in terms of our present analysis what is important to note is the following:

Language may not be the only way to grasp the concept of number. One may overcome the limits of Mundurukú's numerical thinking not only through the medium of some elaborate numerical lexicon but also through the material affordances of knotted strings, notched bones, sticks and pebbles. This is a very important point, especially from the perspective of cognitive archaeology, since the majority of studies arguing in favour of a strong 'language thesis', in most cases, fail to realise or even consider the possibility that a system of counting *words* may not necessarily be the only system of counting and that other semiotic means for representing number may well be used and have similar effects to those one can observe in the case of a well-developed numerical lexicon.

Archaeology and numerocity

As discussed, the human numerical abilities can be seen as being rooted in two core systems with a long phylogenetic history that account for humans' basic 'number sense'. The first system refers to our ability to approximate large numerical magnitudes; the second system, to our capacity to identify the exact numerocity of small numbers of individual objects. Indeed, numerical reasoning, as Feigenson, Dehaene and Spelke (2004, 313) observe, might be easy and transparent when it rests on one of the two core systems, but also hard and counterintuitive when it goes beyond their limits. The making sense of an exact, large cardinal value presupposes cognitive processes that children take many years to learn and that people may perform in different ways in different cultures or even lack altogether. The crucial question then, from a long-term perspective, is "what drives

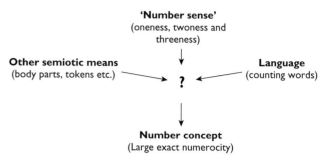

Figure 4.2. How did the sapient mind move beyond approximation?

humans beyond the limits of the core system?" (ibid., 313) (Figure 4.2).

As has been shown previously the possibility, proposed by many researchers, that it is language (the presence or absence of number words) that provided the necessary link that enabled humans to move beyond the threshold of approximation presents a number of problems.

Let me clarify here that I do not dispute the fact that it is language competence that enables above all the development of the verbal symbolic number system essential for the development of exact calculation and higher mathematics. What I argue is that although this may well be the case when verbal number exists in the Vygotskian developmental 'zone of proximal development', it cannot be used to account for the development of numerical thinking in a context where such verbal numerical competence does not yet exist. Despite the evident association between language and exact arithmetic, language lacks in itself the necessary 'representational stability' (Hutchins 2005) that would have made possible such a transition. But if language, the human cognitive artefact par excellence, is not sufficient to do the trick, then what is? Or as S. Dehaene phrases the cultural-evolutionary question: "How did *Homo sapiens* alone ever move beyond approximation?" (1997, 91).

The suggestion I want to make is that in order to answer this question we should look outside the head. More specifically, we need to shift the boundaries of the cognitive system responsible for the development of human numerical cognition beyond the skin. By that of course I do not mean the obvious, namely, that there is a point beyond which we stop looking for answers inside the brain and turn our focus to cultural processes. What I am arguing is that it is in the cross section of those two major components of human cognition that we should be looking for answers: *where brain, body and culture conflate* (Malafouris 2004).

Working to this end a concrete case study might help us focus the issues that arise. One of the best examples that archaeology has to offer in this respect is undoubtedly that of the Near Eastern system of counting discussed by Schmandt-Besserat in her chapter (this volume). In this context, three crucial stages in the developmental trajectory of the Near Eartern concept of number can be identified (Figure 4.3).

The archaeological details of this unique cultural biography of the human 'number sense' embodied in clay and preserved in the archaeological record have been extensively discussed by Schmandt-Besserat in her chapter (also 1992; 1996). It suffices for my purposes here to underline a few major points in relation to each of those three major steps that are particularly relevant to my argument here.

STAGE 1. THE CLAY TOKENS

- Small clay tokens were linked according to their shape (cylinders, cones, spheres etc.) with specific quantities of particular agricultural commodities (e.g., the ovoid stood for a jar of oil).
- Numerosity was expressed in one-to-one correspondence (concrete counting).
- The tokens did not represent numbers (e.g., two, three, four); for instance, there is no token representing 'two' or 'three' jars of oil (even if two and three were certainly numerocities within the range of their basic 'number sense').
- The tokens were not symbols (in the sense of arbitrary signifiers) but enactive signs.

- Each token type counted exclusively a specific category of items (e.g., ovoids could only count jars of oil and jars of oil could only be counted with ovoids).

STAGE 2. THE ENVELOPES

- The envelopes were round, hollow balls of clay, invented to store tokens.
- After the envelope was sealed, equivalent tokens were pressed onto the surface of the envelopes to make their shape and number visible from outside.
- The three-dimensional tokens were reduced to two-dimensional markings.
- The markings on the envelopes were laid according to a standardized format (they were set in straight lines, each line featuring only one kind of sign repeated as many times as needed and in hierarchical order).
- Symbolic equivalence emerged through the property of indexicality.

STAGE 3. THE PICTOGRAPHIC TABLETS

- The images of tokens were traced on the tablet (iconicity).
- The sign for 'jar of oil' was preceded by numerals – signs for 1, 10 and 60.
- The pictographs mark the momentous event when the concept of number was abstracted from that of the item counted.

At first glance what the preceding process can tell us about the role of material culture in the emergence of numerocity is that the use of number expressed in clay (concrete counting) precedes the abstraction and thus conceptualization of number (what in the context of material engagement theory (MET) is referred to as the hypothesis of enactive signification: Malafouris 2005). This basic claim, made also by Ifrah in his *From One to Zero* (1985), resonates with the recurrent find in developmental psychology that young children understand how numbers work before "they have fully mastered the mapping from particular numbers to particular numerocities" (Gelman & Butterworth 2005, 8).

Two closely related questions thus arise, (a) what might be the causal role of this form of meaningful material engagement that we observe in the case of the Near East and (b) how can this causal role be understood against the neurological background of numerocity discussed earlier?

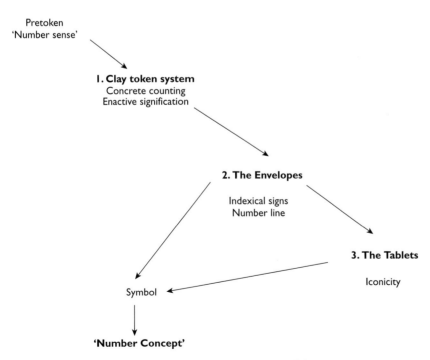

Figure 4.3. Three stages in the developmental trajectory of the Near Eastern concept of number.

I start with the first question. The point to note is that at these early developmental stages – and this applies both from an ontogenetic and a phylogenetic perspective – the use of clay tokens provides the necessary external scaffolding, with a dynamic and constitutive role, for the emergence of arithmetic competence. The process of counting with clay tokens should be seen as an integrative projection between mental – the basic biological approximate 'number sense' (Dehaene 1997) – and physical – for instance, fingers or clay tokens – domains of experience. It is the resulting structural coupling or blend (Fauconnier & Turner 2002; 1998) that brings about the possibility of the meaningful cognitive operation we know as counting and not some innate biological capacity of the human brain. The clay tokens do not stand for numbers, as it may seem; the clay tokens bring forth the numbers and make visible and tangible the manipulation of their properties. What essentially happens in this case – put in very simple terms – is that the vague structure of a very difficult and inherently meaningless conceptual problem – that is, counting – by being integrated via projection with the stable material structure of the clay tokens is transformed into an easier spatiovisual problem. However, spatiovisual problems can be directly manipulated and manually resolved in real time and space. As Schmandt-Besserat observes in her chapter, the tokens made it possible to visualize and manipulate numerocity. Thus the problem – that is, counting – becomes meaningful.

Let me now turn to our second question, that is, how the preceding remarks can be understood against the neurological background of numerocity discussed earlier.

How does the neurological substrate of our evolved 'number sense', which apparently we hold in common with other species, interact with this complex, extended system of 'extraneural' numerical thinking? How can the intraparietal networks of neuronal interaction, necessary for the emergence of true numerocity, be grounded upon a clay foundation?

The image to avoid, as Andy Clark proposes from the perspective of 'active externalism', is one of simple translation from a cultural to a biological realm (2003). Neither brain nor culture, in isolation, will ever answer the question how the intelligent use of clay could ever give rise to the concept of number. I believe that what the case of Near East shows us is *not* some gradual representational process by which our initial embodied, analogical and associative numerical mental engine is externalized and transformed through a series of linear steps, first to a kind of symbolic token-manipulating representational system and then to some sort of computational numerical device. First, tokens are not symbols; they are enactive signs. In particular, the clay token does not stand for or represent the concept of number but instead *brings forth* the concept of number. The enactive sign does not refer to something existing separately from it, but is a constitutive part of what it expresses that otherwise cannot be known. It operates on the principle of participation rather than that of symbolic equivalency (for enactive signification see also Malafouris 2007a, b). Second, numerical cognition is much more than an 'internal' computational mechanism, or else how do we account for such basic phenomena as the 'numerical distance effect'? As far as I know, computers, and the digital logic they instantiate, unlike humans, do not take longer to compare 7 with 8 than 2 with 8.

What instead we should seek to explore are the possible links and bridges between brains, bodies and things that may have caused the critical integration of the different intraparietal areas. In other words, we should be looking for a culturally and practice-effected *reorganisation* (Kelly & Garavan 2005, 1090; see also Poldrack 2000) in the neural connectivity of this region.

Although such a topic demands a far more detailed treatment than the one I can offer within the limits of this chapter, the general outline of my working hypothesis can be stated as follows:

I propose that the process of engaging and grasping number as a clay token may have offered the necessary causal underpinning for the abstraction of number by inducing or reinforcing connections in the intraparietal area. The crucial neurological link in this respect, I suggest, should be seen in the anterior intraparietal (AIP) area. The reason is simple enough. As demonstrated by a number of imaging studies the AIP area is *crucial for the manual tasks of pointing, reaching and grasping three-dimensional objects and tools*. If one adds to the preceding observation the recent finding by Iriki (2005) that even two weeks of tool use leads to the development of additional connections between the temporal-parietal junction and the AIP area in macaques, then one may easily hypothesize, especially from a 'neural constructivist' point of view, about the effects that more than 4,000 years of counting and measuring with clay tokens might have on connectivity between the angular gyrus, ventral intraparietal (VIP) and lateral intraparietal (LIP) (see also Hubbard et al. 2005, 445) areas. Furthermore, this neuroanatomical proximity and functional connectivity between number-related and grasp-related regions in the intraparietal sulcus (IPS) may also be associated with the important – and to a large extent cross-cultural – role of finger knowledge in the development of numerical representations (ibid.). In connection with this, a recent study by Andres et al. (2004) that has shown that the size of grip aperture also has a SNARC-like effect (small numbers are responded to more quickly by closing the hand, and large numbers by opening the hand) may also be seen as indicative of the preceding crucial association.

Conclusion

Although the human brain may be *hardwired for math* (Butterworth 1999), we should keep in mind that the human brain is only a part, albeit a crucial one, of an extended cognitive system where the software very often directly affects the hardware. What the early Holocene archaeological record clearly indicates is that numerical cognition does not necessarily have to be stored in a verbal format, or to activate those brain regions we traditionally associate with language. The meaning of a Neolithic clay token, in a given basic numerical task, does not need a name in order to emerge and be understood; it can be grasped, literally, by the hand that used it. This is possible because of the basic property that constitutes, above anything else, the cognitive efficacy of material culture: things can act as their own best representation and thus provide the missing link between neural and cultural plasticity. This is why a simple Neolithic token can drive the sapient mind beyond approximation. It does the trick by transforming and simplifying the problem of number, enabling the building of neural connections that would have been impossible otherwise. It also does something even more important: it takes care of a part of the problem by itself, thus becoming an inseparable part of numerical cognition, which now extends beyond the brain and into the world.

ACKNOWLEDGEMENTS

I would like to thank Colin Renfrew and Iain Morley for their invitation to contribute to this volume. The research presented is funded by the Balzan Foundation.

REFERENCES

Andres, M., Davare, M., Pesenti, M., Olivier, E. & X. Seron, 2004. Number magnitude and grip aperture interaction. *Neuroreport* 15(18), 2773–2777.

Antell, S. E. & D. P. Keating, 1983. Perception of numerical invariance in neonates. *Child Development* 54, 697–701.

Biro, D. & T. Matsuzawa, 2001. Chimpanzee numerical competence: Cardinal and ordinal skills, in *Primate Origins of Human Cognition and Behavior*, ed. T. Matsuzawa . Tokyo & Berlin: Springer, 199–225.

Brannon, E. M. & H. S. Terrace, 1998. Ordering of the numerosities 1 to 9 by monkeys. *Science* 282(5389), 746–749.

Brannon, E. M. & H. S. Terrace, 2000. Representation of the numerosities 1–9 by rhesus macaques (Macaca mulatta). *Journal of Experimental Psychology: Animal Behavior and Processes* 26, 31–49.

Brannon, E. M. & H. S. Terrace, 2002. The evolution and ontogeny of ordinal numerical ability, in *The Cognitive Animal: Empirical and Theoretical Perspectives on Animal Cognition*, eds. M. Bekoff, C. Allen & G. M. Burhgardt . Cambridge, MA: MIT Press, 197–204.

Butterworth, B., 1999. *What Counts: How Every Brain Is Hardwired for Math*. New York: Free Press.

Calabria M. & Y. Rossetti, 2005. Interference between number processing and line bisection: A methodology. *Neuropsychologia* 43(5), 779–783.

Clark, A., 2003. *Natural-Born Cyborgs: Minds, Technologies and the Future of Human Intelligence*. New York: Oxford University Press.

Davis, H. & R. Pérusse, 1988. Numerical competence in animals: Definitional issues, current evidence, and a new research agenda. *Behavioural and Brain Sciences* 11, 561–615.

Dehaene, S., 1997. *The Number Sense*. New York: Oxford University Press.

Dehaene, S., 2005. Evolution of human cortical circuits for reading and arithmetic: The "neuronal recycling" hypothesis, in *From Monkey Brain to Human Brain*, eds. S. Dehaene, J-R.Duhamel, G. Rizzolatti & M. Hauser. Cambridge, MA: MIT Press.

Dehaene, S. & L. Cohen, 1995. Towards an anatomical and functional model of number processing. *Mathematical Cognition* 1, 83–120.

Dehaene, S. & L. Cohen, 1997. Cerebral pathways for calculation: Double dissociation between rote verbal and quantitative knowledge or arithmetic. *Cortex* 33, 219–250.

Dehaene, S., Dehaene-Lambertz, G. & L. Cohen 1998. Abstract representation of numbers in the animal and human brain. *Nature Neuroscience* 21, 355–361.

Dehaene, S., Piazza, M., Pinel, P. & L. Cohen 2003. Three parietal circuits for number processing. *Cognitive Neuropsychology* 20, 487–506.

Dehaene, S., Spelke, E., Pinel, P., Stanescu, R & S. Tsivkin, 1999. Sources of mathematical thinking: Behavioral and brain-imaging evidence. *Science* 284, 970–974.

Eger, E., Sterzer, P., Russ, M. O., Giraud, A. L. & A. Kleinschmidt, 2003. A supramodal number representation in human intraparietal cortex. *Neuron* 37, 719–725.

Fauconnier, G. & M. Turner, 1998. Conceptual integration networks. *Cognitive Science* 22, 133–187.

Fauconnier, G. & M. Turner, 2002. *The Way We Think: Conceptual Blending and the Mind's Hidden Complexities*. New York: Basic Books.

Feigenson, L., Dehaene, S. & E. Spelke 2004. Core systems of number. *Trends in Cognitive Sciences* 8, 307–314.

Gelman, R. & B. Butterworth, 2005. Number and language: How are they related? *Trends in Cognitive Sciences* 9, 6–10.

Gelman, R. & C. R. Gallistel, 2004. Language and the origin of numerical concepts. *Science* **306**, 441–443.

Gordon, P., 2004. Numerical cognition without words: Evidence from Amazonia. *Science* **306**, 496–499.

Hubbard E. M., Piazza, M., Pinel P. & S. Dehaene, 2005. Interactions between number and space in parietal cortex. *Nature Reviews (Neuroscience)* **6**, 435–448.

Hutchins, E, 2005. Material anchors for conceptual blends. *Journal of Pragmatics* **37**, 1555–1577.

Ifrah, G. 1985. *From One to Zero: A Universal History of Numbers.* New York: Viking.

Iriki, A., 2005. A prototype of *Homo faber*: A silent precursor of human intelligence in the tool-using monkey brain, in *From Monkey Brain to Human Brain*, eds. S. Dehaene, J-R.Duhamel, G. Rizzolatti & M. Hauser. Cambridge, MA: MIT Press, 253–271.

Isaacs, E. B., Edmonds, C. J., Lucas, A. & D. G. Gadian, 2001. Calculation difficulties in children of very low birth-weight: A neural correlate. *Brain* **124**, 1701–1707.

Kelly, A. M. C. & H. Garavan, 2005. Human functional neuroimaging of brain changes associated with practice. *Cerebral Cortex* **15**, 1089–1102.

Lakoff, G & R. E. Núñez. 2000. *Where Mathematics Comes From: How the Embodied Mind Brings Mathematics into Being.* New York: Basic Books.

Lee, K. M., 2000. Cortical areas differentially involved in multiplication and subtraction: A functional magnetic resonance imaging study and correlation with a case of selective acalculia. *Annals of Neurology* **48**, 657–661.

Levy, L. M., Reis, I. L. & J. Grafman, 1999. Metabolic abnormalities detected by H-MRS in dyscalculia and dysgraphia. *Neurology* **53**, 639–641.

Lipton, J. S. & E. S. Spelke, 2003. Origins of number sense: Large-number discrimination in human infants. *Psychological Science* **14**, 396–401.

Malafouris, L., 2004. The cognitive basis of material engagement: Where brain, body and culture conflate, in *Rethinking Materiality: The Engagement of Mind with the Material World*, eds. E. DeMarrais, C. Gosden & C. Renfrew. Cambridge: McDonald Institute for Archaeological Research, 53–62.

Malafouris, L., 2005. Projections in Matter: Material Engagement and the Mycenaean Becoming. Unpublished PhD dissertation, Cambridge University.

Malafouris, L., 2007a. The sacred engagement: Outline of a hypothesis about the origin of human 'religious intelligence', in *Cult in Context, Reconsidering Ritual in Archaeology*, eds. Barrowclough, D. A. & Malone C. Oxford: Oxbow Books, 198–205.

Malafouris, L., 2007b. Before and beyond representation: Towards an enactive conception of the Palaeolithic image, in *Image and Imagination: A Global History of Figurative Representation*, eds. C. Renfrew & I. Morley.

Cambridge: McDonald Institute for Archaeological Research, 289–302.

Moyer, R. S. & T. K. Landauer, 1967. Time required for judgments of numerical inequality. *Nature* **215**, 1519–1520.

Neider, A., 2005. Counting on neurons: The neurobiology of numerical competence. *Nature Reviews (Neuroscience)* **6**, 177–190.

Pesenti, M., Thioux, M., Seron, X. & A. De Volder, 2000. Neuroanatomical substrates of arabic number processing, numerical comparison and simple addition: A PET study. *Journal of Cognitive Neuroscience* **12**, 461–479.

Petersen, S. E., van Mier, H., Fiez, J. A. & M. E. Raichle, 1998. The effects of practice on the functional anatomy of task performance. *Proceedings of the National Academy of Sciences of the USA* **95**, 853–860.

Pica, P., Lemer, C., Izard, V. & S. Dehaene, 2004. Exact and approximate arithmetic in an Amazonian indigene group. *Science* **306**, 499–503.

Pinel, P., Piazza, M., Le Bihan, D. & S. Dehaene, 2004. Distributed and overlapping cerebral representations of number, size, and luminance during comparative judgments. *Neuron* **41**, 983–993.

Poldrack, R. A., 2000. Imaging brain plasticity: Conceptual and methodological issues – a theoretical review. *Neuroimage* **12**, 1–13.

Schmandt-Besserat, D., 1992. *Before Writing. Vol. I, From Counting to Cuneiform.* Austin: University of Texas Press.

Schmandt-Besserat, D., 1996. *How Writing Came About.* Austin: University of Texas Press.

Simon, O., Mangin, J.-F., Cohen, L., Le Bihan, D. & S. Dehaene, 2002. Topographical layout of hand, eye, calculation, and language-related areas in the human parietal lobe. *Neuron* **33**, 475–487.

Varley R. A., Klessinger, N. J. C., Romanowski, C. A. J. & M. Siegal, 2005. Agrammatic but numerate. *PNAS* **102**(9) 3519–3524.

Wynn, K., 1992. Addition and subtraction by human infants. *Nature* **358**, 749–750.

Wynn, K., 1996. Infants' individuation and enumeration of actions. *Psychological Science* **7**, 164–169.

Xu, F. 2003. Numerosity discrimination in infants: Evidence for two subsystems of representation. *Cognition*, **89**, B15–B29.

Xu, F. & E.S. Spelke. 2000. Large number discrimination in 6-month-old infants. *Cognition*, **74**, B1–B11.

Zebian, S., 2005. Linkages between number concepts, spatial thinking, and directionality of writing: The SNARC effect and the reverse SNARC effect in English and Arabic mono-literates, biliterates and illiterate Arabic speakers. *Journal of Cognition and Culture* **5**(1–2), 165–90.

Zorzi, M., Priftis, K. & C. Umilta, 2002. Neglect disrupts the mental number line. *Nature* **417**, 138–139.

5

Numerical cognition and the development of 'zero' in Mesoamerica

John Justeson

Part I. Numeration and numerical cognition

Cognition is a system consisting of representations of knowledge together with the processes that operate on those representations. What is fundamental to *numerical cognition* is the representation of knowledge about number and numeration, and the operations that are performed on them. This section explores features of numeral systems that relate to several different perspectives on these matters within cognitive and linguistic anthropology. It begins with a selection from Greenberg's (1987) findings on cross-linguistic regularities in the structure of numeral systems in spoken languages.

Number words and phrases

One way to explore how number is conceived is through its representation in language. For many linguistic anthropologists, it seems almost inevitable that the grammatical structure of words relating to regularly relevant semantic categories and domains will help to shape and/or be shaped by the ways they process information involving those categories and domains. Whether or not this is so in the case of number, the relevance of its linguistic representation follows from two empirical observations. (1) The vast majority of languages have *numerals* – conventional terms used widely in a speech community to represent specific numbers.[1] (2) Worldwide, numeral systems – the linguistic organizations of terms representing numbers – show great similarity in their basic structure. The major work relevant to this chapter is by Greenberg (1987; see also Stampe 1977, Hurford 1987), who provides 54 generalizations capturing the structures of a wide variety of documented numeral systems. Many of these structural regularities plausibly reflect regularities in mental representations of numbers.

Perhaps surprisingly for us who are accustomed to a notational system that allows us to represent arbitrarily high numbers, all natural languages have some *highest* numeral. The principles by which numerals are formed relate closely to the size of the highest numeral in a language.

Every language with numerals has one or more *basic number terms* – lexical items of fixed form that refer to a particular number of entities, that are used to enumerate entities from diverse semantic fields, and that are not composed of two or more number terms. 'One' is always among the basic number terms.

A few languages have *only* basic number terms and have no conventional expressions for larger numerals, the only standard term for higher numbers of objects meaning something like 'many'. Among these languages, the South American language Botocudo reportedly has the minimum contrast of 'one' versus 'many', while another, Guana, has numerals as high as 'four'; most have terms up to 'two' or 'three' (Greenberg 1987:256).

Most languages, including all that have numerals representing numbers higher than four, have in addition a set of *derived* or *composite* numerals, made up of at least one basic number term and at least one additional element, which may but need not be another number term, whether basic or derived. In composite number terms that are made up of other number terms, the numeral's value can be expressed by a mathematical relationship among the referents of the constituent terms, normally involving addition and/or multiplication. I have not investigated the issue exhaustively, but it appears that, in these languages, every basic number term appears in at least one composite number term.

In several languages whose numeral terminologies are quite small, the only arithmetic relationship involved in composite terms is addition. Among clear cases, the smallest such systems have 'three' as their highest numeral, with 'three' derived from terms for 'one' and 'two'; the largest have numerals up to 'ten' (Greenberg 1987:256–7).[2]

Most languages build up numerals in part by making use of a relationship corresponding to multiplication. Typically, they form composite number terms by juxtaposing some numerals whose values, when multiplied, yield the value of the composite term. A few languages have numeral systems that are basically additive in structure, but with one or two terms expressing some numbers as double or triple some other terms. Otherwise, however – whenever multiplication is systematic, found in a large number of numerals – the system involves a special use of one or more special *base* numbers: up to some point, almost every multiple of a given base is either designated by a basic number term, or by a composite term in which the term for the base is juxtaposed with a term for a multiplier of that base whose referent, multiplied by the referent of the base, yields the value of the term (Greenberg 1987:270). These systems are highly structured: the terms for bases are always basic number terms, and a multiplier is smaller than the base to which it applies.

In languages with a series of bases, each a multiple of the next lower base, composite number terms can be seen as formed of several subterms whose values relate to one another by addition, with at most one subterm representing a number smaller than the smallest base, and with each of the other subterms being a term for a multiple of a different base.

In some systems, every base is a power of the smallest base; this is attested for bases of 4, 10, 12, and 20 (Greenberg 1987:270). Most commonly, the bases are *successive* powers of the smallest base. The essential structure of numerals in these systems is almost identical to that of polynomial expressions in algebra. Any positive integer n can be represented uniquely by a set of integer coefficients c_i, $0 \leq c_i \leq b - 1$ and an integer base $b > 1$, such that, if $b^m \leq n < b^{m+1}$, then there is one set of values for these coefficients that will make

$$n = c_m \, b^m + c_{m-1} \, b^{m-1} + \ldots + c_1 \, b^1 + c_0 \, b^0$$

In spite of the ability of modern mathematicians to represent arbitrarily large numbers, in natural languages there is always a highest base, usually no higher than b^3.

For the most part, the multipliers of the bases are explicitly reflected by the corresponding word, for numbers 1 through $b - 1$, in the linguistic expressions. There are systematic departures from this usage. Cross-linguistically, it is very common that the numeral 1 does not appear linguistically to express a number 1 that is the multiplier of a base. One absolutely consistent linguistic departure from an algebraic formalism using polynomials is that there is no linguistic element corresponding to an algebraic coefficient of zero for a base; if the algebraic expression would use a zero coefficient for a given base, the words for that base and its multiplier are simply not present in the linguistic expression. In fact, no word for zero occurs in *any* composite number term, in any context, in any natural language: "zero is never expressed as part of the numeral system" (Greenberg 1987:255). This is consistent with a view that *zero is not an innate element of human numerical cognition*, but rather has appeared as an extension or addition to the conception of number in some mathematical traditions.

Greenberg's universals have an obvious evolutionary implication: numeral terminologies incorporating more operator relationships arise out of those with fewer as the number of numerals for which there are conventional terms expands. This expansion must be associated with the incorporation of more numbers into the system of conventional number terms, as at least some speakers of the language come to refer routinely to higher numbers in some discourse contexts. The development of more elaborate numeral systems, then, appears to be a side effect of cultural practices and of interpersonal interactions involving them. In principle, such a development need not be unidirectional: numeral systems with simpler terminological structures might emerge out of more elaborate systems, presumably as changing cultural practices lead speakers to regularly use a smaller range of numbers; for example, a group immigrating into a numeral-poor area might adjust in this way.

Language universals and numerical cognition

The regularities established by Greenberg about the ways that human beings talk about numbers seem likely to have emerged from a shared numerical cognition.

The smallest numbers and numerals

Human beings are born with the ability to recognize immediately the difference between one, two, or three objects – with no more processing time required to recognize any among these numbers – while distinguishing among larger numbers of objects requires longer and more elaborate cognitive processing (see, for example, Dehaene 1997). This more elaborate processing consists of something like chunking the numbers of items into two or more groups, each with smaller numbers of items, or of something like counting. Similar capabilities are known for a large number of nonhuman species.

A hardwired capability of this sort is deployed by all visually normal human beings in processing visual information in their environment; distinguishing among such quantities is bound to be a resource that is drawn upon in everyday life. It is this set of numbers of items that can be recognized instantly that occur in numeral systems having only basic number terms, and that are cross-referenced in systems of grammatical number.

Metaphor, embodied cognition, and number

Starting around 1980, cognitive scientists began exploring the idea that much unconscious inference is based on the application of metaphors: a set of understandings of a familiar domain gets used to draw inferences about one less familiar by treating elements and processes from the familiar domain as analogues of features of the unfamiliar domain; understandings of one domain are embodied in understandings of another. This is reflected and enacted in language and other forms of communication and representation: the ways that people speak concretely about some domains are applied to many other domains in which their applicability is a semantic extension.

One recurring resource for such metaphors is the human body. Cross-culturally, number and numeration are widely embodied in cultural practices with a "digit" metaphor: in representing a number by displaying the corresponding number of digits; in "finger counting", displaying or touching a group of digits in sequence; and in adding and subtracting numbers by operations using fingers and hands, and sometimes toes and feet. Accounts of languages with few number words typically report that finger counting or display is used by speakers along with or in preference to the verbal use of numerals, and for indicating much larger numbers than are encoded in their language (see note 2).

The numeral vocabulary of many languages is etymologically related to a body-based system for counting, with smaller number words including or descending from explicit hand and digit references: 3 = 'middle one'; 5 = 'hand'; 6 = 'other hand', or 'other'; 10 = 'completed'; and the like. In others, the numbers 1 through 5 are etymologically opaque basic numerals, while 6 through 9 mean something like '*n* on the other'. Many other languages have structurally similar systems in which words for 6 through 9 combine a basic numeral for 5 with one for 1 through 4, with nothing that etymologically suggests the involvement of the hands or fingers.

An engagement with number through mapping onto the fingers is available to conscious consideration, but much everyday mathematical inference proceeds unconsciously. Lakoff and Nuñez (2000) argue that mathematical concepts surrounding number – including mathematical operations, and their properties such as the associative and distributive laws – can be understood in terms of a metaphor of numbers as collections that is grounded in the neuropsychological ability to distinguish among of collections of small numbers of objects. The grounding metaphors are that

numbers are like collections of comparable objects

the size of a collection is like the size of the number

adding numbers is like merging collections

subtracting is like removing a smaller collection from a larger one

the smallest collection is like 1

These metaphors have consequences that are equivalent to mathematical properties. For example, just as a number's successor is the next larger number, so merging a collection with the smallest collection forms the next larger collection.

Collection metaphors and number terms

Linguistically, the collection metaphor for numbers relates most straightforwardly to terms for numbers that are smaller than bases. The recurrence of numerals for bases in a wide variety of numeral systems suggests that they are fundamental to the organization of numerical cognition when larger numbers are involved. Neuropsychologically, numbers such as bases that are too large to recognize immediately are identified through "chunking", a process of breaking them up into smaller groups of recognizable size. Linguistically, relating numerals for bases to the collection metaphor requires a notion corresponding to chunks of fixed size. Greenberg observed that numeral bases are treated grammatically as analogous to standardized units of measure. This suggests that a collection metaphor is extended in the numerical cognition of some groups to include completed collections of standardized size – in effect, containers, physical tools for working with standardized measures. Inference based on a metaphor in which numbers are treated like containers of objects yields results very similar to those of the collection metaphor, while introducing the concept of a base, or set of bases, corresponding to filled containers. Standardized weights used with scales embody a similar metaphor for amount.

There is striking support for something like this extension in Mesoamerican languages. Numeration in Mesoamerican languages was *vigesimal*, every indigenous language seemingly having had bases of 20, 400, and 8,000. Words for the higher numerical bases, 400 and 8,000, are derived from words for containers or other ways of gathering materials (Table 5.1).[3] The primary semantic basis for words for '8,000' is the normative conception that gunny sacks of cacao held 8,000 cacao seeds. Thus, words for such sacks – and, by extension, women's skirts – were used to mean '8,000'; Lowland Mayans used *pi:k* (earlier *pe:q*, an old word for cacao) and Sapotekos used *(s)su:7ti* for both 'skirt' and '8,000' (Kaufman and Justeson 2007:201). Even some less widely distributed words for '20' were derived from words for containers; a semantically distinct but related case is Mayan *tahb'* 'tumpline', which is used in carrying a bundle.

The collection metaphor captures other linguistic generalizations about numeral systems. For example, in composite numerals whose components are additively related, most commonly the numerals are simply juxtaposed or are linked by an element meaning something like 'and' or 'with'. While some (few) languages

Table 5.1. *Container terms as numeral bases in Mesoamerican languages*

	Colonial Nawatl	Colonial Soke	Lowland Mayan	Colonial Sapoteko
400	**pan-tli** –	**mon7.e** 'something wrapped'	**b'ahk'** '(a) bundle: something strapped on or wrapped'	**ella** –
8,000	**xikipil-li** 'gunny sack'	**tzunu7** 'sack, bag, pocket, cap'	**pi:k < *pe:q** 'cacao' > *'bag' > 'skirt'	**(s)su:7ti** 'bag, skirt'

link such numerals by an element meaning something like 'upon', no language links them with something like 'under' (Greenberg 1987:265).

Zero as number and numeral

The number zero is somewhat difficult to accommodate by modelling numerical cognition on a collection metaphor: the everyday experience of a "collection" is as a grouping of objects, and in the absence of any objects, there is no collection. Similarly, the conceptualization of addition that is associated with this model does not conform with everyday experience when applied to the defining property of zero, that $0 + n = n + 0 = n$. According to this model for numerical cognition, adding one number m to another number n corresponds to the physical process of merging a collection of m objects with one of n objects (or "adding" a group of m objects with one of n objects). In practice, a collection of n objects is rarely if ever produced by merging an empty collection with a collection of n objects; rather, a collection of n objects is simply left unchanged. A number zero, then, is not consistent with the basic number-as-collection metaphor.

Inference based instead on a container metaphor partly captures the additive properties of a numerical zero: the contents of a container with n objects in it can be poured into an empty container, which results in a container having n objects in it; and one might attempt to pour the contents of an empty container into another container, unaware that the first container is in fact empty. These operations correspond to the additive properties of zero. However, for the purpose of numerical problem solving, the metaphor is not meaningful as it is in the case of containers that are not empty. The metaphor is used deliberately to work out the result of adding two numbers together. It seems unlikely that anyone ever thought through the solution to any mathematical problem using the metaphor of an empty container.

Just as zero is not a numeral in natural languages, then, zero does not arise out of what Lakoff and Nuñez argue is an unconscious numerical cognition shared by all human beings: emptiness or nothingness does not correspond to a "natural" number according to the grounding metaphors of numerical cognition. A number zero must have its source in an *extension* of the concept of number. That source can be identified in the conscious practices of mathematical specialists working with mathematical notation – in particular, with positional notation.

Part II. The emergence of zero

This section focuses on one of the most widely heralded achievements of ancient Mesoamerican civilization, the "invention" of an explicit zero – probably in fact more a discovery than an invention. By some accounts, the Mesoamerican development of some such concept was the first in history, but the Babylonian case may well predate it. In any case, the concern of this chapter is not with parochial issues of chronological priority but rather with cognitive issues and developmental processes. With respect to these, the Mesoamerican case bears comparison with well-known instances from the Old World (for which see Chrisomalis 2003).

This section summarizes the author's reconstruction of the Mesoamerican developments. There are so few early records that any such reconstruction must be somewhat speculative. It is nonetheless of interest that early records suggest a particular set of processes as leading to the development of some such construct in Mesoamerica, and specific roles for linguistic and notational practices in these processes. It is not entirely clear that the resulting Mesoamerican concept, which we today associate with the concept of zero, was in fact numerical; there is plausibly a prenumerical phase in the development of zero elsewhere as well.

General considerations on the origin of zero

Instances of the development of a numerical concept of zero suggest that a particular sequence of innovations is always involved.

The number zero arises within a specialized notation for representing numbers. Like body-based counting schemas, notational systems that are regularly used by specialists replace or supplement collections and containers as grounding metaphors or schemas for the number concept in numerical inference. To implement mathematical operations on numbers, mathematical specialists develop algorithms that apply to these representations; these replace or supplement the merging of collections or the contents of containers as metaphors for arithmetic operations. If numerical cognition is a system consisting of the means by which numbers are represented and of the processes that act on those representations, the numerical cognition of these specialists comes to differ from that of people who do not make task-oriented use of such notations.

An abbreviated numerical notation – a system of positional notation – is a precursor to the notational systems with a zero symbol. Positional notation is based explicitly on the numerical vocabulary of a spoken language, with the numerals that modify linguistic base terms being represented in order while the bases themselves are suppressed. Because the representation of numbers in language has no numeral zero, then, the earliest phase of a positional notation system *never* includes a symbol corresponding to this concept.[4]

In some systems of positional notation, such as the khipu, space is allocated for each successively higher base, whether or not there is a numeral modifier of the base in the number word itself. Abstractly, the khipu is a "tabular" system, in which positional numerals are lined up adjacent to one another. With use, efficient algorithms for processing (for example, adding or comparing) adjacent positional numerals promotes an alignment of digits representing modifiers of the same numeral bases; this produces an empty space in association with the position of a base with no modifier.

A number zero only arises within systems of positional notation in which signs occupy the relative position of those bases that do not appear in the corresponding number term. Initially, these marks do not have a numerical interpretation; in the Babylonian tradition, for example, the mark at issue was in origin a word divider. To be reinterpreted as corresponding to a number, the contextual support for the traditional interpretation must be undermined: the distribution of these marks within the context of positional numbers or within the contexts of their origin must be altered before an alternative interpretation is likely to emerge.

Mesoamerican positional notation and the Mayan discovery of zero

I. Basic system of mathematical notation
The first stage leading to the development of the Mayan zero sign was the invention of a tally-like *bar-and-dot*

system of numerical notation. It was known in Mesoamerica at least since the Middle Preclassic period (ca. 600–300 BCE) and may have developed much earlier. This system of notation was used for numerals (and numbers) in a variety of uses, but by far the most common use was to represent dates – mostly, in the pan-Mesoamerican sacred calendar of 260 days, usually called something like "day count" in Mesoamerican languages. A variety of formats for the representation of the sacred calendar are preserved in later screenfold manuscripts; different formats were appropriate to different uses – for example, those that relate other calendrical and astronomical cycles to sacred time – and thus to different algorithms.

2. Time counts
During the Late Preclassic period (about 300 BCE–250 CE), intervals of time in days, months (of 20 days each) and years were among the numeral constructions attested in the hieroglyphic texts of southeastern Mesoamerica; these phrases expressing these intervals are conventionally referred to as *distance numbers*. The notation for these time spans was a direct representation of the linguistic expressions for them, with a numeral followed by a spelling of the word for the period in question, for example, probably the Mayan *ho7=laju:n winik-V:l* 'fifteen months' on Kaminaljuyu Stela 10 (ca. 300 BCE), and *mak tuk-n 7ame7* 'thirteen years' on the epi-Olmec La Mojarra stela (157 CE). Such intervals are sparsely attested (as are hieroglyphic texts in southeastern Mesoamerica in this era); they do not seem to appear among the more numerous chronological statements in Late Preclassic Zapotec hieroglyphic writing.

3. Positional notation
Positional notation developed and spread in southeastern Mesoamerica, among two neighboring groups, epi-Olmecs and Mayans, by (and probably not long before) 36 BCE. It was used only within a specialized calendar system known among epigraphers as the *long count*. This chronological cycle is treated as a succession of katuns in the only indigenous term known to us (colonial Yucatec <u kahlay katunob>); and, just as the "count of days" was 260 days long, so the cycle of katuns was 260 katuns long.

In this calendar, a given date was represented by the amount of time that had passed since a base date in mythological time. Like Mesoamerican numeration generally, long count dates were represented in vigesimal units: of days, months (of 20 days), years (of 360 days), of 20 years (known by epigraphers as *katuns*), and of 400 years (known by epigraphers as *baktuns*). The 360-day year is only known in association with counts, including the long count, in which a 20-year span was a unit. The same word was used for years of 360 days and for years of 365 days, in Mayan at least.

These expressions are effectively a specialized form of time count ("distance numbers") that had been recorded for some 250 years before the first extant long counts, but they differ in two respects. First, the few attested distance numbers in this era do not exceed 13 years; they are appropriate to the affairs of individual human beings. Long counts, anchoring current dates in mythic time, represent spans of millennia.

The other difference is in the notational system. The earliest notation for long count dates was an abbreviation of the linguistic expressions for these time spans, in which the modifiers of the chronological units are recorded, in sequence, but the units themselves are not mentioned – a pure positional notation system. This system agrees with the structure of numerals and chronological expressions in Mije-Sokean languages, such as epi-Olmec; an example is the epi-Olmec long count on a wall panel from Chiapa de Corzo, originally written as a five-digit sequence, **7 16 3 2 13**, which represented the epi-Olmec phrase shown in Table 5.2. (The epi-Olmec words for 'baktun' and 'katun' are unknown, and so are rendered in small capitals in the epi-Olmec version; the epi-Olmec word for 'sixteen' may have been the ancestor of Gulf Sokean *mak ko tujtu* rather than of Soke *yʉk ko tum-ʉ*).

The normal way to express this time span in the earliest Mayan hieroglyphic records would have been "13 days in the 3rd month of the 4th year of the 17th katun of the 8th baktun", which would have been abbreviated as **8 17 4 3 13** rather than **7 16 3 2 13**. But the earliest Mayan long counts in positional notation also used the epi-Olmec rather than the indigenous Mayan format. In all likelihood, then, the positional format of long count notation was developed among epi-Olmecs and was based on their numeral expressions. However, the public display of long counts in positional notation in royal inscriptions seems to have begun almost simultaneously among epi-Olmecs and Mayans; Mayan and epi-Olmec calendar specialists may have jointly worked out the system.

The epi-Olmec pattern of chronological expression was adopted by Mayans in the long count calendar and,

perhaps by extension, in distance numbers generally; native Mayan patterns survived in nonchronological contexts and in other chronological contexts. Once distance numbers involving two or more units are attested, an influence of normal Mayan numeral syntax can be seen in that the smaller units precede the larger – a cross-linguistically rare pattern – but they do not reflect the ordinal/possessive construction of these numeral phrases (e.g., '46' = "6 in the 3rd score"). In the long count, the epi-Olmec unit order was maintained.

Positional notation is the only format known for the long count through 162 CE. At some point, maybe from the beginning, it came to be used for distance numbers as well as for long counts; positional format is used extensively in the mathematical and astronomical tables of Mayan screenfold manuscripts both for long counts and for distance numbers. But the two formats, positional versus linguistically explicit, were applied in contextually distinct ways: the linguistically explicit format for general time intervals continued to be used in textual context.

4. Positional notation without zero

In 125 CE, Takalik Abaj Stela 5 was erected as the first known year-ending monument in Mesoamerica. It bears two aligned long count dates in positional notation, side by side, and a largely illegible hieroglyphic text. The iconography shows it to be Mayan. The monument's long count dates contain just four digits each; they can be transcribed as shown in Table 5.3. (In later positional records, these dates would have been represented as **8 3 2 0 10** and **8 4 5 0 17**.) Supporting this interpretation, the second date was the seating of a new 365-day year, an occasion known to have been celebrated later by rulers.

These positional representations abbreviate the overt linguistic expression of these time spans in exactly the same way that the five-digit notations do: they record all of the expressed numeral modifiers and none of the time periods. As a representation of the linguistic expression, no digits are missing. There is no overt indication of what time period is lacking, and there is only marginally more space between the third and fourth digits to provide guidance. In a tabular format, the alignment of adjacent numerals would have made this clear, and since corresponding digits are precisely aligned in these two

Table 5.2. *Epi-Olmec phrase represented by the sequence 7 16 3 2 13*

wʉs.tʉk=tujtu BAKTUN,	yʉk ko tum-ʉ KATUN,	tuk-ʉ 7ame7,	wʉs.tʉk poy7a,	mak=tuk-ʉ jama
7 baktuns,	16 katuns,	3 years,	2 months,	13 days

Table 5.3. *Transcription of long count dates on Takalik Abaj Stela 5*

	baktuns	katuns	years	months	days	sacred calendar
L:	waxak BAKTUN,	7u:x may,	ka ha7b',		laju:n k'i:n	ho7 ?7o:k
T:	8	3	2	–	10	5 [Coyote]
L:	waxak BAKTUN,	cha:n may,	ho7 ha7b',		wuk=laju:n k'i:n	b'aluk ?chab'a:n
T:	8	4	5	–	17	11 [Earthquake]

adjacent notations, it is likely that the empty slot would have been clear had one of the dates been a five-digit rather than a four-digit notation.

5. Explicit Mayan representations of long count dates

Positional notation continued to be used on epi-Olmec monuments until the time of the last known epi-Olmec long count date (ca. 533 CE). It was almost entirely abandoned by Mayans for monumental display sometime between 125 CE and about 300 CE, although it was evidently maintained in the manuscript tradition. Mayans adopted a new, linguistically explicit notation for the long count that would seem to have been an extension of that used for distance numbers; the choice of positional versus language-based notation for long counts, as for general time intervals, was now functionally associated with tabular versus textual context.

Long count dates expressed in this format would have no ambiguity with respect to dates like those of Takalik Abaj Stela 5; the units of time being modified by the numerals are part of the written representation. This may have been part of the impulse to adopt this notational system, but there could well have been an aesthetic element to the shift as well – the long count in positional notation is visually spare while the remainder of the text involved relatively elaborate groupings of signs, rich in internal detail.

These long counts were highly salient visually: they almost always begin the text in which they occur, and they are characteristically written in sign groups substantially larger than the norm in a given text. They were also highly salient rhetorically: because of its highly parallelistic syntactic structure, which is a major feature of Mesoamerican ritual speech, the long count would give the recitation of the beginning of the text a high performative impact:

(There were) 8 baktuns,
(there were) 12 katuns,
(there were) 14 years,
(there were) 8 months,
(there were) 15 days,
(when) on 13 Eagle, ...

Lounsbury (1990) argues that these expressions were in fact formalized locutions that were based on recitation from written texts encoded in the discrepant notation; this he supports with parallel examples, which are likely to have been transcribed from hieroglyphic originals, recorded in Spanish script in the Yucatec Mayan *Books of Chilam Balam*. The contrast between the syntax of these expressions and those of ordinary Mayan expressions for time intervals may also have been marked them off as out-of-the-ordinary and thus evocative of a special status that would correlate with the social context of their recitation and of their ideological meaning, much like the former effect of Latin in the Catholic Church in reinforcing the "otherness" of the ritual experience.

6. Seeds of an eventual zero

The most prominent dates for the erection of Mayan royal monuments were the ends of katuns. Katuns were the most momentous stations in the long count from the point of view of ritual performance. From the point of view of performative impact of the formal expressions, however, these are the very dates whose recitation would have been the sparest and least satisfying:

(There were) 8 baktuns,
(there were) 14 katuns,
(when) on 7 Lord, ...

Mayans adopted a rhetorical device that obviates this difficulty and arguably renders the parallelism of katun-ending long count dates the most striking of all. After Tikal Stela 29, the next earliest dated Mayan monuments with long count dates were dedicated in 357 CE, on **8 16 0 0 0** – at the end of a katun. This is the earliest attested explicit use of a sign that appeared in the place of zero. The sign that appears in this position is known from later contexts to represent the syllable *mi*. Kaufman (Kaufman with Justeson 2003:1553) reconstructs a Mayan root **mi* meaning something like 'lacking'. These early long count notations can be translated literally as

(There were) 8 baktuns,
(there were) 16 katuns,
there were no years,
there were no months,
there were no days,
                (when) on 7 Lord, ...

This is in fact the literal translation of the first fully explicit long count expressions referring to a katun ending.

The word *mi* in this context is quite unlikely to have also had a numerical interpretation. Mayan numerals constitute a distinguishable subclass of nouns. However, the word *mi* 'lacking' is not a noun, because it cannot be inflected as a noun; in fact, it is grammatically an adjective, here serving syntactically in an adjectival predication.

After this date, only one Mayan monument, Pestac Stela 1, is known to have made use of positional notation; its long count date may be transcribed as **9 11 12 9 mi** (665 CE). This is one of very few Mayan stelae that contain no text beyond the long count date. Long count dates in purely positional notation are otherwise found only within numerical tables in Mayan screenfold manuscripts, which date several centuries later. The nontextual context of Pestac Stela 1 is therefore appropriate to positional notation and is plausibly representative of the way long counts and time intervals were recorded in contemporaneous Mayan screenfold manuscripts.

The use of the sign **mi** in positional notation is a straightforward application of this sign from one pattern in fully explicit expressions of the long count in textual context to another in the abbreviated versions of those expressions in tabular context; the fuller context would have been actively available as an interpretive framework for the use of **mi** in positional notations. Functionally, it may have been treated in positional context as a "place holder", reflecting the presence of a given unit, but under the circumstances one must be skeptical that the sign would have had a numerical (or other nontraditional) interpretation in the abbreviated context.

7. The emergence of zero?

In the screenfold manuscripts that come down to us, the sign **mi** is rare as a place holder in positional notations, whether of long counts or of time intervals. The standard sign used in its place is a lens-shaped sign, with a variety of interior details that suggest it depicts a seashell; Blume (in press) argues convincingly that these depict *oliva* shells. A few of these place holders are more iconic representations of shells, and one is an overt depiction of a conch with the Postclassic form of the sign **mi** as a phonetic complement. This suggests that the shell signs for zero may represent the same word as the Classic zero sign.

The lens-shaped sign does not otherwise occur in the manuscripts or in earlier Mayan hieroglyphic texts; it is functionally specific to positional notation where it corresponds to zero. Since the sign was not used in any other context, there is no intertextual basis for a predicate interpretation of the sign.

In numerical tables, the lens-shaped signs would have been integrated with digits in algorithms for adding or subtracting positional representations of time intervals. In particular, the algorithm for adding adjacent positionally represented numbers was probably always broken down by adepts into the repeated application of a simpler addition algorithm that applies only to aligned numeral symbols that correspond to modifiers of the same base in the linguistic form of a numeral, along with a 'carrying' procedure. A mark that corresponds to the lack of a modifier is readily integrated into such an algorithm; in this case, the specialist simply copies the numerical symbol associated with the same base in the other positional numeral.

This provides a numerical framework for interpreting this sign as a numeral, and thereby for the emergence of a number zero. It is plausible that the vocabulary for the *mathematical operation* of addition might be applied by mathematical specialists to the *algorithmic schema* of adding individual digits. It is not necessarily the case that operations on the nonnumerical marks will be talked about in this way; specialists may make use of terminology that relates to the nonnumerical origins of the marks used in this part of the algorithm. Once the same terminology for the operations comes to be applied by specialists, this sets the stage for a reconceptualization of the algorithm as simply addition, perhaps by a later generation, and thereby to a reconceptualization of the mark as, in this context, the representation for a number.

To know whether Mayans did indeed interpret these signs numerically, we would have to know how these relevant addition problems were expressed in Mayan discourse. Still, the circumstances are as supportive of a numerical zero interpretation as, for example, in Babylonian.

8. Extensions of positional notation

Judging from what we know of their descendants from the 16th century onward, all pre-Columbian Mesoamerican languages appear to have shared the peculiarity that 20 was a base of their numeral system (*vigesimal* numeration). All Mesoamerican languages seem to have had basic number words for 20, 400, and 8,000. Few if any had basic number words for higher powers of 20; correspondingly, for most Mesoamerican languages, the highest number for which there was an indigenous expression was 159,999.

Given these limitations on the numeral vocabulary of Mesoamericans generally, the longest positional numeral

Table 5.4. *Expressions for multiples of 100,000 in the Tecpatán Soke* Vocabulario *of 1733*

Çien mil en numero 100,000	Mac vestec suno comac mone *mak wɨstɨk tzunu7 ko mak mone7*	ten two eight-thousand and ten four-hundred 'twelve 8,000s and ten 400s'
Doçientos mil 200,000	Ips comos chuno *7i7ps ko mos tzunu7*	twenty and five eight-thousand 'twenty-five 8,000s'
Berendt: trecientos mil 300,000	ips co yet co vestec tzuno co mac mone *7i7ps ko wstk tzunu7 ko mak mone7*	twenty and fifteen and two eight-thousand and ten four-hundred 'thirty-seven 8,000s and ten 400s'
Berendt: quinientos mil 500,000	tucips co vestec tzuno co mac mone *tukɨ=7i7ps ko wɨstɨk tzunu7 ko mak mone7*	three twenty and two eight-thousand and ten four-hundred 'sixty-two 8,000s and ten 400s'
Seisçientos mil 600,000	Tocips coyetchuno *tukɨ=7i7ps ko yɨt tzunu7*	three twenty and fifteen eight-thousand 'seventy-five 8000s'
Berendt: setecientos mil 700,000	mactasips co cucay tzuno co mac mone *maktas=7i7ps ko kukay tzunu7 ko mak mone7*	four twenty and seven eight-thousand and ten four-hundred 'eighty-seven 8,000s and ten 400s'
Ochoçientos mil numero 800,000	Mosips tzunu *mos=7i7ps tzunu7*	five twenty eight-thousand '(a) hundred 8,000s'
Noveçientos mil numero 900,000	Mosips comac vestec tzunucoma mone … *mos=7i7ps ko mak wɨstɨk tzunu7 ko mak mone7*	five twenty and ten two eight-thousand and ten 400 '(a) hundred and twelve 8,000s and ten 400s'

Note: Most entries are from the version of Pozarenco's manuscript in the John Carter Brown Library. *Berendt* labels entries from Berendt's (1870) hand copy of another, lost version of the manuscript in place of erroneous entries from the JCB manuscript. That manuscript gives <mone> '400' for seven hundred thousand (700,000), the last word of the expression in Berendt's copy, suggesting that this may have been the only word on a second line in the manuscript from which the JCB version was copied. The JCB version gives thirty-seven 8,000s and fifteen (rather than ten) 400s for three hundred thousand (300,000), a substitution of *yɨt* for *mak*. The JCB version gives fifty (rather than sixty-two) 8,000s and two (rather than ten) 400s – plus an illegible word – for five hundred thousand (500,000), an error for which no simple account can be given. No expression for four hundred thousand (400,000) is given in either version; fifty 8,000s would have been expected.

would have had at most six digits, up to the so-called pictun, or period of 8,000 years (currently read by some epigraphers as *pih* or *pik*). There are indeed several texts that refer to this period. There are also, however, a few Classic period hieroglyphic texts that represent far larger periods of time using an extended vigesimal notation system, with coefficients of at most 19 and including many higher powers of 20. The largest known, from the site of Coba, represents a time period in vigesimal notation with every vigesimal base up to 20^{21} or perhaps 20^{22} years.

There are colonial sources that give terms for numbers greater than 160,000, but these seem to have been manufactured on request by Spanish priests who were gathering vocabulary including that for numbers. A case in point is the 1733 vocabulary of Tecpatan Soke (Pozarenco 1733). Apart from an oversight of 400,000, all multiples of 100,000 up to 900,000 were systematically elicited by a Spanish cleric; see Table 5.4. The term for 100,000 fell within the bounds of the indigenous numeral system, and this term conforms to the structure of native Soke numerals in containing no coefficients higher than 19 for any of the bases. No higher

multiple of 100,000, however, was part of the native system used by everyday people in Mesoamerica. The recorded expressions violate the structures of native Soke numerals, and of a system of strict vigesimal notation. Faced with a need to invent words for higher numbers, indigenous people used words for numbers above 19 as a coefficient modifying their word for '8,000'; the means they used did not involve an extension to the system of vigesimal representation through the invention of terms for higher multiples of 20.

This suggests that the Classic period extensions of the vigesimal system were due to specialists, and that they were probably not current in the population at large.

Terms for three higher powers of 20 are reported by Beltrán from 18th-century Yucatan, <calab> for 160,000; <kinchil> for 1,000,000 (treated by 20th-century writers as intended for 3,200,000); and <alau> for 64,000,000 (Beltrán de Santa Rosa 1746:160). These look like basic number terms, as expected for bases – following the Soke pattern terms like *k'al pìːk*, *b'áːk pìːk*, and *pìːk pìːk* would be expected of Spanish-based neologisms – and Burkitt (1902:457) also reports *kalab'* for 160,000 in Q'eqchi' Mayan. If these terms arose without European influence, however, it seems likely that they arose and were used as part of the practice of mathematical specialists familiar with vigesimal positional notation: Beltrán cites <uac calab catac hopic> 'six 160,000s and five 8,000s' as an alternate term for 1,000,000, which agrees with the structure of numbers as represented in this formal system; it disagrees with indigenous Mayan numeral structure, under which 'five 8,000s in the seventh 160,000' would have been expected.

However, their pre-Columbian pedigree is uncertain, for several reasons. (1) No such terms are reported in earlier lexical or grammatical sources, some of which are massive. (2) The attribution of <kinchil> to the decimal base 1,000,000 suggests Spanish influence; that 'one million' was Beltrán's actual understanding of <kinchil> is suggested by the fact that he gives 'six 160,000s and five 8,000s' as an alternate term for 1 million immediately afterward. (3) The violation of standard Mayan numeral structure in 'six 160,000s and five 8,000s' ultimately reflects non-Mayan influence; while it could result from the practices of mathematical specialists, it could instead reflect European influence in the conception of vigesimal numeration. (4) Burkitt's source for *kalab'* as 160,000 in Q'eqchi' is a religious manuscript containing stories from the Old Testament; the term could have been taken by a Catholic priest from Beltrán since a word for 160,000 was needed to translate the number 675,000 in the Book of Numbers (31:32).

9. The end of zero

The narrow dependence of the zero concept on specialized graphical formats restricted to an elite class of calendar specialists led to a reversal of what is sometimes seen as an inexorable cognitive trend toward increasing abstraction and formalization in mathematical systems. While, in ancient times, an effectively numerical concept of zero received graphical expression in Mayan hieroglyphic texts for more than a millenium, this indigenous construct died out and left no trace in any Mesoamerican language or cultural practice. With the Spanish invasion of Mesoamerica, the practices of the calendar specialists were actively suppressed as instruments and symbols of native identity and resistance to Spanish civil and ecclesiastical authority. This suppression was successful in much of Mesoamerica. The long count was lost everywhere it was known – and lost with it, perhaps, was an indigenous concept of zero.

ACKNOWLEDGMENTS

I first explored the idea that zero had not been invented until after the origins of the long count while on a Tinker Foundation postdoctoral fellowship during 1978–9; I thank the Tinker Foundation for supporting my work that year, the Department of Anthropology at Yale University for hosting me, and the late Floyd Lounsbury for sponsoring me. It was Anthony Aveni's invitation to contribute a paper on ancient Mesoamerican computing practices to an encyclopedia of science (Justeson 2001) that led me to revisit the issue; it was only as I completed work on that paper in 1996 that I recognized that Abaj Takalik Stela 5 lacked coefficients of the month position – although this interpretation had already been entertained by John Graham soon after the discovery of the monument (Graham, Heizer, and Shook 1978:92). Davletshin (2002) later came to a similar interpretation of the dates on this monument. The scenario for the origin of the Mayan zero presented here was posted in brief on September 23, 1997, on Aztlan, a Mesoamericanist listserv, and in more detail than is possible here in a 3-hour presentation in the September 1998 meeting of the Northeast Mesoamerican Epigraphy Group at the University at Albany. I have received helpful comments on this chapter from Terrence Kaufman, Roberto Zavala Maldonado, and two anonymous reviewers.

NOTES

1. Some reports of languages that lack any terms for numbers can legitimately be treated with skepticism, but Everett's (2005) report that the speakers of the Brazilian language Pirahã lack any numeral vocabulary is based on an intimate and detailed knowledge of this language built upon his own field work over a period of 27 years and has been substantiated by subsequent linguistic and ethnographic investigations.

2. Structurally similar systems are reported in which numbers made up exclusively by addition go well past '10'. However, these reports appear to result from accommodations by bilingual speakers of the language to the efforts of foreigners to extract higher numerals. All such "systems" make use of a very small number of basic numerals. Greenberg (1987:257) reports that they are always accompanied by counting (or keeping track) on the hands and feet, while these body-counting systems are often used without corresponding linguistic forms. Some of the reported terms are simply descriptive of the gesture corresponding to a number.

   Lounsbury (1978:761) reports in some detail on one such manufactured system. Bororo has two basic numerals, mito 'one' and pobe 'two'. It appears to have had a conventional numeral for 'three' given the close agreement between the independent results obtained by Lounsbury in 1950 with those gathered in the 1940s by Albisetti, Colbacchini, Rondon, and Faria. Past 'three', the expressions differ, and for these numbers the early reports give rather suspicious expressions, like augere pobe augere pobe augere pobe augere pobe (roughly, 'another pair and another pair and another pair and another pair'), which are accompanied by gesture counting. Lounsbury was able to coax a bilingual Bororo-Portuguese speaker to provide phrases as high as '30', all of them seemingly descriptive of a gestural representation of the elicited number.

3. Words in Mesoamerican languages are written in a practical, Spanish-based orthography. Most letters and digraphs have their usual Spanish pronunciations. Among letters and digraphs not found in Spanish, 7 represents a glottal stop; tz represents a sibilant affricate [ɕ], which sounds like ts; and ʉ, or "barred u", represents a high, central-to-back unrounded vowel, which sounds like the u of put and bush, as pronounced by some southerners and westerners in the United States, and like the u in "just now". In representing the grammatical structure of words, = joins the members of a compound, – joins inflectional affixes to stems, . joins derivational affixes to stems, and + joins clitics to words (clitics are words that do not carry an accent).

4. It is widely assumed that the existence of positional notation presupposes the concept of a numerical zero or even an explicit graphical zero notation. In fact, it is the converse that appears to be true: a system of positional notation seems to be required in order to foster the idea of zero as a quantity that can be manipulated arithmetically. A graphical zero is rather a by-product of the use of a system of positional notation than a precondition for it.

REFERENCES

Beltrán de Santa Rosa, Pedro, 1746. *Arte de el idioma maya reducido a succintas reglas, y semi-lexicon yucateco.* Mexico City: Viuda de D. Joseph Bernardo de Hogal.

Berendt, C. Hermann, 1870. *Vocabulario de la Lengua Zoque: Año de 1733.* Manuscript in the University of Pennsylvania Library.

Blume, A., in press. Maya concepts of zero. In *Proceedings of the American Philosophical Society.*

Burkitt, Robert, 1902. Notes on the Kekchí language. *American Anthropologist* **4**:441–63.

Chrisomalis, S. A., 2003. *The Comparative History of Numerical Notation.* PhD dissertation in Anthropology, McGill University.

Corbett, G. G., 2000. *Number.* Cambridge: Cambridge University Press.

Davletshin, A., 2002. Once upon a time there was no zero: The evolution of the south-eastern Mesoamerican calendric notation system. Abstract, in *Cultural Context from the Archaeoastronomical Data and the Echoes of Cosmic Catastrophic Events: Abstracts Submitted for the SEAC 2002 Tenth Annual Conference, 27–30 August in Tartu, Estonia,* eds. Mare Kõiva, Harry Mürk, and Izold Pustõlnik. Tartu: Estonian Literary Museum, 25–6.

Dehaene, S., 1997. *Number Sense: How the Mind Creates Mathematics.* Oxford: Oxford University Press.

Everett, D. L., 2005. Cultural constraints on grammar and cognition in Pirahã: Another look at the design features of human language. *Current Anthropology* **46**:641–6.

Graham, J. A., R. F. Heizer, and E. M. Shook, 1978. Abaj Takalik 1976: Exploratory investigations. In *Studies in Ancient Mesoamerica, III*, ed. J. A. Graham (Contributions of the University of California Archaeological Research Facility, Number 36). Berkeley, California: Archaeological Research Facility, 85–114

Greenberg, J. H., 1987. Generalizations about numeral systems. In *Universals of Human Language*, vol. 3: *Word Formation*, eds. J. H. Greenberg, C. A. Ferguson, and E. A. Moravcsik. Stanford, California: Stanford University Press, 249–95.

Hurford, J. R., 1987. *Language and Number: The Emergence of a Cognitive System.* Oxford: Oxford University Press.

Justeson, J. S., 2001. Pratiche di calculo nell'antica Mesoamerica. In *Storia della Scienza*, Vol. II, ed. A. F. Aveni. Rome: Istituto della Enciclopedia Italiana, Fondata de Giovanni Treccani, 976–90

Kaufman, T. S., with the assistance of J. S. Justeson, 2003. *A Preliminary Mayan Etymological Dictionary.* Published online at http://www.famsi.org/01051/pmed.pdf.

Kaufman, T. S., and J. S. Justeson, 2007. The history of the word for cacao in ancient Mesoamerica. *Ancient Mesoamerica* **18**(2):193–237.

Lakoff, G., and R. Nuñez, 2000. *Where Mathematics Comes From: How the Embodied Mind Brings Mathematics into Being.* New York: Basic Books.

Lounsbury, F. G., 1978. Maya numeration, computation, and calendrical astronomy. In *Dictionary of Scientific Biography*, vol. 17: *Anonymous Contributors to Science*, ed. C. C. Gillispie. New York: Charles Scribner's Sons, 759–818.

Lounsbury, F. G. 1990. Some aspects of Mayan numeral syntax pertinent to the opening date of Stela 8 of Copán. In *Circumpacifica: Festschrift für Thomas S. Barthel*, vol. 1: *Mittel- und Südamerika*, eds. B. Illius and M. Laubscher. Frankfurt am Main: Peter Lang, 289–301.

Pozarenco, Juan de. 1733. Vocabulario de la lengua Çoque. Manuscript in the John Carter Brown Library, Brown University, Providence, Rhode Island.

Stampe, R., 1977. Cardinal number systems. In *Papers from the Twelfth Regional Meeting*, eds. S. S. Mufwene, C. A. Walker, and S. B. Steever. Chicago: Chicago Linguistic Society, 594–609.

6

Recording measure(ment)s in the Inka khipu

Gary Urton

Introduction

The objective of this chapter is to explore various features of the encoding of information in the *khipu* (Quechua: 'knot'), the knotted-string device used for record keeping in the Inka empire of pre-Columbian South America. Specifically, I will discuss what the testimony concerning khipus contained in Spanish colonial documents, as well as study of museum samples of khipus, can teach us about the types and standards of measurements used by local and state administrators in the Inka empire. Given these objectives, we should be clear from the beginning about the range of concepts and practices connected with 'measure' and 'measurement', at least as these are understood in English. To measure means "to compute, estimate, or ascertain the extent, quantity, dimensions, or capacity of [something], especially by a certain rule or standard" (*Webster's New Twentieth Century Dictionary* 1978). In addition to this dauntingly wide range and variety of activities, measurement involves more abstract concepts and forms of evaluation, including "to estimate by reference to any standard; to judge of the value, extent, magnitude, or greatness of [something/someone]" (*Webster's New Twentieth Century Dictionary* 1978).

Clearly, if our objective here is to discuss the recording of measure(ment)s in the Inka khipus, we will have to find some way to limit the domains of reference, as space will not permit a full consideration of the many and varied principles and activities evoked previously. In fact, there is no need to reduce the subject matter artificially, for we are faced from the outset with a fundamental limitation to our knowledge of and ability to interpret information in these devices. The limitation results from the unfortunate circumstance that we have not yet achieved a complete decipherment of the khipus.

While we can interpret certain signs encoded in these devices, we cannot read the entire messages.

To be somewhat more specific, Spanish observers of colonial era manipulations of khipus inform us that the knotted records contained at least two basic types of information, or sign values: signs standing for numbers and signs standing for identities (i.e., names of people, places, things). While we have known for almost a century how to read khipu numerical sign values in configurations of knots (Locke 1923), we do not know in most cases how to interpret the signs used to signify identities. For example, while we might determine that a specific cord contains knots signing the numerical value '36', we generally cannot say with certainty what such a number referred to – whether to a dimension of a cultivated field, the result of a census count, or another form of measurement. Only in the case of khipus containing either data from astronomical observations organized and recorded in calendrical periodicities (see Urton 2001) or data recorded in the full decimal values used in Inka tribute assignments (see later discussion) can we be relatively certain of the referents of numerical information recorded on khipus. It is important to note in this regard that what we take to be number signs may in some cases have been interpreted as signifiers of identities, as when numbers were used as labels, rather than as magnitudes (see Ascher 2002; Urton 2003 and 2005; Urton and Brezine 2005).[1] Unfortunately, it is not always clear when any given knot configuration recorded on a khipu was meant to be read as a number label rather than as a magnitude; research on this matter is controversial and ongoing.

Given the circumstances outlined, the question arises, What can we say about different types of measurements that might have been recorded on khipus? We can discuss two types of information with a considerable degree of confidence. First, we can detail with considerable specificity what the Spaniards who observed khipus in use in the early years following the conquest (beginning in 1532) had to say about the measurements Inka officials recorded on them. And, second, we can analyze numerical data registered on extant khipu samples. We will find from these two sources of information that we are in fact able to make a number of quite specific suggestions about different types of measure(ment)s that were registered on khipus by local and state administrators.

Before entering into discussions of the various types of data outlined previously, it may be helpful to those not familiar with the Inka khipu to give a brief overview of the structural features and visual characteristics of these remarkable devices.

Khipus and their methods of information registry

According to my own inventory, there are 750+/- khipu samples currently in museums and private collections in Europe, North America, and South America. While some khipus are too fragile to permit study, some 375 samples have been studied closely, and observations on many of these may be viewed at http://khipukamayuq. fas.harvard.edu/. Statistical information pertaining to khipu structures discussed later derives from analyses of data by the Khipu Database project, Harvard University, the home of the Web site noted.[2]

Khipus are knotted-string devices made of spun and plied cotton or camelid fibers. The colors displayed in khipus are the result of the natural colors of cotton fiber and camelid hair or of the dyeing of these materials with natural dyes. The 'backbone' of a khipu is the so-called primary cord, a ca. 0.5 cm in diameter cord to which are attached a variable number of thinner strings, called pendant cords (Fig. 6.1). Khipus contain from as few as one up to as many as 1,500 pendants (the average for 350 of the samples studied to date is 84 cords). Top cords are pendant-like strings that leave the primary cord opposite the pendants, often after being passed through the attachments of a group of pendant strings. Top cords often contain the sum of values knotted on the set of pendant cords they bind together. About one-quarter of all pendant cords have one or more second-order cords, called subsidiaries, attached to them. Subsidiaries may themselves bear subsidiaries, and so on, to produce multiple, branchlike string structures (for an overview of khipu structures, see Conklin 2002).

The majority of khipus have knots tied into pendant, subsidiary, and top strings in tiered clusters in a decimal system of numeration (Locke 1923). Three basic types of knots make up the decimal signing system: figure-8 knots signifying 1s, 'long' knots signifying the values 2–9, and single, or overhand, knots signifying full decimal values (i.e., 10s, 100s, 1,000s). The most thorough and systematic treatment to date of the numerical, arithmetic, and mathematical properties of khipus is Ascher and Ascher's *Mathematics of the Incas: Code of the Quipus* (1997; see also Urton 2003). The Aschers have shown that the arithmetic and mathematical operations used by Inka record keepers included, at a minimum, addition, subtraction, multiplication, and division; division into unequal fractional and proportional parts; and multiplication of integers by fractions (Ascher and Ascher 1997:151–152). It is important to note that khipus were used to record, but not to calculate, numerical values. Values registered on khipus were calculated by means of stones, maize kernels, or other such objects manipulated on the ground (Polo de Ondegardo 1917 [1571]:164; Acosta 2002:343–344; Garcilaso de la Vega 1966 [1609]:124; see also Urton 1998; and Platt 2002) or within what are called *yupanas* ('counters'). The latter are ceramic or stone objects containing compartments representing different subunits or powers of the decimal numeration system (see Gentile and Margarita 1992; Lee 1996; Pereyra 1990; Radicati 2006).

While roughly two-thirds of all khipus studied to date have their knots organized in the decimal manner described, about one-third of samples bear knots scattered across the cords in a nonclustered, nontiered fashion. Researchers are generally of the opinion that such khipus were not records of decimally based quantitative data, but rather, that they contained signs for values and identities consulted in narrative renderings of myths, life histories, event histories (e.g., accounts of battles) laws, and so on (Quilter and Urton 2002). Such narrative renderings of information knotted onto khipus would have employed terms for measurements like those in the second set of definitions given at the beginning of this chapter: representations of the value, extent, magnitude, or greatness of an event or of the actions of an individual in the history of the empire ("The Chankas approached with a *large* and *powerful* army").

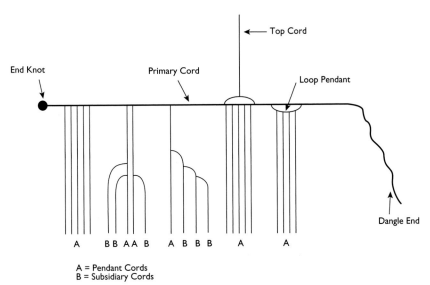

Figure 6.1. Khipu structures.

What kinds of information were recorded on khipus?

From the Spanish chronicles and documents, we learn that the khipu keepers – known as *khipukamayuq* ("knot maker/organizer") – recorded information pertaining to such things as census data and assessments from these of what was owed to the state in the way of labor tribute, including military service and service in state mines; counts of the llama and alpaca herds belonging to the state; and a host of information pertaining to the production, collection, storage, and redistribution of staple goods (maize, potatoes, etc.) and luxury items (e.g., fine textiles, metals, and raw and worked spondylus shell). In addition, the chronicler Garcilaso de la Vega noted that the Inka knew a great deal of geometry because this was necessary for measuring their lands, and adjusting the boundaries and dividing them (Garcilaso de la Vega 1966 [1609]:124). Garcilaso went on to give a more complete accounting of what was recorded on those occasions when the Inka conquered new territory:

> When the Inca had conquered a province he had a record made on his *knots and beads* [i.e., knots] of the pasture lands, high and low hills, ploughlands, estates, mines of metals, saltworks, springs, lakes, and rivers, cotton fields, and wild fruit-trees, and flocks of both kinds, including those that produced wool and those that did not.
>
> All these things and many others he had counted, measured, and recorded under separate headings, firstly the totals for the whole province, and then those for each village and each inhabitant. They measured the length and breadth of the arable land, the cultivable area, and the pasture land. When all the details were known, a full report was made of the whole province. (1966 [1609]:269–270)

When we search the Spanish chronicles and documents for more detailed information concerning possible standard units for measuring distance, length, or weight, as well as capacity measures for liquids, grains, and other substances, or equivalence values used in the exchange of produce (e.g., one unit of corn = X units of potatoes), we find very little specific information. Our best sources on such matters are the colonial dictionaries of native Andean languages. The objective in discussing selected data from these sources later will not be to review all known measures recorded in dictionaries, but rather to identify a few core measuring values and principles and to see how extant khipus might have been used to record them (see Lee 1996; Rostworowski 1960).

According to the Quechua dictionary of González Holguín (1952 [1608]), the general term for measurement was *tupu*. He glosses the term generally as measurement of any thing (*medida de qualquiera cosa*). He also glosses *tupu* as league (*legua*), a Spanish distance measure of approximately three miles. However, in her study of the use of this term as a distance measure in references to the Inka road system, Sanhueza Tohá argues that the *tupu* was of variable length (2004:484 and 486). *Tupuni* is to measure something with a staff (*vara*), or gauge/rule (*medida*), glosses that suggest the existence of standard measuring devices. The phrase denoting the title of the official responsible for measuring land (*allpa*) was *allpa tupuk apu, o cequek apu* ("measurer, or the one who partitions land"). Thus, *tupu* was a measure of length/distance as well as an areal measure. It is unclear what the standard size of an areal *tupu* was in Inka times or whether there even was a standard. Rostworowski documents values for the *tupu* in early colonial sources ranging from such measures as 60 x 50 paces to the amount of land required to support a married couple without children (Rostworowski 1960:15–16). She concludes that the size of the *tupu* was variable and depended on the context of its delineation.[3]

As for subdivisions of the *tupu* used as a land measure, González Holguín notes that half of *huc tupu* ("one *tupu*") was the unit called *checta*; one-quarter of a *tupu* was the *sillcu*; and one-eighth was the *cutmu*. Thus, the normative principle of partitioning *tupus* as reflected in this terminology was the full *tupu* unit successively halved, a process that reflects what was perhaps the most common organizational principle in the Inka state: dualism, or the (repetitive) subdivision of whole units into halves. I would note here, as we will find later, that census accounting and tribute records were organized on a decimal principle, that such values and unit groupings do not appear to have been employed in subdividing length, width, capacity, or other such substance measures.

Several Inka measurements were based on body parts. Examples include the *rikra*, which was equated with the Spanish term *braça* ("arm"), the distance from the midline of the body to the tips of the outstretched fingers of one arm. *Rikra* also indicated the capacity measure of an arm load. Another body part measure was the *ccapi*, glossed as *palmo* ("handspan"). To measure by handspans was termed *ccapani*. The smallest measure was the *yuku*, the distance from the tip of the outstretched index finger to thumb (see Lee 1996; and Rostworowski 1960). Similar body measurements are used in the Andean countryside today, and it has often been supposed that many of the everyday measures and equivalence standards used in highland communities in the ethnographic present were also used in Inka times (e.g., see Valencia Espinoza 1982). While this may have been the case, there is little or no evidence for most such measures in the colonial sources, and I will not enter into an analysis of these issues, given the limitations on space here.[4]

As we are unable to read the subject and topic identities of measurements and other statistical data recorded in khipus, we are therefore uncertain when any given sample might have served as a registry of values drawn from one or another of the common measures mentioned earlier. Nonetheless, careful study of extant khipus allows us to identify samples that display ratios, proportions, and other such numerical values and relations that may result from the recording of standardized measurements (see Lee's discussion of ratios and proportions in Inka architectural measurements, 1996). One straightforward example of such a khipu registry will illustrate the point.

Table 6.1 contains data from a khipu (AS130), in the Museum für Völkerkunde, Berlin, whose provenance is recorded in museum records as "near Lima". The left-hand column in Table 6.1 gives the cord numbers of the 16 pendant cords making up this sample. When a numeral is followed by the designation *s1*, this refers to 'subsidiary 1' of the cord in question (i.e., 1s1 = subsidiary one of cord #1). The column second from the left gives the color codes for the respective cords. The next column to the right, under the heading 'Value', records the reading of the numerical values of knots tied onto cords as interpreted in the standard decimal reading. The information in the column to the far right, 'Alternate Values', shows my calculations of sums of values contained on different cord groupings of khipu AS130.

We see in Table 6.1 that cord #1 contains the value 37 and that it bears a subsidiary cord containing the value 26, giving a total for cord #1 of 63. Next, we note that cords #2 through #12 (including their subsidiaries) contain numerous values between 1 and 3, which total 26, the same value knotted onto subsidiary cord #1s1. Cords #13–#16 and their subsidiaries contain values between 3 and 6 totaling 37, the sum knotted into cord #1 (minus its subsidiary). Thus, cord #1 and its subsidiary carry the same value as cords #2 through #16 and their subsidiaries. While I cannot identify from the information on sample AS130 what substance, or measurement, was recorded on this khipu (though many values in the range of 1–6 may represent census accounts; see Urton 2006), it is clear that some set of items was here being accounted for once as a unitary (actually dual) value: 63 (= 37 + 26) and again as this same pair of values subdivided into two smaller, numerical groupings

Table 6.1. *Khipu record of summation, subdivision, and proportional values*

KHIPU AS130

Cord number	Colour	Value	Alt. values
1	W	37	
1s1	DB:W	26	Cord 1 = 63
2	YB:W	1	
2s1	YB	1	
3	W	1	
3s1	YB	2	
4	YB	2	
4s1	DB:W	2	
5	DB	3	
5s1	YB	1	
6	BS		
7	LB		
8	LB:YG	1	
9	DB-W	1	
10	BS:YB	3	
10s1	YB	3	
11	BS:LB:YG	2	
11s1	YB	1	
12	DB:W	1	
12s1	YB	1	Cords 2–12 = 26
13	YB	4	
13s1	YB	3	
14	DB:W	4	
14s1	YB	4	
15	DB:W	6	
15s1	YB	6	
16	DB:W	5	
16s1	YB	5	Cords 13–16 = 37
			(Cords 2–16 = 63)

of overlapping magnitudes: 1–3 [= 26] and 3–6 [= 37]. The recording and accounting procedures displayed in this example would have been adequate for recording whole values (e.g., of land measures, weights, capacities) divided into numerous subunits, parts, or portions of the whole. These groupings and relations represent a record of quantitative values manipulated in accordance with two different ways of arriving at, or subdividing, the linked sums 26 and 37. The ability to record and manipulate numerical values in the ways shown in this example would have represented the means for recording units of measurements from censuses, or the storage and redistribution of goods in state storehouses (see D'Altroy and Earle 1992).

How often did new information come into khipu accounts?

Once a province had been conquered, its human and material resources counted, and proper order (*buen govierno*) established, regular accounting updates were carried out. Such annual recounts were made of the number of people who had died and been born, changes in the number of camelids in state herds, and other such matters. Our sources generally concur that such local recounts and adjustments were carried out once a year, possibly around November (Cieza de León 1967 [1551]:62; Garcilaso de la Vega 1966 [1609]:273, 326, and 331; Cobo 1983 [1653]:200 and 202; see also Murra 1980:56–57 and 110).

In addition to these annual account adjustments, the state periodically sent inspectors into the countryside to perform complete recounts of the population and of state resources. These large scale, multiyear inspection tours were conducted by the lords of the provinces, the *t'ukrikuq*, accompanied by the local governor, the heads (*caciques*) of each village visited, as well as the local record keepers. The information collected during these multiyear inspection tours was used to make adjustments in the assessment of tribute (see Julien 1988; LeVine 1987). As for the timing of such visits, we are told they occurred either every three or every five years (respectively, Murra [citing a Huamanga source] 1980:109; and Martín de Murúa 2001[1590]:384).

It is important to note that, in the Inka state, 'tribute' took the form of a requirement of labor service – public work time – levied on each tributary in the empire. Garcilaso de la Vega referred to the labor tax as the third law of the Inka state: "that no Indian was ever obliged for any reason to pay anything instead of tribute, but only to pay in labor, with his skill or with the time he devoted to the service of the king and the state" (Garcilaso 1966:273). Every 'taxpayer' (state laborer) was required to work on state projects a specified period of time each year. Using census data recorded on khipus, Inka accountants assessed tribute levels and assigned tasks to different numbers of workers on local projects (e.g., building and maintaining roads, bridges, and storehouses; weaving; guarding the herds of the Inka; see Julien 1988; LeVine 1987; Murra 1982; Urton 2006). In order to understand the types of census accounting units that might have been encoded in the extant khipus, I provide in the following a brief overview of Inka decimal administration. I would stress that the system outlined here is that described in ideal terms by several of the chroniclers; the actual numbers of people in each unit often varied from these ideal numbers (see

the exchange of letters on this question in *Science*, vol. 310, December, 2005:1903–1904).

At the lowest level of the Inka administrative hierarchy, local tributaries were grouped into five accounting units of 10 members each (see Figure 6.2). One member of each group of 10 served as headman, or *chunka kamayuq* ("organizer of 10"). Five such groupings made up a unit of 50 tribute payers under the authority of a *pichqachunka kuraka* ("lord of 50"). Two groups of 50 were combined into a unit of 100 tributaries led by a *pachaka kuraka* ("lord of 100"), and so on, up the decimal hierarchy to the largest named groups, the *hunu*, composed of 10,000 tributaries. Near the top of the administrative hierarchy were the governors, called *t'uqrikuq* (or Toqrikoq, "overseers"), of each of the approximately 80 provinces. Among other duties, the *t'uqrikuq* was responsible for overseeing the collection of census records, as well as for passing the information on up the administrative chain (see Murra 1980:110; Pärssinen 1992:257–287).

The khipu was the principal instrument for recording what was owed and what had been 'paid' – that is, what work had and had not been performed – in state labor. As such, we can expect that perhaps a significant number of extant khipus were produced as records of tribute owed and performed. As I have suggested earlier (1997),

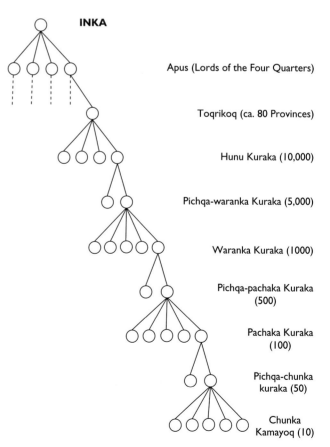

Figure 6.2. Inka decimal administration.

it is likely that khipu accounts of work to be done would have taken the form of notations of full decimal values (e.g., "send 40 workers to repair the bridge"), whereas the accounts of work actually performed would have resulted in a wider and more diverse range of nondecimal values (e.g., "33 workers came to repair the bridge").

As for registries in extant khipus of full decimal values, recent studies of khipu transcriptions from the central Peruvian highlands have shown that, in assigning numbers of tribute laborers to different tasks, Inka accountants derived whole decimal values (e.g., 10, 40, 150) from calculations of standardized percentages of total census counts rounded to whole, decimal numbers. For instance, in a khipu registry from Chupachu, the actual census count of 4,108 households was rounded to 4,000 (= four *waranqas* = 4 x 1000). Labor assignments were then made as percentages of the total: 1 percent = 40 workers; 1.5 percent = 60 workers; and so forth (Julien 1988). The latter represent what the accountants must have regarded as standard measures of sizes of state labor units. There are numerous examples of khipus, all or most of whose numerical information is registered in full decimal units, that may represent registries of just such calculations (see Table 6.2).

Another interesting example, khipu AS161 (Table 6.3), shows two arrangements, or ways of subdividing, a group of 100 (e.g., workers). The first six strings of AS161 contain the nearest equal division of 100 decomposed into six parts (16 + 16 + 17 + 17 + 17 + 17); the last two strings of the sample each contain the value 50. Thus, khipu AS161 could be used as a planning model, or pattern, for subdividing the accounting unit of a group of 100 (*pachaqa*) into two and six subdivisions. Samples such as those detailed in Tables 6.2 and 6.3 could have been used as planning khipus for the organization of decimal labor units in Inka administration.

It is interesting to note in regard to the labor tribute system that the record keepers required means for registering labor debits and credits, which would have constituted forms of measurement in the public labor accounting sector. For instance, Garcilaso de la Vega noted:

> Each craftsman was therefore only obliged to supply his labor and the time needed for the work, which was two months, or at most three. This done, he was not obliged to work any more. However, if there was any work left unfinished, and he wished to go on working of his own free will and see it through, *what he did was discounted from the tribute he owed for the following year*, and the amount was so recorded by means of their knots and beads [i.e., stones for calculating]. (Garcilaso 1966:273; my emphasis)

Table 6.2. *Khipu with all decimal values*

KHIPU AS101 – Part 2 / 1000044		
Cord number	Colour	Value
1	LB	30
1s1	GY	20
2	LB	30
2s1	G0	20
3	LB	70
3s1	G0	50
4	LB	30
4s1	LB:W	20
5	W	70
5s1	KB	30
6	W	70
6s1	KB	30
7	W	90
7s1	KB	40
8	W	70
8s1	KB	30
9	LB:W	30
10	LB:W	30
11	LB:W	70
12	LB:W	30
13	DB:LB	60
13s1	DB:LB	40
14	DB:LB	60
14s1	DB:LB	40
15	DB	120
15s1	DB:LB	60
16	DB	60
16s1	DB:LB	40

Table 6.3. *Khipu with two divisions of 100*

KHIPU AS161 / 1000134			
Cord number	Colour	Value	Alt. values
1	B	16	
2	B	16	
3	B	17	
4	B	17	
5	B	17	
6	B	17	100
7	B	50	
8	B	50	100
		Total: 200	

Garcilaso also noted debit/credit recording measures and accounting techniques in which "the knots showed how much work each Indian had done, what crafts he had worked at, what journeys he had made on the instructions of his ruler or his superiors, and any other occupation he had busied himself with; *all this was deducted from the tribute* he was required to produce" (1966:274–275; my emphasis). Accounting for such arrangements would have required complicated bookkeeping procedures – perhaps similar to those of European double-entry bookkeeping of the time[5] – involving measures of labor debits and credits for tribute workers throughout the empire. Such debit/credit accounting might have taken the form of what we today identify as pairs of 'matching' khipus, perhaps representing audits targeting zero (see Salomon 2004:202).

How was the information on different measurements recorded?

As for the question of what the colonial Spanish sources have to say about how information was actually recorded on khipus, we have several such accounts, which are of varying degrees of usefulness in helping us to interpret extant khipu samples. Such accounts range from the casual, offhanded comment on how information was classified and recorded to fairly detailed explanations (for informative, extended discussions on the latter accounts, see Pärssinen 1992 and Sempat Assadourian 2002). In discussing the khipu accounts kept in the city of Arica, in what is now northern Chile, Martín de Murúa mentions that they used large knots to indicate the towns that the Inka had conquered and small knots to signify the numbers of Indians who had been defeated, and they used black cords to signify the numbers of warriors who had died (Murúa 2001 [1590]:534–535). Garcilaso says that, in conducting censuses of the herds of the Inka, the animals were divided into groups by color; the different groups were then counted and the information was recorded by means of the khipu, "the threads being of the same color as the flocks in each case" (1966:260). He later notes that the animals were also divided up and recorded in terms of the different 'species' to which they belonged (presumably llama and alpaca), as well as by sex (Garcilaso 1966:326). These classificatory differences would likely have been encoded by thread colors on the khipus.

The most probable method for organizing such information is in terms of what is known as 'color banding'. In this type of formatting, cords are grouped by color so that one sees, for example, six dark brown cords followed by six medium brown cords, then six light brown ones,

Figure 6.3. Khipu with colour banding. (Colección Temple/Radicati, Lima, Peru; photo by G. Urton.)

and then six white cords. Different positions within the six strings of the six-cord groupings could have been used to record the counts of specific types of animals of the respective colors (e.g., position #1 = adult female llamas; position #2 = young females; position #3 = adult males). An example of such formatting is shown in Figure 6.3, a khipu from the Santa Valley, on the north-central coast of Peru.

A similar notion appears in Garcilaso's discussion of the recording of tribute, which he says was organized in terms of kind, species, and quality (1966:331). The latter variable – 'quality' – would have involved the use of relative value judgments and corresponding measurement designations (i.e., good, better, best). Garcilaso also says that items that were not entered according to the principle of color symbolism, or color matching (as noted previously), were arranged in an order "beginning with the most important and proceeding to the least, each after its kind, as cereals and vegetables…. In dealing with arms, they placed first those they considered noblest, such as spears, then darts, bows and arrows, clubs and axes, slings, and the other weapons they possessed" (1966:330).

The late John V. Murra (1975) analyzed a transcription of a colonial khipu that was used to record material stolen (*rancheado*) by the Spanish invaders from the old Inka storehouses in Xauxa. In this sample, items were organized according to a principle of hierarchical weighting, or evaluation, producing a classification of 'ethnocategories' in which humans were recorded before animals, llamas were listed first among the animals, maize was the highest-ranked plant, and so on, through a long accounting of categories ranked by native measures of valuation. It is not known how a system of recording ranked types, with ranking within each type, would have been performed. One possible method is what is referred to as 'color seriation' (see Radicati 2006; and Salomon 2004). In this recording technique, cords are organized in repeating color-differentiated sets. For instance, one often finds four-cord sets of strings – dark brown, medium brown, light brown, white – followed by repeating four-cord sets organized in the same color sequencing (see Figure 6.4). In such an arrangement, the order of four-cord sets could reflect the hierarchy of types of objects (first set = humans; second set = animals; third set = arms; etc.). Within the sets, the four positions would rank the members of that type. For instance, for a four-cord set relating to the ranking of arms: dark brown = spears; medium brown = darts; light brown = bows and arrows; white = clubs and axes).

The earlier mention of a khipu that recorded items stolen by Spaniards from an Inka storehouse in Xauxa brings up what was in fact the earliest reference in the Spanish documents pertaining to khipu recording practices. This is the account of Hernando Pizarro, the brother of Francisco Pizarro, the general of the force that invaded Peru, relating to an event that transpired on Hernando Pizarro's expedition from the highlands town of Cajamarca to the coastal pilgrimage site of Pachacamac, in 1533. While traveling along the Inka highway, Hernando Pizarro and his men took several items from an Inka storehouse. Immediately after removing the items, Pizarro reports that the khipu keeper of the storehouse "... untied some of the knots which they had in the deposits section [of the khipu], and [re-]tied them in another section [of the khipu]" (Pizarro 1920:175, 178). Thus, the untying and retying of knots may have been one mode of registry used by at least some khipu keepers. One sees clear evidence of untied knots, such as in the sample from the central coastal site of Chancay, in the Lowe Museum of Art, University of Miami, shown in Figure 6.5. While there

is indeed some evidence of untied knots in extant khipus, it is unclear to what extent the untying of knots was used as a recording strategy in pre-Hispanic times. While Salomon argues that untying knots was a common recording technique in the patrimonial khipus in Tupicocha, I have seen only occasional evidence of the practice in museum samples of khipus. This is a subject of some ongoing controversy among students of the khipus (Salomon 2004:215; Urton 2003:52).

As for the all-important census and tribute records, the Jesuit priest Bernabé Cobo stated in 1653 that

> in order to find out the number of people that there were in each province, including both the natives and the *mitimaes* [transplanted laborers], nobles and plebians, it was ordered that everyone be counted according to age, social position, and marital status; special lists were made of the taxpayers and of those who were exempt, of children, women, and old people.... And a record was made of the exact number of boys, youths, and adult males; and the women were grouped in the same way. Their language has special nouns for each one of these age grades. (Cobo 1983 [1653]:194)

In addition to the various classes and subdivisions of the population outlined by Cobo in the passage cited, he goes on to state that the Inkas made the same division throughout all of their kingdom that they had made in dividing Cuzco into *Hanan* ('upper') Cuzco and *Hurin* ('lower') Cuzco (1983:195). He notes that this dual division of the census data would have been helpful in keeping track of the numbers of people within each 'tribal' (probably *ayllu*) subgrouping. From Cobo's account, we may suppose either that community census data were divided between two different khipus, each recording the census for its respective moiety, or that all of the data from both moieties were recorded twice, once by

Figure 6.4. Khipu with colour seriation. (Museo de Sitio – Puruchuco, Peru; photo by G. Urton.)

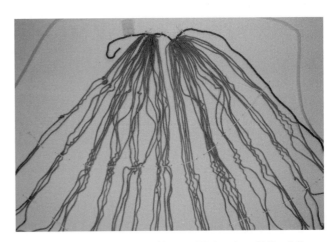

Figure 6.5. Khipu with untied knots. (University of Miami, Lowe Museum of Art; photo by G. Urton.)

the khipu keeper of the upper moiety and again by the khipu keeper of the lower moiety.

In fact, we have testimony in a colonial *visita* (the record of an administrative 'visit', usually made for census purposes) from 1567, which shows that the preferred method of registry – at least in the southeastern quadrant of the empire (i.e., Kullasuyu) – was for the khipu keepers of the provincial moieties each to retain a copy of the full census data from the province as a whole. The document in question is the *visita* of the province of Chucuito, southwest of Lake Titicaca, which was carried out by Garci Diéz de San Miguel (1964 [1567]). At one point in the document, the head (*cacique principal*) of the lower moiety of the province, Martín Cusi, along with his head khipu keeper, Lope Martín Ninara, were asked whether or not the lower moiety census khipu, which dated to the time of the Inka, matched in all respects the khipu that was in the possession of Martín Cari, the *cacique principal* of the upper moiety (see Loza 1998:141, 150). The reply was that, after comparing the two khipus, section by section,

> they [the two khipus] conformed in all their parts/divisions and numbers of Indians in all the towns of *both moieties* [*parcialidades*] *except* that in one section pertaining to the Canas Indians of the town of Pomata the [khipu] of don Martín Cari recorded 20 Indians but that the said don Martín [Cusi] and his quipocamayo said that according to their *quipo* it appeared there were 22 [Canas Indians in Pomata] and that all the other sections [of the two khipus] conformed in the declarations made by the two caciques. (Diéz de San Miguel 1964:74).

We learn several important things about the recording of census figures from this account. First, the khipu keepers for the upper and lower moieties of provinces each retained copies of the census data for the entire province – that is, for both moieties. Second, the census data were recorded in hierarchically organized sections; the census counts for towns were subdivided into figures for the different ethnic groups that made up the town's population. And, third, it was apparently common for the khipu keepers of provincial moieties to check each other's figures. In sum, the information on census khipus from around Lake Titicaca suggests that we might expect to find in the corpus of khipus matching, or paired, samples, one appearing to be a copy of the other (see Loza's discussion of similar accounting organization in upper and lower Huanca; 1998:145–147). In such instances, we ought not be surprised if the two samples do not in fact match exactly in all sections, as was the case with the pair of moiety khipus from Chucuito, which matched

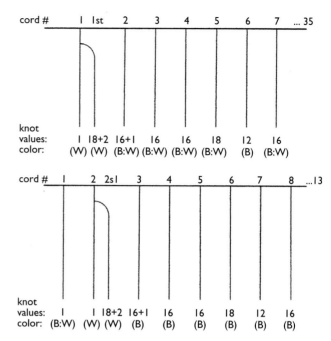

Figure 6.6. A pair of matching khipus.

exactly except for a count of 20 Canas Indians in one of the khipus and 22 in the other.

Several khipus that reflect this (what I term) 'checks and balances' accounting principle have recently been identified in the khipu corpus (see Urton 2005, as well as Quilter's discussion of 'redundancy' in khipu accounts 2002:202). For example, Figure 6.6 displays sections of two khipus that record exactly the same sequence of numbers. The two khipus differ only in terms of their color; such a difference could have marked one sample as pertaining to the upper moiety, the other to the lower. We also have examples, similar to that attested to in the *visita* of Chucuito (earlier), in which, while the values on most cords of two different khipus match, there are small discrepancies in the data recorded on certain of the cords. An example of this type of 'close match' occurs in paired khipus from the Peruvian central coastal site of Puruchuco (Urton and Brezine 2005; see Table 6.4).

Were units of measurement in the khipus standardized?

One issue that emerges from a reading of the various accounts concerning the information collected by the khipu keepers is that record keeping must have been an ongoing, full-time activity throughout the empire. This would have involved great numbers of people assigned to collect, record, and then keep track of information within each community. These data would first have been gathered and organized locally and then forwarded

Table 6.4. *Close match of khipus from Puruchuco*

KHIPU UR064 / 1000263			KHIPU UR068 / 1000262		
Cord number	Colour	Value	Cord number	Colour	Value
1	AB	1	1	AB	1
2	W		2	GG	
3	MB		3	W	
4	GG		4	AB	
5	CB:W		5	KB:W	
6	W		6	W	
7	MB		7	AB	
8	GG	1	8	GG	1
9	CB:W		9	KB:W	
10	W	1	10	W	1
11	AB		11	AB	
12	GG		12	GG	
13	CB:W		13	KB:W	
14	W	3	14	W	3
15	MB		15	AB	
16	GG		16	GG	
17	CB:W		17	KB:W	
18	W	7	18	W	8
18sl	W	1	19	AB	2
19	AB	2	20	GG	1
20	GG	1	21	KB:W	
21	CB:W		22	W	8
22	W	8	23	AB	1
23	MB	1	24	GG	3
24	GG		25	KB:W	1
25	CB:W	1	26	W	56
26	W	56	27	AB	5
27	MB	5	28	GG	4
28	GG		29	KB:W	1
29	CB:W	1	30	W	1,213
30	W	1,212	31	AB	43
31	AB	43	32	GG	64
32	GG	64	33	KB:W	17
33	CB:W	16	34	W	2
33sl	W	1	35	AB	
34	W	2	36	GG	1
35	AB		37	GG:W	
36	GG	1	38	W	8
37	W	8	39	AB	1
38	MB	1	40	GG:AB	1
39	GG:AB:W	1	41	KB:W	
40	CB:W		42	W	8
41	W	8	43	AB	1
42	AB	1	44	GG	3
43	GG	3	45	KB:W	1

to the provincial center, where they would be combined with information from other communities within the province. The resulting information would then be sent or taken to the capital, Cusco. Cieza reported that, every year, the heads of the provinces went with their khipus to Cuzco, where they gave an account of the numbers of people who had been born and those who had died that year in their respective provinces (1967 [1551]:62).

How was recruitment into the 'cadre' of khipu keepers carried out? And to what degree might they have been trained in standardized recording techniques? The answers to these questions depend on the level one is talking about within what was clearly a hierarchy of record keepers. At the lowest, local level, several sources tell us that the record keeping function was performed by old men, cripples, and the incapacitated – that is, by those who were not subject to the annual labor draft (Guaman Poma 1980 [1615]:363 and 365). As these people were longtime residents of their communities, it is likely that they would have been schooled in local traditions of record keeping, which may have differed from those of other distant, or even neighboring, traditions. Such differences might explain Martín de Murúa's observation that "each province, just as it had its own native language also had a new [i.e., different] style of Quipu as well as a new logic [for it]" (Murúa 2001:361).

Murúa's comments raise a question with respect to the degree of standardization, or conventionalization, of the recording techniques and measurements used by khipu keepers throughout the empire. Since the concept of measurement generally implies the existence of a standard unit of measure, how could such standardization have developed within a system in which not just the style but the *logic* of records varied from province to province? We cannot answer this question definitively at the present time. However, it is important to add to this discussion what we learn when we look at how recruitment and training worked at the top of the hierarchy of record keepers. Martín de Murúa provided the following account of a school that was set up in the Inka capital city of Cusco for training state administrators and khipu keepers. These were the sons of nobility and other high-ranking individuals who would later take up important administrative positions in the provinces:

> The Inca ... ordered that the sons of the principal people and the nobility who lived nearby should be taught in a house everything needed in order to be wise and experienced in politics and war. ... Therefore, he set up in his house a school, in which there [were] ... four teachers in charge of the students for different subjects at different times. The first teacher taught first the language of the Inca ... the next [second] teacher taught them to

> worship the idols and the sacred objects [*huacas*] ... . In the third year the next teacher entered and taught them, by use of *quipus*, the business of good government and authority, and the laws and the obedience they had to have for the Inca and his governors ... . The fourth and last year, they learned from the other [fourth] teacher on the cords and *quipus* many histories and deeds of the past ... and of every notable thing that had happened. (Murúa 2001:364; my translation)

Thus, administrative training began with the study of language (probably Quechua, but perhaps Aymara; see Cerrón-Palomino 2004), moved to the inculcation of religious values, and then proceeded through a two-year program of training built around manipulation of the khipus. From Murúa's description, it appears that the students would have been instructed in the statistical measurements associated with 'good governance' during the third year of their schooling and with qualitative and value measurements incorporated in the lessons of Inka history in the fourth year. It is unclear from Murúa's account of the third-year training whether the students learned lessons recited (by the teacher) from khipus, or whether the students learned to manipulate the khipus themselves. I assume it was the latter, as this is stated explicitly for their education in the fourth year ("el cuarto y postrero año, con otro maestro *aprendían en los mismos cordeles y quipos* muchas historias..."; "the fourth and last year, they learned from the other [fourth] teacher on the cords and *quipus* many histories..."). The young men who underwent this program of studies would go on to serve the Inka in prominent positions in the hierarchy of provincial administrative officials. It is quite likely that, as they were trained in the political center by agents of the state, these young noble record keepers would have been schooled in a single, standardized tradition of khipu recording.

From the preceding discussion, we have arrived at two very different views on the standardization of measures and the means of recording them in khipus. I suspect that what we are seeing is a system characterized by the standardization of measures and recording methods at the top, variation among local traditions at the bottom, and a synthesis of these two traditions somewhere midway along the hierarchical chain of record keeping (see Figure 6.2). By a 'synthesis' of traditions, I mean that there may (must?) have been a translation of recording values and methods as information moved up and down the administrative chain. This translation would have operated in a reciprocal fashion; that is, as information moved up the chain of transmission from various locales, it would have arrived at a point at which translation into the 'official code' would have been necessary in order

Puruchuco Accounting Hierarchy

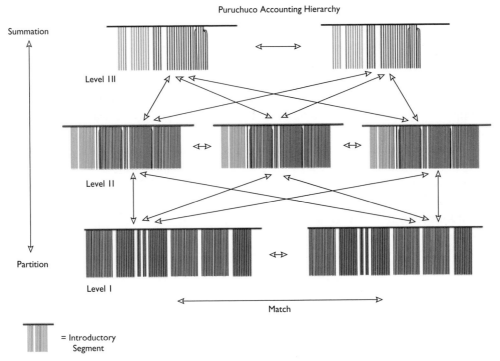

Figure 6.7. The Puruchuco accounting hierarchy.

to combine the accounts and measures from different local sources into a single, official, aggregate accounting. In the other direction, as information moved down the administrative chain, and particularly as it was directed to a specific local community, someone would have had to translate the conventionalized messages from above into the local code, or parlance. In the next section, we will examine a remarkable set of khipus that gives us a glimpse into these processes.

How did information move within the administrative hierarchy?

There is not space to provide a full treatment of the question of where the point(s) of transition and translation may have been located within the hierarchical Inka state administrative structure, as discussed earlier. However, it is important to take note briefly of what we (Urton and Brezine 2005) have recently described as an instance of just such an 'accounting hierarchy' (see Figure 6.7).

Figure 6.7 shows the interrelations among a set of seven khipus that were found, together with 15 other samples, in an urn in a burial located under the floor of a small house near the site of Puruchuco. This site is located in the Rimac Valley, on the central coast of Peru, some 9 km east of the center of present-day Lima, where the river flows between the foothills out onto the broad plain of the Lima valley. Puruchuco has been described

as the 'palace' of a local lord who was subordinate to the Lord of Yschma, the latter of whose political and religious center was the site of Pachacamac, in the nearby Lurin Valley (Villacorta 2005).

The khipu 'accounting hierarchy' from Puruchuco shown in Figure 6.7 operates on two principles: First, khipus on the same level are matching, or 'closely matching' (see previous discussion); thus, each served as a check on the other. And second, the sums of certain groups of four-color seriated cords on Level I, at the bottom of the three-level hierarchy, are recorded on cords of the same color on khipus on Level II, and sums of groups of color seriated cords on Level II are recorded on cords of the same color on Level III. It is important to stress that what I have characterized as the summation of values up the hierarchy can also be characterized (reciprocally) as a division or partition of the larger values recorded on khipus at higher levels to the smaller, multiple values recorded on khipus on the next lower level (for a more detailed discussion, see Urton and Brezine 2005).

The accounting hierarchy from Puruchuco is important for our study of accounting and measurements in the khipus for a number of reasons. First, as we saw in a simpler form in sample AS130 (Table 6.1), the Puruchuco accounting hierarchy shows how khipus could be used either to assemble a sum from numerous, smaller values, or to subdivide a large value into numerous parts, or portions. These reciprocal operations provided the means for accounting for part-whole measures of any number of entities – such as land area, weight, and capacity measures and census and tribute records – in Inka record keeping. Second, this is the first evidence we have from the corpus of extant khipus of the transmission of information between two (or more) khipu samples. Third, the information encoded in the khipus composing this accounting hierarchy was registered by means of color seriation, a method that, as suggested earlier, may have been used in the representation of the hierarchical ranking of values and identities. And, finally, the passing of information up and down the three levels composing the Puruchuco accounting hierarchy provides us with a model of/for how information moved within the hierarchical administrative system of the Inka state, as outlined in Figure 6.2.

Conclusions

We have addressed a number of questions concerning the types or principles of measurement that might have been used in the Inka state, including those for measuring land area, length or distance measures, units and subunits of capacity measures, and a host of data concerning unit groupings, or measures, in census and tribute accounting. We have seen how certain of these measures and administrative groupings are described in the chronicles and how they may have been recorded in the Inka khipus. The central problem in khipu studies today, as it has been since the beginning of the last century, is connecting the ethnohistoric accounts of Inka administrative and 'book'-keeping practices by means of the khipus, on the one hand, with analyses of extant khipus, on the other hand. In the latter case, our ability to interpret khipu numerical data has afforded us considerable insight into Inka administrative principles and practices; however, our continuing inability to interpret the identities of the information recorded on the khipus represents a severe limitation on our ability to gain deeper insights into how the Inka state was organized and how the rich resources – human, animal, mineral, and other – of this great empire were (re-)produced, accounted for, and disposed of (e.g., from work assignments of human labor to the storage and redistribution of goods) by the state.

There is another problem that emerges in relation to our still sketchy understanding of how the Inka administrative apparatus was organized, how actors in the administrative institutions operated, and how administrators themselves interacted with commoners – the *hatunruna* ("great people") – in the countryside. The issue in question concerns the way in which the Spanish chroniclers described the relations of power and the potential for resistance in the Inkaic accounting regime. The ethnohistoric accounts give us a picture of unity and compliance with khipu record keeping on the part of subjects of the Inka in the provinces. Now, it is not just a conceit of postmodern, postcolonial sensibilities that the plans of state apparatchiks are understood often to go awry, or are contested by subjects or 'consumers' at all levels of society. If we assume that this was the case as well in the Inka world (as I do), how are we to evaluate critically khipu accounting practices and their reception and possible rejection by subject populations if we approach the study of these accounting devices and practices through the claims made by Spanish (or Spanish-educated) commentators, virtually all of whose information on these matters came from members of the Inka nobility? Clearly there is the potential for a profound disjunction between the official claims and the (unrecorded) reality of the ways in which people in the provinces may, or may not, have participated in and complied with the Inka accounting program and procedures. If there is, in fact, a disjunction, or distortion, in the official record of the chronicles, the only sources of correction that I am aware of are local documents (e.g., the *visitas*) and careful study of the information encoded in the corpus of extant khipus themselves. The latter is still an uncertain and ambiguous undertaking, given our continuing inability to interpret the identities referenced in the knotted-string accounts.

One important tool that has recently become available for the project identified in the previous paragraph is the searchable database produced by the Khipu Database project at Harvard University. It is hoped that, as work progresses on this and other projects – including the Aschers' studies of khipu mathematics (1997); Salomon's ethnographic research (2004); Conklin's work on the structures of khipus (2002); and Pärssinen and his colleagues' project of transcribing and publishing khipu transcriptions (Pärssinen and Kiviharju 2004) – we will achieve deeper insights into the accounts of khipus contained in the Spanish chronicles and documents. The critical intersection and confrontation we are concerned with here is that between European texts written in alphanumeric script, on one hand, and the records of a civilization that constructed its understanding and representations of the world in supple, colorful knotted threads, on the other.

ACKNOWLEDGEMENTS

I express my sincere appreciation to Professor Colin Renfrew and Dr. Iain Morley for the invitation to participate in the conference 'Measuring the World and Beyond', which was held at the McDonald Institute for Archaeological Research, University of Cambridge, on 13–17 September 2006. I thank as well the other participants in that conference, whose comments and questions were extremely helpful to me as I reworked my presentation for this publication. I thank Carrie Brezine and Jeffrey Quilter for reading and commenting on an earlier draft of this chapter. Thanks also to Brezine for preparing the figures and tables from data in the Khipu Database at Harvard. I alone am responsible for all errors that remain in the chapter. I acknowledge with sincere appreciation the financial support of the National Science Foundation, for research grants over the period 2001–2007 (2001–2004: BCS#0228038; 2003–2004: BCS#0408324; 2006–2007: BCS#0609719) in support of the creation and development of the Khipu Database project at Harvard. I also acknowledge with gratitude additional funds in support of this project over the same period provided by Dumbarton Oaks and the Faculty of Arts and Sciences at Harvard University.

NOTES

1. For example, the nine-digit numbers on U.S. Social Security cards originally indicated such information as the state in which a person was born (since 1972 they have been linked to the Zip code on the application), as well as serially assigned subgroupings of people within that area (http://people.howstuffworks.com/social-security-number2.htm).

2. The Khipu Database (KDB) project was initiated at the Peabody Museum, Harvard University, in 2001. Ms. Carrie J. Brezine, who served as full-time KDB manager from 2001 to 2005, created the entry application for the KDB and has been responsible for all subsequent computer analyses of data on the 350+/- khipus stored in this resource.

3. During the colonial period, the tupu became fixed at 2,200 m2 (Valencia Espinoza 1982:70–71).

4. For an overview of the few known capacity measures in Quechua and Aymara, see Rostworowski (1960).

5. The analysis of the types of accounting methods used in the Inka khipus has received little formal attention to date (see Salomon's extensive data on this topic from his historical and ethnographic studies of the Tupicochan patrimonial khipus; 2004:200–203). The only articles written directly on this topic are a set of three articles published in the *Journal of Accounting Research* (see Jacobsen 1964; Forrester 1968; and Buckmaster 1974). These articles, which have not to my knowledge been referenced in the current spate of khipu studies, focused principally on the question of whether or not the khipus contained a form of double-entry bookkeeping. I am currently at work on an analysis of this question and other related topics concerning khipu accounting and controls (Urton 2009).

REFERENCES

Acosta, J. de, 2002. *Natural and Moral History of the Indies* [1590], edited by J. E. Mangan, with an Introduction and Commentary by Walter D. Mignolo. Translated by Frances López-Morillas. Duke University Press, Durham and London.

Ascher, M., 2002. Reading Khipu: Labels, Structure, and Format. In *Narrative Threads: Accounting and Recounting in Andean Khipu*, edited by J. Quilter & G. Urton. University of Texas Press, Austin, 87–102.

Ascher, M. & R. Ascher, 1997. *Mathematics of the Incas: Code of the Quipus* [1981]. Dover, New York.

Buckmaster, D., 1974. The Incan Quipu and the Jacobsen Hypothesis. *Journal of Accounting Research* **12**, 178–181

Cerrón-Palomino, R., 2004. Aimara as the Inca Official Language. In *Identidad y transformación en el Tawantinsuyu y en los Andes coloniales*, edited by P. Kaulicke, G. Urton & I. Farrington. *Boletín de Arqueología PUCP 8*, 9–22.

Cieza de León, P., 1967. *El Señorío de los Incas* [1551]. Instituto de Estudios Peruanos, Lima.

Cobo, B., 1983. *History of the Inca Empire* [1653]. Translated by R. Hamilton. University of Texas Press, Austin.

Conklin, W. J., 2002. A Khipu Information String Theory. In *Narrative Threads: Accounting and Recounting in Andean Khipu*, edited by J. Quilter & G. Urton. University of Texas Press, Austin, 53–86.

D'Altroy, T. and T. Earle. 1992. Staple Finance, Wealth Finance and Storage in the Inka Political Economy. In *Inka Storage Systems*, edited by T. Y. Levine, pp. 31–61. University of Oklahoma Press, Norman.

Diez de San Miguel, G., 1964. *Visita hecha a la Provincia de Chucuito* [1567]. Ediciones de la Casa de la Cultura del Perú, Lima.

Forrester, D. A. R., 1968. The Incan Contribution to Double-Entry Accounting. *Journal of Accounting Research* **6**, 283.

Garcilaso de la Vega, E., 1966. *Royal Commentaries of the Incas* [1609]. Translated by H. V. Livermore. 2 vols. University of Texas Press, Austin.

Gentile L. & E. Margarita E., 1992. Las investigaciones en torno al sistema de contabilidad incaico estado actual y perspectivas. *Bull. Inst. Fr. Études Andines* **21**, 161–175.

Gonzalez Holguín, D. de, 1952. *Vocabulario de la lengua general de todo el Perú llamada lengua Qquichua o del Inca* [1608]. Universidad Nacional Mayor de San Marcos, Lima.

Guaman Poma de Ayala, F. 1980. *El primer nueva corónica y buen gobierno* [1615], edited by J. V. Murra & R. Adorna. Translated by J. L. Urioste. 3 vols. Siglo Veintiuno, Mexico City.

Jacobsen, L. E., 1964, The Ancient Inca Empire of Peru and the Double Entry Accounting Concept. *Journal of Accounting Research* **2**, 221–228.

Julien, C. 1988. How Inca Decimal Administration Worked. *Ethnohistory* **35**, 257–279.

Lee, V. R., 1996. *Design by Numbers: Architectural Order among the Incas*. Private Publication by V. R. Lee.

LeVine, T. Y., 1987. Inka Labor Service at the Regional Level: The Functional Reality. *Ethnohistory* **34**, 14–46.

Locke, L. L., 1923. *The Ancient Quipu or Peruvian Knot Record*. American Museum of Natural History, New York.

Loza, C. B., 1998. Du Bon Usage des *Quipus* face à l'Administration Coloniale Espagnole (1550–1600). *Population* **1–2**, 139–160.

Murra, J. V., 1975. Las etno-categorías de un khipu estatal. In *Formaciones económicas y políticas en el mundo andino*. Instituto de Estudios Peruanos, Lima, 243–254.

Murra, J. V., 1980. *The Economic Organization of the Inca State*. JAI Press, Greenwich, CT.

Murra, J. V., 1982. The Mit'a Obligations of Ethnic Groups to the Inka State. In *The Inca and Aztec States, 1400–1800: Anthropology and History*, edited by G. A. Collier, R. Renato & J. D. Wirth. Academic Press, New York, 237–262.

Murúa, F. M. de, 2001. *Historia General del Perú* [1590]. Dastin Historia, Madrid.

Pärssinen, M., 1992. *Tawantinsuyu: The Inca State and Its Political Organization*. Studia Historica *43*. Societas Historica Finlandiae, Helsinki.

Pärssinen, M. & J. Kiviharju, 2004. *Textos Andinos: Corpus de textos khipu incaicos y coloniales, Vol. 1.* Instituto Iberoamericano de Finlandia and Universidad Complutense de Madrid, Madrid.

Pereyra, H., 1990. La yupana, complemento operacional de quipu. In *Quipu y yupana: Colección de Escritos*, edited by C. Mackey, H. Pereyra, C. Radicati di Primeglio, H. Rodríguez & O. Valverde. Consejo Nacional de Ciencia y Tecnología, Lima, 235–256.

Pizarro, H., 1920. A los Señores Oydores de la Audiencia Real de Su Magestad. In *Informaciones sobre el antiguo Perú*, edited by H. H. Urteaga. Colección de Libros y Documentos References a la Historia del Perú 3 (2nd series). Sanmartí y Ca., Lima, 6–180.

Platt, T., 2002. Without Deceit or Lies: Variable Chinu Readings during a Sixteenth-Tribute-Restitution Trial. In *Narrative Threads: Accounting and Recounting Andean Khipu*, edited by J. Quilter & G. Urton. University of Texas Press, Austin, 225–265.

Polo de Ondegardo, J., 1917. *Informaciones acerca de la Religión y Gobierno de los Incas*. Colección de Libros y Documentos Referentes a la Historia del Perú 4. Sanmartí y Ca., Lima.

Quilter, J. 2002. Yncap Cimin Quipococ's Knots. In *Narrative Threads: Accounting and Recounting in Andean Khipu*, edited by J. Quilter & G. Urton. University of Texas Press, Austin, 197–222.

Quilter, J. & G. Urton, 2002. *Narrative Threads: Accounting and Recounting in Andean Khipu*. University of Texas Press, Austin.

Radicati di Primeglio, C., 2006. *Estudios sobre los Quipus*, edited and with an introduction by G. Urton. Fondo Editorial Universidad Nacional Mayor de San Marcos, Lima.

Rostworowski de Kiez Canseco, M., 1960. *Pesos y Medidas en el Peru Pre-Hispanico*. Librería y Imprenta Minerva, Lima.

Salomon, F., 2004. *The Cord Keepers: Khipus and Cultural Life in a Peruvian Village*. Duke University Press, Durham and London.

Sanhueza Tohá, C., 2004. Medir, Amojonar, Repartir: Territorialidades y Prácticas Demarcatorias en el Camino Incaico de Atacama (II Región, Chile). *Chungara, Revista de Antropología Chilena* **36**, 483–494.

Sempat Assadourian, C., 2002. String Registries: Native Accounting and Memory According to the Colonial Sources. In *Narrative Threads: Accounting and Recounting in Andean Khipu*, edited by J. Quilter & G. Urton. University of Texas Press, Austin, 119–150.

Urton, G., 1997. *The Social Life of Numbers: A Quechua Ontology of Numbers and Philosophy of Arithmetic*. University of Texas Press, Austin.

Urton, G., 1998. From Knots to Narratives: Reconstructing the Art of Historical Record-Keeping in the Andes from Spanish Transcriptions of Inka *Khipus*. *Ethnohistory* **45**, 409–438.

Urton, G., 2001. A Calendrical and Demographic Tomb Text from Northern Peru. *Latin American Antiquity* **12**, 127–147.

Urton, G., 2003. *Signs of the Inka Khipu: Binary Coding in the Andean Knotted-String Records*. University of Texas Press, Austin.

Urton, G., 2005. Khipu Archives: Duplicate Accounts and Identity Labels in the Inka Knotted String Records. *Latin American Antiquity* **16**, 147–167.

Urton, G., 2006. Censos registrados en cordeles con Amarres. Padrones Poblacionales Pre-Hispánicos y Coloniales Tempranos en los *Khipu* Inka. *Revista Andina* **42**, 153–196.

Urton, G. 2009. Sin, Confession, and the Arts of Book- and Cord-Keeping: An Intercontinental and Transcultural Exploration of Accounting and Governmentality. *Comparative Studies in Society and History* **51**(4), 1–31.

Urton, G. & C. J. Brezine, 2005. Khipu Accounting in Ancient Peru. *Science* **309**, 1065–1067.

Valencia Espinoza, A., 1982. *Pesas y Medidas Inkas*. Cuzco, Peru.

Villacorta Ostolaza, L. F., 2005. *Puruchuco y la Sociedad de Lima: Un homenaje a Arturo Jiménez Borja*. CONCYTEC, Lima.

SECTION II

Materialising the economy

The second section of the book deals specifically with the archaeological identification of the application of measurement to systems of economy and trade. Anna Michailidou opens her consideration of weighing in the Bronze Age Aegean by giving an overview of the occurrence of relative and absolute measurement in Egypt and ancient Greece, where – with an explicit connection between measurement and religion – the invention of systematic weighing was credited to the god Thoth and the hero Palamedes (great-great-great-grandson of Poseidon), respectively. Weighing is attested archaeologically by balances and numerous balance weights, as well as in written sources. The weighing system and activities of the Aegean have to be understood in the context of the other weighing systems and trade activities of the time. Some weights in use in the Aegean and Near East seem to have been deliberately manufactured to act as 'nodal points' for other weighing systems of the period. For example, the Aegean unit of ca. 65.5 grams could have represented 5 Egyptian *deben*, 8 Egyptian *shaty*, and 10 Near Eastern *shekel*.

It seems that many foodstuffs (e.g., grain, flour, pulses, oil, wine) were measured by volume rather than weight (excepting bread, fish, and meat), but that commodities such as metals, yarns, textiles, some wood and ivory, and condiments, dyes, and spices were measured by weight. There were evidently systems in place for the comparison of these two systems too, that is, for the measurement of the weight-value of something offered in exchange for a volume of commodity. Michailidou explores the archaeological evidence for the use of weights from Aegean sites and considers their values, as well as their roles in commercial, palace and burial contexts, and the potential role of expert commodifiers involved in transactions.

Lorenz Rahmstorf's contribution retains the focus on and around the Bronze Age Aegean. His identification of Bronze Age Aegean balance weights amongst those objects previously called only 'pestles' or 'spools' has transformed the interpretation of that type of artefact. Here he discusses the latest results of his work in progress identifying weights from sites in the broader region, and their implications for an understanding of the development and spread of such practices in the Aegean and the Near East. In the first part of the chapter he discusses the likely units of weight in use in different areas, and their relationships with each other, including the Mesopotamian and Syrian shekel and mina, and farther east, with those of the Indus Valley. He goes on to consider the contemporaneous cultural and economic practices likely to have been instrumental in the development and use of these systems, as well as physical and metrical criteria for identifying such objects in the archaeological record.

Mark Kenoyer takes us fully into the Indus Valley itself, presenting the evidence (including new evidence and interpretations from his own excavations) from the Harappan culture for the use of measurement systems, and what such systems can tell us about the prevailing concepts of order and cosmology. He argues for a much longer-term indigenous development of aspects of the urbanised society than has been traditionally presented. Recent excavations at Harappa have revealed that certain artefacts and technologies thought to be diagnostic of later Harappan periods actually have a far longer history and development. These include the production of standardised bricks, cubic weights and the orientation of architecture on the cardinal directions. Kenoyer argues that the cubical stone weights that emerged in the Harappa Phase seem to have been part of a system, along with seals and the great city walls, for the control of trade. Long-distance trade of raw materials and stones used for beads would have required agreed systems for value based on material and/or relative size, and Kenoyer suggests that strings of beads made from these materials may have themselves functioned as standardised exchange units and their production would have involved the use of precise measurements. He goes on to discuss in more detail the use and development of these standardised objects; their possible roles in the control of trade, tithes and taxation; the civic bodies who might have been responsible for the perpetuation of such systems; as well as other symbolic evidence for shared belief systems.

7

Measuring by weight in the Late Bronze Age Aegean: The people behind the measuring tools

Anna Michailidou

Introduction

Κατὰ δὲ Πρωταγόραν τὸν σοφώτατον πάντων χρημάτων ἄνθρωπον μέτρον εἶναι, κατὰ δὲ Θεαίτητον τούτων οὕτως ἐχόντων αἴσθησιν ἐπιστήμην γίγνεσθαι (the doctrine of the great philosopher Protagoras, that man is the measure of all things, and the doctrine of Theaetetus that, since these things are true, perception is knowledge) (Platon, Theaetetus 160 d.9). This quotation may perhaps bring to mind the Egyptian cubit, of the length of a human forearm, and its subdivisions into palms and digits. In architecture, ergonomic requirements, such as the height of a door or the measurements of a staircase, exhibit dimensions related to the human body, whose nature makes them universal and diachronic (cf. Palyvou 2005, 156 with reference to *Modular Man* by Le Corbusier). The technique of measurement by weight is very close to Theaetetus's doctrine that perception leads to knowledge, since everyone can feel which is the heavier of two objects held in the two hands. Thus the mechanism of the balance, which actually predates the invention of weights, in fact reproduces an action performed by the human body itself. In the tomb of Ka-irer, dating to the Old Kingdom of Egypt, there is a scene showing ingots being weighed in a curiously designed balance in the form of woman with arms stretched horizontally (Kisch 1965, 26; Lauer 1976, 77). Furthermore, the most widely occurring largest unit in various metric systems is the heaviest load that a man can comfortably carry on his shoulders, that is, about 30 kilos (Figure 7.1).

Initially, the purpose of a balance was to measure equality. Its first practical use was to confirm two equal parts of the same product, which could then be transported. They could be suspended from the two ends of a long pole resting on the shoulders of the bearer and measured in relation to each other upon distribution.

Figure 7.1. Ox-hide ingot of copper carried by Cretan messenger depicted in an Egyptian tomb painting of the Eighteenth Dynasty (after Karetsou & Andreathaki-Vlazaki 2000, 92, no 67).

The measurement of equality also lies behind the weighing of the deceased's heart in ancient Egyptian iconography. The weight of the heart has to be exactly the same as that of the goddess Maat, who is usually represented by her feather on the other pan of the balance (Faulkner 1985, 34, spell 125). It should be emphasized that this ancient Egyptian concept was different from the *psychostasia (kerostasia)* of the ancient Greeks, because the latter measured the *inequality* that would determine *before his death* the inevitable end of one of the two persons whose fate was being judged (Michailidou 2000a, 146 for references).

Absolute measurement started from the moment when a stone was placed on one of the pans, to balance the commodity placed on the other pan. This provided a visual and more permanent witness to the mass measured, since the stone could be kept and the weighing repeated or the initial result be checked. A survival of this concept is mentioned in an Egyptian papyrus: the tomb robbers keep the stone used as a balance weight when dividing up the

Figure 7.2. The melon-shaped stone weight from Aghia Photia, Crete, with incised Linear A inscription.

spoils from one tomb (Kemp 1991, 248). A special class of noncanonical inscribed weights from Deir el-Medina in Egypt also function as witnesses to standard weights.[1] For instance, we possess a stone with the inscription "*weight of fresh cleaned fish*", the only likely parallel in the Aegean so far found being a melon-shaped stone from Aghia Photia, Crete (Figure 7.2), with the design of a fish and a Linear A inscription on it (Michailidou 2001a, 60–65, 80, figs. 13–18; Alberti 1998).

An advance in the technique of absolute measurement is represented by the use of a series of stones of various interrelated ratios. The invention of a metric system of weight is indeed a cognitive invention,[2] ascribed by the Egyptians to their god Thoth[3] and by ancient Greeks to their hero Palamedes, of the Trojan War (Kakridis 1986). Powell refers to 'metrological organizers' in the Mesopotamian world. Thuraeu-Dangin discusses the two poles in the mechanics of the system, namely, the 'old load', traditionally the maximal weight a man could carry, and the 'new purely conventional unit' invented (in this case the Sumerian Mina).[4] Kopcke claims with regard to the Aegean that "to proclaim standards by which things can be weighed and measured appears to be a time-honoured prerogative of central authority" (Kopcke 1987, 257; Michailidou 2001a, 54). Script and metrology were certainly a means of exercising power in bureaucratic hierarchical societies, where weight-measuring tools were linked with both productive and administrative activities.

1. Material and cognitive measuring equipment

The balance

Up to the Roman period, when the development of the steelyard is attested for the first time, the normal form

of the balance is the simple equal-arm balance with two pans.

Bronze weighing pans are underrepresented at ancient sites for various reasons. They tend to be poorly preserved, their metal was recycled and they were often part of a set of personal belongings. Information on the Aegean in particular is offered by the catalogues of balances by Vandenabeele and Olivier, Petruso and Pare. No truly intact balance has been found; some information on details is perhaps observable on the golden, but nonfunctional balances found in Mycenaean shaft grave III (Vandenabeele & Olivier 1979; Petruso 1992; Pare 1999).[5] The higher number of balances from tombs is a consequence of the fact that grave goods were not normally recycled. More recent finds (e.g., from Mochlos, Crete) have now augmented the samples from settlements (Soles & Davaras 2004; Brogan 2006).

Balance weights

Primarily made of stone, these are a far more common find. The balance weight is in essence the stone that measures (in Akkadian called *abnu* = stone, in Egyptian *inr* = stone). This function is represented in the following text from Deir el-Medina, inscribed on a fragment of stone, whose weight is the witness to the mass of the yarn measured:

> *12 deben, with the weight of two stones, the weight of the yarn of PN* (Michailidou 2001a, 65, which features more on the role of stone in practical processes, plus the relevant bibliography)

In contrast to Egyptian and Near Eastern balance weights, the so-called Minoan or Aegean balance weights (Figure 7.3) are of a distinctive discoid shape, very often made

Figure 7.3. Lead discoid-shaped balance weights from the settlement of Akrotiri on the island of Thera.

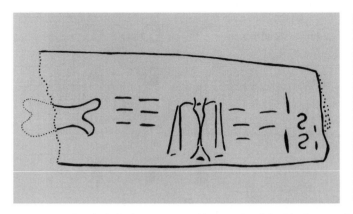 

Figure 7.4. On the left, the Linear B tablet KN Oa 730 with the record of ingots, 60 in number, followed by the sign for the balance functioning as metrogram for one talent in Linear B script (after CoMIK, vol. I). On the right, the sign for the balance in Linear A script.

of lead and as a rule uninscribed, although sometimes marked with signs, some of them being related to the mass of the weights (Petruso 1992, 61). Balance weights of stone, whether discoid or of some other shape, are also in use in the Aegean of the Late Bronze Age, naturally so, since stone is the appropriate material for precision weighing.

Only occasionally are balance weights found in a set and even more rarely together with their scale pans. Petruso, Michailidou, Alberti and Aravantinos provide details on the social context of balance weights in the Aegean era. Such weights derive from palaces; settlements, especially ports; sanctuaries and tombs (Alberti 2003; Aravantinos in Aravantinos & Alberti 2006; Michailidou 1999; Petruso 1992; see also Alberti, Ascalone & Peyronel 2006) and are also found in shipwrecks (Bass 1997; Pulak 2000) .

Written sources

Records of weight, balance weights and the weighing process itself are attested in texts from the Near East and Egypt. In the Aegean, however, in texts of the Linear B script, the only evidence provided concerns the recording of quantities of certain products, found following special ideograms-metrograms denoting units of weight (cf. Petruso 1992, 19, table 1). Linear B ideogram *118, a pictogram of the balance (Figure 7.4), is the sign for the largest unit of weight, the so-called talent (of around 30 kilos weight). There are no similar metrograms in the Linear A script, perhaps apart from the sign of the balance (Michailidou 2000a, 133), which only on four occasions is isolated and followed by numbers;[6] in most of the Linear A tablets this sign is part of a word, though often occurring at the end of the word. However, the existence of klasmatograms, in both Linear A and the Cretan hieroglyphic scripts (Bennett 1950; 1980;

Karnava 2001), is a secure indication of the presence of measuring, as opposed to mere counting. It is most probable that the basic ratios remained the same and that it was only the mode of recording that changed from the Linear A, which features fractions of a larger unit, to Linear B, which involves multiples of integer fractional quantities, represented by the metrograms (Michailidou 2004, 317–318 with views for and against this view).

The metric system

The Minoan/Aegean unit of 61–65.5 grams is the distinctive unit of the Late Bronze Age Aegean, particularly in Crete and the Cyclades during the New Palace era (Evans 1906; Caskey 1969; Parise 1971; Petruso 1992; Michailidou 1990; for a chronological panorama of all the Bronze Age period, see Alberti 2005). Other units have been proposed for previous periods in certain areas (Petruso 1978; Rahmstorf 2003; 2006) or for the Late Mycenaean period (Petruso 2003).[7] As Andrew and Sue Sherratt have rightly pointed out, "Aegean civilization was undoubtedly culturally independent, in that it retained its own languages and developed its own style; but its growth can only be understood in the context of its interaction with these larger economic structures", that is, the Levant, Mesopotamia and Egypt (Sherratt & Sherratt 1991, 355). Whilst there were differences in the metric systems used in these areas, certain equivalences between foreign systems facilitated accounting and interregional trade. The best example is provided by Ugarit, where the 'Western Syrian' mina of 470 grams represented the meeting point for four metric systems, with the differences beginning at the level of its division into shekels (Parise 1984; for more references to this subject cf. Michailidou 2004, 316–317; see also Rahmstorf, this volume; particularly instructive on the subject of metrological interconnections is the article by Zaccagnini

Figure 7.5. A stone balance weight from Akrotiri on Thera of the weight-value of the Syrian mina.

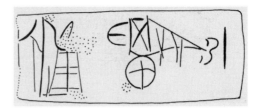

Figure 7.6. The Linear B tablet KN Sc 245+5064 displaying the ideogram for chariot, followed by one digit (after CoMIK, vol. I).

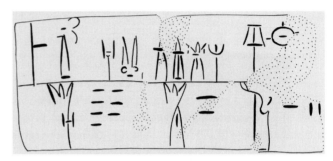

Figure 7.7. The Linear B tablet KN F(2) 852+8071. At the extreme top right is the numeral sign for 10,000 immediately preceded by the ideogram for grain (after CoMIK, vol. I).

1999–2001). With regard to the Aegean system, balance weights of this system have been found in Ugarit (Courtois 1990, 121), possibly also one weight in the Uluburun wreck (Pulak 2000, 264), while the Syrian mina itself is present at Akrotiri (Figure 7.5). The so-called Minoan or Aegean standard of 65.5 grams was defined by Evans as the fifth multiple of the Egyptian unit of gold (13 grams) and by Zaccagnini as the 10th multiple of a Near Eastern shekel of 6.5 grams (Evans 1906; Parise 1971; 1981; Zaccagnini 1986; De Fidio 1998–1999; Michailidou 2004). With regard to any *intentional* equivalences between the various systems of weight, the Minoan unit of 61–65 grams could have acted as a control on the value of both gold (that is, five Egyptian *deben* of gold of ca. 13 grams) and silver (eight Egyptian *shaty* of silver of ca. 7.6 grams), while the heavier unit of 67 grams was equivalent to eight Babylonian shekels, of 8.40 grams. It seems that particular weight-values functioned as keys to interconnections among the various systems of weight and that actual balance weights were intentionally manufactured of these values (e.g., Michailidou 2004, 317; for correlating weighing systems and the masses of metal artifacts see also Lassen 2000; Michailidou 2001b).

2. Commodities to be measured by weight

Accounting of commodities, whether in production, storage or circulation of any kind, is commonly attested in Near Eastern texts, whether in administrative or private archives, and even in letters. In Aegean Linear B tablets, men and women are counted, as are animals, domestic equipment, weapons and chariots (Figure 7.6). The numerals used consist of signs denoting the digit (vertical stroke), the decade (horizontal stroke), the hundred (circle) and the thousand, all of them common in both the Linear A and Linear B scripts. Only in Linear B is there a specific sign denoting the unit of 10,000 (Figure 7.7), a fact that suggests that Mycenaean bureaucrats needed to record greater volumes than did the Minoans. This may be one of the reasons why the Minoan unit, of 61–65.5 grams, though incorporated as a value in Mycenaean accounts (Aravantinos 1995; Petruso 2003), in Chadwick's view, concealed behind the recorded quantity P 3 (Chadwick 1976, 104), is replaced by the recording unit of ca. 1,000 grams, that is the Mycenaean double mina (the so-called metrogram M), a value frequently employed in Anatolia and the Near East also.

For commodities exchanged in long-distance trade, we have the archaeological evidence derived from shipwrecks. Especially helpful in this discussion is the Uluburun wreck, since, in Pulak's view, its load may represent a royal gift destined for some Mycenaean port (Pulak 2005a, 295). How was the merchandise on board measured? Almost 151 balance weights were also found on board. On the basis of textual evidence we suggest that the domed, heavier weights were not used for foodstuffs in general, since commodities such as barley, wheat, flour, pulses, oil, wine, beer and figs are commonly reckoned in various Near Eastern texts by volume, rather than by weight. On the other hand, ivory would be counted when transported or

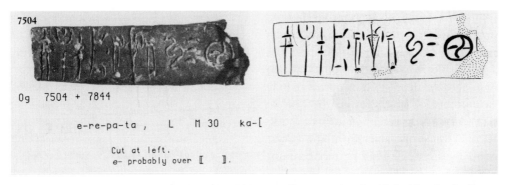

Figure 7.8. The Linear B tablet KN Og 7504+7844 recording one talent (or 30 double minas) of ivory, recorded as *e-re-pa-ta* (after CoMIK, vol. III).

Figure 7.9. Linear B tablets KN Np (2) 860 and Np (2) 861 displaying the ideogram for saffron (extreme left), followed by metrograms for weight and numerals (P 4 and N 1) (after CoMIK, vol. I).

stored as a whole elephant tusk but be measured by weight as fragments (as found in Uluburun: Yalçin, Pulak & Slotta 2005, 583, fig. 83) because ivory is recorded by weight (Figure 7.8) in a tablet from Knossos (Trantalidou 2001, 276; also Pare 1999 with reference to Herodotus's mention of 20 big elephant tusks). A good piece of evidence in this direction is the discovery of balance weights along with half-worked ivories in the so-called Ivory Workshop at Thebes, of LH IIIB1 date (Aravantinos in Aravantinos & Alberti 2006). Taking into account additional evidence from Near Eastern texts, we may conclude that several commodities were accounted by weight, these being metals, wool and goat's hair, linen (possibly also counted in bundles: Chadwick 1976, 153–154), yarn, textiles (e.g., when tested in relation to the raw material used, otherwise officially recorded by numbers), ropes (apart from cases involving measuring of length), alum, wood (occasionally, otherwise mostly counted by pieces), ivory, precious stones, hides (sometimes, otherwise mostly counted, see Trantalidou 2001, 277–87); also some condiments, perfume and dyes (Sarpaki 2001) such as ponikijo, red safflower and saffron (Figure 7.9), the majority of the rest being measured by volume. Also weighed are celery, wax and tendons. As for foodstuffs, there were only some cases of loaves being recorded by weight (they were normally counted), fish (which are normally counted or measured by volume) and possibly meat.

3. Activities involving weighing

The process of weighing is attested in Near Eastern texts as part of economic activities related to manufacture, transportation/transmission and exchange at various levels.[8] In the Aegean Linear B texts, the *ta-ra-si-ja* mode of production[9] is based on the weighing of the raw material distributed to artisans and then of the finished products delivered by the craftsmen. This system was used in the production of textiles, in bronze working and chariot wheel production. Otherwise, fewer details regarding weighing are recorded in the Linear B texts (Michailidou 2001b).

With regard to long-distance transportation, in antiquity ships or caravans of donkeys and mules were used. The Old Assyrian traders transporting tin and textiles to Asia Minor employed their own balance weights to check their merchandise, but they also counted it by donkey loads.[10] Each donkey carried 65 kilos, divided into two packets, which meant that the net merchandise was two talents plus an extra amount for various expenses. Today villagers in Crete often calculate 50 kilos for each side of the donkey, but distances in Crete are shorter.

Weight in transportation was a factor that also influenced units of volume. This accounts for why the largest pure unit of dry measure in the Linear B texts, which is always indicated by the particular dry-commodity ideogram itself (Figure 7.10), consists of 10 units of 9.6 litres, that is, 96 litres, whilst the largest liquid measure, again denoted by the relevant ideogram of the commodity, equals only three units of 9.6 litres, that is, 28.8 litres (Palaima 2005, 269; for other absolute values cf. also Chadwick 1976, 106). The weight of a litre of oil, a little lighter than the water equivalent of 1 l. = 1 kg, is much heavier than a litre of wheat. The largest unit of volume of a commodity, whether dry or liquid, was in fact the content of a standard sack made of some material such as leather, wool, goat hair, or of a jar or a basket.[11] The most typical jars used in long-distance marine trade as containers of organic materials or manufactured items are the Syro-Canaanite jars, the Cypriot jars and the Aegean stirrup-jars made in standard volumes, which allowed one to estimate the quantity transported merely by counting the number of jars.[12] Standardization of stirrup-jars is also found in the large quantity of 1,800 jars recorded in one Linear B tablet from the palace archive of Knossos (Figure 7.11). Most pottery containers, of course, could be used during their life to convey different commodities. Herodotus (III.6) explains that though wine was imported to Egypt from Greece and Phoenicia, no wine jars were found because people in Egypt gathered the containers after use in Memphis, filled them with water and sent them to the Syrian desert. In connection with this, Rutter makes the interesting remark that the Aegean stirrup-jars carried by the Uluburun ship were in fact in secondary use (cited in Bachhuber 2006, 347). Moreover, their fabric points to a variety of different production centers, mostly on Crete (Pulak 2005a, 297, citing Day 1999, 68), whence they very probably made their first journey, containing oil or wine.

Linear B tablets, given that they function only as "system-internal mnemonic texts" (Palaima 2005, 274, n. 15), do not contain information on long-distance trade; the only – indirect – evidence is some references to ship construction and manning of ships or some records of foreign names of commodities or 'ethnic' names of individuals or groups (Palaima 1991). In Malcolm Wiener's view, texts related to long-distance expeditions will have been written on materials other than clay, more suitable for surviving storage over the longer period needed for such expeditions (cf. Wiener 1999).

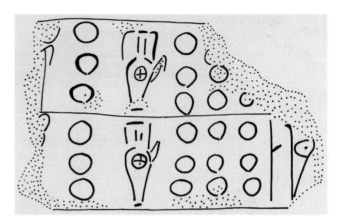

Figure 7.11. The Linear B tablet KN K 700 displaying the account for 1,800 stirrup-jars in two entries of 900 each (after CoMIK, vol. I).

Turning to pictorial evidence, we note that, in spite of the rich repertoire in Aegean wall paintings, there exists no surviving depiction of weighing. This is only partially to be explained by the Aegean avoidance of subjects drawn from everyday activities. The only exception so far comes from a little farther afield, from the island of Cyprus, on a vase from Enkomi (see Pare 1999, 474–476 for a summary of the various views on this depiction). Strangely enough, representation of weighing is also extremely limited in Near Eastern iconography (there are very few on seal iconography: e.g., *OIP* 47, no. 42). On the other hand, however, scenes of craftsmen weighing, accompanied by captions, are abundant in Egyptian iconography, in relation to gold measuring and jewellery making. Weighing tools depicted as being employed in industry were either the large freestanding balance, with balance weights shown nearby, or the smaller portable balance. Such portable balances are also depicted in the hands of traders, as is the case of an Egyptian who receives, either for his own or his master's account, the merchandise offered by a Syrian (in a scene from the tomb of Kenamun, Eighteenth Dynasty: Kemp 1991, 253–254, fig. 86). In this scene it is clear that what is to be weighed by the Egyptian is the product given in exchange, rather than the jar of wine. Thus balance weights were necessary both for measuring the mass of the merchandise offered and for estimating the value of the means of payment in return, presumably consisting here of metal or spices (Kemp 1991, 253; James 1984, 256). It is no surprise that the only mathematical problem presented in the Rhind Mathematical Papyrus referring to weighing (no. 62) deals with this subject of the evaluation of metals (Robins & Shute 1987, 50).

So, we now turn to the importance of weighing activity in the evaluation of commodities. Recalling once more that Πάντων χρημάτων μέτρον ἄνθρωπος

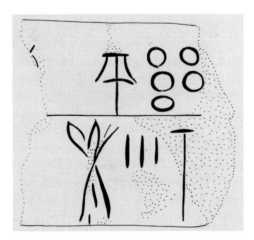

Figure 7.10. The Linear B tablet KN F(2) 853+5947+6035 recording quantities of grain (500+) and olives ((3 and 1/10 +) measured in units of capacity for dry commodities (after CoMIK, vol. I).

('man is the measure of all things') and that Χρήματα (lit. 'money') means 'that of which I am in need' (ἔχω χρεία) and thus πράγματα, ἀγαθά ('property', 'goods', 'wealth'), we can now proceed to the phrase that χρήματα δὲ λέγομεν πάντα ὅσων ἡ ἀξία νομίσματι μετρεῖται ("wealth we call all that deserve to be measured by coins") (Aristotle, *The Nikomachean Ethics* IV, 1,2). Hence the variation in the meanings of the words 'money', 'currency' and 'coinage' becomes comprehensible. In pre-coinage societies, such as the Bronze Age Aegean and its neighbours, we are dealing with the commodities that were in demand, and it has rightly been noted that "what was spreading can be summarized as consumer demand" (Sherratt & Sherratt 1991, 355–356). Certain commodities became trade goods par excellence and they were actually occasionally used as means of payment. The cheapest of these was barley, measured in volume, and the most universally acceptable were metals, measured by weight, with silver serving also as a denominator of value. James rightly points out that even in Egypt, where the barter system involved goods being traded against goods, 'value' came in time to mean 'metal value', which he defines as an almost monetary conception (James 1984, 257).

Anna Sacconi has recently put forward the view that monetary indications are present in some of the Linear B texts (Sacconi 2005). I have also recently suggested that Minoan economy was partly a monetary, albeit precoinage, economy. For instance, nonfunctional metal axeheads, in particular when made of precious metals, may have functioned as gifts made by the state in return for services, and therefore as means of payment. Axeheads cut from copper plate, such as those found in the sanctuary of Juchtas on Crete, may have functioned as cheaper forms of currency. In both instances small axeheads are perhaps definable as *sacred* money (Michailidou 2003; 2005, 22, fig. 9).

To return to activities more humble than the estimation of the exchange value of merchandise: many aspects of everyday life would be unknown to us, had not the texts survived. In industry wax, for instance, was weighed:

7 minas of wax for coating the doors

was the amount needed for a matrix (?) for the construction of a bronze door, while bitumen (measured by weight) and whitewash were also used for doors, the latter being measured in volume or weight (1–1½ kg for one door) (Salonen 1961, 115–116). In the Assyrian Lexicon under the entry for 'whitewash' (*gassu*), there is a comment on magic drawings relating to a particular text:

with whitewash I drew (a picture of) the Fighting Twins inside the Door (CAD, sv *gassu*: text: *AoF* XIV 150.215 f)

This recalls the Theran wall painting of the fighting twins (Doumas 1992, Pl. 79), which, located as it is on the upper floor between two doors, perhaps had the semiotic meaning of guarding the entrances to the private room and to the room with the depositories. In the following section we will look more closely at the material and textual evidence from Thera, which will enable us gradually to progress from the tools of measurement themselves as found, to their owners, as hypothesised.

4. Akrotiri on Thera: A settlement case study

Akrotiri was a settlement of an urban character, which flourished around the middle of the second millennium (LM IA), during the period when the Cretan Linear A script and the 'Minoan' metric system of weight were expanding. This site enjoys the advantage of not belonging directly to the Minoan palace system or to the – later – Mycenaean bureaucratic environment. Moreover, a significant quantity of the original household equipment has survived, protected by the layers of pumice produced during the eruption of the volcano.

Regarding the distribution of lead weights in this settlement, several points are to be noted. Apart from the fact that weights have been found in almost every building, there is the particular feature whereby whole groups of weights have been found in the same house, sometimes even in the same room. Such is the case of the West House, where 26 discs were found in the storeroom of the upper floor. This group also incorporates a lead weight of 3 kilos, that is, of the same value as that of the particular Mycenaean unit for wool (LANA). In the same house, the great number of loom weights, over 400, indicates that a weaving workshop functioned on the upper floor. Thus these 26 balance weights may have been used for weighing wool (Tzachili 1990; Michailidou 1990). Tzachili emphasizes that traces of measuring are a strong indication that the producer is not the same person as the consumer, because people rarely count goods if they produce them for their own consumption (Tzachili 2001b, 178). In Tzachili's view, cloth making at Akrotiri was the work of specialized weavers, which accounts for the fact that loom weights are not found in every house (Tzachili 1990, 385). To date, at least three weaving workshops have been identified on the upper story of three houses, whilst in two of them collections of lead weights have also been found (Michailidou 1990, 417–418).[13] Thus

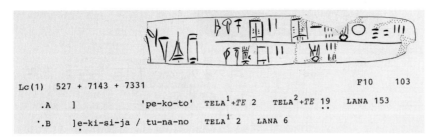

Lc(1)   527 + 7143 + 7331   F10   103

  .A   ]   'pe-ko-to' TELA^1+*TE* 2   TELA^2+*TE* 19   LANA 153

 `.B   ]e-ki-si-ja / tu-na-no   TELA^1 2   LANA 6

Figure 7.12. The Linear B tablet KN Lc (1) 527+7143+7331 with entries for textiles TELA + *TE* amd TELA *tu-na-no*, followed by the unit of wool (LANA) in quantities required for these qualities of cloth (after CoMIK, vol. I).

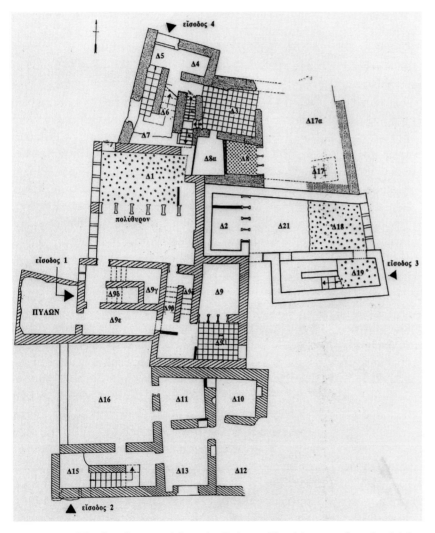

Figure 7.13. The four houses of Complex Delta at Akrotiri, upper floor level (after Michailidou 2001c). The tablets were found in the storeroom below the room Δ 18, in the House with entrance 3 on its eastern side.

cloth producers were able to weigh the raw material for themselves, as they did perhaps in some connection to the type of cloth in demand. The range in quantity of wool needed for particular types of textiles is confirmed by the Mycenaean Linear B tablets. We have, for example, three units of wool (LANA) for the cloth TELA *tu-na-no* or 7 units of wool for the cloth TELA + *TE* (Figure 7.12). Some varieties of cloth are known even from Linear A texts (as TELA + *KU* and TELA + *ZO*), whilst a new unknown variety (TELA + *SE*) is recorded at Akrotiri, attested by Boulotis on the Linear A tablet THE 8 found in one of the four houses of Complex Delta (Figure 7.13). Another fragment of a tablet from the same house records about 46 sheep. It would seem, then, that only the record of quantities of wool, not in any case a frequently attested activity in Linear A, is missing or not preserved (Boulotis 1998; 2008, 82).[14] Boulotis emphasizes the point that, if one were right in supposing that the occupant of this house supplied the wool from his flocks, thereafter receiving and recording the textiles on tablets kept in his own house, this situation would indicate a pre-stage of the *ta-ra-si-ja* mode of production, known to us only from the later Mycenaean archives (Boulotis 2008, 86). Textiles were recorded by numbers on the Linear B tablets (e.g., Tzachili 2001b), as they also were in the fewer instances on Linear A tablets. However, it is in Akrotiri itself that the only record in Linear A of a great number of textiles (200+) has been found. Tzachili has emphasized that evidence for weaving is concentrated in ports. We may then wonder to what extent cloth production at Akrotiri was export oriented.

We may recall here the trade mechanisms of the Old Assyrian traders. A number of the textiles sent from Assur were locally produced in their households, but other varieties, namely, the famous Accadian textiles, were imported to Assur, thereafter to be sent to Asia Minor via the same caravans. In Veenhof's view (Veenhof 1972), production only played a limited role in the trade, which hence consisted essentially of linking separate but somehow complementary markets. In such a case, Akrotiri may also have functioned as a port of entry and transit depot for merchandise arriving from elsewhere, such as Crete, since the occupant of the house with the tablets was in contact with Crete, as indicated by the sealings, that is, flat-based nodules, on Cretan clay found in the same house. There are reasons for believing that the whole Complex Delta was inhabited by merchants (Michailidou 2008, 247–249; Boulotis 2008):

Lead weights were found in all four houses of this complex, together with three balances in two of the houses (for more detail see Michailidou 2008, 49). Two of the balances are from a basement storeroom with exotic material, that is, two ostrich eggs, and the balance weight of the weight-value of a Syrian mina was also found in this room (Figure 7.5), according to the late Emily Spyridon Marinatos. In another house of the same complex, the heaviest lead balance weight with a bronze handle was found, 15 kilos in weight, to be considered as a half-talent. As pointed out elsewhere, "the concentration of examples of writing observed in at least three out of the four houses in Complex Delta is possibly related to the particular finds in the storerooms of these houses and, in my view, these finds suggest that the occupants may have been businessmen or merchants. These were probably the people who came into contact with Crete (receiving and reading the sealed correspondence) and with other parts of the Mediterranean, as well" (Michailidou 2000–2001 with the discussion on the subject of literacy at Akrotiri). One may also quote the article by C. Michel, "Les marchands et les nombres", in relation again to the Old Assyrian traders, in particular with regard to the letter of a trader's son living and working in Assur, where he is also being trained in script. Evidence for the intellectual equipment required of traders is certain school texts among the Kültepe tablets that deal with problems of equivalence among commodities (Michel 1998).

Besides the involvement of people of the settlement in long-distance trade, we also need to consider measuring in their intracommunity exchanges (for other ways of practical accounting, cf. Tzachili 2002–2003). Though we lack any letters, apart from a temporary note on an 'ostrakon' of unknown purpose (Michailidou 1992–1993), we may expect for Akrotiri something similar to Renger's view for Mesopotamia: "More or less everything that played a role in the daily life of the inhabitants of Ancient Mesopotamia changed hands.... According to the letters, the following goods or objects were bought: barley, flour, oil, beer, dates, and fish, as well as more unusual foodstuffs, – such as wild doves, locust, duck-eggs –, wool, garments, shoes or sandals, oxen, sheep, and a variety of raw materials" (Renger 1984, 102, 106). In Akrotiri, capacity measures certainly facilitated the exchanges of dry and liquid agricultural staples and foodstuffs such as grain, flour,

pulses, figs, olives, wine and oil. Such products could be reckoned thanks to the number of standardized pots (studied so far: cf. Doumas and Constantinides 1990; Katsa-Tomara 1990; more recently Younger 2003) and possibly recorded by the Linear A klasmatograms.[15] The heavier balance weights were capable of estimating wool masses, whilst the lighter ones, most probably of stone, may have measured the mass of precious commodities, for example, saffron, as is the case in the Linear B evidence (Figure 7.9), since saffron was gathered in the island itself, as is shown by the evidence from frescoes. A rounded sherd from Akrotiri, which bears – in my view – a postfire Linear A sign and was found in the Mill Room entrance of one of the houses of Complex Delta,[16] may have been a token perhaps functioning like the 'noduli' of the Minoan administrative system (Michailidou 2000–2001, 22–23; Weingarten 1986 suggests that noduli are dockets, i.e., receipts for work done). Abundant quantities of similar rounded sherds, not, as a rule, inscribed, come from various parts of the settlement. They may have been used as counters or tokens for intracommunity exchanges.

5. The owners and users of the weighing equipment

In settlements

To summarize our evidence from Akrotiri: lead balance weights of the Minoan/Aegean standard were found in various situations and locales:

1. They were found in almost all buildings. Thus all inhabitants may have made use of them in relation to activities involving commodities measured by weight (cf. sections 2–3).
2. In certain houses they were found in clusters, along with loom weights, suggesting that they played a particular role in textile production.
3. They were more usually found without the balance. Lead weights may not always have been used on bronze pans, and there may also have been balances of wood or basketry. Alternatively, some bronze balances may not have been left behind by the departing inhabitants. We know from Old Babylonian texts that balances were indeed often included in inherited property.
4. In particular, in the four houses of Complex Delta, weights and balances may be the property of merchants (cf. section 4).
5. Stone weights were also found. They are most appropriate for precision weighing, especially in small-scale

pans. The building called Xeste 3, adorned with the frescoes of crocus gatherers (Doumas 1992, 127 *ff*) and regarded by Doumas as being of a public character, yielded a marble weight possibly representing the imported 'Minoan' standard. Moreover, a half-fragment of a barrel-shaped hematite weight from one of the houses of Complex Delta was purposely adapted to one-third of the Minoan unit (this balance weight is of a non-Minoan shape and material: Michailidou 2006, 238–241, figs. 2 and 3).

Thus the textile producer himself presumably measured the raw material he received and then the product he produced. To gain some idea of the quantities in the chain of production, we will use Killen's results from the Linear B evidence, which, however, cannot be absolutely applied to the data from the Linear A. Since the amount of wool produced per sheep varied depending on gender, culture and time, we can present only a working hypothesis. Thus, with regard to the 46 sheep mentioned in the tablet from Complex Delta, we attempt to calculate the greatest possible production of their wool, based on the four sheep to one LANA ratio of the Linear B evidence: it will have corresponded to 11½ LANA or 34½ kilos, enough quantity for the produce of, for example, 17 *pa-we-a ko-u- ra* (of 2 kilos each). If, instead, we choose the quality TELA + *KU* because this, unlike the previous case, is actually recorded in Linear A texts, then the result will be 11 textiles, of 1 wool unit (3 kilos) each (for the preceding textiles and wool see, for instance, Killen 2001, 172). We do not know the wool amount needed for the newly attested quality TELA + *SE*, or whether indeed these textiles were of wool (Boulotis 2008, 82, refers also to the possibility that they were of silk but ultimately retains the view that they were of wool).

The user/owner of the half-talent balance weight, who was apparently living, or working, in the next house of the same complex, was able to measure by himself, perhaps by means of some wooden balance that has not survived, five units of wool (received from his neighbor?). He could also have measured a half-ingot of copper. A fragment of copper ingot has been found in Akrotiri weighing three kilos. However, a copper half-ingot of 15 kilograms was found at Mochlos, on Crete, another settlement where many balance weights and at least five sets of bronze scale pans were recovered from a variety of contexts within the LM IB community. Coming from the ceremonial centre, several town houses, the artisans' quarters and a rural farmstead, they thus testify, in the view of the excavators, to the role they played in the trade of raw materials and the production and exchange of goods (Brogan 2006; for evidence from the settlement of Poros, Crete, see Dimopoulou 1997). Of the older

Figure 7.14. Lead weight from Mochlos with incised Linear A inscription (after Karetsou 2000, 136, fig. 17).

finds by Sieger, we may also mention here the inscribed lead weight (Figure 7.14), there being a slight possibility, on the basis of Egyptian parallels, that the Linear A inscription may be connected with ownership of the object. Such a hypothesis cannot be proved, of course, and, besides, in the Aegean there was no tradition of inscribing balance weights (Olivier 1989; Michailidou 2001a, 66).

In palaces

The invention of standards for measuring goods was the task of central authorities. Thus a stone 'anchor' of the weight-value of a talent from the palace at Knossos is certainly a candidate for identification as an official weight standard (Petruso 1992, Pl. 7, no. 73; Michailidou 2001a, and references therein). Since no evidence of the weighing process itself exists in the palatial Mycenaean archives, we turn to the examples in Egyptian iconography, where at least two persons are involved: the specialist(s) who deals with the function of the balance and the scribe reckoning the result. An official depicted on a large scale, who is the owner of the tomb, is frequently found inspecting the process as part of the various economic activities for which he is responsible. In the view of Vercoutter, the title *the Scribe who counts the Gold* is applied to either a person working in workshops or one who is participating in the pharaonic expeditions to gold mines. Graffiti such as *the scribe who counts the gold Anupenhab* complement captions such as *the scribe who counts the gold Harnufe*r found placed over the head of the scribe in the painting from the tomb of Huy, viceroy of the Pharaoh in Nubia (Vercoutter 1959). When a weighing scene is subsequently depicted in the ideological domain (Faulkner 1985, 34), the god Thoth takes the place of the scribe and the god Anoubis the place of the balance specialist, while 14 gods and goddesses are depicted witnessing the judgment (Vercoutter 1959; Michailidou 2000a, fig. 28).

More information on persons participating in weighing in the palace environment is to be gained from texts from Mari. The following are recorded as participating in a proper weighing process:[17]

1. One or two specialist/s in handling the balance, usually a worker in precious metals or possibly an administrator (Joannès 1989, 127–128, nn. 63–64).
2. The scribe reckoning the result, who was only a specialist in script. He gives various details of the process of weighing, for instance, the occasional use of a counterweight.
3. One or more persons, named *ebbû* (translated in French by Cecil Michel as the 'Prud'Homme'), are on occasion mentioned as supervising, with a view to ensuring the exactness of the weighing process.

We learn from these texts that the heavier weights used were made of lead, which is so commonly found in the Aegean, although not present in the archaeological record from Mesopotamia (cf. also Ratnagar 2003, 84). The highest weight-value mentioned for a balance weight is 10 minas (5 kg); the highest quantity weighed is 25 minas (12.798 kg). For weights greater than this, a second weighing, a third, and so on, were performed, while the lightest quantity weighed is 135 grains (6.21 grams).

We also learn about the origin of some of the balance weights. We hear of "weights of the royal service", "weights of the market", in one case "weight of the sanctuary" and weights of certain named persons. When traveling, the king of Mari took with him both balances and weights and the balance specialists themselves, who were more probably jewellery makers. During the journey (e.g., to Ugarit) they weighed the precious objects given or received. Balance specialists and their tools are also following the Mari army to Babylon. Exactness in weighing, to a degree of one shekel, was required at all stages of metal technology and was also regarded as indicative of the "valeur morale d'un fonctionnaire". This thus accounts for why the origin of the weights is mentioned (that is, whether it belongs to the royal service or not) and the presence of the *ebbû* ('honest men' or connoisseurs) is required (Joannès 1989, 127, n. 62).

The funerary context

Any attempt to conceive the meaning of weighing tools in tombs always leads to consideration of the semiotic or/and symbolic role of such tools. They were deposited in both male and female burials and were most common during the LH II, LH II-III in the Mainland and LM III in Crete (Alberti 2003). The most frequent find is the balance. Only in three or four cases is this found along with weights, although few tombs have produced only weights. The balances are carefully made and functional, and, in Alberti's view, the wide dimensional range of the pans (4.5–17.7 cm) indicates the ability to weigh masses from less than 15 grams to ca. 3 kilos (Alberti 2003). They are generally found in well-defined tombs with fairly rich grave goods. According to Pare, "it is most likely that they generally did not enter the graves invested with any profound symbolic meaning, but instead comprise elements of the deceased's personal possessions" and this leads him to the interesting conclusion that "scales and sets of weights were possessions fairly common among high status individuals in the Aegean between the 17th and 12th cent. B.C.... These people do not seem to have had a specialist function: craftsmen's tools are not found among the grave-goods, and there is no evidence for specialist merchants in the Bronze Age Aegean" (Pare 1999, 474–476). As will be considered at the end of this chapter, I think that some of these persons may have performed specialist functions. However this may be, Pare's view of them as owners of measuring tools is certainly very important.

On shipboard

Weighing tools from wrecks are "of great value due to their contemporaneous use as functioning sets within related commercial context at the time of the ship's sinking" (Pulak 2006, 47). At the same time they are more difficult to interpret, since "every item found on a ship was carried onto that ship for a purpose" (Bass 2006, 85). The explanation suggested by Bass for the Cape Gelinodya wreck of the 12th century, that it may have belonged to a private trader, a species of an itinerant smith using the 65 balance weights found on board, mostly based on a Syrian standard (Bass 1991, 73), may be consonant with the explanation offered by Stieglitz for the presence of length-measuring instruments of the itinerant architect on board a fifth-century BC ship (Stieglitz 2006, 203). Of the 151 balance weights from the Uluburun wreck, at least seven sets (of which four display sphendonoid and three domed weights) were based on the current Syrian (and Cypriote) norm of ca. 9.3 grams. Two additional sets based on a unit mass of 7.4 grams and 8.3 grams were also present. Three pairs of scale pans were found, one or two being inside a wooden box (Pulak 2000; also 2005b). Thus, at least three merchants, possibly four, who may have been Syrians or Cypriots, will have been aboard the ship, in Pulak's view, each one being equipped with a sphendonoid set for accurate weighing of small valuable commodities, and one domed set for weighing bulkier merchandise. Pulak suggests that the merchants on board used their weights at the ports in order to estimate the value of the items received in exchange for the merchandise they delivered (Pulak 2000). However, in the Egyptian painting depicting the Syrian traders, we apparently see the opposite, if, of course, we take the depiction literally (as the bibliography stated does) and provided that the balances here are not confined to a semiotic role, intended to underline the role of the holder as trader. Pulak further suggests that two Mycenaeans on board "acted as emissaries or envoys, accompanying a cargo of reciprocated 'gift exchange' to the Aegean" and that "they may have been the 'messengers' of ancient literary sources, returning from a 'diplomatic' mission to the Near East", naturally causing one to reflect upon their possible position in the palatial administration (Pulak 2005a, 308). He rejects the idea that they are merchants, because as merchants they would have carried their own balance weights. We are immediately confronted with the amorphous problem of how to define a Bronze Age merchant in the Aegean.[18] Thus we raise here two points for further discussion: a) On Homer's definition these Mycenaeans may have been called *émporoi*, the term primarily meaning "passengers travelling on a ship they do not own," and b) these two persons perhaps need not have carried with them on board the so-called Aegean standard weights, because any accurate weighing of the merchandise that employed the home standard will have taken place at the port of destination,[19] as has been convincingly suggested for the estimation of weight of the copper ingots (Zaccagnini 1986; Pulak 2000, 138).

Questions for further research

From this review of the evidence, the current discussion on weight metrology and relations of production evidently leads to some further questions regarding the Aegean era:

> Should we look for the use of state balance weights as against others, such as 'weights of the Market' or 'weights of the Land' (in Old Assyrian texts: Zaccagnini 2000), and to what extent would the privately owned weights have been acceptable in transactions related to the obligations to the central authorities?

In Egyptian pharaonic art and in particular in the Mari Archives relating to metals, we have remarked upon a division of labour between the person operating the balance and the scribe recording the result, together with the person(s) of higher rank inspecting the process, with a view to guaranteeing the result. The scribe is not named or even mentioned in the Linear B tablets, but is attested palaeographically. If the scribe is not the one, who then would have been the balance specialist? On the basis of the Mari evidence, it may have been the metal worker in precious metals, for instance, a *ku-ru-so-wo-ko*, or any experienced metal worker, since the virtues required for such a job are experience and loyalty.

In such a case, in response to Pare's remark that the persons buried with weighing tools do not seem to have had any specialist function, one might suggest that they were 'specialists of the balance'. Some of them were of a certain status (and in possession of the balances) and therefore seem closer to the conception of the connoisseurs on the Mari tablets.

If Dimitris Nakassis is correct in suggesting that among the *ka-ke-we* of the Mycenaean tablets there were persons of high status participating in the palatial economy, sometimes acting as entrepreneurs in the acquisition of foreign raw materials (Nakassis, forthcoming), they would perhaps be the appropriate persons to escort royal expeditions under the pretext of 'royal gifts', in particular when metal (either as raw material or prestige items) was the merchandise in demand, as was most often the case.

The Mycenaean envoys on the ship of Uluburun have been regarded as not being merchants on the grounds that the balance weights on board do not fall into the Aegean system. Perhaps, however, we should recall that at this time other systems were also functioning.[20] Apart from Ugarit, where five metric systems of weights were in use at the same time (Courtois 1990), there is Petruso's suggestion that some of the balance weights from Boeotian Thebes are based on another standard of 9.65 grams, not so far from the 9.4 and 9.3 standard of the weights on the ship (Petruso 2003). To quote also Alberti and Aravantinos: "the evidence of Thebes illustrates the cohabitation and the combination of shapes and standards of different weighing traditions ('Minoan', 'Mycenaean' and Levantine) in a Mycenaean palatial centre" (Aravantinos & Alberti 2006, 310–311). If, for the sake of argument, Thebes was the final destination of the ship's load, could the commodities have been checked on arrival by the same Levantine/Syrian standard? In any case the inhabitants of the Aegean were not ignorant of the Syrian standard, as a consequence of the spread of the Syrian mina (Zaccagnini 2000).

From Near Eastern texts we do hear of the merchant who carries his own balance weights in his leather bag. Would, however, these weights always have been those of his *home* metric system, if they accompanied him on a journey to procure merchandise from lands employing another metric system? A *merchant* of Ur receives copper in Dilmun measured by the Dilmun weight, although, when he is back home, the amount is converted according to the Ur standard (Roaf 1982). The Syrian/Cypriot standard was the dominant system of the lands where the ship was loaded (lands where the other two standards attested aboard were also in use).

In our search for merchants, we should recall that their status need not have been the same everywhere and throughout time.[21] The fact that this trade is not specifically mentioned in the Linear B tablets probably indicates that in the Mycenaean era there was not a permanent division of labour in this domain.[22] I agree with Pulak that the Mycenaeans on board may have acted as messengers,[23] perhaps like the Cretan who acquires tin at Ugarit, as reported by a well-known tablet from Mari. They could have been, however, of any profession that gave them the required ability and knowledge, in particular with regard to *guaranteeing* the quality of the royal gift, perhaps as connoisseurs under the aegis of the ruler expecting the gift, and possessing a status similar to that of the *ebbû* as mentioned in the Mari tablets (Michel 1990). For, in Michel's view, the *ebbû* are the experts in the domain in which they operate. They know the techniques used by the artisans in weighing and are trained in calculations relating to the estimation of value of the transported merchandise, and they are also able to convert values between different systems of measure. Thus, when one such person goes to estimate a load of tin arriving by caravan, before King Zimri-Lim is to receive it, he is defined by Michel as "acheteur officiel du palais de Mari", therefore "un marchand" (Michel 1990, 212).[24] We should add also that any expert was nominated by the king for a certain task or a certain period, and, more importantly, that he was very seldom acting alone. In fact, very frequently two or more names are recorded as *ebbû* appointed by the king for the same task, which means that the presence of *two* Mycenaeans might be justified in the conduct of such transactions. The *ebbû* were also sent to act as arbitrators and their high status seems to have been of the level of the high rank ascribed by the excavator to the Mycenaeans and some of the Syrians aboard.[25] Do we perhaps have specially appointed experts/arbitrators from both ends of the journey made by the royal gift? In such a hypothesis, the absence of the 'Aegean' system – only one among the metric systems of the time – is perhaps not the decisive factor in our attempt to define the role of the messengers aboard the ship.

NOTES

1. According to Valbelle (1977) they were used '*pour une opération particulière*', as, for instance, for checking the weight of a bronze tool returned by one of the workers.

2. Colin Renfrew has defined the study of weight metrology as one of the tasks of the so-named archaeology of the mind: Renfrew 1983. See also Renfrew and Zubrow 1994.

3. For more on this subject see Michailidou 2000a.

4. The metrological organizers should have the ability of combining three factors: the numerical system at use, the heaviest load in practice and the mean value of the weight of the grain of barley (the lightest unit of the Mesopotamian system): Powell 1971, 209; Thuraeu-Dangin 1921.

5. We must note here that the Vapheio balance as displayed in the National Archaeological Museum at Athens is not intact but partially reconstructed, as I have been kindly informed by Dr. Lena Papazoglou.

6. In Linear A tablets *HT* 12, 24β, 38 and *KN* 2: GORILA V, 273.

7. With a distinction among the Early Mycenaean (closer to Minoan or Syrian units) and Late Mycenaean (perhaps closer to the Hittite unit).

8. We need not enter here into the subject of the 'marketless economy' (cf. more recent discussion in Clancier, Joannès, Rouillard & Tenu 2005) since even then, the activities involved in distribution, reciprocity, etc., would also require measuring.

9. The fundamental work on this subject is Duhoux 1976.

10. For this reason there is a view that *o-no* in the Linear B tablets might refer to donkey loads, but this view is not widely accepted and this word is currently connected with the concept of buying: cf. references cited in Michailidou 1999 and Sacconi 2005.

11. As was the rule for immediate neighbours to the east; to quote here Michel 2006, 7: "Tel est le cas des céréals généralement commercialisées en sacs et en jarres, de contenance standard. L' usage de ce système dans la documentation paléo-assyrienne semble de pratique courante pour tout compte d' objets ou de produits definies par une seule unitée. L' emploi d' une système decimal reposant sur un principe additif en Anatolie et en Syrie du nord rappelle la notation numérique minoenne contemporaine attesté par le linéaire A. Le systeme adopté plus tard par le hittite hiéroglyphique est identique".

12. The Syro-Canaanite jars from the Uluburun wreck fall into three distinguishable clusters of about 26.7 litres., 13 litres and 6.7 litres (Pulak 2001).

13. In the third weaving workshop, the excavation has not advanced in lower levels, so there is a small chance lead weights will appear in the future.

14. See also Michailidou 2008, 255–257.

15. One may agree with Perna (2003, 346) about the use of the same fraction to denote the volume of either a liquid or a dry material or a commodity's weight. With regard to the Phaistos tablet PH 8, to agree with him about the use

of fractions to denote the weight of the vessels registered would also imply that the metal vases recorded were standardized by weight and not by size, in itself a very important notion (cf. for the Mycenaean vases: Michailidou 2001b, Table 2). So, it is particularly important that the fraction inscribed before firing on a small jug from Mallia is regarded by Pelon as a sign of a unit of measure of capacity, because, since this jug is of clay, in this case we may be sure that it is not the weight that is meant by it (as also Perna 2003, 346).

16. Michailidou 2000–2001, 11–13. It must be pointed out here that like the weaving workshops, mill installations were not present in every house, the latter being a more important factor since in this case we are dealing with fixed architectural elements that indicate a primary space function: Michailidou 2001c, 379–380.

17. The whole paragraph here is based on Joannès 1989.

18. For more on the subject of merchants see Michailidou 2000b and in particular Michel 2005, 128.

19. Pulak himself ends his article on balance weights with the following: "On reaching the port of destination, the cargo and other merchandise would undoubtedly have been subjected to precise counting and reweighing with weights based on the Aegean mass system" (Pulak 2000, 264).

20. During the Late Bronze Age the integration of the weighing systems is almost complete, especially in the Levant: Alberti & Parise 2005, 381–382 and references therein.

21. For instance, the term *tamkārum* is not used for an official function in Old Assyrian evidence (contrary to Old Babylonian or Nuzi evidence): Michel 2005, 128.

22. For more remarks on the name of the profession see Michailidou 2000b.

23. 'Messengers' are occasionally synonymous with 'merchants' in letters of Amarna, sent by the king of Alashiya (e.g., indicatively Bachhuber 2006, 551 with references).

24. There are also cases of his being not a specialist but an eminent person who was a reliable arbitrator.

25. Pulak (2005a, 296 and 309) ascribes the highest-ranking position in the palatial administration to the Mycenaean envoys and ascribes an elite status to the Syro-Canaanite (or Cypriots?) merchants.

REFERENCES

Alberti, M. E., 1995. Ayia Irini: Les poids de balance dans leur context, *Numismatica e Antichità Classiche* **24**, 9–37

Alberti, M. E., 1998. A Stone or a Weight ? The Tale of the Fish, the Melon and the Balance, *ANNALI* **45**, 9–22

Alberti, M. E., 2003. Weighing and Dying between East and West. Weighing Materials from LBA Aegean Funerary Contexts, *METRON, Aegaeum* **24**, Liège, 277–284

Alberti, M. E., 2005. I sistemi ponderali dell' Egeo nell' Età del Bronzo. Studi, storia, pratica e contatti, *ANNUARIO* **81**(2003), 597–640

Alberti, M. E., E. Ascalone & L. Peyronel (eds.), 2006. *Weights in Context, Bronze Age Weighing Systems of Eastern Mediterranean*, Proceedings of the International Colloquium, Roma 22–24 November 2004, Istituto Italiano di Numismatica, *STUDI E MATERIALI* 13, Roma

Alberti, M. E. & N. Parise, 2005. Towards an Unification of Mass-Units between the Aegean and the Levant, *EMPORIA, Aegaeum* **25**, Liège, 381–391

Aravantinos, V., 1995. Old and New Evidence for the Palatial Society of Mycenaean Thebes: An Outline, *POLITEIA, Aegeaum* **12**, Liège, 613–622

Aravantinos, V. & M. E. Alberti, 2006. The Balance Weights from the Kadmeia, Thebes, M. E. Alberti, E. Ascalone & L. Peyronel (eds.), 2006, 293–313

Bachhuber, C., 2006. Aegean Interest on the Uluburun Ship, *AJA* **110**, 345–363

Bass, G. F., 1967. *Cape Gelidonya: A Bronze Age Shipwreck.* Transactions of the American Philosophical Society 57, Part 8, Philadelphia

Bass, G. F., 1991. Evidence of Trade from the Bronze Age Shipwrecks, N. H. Gale (ed.), *Bronze Age Trade in the Mediterranean*, Papers Presented at the Conference Held at Rewley House, Oxford, December 1989, *SIMA* 90, Jonsered

Bass, G. F., 1997. Prolegomena to a Study of Maritime Traffic in Raw Materials to the Aegean during the Fourteenth and Thirteenth Centuries B.C. TEXNH, *Aegaeum* **16**, Liège, 153–170

Bass, G. F., 2006. Review of G. F. Bass, S. D. Matthews, J. R. Steffy & F. H. van Doorninck, *Serce Limani, An Eleventh-Century Shipwreck,* Vol.1: *The Ship and Its Anchorage, Crew, and Passengers, BASOR* 341, 84–86

Bennett, E. L., 1950. Fractional Quantities in Minoan Bookkeeping, *AJA* **54**, 204–222

Bennett, E. L., 1980. Linear A Fractional Rectractation, *Kadmos* **19**, 12–23

Boulotis, C., 1998. Les documents en Linéaire A d' Akrotiri, Thera: Remarques préliminaires, *BCH* **122**, 407–411

Boulotis, C., 2008. The Linear A Tablets from Akrotiri (THE 7–12): Aspects of the Economic Life in the Settlement (in Greek), Chr. Doumas (ed.), Ακρωτήρι Θήρας. Τριάντα χρόνια έρευνας, 1967–1997, Επιστημονική συνάντηση 19–20 Δεκεμβρίου 1997, Βιβλιοθήκη της εν Αθήναις Αρχαιολογικής Εταιρείας αρ. 257, Αθήνα, 67–94

Brogan, T. M., 2006. Tipping the Scales: Evidence for Weight Measurement from the Wider Neopalatial Community at Mochlos, M. E. Alberti, E. Ascalone & L. Peyronel (eds.), 2006, 265–292

CAD, 1956–. *The Assyrian Dictionary at the Oriental Institute of the University of Chicago*, Chicago

Caskey, M. E., 1969. Lead Weights from Ayia Irini in Keos, *ArchDeltion* **24** A, 95–106

Chadwick, J., 1976. *The Mycenaean World*, Cambridge

Clancier P., F. Joannès, P. Rouillard & A. Tenu (eds.), 2005. *Autour de Polanyi: Vocabulaires, théories et modalités des échanges*, Paris

CoMIK: J. Chadwick, L. Godart, J. T. Killen, J.-P. Olivier, A. Sacconi & I. A. Sakellarakis, *Corpus of Mycenaean Inscriptions from Knossos*, Vol. I–IV, *INCUNABULA GRAECA* LXXXVIII, Roma 1986–1998

Courtois, J. C., 1990. Pois, prix, taxes et salaires à Ougartit (Syrie) au II e millénaire, R. Gyselen (ed.), *Res Orientales II*, Paris, 119–127

Day, P. M., 1999. Petrographic Analysis of Ceramics from the Shipwreck at Point Iria, W. Phelps, Y. Lolos & Y. Vichos (eds.), *The Point Iria Wreck: Interconnections in the Mediterranean ca. 1200 BC*, Proceedings of the International Conference, Island of Spetses, 19 September 1998, Athens, 59–76

De Fidio, P., 1998–1999. On the Routes of Aegean Bronze Age Wool and Weights, J. Bennet & J. Driessen (eds.), *A-na-qo-ta. Studies Presented to J. T. Killen*, Salamanca, 31–37

Dimopoulou, N., 1997. Workshops and Craftsmen in the Harbour-Town of Knossos at Poros-Katsambas, *TEXNH, Aegaeum* **16**, Liège, 433–438

Doumas, C., 1992. *The Wall Paintings of Thera*, Athens

Doumas, C. & A. G. Constantinides, 1990. Pithoi, Size and Symbols: Some Preliminary Considerations on the Akrotiri Evidence, D. Hardy et al. (eds.), *Thera and the Aegean World* III, Vol. 1, London, 40–43

Duhoux, Y., 1976. *Aspects du vocabulaire économique mycénien (cadastre-artisanat-fiscalité)*, Amsterdam

Evans, A. J., 1906. Minoan Weights and Mediums of Currency from Crete, Mycenae and Cyprus, *Corolla Numismatica*, Oxford, 336–367

Faulkner, R. O., 1985. *The Ancient Egyptian Book of the Dead*, London

GORILA: L. Godart & J.-P. Olivier, *Recueil des inscriptions en Linéaire A, EtCrét* XXI, Vol. 1–5, Paris 1976–1985

James, T. G. H., 1984. *Pharaoh's People: Scenes from Life in Imperial Egypt*, London

Joannès, F., 1989. La culture matérielle à Mari (IV): Les méthods de pesée. A propos d'un ouvrage recent, *RA* **83**, 113–151

Kakridis, I. T., 1986. *Greek Mythology, the Trojan* War, Athens, Ekdotike Athenon

Karetsou, A. (ed.), 2000. Κρήτη – Αίγυπτος. Πολιτισμικοί δεσμοί τριών χιλιετιών, Μελέτες, Αθήνα

Karetsou, A. & M. Andreathaki-Vlazaki (eds.), 2000: Κρήτη – Αίγυπτος. Πολιτισμικοί δεσμοί τριών χιλιετιών, Κατάλογος, Αθήνα

Karnava, A., 2001. Fractions and Measurement Units in the Cretan Hieroglyphic Script, A. Michailidou (ed.), *Manufacture and Measurement: Counting, Measuring and Recording Craft Items in Early Aegean Societies*, ΜΕΛΕΤΗΜΑΤΑ 33, Athens, 45–51

Katsa-Tomara, L., 1990. The Pottery-Producing System at Akrotiri: An Index of Exchange and Social Activity, D. Hardy et al. (eds.), *Thera and the Aegean World* III, Vol. 1, London, 31–40

Kemp, B. J., 1991. *Ancient Egypt: Anatomy of a Civilization*, London

Killen, J., 2001. Some Thoughts on *ta-ra-si-ja*, S. Voutsaki & J. Killen (eds.), *Economy and Politics in the Mycenaean Palace States*, Cambridge, 161–180

Kish, B., 1965. *Scales and Weights: A Historical Outline*, New Haven and London

Kopcke, G., 1987. The Cretan Palaces and Trade, R. Hägg & N. Marinatos (eds.), *The Function of the Minoan Palaces*, Athens, 255–259

Lassen, H., 2000. Introduction to Weight Systems in the Bronze Age Mediterranean: The Case of Kalavassos-Ayios Dhimitrios, C. F. E. Pare (ed.) *Metals Make the World Go Round*, Oxford, 233–246

Lauer, J. P., 1976. *Saqqara: The Royal Cemetery of Memphis*, London

Lolos, Y., 1999. The Cargo of Pottery from the Point Iria Wreck: Character and Implications, W. Phelps, Y. Lolos & Y. Vichos (eds.), *The Point Iria Wreck: Interconnections in the Mediterranean ca. 1200 B.C.*, Athens, 43–58

Michailidou, A., 1990. The Lead Weights from Akrotiri: The Archaeological Record, D. Hardy et al. (eds.), *Thera and the Aegean World* III, vol. 1, London, 407–419

Michailidou, A., 1992–1993. Ostrakon with Linear A Script from Akrotiri (Thera): A Non-Bureaucratic Activity? *Minos* **27**, 7–24

Michailidou, A., 1999. Systems of Weight and Social Relations of 'Private' Production in the Late Bronze Age Aegean, A. Chaniotis (ed.), *From Minoan Farmers to Roman Traders*, Stuttgart, 87–114

Michailidou, A., 2000a. Ο ζυγός στη ζωή των κατοίκων του Αιγαίου και της Αιγύπτου, Α. Καρέτσου (επ.) Κρήτη – Αίγυπτος. Πολιτισμικοί δεσμοί τριών χιλιετιών, Μελέτες, Αθήνα, 128–149

Michailidou, A., 2000b. Auf den Spuren der Händler in de Ägais: Waagen, Gewichte und ihre theoretischen Zusammenhänge, H. Siebenmorgen (ed.), *Im Labyrinth des Minos, Kreta, die erste europäische Hochkultur*, Munchen 222, 191–210

Michailidou, A., 2000–2001. Indications of Literacy in Bronze Age Thera, *Minos* **35–36**, 7–30

Michailidou, A., 2001a. Script and Metrology: Practical Porcesses and Cognitive Inventions, A. Michailidou (ed.), *Manufacture and Measurement: Counting, Measuring and Recording Craft Items in Early Aegean Societies*, ΜΕΛΕΤΗΜΑΤΑ 33, Athens, 53–82

Michailidou, A., 2001b. Recoding Quantities of Metal in Bronze Age Societies in the Aegean and the Near East, A. Michailidou (ed.), *Manufacture and Measurement: Counting, Measuring and Recording Craft Items in Early Aegean Societies*, ΜΕΛΕΤΗΜΑΤΑ 33, Athens, 85–119

Michailidou, A., 2001c. *Akrotiri on Thera: The Study of the Upper Storey of the Buildings* (in Greek), Athens

Michailidou, A., 2003. Measuring Weight and Value in Bronze Age Economies in the Aegean and the Near East: A Discussion on Metal Axes of No Practical Use, *METRON, Aegaeum* **24**, Liège, 301–314

Michailidou, A., 2004. On the Minoan Economy: A Tribute to 'Minoan Weights and Mediums of Currency' by Arthur Evans, *Knossos. Palace, City, State, BSA Suppl.* **12**, 311–321

Michailidou, A., 2005. *Weight and Value in Pre-Coinage Societies: An Introduction*, ΜΕΛΕΤΗΜΑΤΑ 42, Athens

Michailidou, A., 2006. Stone Balance Weights? The Evidence from Akrotiri on Thera, M. E. Alberti, E. Ascalone & L. Peyronel (eds.), 2006, 233–263

Michailidou, A., 2008. *Weight and Value in Pre-Coinage Societies. Volume II: Sidelights on Measurement from the Aegean and the Orient*, ΜΕΛΕΤΗΜΑΤΑ 61, Athens

Michel, C., 1990. La culture matériel à Mari III. *Ebbum et Ebbûtum. MARI* **6**, 181–214

Michel, C., 1998. Les marchands et les nombres: l'exemple des Assyriens à Kaniš, *Intellectual Life of the Ancient Near East, CRRAI* **43**, Prague, 249–267

Michel, C., 2005. Le commerce privé des Assyriens en Anatolie: un model du commerce archaique selon K. Polanyi, in P. Clancier, F. Joannès, P. Rouillard & A. Tenu (eds.), 121–133

Michel, C., 2006. Calculer chez les marchands Assyriens au début du IIe millénaire av. J.-C., www.dma.fr/cultuemath/histoire

Nakassis, D., forthcoming. *Individuals and the Mycenaen State,* Ph.D to be submitted, Chapter 5 (I am most grateful for the permission to consult this chapter)

Olivier, J.-P., 1989. La disque de Mokhlos: Une nouvelle inscription en Linéaire A sur un poids en plomb, HM 83/MO Zf 1, *Kadmos* **28**, 137–145

Palaima, T. G., 1991. Maritime Matters in the Linea B Tablets, *Thalassa*, Aegaeum 7, Liège, 273–310

Palaima, T. G., 2005. Mycenaean Ideograms and How They Are Used, M. Perna (ed.), *Studi in onore di Enrica Fiandra*, Napoli, 267–283

Palyvou, K., 2005. *Akrotiri Thera: An Architecture of Affluence 3,500 Years Old*, Philadelphia

Pare, C., 1999. Weights and Weighing in Bronze Age Central Europe, *Eliten in der Bonzezeit,* Mainz am Rhein, 421–514

Parise, N. F., 1971. Un'unità ponderale egea a capo Gelidonya, *SMEA* **14**, 163–170

Parise, N. F., 1981. Mina di Ugarit, mina di Karkemish, mina di Khatti, *DdA* **3**, 155–160

Parise, N. F., 1984. Unità ponderali e rapporti di cambio della Siria di Nord, A. Archi (ed.), *Circulation of Goods in Non-palatial Context in the Ancient Near East, INCUNABULA GRAECA* 82, Roma, 125–138

Perna, M., 2003. Ideograms of Vases and Fractions in Linear A Script, *METRON, Aegaeum* **24**, Liège, 343–347

Petruso, K. M., 1978. *Systems of Weight in the Bronze Age Aegean*, Ph.D. Diss. Indiana University

Petruso, K. M., 1992. *Keos VIII: Ayia Irini: The Balance Weights*, Mainz am Rhein

Petruso, K. M., 2003. Quantal Analysis of Some Mycenaean Balance Weights, *METRON,* Aegaeum 24, Liège, 285–291

Powell, M., 1971. *Sumerian Numeration and Metrology*, Ann Arbor, Michigan

Powell, M., 1995. Metrology and Mathematics in Ancient Mesopotamia, J. M. Sasson (ed.), *Civilizations of the Near East*, Vol. 5, New York, 1941–1957

Pulak, C., 1998. The Uluburun Shipwreck: An Overview, *IJNA*, **27**, 188–224

Pulak, C., 2000. The Balance Weights from the Late Bronze Age Shipwreck at Uluburun, C. Pare (ed.), *Metals Make the World Go Round*, Oxford, 247–266

Pulak, C., 2001. The Cargo of the Uluburun Ship and Evidence for Trade in the Aegean and Beyond, L. Bonfante & V. Karageorghis (eds.), *Italy and Cyprus in Antiquity 1500–450 B.C.*, Nicosia, 13–60

Pulak, C., 2005a. Who Were the Mycenaeans aboard the Uluburun ship? *EMPORIA, Aegaeum* **25**, Liège, 295–310

Pulak, C., 2005b. Das Schiffswrack von Uluburun, U. Yalçin, C. Pulak & R. Slotta (eds.), Bohum, 55–102

Pulak, C., 2006. The Balance Weights from Uluburun and Cape Gelidonya Shipwrecks, M. E. Alberti, E. Ascalone & L. Peyronel (eds.), 2006, 47–48 (Summary)

Rahmstorf, L., 2003. The Identification of Early Helladic Weights and Their Wider Implications, *METRON*, Aegaeum **24**, Liège, 293–297

Rahmstorf, L., 2006. In Search of the Earliest Balance Weights, Scales and Weighing Systems from the East Mediterranean, the Near and Middle East, M. E. Alberti, E. Ascalone & L. Peyronel (eds.), 2006, 9–45

Ratnagar, S., 2003. Theorizing Bronze-Age Intercultural Trade: The Evidence of the Weights, *Paleorient* **29/1**, 79–92

Renfrew, C., 1983. Divided We Stand: Aspects of Archaeology and Information, *AmerAnt* **48**, 3–16

Renfrew C. & E. B. W. Zubrow (eds.), 1994. *The Ancient Mind: Elements of Cognitive Archaeology*, Cambridge

Renger, J., 1984. Patterns of Non-Institutional Trade and Non-Commercial Exchange in Ancient Mesopotamia at the Beginning of the Second Millennium B.C., A. Archi (ed.), *Circulation of Goods in Non-Palatial Context in the Ancient Near East*, Roma, 31–123

Renger, J., 2005. K. Polanyi and the Economy of Ancient Mesopotamia, in P. Clancier, F. Joannès, P. Rouillard & A. Tenu (eds.), 45–65

Roaf, M., 1982. Weights on the Dilmun Standard, *Iraq* **44**, 137–141

Robins, G. & C. Shute, 1987. *The Rhind Mathematical Papurys*, London

Rutter, J. B., 1999. Cretan External Relations during LM IIIA2-B (1370–1200 B.C.): A View from the Messara, W. Phelps, Y. Lolos & Y. Vichos (eds.), *The Point Iria Wreck: Interconnections in the Mediterranean ca. 1200 B.C.*, Athens, 139–186

Sacconi, A., 2005. La 'monnaie' dans l' économie mycénienne: Le témoignage des textes, *EMPORIA, Aegaeum* **25**, Liège, R.69–74

Salonen, A., 1961. *Die Türen des alten Mesopotamien*, Helsinki

Sarpaki, A., 2001. Condiments, Perfume and Dye Plants in Linear B: A Look at the Textual and Archaeobotanical

Evidence, A. Michailidou (ed.), *Manufacture and Measurement: Counting, Measuring and Recording Craft Items in Early Aegean Societies*, ΜΕΛΕΤΗΜΑΤΑ 33, Athens, 195–265

Sherratt, A. & S. Sherratt, 1991. From Luxuries to Commodities: The Nature of Mediterranean Bronze Age Trading Systems, N. H. Gale (ed.), *Bronze Age Trade in the Mediterranean*, Jonsered, 351–386

Soles, J. S. & C. Davaras (eds.), 2004. *Mochlos IC*, Philadelphia

Stieglitz, **R. R.** 2006. Classical Greek Measures and the Builder's Instruments, *AJA* 110, 200–203

Thuraeu-Dangin, F., 1921. Numération et métrologie Sumériennes, *RA* **18**, 123–135

Trantalidou, K., 2001. Producing and Recording Leather and Other Animal Products, A. Michailidou (ed.), *Manufacture and Measurement: Counting, Measuring and Recording Craft Items in Early Aegean Societies*, ΜΕΛΕΤΗΜΑΤΑ 33, Athens, 267–317

Tzachili, I., 1990. All Important yet Elusive: Looking for Evidence of Cloth-Making at Akrotiri, D. Hardy et al. (eds.), *Thera and the Aegean World* III, Vol. 1, London, 380–389

Tzachili, I., 2001a. Circulation of Textiles in the Late Bronze Age Aegean, A. Michailidou (ed.), *Manufacture and Measurement: Counting, Measuring and Recording Craft Items in Early Aegean Societies*, ΜΕΛΕΤΗΜΑΤΑ 33, Athens, 167–175

Tzachili, I., 2001b. Counting and Recording Textiles in the Mycenaean Archives of Knossos, A. Michailidou (ed.), *Manufacture and Measurement. Counting, Measuring and Recording Craft Items in Early Aegean Societies*, ΜΕΛΕΤΗΜΑΤΑ 33, Athens, 177–193

Tzachili, I., 2002–2003. The Clay Cylinders from Akrotiri, Thera: A Non Literate Alternative Way of Accounting? *Minos* **37–38**, 7–76

Valbelle, D., 1977. *Catalogue des poids à inscriptions hiératiques de Deir el-Medineh*, FIFAO, Cairo

Vandenabeele, F. & J.-P. Olivier, 1979. *Les idéogrammes archéologiques du Linéaire B*, EtCrét. 29, Paris

Veenhof, K. R., 1972: *Aspects of Old Assyrian Trade*, Leiden

Vercoutter, J., 1959. The Gold of Kush: Two Gold-Washing Stations at Faras East, *Kush* 7, 12–153

Weingarten, J., 1986. Some Unusual Minoan Clay Nodules, *Kadmos* 25, 1–21

Wiener, M., 1999. Present Arms, Oars, Ingots: Searching for Evidence of Military or Marine Administration in LM IB, *POLEMOS, Aegaeum* **21**, Liège, 411–421

Yalçin, U., C. Pulak & R. Slotta, (eds.), 2005. *Das Schiff von Uluburun: Welthandel vor 3000 Jahren*, Bochum

Younger, J. G., 2003. Calculating Vessel Volumes, *METRON, Aegaeum* **24**, Liège, 491–2

Zaccagnini, C., 1986. Aspects of Copper Trade in the Eastern Mediterranean during the Late Bronze Age, M. Marazzi, S. Tusa & L. Vagnetti (eds.), *Traffici micenei nel Mediterraneo.* Taranto, 413–424

Zaccagnini, C., 1999–2001. The Mina of Karkemiš and Other Minas, *State Archives of Assyria Bulletin* **13**, 39–56

Zaccagnini, C., 2000. A Note on Old Assyrian Weight Stones and Weight System, S. Graziani (ed.), *Studi sul Vicino Oriente Antico, dedicati alla memoria di Luigi Cagni*, Napoli, 1203–1213

8

The concept of weighing during the Bronze Age in the Aegean, the Near East and Europe

Lorenz Rahmstorf

The concepts applied in prehistoric societies and early civilisations to quantify the number of things and their length (including speed and distance), volume and weight offer an important and direct understanding of the minds of the ancient people, the organisation of their societies and their contacts with the neighbouring cultures. However, analysing early quantification has never played a major role in archaeology. This is partly a result of the difficult evidence one is facing: the detection of ancient measurement in the archaeological record is surely one of the greatest difficulties to be overcome in the study of early quantification. This also holds true for early weight metrology. Nevertheless, the importance of this topic and its relevance for early societies have been acknowledged by more and more scholars in recent years. More detailed empirical work is needed before the establishment of broad theories and reconstructions becomes possible. For example, there are still many questions about the spread and adoption of the various weighing systems used in the eastern Mediterranean, in the Near and Middle East and in Europe during the Bronze and Iron Ages. It is still a matter of debate as to the earliest date from which weights were known and used in some parts of the world.[1] Despite such shortfalls in research, some basic topics need to be and can already be addressed in the course of this work and we should keep in mind the following questions:

1. What objective criteria are there to indicate with certainty that a special group of artefacts are weights?
2. Are there recurring traits in the appearance and actual shaping of weights? Why were certain shapes, materials, surface treatments, and so on, chosen?
3. Was the concept of weighing invented at one place and did it spread from there, or are independent inventions at various places possible?

4. Is the concept of weight and weighing connected to a certain degree of development in societies, and to other major changes, like intensive metallurgy, long-distance trade and urbanisation?

My research on such questions started when I identified Early Bronze Age balance weights from the Aegean region from the third millennium BC. In this chapter I would like to discuss the units of weight and their implications for the Aegean and the Near East in the third millennium BC, in particular with regard to the questions posed previously. At the end of this contribution I will turn to evidence for weighing in central Europe during the second millennium BC, as the archaeological evidence for weighing from Bronze Age Europe has received little note and discussion so far.

Earliest balance weights in the Aegean, Anatolia and Syria in the third millennium BC

In 2001 I identified markings on three spool-shaped to cylindrical objects from Tiryns that stand in logical relations to each other (Rahmstorf 2003a). Two spools bear one marking/drilling and weigh 9.1 g and the third spool exhibits four markings and weighs 37.6 g, implying a unit of 9.1–9.4 g (Figure 8.1: 2–4). Further study of similar objects from Tiryns revealed markings on two more objects. The marking on one spool-shaped object made out of spondylus (Figure 8.1: 1) was hidden under some dirt in the depression. While drawing the object of Figure 8.1: 5, I became aware of the six parallel incisions. Both emphasize again a unit of slightly above 9 g.[2] In addition, further sampling of such objects from other Aegean Early Bronze Age sites supported the assumption that these 'pestles' – as they were called until then – were in fact balance weights. Such objects, often made from attractive stone material and spondylus (like Figure 8.1: 1), are typical finds in Early Bronze Age (EBA) II (ca. 2800/2700–2300/2200 BC) contexts on the Greek mainland and Aegean islands. Sporadically they even appear in Anatolia (Troy, Kusura, Tarsus – see later discussion). So far, these objects have been identified by most archaeologists as pestles, even if in most cases they do not have any traces of wear (Rahmstorf 2006a, 74–75). In published commentaries on the new interpretation of these objects as balance weights, it has been pointed out that further research is necessary on this subject.[3] This further research, which gives strong support for the widespread use of similar weighing standards, will be presented here.

Through a current research project I aim to sample the weights of all the objects known from around 50

Figure 8.1. Spool-shaped balance weights from Tiryns with markings. 1: LX 38/80 b1314 IXf R 10 (8.9 g); 2: LXI 39/96 a1349 XVIIa (9.1 g); 3: LXV 38/21 a1587 VII (9.1 g); 4: LXI 53/44 a2604 Ia (37.6 g); 5: LXIV 38/57 e1587 Ofl.IX (55.1 g). Scale 1:1.

sites in the Aegean and Anatolia systematically. This research has not yet been completed, but from around half of these sites data have been sampled: so far these constitute ca. 200 spool-shaped weights and ca. 30 haematite balance weights and other possible weights in different shapes and materials. These objects weigh between 2.7 g and 3,790 g, but more than 90 percent weigh less than 100 g. Although the sampling is yet to be completed, this sample is large enough to be subject to statistically significant analyses. So far, it has been possible to detect a unit (also called shekel or standard) of 9.4 g or slightly lighter, which all marked examples from Tiryns suggest, either by representing the unit itself or by being multiples of it (fractions of this unit also occur). More than two-thirds of the total sample of objects can be assigned to this unit, but seemingly not all, unless one allows an extremely large range of error. In 2003, I assumed that another unit of 8.3–8.4 g is represented in the sample (Rahmstorf 2003a, 295 pl. LXIIa), which would be the shekel well known from Mesopotamia. I later realized that a set of six spool-shaped weights now in the Goulandris Museum (Rahmstorf 2006a, 76 fig. 13, 12–17; 16) seems to be based on a unit around 7.8 g. Finally, another strong cluster seemed to peak in the sample between 11.5 and 12 g. It seemed to become confusing: were there two, three or even four units used at the same time? And how could one verify this? Could it be that not all such objects were balance weights?

With this intuitive approach I asked myself whether there could already have been various units used in the

EBA Aegean that, unfortunately, were lying very close to each other making definite assignment difficult. Considering a usual deviation of +/– 5 percent of the mass of balance weight in relation to the intended weight, it becomes clear that there is considerable possible overlap when one wants to assign an actual balance weight to a certain unit. Matters were not as easy as I had hoped in the beginning. While most of the spool-shaped balance weights can obviously be assigned as a multiple or fraction of the unit of 9.4 g, there seem also to be other units present. The haematite EBA balance weights, which were the only balance weights known from the EBA Aegean prior to the identification of the spool-shaped 'pestles' as balance weights, from Poliochni on Lemnos and Troy in northeast Aegean support such a notion: there, the unit of 9.4 is strongly represented, as C. Petruso has demonstrated (Petruso 1978, 40–50: System I), but again a good portion of the complete sample of weights from these two sites cannot be assigned to this unit (see also Lindsten 1943).

Thanks particularly to the publications of N. Parise (Parise 1970–1971; Parise 1981; Parise 1984) and D. Arnaud (Arnaud 1967), since the late 1960s it has become clear that in Late Bronze Age (LBA) Syria the mina was divided into three different units or shekels (Table 8.1). Parise called them the mina of Karkemish (470 g: 60 = 7.83 g), the mina of Ugarit (470 g: 50 = 9.4 g) and the mina of Hatti (470 g: 40 = 11.75 g). Generally the conversion of the weighing systems was achieved in a relation 4:5:6. In Table 8.2 are collated all marked or

Table 8.1. *The conversion of units (talent, mina and basic units) in LBA Syria according to N. Parise (1984)*

T	28200	1				
M	470	60	1			
H	11.75	2400	40	1		
S	9.4	3000	50	5/4	1	
K	7.83	3600	60	3/2	6/5	1

Note: t = talent; m = mina; h = Hittite/Hatti unit of 11.75 g; s = Syrian/Ugaritian/Egyptian (qedet) unit of 9.4 g; k = unit of Karkemiš of 7.83 g.

inscribed balance weights of the third millennium from sites in the Aegean, Syria and Mesopotamia that are published to date. Recent findings of a good sample of EBA balance weights found at Ebla and more occasionally at other Syrian sites made it obvious that the mina of 470 g was already known during the third millennium BC in this region. This is obvious from two inscribed or marked weights, one from Ebla (Archi 1987, 58 fig. 2, 21 = Table 8.2: 'Ebla 2') and one from Tell Sweyhat (Holland 1975, fig 1 = Table 8.2: 'Tell Sweyhat'), even if other possible minas' weights are much more difficult in their assignment (Archi 1987, 58–59 fig. 2, 22–25 = Table 8.2: 'Ebla 3–6'). The Ebla weights are dated to the Syrian EBA IVA, which can be paralleled with late EBA II (Lerna III D) in the Aegean; the weight from Tell Sweyhat belongs to the Akkadian period, which is largely simultaneous with the latest EBA II and the transitional phase to EBA III in the Aegean. In addition, all units of weight mentioned in regard to the EBA weights from the Aegean and Anatolia were also well known from Early Bronze Age Syria. There is a marked weight with six incisions from Ebla representing the unit of 11.75 g (Table 8.2: 'Ebla 1'). Other completely preserved balance weights without any markings from Ebla make it obvious that besides the 11.75 g unit (Archi 1987, 56 fig. 1, 8–9: 11.4 g; 12.02 g), the 7.83 g unit (Archi 1987, 55 fig. 1, 4: 7.9 g) and the 9.4 g unit (Archi 1987, 55 fig. 1, 5–6: 9.2 g; 9.4 g) were also present. Others represent all three units (Archi 1987, 53, 57 fig. 1, 18: 141.9 g = 18 x 7.88 g = 15 x 9.46 g = 12 x 11.825 g), demonstrating that these different weighing systems and their elegant conversion were already used during the third millennium BC. At Ebla the unit 8.33 g appears not to exist in the sample. But it is known in northeast Syria at Tell Brak (Oates 2001, 265 fig. 485, 34 = Table 8.2: 'Tell Brak 2'), as well as in Cilicia, as we will see from the evidence from Tarsus (later). This unit was especially at home in Mesopotamia, where a mina of 500 g was in use that was divided into 60 shekels of 8.33 g. In the mid-third millennium balance weights based on this unit were excavated at Tepe Gawra in northern Mesopotamia (Speiser 1935,

90 pl. XLIII, 4–5. 7 = Table 8.2: 'Tepe Gawra 1–4'). The Mesopotamian unit of 8.33 g does not easily fit into the calculations with a mina of 470 g, but if one divides this mina by 55, this results in a unit of 8.55 g – possibly a heavy Mesopotamian shekel (?). Other finds from EBA Syria imply again the use of the 9.4-g unit, as is probably the case at Tell Munbaqa (Czichon & Werner 1998, 97 pl. 92, 869 = Table 8.2: 'Tell Munbaqa') and clearly at Tell Brak (Oates 2001, 265 fig. 485, 35 = Table 8.2: 'Tell Brak 1'). They also indicate the use of the 11.75-g unit, and probably the 7.83-g unit at Tell Beydar, too (Milano 2004, 2–3 fig. 1. 3 = Table 8.2: 'Tell Beydar 1–2'), even if this remains complicated (cf. discussion in Milano 2004).

The 19 marked balance weights including the 5 from Tiryns are, of course, only a small portion of the corpus of weights from the eastern Mediterranean and upper Mesopotamia dating to the third millennium BC. Several hundred, probably around 500, unmarked balance weights can now be named from around 60 EBA sites in the eastern Mediterranean (Rahmstorf 2006a, fig. 11),[4] including all spool-shaped weights and some other balance weights from Anatolian sites not identified before. This is a dramatic increase compared to the only ca. 100 haematite weights known from the eastern Mediterranean only a few years ago, from Troy, Poliochni, Tarsus, Ebla, Tell Sweyhat and Tell Munbaqa. Most recently, in late September 2006, I was able to restudy the balance weights from the old excavations by H. Goldman and her team at Tarsus, thanks to the kindness of Prof. Dr. A. Özyar. Tarsus has always been of special interest to me as not only haematite weights, but also spool-shaped objects/balance weights have been found. These four spool-shaped weights (Figure 8.2) are in fact those found the farthest east. They had already been compared by Goldman to the Aegean examples, and two of them were illustrated by chance on the same plate right below the haematite weights (Goldman 1956, 275 fig. 420, 108–109). The two illustrated are slightly damaged but because of their symmetrical shape the reconstruction of the original weight is easy: the calculated density

Table 8.2. *The 21 marked or inscribed balance weights of the third millennium from seven sites in the Aegean, Syria and Mesopotamia published to date*

Site	Weight	Markings	Proposed unit	Calculation
Tiryns 1	9.1 g	1 circle	9.4 g	9.1 x 1 = 9.1 g
Tiryns 2	9.1 g	1 dot	9.4 g	9.1 x 1 = 9.1 g
Tiryns 3	8.9 g	1 dot	9.4 g	8.9 x 1 = 8.9 g
Tiryns 4	37.6 g	4 dots	9.4 g	9.4 x 4 = 37.6 g
Tiryns 5	55.1 g	6 incisions	9.4 g	9.18 x 6 = 55.1 g
Ebla 1	68.7 g	6 incisions	11.75 g	11.75 x 6 = 70.5 g
Ebla 2	467.5 g	1 groove	1 mina	470 : 60 = 7.83 g 470 : 55 = 8.55 g 470 : 50 = 9.4 g 470 : 40 = 11.75 g
Ebla 3	574.3 g	1 groove and 5 incisions	9.4 g (564 : 60) 11.48 g (574 : 50) 8.2 g (574 : 70)	470 + 470/5 = 470 + 94 = 564
Ebla 4	666.1 g	1 groove and 4 incisions	9.51 g (666 : 70) 13.32 g (666 : 50) 8.33 g (666 : 80)	470 + 470/4 = 470 + 117.5 = 587.5 g
Ebla 5	860 g	2 grooves	2 minas?	470 x 2 = 940 g
Ebla 6	1332 g	3 grooves	3 minas?	470 x 3 = 1,410 g
Tall Munbaqa	47.9 g	L-shaped groove	7.83 g 8.55 g 9.4 g 11.75 g	6 x 7.83 = 47 g 5.5 x 8.55 = 47 g 5 x 9.4 = 47 g 4 x 11.75 = 47 g
Tell Sweyhat	472.2 g	inscribed with: 1 mina	1 mina	470 : 60 = 7.83 g 470 : 55 = 8.55 g 470 : 50 = 9.4 g 470 : 40 = 11.75g
Tell Beydar 1	2.60 g	6 incisions	7.83 g?	470 : 60 = 7.83 g 7.83 : 6 = 1.305 g x 2 = 2.61 g
Tell Beydar 2	3.05 g	4 incisions	11.75 g	470 : 40 = 11.75 g 11.75 : 4 = 2.94 g
Tell Brak 1	46.92 g	5 incisions	9.4 g	470 : 50 = 9.4 g 9.4 x 5 = 47 g
Tell Brak 2	25.03 g	3 incisions	8.33 g	500 : 60 = 8.33 g 8.33 x 3 = 25 g
Tepe Gawra 1	16.68 g	2 incisions	8.33 g	500 : 60 = 8.33 g 8.33 x 2 = 16.66 g
Tepe Gawra 2	17.7 g	2 incisions	8.33 g?	500 : 60 = 8.33 g 8.33 x 2 = 16.66 g
Tepe Gawra 3	65.5 g	8 incisions	8.33 g	500 : 60 = 8.33 g 8.33 x 8 = 66.66 g
Tepe Gawra 4	82.9 g	10 incisions	8.33 g	500 : 60 = 8.33 g 8.33 x 10 = 83.3g

Source: Data taken from Archi 1987, Czichon & Werner 1998, Holland 1975, Milano 2004, Oates 2001 and Speiser 1935.

of the material is multiplied by the volume of the displaced water when the object with its reconstructed original volume (added in plasticine) is placed in a measuring jug. This standard method was also used by C. Pulak for the weights from the Uluburun shipwreck (Pulak 2000). Only recently was I able to apply this method to all chipped or fragmented spool-shaped weights. The results of these reconstructions are not, of course, highly precise, but taking into account some notion of their range of error, they greatly enrich the database.

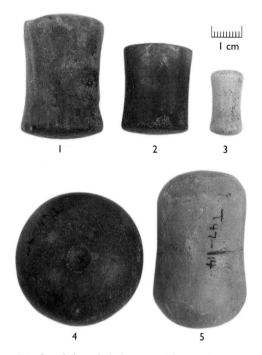

Figure 8.2. Spool-shaped balance weights and a 'macehead' from EBA II Tarsus. 1: no. 109, 45.8 (-) g = 46.5–47.8 g rec.; 2: no. 108, 24.7 g = 27.8 g rec.; 3: no. 111, 4.5 g; 4: no. 77, 79.4 g; 5: no. 110, 79.5 g. Numbers according to Goldman 1956. Scale 1:1.

The Tarsus spool-shaped weights[5] weigh 4.5 g (Goldman 1956, 275 no. 111 = Figure 8.2: 3), 24.7 (-)g = rec. 27.8g (Goldman 1956, 275 no. 108 = Figure 8.2: 2), 45.8 (-)g = rec. 46.5–47.8 g (Goldman 1956, 275 no. 109 = Figure 8.2: 1) and 79.5 g (Goldman 1956, 275, no. 110 = Figure 8.2: 5). The objects of Figure 8.2: 1–3 could again nicely represent the unit of 9.4 g with the multiples ½, 3 and 5. Only the object of Figure 8.2: 5 seems to be another unit, possibly 10 times 7.95 g (= the unit of 7.83 g). The objects of Figure 8.2: 1–2, 5 were all found together in Room 114 of the EBA II Tarsus, although it is not clearly stated in which of the two levels of Room 114 (Goldman 1956, 14–15 plan 4–5). The small spool-shaped weight (Figure 8.2: 3) was found on the street separating the northern row, with rooms like 114, from the southern row, with rooms like 117. In the latter room there was also excavated an object that Goldman called an "unfinished macehead" (Goldman 1956, 274 fig. 420, 77 = Figure 8.2: 4), a flattened spherical object with an unfinished drilling hole, which weighs 79.4 g. This 'macehead' is in its reddish colour rather similar to the object of Figure 8.2: 1. What is striking is the similarity of its mass to that of the object of Figure 8.2: 5 (79.5 g), which in fact seems to be marked with a horizontal incision (the first '1' of the excavation number written on it [T47–114] is inked in this lineal depression). It could be that the drilling hole on the 'macehead' is not unfinished but is in fact a marking rather similar to the line

incision on the spool-shaped weight. So both objects might be marked balance weights of similar mass (and by that rationale should probably be included in Table 8.2). Whether or not this is the case regarding the 'macehead', the weighing of these spool-shaped objects found farthest east showed that they are balance weights that can be easily assigned to units already mentioned.

The haematite weights from Tarsus have already been discussed by H. Goldman and M. Lang in the original publication (Goldman 1956, 266–268 fig. 420, 117–128 = Figure 8.3).[6] Their assignment to one or more units remains difficult despite the fact that 11 of them were found together on the floor of Room 74 (Goldman 1956, 33 plan 10). To me, they seem to represent at best the unit of 8.33 g, as I have argued elsewhere (Rahmstorf 2006a, 72; Rahmstorf 2006b; but compare Petruso 1978, 61–64). Nearly all haematite balance weights from Tarsus are found in EB III levels; only the weight of Figure 8.3: 1 is said to derive from an EB I context, but because it is a single occurrence in EB I levels it remains to be proven that it was not dislocated through site formation and excavation processes. Interestingly, it might be that at Tarsus the spool-shaped balance weights were used at an earlier stage (EB II) and were later replaced by haematite balance weights (EB III).

This intuitive approach using marked balance weights and looking for clusters around certain masses in a sample of artefacts forms the most obvious way to deduce the underlying units. It is often supported by the metrological-historical approach using written evidence from contemporaneous and later texts, as well as balance weights from later periods. The third possible approach is noninductive and uses mathematical methods to demonstrate the probability of possible units. Mathematical-statistical methods have seldom been used so far for the evidence of the Near East. K. Petruso has applied them to the Minoan balance weight from the second millennium (Petruso 1992: 32–33, 71–75). In this contribution I would like to show how well the mathematical-statistical approach proves and verifies the results obtained so far. To date, I have sampled the mass of 202 spool-shaped balance weights from the Aegean and Anatolia, of which 180 complete or reconstructed objects could be used for metrological calculations. To this set of data I have applied the so-called Kendall formula, which was originally formulated by the Cambridge statistician D. G. Kendall (Kendall 1974).[7] It aims to identify quanta in a set of numerical data ('hunting quanta'). This is a perfect method for verifying the existence of certain units in a sample. Balance weights are an ideal source, as every completely preserved balance weight can be treated as one secure piece of data, whereas, in contrast, the data selection for quantal analysis

Figure 8.3. Haematite balance weights from EBA I (?) and EB III Tarsus. 1: no. 117, 10.1 g; 2: no. 118, 99.9 g; 3: no. 130, 12.4 g; 4: no. 119, 48.6 g; 5: no. 123, 22.5 g; 6: no. 124, 18.6 g; 7: no. 125, 20.3 g; 8: no. 129, 7.1 g; 9: no. 120, 16.6g; 10: no. 122, 32.8 g; 11: no. 128, 5.2 g; 12: no. 126, 8g. Numbers according to Goldman 1956. Scale 1:1.

in architecture remains a big problem. Quantal analysis based on the Kendall formula has been attempted in seeking the unit of length in Minoan architecture and a result has been proposed (Cherry 1983). But the internal problems of data selection from ancient building plans seem to preclude our obtaining any reasonable results, as "an immediate difficulty is deciding what data are pertinent to the problem" (Fieller 1993, 286). We do not have this problem with balance weights.

The result from the application of this technique to the spool-shaped weights (sample size: 180) is surprisingly clear: there are explicit peaks in the distribution of possible units between 5 g and 15 g at ca. 7.83 g, 8.54 g, 9.4 g, and 11.75 g (Figure 8.4). This means that all units known from EBA Syria are also present in the EBA Aegean and possibly also in Anatolia (so far, I have only been able to sample weights from Tarsus). The largest spool-shaped object from the Aegean, an 18-cm-long 'pestle' from deposit BO from Room ED.4 at EBA II Aghia Irini on Kea (Wilson 1999, pl. 38, SF-115), demonstrates the use of the different units at the same time. This huge object weighs 3,790 g, which can be divided by 480, 440, 400 and 320, resulting in units of 7.86 g, 8.61 g, 9.48 g and 11.84 g. In Table 8.3 the common multiples of all four units are shown: at 94, 188, 376 and 470, and so on. For the units 7.83, 9.4 and 11.75 there are common multiples at 47, 141, 235, and so forth. Common multiples of the units 7.83 and 11.75 are situated at 23.5, 70.5, 117.5, 164.5, et cetera. The sample of

the actual balance weights underlines these results: there are clusters around special numbers – 'meeting points' – of the various units. Some examples may be given: 19 weights vary around 44.7 and 49.6, representing 6, 5 or 4 times the units 7.83, 9.4 and 11.75. Two weights from EBA II from the important settlement of Kastri on Syros weigh exactly the same as each other: 70.4 g. This would be 6 x 11.75 g, or 9 x 7.83 g. The 20 heaviest spool-shaped weights known to me (Rahmstorf 2006a, Fig. 17, state of research: 9/04) cluster at important common multiples at 94 g, 103 g, 117.5 g, 141 g and 188 g. In addition 156.67 g occurs in two weights representing a third of a mina of 470 g; 117.5 g is not only 15 x 7.83 g, and 10 x 11.75 g, but also a quarter of a mina. The common multiple of all four units at 188 g may well also be reinforced by indirect evidence for weighing, highlighted by Renfrew (1972, 408–409): at least one pair if not all three silver bullion bars from Troy IIg might originally have weighed or have been intended to weigh 188 g, that is, 20 x 9.4 g or 16 x 11.75 g, 22 x 8.54 g, 24 x 7.83 g. This accords with Petruso's suggestion that "it is quite likely that the bars were each evaluated for manufacture and/or sale at 18 or, more likely, 20 shekel" (Petruso 1978, 50).

With this evidence at hand it seems to me obvious that the people in the EBA Aegean were using exactly the same units or shekels as in EBA Syria. The cognitive and strategic abilities must have been very similar in both regions when the way of calculating was

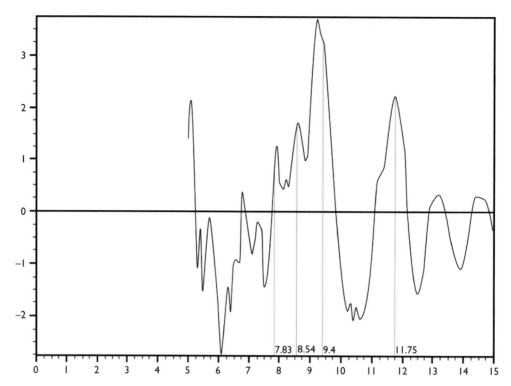

Figure 8.4. Applying the Kendall formula on spool-shaped balance weights (n = 156) from the EBA Aegean: peaks at 7.9, 8.55, 9.25 and 11.75. State of applied data: November 2006. Programme: Matthias Zimmer.

identical. Even more substantially than other archaeological evidence for distribution of artefacts in the eastern Mediterranean it shows how intensive the contacts must be conceived to have been. It seems to me that the appearance of weights, scales and weighing systems in the Aegean is connected to the spread of Near Eastern innovations. Various classes of artefacts, such as certain types of pottery vessels, pigment containers and roller-impressed pottery, which are at home either in Anatolia, Syria or generally the eastern Mediterranean, are also found in the EBA II Aegean. In a recent contribution I tried to show that collectively this constitutes a spread of technological (potter's wheel), economical (balance weight metrology, administrative use of seals) and social (the importance of colour pigments, luxury oils, drinking rituals and certain shapes of drinking vessels) innovations and ideas from a Near Eastern (Mesopotamia/ Syria) core region (Rahmstorf 2006a).[8] Nevertheless, the genuine contribution of the Aegean people to the emergence of their civilisation (Renfrew 1972) shall not be discounted. However, while the peoples of the Aegean were certainly not only receptive and passive but highly innovative on their own (demonstrated for example in their own choice of the shape and material of the balance weights in contrast to the Near Eastern haematite weights), those influences must have had an important impact on the development of the Aegean societies.

For a long time, the Mesopotamian relations to the east, to the Harappan culture, have also been known through the evidence from balance weights (most recently: Ascalone & Peyronel 2003; Ratnagar 2003; Rahmstorf 2006b; see also Kenoyer, this volume). In the Harappan culture the cubic weights were based on a system with a main unit of ca. 13.7 g (the fractions $\frac{1}{16}$, $\frac{1}{8}$, $\frac{1}{4}$, $\frac{1}{2}$, and multiples 2, 4, 10, 20, 40, 100, 200, 400 of this basic unit are obvious, see Hendrickx-Baudot 1972). Now it should be concluded that the Syro-Mesopotamian relations reached out very far to the west as well. Similar units (shekels) and weighing systems were adopted in upper Mesopotamia/Syria, Anatolia and the Aegean. This innovation spread as far west as the Ionian islands, where a spool-shaped balance weight was found in Round-grave 23 in the rich cementery of Steno/Nidri on Lefkas in the islands (Kilian-Dirlmeier 2005, 34, 123 fig. 90 pl. 25, 3 bottom; 71, 6 – not yet weighed). On a typological and morphological basis the Aegean weights were spool-shaped; the Near Eastern weights were often sphendonoid, spindle- or barrel-shaped and made out of haematite (but other stone material and shapes were also in use); and the Harappan weights were mostly cubic. The distribution of the earliest weights between the Aegean and western India during the third millennium reveals around 100 sites (Figure 8.5). The three different types (but note that the Near Eastern type is the least

Table 8.3. *Multiples and common denominators of basic units*

	7.83	8.54	9.4	11.75
1 x	7.83	8.54	9.4	11.75
2 x	15.67	17.09	18.8	*23.5*
3 x	*23.5*	25.63	28.2	35.25
4 x	31.33	34.18	37.6	**47**
5 x	39.16	42.72	**47**	58.75
6 x	**47**	51.27	56.4	*70.5*
7 x	54.83	59.81	65.8	82.25
8 x	62.67	68.36	75.2	**94**
9 x	*70.5*	76.90	84.6	105.75
10 x	78.33	85.45	**94**	*117.5*
11 x	86.16	**94**	103.4	129.25
12 x	**94**	102.54	112.8	**141**
14 x	109.67	119.63	131.6	*164.5*
15 x	*117.5*	128.18	**141**	176.25
16 x	125.33	136.72	150.6	**188**
18 x	**141**	153.81	169.2	211.5
20 x	156.67	170.90	**188**	**235**
21 x	*164.5*	179.45	197.4	246.75
22 x	172.33	**188**	206.8	258.5
24 x	**188**	205.09	225.6	**282**
25 x	195.83	213.63	**235**	293.75
30 x	**235**	256.36	**282**	352.5
32 x	250.66	273.45	300.8	**376**
33 x	258.5	**282**	310.2	387.75
36 x	**282**	307.63	338.4	423
40 x	313.33	341.81	**376**	**470**
44 x	344.66	**376**	413.6	**517**
48 x	**376**	410.18	451.2	**564**
50 x	391.66	427.27	**470**	587.5
55 x	430.83	**470**	**517**	646.25
60 x	**470**	512.72	**564**	705

Note: Common multiples of 7.83, 9.4, 11.75 and 7.83, 8.54, 9.4, 11.75 are in bold; common multiples of 7.83 and 11.75 are in italic.

homogeneous in shape and material used) overlap in the distribution, demonstrating also the overlap of the various units used during this time. The absolute number of different units used seems to be rather small; probably only five units were used (7.83 g, 8.33–8.54 g, 9.4 g, 11.75 g, 13.71 g). But more research is certainly needed, especially for the Mesopotamian and Middle Asian evidence. The spheres of interaction in Near Middle East connecting Mesopotamia with the Indus Valley have been studied for some time (Lamberg-Karlovsky 1972; Lamberg-Karlovsky & Tosi 1973). In addition, the spheres of interaction that were putting the Syrian city cultures with centers at Ebla, Tell Brak/Nagar and Mari

in contact with the Anatolian and Aegean world should receive more attention in the future.

The widespread use of similar metrological standards enabled communities to fix precise values to precious amorphous materials like metals, stones or colour pigments, which were not countable like cattle or measurable in uniformly shaped vessels (by volume) like cereals. It is certainly no coincidence that the strong increase in metal production only appeared during the third millennium BC with the EBA.[9] The advanced processing of valuable metals like gold, silver and tin emerged during the third millennium BC at the same time as the use of balance weights and similar weighing systems was spreading. Around 2600 BC weight metrology was integrated into cultures between the Aegean and northwestern India (Rahmstorf 2006b; Kenoyer, this volume). Also the administrative use of seals became common in this vast geographical region during the third millennium. Simultaneously a strong increase in the use of tin in Mesopotamia and neighouring cultures is identifiable with the beginning of Early Dynastic III (Rahmstorf in press). Further evidence is indicated by the distribution of certain specific types of jewellery and precious raw materials such as lapis lazuli. Aruz has recently shown this regarding the so-called quadruple spirals, the flat beads with tubular midrib and the etched carnelian beads (Aruz 2003, fig. 72–74). Her maps, with some additions, plus the distribution of lapis lazuli during the third millennium, are illustrated in Figure 8.6. One could argue that balance weights, tin bronzes, the adminstrative use of seals and some specific types of elite jewellery and precious materials distribute rather similarly in the vast area between the Aegean and northwestern India in the third millennium. This geographical area was the home of the early advanced cultures in Egypt, Syro-Mesopotamia and Pakistan/northwestern India as well as of many urban or protourban cultures in the regions between or at the peripheries. Through the spread of similar economic strategies (sealing practice, metrology, advanced metallury with various complex techniques such as alloying, cupellation and granulation) regions at the periphery became transformed. Autonomous developments and achievements should not be discounted in the regions at the margins, however; the demand for precious materials such as silver, gold, tin and precious stones (lapis lazuli, cornelian, etc.) as prestigious elite items in the centres of the advanced cultures established contact between regions that were not (or not on such a scale) in contact with each other during the fourth millennium. Through various spheres of interaction the interlinking of regions with neighouring regions facilitated the spread of innovations and materials, especially of amorphous materials

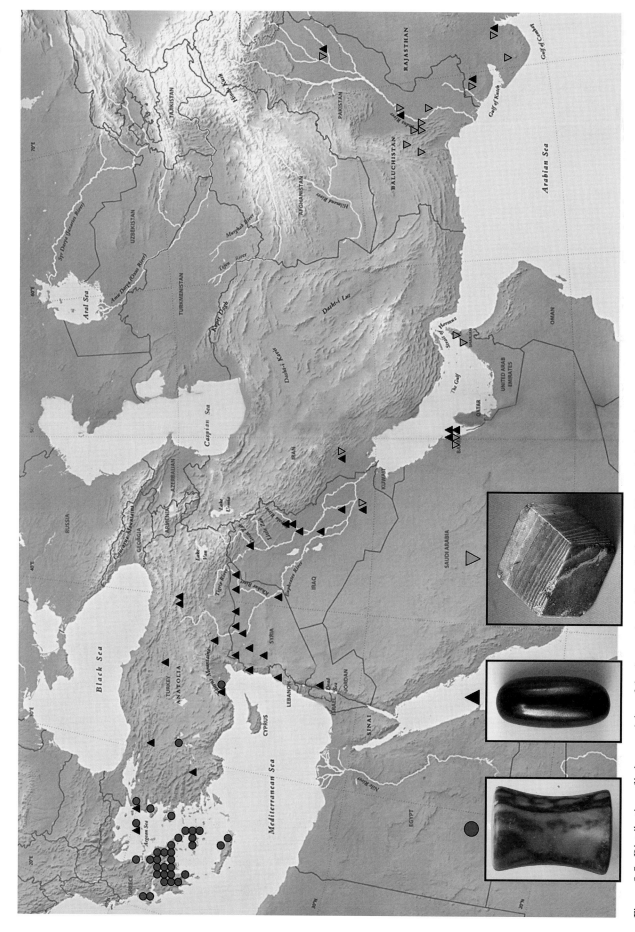

Figure 8.5. Distribution of balance weights of the Aegean (spool-shaped), the Near Eastern (sphendonoid haematite and other types of weights) and the Harappan types (cubic and other shapes) in the third millennium BC.

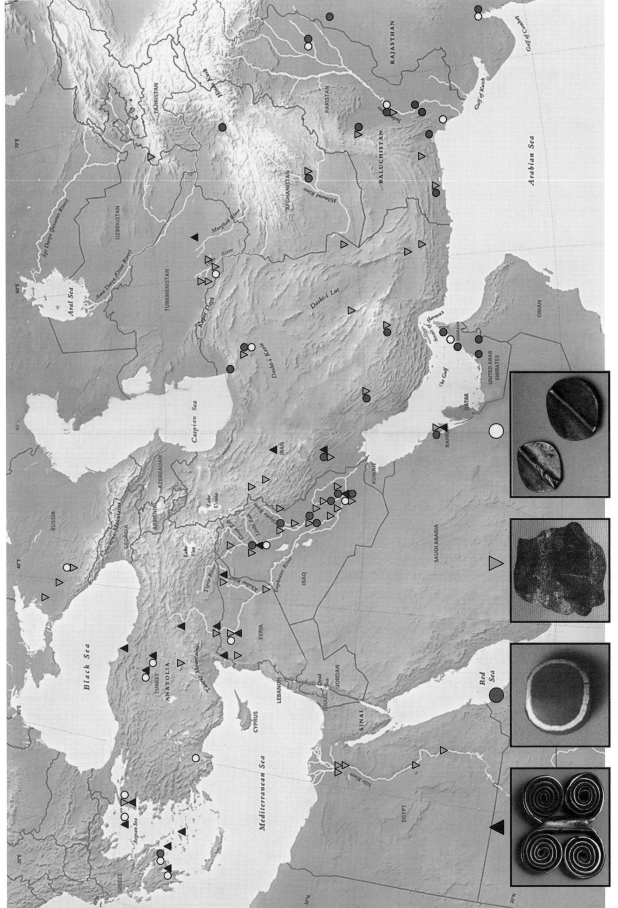

Figure 8.6. Distribution of quadruple spirals, etched cornelian beads, lapis lazuli and flat beads with tubular midrib in the third millennium BC. Based on map and data from Aruz 2003 with additonal evidence.

like metals or stones that could now be weighed according to standards (units of weight) used in similar ways in various regions. These contacts reached an optimum between ca. 2500 and 2200 BC at least for the regions west of Mesopotamia. The chronological interlinking of all this evidence certainly needs further intensive detailed work, which cannot be provided in this short contribution.[10]

The adoption of weighing in central Europe during the Bronze Age

After the establishment of weight metrology during the third millennium it persisted in the eastern Mediterranean and the Near East. In the Aegean it is still difficult to perceive what happened in regard to the use of balance weights after the breakdown of the complex EBA II culture around 2250 BC. On Crete very few balance weights are found from the Old Palace period during Middle Bronze Age (Alberti 2000). With the New Palace period on Crete we get much more evidence mainly from lead discoid balance weights, which are known from a good many sites on Crete and the Cyclades (Petruso 1992). They were based on a unit of 60–65 g (mean around 61 g). There are multiples of 2, 4, 6, 8, 12, 16 and 24 times as well as fractions of ¼, ⅓, ½ and ⅔ known to form the Minoan weighing system (Petruso 1992). From the Mycenaean Palace period of the 14th and 13th centuries BC, we have a much more limited corpus of balance weights so far. Discoid lead weights are not common on the mainland and only a few dozen stone weights of various shapes (sphenonoid, discoid, square-shaped, etc.) have been found or published so far, for example, at Thebes and Tiryns on mainland Greece (Aravantinos 1995; Alberti 2003, fig. 3; Rahmstorf 2008a, 153–163 pl. 57; 93, 1). Some of these weights can be assigned to the Minoan system, but other units than the 61-g unit are also present. So far, the complexity of the Mycenaean systems of weight seems not to be understood completely. For example, the EBA II spool-shaped balance weights discussed earlier also appear in Mycenaean graves and settlements (e.g., at Midea: Demakopoulou, Divari-Valakou, Åström & Walberg, 1997–1998, 57–58, 66 fig. 50) in seemingly closed contexts so that the question arises as to whether they were only picked up out of curiosity by Mycenaeans when they were disturbing earlier EH sites during construction – or whether they were still used in a similar way 1,000 years later! The latter point cannot be easily dismissed as the main unit of 9.4 g was still in widespread use during the LBA in the eastern Mediterranean (e.g., in the sample of weights

from Uluburun: Pulak 2000). Here only an examination of all contexts might offer some solution.

Most interestingly, balance weights also appear at this time in continental Europe (outside the Aegean) for the first time.[11] Some look just like normal pebbles, like the ones from Bordjoš in the northern Serbian Banat. But their identification as balance weights cannot be questioned as they were found together in a storage pit with a beam of a scale, some other finds and pottery of the Gáva-Belegiš II-group, dating the complex to Hallstatt A1, that is, the (earlier?) 12th century BC (Medović 1995). Any assignment of the pebbles' weights, which are 17 g, 51.2 g, 54.4 g, 55.7 g, 62.7 g, 86.7 g, 122.2 g and 183.7 g, to a unit or even a known unit seems difficult, but some correspondence to the Minoan system might not be completely out of the realm of possibility (fractions and multiples of ¼, ¾, ¾?, ¾?, 1, ³⁄₂, 2, 3 of c. 61g). The case of Bordjoš also serves to suggest that we may not expect weights in standardized shapes in Bronze Age Europe like those we know from the Bronze Age Aegean, the eastern Mediterranean, and the Near and Middle East. Probably many such simple pebble weights have not yet been identified in other parts of prehistoric Europe. In central Europe rectangular metal balance weights are known thanks to an important study by C. Pare (1998). Pare was able to assemble evidence from more than a dozen sites mainly in eastern France and southern Germany. These are graves of the central European Recent Bronze Age (Bronze D = ca. 13th century BC), which contained weighing equipment (weights and scales) possibly stored in pouches. This research demonstrated clearly that the concept of weighing was known in central Europe at least from the 13th or late 14th century BC. The total number of weights is small, and even fewer (around 20–25) can be used for metrological calculations. It is obvious that they are all light weights, never weighing more than around 60 g. In most cases only one or two weights are found together in one grave; only in the case of the grave of Steinfurth (Figure 8.7) in the north of Frankfurt were a set of eight weights found together. The limited number known means it is difficult to make definite claims about the units in use. Pare assumed these central European weights were oriented on the Minoan system, being mainly fractions of the Minoan unit of around 61 g (Pare 1998, 487–493 fig. 36 tab. 4–7). The two weights from Gondelsheim near Karlsruhe (Pare 1998, 434–436 fig. 11, 1–2) could represent one times the unit (60.7 g) and the fraction of ⅛ (7.5 g), and the six weights of different shapes from Richemont-Pépinville near Metz (Pare 1998, 442–444 fig. 17, 2–5. 7–8) might illustrate the fractions of ¹⁄₁₆, ⅛, ¼, ⅓ and twice ⅔ of the Minoan unit (but what is the

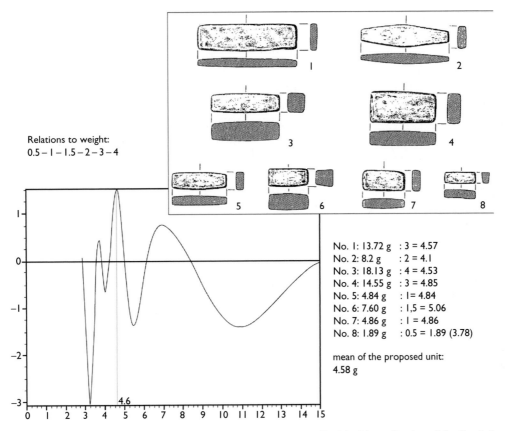

Relations to weight:
0.5 – 1 – 1.5 – 2 – 3 – 4

No. 1: 13.72 g : 3 = 4.57
No. 2: 8.2 g   : 2 = 4.1
No. 3: 18.13 g : 4 = 4.53
No. 4: 14.55 g : 3 = 4.85
No. 5: 4.84 g   : 1 = 4.84
No. 6: 7.60 g   : 1,5 = 5.06
No. 7: 4.86 g   : 1 = 4.86
No. 8: 1.89 g   : 0.5 = 1.89 (3.78)

mean of the proposed unit:
4.58 g

Figure 8.7. Balance weights from Steinfurth, Hesse, in Germany (Bz D) with application of the Kendall formula. Drawing of the objects after Pare 1998.

weight weighing 55 g, Pare 1998, fig. 17, 6?). However, if this is correct, it cannot be applied to the set of weights from Steinfurth, which seems to be a logical series of weights based on a unit of ca. 4.6 g (Figure 8.7). Although Pare might be correct in his conclusions that many of the central European metal weights of the Recent Bronze Age derived their unit from the Aegean, this seems not to hold true for all of them. Probably, the range of possible shapes of the weights demonstrates the lack of a central political authority that might have achieved more standardisation in morphology as well as in units. Also interesting is Pare's assumption that the oval or angular amygdaloid block weights can be linked, as a flattened version of the stone sphendonoids, to the Aegean and the eastern Mediterranean. Such shapes in metal are not known from the Aegean. However, there are three small bronze objects found together in Room 190 in the LH III B1 lower citadel of Tiryns that have a flat rectangular shape and weigh 7.4 g, 8.2 g and 10.3 g (but note the very small modern borehole on each of them carried out for material analyses) (Rahmstorf 2008b, cat. nos. 435, 436, 438).

The central European weights known so far show that the concept of weighing was adopted in this region during the Mycenaean Palace period of the 14th and 13th centuries BC at the latest. The underlying unit was probably also derived from the Aegean. Nevertheless, the lack of uniformity and the existence of other units in addition hint at the idea that there were also strong local developments going on without any tie to the Aegean. But again, because of the general similarities, it seems hardly possible that the concept of weighing was developed independently in central Europe.

Conclusions

We should now discuss the four questions posed in the introduction. Beginning with the first question, What are the objective criteria enabling us to conclude with certainty that a special group of artefacts might be weights? I hope that I have been able to demonstrate that various pieces of evidence need to be reflected upon before one can conclude with certainty that a class of objects are balance weights. Three lines of evidence must be present:

• The weighing system must be intuitively understandable. As Petrie (1926, 7; compare Petruso 1992, 9) has already argued, "in general we should not accept any multiple which is unlikely, such as 11, 13, 23, 28,

33, 46". Likely multiples are, for example, 2, 3, 4, 5, 10, 12 and 60 and the "interim useful and practical factors which could have been derived from them (e.g. 6, 8, 20, 24, 30, 32)" (Petruso 1992, 9; compare also Fieller 1993, 286). If it is not intuitively understandable, it will not have been practical for the ancient users.

- Any possible weighing system should be made more convincing through the application of mathematical-statistical methods, for example, the Kendall formula earlier, hinting at the units already derived through the intuitive approach.
- Any weighing system needs to be verified through the archaeological evidence, in the form of finds of balance weights and (parts of) scales. The weights should form a uniform group of artefacts by their material, their shape, their surface treatment, and so on. The possible balance weights should appear in groups indicating their use in sets.

What are recurring traits in the appearance and actual shaping of weights, and why were certain shapes, materials, and surface treatments chosen? In the Aegean the picture is rather clear: the spool-shaped or cylindrical weights are the only type present. Only at Poliochni and Troy, that is, at sites where a strong Anatolian influence is obvious, are the sphendonoid or ovoid weights made out of haematite, which are so typical for the Near East, even if other types exist there, present. The Aegean spool-shaped weights are often made of very attractive material such as beautiful veined marble. They quite often are made out of spondylus shell as well. Why the Aegean people chose such a shape is difficult to explain. There might be two reasons that are somehow connected. First, the spool-shaped objects are present in the Aegean from the beginning of the Neolithic. These are spools or cylinders made out of badly baked clay, which are most probably loom weights. They hung on the warps of warp-weighted looms (Rahmstorf 2003b, fig. 18; Rahmstorf 2005, pl. 22, 2). These clay spools seem to have been used only for textile production through many millennia, but seemingly never as balance weights. However, the special shape was probably connected to the idea of a hanging weight in the minds of the Aegean people. It is a peculiarity of Bronze Age Aegean inhabitants that they often chose a shape for an innovation or new artefact according to their own taste and experience. Connected to this might have been a practical reason. So far, no pans of scales are known from the EBA, while balance beams made out of bone have been excavated at Poliochni and Troy (Rahmstorf 2006a, fig. 10, 24–25; Rahmstorf 2006b, figs. 3, 5.7). Instead scale pans have been found at sites in Early Dynastic Mesopotamia

(Rahmstorf 2006b, fig. 3, 1–3). The different shape of the balance weights was probably the reason behind this. The sphendonoid or ovoid weights of the Near East could only be placed in pans while the spool-shaped weights could be placed in loops hanging from the beam.

It is obvious that there were standardized shapes for balance weights, like the spool-shaped balance weights in the EBA Aegean, the sphendonoid or duck-shaped balance weights in the Near East and the cube-shaped balance weights of the Harappan culture, even if there was still some variation possible in these regions. Far less uniformity in the morphology of the balance weights, as well as the weighing system and the units used, can be expected outside cultures that seem to have been organized chiefdoms with some hierarchy (such as the EBA Aegean [see Alram-Stern 2004, 520–521 for further references] and Anatolia), or with a statelike level of organisation and defined social hierarchies – with mechanisms of control by "both kin-based and class-based institutionalized power" (Akkermans & Schwartz 2003, 239 regarding the Eblaite state) – such as Mesopotamia and EBA western Syria (but see also Cooper 2006, 61–68). Variation and little uniformity are demonstrated by the evidence of the first balance weights from central Europe of the later second millennium BC. However, one should keep in mind that there is still little empirical data for early (Bronze and Iron Age) balance weights in Europe outside the advanced Mediterranean cultures. It is likely that more data will emerge when 'suspicious' artefacts are sampled more rigorously in various regions of prehistoric Europe in the future. So far, to my knowledge, the limited evidence does not allow the assumption that similar units were used in various other regions of temperate and Mediterranean Europe as, for example, R. Peroni (1998) implies.

Finally, I hope to have also given some insights regarding questions 3 and 4 of the introduction. Through the closely contemporaneous appearance of balance weights from ca. 2600 BC in the vast region between the Aegean and western India, it seems to be rather unlikely that the concept of weighing relative to a standardised unit was independently invented in various places at more or less the same time. The similar units used across vast geographical areas make it much more likely that weighing was invented at one place and spread from there to other regions, even if it remains for further study to explain how and why this became possible. The complexity of the innovation with its requirement of basic mathematical knowledge makes the existence of "change agents as linkers" (Rogers 2003, 368) likely. Also some central authority might be expected in order to establish and certify one or several units. It seems to be reasonable to assume the existence of both – change agents as well as authority, perhaps unified in a certain group of people – already in place in the EBA Aegean. Only with such ingredients in a given society could stable and continuous trade relations be established with neighbouring societies. The overlap of probably only five different units used over great distances demonstrates the interlinking of various urban or proto-urban societies in exchange relations. Each region had its specific material culture but was incorporated in various spheres of interaction. These can be demonstrated by mapping those special artefacts and special materials that have a greater spacial distribution. The balance weights were the medium by which the precise exchange of precious amorphous materials like (certain) metals became possible within and beyond certain spheres of interaction. Special artefacts like certain types of precious jewellery (Figure 8.6) illustrate these trade relations over long distances (Aruz 2003; Rahmstorf in press).

The first appearance of balance weights in central Europe, considerably later, seems once again to be connected to contact with an area (the Aegean) with established weight metrology. In central Europe, however, little evidence for any centralised and stable authority – if any – can be deduced from the archaeological record. It is suggested that "small groups of people would have produced a multitude of small leaders" and "generalised groupings would by comparison have been relatively weakly bonded together, at a more distant kinship level" (Harding 2000, 422). This resulted in little uniformity in the morphology of the weights, as well as the weighing systems used. By this, I intend to imply that the emergence of the concept of standardised weight and the activity of weighing itself was in the first place dependent upon a certain degree of development in societies. This was most probably connected to other major changes like the development of complex metallurgy (alloying in metal work, intensive usage of precious metals and other amorphous materials) and further to urbanisation and intensive long-distance trade.

Addendum September 2009

Since the completion of this contribution in November 2006 I have reached further understanding of the basic units described previously, which shall be described here shortly. As shown earlier, N. Parise first demonstrated some of the relations of the basic units 7.83, 9.4 and 11.75. They can be divided into fractions; for example, 6/5 of 7.83 results in 9.4 and 5/4 of 9.4 are 11.75 (Table 8.1). However, the logical basis of the numerical relations was not fully understood by Parise. All relations among the three basic units can be expressed in the co-prime fractions 3/2, 2/3, 5/4, 6/5 and 5/6. The three basic units have the lowest common multiple at 47 (4 x 11.75 = 5 x 9.4 = 6 x 7.83). Through the fractional expression of the interrelations of the three numbers we can in fact define the original numbers the ancient people used as their units. Two points need to be considered here: first, the ancient people surely used integers instead of the impractical decimal fractions, and, second, the units we measure today are given in modern grams, not in the ancient measuring unit. Through the fractional expression of the basic units we can reveal the original numbers of the ancient measuring unit: the convergence from one unit to the next is based on fractions that have the denominator 2, 3, 4, 5 and 6. Sixty is the smallest number divisible by every number from 2 to 6. The ratios of the three different units can be expressed as fractions of 60. Hence, the impractical decimal fractions 7.83, 9.4 and 11.75 were indeed the integers 10, 12 and 15 (Table 8.4). Important common multiples of 7.83, 9.4 and 11.75 are 47 g (= 60) and multiples of it, especially at 470 g (= 600, the mina) and 28200 g (= 36000, the talent). With this knowledge

Table 8.4. *The convergence of the basic units used between the eastern Mediterranean and the Indus valley*

Units	7.83	[8.616]	9.4	11.75	13.7083	47
Relation of 7.83 to other units:	100%	110%	120%	150%	175%	600%
	1	11/10	6/5	3/2	7/4	6
	60/60	66/60	72/60	90/60	105/60	360/60
Relation of 9.4 to other units:	83.3%	91.6%	100%	125%	136.6%	500%
	5/6	13/15	1	5/4	5/4	5
	50/60	c. 52/60	60/60	75/60	c. 82/60	300/60
Relation of 11.75 to other units:	66.6%	73.3%	80%	100%	116.6%	400%
	2/3	11/15	4/5	1	7/6	4
	40/60	44/60	48/60	60/60	70/60	240/60
Real number:	10	[11]	12	15	17.5	60

Table 8.5. *Some multiples and common denominators of basic units: 7.83 (= 10), 9.4 (= 12), 11.75 (= 15) and 13.71 (= 17.5)*

	10	12	15	17.5
1 x	10	12	15	17.5
2 x	20	24	30	35
3 x	30	36	45	52.5
4 x	40	48	60	**70**
5 x	50	60	75	87.5
6 x	60	72	90	*105*
7 x	**70**	84	*105*	122.5
8 x	80	96	120	**140**
10 x	100	120	150	175
12 x	120	144	180	<u>**210**</u>
14 x	**140**	168	<u>**210**</u>	245
15 x	150	180	225	262.5
16 x	160	192	240	**280**
18 x	180	216	270	*315*
20 x	200	240	300	**350**
21 x	<u>**210**</u>	252	*315*	367.5
24 x	240	288	360	<u>**420**</u>
25 x	250	300	375	437.5
28 x	**280**	336	<u>**420**</u>	490
30 x	300	360	450	*525*
32 x	320	384	480	**560**
35 x	**350**	<u>**420**</u>	*525*	612.5
36 x	360	432	540	**630**
40 x	400	480	600	**700**
42 x	<u>**420**</u>	504	**630**	*735*
44 x	440	528	660	770
45 x	450	540	675	787.5
48 x	480	576	720	**840**
49 x	**490**	588	*735*	857.5
50 x	500	600	750	875
54 x	540	648	810	*945*
56 x	**560**	672	**840**	980
60 x	600	720	900	<u>**1050**</u>

Note: Common multiples of 10 and 17.5 are in bold, of 15 and 17.5 in italic, of 10, 15 and 17.5 in bold and underlined, and of 10, 12, 15 and 17.5 in bold with double underlines.

we can 'translate' the numbers of Table 8.3 into the real numbers used (Table 8.5).

It seems that the exceptional fractional qualities of the number 60 were fully understood by the middle of the third millennium BCE and therefore 60 was chosen as the basis of weight metrology during the EBA in the eastern Mediterranean (Syria, Anatolia, Aegean) and in southern Mesopotamia. It is important to note that the basic unit (shekel) of ca. 8.33 g of southern Mesopotamia

is not really adjustable to the system of the units 7.83, 9.4 and 11.75. Only when calculating with a slightly heavier shekel at 8.616 could it be placed at 11 in the eastern Mediterranean sexagesimal system (Table 8.4). This rather crude adjustment within the Aegean might explain the peak at ca. 8.6 in Figure 8.4. Possibly the sexagesimal system of the eastern Mediterranean (7.83, 9.4 and 11.75) and the sexagesimal system of Mesopotamia (8.33) were competitive independent schemes and used different relative numbers for the real weight. In addition to these results, it is a big surprise that the basic unit of the Harappan culture of ca. 13.7 g (Hendrickx-Baudot 1972) fits precisely into the eastern Mediterranean sexagesimal system when it is placed at exactly 13.7083. It stands then in a relation of 105/60 to 7.83, hence is 17.5, at least in the conversion to the sexagesimal system of the eastern Mediterranean. The Harappans were surely using an integer and not the impractical decimal fraction 17.5. However, its mass could easily be converged to the eastern Mediterranean sexagesimal system. It cannot be assessed here what consequences these results imply for the scale and intensity of cultural interrelations between the mentioned regions.

ACKNOWLEDGEMENTS

I would like to thank Dr. I. Morley and Prof. C. Renfrew for the invitation to the Measuring the World and Beyond conference. For funding of research trips to Greece and Turkey in November 2005 as well as in January and August–September 2006 I would like to express my gratitude to the Institute for Classical Studies, University of London, and the Fritz Thyssen Stiftung, Köln. I am especially thankful to Prof. A. Özyar, who allowed me to study the balance weights from Tarsus-Gözlükule that are presented here. The results presented were only made possible through the permisson and the kind cooperation of many individuals and institutions responsible for the archaeological material from the 25 sites and museums I have visited so far. All will be thanked in the forthcoming final publication on the EBA balance weights, but special thanks are already due to Dr. L. Papazoglou-Manioudaki and K. Paschalidis at the Nationalmuseum at Athens. I am also thankful to Dr. Thomas Link (Würzburg) for graphically improving the figures and to Matthias Zimmer (Mainz) for writing the computer programme on which Figure 8.4 is based.

NOTES

1. During the Measuring the World and Beyond conference it became clear that this seems to be an open question in New World archaeology. There are some ancient Peruvian scales known (Kisch 1965), but are they pre-Columbian or not? For example, the mass of a set of stone weights found together with a scale from Hacienda de Sagrario was based on the

Spanish *onza* (Nordenskiold 1930), but are there securely dated weights from pre-Columbian contexts? It would be very important to know whether the concept of weighing existed in America before the arrival of the Spaniards.

2. The object of Figure 8.1: 1 was found in a LH III B context, raising again the question of later similar use of such objects. The object of Figure 8.1: 5 was found in R 196 of phase 8b in EH II Late. Compare Rahmstorf 2006b, fig. 4, C. At that time – that article was written in May 2005 – I was not yet aware of this further marked object from this context.

3. The few published statements showed some reservations, even if, as was specially pointed out by E. Alberti, these results would be very important for the origins of weighing systems in the eastern Mediterranean when confirmed through further research. See Alberti 2003, 609. For other comments see Alram-Stern 2004, 392, 596 and Alberti and Parise 2005, 382.

4. See Kilian-Dirlmeier 2005, 167–169, for five additional sites with spool-shaped weights in the Aegean.

5. Please note: (-) = fragmented; rec. = reconstructed original weight.

6. Goldman 1956, 267, 275 no. 121 and no. 127 could not be located in the new Tarsus depot but probably will be found in the future. Instead of these, two other haematite weights are shown in Figure 8.3: 3, 8, which were not displayed by Goldman (Goldman 1956, 275, no. 129–130).

7. I would like to thank Matthias Zimmer (Mainz) for writing the computer programme.

8. This article is also accessible on the Internet: http://www.atypon-link.com/WDG/doi/abs/10.1515/PZ.2006.002.

    Note that the maps of Figures 3 and 9 were printed as the old version due to a fault of mine and do not correspond with lists no. 1 and 4. The correct versions of the figures can be obtained from me: rahmstor@uni-mainz.de.

    For similar conclusions regarding the importance of the trade relations during the Aegean later EBA II and the Anatolian EBA III see now also Şahoğlu 2005.

9. It would be very interesting to know whether any means of weight quantification were used in cultures with earlier intensive use of metals such as during the Copper Age in the Balkans (for example, at Varna).

10. In this short article no reference can be given to all the sites mapped in Figures 8.5–8.6. This will be covered in a future work.

11. The balance weights from the North Italian Terramare culture and the metrological significance of the Central European EBA *Ösenringe* (neckrings with flat-hammered rolled ends) cannot be discussed in this short contribution. See Cardarelli, Pacciarelli & Pallante 2001; Lenerz-de Wilde 1995.

REFERENCES

Akkermans, M. M. G . & Schwartz, G. M. 2003. *The archaeology of Syria: From complex hunter-gatherers to early urban societies (ca. 16,000–300 BC).* Cambridge: Cambridge University Press.

Alberti, M. E. 2000. Les poids de Mallia entre les premiers et seconds palais: Un essai de mise en contexte. *Bulletin de Correspondance Hellénique* **124**, 57–73.

Alberti, M. E. 2003. I sistemi ponderali dell'Egeo nell'età del bronzo: Studi, storia, pratica e contatti. *Annuario della Scuola Archeologica Italiana di Atene e delle Missioni italiane in Oriente* **81**, 597–640.

Alberti, M. E. & Parise, N. 2005. Towards a unification of mass-units between the Aegean and the Levant, in *Emporia: Aegeans in the Central and Eastern Mediterranean. Proceedings of the 10th International Aegean Conference, Athens, 14–18 April 2004,* eds. R. Laffineur & E. Greco (Aegaeum 25.) Liège: Université de Liège, 381–392.

Alram-Stern, E. 2004: *Die ägäische Frühzeit. 2. Serie Forschungsbericht 1975–2002. 2. Band. Die Frühbronzezeit in Griechenland mit Ausnahme von Kreta* (Österreichische Akademie der Wissenschaften. Philosophisch-historische Klasse. Veröffentlichungen der mykenischen Kommission 21). Wien: Verlag der Österreichischen Akademie der Wissenschaften.

Aravantinos, V. 1995. Μυκηναϊκά σταθμά από την Θήβα. Σύμβολοι στη μελέτη του Μυκηναϊκού μετρικού συστήμταος, in *Β΄ Διεθνές Συνέδριο Βοιωτικών Μελετών, Λειβαδιά, 6–10 Σεπτεμβρίου 1992,* ed. C. Christopoulou, Athen, 97–137.

Archi, A. 1987. Reflections on the system of weights from Ebla, in *Eblaitica: Essays on the Ebla Archives and Eblaite Language. Vol. I,* eds. C. H. Gordon, G. A. Rendsburg & N. H. Winter. Winona Lake, Ind.: Eisenbrauns, 47–89.

Arnaud, D. 1967. Contribution à l'Étude de la métrologie syrienne au IIe millénaire. *Revue d'Assyriologie* **61**, 151–169.

Aruz, J. 2003. Art and interconnections in the third millennium B.C., in *Art of the First Cities: The Third Millennium B.C. from the Mediterranean to the Indus,* eds. J. Aruz & R. Wallenfels. New Haven, Conn.: Yale University Press, 239–250.

Ascalone, E. & Peyronel, L. 2003. Meccanismi di scambio commerciale e metrologia premonetaria in Asia Media, Valle dell'Indo e Golfo Persico durante l'età del bronzo: Spunti per una riflessione sulle sfere di interazione culturale. *Contributi e Materiali di Archeologia Orientale* **9**, 339–438.

Cardarelli, A., Pacciarelli, M. & Pallante, P. 2001. Pesi e bilance dell'età del bronzo italiana, in *Ponder: Pesi e misure nell'antichità,* eds. C. Corti & N. Giordani. Firenze: Libra '93; 33–58.

Cherry, J. 1983. Putting the best foot forward. *Antiquity* **57**, 52–56.

Cooper, L. 2006. *Early Urbanism on the Syrian Euphrates.* New York: Routledge.

Czichon, R. M. & Werner, P. 1998. *Tall Munbāqa-Ekalte I. Die bronzezeitlichen Kleinfunde* (Wissenschaftliche Veröffentlichungen der Deutschen Orient-Gesellschaft 98). Saarbrücken: Saarbrücker Druckerei und Verlag – SDV.

Demakopoulou, K., Divari-Valakou, N., Åström, P. & Walberg, G. 1997–1998, Excavations in Midea 1995–1996. *Opuscula Atheniensia* **22–23**, 57–90.

Fieller, N. R. J. 1993. Archaeostatistics: Old statistics in ancient contexts. *Statistician* **42**, 279–295.

Goldman, H. 1956. *Excavations at Gözlü Kule, Tarsus. Volume II. From the Neolithic through the Bronze Age.* Princeton, N.J.: Princeton University Press.

Harding, A. F. 2000. *European Societies in the Bronze Age.* Cambridge: Cambridge University Press.

Hendrickx-Baudot, M. P. 1972. The weights of the Harappa-culture. *Orientalia Lovaniensia Periodica* **3**, 5–34.

Holland T. A. 1975. An inscribed weight from Tell Sweyhat, Syria. *Iraq* **37**, 75–76.

Kendall, D. G. 1974. Hunting quanta. *Philosophical Transactions of the Royal Society of London. Series A, Mathematical and Physical Sciences* **276**, 231–266.

Kilian-Dirlmeier, I. 2005. *Die bronzezeitlichen Gräber bei Nidri auf Leukas: Ausgrabungen von W. Dörpfeld 1903–1913* (Römisch-Germanisches Zentralmuseum, Monographien Band 62). Mainz: Verlag des Römisch-Germanischen Zentralmuseums.

Kisch, B. 1965. *Scales and Weights: A Historical Outline* (Yale Studies in the History of Science and Medicine, vol. 1). New Haven, Conn.: Yale University Press.

Lamberg-Karlovsky, C. C. 1972. Trade mechanisms in Indus-Mesopotamian interrelations. *Journal of the American Oriental Society* **92**, 222–229.

Lamberg-Karlovsky, C. C. & Tosi, M. 1973. Shahri-i Sokhta and Tepe Yahya: Tracks on the earliest history of the Iranian plateau. *East and West* **23**, 21–53.

Lenerz-de Wilde, M. 1995. Prähistorische Zahlungsmittel in der Kupfer- und der Bronzezeit Mitteleuropas. *Fundberichte Baden-Württemberg* **20**, 229–347.

Lindsten, E. 1943. Vorgeschichtliche Gewichte aus Troja. *Acta Archaeologica* **14**, 91–105.

Medović, P. 1995. Die Waage aus der frühhallstattzeitlichen Siedlung Bordjoš (Borjas) bei Novi Bečei (Banat), in *Handel, Tausch und Verkehr im bronze- und früheisenzeitlichen Südosteuropa*, ed. B. Hänsel (Südosteuropa-Schriften Band 17 = Prähistorische Archäologie in Südosteuropa Band 11). München-Berlin: Südosteuropa-Gesellschaft e.V., 209–218.

Milano, L. 2004. Weight stones from Tell Beydar/Nabada. *Kaskal* **1**, 1–7.

Nordenskiold, E. 1930. The ancient Peruvian system of weights. *Man* **30**, 215–221.

Oates, J. 2001. The stone objects, in *Excavations at Tell Brak. Vol. 2: Nagar in the Third Millennium BC*, eds. D. Oates, J. Oates & H. McDonald. Oxford: McDonald Institute for Archaeological Research.

Pare, C. F. E. 1998. Weights and weighing in Bronze Age Central Europe, in *Eliten in der Bronzezeit. Ergebnisse zweier Kolloquien in Mainz und Athen* (Römisch-Germanisches Zentralmuseum, Monographien Band 43, 2). Mainz: Verlag des Römisch-Germanischen Zentralmuseums, 421–514.

Parise, N. F. 1970–1971. Per uno studio del sistema ponderale ugaritico. *Dialoghi di Archeologia* **4–5**, 3–36.

Parise, N. F. 1981. Mina di Ugarit, mina di Karkemish, mina di Khatti. *Dialoghi di Archeologia* **3 (Nuova Serie)**, 155–160.

Parise, N. F. 1984. Unità ponderali e rapporti di cambio nella Siria del Nord, in *Circulation of Goods in Non-palatial Context in the Ancient Near East*, ed. A. Archi (Incunabula Graeca LXXXII). Roma: Editione dell'Ateneo, 126–138.

Peroni, R. 1998. Bronzezeitliche Gewichtssysteme im Metallhandel zwischen Mittelmeer und Ostsee, in *Mensch und Umwelt in der Bronzezeit Europas (Man and Environment in European Bronze Age)*, ed. B. Hänsel. Kiel: Oetker-Voges Verlag.

Petrie, W. M. F. 1926. *Glass Stamps and Weights. Ancient weights and measures: illustrated by the Egyptian Collection in University College, London* (British School of Archaeology in Egypt, nos. 39–40). London: Joel L. Malter.

Petruso, K. M. 1978. *Systems of Weight in the Bronze Age Aegean.* Diss. Indiana University.

Petruso, K. M. 1992. *Keos. Vol. VIII: Ayia Irini: The Balance Weights: An Analysis of Weight Measurement in Prehistoric Crete and the Cycladic Islands.* Mainz: Philip von Zabern.

Pulak, C. 2000. The balance weights from the Late Bronze Age shipwreck at Uluburun, in *Metals Make the World Go Round: The Supply and Circulation of Metals in Bronze Age Europe. Proceedings of a Conference held at the University of Birmingham in June 1997*, ed. C. F. E. Pare. Oxford: Oxbow, 247–266.

Rahmstorf, L. 2003a. The identification of Early Helladic balance weights and their wider implications, in *Metron: Measuring the Aegean Bronze Age. Proceedings of the 9th International Aegean Conference. Yale University 18–21 April 2002*, eds. K. P. Foster & R. Laffineur (Aegaeum 24.) Liège 2003: Université de Liège, 293–300.

Rahmstorf, L. 2003b. Clay spools from Tiryns and other contemporary sites: An indication of foreign influence in LH III C?, in Περιφέρεια του Μυκηναϊκού Κόσμου: Β΄Διεθνές Διεπιστημονικό Συμπόσιο/The Periphery of the Mycenaean World. 2nd International Interdisciplinary Colloquium, 26–30 September, Lamia 1999, eds. N. Kyparissi-Apostolika & M. Papakonstantinou. Lamia: ΥΠΟΥΡΓΕΙΟ ΠΟΛΙΤΙΣΜΟΥ, 397–415.

Rahmstorf, L. 2005. Ethnicity and changes in weaving technology in Cyprus and the eastern Mediterranean in the 12th century BC, in *Cyprus: Religion and Society from the Late Bronze Age to the End of the Archaic Period. Proceedings of an International Symposium on Cypriote Archaeology, Erlangen, 23–24 July 2004* eds. V. Karageorghis, H. Matthäus & S. Rogge. Möhnesee-Wamel: Bibliopolis, 143–169.

Rahmstorf, L. 2006a. Zur Ausbreitung vorderasiatischer Innovationen in die frühbronzezeitliche Ägäis. *Prähistorische Zeitschrift* **81**, 49–96.

Rahmstorf, L. 2006b. In search of earliest balance weights, scales and weighing systems from the Eastern Mediterranean, the Near and Middle East, in *Weights in Context: Bronze Age Weighing Systems of Eastern Mediterranean: Chronology,*

Typology, Material and Archaeological Contexts. International Colloquium, Rome, 22–24 November 2004, eds. M. E. Alberti, E. Ascalone & L. Peyronel (Studi e Materiali 13). Rome: Istituto Italiano di Numismatica, 9–45.

Rahmstorf, L. 2008a. *Kleinfunde aus Tiryns: Terrakotta, Stein, Bein und Glas/Fayence vornehmlich der Spätbronzezeit* (Tiryns. Forschungen und Berichte XVI). Wiesbaden: Dr. Ludwig Reichert Verlag.

Rahmstorf, L. 2008b. *Kleinfunde aus Tiryns: Terrakotta, Stein, Bein und Glas/Fayence vornehmlich der Spätbronzezeit* (Tiryns. Forschungen und Berichte XVI) [Elektronischer Katalog]. http://archiv.ub.uni-heidelberg.de/propylaeumdok/volltexte/2008/91/

Rahmstorf, L. in press. Die Nutzung von Booten und Schiffen in der bronzezeitlichen Ägäis und die Fernkontakte der Frühbronzezeit, in *Der Griff nach den Sternen. Wie Europas Eliten zu Macht und Reichtum kamen. Internationales Symposium, Halle*, Feb. 16–21, 2005, eds. F. Bertemes & H. Meller.

Ratnagar, S. 2003. Theorizing Bronze-Age intercultural trade: The evidence of the weights. *Paléorient* **29/1**, 79–92.

Renfrew, C. 1972. *The Emergence of Civilisation: The Cyclades and the Aegean in the Third Millennium B.C.* London: Methuen.

Rogers, E. M. 2003. *Diffusion of Innovations.* 5th ed. New York, London, Toronto and Sydney: Free Press.

Şahoğlu, V. 2005. The Anatolian trade network and the Izmir region during the Early Bronze Age. *Oxford Journal of Archaeology* **24**, 339–361.

Speiser, E. A. 1935. *Excavations at Tepe Gawra, Vol. I: Levels I–VIII.* Philadephia: University of Pennsylvania Press.

Wilson, D. E. 1999. *Keos IX: Ayia Irini: Periods I–III: The Neolithic and Early Bronze Age settlements. Part 1: The Pottery and Small Finds.* Mainz: Philip von Zabern.

9

Measuring the Harappan world: Insights into the Indus order and cosmology

J. Mark Kenoyer

Introduction

The origins of certain types of weights and measures in South Asia can be traced back to the earliest cities of the Indus civilization. This chapter presents an overview of the types of artefacts that inform us about ancient Harappan measurement systems, in order to gain insight into their concepts of order and cosmology. The main focus is on recent discoveries at the site of Harappa, Pakistan, where detailed measurements have been made of a wide range of artefacts in an attempt to understand better the standardization and regional variation of Indus measurement systems.

The Indus civilization or Harappan culture refers to the first urban society that emerged in the greater Indus valley of Pakistan and northwestern India, between 2600 and 1900 BCE (Figure 9.1). After its discovery in the 1920s, in the course of excavations at the sites of Harappa and Mohenjo-daro (now in Pakistan), the Indus civilization was widely thought to have been one of the most highly organized urban societies in the third millennium BCE. This perception was based in part on general impressions about the layout of city streets, and the similarities of brick and weight sizes throughout the greater Indus valley. The north-south and east-west layout of the architecture and city streets, along with the relatively uniform proportions of baked bricks,

was thought to reflect concepts of order, cosmology and standardization imposed by the rulers of the Indus cities. The most widely cited evidence for rigid standardization was the use of cubical stone weights whose "constant accuracy" was thought to reflect "civic discipline" (Wheeler 1968:83). These weights represented a "well defined system unlike any other in the ancient world" (ibid.). The pervasive nature of Indus ideology, order and standardization was further reinforced by the discovery of additional Harappan sites in the highlands of northern Afghanistan, in Kutch and Gujarat, and scattered along the now dry bed of the Saraswati-Ghaggar-Hakra River, which flowed to the east of the Indus.

Although some earlier excavators assumed that the emergence of the Indus cities was the result of migration or indirect influence from Mesopotamia through the western highlands of Baluchistan, it soon became evident that the Indus civilization was the result of indigenous processes. Their distinctive urban society was thought to have emerged suddenly, within a span of 100 to 200 years, beginning around 2600–2500 BCE,

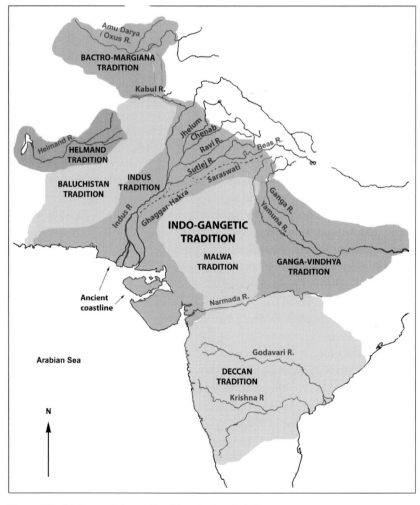

Figure 9.1. Major traditions of prehistoric South Asia.

and then disappeared rapidly around 1900 BCE (Jansen 1993; Possehl 2002). The distinctive features that are thought to have emerged rapidly are new styles of pottery and metal vessels, baked brick architecture and town planning, brick-lined wells, terracotta carts and triangular terracotta cakes, the distinctive stamp seals, standardized weights, and writing (Possehl 2002:51). Although it is not explicitly stated, this rapid development assumes that measurement systems were also rapidly standardized and adopted throughout the greater Indus valley region, an area of almost 680,000–800,000 km², comprising more than 1,500 settlements.

A different view, which will be explored in more detail in this chapter, argues that many diagnostic features of Indus urbanism had been developing for hundreds, if not thousands, of years prior to the construction of the first fired brick building or the manufacture of standardized cubical chert weights. After a brief introduction to the chronology and terminology, I will present an overview of the types of artefacts that inform us about ancient Harappan measurement systems, and how these artefacts changed or remained the same over time. The main focus will be on recent discoveries at the site of Harappa, Pakistan, where detailed measurements have been made of a wide range of artefacts in an attempt to understand better the standardization and regional variation of Indus measurement systems. In the absence of a script that can be read, these data provide an important perspective from which to investigate ancient Indus concepts of order and cosmology.

Chronology and general overview

Although the terms *Indus civilization* and *Harappan culture* are widely used in the literature, a more comprehensive term, the *Indus Tradition* (or *Indus Valley Tradition* (Shaffer 1992)), includes the wide range of human adaptations in the greater Indus region over a long span of history, approximately 10,000 to 1000 BCE (Kenoyer 2006a). This tradition did not evolve in isolation, and three other major cultural traditions relating to the initial emergence of Indus urbanism can be identified for the northwestern subcontinent: the Baluchistan, Helmand and the Bactro-Margiana Traditions (Figure 9.1). The Indus Tradition can be subdivided into eras and phases that are roughly correlated with major adaptive strategies and regional material cultural styles (Table 9.1).

The Neolithic or Early Food Producing Era (circa 7000–5500 BCE) has been documented primarily at the site of Mehrgarh, Pakistan (Jarrige and Meadow 1980; Jarrige et al. 1995) (Figure 9.2). The transition from hunting-foraging to settled agropastoralism is well documented at Mehrgarh during the course of the Early Food Producing and Regionalization Era. Wheat and barley agriculture and the herding of domestic cattle, along with sheep and goats, became the primary subsistence base at Mehrgarh. These same plants and animals provided the foundation for the development of larger towns and eventually cities in the Indus region.

Beginning from the earliest occupation layers, Mehrgarh has evidence for the use of hand-formed mud bricks and well-laid-out compartment buildings. During the Neolithic Period, the mud bricks of Mehrgarh varied in size (28 to 42 cm in length) and proportion (the average is 1:.6:5.2). Although there is no rigid uniformity in the orientation of buildings, they tend to fall along the cardinal directions (Jarrige et al. 1995). In addition to a well-developed architectural tradition, a wide range of crafts, such as bead making, stone working and shell working, were being developed (Jarrige 1991). These crafts continued in later periods at Mehrgarh and are found at other early sites. After 5500 BCE, pottery making and metallurgy became widespread throughout the Indus region, and distinctive regional artefact styles can be defined on the basis of surface treatment and shape as well as manufacturing technique (Mughal 1990; Shaffer 1992).

During the Regionalization Era (5500–2600 BCE), small villages became established in agriculturally rich

Table 9.1. *Indus tradition chronology: Harappa and early Mehrgarh*

Localization Era	
Late Harappan Phase	ca. 1900 to 1300 BCE
Harappa: Periods 4 and 5	*1900–1700 BCE*
Integration Era	
Harappan Phase	2600 to 1900 BCE
Harappa: Period 3C, Final	*2200–1900 BCE*
Harappa: Period 3B, Middle	*2450–2200 BCE*
Harappa: Period 3A, Initial	*2600–2450 BCE*
Regionalization Era	
Early Harappan (several phases)	ca. 5500 to 2600 BCE
Harappa: Period 2, Kot Diji Phase	*2800–2600 BCE*
Harappa: Period 1, A &B, Ravi/ Hakra Phase	*>3500–2800 BCE*
Mehrgarh, Period III	*4800–3500 BCE*
Mehrgarh, Period II	*5500–4800 BCE*
Early Food Producing Era	
Neolithic – Mehrgarh Phase	ca. 7000 to 5500 BCE
Mehrgarh, Period 1, Nonceramic	*7000–5500 BCE*

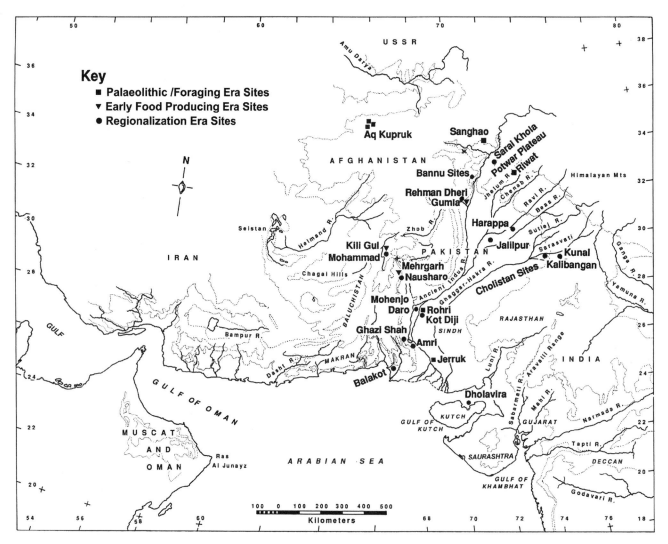

Figure 9.2. Early Food Producing and Regionalization Era sites.

areas and larger villages grew up along the major trade routes linking each geographical region and resource area. The term *Early Harappan* is used to refer to the earlier phase of cultural development that preceded the rise of cities such as Mohenjo-daro and Harappa (Mughal 1970). Mughal's reanalysis of artefacts from stratigraphic layers at the site of Kot Diji clearly demonstrated that many of the so-called diagnostic artefacts of the later Indus cities were already present between 3300 BCE and 2800 BCE, such as distinctive painted pottery, terracotta carts, triangular terracotta cakes, and well-laid-out mud-brick architecture oriented in the cardinal directions. More recently, excavations of the Early Harappan (Kot Diji Phase, 2800–2600 BCE) layers at the site of Harappa have revealed other examples of diagnostic artefacts including stamp seals, clay sealings, a form of Early Indus script, writing on pottery, and even a cubical limestone weight conforming to the later weight system (Meadow and Kenoyer 1997; 2001; 2005; Kenoyer and Meadow 2000; Kenoyer 2005; 2006b).

Sites, such as Harappa, grew to more than 25 hectares in area and were often divided into two walled sectors (Flam 1981; Mughal 1990; Kenoyer 1998). The manufacture of mould-made standardized mud bricks (1:2:4 ratio) for building city walls and domestic architecture began during this period. Small bricks were used for domestic structures, while larger bricks were used in platforms and city walls. Streets, city walls and domestic architecture were oriented to the cardinal directions and settlement planning was maintained over hundreds of years. The layout and maintenance of streets at Harappa and numerous other sites throughout the greater Indus region can be closely associated with the increased use of bullock carts for transport of heavy commodities into the settlements during the Kot Diji Phase.

Regional settlement patterns, along with site layout and the elaboration of specialized crafts, can be linked to the emergence of stratified socioeconomic and political organization systems associated with early urbanism

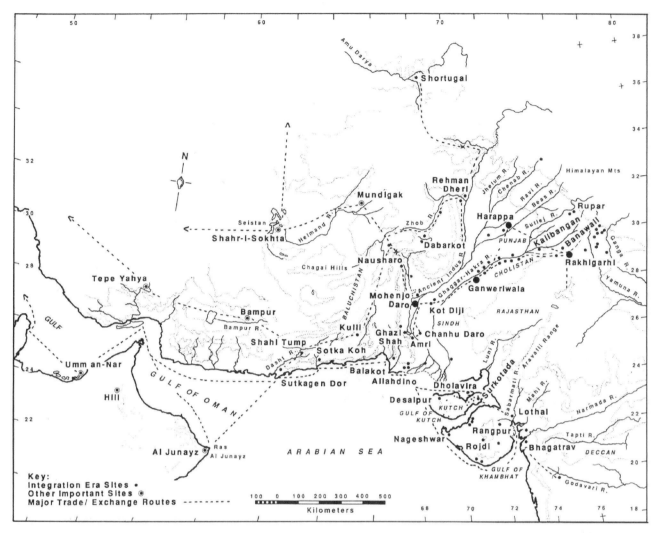

Figure 9.3. Integration Era, Harappa Phase sites.

(Kenoyer 2000, 2006a). These discoveries from Mehrgarh, Kot Diji and Harappa provide conclusive evidence that many of the diagnostic features of the later Indus cities, including systems for control and measurement, were already widespread during the Early Harappan Period, with roots extending back to the Neolithic Period.

The term *Indus civilization* or *Harappa culture* generally refers to the Integration Era, *Harappa Phase*, which dates from around 2600–1900 BCE and represents the major phase of state-level development and urbanism. Cities such as Harappa, Mohenjo-daro, Rakhigarhi, Dholavira and Ganweriwala grew to their largest extent during this 700-year time span. On the basis of radiocarbon dates from Harappa and other sites, the Harappa Phase can now be divided into three subphases as revealed by changes in pottery, use of seals and architecture: Periods 3A (2600–2450 BCE), 3B (2450–2200 BCE) and 3C (2200–1900 BCE). The term 'mature' Harappan Period (or Mature Harappan) is used by some scholars to refer to the entire 700-year time span.

However, many of the diagnostic artefact types associated with the so-called mature Harappan Period, such as painted pottery, pointed base goblets, stone sculptures and figurines, narrative seals, and elaborate jewelry, actually only occur during the last half of this period.

It is during the Harappa Phase that mould-made fired brick become widely used in urban architecture, and standardized cubical chert weights are found throughout the greater Indus region and beyond. Massive mud brick walls surrounded most large settlements and appear to have functioned primarily for control of trade access into the cities. Devices for control of trade, such as seals and weights, are concentrated near gateways and in craft areas located near the gateways or along major streets. While the massive walls could have served as formidable defenses, there is no evidence for major conflict or warfare at any major center.

As will be discussed in more detail later, measurements have been made of all categories of artefacts from all periods of occupation at the site of Harappa. While

there is some degree of standardization in terms of artefact proportions, such as the ratios of brick thickness to
width to length (1:2:4), there is little evidence for rigorous standardization within the site itself. Generally
speaking, when the data from Harappa are compared
to evidence from other Indus sites, it appears that there
is a degree of standardization within some artefact categories, particularly cubical chert weights, and a widespread use of similar proportions for other categories of
artefacts, such as beads, bricks and pottery. However,
on closer examination there appears to be considerable
regional variation in most categories of objects throughout the greater Indus valley.

There is no evidence for hereditary monarchies or the
establishment of centralized territorial states that controlled the entire Indus region, and there is a conspicuous absence of central temples, palaces and elaborate
elite burials that are characteristic of elites in other early
urban societies in Mesopotamia, Egypt and China. The
largest urban centers such as Mohenjo-daro, Harappa
and Dholavira may have directly controlled their surrounding hinterland and were clearly being ruled by
influential elites. The Indus elites would have included
merchants, landowners and religious leaders, who would
have competed for dominance in different areas of the
cities. Smaller towns and villages may have been run by
corporate groups such as town councils or individual
charismatic leaders. Hierarchical social order and stratified society are reflected in architecture and settlement
patterns, as well as artefact styles and the organization of
technological production. In the absence of an organized
military or centralized hereditary elite, internal trade and
exchange and a shared ideology appear to have been the
primary mechanisms for integrating the diverse settlements and communities of the greater Indus valley. The
specifics of the Indus ideology will only be understood
after we have been able to decipher their writing, but
the material representation of this ideology as reflected
in patterning of material culture, and measurement, is
something that we can study.

Early Harappan measurement systems: Ravi and Kot Diji Phase

During the Ravi Phase occupation at Harappa (>3500–
2800 BCE) there is no clear evidence for the use of
standardized measurement systems, such as weights or
linear measures, but the lack of evidence may be due in
part to the relatively small excavation area exposed so
far (Kenoyer and Meadow 2000). There are, however,
several categories of artefacts that demonstrate the

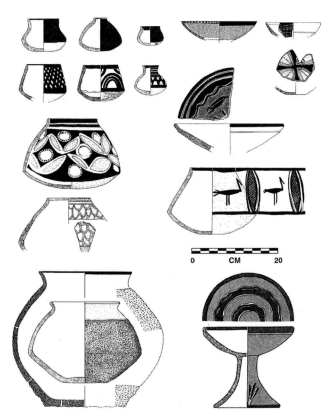

Figure 9.4. Ravi Phase pottery.

beginnings of standardization in terms of pottery making, spinning and presumably weaving, bead making and
brick making. Further excavations are needed to confirm
the patterns seen from the small samples reported later,
but they do provide a point of comparison for what is
seen in later periods at the site.

Pottery vessels with similar shapes were produced
in a range of sizes that were probably developed with
regard to functional features. Cooking pots with low
center of gravity and external projecting rims were probably designed for preparation of liquid foods and cooking over small wood fires. The different sizes of pots
may relate to the types of food being cooked or stored,
the number of people being fed from a single pot or the
optimal size of a vessel for carrying or dispensing liquid.
Although some vessels may have been used as measures
to hold liquid or grain, there is no evidence for precise
standardization during the Ravi phase. Because of the
fragility of terracotta, most measures in later historical
periods were made of wood or metal, so it is not surprising that terracotta measures were not used in the prehistoric period either.

One category of artefact that reveals a degree of standardization, which can also be linked to function, is
spindle whorls. Although the sample size for complete
spindle whorls from the Ravi Phase is not large (n = 6),

there appears to be a range of sizes that suggests two basic weights of thread being spun. The smaller category weighs around 16.6 grams while the larger size is around 28.4 grams (Table 9.2a). Although the sample is small, it appears that similar spindle whorl sizes and weights were used in the subsequent Kot Diji Phase. The larger two categories are roughly the same as those seen during the Ravi Phase, being 23.13 grams and 30.46 grams (Table 9.2b). However, two smaller categories of spindle whorls appear during the Kot Diji Period, and they could indicate the production of finer threads for higher-quality fabrics. Impressions of plain weave textiles with relatively fine threads have been found on terracotta beads. The thread impression is approximately 0.2 mm wide, and the fabric was loosely woven with an open weave of approximately 11 threads per centimeter. A variety of polished bone tools (pickers and separators) that may have been used in weaving have been found in

association with the spindle whorls. Although we do not know the type of looms being used, they were probably simple backstrap looms similar to those used in many traditional communities in South Asia even today. Such looms result in specific lengths and widths of textiles that are often used as a standard form of exchange.

Although there are terracotta beads/whorls within these same weight ranges during the later Harappa Phase, they do not fall into clear categories, and on the basis of the analysis of surface wear and cord marks, most of the terracotta beads/whorls found in the Harappa Phase at Harappa appear to have been used as net weights or loom weights and not as drop spindles. Harappan Phase spinning is thought to have been done with a spinning wheel rather than with drop spindles (Kenoyer 2004). The use of spinning wheels also results in finer and more uniform threads, which were being woven into plain textiles.

Figure 9.5. Ravi and Kot Diji Phase spindle whorls.

Table 9.2. *Early Harappan spindle whorls*

a. Ravi Phase spindle whorls

Size category	Average length	Average diameter	Average weight (gram)	Average ratio	Sample size
Small					
Medium	22.85	30.68	16.60	1.38	4
Large	26.67	39.15	28.40	1.47	2

b. Kot Diji Phase spindle whorls

Size category	Average length	Average diameter	Average weight (gram)	Average ratio	Sample size
Smallest	12.79	24.00	5.90	1.88	1
Small	22.66	30.23	13.90	1.41	3
Medium	32.26	42.96	23.13	1.78	4
Large	30.34	35.96	30.46	1.19	3

Terracotta and stone beads

During the Ravi and later Kot Diji Phases, a wide range of terracotta and stone beads were produced for local use and possibly for regional trade. While terracotta is locally available, other types of raw materials, such as steatite, carnelian, chert, jasper, lapis lazuli and amazonite, were being taken to the site from great distances. The early traders and craftsmen must have developed a mechanism for establishing value and trades of these raw materials as well as the finished beads. In this early period, small lumps of lapis lazuli or agate nodules may have been traded through barter or based on relative size. Strands of finished beads, or even individual beads, also may have been used as a form of standardized exchange, but preliminary analysis of the measurements and weights of Ravi and Kot Diji Phase beads do not demonstrate clear patterns of standardized bead sizes. The bead types include short or long cylindrical, bicone or barrel shapes with similar proportions of length to diameter, but the absolute range of sizes is quite continuous. This is not surprising, as the conservation of valuable raw materials would result in the manufacture of beads from any size of stone fragment.

Nevertheless, the technology involved in bead making would have required the use of precise measurements by craftsmen in order to prepare tools, such as saws and drills, as well as the finished beads themselves. For example, soft steatite taken to the site from various possible sources in the

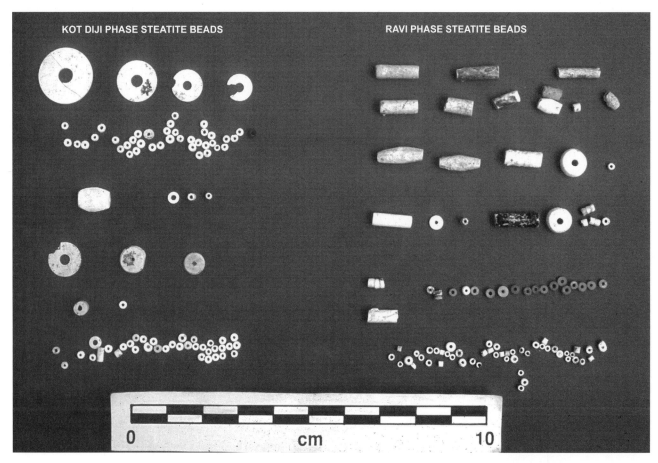

Figure 9.6. Ravi and Kot Diji Phase steatite beads.

northern Indus Valley or Baluchistan (Law 2002, 2005) was used to make a wide range of bead types. The soft stone was sawn into uniformly thin sheets (circa 1 to 2 mm thick) with an equally thin (0.75 to 1.1 mm), finely serrated copper blade. These thin sheets were snapped into tiny rectangular chips and then drilled with a copper drill that ranged from 0.75 to 1.1 mm in diameter. The beads were strung on fine cotton or woolen thread and ground to various diameters to create necklaces composed of beads either with uniform diameters or sometimes in graduated sizes. After final shaping the beads were fired at high temperatures (900° to 1000° Celsius) and glazed to make them white or blue-green colour.

During the Ravi Phase, extremely small steatite microbeads were produced, with measurements as small as 0.75 mm in length and 1.1 mm in diameter, and a minimal weight of 0.003 g. Over 6,100 microbeads would have been required to create a strand long enough to drape around the neck (61 cm or 24 inches). Experimental replication of such beads has been undertaken, but the total time needed to produce such a strand of beads is difficult to estimate because of breakage of beads in the course of manufacture. The firing of the beads to harden them would have taken a full day, and then it may have taken considerable time to restring and polish the beads.

Needless to say, a string of steatite microbeads clearly represents a considerable amount of time and effort, and it is not unlikely that standard lengths of strung microbeads may have been used in trade and exchange.

Although it is not possible to determine how the prehistoric craftsmen measured thin slices of steatite or determined how thin to grind the beads once they were strung on a thread, it is evident that they were able to deal with extremely small units of value. This issue will be addressed later in the discussion of the Indus weight system, which may have evolved alongside or in conjunction with crafts such as stone bead making.

The tradition of microbead production reached its height during the Harappa Phase with the manufacture of beads that were about the same lengths as the early Ravi beads (0.75 to 1.13 mm) but were reduced in diameter to 0.75 to 0.85 mm. These Harappan microbeads weigh around 0.0004 to 0.0006 g and may have been threaded on fine wool or possibly silk thread, which can be spun much thinner and is stronger than cotton thread. What appears to be silk thread preserved inside copper wire beads has been found at Harappa dating to around 2450 BCE. This silk probably derives from the wild silk moth (*Antheraea* sp.) that is found in the Indus valley and other regions of South Asia (Kenoyer 2004).

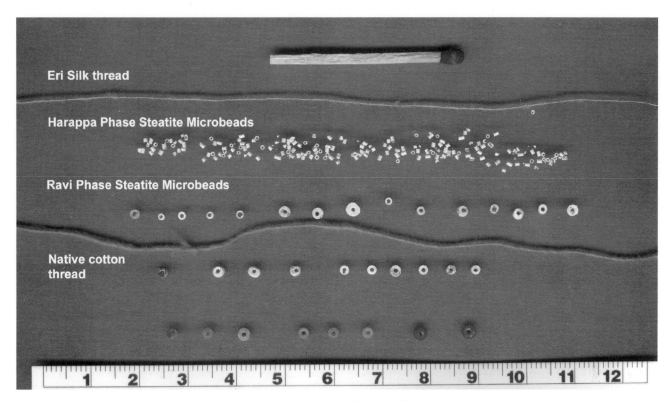

Figure 9.7. Steatite microbeads: Ravi and Harappan Phase.

Figure 9.8. Ravi Phase mud bricks.

Architecture and bricks

The use of mud bricks was already well established in the Indus valley region as early as 7000 BCE, but so far only a few scattered mud bricks have been found from the earliest Ravi levels (Period 1A) and a fragmentary north-south oriented wall from the later Ravi levels (Period 1B). The small dump of burned and partly vitrified mud bricks from Period 1A suggests that they were being made at the site for use in kilns or hearths and possibly also for the construction of houses. These earliest mud bricks were hand formed and therefore do not have uniform shapes. Only two relatively complete examples and about two dozen fragments were recovered. The complete mud bricks were slightly wedge shaped, measuring 4.5 cm thick and 17.5

cm long. The wide end is 9 cm and the narrow end is 5.5 cm. The ratio for the brick, using the wide end, is 1:2:4, which is the basic proportion that becomes standard during the subsequent periods at Harappa and throughout the Indus valley in general. In excavations conducted in 1996, a fragmentary wall dating to the final Ravi Phase (Period 1B) was made of large mud bricks, 11 x 23 x 40 cm. This wall was oriented north-south and confirms the pattern indicated by the posthole structures of 1A.

The sizes of Kot Diji Phase mud bricks at Harappa are very similar to those made during the Ravi Phase, but they were much more uniform because they were mould made. Mud brick was used to build domestic structures as well as to construct platforms and city walls. Large mud bricks, measuring 10 x 20 x 40 cm, were used in the construction of the Early Harappan city walls around Mound AB and Mound E. On the basis of the different colours and compositions of the clay used in the city walls, it appears that the mud bricks were being made locally as well as in the surrounding hinterland. Each mound had its own distinct wall, and each wall had different colours of clay bricks, but the size of bricks is highly regular (Kenoyer 1991). This indicates that a standardized concept of measurement was being used by the people making bricks locally as well as in the surrounding villages.

The large-size mud bricks, 10 x 20 x 40 cm, were occasionally used for house foundations or platforms, and though there is some variation in the absolute brick measurements (e.g., 10 x 20 x 30 or 10 x 18 x 36 cm) and proportions, most have the ratio of 1:2:4. Divider walls and some of the upper structures were made of a smaller-size mud brick measuring approximately 7 x 12 x 24 cm to 7 x 14 x 28 cm (also 1:2:4 ratio).

Because of the limited exposure of Kot Diji Phase occupations at Harappa, it is not possible to get a full layout of houses, but they were generally oriented with the cardinal directions and situated along wide unpaved streets. On Mound AB, the north-south street measures approximately 5 meters wide. The house walls range in width from 7 cm, which is the width of one mud brick, to more than 1 meter wide for foundation or platform walls.

The long continuity in building orientation and brick sizes, from the Ravi through the Kot Diji Phase occupations, cannot be coincidental and must be linked to deeply held socioreligious beliefs associated with settlement organization. The orientation of houses according to the cardinal directions can be done using the morning and afternoon shadows cast by a stick placed in the center of a circle. More complex methods involve sighting on the stars or constellations that rise in the east or set in the west. The 'north star' at around 2300 BCE was a very dim star called Draconis, and it is unlikely that it was used for sighting during the pre-historic period (Parpola 1994). Astronomers calculate that the Pleiades would have arisen in approximately this same spot during each vernal equinox from 2720 to 1760 BCE, and this may have been the constellation used for orientating Early Harappan as well as Harappan buildings (ibid.).

Geometric button seals

While it is possible to speculate about the cosmological significance of building orientation and street layout, the discovery of geometric designs carved on bone or steatite button seals provides a more direct indication of specific ideologies related to space and organization. The earliest carved bone seal from the Ravi Phase is fragmentary but appears to represent one arm of the swastika motif that becomes widespread during the later Harappan Period. The swastika diagram can be interpreted as an effort to create order out of chaos. By dividing chaos into four quarters and turning it in the right direction, order, balance and progress are achieved. In later Hindu iconography, the swastika symbol is associated with Lakshmi, the goddess of wealth, and it is used as a good luck symbol to give wealth and success to the user.

Other geometric symbols found in the Kot Diji Phase occupations include circle and dot motifs, stars and stepped cross designs. All of these symbols can be associated with cosmic order and attempts by humans to give this order to their daily lives. Similar geometric seals have been found at Kot Diji Phase settlements throughout the greater Indus region, and the same designs also appear on painted pottery. The implication of these repeated patterns is the emergence of a repertoire of graphic symbols that appear to reflect a shared set of beliefs. Similar widespread use of images of

Figure 9.9. Cubical stone weight and seal impression: Kot Diji Period.

horned anthropomorphic deities and terracotta animal and human figurines also indicates shared ideology during the Early Harappan Period.

Cubical stone weights

Although the use of standardized brick sizes is a clear indication of a well-defined measurement system, the most important indicator of standardization is seen in the system of weights that first appears at Harappa

Figure 9.10. Cubical stone weights: Harappan Period.

during the Kot Diji Phase around 2800–2600 BCE. Two cubical stone weights have been found at Harappa, one from Mound AB (Trench 39 N) and the other from Mound E (NW corner, Trench 52). The stone weight from Mound AB was found stratigraphically associated with well-dated hearths (2800 to 2600 BCE) (Meadow and Kenoyer 2005) and with indicators of administrative control, such as geometric button seals, a clay sealing and a broken seal featuring an elephant. The weight was made from yellow limestone, measures 9.7 x 9.5 x 7.1 mm and weighs 1.7 grams. This weight belongs to the 'B' category or 2nd ratio of Indus weights as defined by Hemmy (Marshall 1931: 591, Table III) (see Table 9.3).

The second cubical stone object has slightly rounded edges and one polished face and appears to have been a weight that was subsequently used as a hammerstone or pestle. This artefact was made of white quartzite and weighs 102.95 grams, which corresponds to the J category of Hemmy and the 160th ratio (see Table 9.3). The fact that one weight was found within the walled areas of Mound AB, and the other within the walled area of Mound E, suggests that both of the Early Harappan settlement sectors at Harappa were using the same basic weight standard. This pattern continues in the later Harappan Period, when weights of the same standard are found in all of the walled sectors of the site and at other Indus sites throughout the region.

Table 9.3. *Indus cubical weights from Harappa and Mohenjo-daro*

(New) Designation	Ratio	HARP Average weight	Vats Average weight	Mackay Mohenjo-daro	HARP No. of specimens	Vats No. of specimens	Mackay Mohenjo-daro
(AAA)	1/3	0.30			2		
(AA)	2/3	0.60			1		
A	1	0.86	0.95	0.87	7	1	5
(A′)	1 1/3	1.25			8		
B	2	1.78	1.66	1.77	13	12	13
Q	1/3 x 7	2.10			4		
C	1/3 x 8		2.66	2.28		4	2
D	4	3.52	3.50	3.43	12	20	31
E	8	6.61	6.83	6.83	8	27	45
F	16	13.86	13.67	13.73	10	28	91
(F′)	18	15.50			1		
G	32	26.70	27.06	27.41	7	59	94
H	64	51.97	54.73	54.36	3	18	23
J	160	120.81	130.38	136.02	4	18	11
K	200			174.50			1
L	320	225.50		271.33	1	1	4
M	640			546.70			1
N	1,600			1,417.50			3

Many scholars have speculated on the origin of the Harappan weight system, and it is thought to have been derived from grains (Marshall 1931), such as wheat (0.048 grams) or barley (0.064 grams), or edible seeds, such as mustard or mung bean (*masha*). One poisonous seed that is widely referred to in ancient Indian texts on weights is the black and red seed (*gunja*) of the wild licorice plant (*Abrus precatorius*) (Marshall 1931; Mainkar 1984). This seed weighs between 0.109 and 0.113 grams and approximately 8 seeds would correspond to the 1st Indus weight ratio or 0.871 gram, as defined by Hemmy (Marshall 1931). Since the actual weight of these grains varies depending on where they are grown or the amount of water they receive, it is difficult to determine which of them was used to define the original Indus weight system. Regardless of what the base weight was, the system developed by the Early Harappans became widely adopted during the Harappan Period.

Harappa Phase measurement

Although the basic systems of measurement needed for the functioning of large towns had already been established in the Early Harappan Period, the pervasive use of these systems throughout the greater Indus region is only seen during the Harappan Period, from around 2600 to 1900 BCE. Contrary to views taken by many scholars, I do not feel that this adoption was rapid or explosive, but that it happened gradually, over the course of 200 or 250 years, between 2600 and 2450 BCE.

Harappan stone weights

The basic weight system that evolved during the Early Harappan Period became more refined and varied during the Harappan Phase. Extensive studies of weights at Mohenjo-daro, Harappa and Chanhu-daro have been summarized in the early excavation reports (Marshall 1931; Mackay 1938, 1943), but the excavations at Harappa have revealed the presence of several additional weight categories that were not reported previously (Table 9.3). Weights were used with matched scale pans, which were made of copper/bronze and occasionally of terracotta. Two sets of scale pans, along with a bronze cross-beam, a broken arrow-shaped pointer and a hook and chain, were discovered in 1996 in the course of conservation work on Mound F at Harappa (Nasir 2001). The scale pans were made in two sizes; one set is around 6 cm in diameter with three holes for hanging the plate evenly, and the larger set is around 63 cm in diameter. These sizes would be appropriate for the small and medium sizes of Indus weights but not the largest ones.

The first seven Indus weights double in size from 1:2:4:8:16:32:64. There are exceptions to this general pattern, with some anomalous categories such as the 8/3 ratio (approximately 2.28 grams). The most common weight is the 16th ratio, which is approximately 13.7 grams. At this point the weight increments change to a decimal system where the next largest weights have a ratio of 160, 200, 320, and 640. The next jump goes to 1,600, 3,200, 6,400, 8,000, and 12,800. The largest weight found at the site of Mohenjo-daro weighs 10,865 grams (approximately 25 pounds), which is almost 100,000 times the weight of the 'gunja' seed.

The new categories of weights found at Harappa have been designated using a modification of Hemmy's system. Categories AAA, AA and A′ and F′ conform to the earlier categories or represent slight variations (Table 9.3). Categories AAA (0.3 gram) and AA (0.6 gram) are quite small and they may have been missed by the earlier excavators because they did not screen all of the excavation areas. Categories A′ and F′ may simply be anomalies. A comparison of weights from different areas of Harappa itself indicates that all of the cubical weights from the entire Harappa Phase conform to one single system.

In addition to cubical weights, a new style of weight was introduced in the latest phase of the Harappan Period, Period 3C. These weights were generally made from agate or chalcedony and were truncated spheres, with two flat opposing surfaces to prevent them from rolling away. The truncated spherical weights generally conform to the same system as the cubical chert weights. Their shape variation may have had some ritual or cultural significance, but they are found in all the major mounds at Harappa, as well as at Mohenjo-daro (Mackay 1938), Chanhu-daro (Mackay 1943), Lothal (Rao 1979) and even the small site of Rojdi (Possehl and Raval 1989).

During the Harappan Phase cubical stone weights were predominantly made from a distinctive variety of banded chert obtained from the Rohri hills in Sindh. While some weights were made from agate, granite or other patterned stones, the chert varieties are the most widely distributed throughout the city and the Indus region in general. Distinctive manufacturing debris for cubical chert weights has been found in the agate bead making areas of the site. In addition, some perfectly spherical agate balls that may be unfinished weights of the second type have also been found in association with bead making areas. This pattern suggests that bead makers were also involved in the preparation of the highly standardized weights.

Most scholars assume that these weights were used for everyday market exchange, with the smaller weights being used for precious stones and metals, perfumes and valuable medicines. The larger weights are thought to have been used for grain or large quantities of goods. The fact that there are relatively few weights given the size of the cities and market areas suggests that this explanation is probably not valid. It is much more probable that the weights relate to taxation or tithing. The recent excavations at Harappa reveal that the highest concentration of weights is located in association with gateway areas or in craft production areas, where goods entering the city may have been weighed and taxed. Furthermore, many of the smaller sites such as Allahdino have only a single set of weights in the middle range of values, while only the largest sites such as Mohenjo-daro and Harappa have one or two extremely large weights.

Some scholars have proposed a different grouping of the weights by combining all the weights from Mohenjo-daro, Harappa, Chanhu-daro and Lothal and recalculating the averages (Mainkar 1984). This approach assumes that the entire system was centrally standardized and obscures the presence of regional variation. Ongoing studies suggest that each major city had its own internal system of weights that was highly standardized, with general comparability to weights used in other cities, but that there was a certain degree of regional variation. More precise measurements and the examination of weights to determine their condition (chipped or worn) need to be undertaken to investigate this theory fully.

Even if the weights are not absolutely standardized throughout the Indus region, there is a general standard that was followed by all the Indus settlements. One of the key questions that remain to be answered is who was responsible for maintaining the general standardization of the Indus weights over such a large area and for over 700 years. This standardization could not have been simply the result of a shared belief, but must have been rigorously maintained by people who were most concerned with the profits or benefits of using the weights. Rather than political or ideological elites, merchant communities and traders may have been the primary agents in maintaining weight standardization. This interpretation is supported by the fact that the use of cubical stone weights disappeared at the end of the Harappan Period, but the actual system of weights continued to be used during the Early Historical Period and is still used today throughout South Asia (Marshall 1931; Mainkar 1984). Other artefacts associated with Indus political authority as well as trade and ideologies are inscribed seals, many of which included animal symbols such as the 'unicorn' or other totemic animals. At the end of the Indus cities,

Figure 9.11. Harappan bricks.

the Indus script and the use of seals with the unicorn motif do disappear and never emerge again in the Early Historic Period.

Harappan linear measurements and brick sizes

On the basis of two rare discoveries of what have been referred to as scales, combined with careful analysis of architectural features, the earlier excavators calculated that there were two systems of linear measurement at use in the Indus cities, the foot (13.2 inches or 33.35 cm) and the cubit (20.8 inches or 52.83 cm) (Marshall 1931; Mackay 1938; Vats 1940). A fragmentary bonze rod (1.5 inches long) with incised lines found at Harappa is thought to have been a measuring tool, with four divisions that average 0.37 inch or 0.93 cm (Vats 1940: 365–366). An incised shell plaque from Mohenjo-daro had five divisions of 1.32 inches or 3.35 cm (Mackay 1938: 404–405). These measuring devices made of bronze and shell may have been prepared for some special occasion or elite consumer, but the average person living in these cities probably used other means of measurement.

One of the most common measurements in traditional South Asian culture is the width of the hand (four finger widths or *angula* – approximately 7 to 9 cm). Other measurements include various types of hand spans, the distance from the elbow to the tip of the finger (cubit), the foot, two feet, a pace, the distance between the tips of the fingers of both outstretched arms and the vertical distance from the feet to the tip of the hands stretched above the head. The hand measurement is perhaps the most relevant for understanding Harappan architecture, because it is basically the same as the thickness of a wet mud brick.

Experiments with mud brick manufacture show that the wet clay shrinks around 0.5 cm in thickness and width and up to 2 cm in overall length. If a mud brick is made with the width of the hand for thickness, and double that for width, and double that for length, one ends up with a brick that measures 8 x 16 x 32 cm. After drying, the brick will measure 7.5 x 15.5 x 30 cm, and when a brick is fired there is even more shrinkage. This system of measurement is the most likely explanation for the standardized brick shapes, and the proportions are evidence of a specific cultural choice that also has an optimal benefit for architectural constructions.

In the past, the uniformity of brick ratios was thought to represent the presence of a strong centralized government that enforced strict building codes, but this interpretation is no longer supported, though it still appears in much of the secondary literature. The brick ratios clearly reflect a style of technology (Lechtman 1977) that has its roots in the Early Harappan Period and was spread throughout the Indus region. Concepts of measurement and proportion were probably linked to rituals or ideology and passed down from one generation of builders to the next. Given the fact that the bricks are based on specific proportions it is not surprising that similar proportions are reflected in the rooms of houses, in the overall plan of houses and in the construction of large public buildings (Jansen 1991).

The continuities of mud brick from the Early Harappan to the Harappan Period are evidence of cultural continuity in terms of measurement systems, as well as cultural choice regarding overall brick proportions that are optimal for the construction of specific types of buildings.

Fired bricks

The most significant change between the Early Harappan and the Harappan Phase is the introduction of fired bricks. Although some excavators report the use of fired brick during the Early Harappan Period, for example, the construction of fired brick drains at Kalibangan (Lal 1979), most Early Harappan sites did not use this type of building material. Even at Harappa, fired bricks did not appear suddenly at 2600 BCE, but were introduced gradually for construction of drains and eventually buildings, after the beginning of Period 3A. The size of fired bricks corresponds to the smaller size of unfired mud bricks used for domestic architecture. The earliest fired bricks produced at Harappa measure around 7 x 14 x 28 cm (1:2:4 ratio). Unlike mud bricks, which tend to crumble if they are reused for later constructions, fired bricks and brick rubble can be reused repeatedly for hundreds of years. In fact, many modern houses in Harappa town have been constructed with ancient bricks looted from prehistoric buildings. This reuse of fired bricks has made it difficult to determine whether there were changes in brick size over time.

However, careful documentation of brick walls and rebuilt structures in the gateway area of Mound E and ET indicates that there may in fact be changes in absolute brick size over time. The earliest pristine structures in the gateway area date to around 2450 BCE (Period 3B) and were constructed with finely made bricks, measuring 7 x 14 x 28 cm. By the final phase of construction, circa 2000 to 1900 BCE (Period 3C), the walls were being made with relatively small bricks, measuring

Figure 9.12. Harappan well bricks.

Figure 9.13. Harappa: Reconstruction of city walls and gateway, Mound E and ET. Painting by Chris Sloan.

around 5 x 12 x 24 cm. The overall ratio of the bricks remained the same, but the absolute measurements had changed.

Comparison of the absolute measurements of fired bricks is an ongoing project that requires more rigorous dating of structures and the periodization of the bricks, but preliminary studies indicate that there is variation in the absolute brick sizes between the major sites.

Well bricks

One new type of brick that was not found in the Early Harappan Period at Harappa is the wedge-shaped brick that was used to construct cylindrical wells. Although there are not many wells at the site, examples of wells along with different sizes of well bricks have been found on all of the major mounds. One well on Mound AB measured 1.2 meters internal diameter. The bricks were 26 cm long and 36 bricks were used to construct each course (Dales and Kenoyer 1989). One interesting feature of these bricks is the presence of two vertical lines on the outside edge of each brick. This suggests that all the bricks for this well were prepared on commission in order to fit together precisely. Other wells at Harappa range in diameter from 1 meter to as much as 2 meters, and the wedge-shaped bricks for each size of well have been prepared precisely to ensure a tight fit.

City walls and streets

During the Harappa Period, the massive city walls were made of large mud bricks (10 x 20 x 40 cm) faced with small fired bricks (7 x 14 x 28 cm). Although there is evidence of general city planning, the city walls were not standardized in terms of their orientation or size. The original layout of the city walls around each mound is impossible to determine because of the fact that they were rebuilt and repaired numerous times. However, in a few excavation areas, it was possible to cut through the wall and define what a portion of it looked like. On Mound E, the original Early Harappan city wall measures 2 meters wide and has been traced for over 15 meters. The subsequent rebuilding directly on top of the earlier wall was 2.5 meters wide, but the height of this wall is not known. The later Harappan city wall was offset to the east but was oriented along the same alignment, 10° west of true north. The earliest Harappan city wall was 2.5 meters wide and appears to have been built up against the Early Harappan mound as a revetment wall. The exterior of the wall is battered at a very small angle of 5°. Along the south side of Mound E, the city wall is freestanding and is 5.4 to 6.5 meters wide on either side of the southern gateway, but at the gateway the width increases to 8.0 to 8.4 meters. The gateway itself is relatively narrow, 2.8 meters wide, just enough for one ox cart to pass through, but the main street leading north into the center of the city is 5 meters wide, allowing for two-way cart traffic. This pattern of a narrow gateway and wider internal streets is also seen to the east, where a major gateway with an entrance of 2.6 meters was constructed at the edge of Mound E and ET (Figure 9.13).

Major streets transect the city from east to west and north to south as well as along the interior and exterior of the city walls. Most of these streets are 4 to 5 meters wide, though some are even wider. On the basis of these few examples it is evident that the layout of streets, gateways and walls of Harappa, and Indus cities in general, was based more on functional aspects of access and movement. Gateways were narrow to control access, while interior streets were wider to allow free flow of traffic and quick access to all major neighborhoods.

Conclusion

The preceding discussion has attempted to provide new data and interpretations on the nature of measurement in the Indus civilization, with specific reference to the site of Harappa. In contrast to many earlier generalizations about the rigorous standardization and state control, much of the standardization seen in various crafts and measurement systems is related to proportions rather than absolute measurements. Where there is a degree of standardization, as in the case of bricks or even of stone weights, it is possible that the basic measurements themselves are at the root of the standardization and not some type of overarching authoritarian political or economic force. The width of hands or the weight of specific types of grains would have been generally uniform throughout the greater Indus valley, and consequently the measures derived from them would have been relatively uniform. This explanation does not however negate the importance of a shared system of measurement between the major cities and the smaller rural sites. There clearly was some form of unifying ideology that ensured the continued use of a shared system of measurement and weights for over 700 years during the Harappan Period.

Future directions for research on Indus weights and measures need to focus on refining the chronology of the use of specific measures both within each site and at a regional level. A higher degree of precision may allow more concrete interpretations that could be linked to socioeconomic and political control by elites. What is even more important to note is that after around 1900 BCE, the use of cubical stone weights disappeared from the Late Harappan settlements, but the basic weight system used by the Indus cities reemerged during the Early Historic Period in the northern subcontinent during the second phase of urbanism, beginning around 600 BCE (Kenoyer 1997). Finally, in later historical periods in South Asia, there is evidence for minor changes in weight ratios and brick proportions that were established and maintained by the ruling elites as a means to control and benefit from regional exchange. The precise nature of this continuity between the Indus and Early Historic Period remains to be fully investigated using more precise studies of Early Historic and Historical Period weights recovered from archaeological excavations.

ACKNOWLEDGEMENTS

First, I would like to extend my thanks to the organizers of the Mesuring the World and Beyond conference for inviting me to participate in this important dialogue on ancient measurement systems. My work on the weights of Harappa results from my long research at the site as part of the Harappa Archaeological Research Project in collaboration with the Government of Pakistan, Department of Archaeology and Museums. Support for this research has come from a number of different U.S. institutions, including the National Science Foundation, National Endowment for the Humanities, Smithsonian Institution, Peabody Museum of Archaeology and Ethnology of Harvard University, the American School of Prehistoric Research, the University of Wisconsin, and the Kress Foundation. Donations from private individuals have also been extremely helpful. I would like to thank my codirector, Richard Meadow, and all of the HARP team members for their efforts in excavation and artefact documentation that make this research possible.

REFERENCES

Dales, G. F. & J. M. Kenoyer, 1989. Excavation at Harappa – 1989. *Pakistan Archaeology* **25**: 241–280.

Flam, L., 1981. *The Paleography and Prehistoric Settlement Patterns in Sind, Pakistan (ca. 4000–2000 B.C.).* PhD. Philadelphia: University of Pennsylvania.

Jansen, M., 1991. The Concept of Space in Harappan City Planning – Mohenjo-Daro, in *Concepts of Space: Ancient and Modern*, ed. K. Vatsyayan. New Delhi: Abhinav, 75–81.

Jansen, M., 1993. *City of Wells and Drains, Mohenjo-Daro: Water Splendor 4500 Years Ago.* Bonn: Verlag und Vertieb.

Jarrige, J.-F., 1991. Mehrgarh: Its Place in the Development of Ancient Cultures in Pakistan, in *Forgotten Cities on the Indus*, eds. M. Jansen, M. Mulloy & G. Urban. Mainz am Rhein: Phillip von Zabern, 34–49.

Jarrige, C., J.-F. Jarrige, R. H. Meadow & G. Quivron (eds.), 1995. *Mehrgarh Field Reports 1975 to 1985 – From the Neolithic to the Indus Civilization.* Karachi: Dept. of Culture and Tourism, Govt. of Sindh and the French Foreign Ministry.

Jarrige, J.-F. & R. H. Meadow, 1980. The Antecedents of Civilization in the Indus Valley. *Scientific American* **243**(2): 122–133

Kenoyer, J. M., 1991. Urban Process in the Indus Tradition: A Preliminary Model from Harappa, in *Harappa Excavations 1986–1990*, ed. R. H. Meadow. Madison, WI: Prehistory Press, 29–60.

Kenoyer, J. M., 1997. Early City-States in South Asia: Comparing the Harappan Phase and the Early Historic Period, in *The Archaeology of City-States: Cross Cultural Approaches*, eds. D. L. Nichols & T. H. Charlton. Washington, DC: Smithsonian Institution Press, 51–70.

Kenoyer, J. M., 1998. *Ancient Cities of the Indus Valley Civilization*. Karachi: Oxford University Press.

Kenoyer, J. M., 2000. Wealth and Socio-Economic Hierarchies of the Indus Valley Civilization, in *Order, Legitimacy and Wealth in Early States*, eds. J. Richards & M. Van Buren. Cambridge: Cambridge University Press, 90–112.

Kenoyer, J. M., 2004. Ancient Textiles of the Indus Valley Region, in *Tana Bana: The Woven Soul of Pakistan*, ed. N. Bilgrami. Karachi: Koel, 18–31.

Kenoyer, J. M., 2005. Bead Technologies at Harappa, 3300–1900 BC: A Comparison of Tools, Techniques and Finished Beads from the Ravi to the Late Harappan Period, in *South Asian Archaeology 2001*, eds. C. Jarrige & V. Lefèvre. Paris: Editions Recherche sur les Civilisations, Vol. 1: 157–170.

Kenoyer, J. M., 2006a. The Origin and Character of Indus Urbanism: New Perspectives and Challenges, in *Early Cities: New Perspectives on Pre-Industrial Urbanism*, eds. J. Marcus & J. A. Sabloff. Washington, DC: National Academy of Sciences.

Kenoyer, J. M., 2006b. The Origin, Context and Function of the Indus Script: Recent Insights from Harappa, in *Proceedings of the Pre-symposium and the 7th ESCA Harvard-Kyoto Roundtable*, eds. T. Osada & N. Hase. Kyoto: Research Institute for Humanity and Nature, RIHN, 9–27.

Kenoyer, J. M. & R. H. Meadow, 2000. The Ravi Phase: A New Cultural Manifestation at Harappa, in *South Asian Archaeology 1997*, eds. M. Taddei & G. De Marco. Rome/Naples: Istituto Italiano per l'Africa e l'Oriente/Istituto Universitario Orientale, 55–76.

Lal, B. B., 1979. Kalibangan and the Indus Civilization, in *Essays in Indian Protohistory*, eds. D. P. Agrawal & D. K. Chakrabarti. Delhi: B.R., 65–97.

Law, R. W., 2002. Potential Steatite Source Areas of the Indus Valley Civilization, in *Proceedings of the International Colloquium on Indus Civilization, April 6th–8th, 2001*, ed. M. A. Halim. Islamabad: UNESCO, 158–169.

Law, R. W., 2005. Regional Interaction in the Prehistoric Indus Valley: Initial Results of Rock and Mineral Sourcing Studies at Harappa, in *South Asian Archaeology 2001*, eds. C. Jarrige & V. Lefèvre. Paris: Editions Recherche sur les Civilisations, Vol. 1: 179–190.

Lechtman, H., 1977. Style in Technology – Some Early Thoughts, in *Material Culture: Styles, Organization and Dynamics of Technology*, eds. H. Lechtman & R. S. Merrill. St. Paul, MN: West, 3–20.

Mackay, E. J. H., 1938. *Further Excavations at Mohenjo-daro: Being an Official Account of Archaeological Excavations at Mohenjo-daro Carried Out by the Government of India between the Years 1927 and 1931*. New Delhi: Government of India.

Mackay, E. J. H., 1943. *Chanhu-Daro Excavations 1935–36*. New Haven, CT: American Oriental Society.

Mainkar, V. B., 1984. Metrology in the Indus Civilization, in *Frontiers of the Indus Civilization*, eds. B. B. Lal & S. P. Gupta. New Delhi: Books and Books, 141–151.

Marshall, J. H., 1931. *Mohenjo-daro and the Indus Civilization: Being an Official Account of Archaeological Excavations at Mohenjo-daro Carried Out by the Government of India between the Years 1922 and 1927*. London: A. Probsthain.

Meadow, R. H. & J. M. Kenoyer, 1997. Excavations at Harappa 1994–1995: New perspectives on the Indus script, craft activities and city organization, in *South Asian Archaeology 1995*, eds. B. Allchin and R. Allchin. New Delhi: Oxford & IBH, 139–172.

Meadow, R. H. & J. M. Kenoyer, 2001. Recent Discoveries and Highlights from Excavations at Harappa: 1998–2000. *INDO-KOKO-KENKYU Indian Archaeological Studies* **22**: 19–36.

Meadow, R. H. & J. M. Kenoyer, 2005. Excavations at Harappa 2000–2001: New insights on Chronology and City Organization, in *South Asian Archaeology 2001*, eds. C. Jarrige & V. Lefèvre. Paris: Editions Recherche sur les Civilisations, 207–225.

Mughal, M. R., 1970. *The Early Harappan Period in the Greater Indus Valley and Northern Baluchistan*. Philadelphia: University of Pennsylvania, Dept. of Anthropology.

Mughal, M. R., 1990. Further Evidence of the Early Harappan Culture in the Greater Indus Valley: 1971–90. *South Asian Studies* **6**: 175–200.

Nasir, H., 2001. Rare Discovery of Copper/Bronze Objects from Harappa. *Archaeological Review* **8**(10): 119–131.

Parpola, A., 1994. *Deciphering the Indus Script*. Cambridge: Cambridge University Press.

Possehl, G. L., 2002. *The Indus Civilization: A Contemporary Perspective*. Walnut Creek, CA: AltaMira Press.

Possehl, G. L. & M. H. Raval (eds.), 1989. *Harappan Civilization and Rojdi*. New Delhi: Oxford & IBH and AIIS.

Rao, S. R., 1979. *Lothal: A Harappan Port Town (1955–62), Vol. 1*. New Delhi: Archaeological Survey of India.

Shaffer, J. G., 1992. The Indus Valley, Baluchistan and Helmand Traditions: Neolithic through Bronze Age, in *Chronologies in Old World Archaeology*, 3rd ed., ed. R. Ehrich. Chicago: University of Chicago Press, Vol. 1: 441–464.

Vats, M. S., 1940. *Excavations at Harappa: Being an Account of Archaeological Excavations at Harappa Carried Out Between the Years of 1920–21 and 1933–34*. Delhi: Government of India Press.

Wheeler, R. E. M., 1968. *The Indus Civilization*, 3rd ed. Cambridge: Cambridge University Press.

SECTION III

Dimensions and belief

Remaining initially in the Indus Valley, Section III focuses on relationships between measurement, architecture, cosmology and belief systems. Some of the key finds of the earliest excavations at the Indus Valley city of Mohenjo-Daro consisted of weight and linear measurement systems. Drawing upon his own and others' recent work at the site, Michael Jansen outlines the nature of these systems and their relations to architectural structure. These can be considered in terms of their orientation, the dimensions of their constituent rooms, and the dimensions of the bricks from which they were constructed. The bricks maintain a consistent ratio of dimensions and were made in standardised moulds, with the average size being derived from the width of the hand. There appear also to be two different orientation systems, one of which orientates to the cardinal points, although these two systems may actually be related and orientated towards different elements or periods of the same celestial system. Indeed, the 'great ring stones' found at the site have been identified as 'calendar stones', not only part of a calendrical system but also serving the function of astronomical observation instruments associated with the cosmology of the region. Jansen highlights the need for cross-site comparisons within the Indus Valley if we are to understand better the significance of the measurement and orientation systems in use at Mohenjo-Daro.

Half a world away, Saburo Sugiyama elaborates on the use of standardised measure in the creation of the architecture of the Mesoamerican city of Teotihuacan, Mexico. His extensive work at the site has included comprehensive systematic measurement of the architecture and layout of the city, and after discussing the identification and use of the 'Teotihuacan Measurement Unit' (TMU) Sugiyama elaborates the implications of this unit for the relationship between the monumental architecture and calendrical and cosmological numerocities.

This includes an overview of his recent excavations of the Moon Pyramid and its evolving relations with the rest of the complex. A number of calendrical and cosmological sequences are incorporated into the dimensions and orientation of the city, including the positions of the Sun and Pleiades; cycles of Venus, 260 days and 365 days; and the Mayan 'Long Count' calendar. These dimensional and orientational findings are complemented by archaeological material betraying similar concerns. For Sugiyama the Mesoamerican calendrical systems constituted architecturally encoded value systems within which the people lived and interpreted their material world. These could be manifest in the structure of the cities themselves, and it seems that Teotihuacan may represent just such a cosmogram.

Moving to the later, Aztec, period in Mexico John E. Clark examines the architectural features of the ritual precinct of the city of Tenochtitlan and their relations to sacred time. Clark uses established Aztec units of measurement to propose dimensions for structures that are imperfectly preserved and reconstructs the ceremonial precinct of the city. As is the case in many traditional measuring systems, the Aztec system related to human bodily dimensions, with different units used for different purposes. Aztecs could use their measuring systems both to describe objects and to plan them and could transfer measurements between paper plans and the real world. Working backwards (relative to the usual procedure) from known units to building dimensions, Clark asks the important question of whether we would identify these units archaeologically if we did not know them, and what degree of error margin it is reasonable to expect in representations of sacred or significant numbers.

Clark's analysis of the known-unit dimensions of the precinct, from the remaining archaeology and early conquest maps of the site, allows him to conclude that dimensions of celestial and/or ritual time were indeed incorporated into the structures and sacred space. He makes the important point that for each of the obviously significant counts incorporated there are myriad other counts of whose relative significance we have no idea. The meaning and significance – for the experience of different sectors of the population – of these and the counts obviously associated with calendar and time still require investigation.

Kate Spence explores the significance and interpretation of the orientation of Egyptian burial over the course of the predynastic, dynastic and New Kingdom periods, and its relationship with terrestrial and cosmological considerations. Initially the river Nile constituted an important orientating feature for burials, which thus varied from region to region in their orientation relative to cardinal points. Cosmological considerations in such orientation encompassed both the tangible terrestrial world and the intangible realms that were perceived to relate to it. Over time there seems to have been a change in the perception of the grave, from its being considered to lie in the land of the living to instead being located in the land of the dead. With this also occurred a change in the orientation of the body, and an apparent change in the perceived role of the body, as it began to be considered a mediator between the realms of the living and the dead. There was also a shift from the riverine orientation to cardinal orientation during the dynastic period, and this period sees the creation of pyramids orientated extremely precisely to cardinal north. Spence goes on to explore how the precise alignment of the dynastic pyramids was achieved by celestial orientation and measurement techniques, and the nature of their relationship with time and perceptions of the 'eternal' circumpolar stars.

10

Architectural measurements in the Indus cities: The case study of Mohenjo-Daro

Michael Jansen

To date, the major corpus of published information on Indus architecture is still that from the early excavations in the 1920s and early 1930s of Mohenjo-Daro (Mackay 1938; Marshall 1931). With the later excavations by Wheeler (Wheeler 1953) and Dales (Dales &

Kenoyer 1986) no major data of physical remains could be added, except the Granary and some fortification in the citadel area reported by Wheeler (excavated in 1947 and 1950, respectively), and a low-lying area with a slope situated at the western edge of the 'lower City', west of HR area (UPM area) (see Figure 10.1), excavated in 1964 by George Dales. In terms of the conception of the interpretation of the Indus Valley Civilization, both excavations were important, as Mortimer Wheeler discovered the "centralized economic Priest-King system" of this civilization, represented by the 'State Granary'. He also foresaw the great importance of his deep dig (1950), which clearly indicated a gigantic substructure of the citadel. This surrounded, at least, the whole western part of the settlement, as was demonstrated later by the German Research Project at Mohenjo-Daro (1982–84). Today we know that the visible part of Mohenjo-Daro, covering approximately 100 hectares, only represents the 'tip of the iceberg'; in 1989, within the UNESCO Campaign programme for its protection against the Indus floods and for the stabilisation of the Indus River

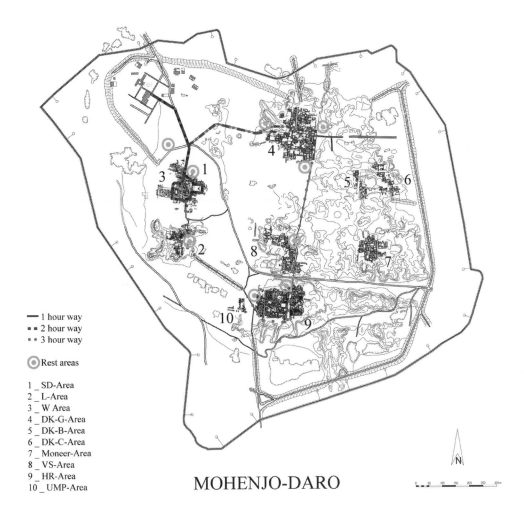

— 1 hour way
▪▪ 2 hour way
▪▪ 3 hour way

◉ Rest areas

1 _ SD-Area
2 _ L-Area
3 _ W Area
4 _ DK-G-Area
5 _ DK-B-Area
6 _ DK-C-Area
7 _ Moneer-Area
8 _ VS-Area
9 _ HR-Area
10 _ UMP-Area

MOHENJO-DARO

Figure 10.1. Map of Mohenjo-Daro with different tourist paths and the excavated areas (numbers 1–10).

banks, large spurs were built into the Indus bed. While digging the foundation trenches with heavy machinery, some 2 metres below the surface (46 m above mean sea level), urban fabric was traced[1] consisting of houses, lanes, wells and bathing platforms. This area is more than 1,500 metres away from the centre of the Lower City. The two observations, of a settlement horizon at least 7 metres below the present surface, and of the horizontal extent of the settlement underneath the present surface in an eastern direction to at least 1,500 metres, allow the conclusion that there is a much larger settlement area than is visible today.

Dales's excavation was important insofar as he indirectly disproved his and Robert Raikes's 'flood theory' (Raikes 1965). His expected 'quay', the ancient harbour of Mohenjo-Daro, turned out to be a stepped architectural feature with another large north-south-running street, parallel to the main street axis of the centre but almost seven meters deeper, showing synchronism of urban context at different heights. This could be exemplarily proven by a sloping drain (unpublished, author's notes 1979), and as such contradicted (with many more examples) the whole traditional structural chronology as developed by Marshall and Mackay on which the chronology of small finds and architectural remains has been based until today.

As a summary of the observations mentioned we can state that our knowledge is still quite uncertain not only of the physical macrostructure of Mohenjo-Daro but also of its socioreligious cultural interpretation. Any chronological interpretation (especially of pottery, seals and figurines) has to take into consideration that the attributed dating is uncertain.[2] As a consequence of the latest request (2006) by the World Heritage Centre UNESCO, Paris, a reinvestigation of the underground limits of the sites will be necessary to identify an appropriate buffer zone for the World Heritage Site.

With an excavation ban imposed on the site in the seventies, at the suggestion of UNESCO as a part of the UNESCO Campaign, no further information could be collected by excavation.

Instead, detailed surface surveys and geophysical testing in the early eighties (Cucarzi 1984; Jansen & Urban 1984a; Vidale 1987), carried out by the joint German-Italian Mission, ultimately added substantially to the understanding of Mohenjo-Daro.

The earliest treatments of measurement at Mohenjo-Daro were published in the excavation reports by Marshall (1931) and Mackay (1938). Mackay dedicated a special chapter (XVIII) to the "System of Weights at Mohenjo-Daro" written by A. S. Hemmy (Hemmy 1938). His chapter comprises (1.) General observations; Groups and ratios; Aberrant weights (601); (2.)Correlation with Babylonian system; Early Egyptian weights (604); (3.) Materials: Differences between later and earlier weights (605) and (4.) Accuracy of weights: Tabulation of weights; Appendix II. In table III (602) Hemmy observed for the first time a weight ratio of 1, 2, 4, 8, 16, 32, et cetera. In appendix II (672) he gives a relation to Egyptian and Susian Weights.

Linear measurement was first investigated by R. C. A. Rottländer (Rottländer 1984). Here he also refers to an analysis by W. Graf (Graf 1976). One of the results is the identification of what Rottländer calls the 'Indus Foot' of 345.55 mm (Rottländer 1984:203). He also gives values for the 'Foot of Nippur' (276.43 mm) and the 'Egyptian Royal Cubit' (523.60 mm). A detailed collection of pre-metric units of length is given in a list at the end of his paper (Rottländer 1984:205). He calculated the 'Indus Foot' from measures given by the author taken primarily from bricks.[3]

As can be observed, bricks in Mohenjo-Daro have different sizes but always maintain the same ratio of proportions of 1:2:4, if approximately 1 cm is added to the actual measure of height and width allowing for the join between bricks. This gives the same proportions as our modern bricks (*Einhandziegel*) (6.25 x 13.5 x 28.0 cm), which constitute a prefabricated rationalized construction unit that can be added to all directions. This makes possible the 'English Bond' (*Blockverband*), which was already in use in Mohenjo-Daro during the 'Mature' Period. The brick construction technology, rather than the brick size, is, according to our observation, the best indicator by which to differentiate between the 'Mature' and 'Late' period in Mohenjo-Daro. Interpreted socio-economically, it is a society that developed a highly rationalized building technology, utilizing only one module for its buildings, the standard brick, prefabricated in moulds and with the possibility of being added to in all directions. The average size, like that of our bricks, was obviously developed out of the width of the hand (palm) to allow rationalized application. If a standard unit of linear measurement was developed, it should be identifiable in brick size as the brick was the basic unit for any building construction. Further research into size/standards is required. Within Indus research no comparative study regarding building technology and standards amongst the different sites has so far been carried out.

Within research into the architectural structures themselves in Mohenjo-Daro, the problem occurs that the traditional house analysis of Marshall and Mackay follows their pattern of stratigraphy, based on horizontal strata, a method heavily criticized by Wheeler (Wheeler 1954). Our research (1979–1986) clearly indicates that the stratigraphy of Mohenjo-Daro is much more complex. Sometimes structures with a difference of height of more than 2 metres belong to one occupation period (e.g., house VI, HR area). The first attempts at formulating a house typology were made by Anna Sarcina (Sarcina 1979). Because of the lack of additional information regarding the complex morphology of the urban development, this approach did not take into consideration the previously mentioned problem of stratigraphy. Another attempt was made by me (Jansen 1983b). Besides the morphological analysis (house VIII, HR B area) a size-proportion diagram was developed, recording each room by its area (square metres) and by its dimensions (length by width in metres). Recording the data of each room in a diagram (x coordinate A x B, y coordinate A/B), a specific pattern occurs by which a typology can be developed (Jansen 1983b:49). As the diagrams (Jansen 1983b:49) show, there is a concentration in analyzed houses (HR A area, house 8, 7, 6A, 1 and MN B4) of rooms with dimensions between 3.0 and 8.0 m and area between 5 and 10 m². House HRA 1 shows a clear deviation from the otherwise similar patterns of the other structures, which, along with the placement of objects within it, led to the conclusion that this structure might have a sacred function. In addition, the analysis of the Great Bath shows a clear divergence from the 'residential pattern' (Jansen 1983a; Jansen 1983b).

In addition to size and proportion, the conception of access to the rooms within one habitation unit can be analyzed. In this regard rooms can be categorised into three types: rooms connected to the public access (outside), transit rooms (with more than one access) and terminal rooms (only one access, interior) (Jansen 1983b:48). It can be assumed that the terminal rooms are those of greatest privacy (here only defined as most distant from 'public' space) and the ones directly connected to the public access are the least private ones. The analysis would be completed once small finds could be relocated to check whether there is a coincidence between the room analysis (space typology) and the individual assemblage of objects. With the availability of the field book data for Mohenjo-Daro at RWTH Aachen and with the completion of the morphological structural analysis this research should provide us with a differentiated understanding of the 'resident behaviour' in Mohenjo-Daro, which, then, could be the basis for a cross-cultural comparative analysis with other Indus sites.

Regarding the 'settlement behaviour' one provisional analysis has been carried out in relation to the orientation system of buildings. In area HR B different buildings and clusters show a different orientation, which might coincide with a change of orientation over

time. According to initial macromorphological studies a shift of structures' orientation can be observed from an almost due north orientation in earlier times to north-north-east in later times. This shift results in nonorthogonal forms of street corners in area HR.

In extension of Wheeler's 'grid plan' a short analysis of the axial systems has been carried out (Wanzke 1987). Wanzke's careful documentation, including of the orientation of 'First Street', shows within the different excavations (DKGNorth, South, VS area, HR area) a deviation of more than 3 gon (Wanzke 1987). In his summary he lists the different streets and lanes with their precise orientation. Their deviation again shows a diversity that needs further explanation and that can only be interpreted once the proper time-space relation for this most important site is properly established. Figures 11 and 14 in his paper list the following axes with their orientation:

– the axes of the main access routes in the areas SD, L, HR, VS, Dales, DK-B+G show a divergence of 7–10 gon towards east;

– the topographical axes 6 and 7 and the Moneer and DK-C axes are orientated exactly towards the cardinal points;

– the north-south axis in the Moneer area continues southwards through the east-west depression;

– the street axis DK-B continues right through to the east of HR-area;

– the street axis of Dales's area is clearly discernible through brickwork that emerges on the surface 300 m south of it;

– the topographic axes that run parallel to the HR street axis to the east and west of it are about 190 meters apart from each other.

Thus we can define two different axis systems in Mohenjo-Daro: System 1 is characterized by a noticeable shift in orientation of ca. 8 gon clockwise, rectangular crossings of the axes and partly identical distances between the latter. System 2 is characterized by an exact orientation to the cardinal points but does not occur as often as system 1. (Wanzke 1987:34)

Wanzke speculated about a probable celestial orientation point and identified Thuban of the Draco constellation, which in 2000 BC was close to the North Star (Wanzke 1987:34). Unfortunately, our research in this respect has not been continued. It would be important to collect the orientation systems of the different Indus sites to identify a probable celestial orientation system. Their different east-west position might, with the according north-south orientation, point towards a single celestial orientation.

Little research has been carried out in relation to other astronomical approaches. One exception is that of Erkka Maula (Maula 1984), following a visit to the site during our work. At that time we had documented the 'ring stones' that are now located in the Mohenjo-Daro museum. After study of them, Maula drew the conclusion that they are 'calendar stones'. "It is suggested that both types of 'great ring stones' serve not only as the earliest known calendric instruments in history, but also as observational instruments in naked eye astronomy, suitable for studying sunsets and sunrises, heliacial rising and settings of other heavenly bodies, and planetary phenomena. Together with 'linga stones', they can be associated with vestiges of the Indus Valley cosmology" (Maula 1984:159).

Conclusion

Discussing "Measuring the World and Beyond: The archaeology of early quantification and cosmology" and here in particular "architectural measurements in the Indus cities", we have to admit that the state of research in the Indus is still quite fragmentary. With the Indus Civilization one of the three earliest civilizations of humankind and with Mohenjo-Daro one of the best preserved archaeological locations of the third millennium we are dealing with a very important phenomenon, which we hardly understand. Here, as elsewhere, we are dealing with the problems associated with interpreting excavations and their reports, almost a decade old, and the need to return to the factual roots to allow new interpretations. Thanks to the excellent recording by the first excavators, some reinterpretation is feasible. Besides the published reports we have the full corpus of field books, allowing us to relocate objects in their structural context. With more than 8,000 old photographs (Sind Volumes) the visualisation of the past setting is excellent. There is hope, within the limits of the World Heritage Programme, to continue with further research at the site, such as identifying the actual settlement limits.

There is still a large gap between the recording of the physical setting and its cultural interpretation, not to mention 'measuring the world beyond'. Compared to that of Egypt and Mesopotamia we know nothing about the distribution of power within the triadic relation of 'profane', 'profane-elitary' and 'sacred'. Without decipherment of the writing and without adequate texts, our interpretation of 'cultural culture' can only be indirectly derived from careful examination of the 'material culture'. And in this area, archaeologists still concentrate primarily on stylistic questions and pottery analysis. As we do understand, the macrocontext of 'urbanity' remains a precious resource in need of further attention.

NOTES

1. The emergency excavation was carried out by M. A. Halim, Department of Archaeology and Museums, Government of Pakistan (DoAM), and is not yet published. Photographic documentation is available with GRM, RWTH Aachen.
2. With the unpublished field books of the excavators, showing the depth position of all objects in absolute measures, a reinterpretation would be feasible.
3. Some brick measurements: 11.75 x 5.75 x 2.75 (Mackay 1938:163 footnote 3), mud bricks 15 x 8 x 3.5, 15 x 7 x3.5, 14.85 x 7.3 x 3.45 (Mackay 1938:170). A huge corpus of data at RWTH Aachen still is waiting for detailed analysis and is not included in this research.

REFERENCES

Cucarzi, M., 1984. Geophysical Investigations at Mohenjo Daro. In *Interim Reports*. Vol. 1. *Reports on Field Work Carried Out at Mohenjo Daro Pakistan 1982–83*, eds. M. Jansen & G. Urban. IsMEO Aachen-University Mission, Aachen, 191–200.

Dales, G. F. & J. M. Kenoyer, 1986. *Excavations at Mohenjo-Daro, Pakistan: The Pottery.* University Museum, University of Pennsylvania, Philadelphia.

Graf, W., 1976. Maß und Zahl in der Induskultur im Lichte der vergleichenden Musikwissenschaft. In *Archaeologia Austriaca Beiheft* 14, ed. R. Pittioni, 461.

Hemmy, A. S., 1938. System of Weights at Mohenjo-Daro. In *Further Excavations at Mohenjo-Daro*, 2 vols., ed. E. J .H. Mackay. Government of India Press, Delhi, 601–612, plus Appendix II 672–78.

Jansen, M., 1983a. *Dokumentation in der Archologie: Techniken, Methoden, Analysen.* Veröffentlichungen der Seminarberichte vom 5.–6. Dezember 1981. Veröffentlichungen des Geodätischen Instituts der RWTH Aachen, Nr. 34.

Jansen, M., 1983b. An Approach towards the Replacement of Artifacts into the Archaeological Context of the Great Bath in Mohenjodaro. In *Dokumentation in der Archologie: Techniken, Methoden, Analysen.* Veröffentlichungen der Seminarberichte vom 5.–6. Dezember 1981. Veröffentlichungen des Geodätischen Instituts der RWTH, Aachen, 43–70.

Jansen, M. & G. Urban, 1984a. *Interim Reports.* Vol. 1. *Reports on Field Work Carried Out at Mohenjo Daro, Pakistan 1982–83.* IsMEO Aachen-University Mission, Aachen.

Jansen, M. & G. Urban, 1987. *Interim Reports.* Vol. 2. *Reports on Field Work Carried out at Mohenjo-Daro, Pakistan 1984–86.* IsMEO Aachen-University Mission, Aachen.

Mackay, E. J. H., 1938. *Further Excavations at Mohenjo-Daro.* 2 vols. Government of India Press, Delhi.

Marshall, S. J., 1931. *Mohenjo-Daro and the Indus Civilization.* 3 vols. Arthur Probsthain, London.

Maula, E., 1984. The Calendar Stones from Mohenjo Daro. In *Interim Reports.* Vol. 1. *Reports on Field Work Carried Out at Mohenjo Daro, Pakistan 1982–83*, eds. M. Jansen & G. Urban. IsMEO Aachen-University Mission, Aachen, 159–170.

Raikes, R. L., 1965. The Mohenjo-Daro Floods. *Antiquity* **39**, 126–203.

Rottländer, R. C. A., 1984. The Harappan Linear Measurement. In *Interim Reports.* Vol. 1. *Reports on Field Work Carried Out at Mohenjo Daro, Pakistan 1982–83*, eds. M. Jansen & G. Urban. IsMEO Aachen-University Mission, Aachen, 201–205.

Sarcina, A., 1979. A Statistical Assessment of House Patterns at Mohenjo Daro. *Mesopotamia Torino 13–14*, 155–199.

Vidale, M., 1987. Some Aspects of Lapidary Craft at Moenjodaro in the Light of the Surface Record of the Moneer South East Area. In *Interim Reports.* Vol. 2. *Reports on Field Work Carried out at Mohenjo-Daro, Pakistan 1984–86*, eds. M. Jansen & G. Urban, Aachen, 113–149.

Wanzke, H., 1987. Axis Systems and Orientation at Mohenjo-Daro. In *Interim Reports.* Vol. 2. *Reports on Field Work Carried out at Mohenjo-Daro, Pakistan 1984–86*, eds. M. Jansen & G. Urban, Aachen, 33–44.

Wheeler, Sir M., 1953. *The Indus Civilization.* Cambridge University Press, Cambridge.

Wheeler, Sir M., 1954. *Archaeology from the Earth.* Oxford University Press, Oxford.

11

Teotihuacan city layout as a cosmogram: Preliminary results of the 2007 Measurement Unit Study

Saburo Sugiyama

Introduction

Teotihuacan, an ancient and highly planned city in the Mexican Highland, has been the focus of varied archaeological inquiries. Those related to its genesis, including the causal factors behind the foundation of such a populous city at this particular location, are of concern not only to Mesoamericanists, but also to those who pursue general themes related to state formation, preindustrial urbanism, or the evolution of human cognitive systems. Ideological factors and an innovative system of urban planning were formulated and applied on a grand scale at Teotihuacan, as is suggested by its unique city layout, unprecedented monumental architecture, and consistent spatial orientations. Here I discuss an indigenous measuring system that the Teotihuacanos could have used to create their precise city layout and major constructions. With newly available data I identify a measurement unit used in Teotihuacan. I present my preliminary interpretations of the ideological principles underlying Teotihuacan's urban arrangement and suggest how the ruling groups of this city conceived their world in time and space and materialized their worldview in city planning. Teotihuacan is a source of exceptionally comprehensive data relevant to better understanding the cognitive structures of ancient Mesoamerican societies, compiled through the extensive excavation and consolidation of the city's major monuments, which are maintained for our benefit by the Mexican National Institute of Anthropology and History (INAH).

Many of the structures visible today at the city were built in highly symmetric relation to each other along the north-south axis (Avenue of the Dead) at the latest by approximately 250 AD, though initial construction stages with significantly different spatial distributions

may have begun at least one century earlier (Millon 1973; Millon et al. 1973; Sugiyama 2003). In spite of the large corpus of information from the city's apogee, we are critically lacking data from its initial stages, which would allow us to better examine issues related to its genesis and early transformation processes. According to our current ceramic chronology and C14 data, among the few known early constructions were the city's three major monuments: the Sun Pyramid, the Moon Pyramid, and a large ceremonial complex, called the Citadel, with its main structure the Feathered Serpent Pyramid (FSP) (Figure 11.1). Many architectural complexes and residences seem to have been integrated in later periods, symbolically and functionally, into the original city layout identified (Cowgill 1992; Millon 1973; Rattray 2001). Intensive excavations indicate that three early building complexes underwent active remodeling, enlargement, or destruction activities throughout the city's history, often covering early constructions. However, the city's basic spatial arrangement evidently endured until its collapse around AD 600 (Millon 1988; Cowgill 1996; Sugiyama 2003).

Extensive explorations of these three monuments began in the early 20th century when precise and systematic recording methods had not yet been established (e.g., Batres 1906; Gamio 1922; Salazar 1970). Therefore, the original excavation data from these projects are scarce, fragmentary, or often inaccurate. However, two large projects to reexplore the FSP in 1988–89 and the Moon Pyramid in 1998–2004 are providing new architectural and chronological information (Cabrera, Sugiyama, and Cowgill 1991; Sugiyama 2004; 2005; Sugiyama and Cabrera 2003; Sugiyama and López 2006; 2007). The Sun Pyramid was also excavated recently by an INAH project that completely uncovered its façades and basal platform (Matos 1995). Here, I will synthesize these more accurate and extensive excavation data to interpret contextually the indigenous quantification system at Teotihuacan.

Since the early 1980s I have been analyzing the dimensions and locations of Teotihuacan's major monuments, plazas, residential compounds, large canals, and other major architectural compounds, as well as the distances along their axes and borders, in the hope of identifying a measurement unit or units used in the city. Initially, I used maps elaborated with aerial photos on a scale of 1:2,000 by the Teotihuacan Mapping Project (TMP) directed by René Millon (1973; Millon et al. 1973) and detailed architectural plans I made with plaintable and alidade at 1:100 scale as part of the Proyecto Arqueológico Teotihuacán 1980–82, directed by Rubén Cabrera of INAH (Cabrera, Rodriguez, and Morelos

Figure 11.1. Aerial view of the Teotihuacan central zone, viewed from the south (photo by S. Sugiyama).

1982a; 1982b; 1991; Sugiyama 1982). In spite of certain difficulties mentioned later, I hypothetically proposed that ancient city planners used a unit equivalent to 83.0 cm, which I named the Teotihuacan Measurement Unit or TMU (Sugiyama 1983; 1993). Previous studies on the topic by other researchers and ethnohistoric records pertaining to Aztec units of measurement also contributed to my study, providing corroborating lines of evidence that gave me the confidence to proceed along this line of inquiry. Over the two decades since my initial research, I have intermittently advanced my study with new excavation data, particularly from recent extensive excavations at the Moon Pyramid and precise quantitative information from the ongoing three-dimensional mapping project I coordinate (Sugiyama and Cabrera 2007). In this chapter, I present new data that bolster my proposed 83.0-cm unit and reinterpret ideological principles that were fundamental to Teotihuacano elites in building and modifying public architecture.

I first present very briefly the Mesoamerican world-view, which was reflected in the Teotihuacan city layout. Then I describe how I reached 83.0 cm as a critical unit of measurement for Teotihuacan, discussing methodological issues and the difficulties in precisely defining the indigenous measuring system archaeologically. After I describe the degree of the precision of our maps, I examine the degree of precision with which Teotihuacan constructors carried out building projects. Then, I analyze specific distances from monumental constructions to suggest that coherent space management programs were functioning in city planning. I conclude that the city layout appears to have been elaborated fundamentally to express a Mesoamerican cosmogenic division of time and space with calendrical, astronomical, or cosmological significance, and that rulers apparently proclaimed divine rulership through the production, reproduction, and use of monuments and cosmic symbols harmoniously integrated into the urban landscape at Teotihuacan.

Mesoamerican worldview

A fundamental characteristic of Mesoamerican culture was that intricate calendrical systems mediated decisive political, military, and social events with regard to astronomical cycles (Shele and Freidel 1990; Schele and Miller 1986). The 365-day solar calendar system, divided into 18 months of 20 days plus 5 liminal days, was used as a principal cycle of time. Since many natural phenomena and related human activities depend on the Sun's cycle and annual environmental changes, rituals related to seasonal events, like those connected to agriculture, were carried out according to this solar calendar (Sahagún 1951: Book 2). In addition to this calendar, the Maya elaborated larger cycles using their civil year, or *tun*, of 360 (20 x 18) days. These included the *katun*, a period of 20 times 360-day years, and *baktun*, 400 times 360-day years, as part of an elaborate system of reckoning time called the Long Count (Justeson 1989: 77).

Another important calendar was the 260-day ritual calendar. Called *tonalpohualli* by the Aztecs and *tzolkin* by the Maya, this cycle comprised 20 day-signs, combined with a prefix number from 1 to 13; thus, specific days were designated by a number and a name and reappeared every 260 days. Although its origin is not yet well understood, it is well documented that this calendar had long been the system used for rituals and divination. The solar calendar and the ritual calendar were combined to make a larger cycle, called the Sacred Round. This cycle is completed in 52 years of the 365-day solar calendar, or 73 'years' of the 260-day cycle (365 x 52 = 260 x 73). The cycle is well documented in Maya and Postclassic Central Mexico and was often used to record historical events.

Lunar cycles (29.43 days) were also recorded and figure prominently in Mesoamerican mythology, astrology, and more elaborate calendar rounds. Special attention was paid to eclipse cycles (173.31 days); for example, the Aztecs observed solar eclipses with great fear and often sacrificed people to avoid their potentially malevolent consequences (Closs 1983; Sahagún 1953: Book 7: 8–9). Solar eclipses were also important, and Mesoamerican civilizations noted that three eclipse cycles exactly coincide with two cycles of the 260-day ritual calendar year (173.31 x 3 = 260 x 2). Venus cycles (584 days) received special attention due to the brightness and uniquely changing appearance of the planet; it emerges periodically as morning or evening stars for certain periods (236 and 250 days, respectively, according to natives' records; Justeson 1989: 79) and disappears between them. Venus cycles were also significant in formulating a larger cycle with the solar cycle (584 x 5 = 365 x 8 = 2,920 days). Even more importantly, it also forms a larger cycle with the solar cycle and the ritual calendar (584 x 65 = 365 x 104 = 260 x 146 = 37,960 days). At Teotihuacan, however, there is no recorded data pertaining directly to these astronomical observations or calendrical systems, except for a limited number of pictographic references suggesting that the ritual calendar was functioning in the city (Caso 1937).

Spatial dimensions were divided along horizontal and vertical scales in Mesoamerica. Horizontal divisions of the world comprised four quarters plus a center, each of them being associated with specific ritual meanings, colours, gods, birds, and trees (e.g., *Codex Fejérváry Mayer* 1971: 1). Space and time were intimately related and combined; thus, Mesoamerican days, months, years, and centuries were assigned to the four directions with divinatory associations (e.g., Coe 1981: 161; Kubler 1962; León-Portilla 1963: 55–56). The primacy of the east-west direction in the arrangement of space apparently derived from the movement of celestial objects, such as the path of the Sun, Moon, Venus, the Pleiades star cluster, and other specific planets or constellations. This primacy can be observed in 16th-century Mesoamerican maps depicting east at the top, as well as by the fact that the principal pyramids at many centers in Mesoamerica face toward the west. At Teotihuacan, two of the three major monuments – the Sun Pyramid and the Feathered Serpent Pyramid – face west, evidently reflecting the celestial axis in an east-west direction. However, no evidence of the east-west axis in the city's earthly layout has been reported archaeologically.[1] Teotihuacan may not have been divided into four sections like the urban plan of Tenochtitlan; instead, the city's public buildings were purposefully and explicitly elaborated solely along the Avenue of the Dead in the north-south direction.

Native divisions of time and space, the movements of celestial objects, and the cycles of other natural phenomena seem to have been deeply rooted in the creation myth of the gods and mankind. The most fundamental account describes a contract with the gods at the time of creation of the universe, the Sun, the Moon, the Earth, and mankind (Sahagún 1952: Book 3: 1–9). For native Mesoamericans, time and space began at a certain moment in a specific place. The Maya believed, for reasons unknown to us, that the universe began August 12, 3114 BC, and they recorded particular historical and mythohistorical events with reference to this first day in the Long Count. August 12 was also given special attention at Teotihuacan and was integrated in the city layout, as I describe later, indicating that Teotihuacan had cosmogenic significance from its foundation.

According to the Mesoamerican worldview, humans and the world came into existence through the self-sacrifice of the gods; as a consequence, humans were obliged to feed the gods by human sacrifice in order to sustain the universe. The Aztecs, arriving in the Mexican Central Valley about 800 years after the collapse of Teotihuacan, believed that the ruined city was the place where the present world and mankind were created by the self-sacrifice of the gods and conceived the ruined city as the place where time began (*Codex Chimalpopoca* 1992). This legend might have been created during the Aztec period; however, we do not know how deep its origins may extend back toward Teotihuacan times.

We know from written records, images, and symbols, as well as archaeological evidence, that the Aztecs and Maya often practiced human sacrificial rituals on an institutionalised scale. Recent excavations at the Feathered Serpent Pyramid and the Moon Pyramid at Teotihuacan have documented that the city's government also carried out human sacrificial rituals repeatedly in association with the construction, enlargement, or modification of important state monuments (Cabrera et al. 1991b; Sugiyama 2005). The manner in which Teotihuacanos buried sacrificial victims and associated symbolic offerings confirms that human sacrificial rituals were fundamentally undertaken with calendrical or cosmological significance (López et al. 1991; Sugiyama and López 2007). Although I do not discuss the topic here, the mortuary programs, including sacrificial victims and rich symbolic offerings discovered at the major monuments, were evidently integrated into the cosmograms that I propose later through this measurement unit study (Sugiyama 2005).

Defining the Teotihuacan Measurement Unit (TMU)

Mesoamerican religious centers with monumental architecture existed by the Early Formative period (1200 BC–800 BC). An indigenous measuring system used to divide sacred space in these centers should also have been functioning at the same time, since these large-scale construction projects would have been impossible without it. I believe that certain units of measurement lasted, evolving through more than two millennia, until the time of Spanish conquest, when the Spanish measurement system was abruptly introduced and quickly replaced indigenous ones. Postconquest ethnohistoric information simply indicates that the measurement unit proposed here falls within the range of units that the Aztecs used at the time of the conquest.

Several researchers have proposed various measurement units used by the Aztecs. The terms used for them clearly indicate that measurement systems developed with reference to the human body. Castillo (1972) examined Nahua terms for different body parts and proposed that standard units were used, including *Cemacolli*: shoulder to finger (0.8 m), *Cenyollotli*: heart to finger (0.9 m), *Cennequetzalli*: standing height (1.6 m), and *Cémmatl*: toe to finger in extended body position (2.5 m). Other units suggested by other researchers include foot size, 27.5–28 cm (Caso 1928), and 82.5 cm (Edward Calnek personal communication 2006). John E. Clark deals with the issue in great detail in this volume; therefore, I do not discuss it further. It is worth pointing out, however, that studies using only ethnohistoric data cannot confirm the correspondence of each unit of the Aztecs or other Mesoamerican societies precisely to the metric system. The present study was based on archaeological information, independent of that suggested by the ethnohistoric data. A significant difference between Aztec and Teotihuacano units can be expected, as the time gap between these two civilizations is nearly one millennium. Additionally, it is likely that several units were in use and that these included regional variations.

The unit I propose here was not achieved instantaneously by simple 'discovery' or by applying a simple hypothesis-testing procedure or statistical program. I followed a long process of approximating the unit, combining inductive and deductive approaches, and the integration of detailed excavation contexts with quantitative data. The study was enhanced significantly as I became increasingly familiar with ancient technologies, site formation processes, and the natives' error range for construction, over more than two decades of topographic survey experience at many Mesoamerican sites. Consequently, I believe that the approach adopted is a logical and effective strategy for this kind of complicated decipherment, as far as the results can be tested scientifically.

One of the fundamental problems for this kind of study is the degree of precision in the maps that are currently available. Previously, several researchers have proposed measurement units used at Teotihuacan including 80 cm (Almaráz 1865: 212–213), 80.5 cm (Drewitt 1987; Drucker 1977), 60 m (Séjourné 1966), 57 m and 322 m (80.5 cm x 400) (Drewitt 1967; 1987). John E. Clark (personal communication 2006) suggests that various units were functioning simultaneously, as was the case for the Aztecs. However, the quality and quantity of data used in previous research have often been critically limited by the accuracy of architectural plans and site maps. Many architectural plans are incomplete or not sufficiently accurate for this type of study, in which fractions are crucial. Reconstruction plans of unexcavated structures are simply not reliable, although many of the researchers listed previously have imprudently relied on them. General plans elaborated by the TMP directed by René Millon (1973) are highly accurate with many detailed features, invaluably useful for spatial analyses of the whole city layout. However, the scale applied (1:2,000) is simply not fine enough for architectural analyses. In 1999 we began an intensive three-dimensional mapping survey of the city in order to elaborate maps precisely locating architectural elements within the citywide spatial/temporal framework. Consequently, the problem of a lack of precision has been significantly diminished.

It is also difficult to understand how and which part of a particular structure Teotihuacanos actually measured because of the complexities of architectural layouts and superimposed modifications that covered or destroyed original structures. Especially complicated features at the residential compounds, often from several different construction stages that are exposed today as a single unit, make it difficult or impossible to determine the original measurements. It is also possible that the entire city was laid out using several measurement units, which also might have changed significantly through time. It is a common feature worldwide that even supposedly consistent measurement units, such as the English 'foot', change gradually over hundreds of years. In addition, it is also likely that Teotihuacan's builders simply were not concerned with measurements in many instances because other variables had already determined the space available. It is also unrealistic to suppose that Teotihuacanos always measured in whole units, without using fractions.

In spite of these difficulties, I still believe that coherent use of measurement unit(s) can be detected and verified with a certain margin of error at Teotihuacan. In this study, I propose a unit (83.0 cm) induced from and applied to the major monuments constructed specifically during AD 150–250. The underlying idea is that the early monumental structures probably reflect the original plan more explicitly than later constructions, conditioned as these were by earlier ones and other variables. In this way, we may also eliminate confusion derived from changes of the unit that might have occurred through time. Most importantly, I apply the same unit to the most fundamental points or lines that Teotihuacano builders must have taken into account to trace the basic lines of the city layout accurately. I analyse the axes and dimensions of the contemporaneous three major monuments

in relation to the north–south axis of the Avenue of the Dead: an interior pyramidal platform found in the Moon Pyramid (Building #4) built around AD 200–250; the Sun Pyramid at its original size constructed by AD 150 (Millon et al. 1965); and the Citadel complex with the FSP (Sugiyama 2005) built around AD 200–250. We now have sufficient data to assert that the creation of the urban structure observable today began apparently with a master plan (Sugiyama and Cabrera 2007), and that these three monuments were erected at the latest by AD 250 and were functioning contemporaneously for the subsequent centuries.

Besides these main alignments, distances used repeatedly at various central locations were also given special attention. In fact, my search for the TMU began at the main sculpted facade of the FSP (Figure 11.2). It was noted in 1981 that the width of a balustrade at the FSP (1.66 m) is almost half of the distance (average 3.29 m) between head sculptures jutting regularly from the west façade, and one-eighth of the width of the staircase (13.06 m). The side dimension (approximately 65.7 m on the south side) of the lowest platform of the FSP is nearly 40 times the same distance (1.66 m x 40 = 66.4 m), although the exact corners have been destroyed and cannot be measured precisely. Very similar distances were also obtained from the Adosada Platform at the Moon Pyramid, as described later. These data from the FSP and the Moon Pyramid originally led me to suggest that a unit of approximately 83 cm was used at Teotihuacan (Sugiyama 1983).

The next step was to apply these possible units to many other structures or distances between monuments, plazas, and other divisions of space. For this purpose, I made several grid sheets with 80.0- to 85.0-cm intervals on tracing paper, also taking into account what other scholars had proposed, and overlapped them with detailed architectural plans I made at a scale of 1:100 for the Proyecto Arqueológico Teotihuacan 1980–82 (Sugiyama 1982). During this phase of constant testing of hypothesized units, I reached a tentative conclusion that around 83.0 cm was a possible unit most applicable to many architectural compounds. However, I still could not conclusively assert its appropriateness statistically using accurate data since the mapping project had not yet concluded completely, and the unit proposed did not fit in many other cases.

The study during the early 1980s was enhanced significantly when I applied 83.0 cm to the Sun Pyramid (Figure 11.3). During the testing process of the hypothesized unit, it unexpectedly became evident that the original length of a side of the Sun Pyramid corresponds to 260 TMU with less than 1 m of error, according to the

Figure 11.2. The main façade of the Feathered Serpent Pyramid (photo by S. Sugiyama).

dimensions given in the map made by the TMP (Millon et al. 1973). As was outlined previously, 260 was one of the most important calendar numbers in Mesoamerica, as it represents the number of days in the ritual calendar used by all cultures in the region. Applying the same unit to the Citadel complex, numbers associated with Venus were discernible. The association of the Citadel with the planet is clear, since its main temple was adorned with an elaborate sculptural program incorporating the Feathered Serpent, the Mesoamerican deity personifying the planet Venus.

One of the reasons for proposing an 83.0-cm unit for Teotihuacan is that only this unit coherently conforms to the dimensions of the major constructions at Teotihuacan, consistently relating them to important numbers in Mesoamerican calendrical systems or cycles of celestial bodies. I should mention that the total measurements derived from many construction units I do not mention here do not accord well with the TMU, and further data on them are still to be recovered by our ongoing mapping project. Nevertheless, the conformities among my proposed TMU, the dimensions of major structures, and important numbers in Mesoamerican astronomy and astrology are too

numerous to be considered accidental. They support the proposition that Teotihuacan was planned with cosmic encoding or as a cosmogram involving these important numbers.

Applying TMU to the major monuments and city layout

I consistently use 83.0 cm as a unit of measurement for all cases described later. I analyze the three-dimensional maps using AutoCAD software, with measurements collected by digital transit (Total Station) and low-altitude aerial photos (Sugiyama and Cabrera 2003; 2007). We have been recording all available architectural features, differentiating original, consolidated, or reconstructed walls (Figure 11.4). Our survey indicates that the reference points we established in the field may be subject to a few centimetres of deviation, while actual architectural points within the 2.3-km-long central area surveyed along the Avenue of the Dead show several centimetres of error. Much larger errors, of several tens of centimeters, but less than one metre in most cases, may occur because of the incompleteness of excavation data or inaccuracy in

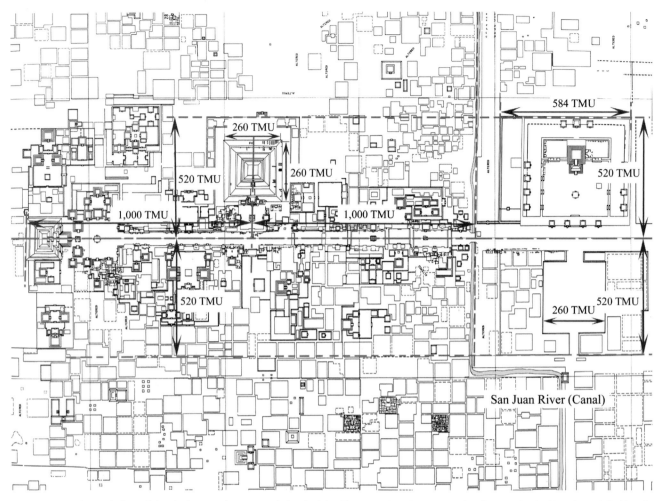

Figure 11.3. General plan of the city's central zone, made by the Teotihuacan Mapping Project (Millon et al. 1973) and modified by the author. Possible measured distances, indicated in TMU, were proposed in 1993 (Sugiyama).

reconstructed architecture. Ambiguity remains particularly when we cannot precisely measure original features; for example, the edges of talud (sloped) walls connected with the original floor are often covered, and therefore raised, by later floor construction or are destroyed completely. In these cases I have hypothetically reconstructed missing or original sections, based on available contextual information, to calculate the most probable points. Any measurements taken from other sources are indicated in each corresponding place; otherwise, the numbers listed in this chapter are measurements taken from our three-dimensional maps with the error range described earlier. The listed distances between certain points of structures or axes were always measured horizontally and parallel to the city's north-south or east-west axis. I tried to choose points that seemed to me to be the most accurate and representative considering local contexts and current preservation conditions.

Our more accurate maps make it possible to identify the level of precision that Teotihuacanos applied to

their constructions. I examine their accuracy using an AutoCAD map of the Moon Plaza complex and hypothetically propose that similar-sized platforms were symmetrically located with respect to the north-south axis of the city and were intentionally calculated and constructed. Recovering precise data from these structures, it is possible to interpret the range of differences in their size or location as being indicative of indigenous errors or accuracy of the Teotihuacan constructors. For this purpose I use medium-size structures surrounding the Moon Plaza, Structures 1 & 7, 3 & 9, 4 & 10, and 5 & 11, which were evidently distributed intentionally as pairs in terms of location and size (see Figure 11.7, later in the chapter, for their locations). Table 11.1 shows the differences in the widths of the main façades and the staircases between paired constructions, both at the lowest and second platform levels. We should particularly consider data from each second platform level, which more often preserves the original floor than does the first level of each structure, which lacks accurate data

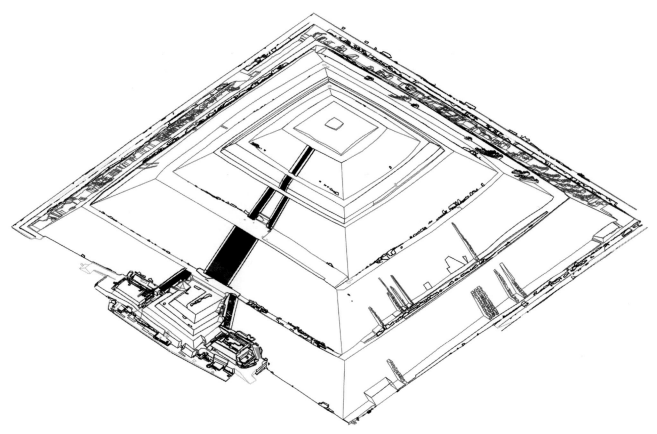

Figure 11.4. 3D map of the Sun Pyramid, created with AutoCad. The data were recovered with Total Station in 2004–2006 by the Moon Pyramid Project.

Table 11.1. *Comparative data on the size of paired platforms in the Moon Plaza*

	First platform	Difference	Second platform	Difference	Staircase	Difference	Staircase at second platform	Difference	a: Staircase b: At second platform
Str. 2	32.11				9.46				
Str. 1	36.01	0.43	31.89	0.34	9.19	0.00	9.15	0.07	a: −0.35
Str. 7	35.58		31.55		9.19		9.22		b: −0.21
Str. 3	32.57	0.36	28.51	0.02	9.47	0.22	9.50	0.11	a: 0.18
Str. 9	32.21		28.54		(9.25)		9.39		b: 0.04
Str. 4	38.76	0.93	34.69	1.23	9.95	0.10	9.99	0.16	a: −0.34
Str. 10	39.70		35.92		9.86		9.83		b: −0.47
Str. 5	31.54	0.81	28.21	0.37	10.39	1.09	9.73	0.51	a: −0.73
Str. 11	32.35		28.58		(9.31)		9.22		b: −0.15

Note: Width in metres; from the three-dimensional plan created by the Moon Pyramid Project.

on the corresponding plaza floor. The differences were 2, 7, 10, 16, 34, 37, 51, and 122 cm (34.9 cm in average). However, it is possible that Structures 4 & 10 were constructed differently or that the latter was enlarged later, in which case 22 cm can be considered the average error range for the medium-sized constructions (about 32 m wide).

Locational data also suggest that Teotihuacan's builders erected public structures at a specific location to keep them in a symmetrical relationship with respect to the city's north-south axis. Table 11.2 shows the distance from the north-south axis recorded by the TMP (Millon et al. 1973) to the midpoint of centrally located structures or paired constructions in the Moon

Table 11.2. *Deviation from two north-south axes of the Avenue of the Dead to the midpoint of central structures or to the midpoint of paired platforms at the Moon Plaza*

	A	B
Moon Pyramid (N. corners)	−0.48	−0.11
Intermediate platform (N. corners)	−0.45	−0.08
Intermediate platform (S. corners)	−0.43	−0.06
Adosada Platform (N. corners)	−0.30	0.07
Adosada Platform (S. corners)	−0.42	−0.05
Staircase at the Adosada Platform (N. corners)	−0.45	−0.08
Staircase at the Adosada Platform (S. corners)	−0.47	−0.10
Structure 36 (N. corners)	−0.38	−0.01
Structure 36 (S. corners)	−0.44	−0.07
Structure 44 (N. corners)	−0.21	0.16
Structure 44 (S. corners)	−0.31	0.06
Structure 1 (SE corner) and Structure 7 (SW corner)	−0.27	0.10
Structure 3 (SE corner) and Structure 9 (SW corner)	(0.23)	(0.60)
Structure 4 (SE corner) and Structure 10 (SW corner)	−0.41	−0.04
Structure 5 (SE corner) and Structure 11 (SW corner)	−0.15	0.22

Note: In metres. The SW corner of Structure 9 was covered with a later construction; therefore, deviation cannot be measured precisely. (A: distance from TMP's axis; B: distance from new axis set parallel to, and 37 cm west of, TMP's axis.)

Plaza. The differences consistently indicate that the north-south axis originally set by Teotihuacanos was about 37 cm (average deviation) west of, and parallel to, the axis identified by the TMP, and that midpoints measured fall within ±10 cm of the original axis. These sample data from the Moon Plaza clearly demonstrate exceptionally high accuracy of Teotihuacan architectural engineering and strong intentionality in the location of constructions, which may also have been applied to other architectural units and the whole city layout. The information also provides reasons for interpreting our quantitative data described later and a basic guideline we should follow regarding indigenous error margins.

The Pyramid of the Sun

I observed in 1993 that the Sun Pyramid was evidently set at the exact centre of the entire city layout (Figure 11.5). The east-west axis of the pyramid seems to have been the central line between the northern edge of the

Moon Pyramid and the southern edge of the San Juan River (Grand Channel). If so, the Citadel and the Great Compound would have been exceptional complexes outside this central zone (Sugiyama 1993). The fact that the distance between the east-west axis of the Sun Pyramid and each of these border lines approximately corresponds to 1,000 TMU strongly indicates that this was the center for the urban plan, from which other structures were measured and placed correspondingly. As I explain later, this coincidence may not have been the only factor underlying the whole city layout, as other principles also seem to have been involved. At any rate, the Sun Pyramid was apparently an initial point from which to trace the city's growth and development, as suggested by its early construction date, its location, and its being the largest of all the monuments in the city.

The Sun Pyramid was extensively excavated, consolidated, and partially reconstructed by Batres in 1906, resulting in the monument we observe today. We now know that its upper section and the main (western) façade of the Adosada Platform added on the pyramid's western façade were erroneously reconstructed (Millon 1973). Later research by Millon and others (Millon et al. 1965) inside the archaeological tunnels excavated into the pyramid by Noguera (1935) and Pérez (1935) suggested that the pyramid might contain an earlier platform; however, little is known about this suggested structure. The next stage of construction of the Sun Pyramid seems to have comprised four stepped platforms with a nearly square footprint. The lowest platform on its north, east, and south sides clearly demonstrates that there were at least two architectural stages (Figure 11.4). Our mapping survey in 2006 provides more precise data: the north, east, south, and west sides of the older/smaller pyramid measure 214.63 m (258.59 TMU), 215.15 m (259.22 TMU), 215.72 m (259.90 TMU), and 210.50 m (253.61 TMU), respectively (Figure 11.5). Except for the western façade, which features unclear overlapping construction, the sides are close to 260 TMU. This earlier building was dated to the Tzacualli phase, which, according to Millon (1973), corresponds to AD 1–150. The figures suggest that the original dimensions were probably determined to symbolize the most important ritual cycle of 260 days.

The north, east, south, and west sides of the later building completely covering the earlier one measure 221.43 m (266.78 TMU), 223.75 m (269.58 TMU), 224.24 m (270.17 TMU), and 221.53 m (266.90 TMU), respectively, and were dated by Millon (1973) to the Xolalpan phase (AD 400–500 or later). We do not know the reason for this significant unevenness on the four sides, but the dimensions of the enlarged façades in TMU do not appear significant.

The intention to shape the older monument to specific dimensions can be confirmed by the fact that the distance between the city's north-south main axis and the east limit of the Sun Pyramid compound is exactly double the side dimension of the older Sun Pyramid (Figure 11.5). This monument was surrounded by a long, wide platform on its north, east, and south sides. This evidently formed the Sun Pyramid compound, as extensive excavations by Matos (1995: 312–329) demonstrated, although we lack datable information with which the platform can be correlated with the pyramid chronologically. On the east side of the East Platform there are two overlapping walls that delimit the Sun Pyramid compound; the earlier one is located 429.26 m (517.18 TMU) from the city's axis, whereas the later wall is 431.27 m (519.60 TMU) from the axis. The number 520 was important not only

because it is double 260, but because it is also three times the eclipse cycle, which is 173.31 days. As mentioned in the introduction it is widely known that Mesoamerican peoples paid particular attention to eclipse phenomena, especially the Aztecs, who treated them as omens (Sahagún 1954) and recorded their cycle (Aveni 1980). The fact that the solar eclipse cycle can also be found at the Moon Pyramid, as described later, strengthens the notion that the Teotihuacan people were also aware of this cycle and incorporated it into the most conspicuous monument complex and entire city layout.

The Pyramid of the Moon

Until 1998 the Moon Pyramid had been the least explored monument in Teotihuacan. It was explored

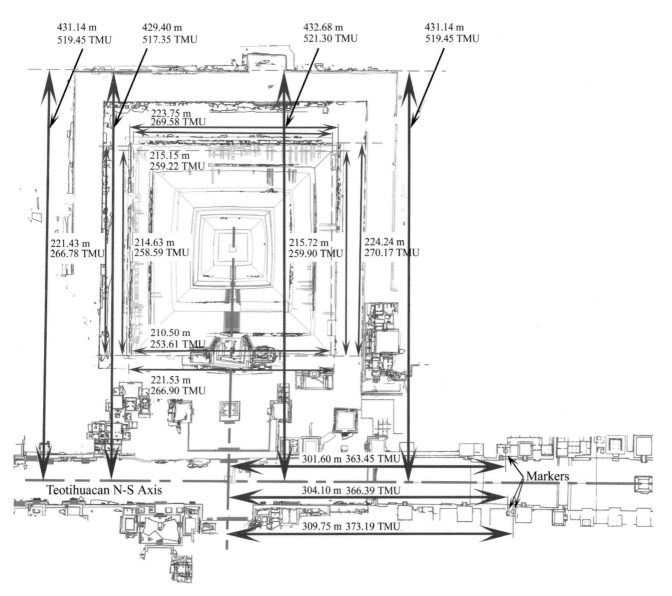

Figure 11.5. Plan of the Sun Pyramid complex with the Avenue of the Dead, from a three-dimensional map created with AutoCad by the Moon Pyramid Project.

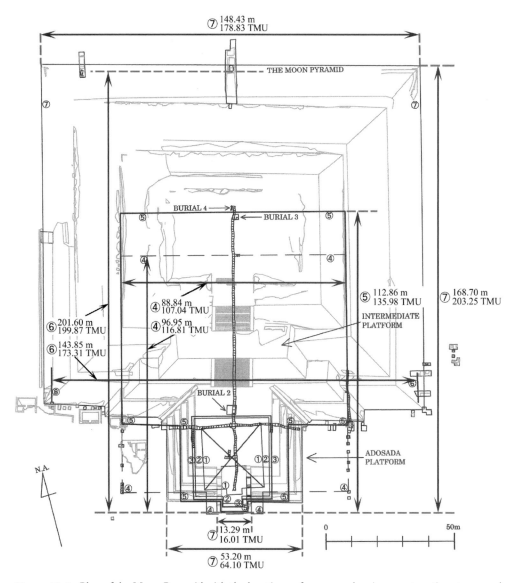

Figure 11.6. Plan of the Moon Pyramid with the locations of seven overlapping construction stages and measurements in TMU, from a three-dimensional map created with AutoCad by the Moon Pyramid Project.

intensively during the last decade by an international project directed by the Mexican archaeologist Rubén Cabrera and me (Sugiyama and Cabrera 2003; 2007). Tunnel operations within the pyramid's nucleus have discovered an elaborate architectural sequence, including seven overlapping monumental constructions and five burial complexes of sacrificed individuals and sacred animals associated with rich offerings (Sugiyama and López 2007).

The superimposed structures were designated Buildings 1 to 7, numbered from the earliest to latest (Figure 11.6). Our excavations and the three-dimensional mapping of the Moon Plaza complex provide precise architectural information for each building, associated with chronological data. Building 1, the oldest

monument found to date at Teotihuacan (dated to the Patlachique phase), is a square pyramidal platform measuring 23.5 m (28.31 TMU) at its base. The location of the Moon Pyramid was evidently chosen around the beginning of the city's history, circa AD 100, prior to the establishment of the currently observable urban grid system.

During the first three enlargement phases (Buildings 1 to 3) the monument was a square pyramidal platform with stepped *talud* façades that were elaborated gradually on a modest scale, retaining the same architectural style. The east-west width of Buildings 2 and 3 measures 29.3 m (35.30 TMU) and 31.3 m (37.71 TMU), respectively, at the base. In sharp contrast, the erection of Building 4 during the early third century AD, nine times larger than its immediate predecessor, seems to imply a substantial growth in manageable resources and increased political centralization. Its east-west dimension was widened to 88.84 m (107.04 TMU), while the north-south dimension became 96.95 m long (116.81 TMU). The grid system visible today was apparently established by the time of Building 4's construction during AD 200–250, at the latest. This was approximately when the Citadel and the FSP were constructed (the end of the Miccaotli phase). This evidently represents the time of the establishment of the major monumental constructions. The dimensions of Building 4 do not correlate with any significant calendrical or astronomical numbers. However, it is intriguing that the number is close to 105, which represents the complement period to the 260-day calendar forming a solar year cycle (105 + 260 = 365); as is discussed later, one of the most striking findings here for the TMU proposal is that the whole north-south distance of the central ceremonial zone by that time, the distance between Building 4 and the Citadel, corresponded to nearly 2,600 TMU – the ritual calendar times 10.

Building 6 represents another substantial enlargement program at the Moon Pyramid. We can safely conclude that Building 6 had almost the same form and size as the Moon Pyramid visible today, but the east-west dimension grew to approximately 143.9 m. We see here again certain intriguing numbers applied to this enlargement program. The north-south dimension of Building 6 (201.6 m) seems to have reached 200 TMU, although its northern and southern edges cannot be precisely determined. Meanwhile, according to accurate excavation data, the east-west dimension became 173.31 TMU, which is exactly the number of the solar eclipse cycle. These two numbers seem to have been derived from Mesoamerican astronomical and numbering systems, if the proposed TMU was utilized.

Building 7 comprises most parts of the façades of the currently visible Moon Pyramid – the main body, the intermediate platform, and the Adosada platform, constructed simultaneously and together forming a single architectural unit. It is noteworthy that the width of the staircase, 13.29 m (16.01 TMU), was close to that of the staircase at the FSP (13.06 m; 15.73 TMU), and one-quarter of the whole width of the Adosada platform's east-west dimension at the Moon Pyramid (53.20 m; 64.10 TMU). The pyramid was, by then, a part of the Moon Plaza compound (Figure 11.7). Many pieces of evidence of later constructions and modifications in surrounding areas after the erection of Building 7 indicate that the monument functioned until the collapse of the city. However, the complicated symmetrical spatial distribution of surrounding midsized temples does not

provide any clear evidence of significant measurements, except for the east-west distances between Structures 4 & 10, paired pyramids facing each other across the central low platform in the Plaza; this distance (143.18 m; 172.51 TMU) again corresponds approximately to the solar eclipse cycle, 173.31 days.

The Citadel and the Feathered Serpent Pyramid

The Citadel was located at the southern edge of the central ceremonial zone, although it lies near the centre of the whole urban area, in which ceramics and other artefacts cover the surface (Millon et al. 1973). The extensive excavation by INAH confirmed that the Citadel, as its name indicates, was truly a fortified ceremonial center with thick high walls surrounding the central vast plaza area (Figure 11.8). To the north, excavation data show that an additional area was attached, perhaps for secondary uses of ritual significance or simply for functional activities (Rodríguez 1982; Múnera 1985).

As mentioned previously, the unmistakable eastern limit of the Citadel is located at 433.17 m (521.89 TMU) from the city's north-south axis; the distance seems to be too close to that of the space between the eastern edge of the Sun Pyramid compound and the city's axis to be accidental. It can therefore be concluded that the Citadel complex and the Sun Pyramid complex were consciously constructed in association with one another, to imply a special calendar number, twice 260 days, or thrice 173.31 days.

The most interesting numbers are from the total width of the Citadel complex. The total north-south measurement is 482.58 m (581.42 TMU), which is 2.5 units short of the cycle of Venus in days. Considering the accuracy demonstrated by the Teotihuacanos in the exact spatial distribution of the buildings, this implies there is an as-yet-unknown motivation for using this shorter measurement. In turn, the north-south width of the Citadel complex, 403.86 m (486.58 TMU) or 404.59 m (487.46 TMU), accords well with the number of days in which Venus was recorded visible by natives as either a morning or evening star (236 + 250 = 486 days). The association of the Citadel with the Venus cycle is clear, as indicated by the sculptures of the Feathered Serpent present, a symbol of Venus, and pictographic data on this sacred creature (López et al. 1991). Besides these primary numbers or distances found in the Citadel, there were no clear distinctive features or numbers implied by TMU.

The FSP was a complex building that comprised monumental architecture, sculptural programs, and a mass-sacrificial complex of more than 137 individuals

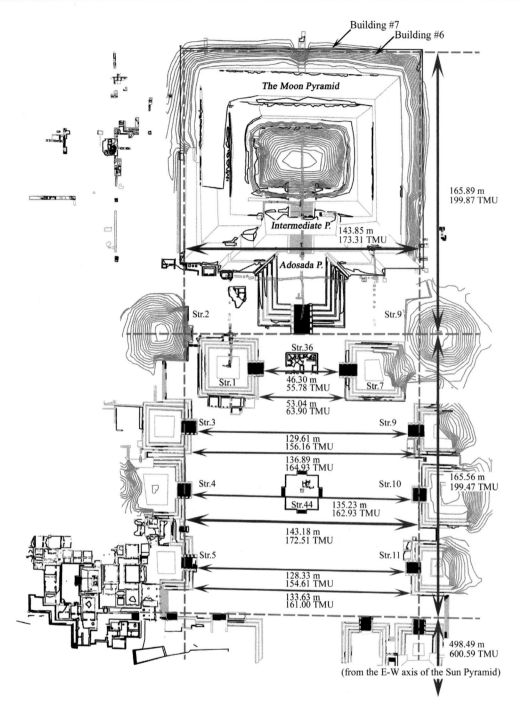

Figure 11.7. Plan of the Moon Plaza complex with measurements in TMU, from a three-dimensional map created with AutoCad by the Moon Pyramid Project.

integrated into the building in order to express calendrical themes explicitly. The TMU was deduced from this unique and highly symmetrical monument, as previously described; however, besides the correspondences listed earlier, the building exhibits no specific measurement unit system. For more sound explanations regarding its underlying significance and related numbering system further data and analytical studies are required, not only of architectural dimensions, but also of the complicated sculptural and mortuary programs.

Relation of three major monuments along the Avenue of the Dead

The three major monuments discussed were constructed by AD 150–250 (the Miccaotli phase) as the principal structures presumably within a master plan, although some of them may have existed earlier than others (Figure 11.9). This was a time of major monumental constructions that were apparently orchestrated by the state across the city; therefore, these activities would

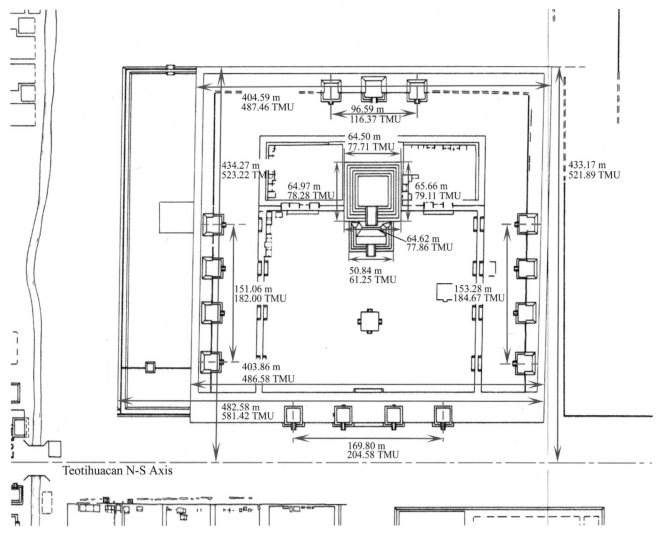

Figure 11.8. Plan of the Citadel complex with measurements in TMU, traced from Millon et al. (1973) with modification.

have been related to each other symbolically and functionally. The TMU study indicates that there were several fundamental alignments along which the locations of the three monuments were determined. One is the whole space of the central ceremonial zone running in a north-south direction, delimited by the Moon Pyramid to the north and the Citadel to the south. The distance (2,156.86 m; 2,598.63 TMU) between the northern limit of Building 4, uncovered and precisely measured through our tunnel exploration, and the unquestionable south edge of the Citadel coincides with 2,600 TMU, 10 times 260 (or 13 x 20 x 10). Although this central ceremonial zone was not apparently divided with a grid system of 260 TMU in a simplistic way, this coincidence should not be considered accidental. Whether the TMU is a valid measure or not, the distance coincides to 10 times the width of the older Sun Pyramid, so clear proportional relations exist.

It seems that there was an additional calendrical principle integrated in the city's spatial structure of this period in the north-south direction. The distance between the two east-west axes of the Sun Pyramid and of the Citadel (1,194.99 m; 1,439.75 TMU) corresponds to nearly 1,440 TMU, or 4 times 360 (20 x 18). We know that the Mesoamerican Long-Counting system, recorded in Maya regions, consisted of multiples of 20, 18, 20, 20, so on, so that 20 x 18 remains close to the solar year. At Teotihuacan, we have not deciphered a numeric system or calendar complexes mainly because we have not decoded the writing system used at the city, although we can suspect that pan-Mesoamerican numbering systems including the Long Count system were in use at this planned city. For the Aztecs, 360 days meant one solar year, though they used to add 5 supplementary liminal days, on which human activities were limited, to fit to the 365-day solar cycle.

There is another line of evidence that supports the TMU proposition and the argument described. Pecked-cross petroglyphs uncovered along the Avenue of the Dead seem to have recorded 365-day cycles. Petroglyph

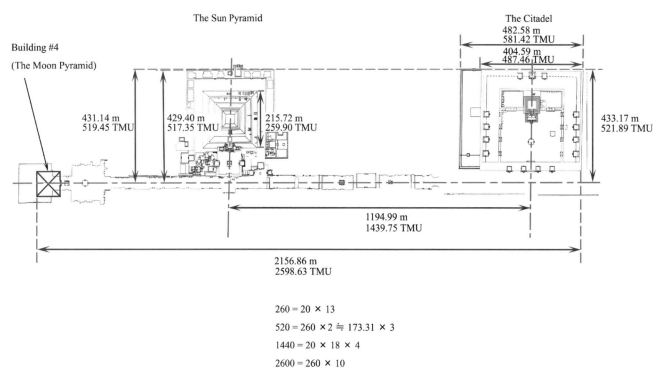

Figure 11.9. General plan of the Teotihuacan city layout in AD 200–250 (end of the Miccaotli phase), traced from Millon et al. (1973) with modification.

#1 in a room east of the Avenue was located at 301.60 m (363.45 TMU) from the east-west axis of the Sun Pyramid, while #2 and #3 were found at 304.10 (366.39 TMU) and 309.75 m (373.19 TMU), respectively, from the same axis, in a room west of the Avenue (Figure 11.5). These data suggest that the space division of the Avenue in the north-south direction was primarily determined in relation to the 260-day calendar, solar cycle, and Venus cycle, stressing again the highly integrated concern of Teotihuacanos with astronomical movements.

The TMU study further suggests that a modification program was carried out around AD 350, defined as the end of the Early Tlamimilolpa phase, reflecting changing meanings or innovative calendrical or cosmological significance (Figure 11.10). In the Citadel complex, a new building called an Adosada platform was built covering the principal façade of the Feathered Serpent Pyramid. Since destruction and looting activities may have been involved in this radical modification, the change recorded in archaeological materials would have had sociopolitical and/or religious implications (Sugiyama 1998). It is not possible to suggest, at present, any new ideological factors from the TMU study, as the construction data from the Adosada Platform and the remodeled 'Palaces' in the Citadel do not coincide with any significant numbers.

At the Moon Pyramid complex, Building 6 was erected as a part of a substantial enlargement program during the same period (Figure 11.7). Distances from the east-west axis of the Sun Pyramid to the southern limit of the Moon Plaza, the south edge of the staircase at the Adosada platform of the Moon Pyramid, and the possible northern limit of Building 6 measure almost 600, 800, and 1,000 TMU (498.49, 664.05, and 829.94 m), respectively. We observed at the Moon Pyramid and other major complexes that staircases are consistently included in the measurements of the building; this being the case, these points apparently served to trace the most fundamental lines for city-layout divisions. Minimal fractions support the idea that these reference points with equal distances, or multiples of them, were not accidental; more probably they would have been measured to demarcate the structural landscape. More importantly, the east-west width of Building 6 seems to have been determined to correspond exactly to the number of days of a solar eclipse cycle, as discussed previously (143.85 m or 173.31 TMU). This particular celestial number was suggested to have already been in use on the basis of the number 520 obtained at the Sun Pyramid and Citadel complexes. These coherent data suggest that the solar eclipse cycle was known in Teotihuacan since its early occupation and formed a principal spatial structure of the city's layout. The data from repeated enlargement or remodeling programs in later periods also indicate that ruling groups actively tried to supplement or modify at a citywide level calendrical and cosmological significance originally established in an early time in the monuments' lives.

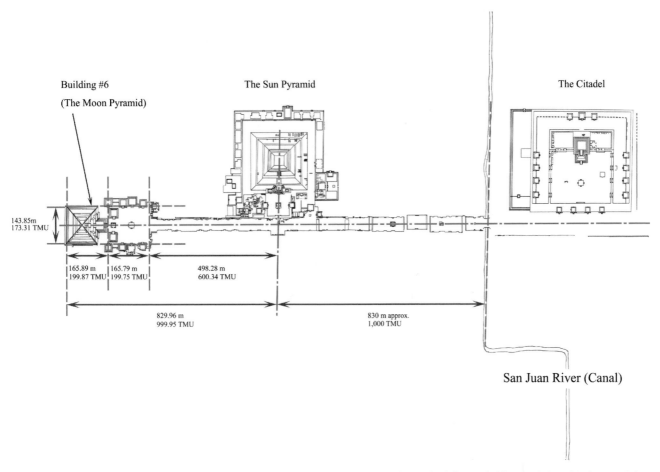

Figure 11.10. Reconstruction plan of the Teotihuacan city layout around AD 350 (end of the Early Tlamimilolpa phase), traced from Millon et al. (1973) with modification.

Preliminary conclusion regarding Teotihuacan cosmograms

It is well known that there were elaborate calendar systems in Mesoamerica, probably dating from the earliest civilizations in the region. Many scholars describe Mesoamericans as people obsessed with astronomy and rituals related to the passage of time. Ethnohistoric and epigraphic information indicates that various time-reckoning systems functioned simultaneously in different social contexts, and that the passage of time was explicitly marked by politico-religious events including human sacrifice and the wars that obtained captives for such rituals. For Mesoamerican peoples, calendrical cycles were not just time-reckoning devices; they also constituted an essential value system to be encoded as sacred cosmograms within which people conceived, measured, and interpreted the material world to locate themselves in time and space and to predict their futures.

The indigenous Mesoamerican concern with the passage of time is widely recorded in monuments, sculptural programs, inscriptions, murals, symbols, and manuscripts from the region. At Teotihuacan, where writing systems have not yet been decoded, similar concerns by ruling groups have not previously been specifically identified, though some researchers propose them intuitively or hypothetically in more tenuous terms (Coe 1994; Coggins 1993; Millon 1993). If the TMU proposition is accurate, numbers indicated by the TMU would demonstrate that the city layout of Teotihuacan was fundamentally created to represent a Mesoamerican cosmogram quantitatively and spatially with precise space divisions integrated. Basically, all important calendrical cycles and conspicuous astronomical movements were in fact recorded and materialized architecturally in the city layout.

Although the precise data available are still incomplete, I have listed possible significant numbers integrated in the urban space, such as (105), 173.3, 200, 260 (20 x 13), 360 (20 x 18), 365, 486, 520 (260 x 2 = 173.3 x 3), 584, 600, 800, 1,000, 1,440 (20 x 18 x 4), and 2,600 (260 x 10). These numbers can be divided or combined in various ways or can be represented in different indigenous measurement units, as was the case with Aztec units (Castillo 1972; John E. Clark, this volume).

However, they were related to each other, and here I have only applied what was likely a basic unit. Our ongoing survey project will provide more comprehensive and holistic interpretations with solid data to address such issues in the near future. The following are preliminary comments with different kinds of supporting data at this initial stage.

The proposed almanac integrated into the urban spacing can be reinforced by the data regarding the city's orientations. The north-south central line of the Avenue of the Dead was only one principal axis of the city represented in the city layout. The axis was apparently orientated upward to the top of Cerro Gordo ('Fat Mountain'), the highest mountain of the Teotihuacan Valley (Figure 11.1) (Tobriner 1972). Logically, other constructions in the city, even those distant from the Avenue of the Dead, followed in close relation to this central north-south axis. This upward orientation to the north may also have been significantly related to the cardinal direction north situated 15.5 degrees west of this axis. Contrastingly, the city's east-west orientation of all constructions was related to the astronomical movements of the Sun and Pleiades, as has been documented by detailed archaeoastronomical studies (Aveni 1980; Dow 1967; Drucker 1977; Malmstrom 1978; Millon 1981; 1993). The Sun set on the western horizon exactly following the direction of the city's east-west axis on August 12 and April 29. These two dates separate a year into two periods lasting 105 and 260 days, the latter of which coincides perfectly with the ritual calendar. August 12 was also important as the legendary day of the beginning of time, presumably in 3114 BC for the Maya. The Pleiades, well recorded as an important constellation in Mesoamerica, was also centrally related to the city's east-west axis, as this important star cluster set on the same spot on the western horizon at Teotihuacan around May 18, when the Sun passes the zenith at noon (Aveni 1980; Millon 1981, 1993: 35). These data of architectural orientations strongly demonstrate that the urban plan was shaped since its inception explicitly to express cosmogenic time and space conceptualized by the city's leaders; the data also support the TMU study, which independently indicates that cosmogenic meanings were integrated into built space. The urban plan of Teotihuacan was apparently created intentionally to materialize a worldview conspicuously through quantification of time and space under the logic set by celestial movements.

One of the fundamental findings of the TMU study is that the 260-day ritual calendar was centrally incorporated into the city layout. The distance corresponding to 260 TMU (the original size of the Sun Pyramid) was evidently the basic unit for the subdivision of urban space in both its north-south and east-west directions. The Sun Pyramid and perhaps the Great Compound (interior plaza) located in front of the Citadel (Figure 11.3) obviously represented this ritual calendar. The TMU study also suggested that the size of two major monuments of the city, the Sun Pyramid (260 days) and Building 4 at the Moon Pyramid (105 days), complementarily represented a solar cycle (365 days).

It is most likely that the unit 260 was also applied to subdivide the core area in a north-south direction at an early time of urban planning. The sacred space delimited by the Moon Pyramid (Building 4) and the Citadel was set corresponding to 10 times the 260-day calendar in a north-south direction. Further, the distance between the central north-south axis and the east limit of two large monumental complexes coincides with 520-day cycles. The TMU study suggested that the 260-day cycle was fundamentally created in relation to the solar eclipse cycle (260 x 2 = 173.31 x 3).

The study also suggests that the Long Count Calendar system in the Maya area was functioning at Teotihuacan. If the TMU correspondence to our metric system is correct, the distance between the Sun Pyramid and the Citadel (1,440 TMU = 20 x 18 x 4) can hardly be considered accidental. It may be worth remembering that 8 times the solar calendar cycle (4 x 2), namely, one round trip between the monuments, formed a larger period in combination with five Venus cycles. Although 365 days, instead of 360 days, is used in this instance, identification of possible meanings associated with these monuments (the Sun Pyramid possibly with the Sun, and the Citadel with Venus) would stimulate further analysis and interpretation.

A corresponding range of motivations of Teotihuacanos to materialize their unique cosmogram can be elucidated by analyzing different kinds of archaeological materials, particularly ritual objects set in mortuary contexts like those we found at the Feathered Serpent Pyramid and the Moon Pyramid. We demonstrated that at the Feathered Serpent Pyramid more than 137 individuals were sacrificed and buried with exceptionally rich offerings in dedication to its construction, and that the spatial distribution of interments of the individuals in groups of 4, 8, 9, 18, and 20 unquestionably demonstrates the Teotihuacanos' profound concerns regarding calendrical and/or cosmological meanings (López et al. 1991; Sugiyama 2005).

Our recent exploration of sacrificial burials at the Moon Pyramid and subsequent analyses of mortuary contexts and associated material studies also indicate that sacrificial rituals at the monuments were essentially related to a cosmogram of calendrical and astronomical significance (Sugiyama and López 2007). Our ongoing analyses of the symbolism associated with monumental architecture, sculptures, burials, and other kinds of symbolic materials should enhance our understanding of an ancient cognitive system of time and space, and related social institutions. Sacred rulership was apparently responsible for the meaningful manipulation of monumental constructions and the control of people who built them; rulers thus proclaimed their earthly political power to create, maintain, and modify cosmograms materialised in the city layout, beginning during the inception of Teotihuacan as a great city.

ACKNOWLEDGEMENTS

I am very thankful to Colin Renfrew and Iain Morley of the McDonald Institute, Cambridge University, for the invitation to the Measuring the World and Beyond symposium and for their invaluable comments, encouragement, and patience. Discussions with the participants, particularly Anthony F. Aveni, John Justeson, and John E. Clark, were very helpful in enhancing the chapter presented here. The Moon Pyramid Project, under the auspices of which the mapping survey was carried out taking measurements for this chapter, was supported by the Japan Society for the Promotion of Science, the National Science Foundation, National Geographic Society, and Arizona State University funding, among others, and authorized by the National Committee of Archaeology in Mexico (Consejo de Arqueología). Maps I used for this study were elaborated by the Moon Pyramid Project members, including Hironori Fukuhara, Ivan Hernandez I., Shigeru Kabata, Yuko Koga, Hironori Kotegawa, Hirotsugu Makimura, Tatsuya Murakami, Erick Valle P., and Osamu Yoshida. I must express my gratitude to Peter Jiménez of INAH, who encouraged me to pursue the issue with invaluable suggestions. I am also indebted to David Carballo and Nawa Sugiyama for their English corrections and comments on this chapter, and to Hironori Fukuhara for preparing the figures and tables used in this chapter.

NOTE

1. Millon (1973) and his associates proposed that there were East and West Avenues, crossing the Avenue of the Dead at the area of the Citadel and the Great Compound. However, archaeological data seem to deemphasize, if not disprove, the Avenues hypothesized as the main east-west axis.

REFERENCES

Almaráz, R. 1865 Apuntes sobre las pirámides de San Juan. In *Memoria de los trabajos ejecutados por la comision científica de Pachuca en el año de 1864*, pp. 349–358. Ministerio de Fomento, México, D.F.

Aveni, A. F. 1980 *Skywatchers of Ancient Mexico*. University of Texas Press, Austin and London.

Batres, L. 1906 *Teotihuacán ó la Ciudad Sagrada de los Tolteca*. Imprenta de Hull, México, D.F.

Cabrera C., R., I. Rodríguez G., and N. Morelos G. 1982a *Teotihuacan 80–82: Primeros resultados*. Instituto Nacional de Antropología e Historia, México, D.F.

Cabrera C., R., I. Rodríguez G., and N. Morelos G. 1982b *Memoria del Proyecto Arqueológico Teotihuacán 80–82, Vol. 1*. Instituto Nacional de Antropología e Historia, México, D.F.

Cabrera C., R., I. Rodríguez G., and N. Morelos G. 1991 *Teotihuacan 1980–1982: Nuevas interpretaciones*. Instituto Nacional de Antropología e Historia, México, D.F.

Cabrera C., R., S. Sugiyama, and G. L. Cowgill 1991 The Temple of Quetzalcoatl Project at Teotihuacan: A Preliminary Report. *Ancient Mesoamerica* 2 (1): 77–92.

Caso, A. 1928 Las medidas del calendario azteca. *Revista Mexicana de Estudios Historicos*, Tomo II, Num. 4, pp. 128–137, México, D.F.

Caso, A. 1937 ¿Tenían los teotihuacanos conocimiento del tonalpohualli? *El México Antiguo* IV: 131–143.

Castillo F., V. M. 1972 Unidades nahuas de medida. *Estudios de Cultura Náhuatl* 10: 195–223.

Closs, M. P. 1983 Cognitive Aspects of Ancient Maya Eclipse Theory. In *World Archaeoastronomy*, ed. A. F. Aveni, pp. 389–415. Cambridge University Press, Cambridge.

Codex Chimalpopoca. 1992 *History and Mythology of the Aztec: Codex Chimalpopoca*, trans. J. Bierhorst. University of Arizona Press, Tucson.

Codex Fejérváry Mayer. 1971 *City of Liverpool Museums*. Akademische Druck-U. Verlagsanstalt, Graz.

Coe, M. D. 1981 Religion and the Rise of Mesoamerican States. In *The Transition to Statehood in the New World*, eds. G. D. Jones and R. R. Kautz, pp. 157–171. Cambridge University Press, Cambridge.

Coe, M. D. 1994 *Mexico from the Olmecs to the Aztecs*. Thames and Hudson, New York.

Coggins, C. 1993 The Age of Teotihuacan and Its Mission Abroad. In *Teotihuacan: Art from the City of the Gods*, eds. K. Berrin and E. Pasztory, pp. 140–155. Thames and Hudson and the Fine Arts Museums of San Francisco, New York.

Cowgill, G. L. 1992 Toward a Political History of Teotihuacan. In *Ideology and Pre-Columbian Civilizations*, eds. A. A. Demarest and G. W. Conrad, pp. 87–114. School of American Research Press, Santa Fe.

Cowgill, G. L. 1996 Discussion. *Ancient Mesoamerica* 7 (2): 325–331.

Dow, J. W. 1967 Astronomical Orientations at Teotihuacan, a Case Study in Astro-Archaeology. *American Antiquity* 32: 326–334.

Drewitt, R. B. 1967 Planeación en la Antigua Ciudad de Teotihuacan. In *Teotihuacan, Onceava Mesa Redonda*, pp. 79–94. Sociedad Mexicana de Antropología, México, D.F.

Drewitt, R. B. 1977a Precolumbian Mesoamerican Measurement Systems: Unit Standards for Length. Paper presented at the 76th Annual Meeting of the American Anthropological Association, Houston.

Drewitt, R. B. 1977b A Solar Orientation Framework for Teotihuacan. Paper presented at the XV Mesa Redonda of the Sociedad Mexicana de Antropología, Guanajuato.

Drewitt, R. B. 1987 Measurement Units and Building Axes at Teotihuacan. In *Teotihuacan: Nuevos Datos, Nuevas Síntesis, Nuevos Problemas*, eds. E. McClung de Tapia and E. C. Rattray, pp. 389–398. Universidad Nacional Autónoma de México, México, D.F.

Drucker, R. D. 1977 A Solar Orientation Framework for Teotihuacan. Paper presented at the XV Mesa Redonda of the Sociedad Mexicana de Antropología, Guanajuato.

Gamio, M. 1922 *La población del Valle de Teotihuacán*. 3 vols. Secretaria de Agricultura y Fomento, México, D.F. (Republished in 1979. 5 vols. Instituto Nacional Indigenista, México, D.F.)

Gamio, M. 1983 Ancient Maya Ethnoastronomy: An Overview of Hieroglyphic Sources. In *World Archaeoastronomy*, ed. A. F. Aveni, pp. 76–129. Cambridge University Press, Cambridge.

Justeson, J. S. 1989 Ancient Maya Ethnoastronomy: An Overview of Hieroglyphic Sources. In *World Archaeoastronomy*, ed. A. F. Aveni, pp. 76–129. Cambridge University Press, Cambridge.

Kubler, G. 1962 *The Shape of Time*. Yale University Press, New Haven.

León-Portilla, M. 1963 *Aztec Thought and Culture: A Study of the Ancient Nahuatl Mind*. University of Oklahoma Press, Norman.

López A., A., L. López L., and S. Sugiyama. 1991 The Temple of Quetzalcoatl at Teotihuacan: Its Possible Ideological Significance. *Ancient Mesoamerica* **2** (1): 93–106.

Malmstrom, V. H. 1978 A Reconstruction of the Chronology of Mesoamerican Calendrical Systems. *Journal of the History of Astronomy* **9** (2) (25): 105–116.

Matos M., E. 1995 *La Pirámide del Sol, Teotihuacan*. Artes de México, Instituto Cultural Domecq, A.C., México, D.F.

Millon, R. 1973 *Urbanization at Teotihuacan, Mexico. Vol. 1: The Teotihuacan Map. Part One: Text*. University of Texas Press, Austin.

Millon, R. 1981 Teotihuacan: City, State, and Civilization. In *Supplement to the Handbook of Middle American Indians. Vol. 1: Archaeology*, eds. V. Bricker and J. Sabloff, pp. 198–243. University of Texas Press, Austin.

Millon, R. 1988 The Last Years of Teotihuacan Dominance. In *The Collapse of Ancient States and Civilizations*, eds. N. Yoffee and G. Cowgill, pp. 102–164. University of Arizona Press, Tucson.

Millon, R. 1993 The Place Where Time Began. In *Teotihuacan: Art from the City of the Gods*, eds. K Berrin and E. Pasztory, pp. 17–43. Thames and Hudson, The Fine Arts Museums of San Francisco, San Francisco.

Millon, R., B. Drewitt and A. A. Bennyhoff. 1965 The Pyramid of the Sun at Teotihuacán: 1959 Investigationes. In *Transactions of the American Philosophical Society*, New series, vol. 55, part 6. American Philosophical Society, Philadelphia.

Millon, R., B. Drewitt, and G. L. Cowgill. 1973 *Urbanization at Teotihuacan, Mexico. Vol. 1: The Teotihuacan Map. Part Two: Maps*. University of Texas Press, Austin.

Múnera B., L. C. 1985 Un taller de cerámica ritual en la Ciudadela, Teotihuacan. B.S. thesis, the Escuela Nacional de Antropología e Historia, México, D.F.

Noguera, E. 1935 Antecedents y relaciones de la cultura teotihuacana. In *El México Antiguo*, tomo III, nums. 5/8, abril, pp. 3–89. México, D. F.

Pérez, J. R. 1935 Exploracion del tunel de la Piramide del Sol. In *El México Antiguo*, tomo III, nums. 5/8, abril, pp. 91–95. México, D.F.

Rattray, E. C. 2001 *Teotihuacan: Ceramics, Chronology and Cultural Trends*. University of Pittsburgh and Instituto Nacional de Antropología e Historia, México, D.F.

Rodríguez G., I. 1982 Frente 2. In *Memoria del Proyecto Arqueológico Teotihuacan 80–82*, eds. R. Cabrera C., I. Rodríguez G., and N. Morelos. G., pp. 55–73. Instituto Nacional de Antropología e Historia, México, D.F.

Sahagún, Fernando B. 1950–1982 *Florentine Codex: General History of the Things of New Spain*, trans. A. J. O. Anderson and C. E. Dibble. School of American Research and the University of Utah, Santa Fe.

Salazar O., Ponciano. 1970 *Proyecto Teotihuacan: Temporadas IV y V, Años 1962–1964, Zona de Trabajo Numero I: Plaza de la Luna*. Unpublished manuscript in Archive of Instituto Nacional de Antropología e Historia, México, D.F.

Schele, L. and D. Freidel. 1990 *A Forest of Kings: The Untold Story of the Ancient Maya*. William Morrow, New York.

Schele, L. and M. E. Miller. 1986 *The Blood of Kings: Dynasty and Ritual in Maya Art*. G. Braziller, New York.

Séjourné, L. 1966 *Arquitectura y Pintura en Teotihuacan*. Siglo Veintiuno, México, D.F.

Sugiyama, S. 1982 Los trabajos efectuados por la Sección de Topografía. In *Memoria del Proyecto Arqueológico Teotihuacán 80–82*, eds. R. Cabrera C., I. Rodríguez G., and N. Morelos G., vol. 1, pp. 467–475. Instituto Nacional de Antropología e Historia, México, D.F.

Sugiyama, S. 1983 Estudio preliminar sobre el sistema de medida teotihuacana. Paper presented at the Round Table of Sociedad Mexicana de Antropología, Taxco.

Sugiyama, S. 1993 Worldview Materialized in Teotihuacan, Mexico. *Latin American Antiquity* **4** (2): 103–129.

Sugiyama, S. 1998 Termination Programs and Prehispanic Looting at the Feathered Serpent Pyramid in Teotihuacan, Mexico. In *The Sowing and the Dawning: Termination, Dedication, and Transformation in the Archaeological and Ethnographic Record of Mesoamerica*, ed. S. Mock. University of New Mexico Press, Albuquerque.

Sugiyama, S. 2003 Governance and Polity at Classic Teotihuacan. In *Mesoamerican Archaeology: Theory and Practice*. Blackwell Studies in Global Archaeology, eds. J. Hendon and R. Joyce, pp. 97–123. Blackwell, Oxford.

Sugiyama, S. 2004 *Voyage to the Center of the Moon Pyramid: Recent Discoveries in Teotihuacan*. Arizona State University and INAH, México, D.F.

Sugiyama, S. 2005 *Human Sacrifice, Militarism, and Rulership: Materialization of State Ideology at the Feathered Serpent Pyramid, Teotihuacan.* Cambridge University Press, Cambridge.

Sugiyama, S. and R. Cabrera C. 2003 Hallazgos recientes en la Pirámide de la Luna. *Arqueología Mexicana* **XI** (64): 42–49.

Sugiyama, S. and R. Cabrera C. 2007 The Moon Pyramid Project and the Teotihuacan State Polity: A Brief Summary of the 1998–2004 Excavations. *Ancient Mesoamerica* **18**: 109–125.

Sugiyama, S. and L. López L. eds. 2006 *Sacrificios de consagración en la Pirámide de la Luna.* CONACULTA-INAH/ Arizona State University, México, D.F.

Sugiyama, S. and L. López L. 2007 Dedicatory Burial/ Offering Complexes at the Moon Pyramid, Teotihuacan: A Preliminary Report of 1998–2004 Explorations. *Ancient Mesoamerica* **18**: 127–146.

Tobriner, S. 1972 The Fertile Mountain: An Investigation of Cerro Gordo's Importance to the Town Plan and Iconography of Teotihuacan. In *Teotihuacan: XI Mesa Redonda*, pp. 103–116. Sociedad Mexicana de Antropología, México, D.F.

12

Aztec dimensions of holiness

John E. Clark

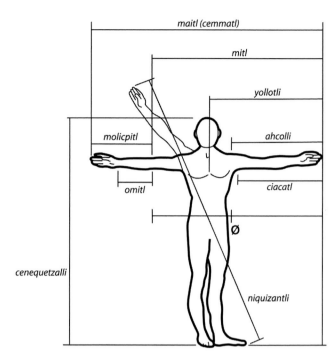

Figure 12.1. Aztec units of measure and their body referents (redrawn with significant modifications from Castillo 1972:219, fig. 8).

In this chapter I investigate the possibility that the Aztecs constructed their ritual precinct at Tenochtitlan along the dimensions of sacred time. Saburo Sugiyama makes this point for Teotihuacan (1993; 2005; this volume), and I have made similar claims for even earlier centers (Clark 2001; 2004a, b). These proposals for Mesoamerican centers have relied on analyses of archaeological data to infer ancient units of measure and their numerical modularities. I reverse the procedure here and start with verified Aztec units of measurement and deploy them to propose numerical values for the dimensions of palaces, temples, and plazas. Discussion is organized in three parts. I first summarize the Aztec system of linear measurements. Next follows my evaluation of the dimensions of two palaces known from early historic records. Finally, I analyze the most current information for the ceremonial precinct of Tenochtitlan (now downtown Mexico City) in light of different native units of measure. These two applications of native measures to public architecture support the premise that the Aztecs, as did earlier Mesoamericans, built their sacred center to accord with the dimensions of sacred time.

Aztec linear units and their metric values

Aztec linear measures were calibrated to the human body, and in ways similar to the Spanish system to which it was later correlated. Both the Spanish and the Aztecs emphasized various arm measures, particularly the *braza*. A braza was two *varas* long. The Aztec equivalents to the Spanish braza and vara were the *maitl* ('hand', the measure between the outstretched hands) and *yollotli* ('heart', the measure from the center of the chest to an outstretched hand). The principal Aztec measures and their somatic referents are shown in Figure 12.1. Signs known for different units are illustrated in Figure 12.2. Most of these units have long been appreciated. One of the better descriptions of Aztec mensuration is still Daniel Brinton's (1885) exposition of Mesoamerican units of measure. Missing in his study, however, is an argument for the metric values of these units. The historic sources for Mexico and Spain allow us to relate the Aztec system to the 15th-century Castillian system, and hence to modern systems of measurement (see Clark 2008 for detailed discussion). The metric values listed in Table 12.1 are based on the reported correspondence of the Aztec *yollotli* to the Castillian vara of 83.59 cm (see Castillo 1972; Clark 2008).

Aztec mensuration has been a research concern to historians and archaeologists interested in subsistence economy. Early documents and maps describe the size and quality of agricultural fields and list field dimensions in Aztec units. To make use of these sources, one needs to know the metric values (at least approximately) of these units for both cultures (see Harvey and Williams 1980). Different correlation values have been proposed.

The clear starting point for correlating Aztec and Spanish linear units was provided by the native historian Don Fernando de Alva Ixtlilxóchitl in his description of the immense palace complex built by his fifth great-grandfather, Nezahuacóyotl, king of Texcoco (Ixtlilxóchitl 1975:9).

"These houses were in length from east to west four hundred and eleven and a half [native] measures,

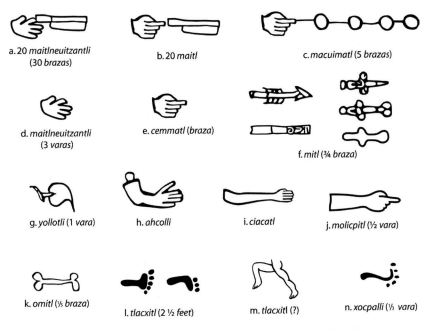

a. 20 *maitlneuitzantli* (30 *brazas*)

b. 20 *maitl*

c. *macuimatl* (5 *brazas*)

d. *maitlneuitzantli* (3 *varas*)

e. *cemmatl* (*braza*)

f. *mitl* (¾ *braza*)

g. *yollotli* (1 *vara*)

h. *ahcolli*

i. *ciacatl*

j. *molicpitl* (½ *vara*)

k. *omitl* (⅙ *braza*)

l. *tlacxitl* (2 ½ feet)

m. *tlacxitl* (?)

n. *xocpalli* (⅓ *vara*)

Figure 12.2. Symbols of Aztec units of measure (from Clark 2008:fig. 3).

Table 12.1. *Aztec linear measures and their metric values*

Unit	Description*	Length
matlacicxitla	*maltacicxitlatamachiualoni* 'measure of 10 feet' (S:258)	2.786 m
maitlneuitzantli	3 varas	2.508 m
tlalquahuitl	'wooden measuring rod' (S:604), 3 varas	2.508 m
niquizantli	vertical braza, 2.5 varas	2.090 m
maitl	'hand' (S:250); horizontal braza, 2 varas	1.672 m
cenequeztzalli	'stature' (S:83), height of a man	1.60 m
mitl	'arrow, dart' (S:14, 80; M:57), 1.5 varas	1.254 m
yollotli	'heart' (S:199), 1 vara	83.59 cm
ahcolli	'shoulder' (S:14)	77.5 cm
ciacatl	'armpit' (S:109)	72.0 cm
tlacxitl	'step' (C:200, 201)	69.65 cm
molicpitl	'elbow' (S:285), ½ vara	41.80 cm
matzotzopaztli	'forearm' (S:263)	38.6 cm
omitl	'bone' (S:357)	33.44 cm
xocpalli	'foot print' (S:777), *tlacxitamachihualoni*, foot length (S:583)	27.86 cm
macpalli	'palm of the hand' (M:51), cuarta, 1/4 vara	20.90 cm
Cenmiztitl	'jeme' (C:220; M:118)	18.0 cm
centlacol icxitl	'half a foot' (S:85)	13.93 cm
mapilli	'finger of the hand' (M:37; S:255)	1.74 cm

*Sources: C (Castillo 1972), M (Molina 1977), S (Siméon 1977).

which reduced to our [Spanish] measures make twelve hundred and thirty-four and a half yards (*varas*), and in breadth from north to south three hundred and twenty-six measures, which are nine hundred and seventy-eight yards" (Brinton 1885:203, citing Lord Kingsborough; see Chavero 1952, vol. 2, chapter 36; Ixtlilxóchitl 1975:II:93; Castillo 1972:213; Harvey and Williams 1980:note 15; Williams and Harvey 1997:27)

Each Aztec unit was three Spanish varas in length. Other sources indicate that the varas were the Castillian vara (a.k.a. the vara of Burgos) 83.5905 cm long (Borah and Cook 1958:11; Carrera Stampa 1949:10–11; Castillo 1972; Clavijero 1976:161; Galván Rivera 1883:157; Guillemin-Tarayre 1919:502–03; Hamilton 1965:169; Orozco y Berra 1880), so the Aztec unit employed in building Nezahuacóyotl's palace complex was 2.5077 m long. By this correlation, the palace complex measured 1,031.92 m by 817.51 m and spread over 84.36 ha.

Dimensions of two Aztec palaces

My exploration of Aztec architecture starts with Nezahuacóyotl's palace at Texcoco. The dimensions of this compound listed in native counts are 411.5 units east to west, and 326 units north to south. As commented on by Brinton (1885:205), these numbers 'are strikingly irregular' and violate basic assumptions of inductive metrology as advocated by W. M. Flinders Petrie (1877; 1879) and others. The palace dimensions are not listed in whole numbers, round numbers, or simple numbers. Other assumptions of inductive metrology are also violated. Aztec house and field dimensions in early colonial documents are compound numbers consisting of the distance in standard units of measure, plus the fractional remainder of the last, incomplete measure listed in different units (see Matías 1984; 1989). One must understand the relationships among different kinds of units to work the system because fractions are expressed as whole numbers of a different unit (Table 12.1). The unit used as the 'standard' also varied according to the items described, with longer units (*tlalquahuitl*) favored for large plots of land and smaller ones (*maitl*) for houses. Even smaller units would be appropriate for measuring cloth and other items (see Matías 1984). Distances on

Table 12.2. *Dimensions of Nezahualcoyotl's Palace in different Aztec measures*

Units	Length	Width	Diagonal	Perimeter
meters	1,031.92	817.51	1,316.5	3,698.9
tlalquahuitl (2.508 m), 3 vara	411.5	326	525	1,475
mitl (1.254 m), ½ tlalquahuitl	823	652	1050	2,950
yollotli (83.95 cm), 1 vara; ½ maitl	1,234.5	978.1	1574.9	4,425
maitl (1.672 m), 2 vara	617.2	488.9	787.4	2,212.3
niquizantli (2.090 m), 2.5 vara	493.7	391.2	629.9	1,769.8

early land maps are never shown by subtracting a fractional unit from a total length (see Harvey and Williams 1980; Williams and Harvey 1997).

It will be instructive to examine Nezahuacóyotl's palace for its spatial patterning and distance counts before analyzing a second Texcoco palace and the Sacred Precinct at the Aztec capital, Tenochtitlan. Nezahuacóyotl's palace is the only complex for which precise information of the number of native units and their Spanish equivalents is explicit. The following analyses of his palace, and the other compounds, take account of two caveats. First, Aztec mensuration was and is capable of fine measurements down to fractions of the width of a fingernail (see Wiercinski 1980). It was as precise as its Spanish counterpart at the time and was used with greater precision in measuring land (Harvey and Williams 1980:504). Aztec units could be used to describe the dimensions of objects or to plan these objects in the first place.

Plans made on paper could be transferred to the ground, and vice versa. Whether or not the distances recorded for Nezahuacóyotl's palace correspond to the original, intended dimensions of its builders or are later descriptions of them by others will never be clear. The second caution is that in evaluating archaeological exercises of inductive metrology, such as for Teotihuacan (Sugiyama, this volume), we should approach Aztec archaeology in similar ways and with similar questions. Some key dimensions of buildings are not immediately obvious, such as the diagonals of quadrangles, diameters of round buildings, and the perimeters of these buildings.

Returning to Nezahuacóyotl's palace, I presume the description is accurate but cannot presume that the units recorded were necessarily the ones used in planning and constructing the complex. The fact that the dimensions are given in the same measurement unit is a good sign that it may be both. I do not detect any obvious calendar cycles in these dimensions. If the compound was rectangular, it would have had a diagonal of 525 units and a perimeter of 1,475 units. The same dimensions expressed in other Aztec linear units would give the counts listed in Table 12.2. None of these numbers appears ritually

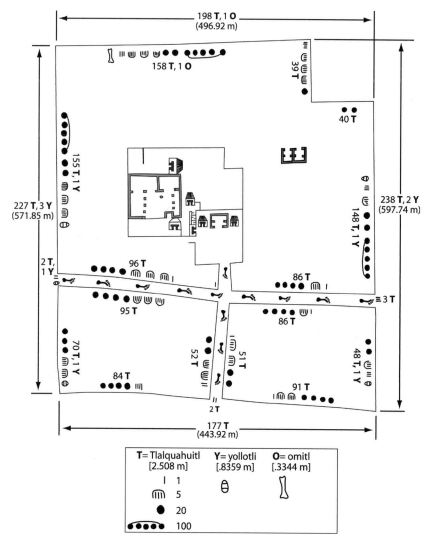

Figure 12.3. The Oztoticpac palace and its dimensions (redrawn from Cline 1966:80, fig. 4).

significant in the ways described by Sugiyama (this volume) for Teotihuacan. His vara or *yollotli* measure of 83 cm would provide a multiple of 3 for the dimensions given by Ixtlilxóchitl for Nezahuacóyotl's palace.

Conversion into *maitl* units would also be a simple operation. The *niquizantli* measure provides more interesting numbers because it is a more complex fraction of the standard *tlalquahuitl* unit. An important question is how archaeologists would interpret these dimensions were they to recover them through excavation. The extrapolated diagonal of the palace compound in *tlalquahuitl* (assuming it was rectangular) is just slightly longer than 2 x 260 units (525 instead of 520). The perimeter is 4 times 368.8, a credible solar year count. The estimated perimeter distance for the original measures in *niquizantli* units of 2.09 m gives a perimeter of 1,769.8 units, or 3 x 590 – a close approximation of the average Venus count (584). The numbers for the *mitl* units are of special interest because the original description implies this dimension with its half *tlalquahuitl* count (i.e., 411.5). The diagonal of the compound in *mitl* units is 1,050, very close to 4 x 260 (1,040), with 260 being the number of days in the ritual calendar (see Aveni 2001 for descriptions of Mesoamerican timekeeping and calendars). The palace dimensions are within measurement error (both ancient and modern) of these special numbers, so a critical question for future studies should be the acceptable degree of error and its effect on retrieving correct ancient dimensions and counts (see Petrie 1887).

None of these measures is compelling evidence that Nezahuacóyotl's palace compound was built to calendar counts or astronomical cycles. Information is also lacking on the layout of his palace complex, so the question cannot be resolved with the extant data.

Much more information is available for the Oztoticpac palace compound built a century later in the same Texcoco kingdom (see Cline 1966). It consists of two native maps with the perimeter dimensions specified, including the width of the various roads. The maps list exactly the same dimensions and allow one to verify counts, proportions, and geometry. As shown in Figure 12.3, palace dimensions are listed in vigesimal notation, with the main unit understood rather than represented with a separate symbol. Each black circle equals 20 units, and each vertical bar equals 1 unit. Both are clustered in groups of 5 units. As with Nezahuacóyotl's palace, the main unit of Oztoticpac palace is presumed to be the 2.508-m-long *tlalquahuitl*. Fractional distances shorter than this are shown as hearts (*yollotli*) and bones (*omitl*). The footprints on the map represent paths of travel rather than measured

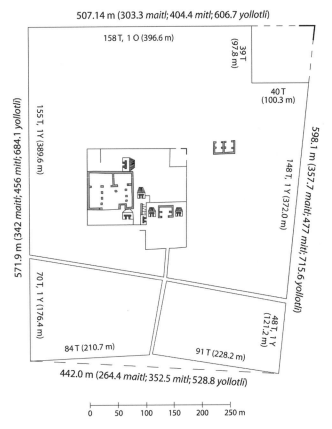

Figure 12.4. The Oztoticpac palace adjusted to scale.

paces. The palace plan shows the basic configuration of the compound and the lengths of its major segments. Figure 12.4 portrays the same compound adjusted according to the native measurements listed. For convenience, in making the scalar adjustments I started with a right angle in the northwest corner. I also projected the lines to show the missing northeast corner. Notice that the adjusted drawing is very close to the original proportions.[1] Figure 12.4 lists the dimensions of the sides of the compound in different Aztec units. No information is provided for the size of the palace buildings at the center of the compound, but analyses described later indicate they may be to scale.

None of the individual *tlalquahuitl* dimensions listed on the perimeter appears to be a ritually significant number in terms of Mesoamerican calendars. As with Nezahuacóyotl's palace, one needs to consider the same length intervals in light of other units of measurement. As viewed as a complete quadrangle (Figure 12.4), the perimeter of the compound is 2,119.2 m, or 845 *tlalquahuitl* or 2,535 *yollotli* (7 x 362) long. This last number is 15 *yollotli* too long for seven 360 counts and 20 *yollotli* too short for seven 365 counts. However, if one allows for a 2-*tlalquahuitl*-wide road around the compound (the width of the roads running through the compound), the perimeter would be 2,139.26 m, or 2,559.2 *yollotli* (7 x 365.6). This is an accurate estimate of the tropical year and lends credence to the observed possible solar count in the perimeter of Nezahuacóyotl's palace. The eastern edge of the Oztoticpac compound is 598.13 m long, or 715.6 *yollotli* (2 x 357.8). If one compensates for a surrounding road, this would be 603.1 m, or 721.6 *yollotli* (2 x 360.8). Solar counts appear to have been involved with the perimeter measures, and other spacing within the compound (see later discussion).

The same dimensional data for the Oztoticpac palace allow one to check the basic geometry and proportions of the compound. It was trapezoidal rather than rectangular. Supplying the missing northeast corner and bridging the inward converging edges of the southern end give the perimeter counts just mentioned. Two striking features are the unusual angles of the roads and the compound's tapered sides. The roads partition the compound asymmetrically. As illustrated in Figure 12.5, the three longest sides are divided into fourths, fifths, and sixths by the roads and their implied extensions. The roads also intersect the western and northern sides at the

golden ratio (phi = 1.618) – a venerable Mesoamerican practice evident at Teotihuacan, La Venta, and numerous other ceremonial centers (see Clark 2001; Martínez del Sobral 2000; Mora-Echeverría 1984). In sum, the listed dimensions and segmentation of the Oztoticpac palace compound exhibit special counts and proportions in overall configuration. These are repeated in the inner courtyard and its buildings. Such segmentation had to be planned and constructed. Extension of the sides of the inner court and main buildings (indicated with dashed lines) shows an intriguing series of vigesimal fractions for each side. Starting with the right side and proceeding counterclockwise, the compound boundaries are each divided into twentieths in a consecutive series: 7 + 13, 8 + 12, 9 + 11, and 10 + 10. Division of the right edge into 7/20 plus 13/20 is particularly interesting because the Mesoamerican divinatory calendar of 260 days is based on the permutation of 13 numbers and 20 named days, with the same combination of named number and named day occurring every 260 days. The compound displays a sophisticated series of overlapping partitions that would have required great planning. The fact that many segments also conform to special numbers only increases the level of difficulty involved in planning and building the compound.

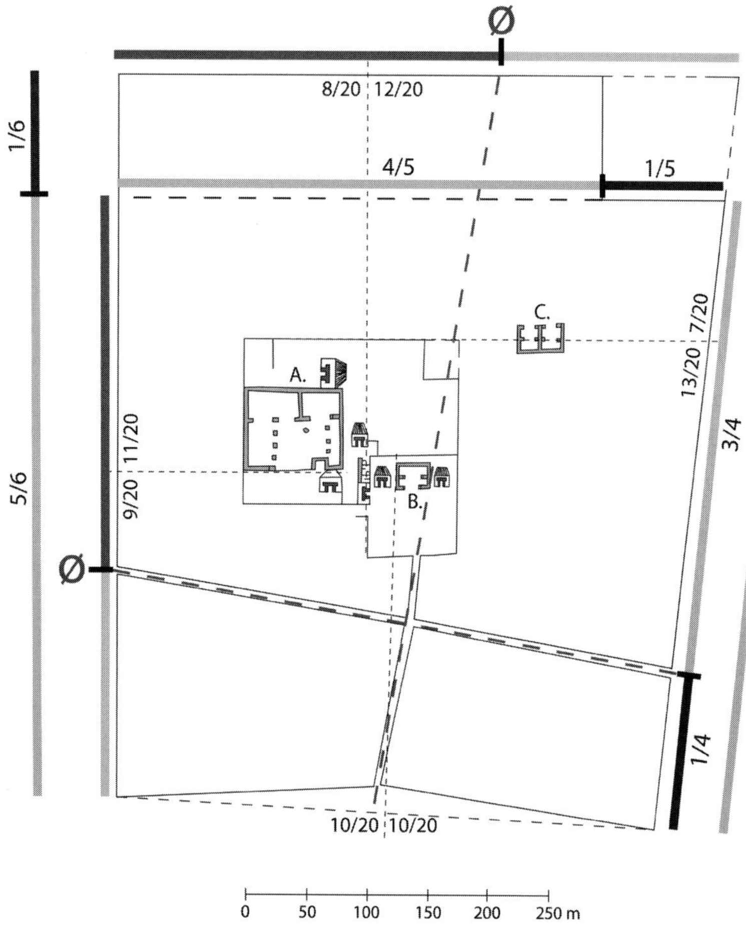

I first approached the Oztoticpac palace map with the presumption that it was not to scale, but after checking the dimensions of the innermost court and buildings, I believe it is accurate enough for detailed analysis. I calculated the metric scale for the map on the basis of the outer dimensions given in Figure 12.3 and used this scale to calculate the size of its other features. A simple check of the inner compound showed that it is within a hand span or two in each major dimension to the *yollotli* counts shown in Figure 12.6. These surprised me because the dimensions are in the same unit and close to round numbers, suggesting that the original drawing is precise. The same is true of the relationship of the compound perimeter to the inner court and palace. The results show multiple uses of solar (360, 365), lunar (354), Mercury (116), Venus (584), Saturn (378), Jupiter (399), and Mars (780) counts, as well as the ritual calendar count at various scales (130, 260, 520,

Figure 12.5. The general proportions of the Oztoticpac palace.

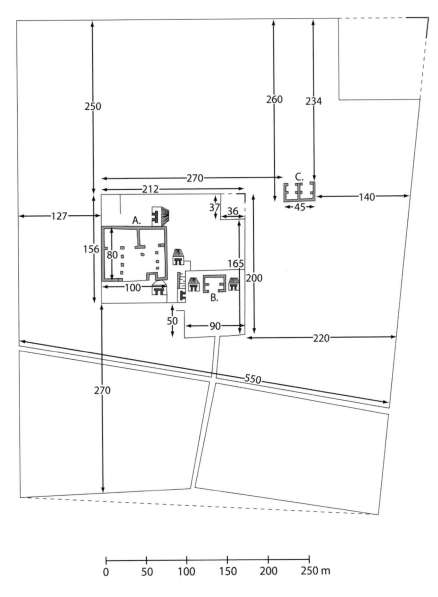

Figure 12.6. The Oztoticpac palace in *yollotli* units.

by random chance? Few or none. The elevated number of significant interval distances at different scales between significant points in the compound goes well beyond chance. The data demonstrate site planning according to special counts and distances. The lengths of many of the intervening spaces are prescribed by the listed dimensions on the map and set mathematically, such as the lengths of sides, diagonals, and perimeters. Others result from the intersections of various diagonals with the corners of major buildings, with the corners of the central courtyard, or with lines projected from the sides of buildings or the central compound. Not all points within the compound were equally valued. I only considered distances between points marked by significant architectural features. In the central compound I evaluate the locations of the three buildings shown as foundations (labeled as A, B, and C) rather than their associated buildings drawn in frontal view. Building A looks like the palace proper. Buildings B and C appear to be temples that face opposite directions; cardinal directions are not specified on the map.[2] One caution for contemplating these results is to remember that the dimensions of the buildings of the inner court are only recorded on the original map artistically and not with listed dimensions. As apparent in Figure 12.3, more care was taken in drawing the inner courtyard and its buildings than with the outer perimeter and its roads. With these reservations, my analysis of the Oztoticpac map shows evidence of planning, geometric proportions, and the use of special distance counts in the manner described by Sugiyama (this volume) for earlier Teotihuacan. The most significant calendar dimensions relate to the spacing of buildings within the compound rather than the buildings themselves. The spacing is not random.

These spatial analyses are more easily illustrated than described. I approached the question of architectural planning from two different directions. The first was to calculate the distances between all points I thought significant and to convert these metric values into Aztec units at various scales to see whether they conformed to special counts (Figure 12.6). I did this exploratory

780). Many other counts are also attested. Both the inner and greater palace compounds lack an upper right corner about 40 units square – but in different Aztec units. These squares are fractal. Calendrical and ritual counts are also represented at different scales, meaning different measurement units. The calendrical counts linking various features of this compound are redundant, impressive, and significant. A few illustrative examples will suffice to show how different 'counted' dimensions link together significant features.

One possible objection to the exploratory analysis to follow is that there are enough buildings and corners in the palace compound that one is bound to discover some line segments of a desired length that will connect some of them. How many connection lines of 'calendrical' length between significant points should one expect work by hand with a simple compass, ruler, and calculator. In a second round, I started with hypothetical Aztec units, calculated their length in meters, converted them to the scale of the map, and checked to see whether they were represented in the palace compound in a significant way. I began with the counts Sugiyama describes for Teotihuacan (i.e., 260, 360, 365, 520, and 584). Only later did I check for other planetary cycles and their counts in the layout of the Oztoticpac palace. I obtained the numbers for the synodic periods of planets from Anthony F. Aveni's (2001:87) work on ancient Mesoamerican astronomy. These exercises were exploratory and not precise. The final numerical precision shown in the following illustrations was calculated with the aid of a computer drawing program.

Figures 12.7 through 12.9 illustrate significant dimensions for different temporal cycles in vara or *yollotli* units. An unanticipated feature of the analysis is that the different solar, lunar, planetary, and 260 ritual counts converge on different features and buildings, thereby suggesting that the counts by which they were plotted and built were related to their purpose and meaning. A few comments on each illustration will demonstrate the promise of the Oztoticpac map and metrological analysis based on Aztec linear units of measure. Of the many correlations, I only illustrate solar and Jupiter counts here.

The lower boundary of the greater compound, as projected as a straight line, is 352.5 *mitl*, or just 1.88 m short of 354. Curiously, if one measures the actual perimeter of the indentation (see Figure 12.3), it measures 443.92 m (the 177 *tlalquahuitl* on the original map). This is precisely 354 *mitl*. The upper edge of the compound is 404.4 *mitl* long, a close approximation of the 399 Jupiter count, or to a 400 count in the vigesimal system. In this same series, the southern road dividing the compound is 367.3 *mitl* long, so moving from the lower to upper margin (likely west to east in real space), the three major segments in *mitl* units represent the Moon, Sun, and Jupiter – within a very small degree of measurement error. These distances are of special interest because they link Buildings A, B, and C to each other.

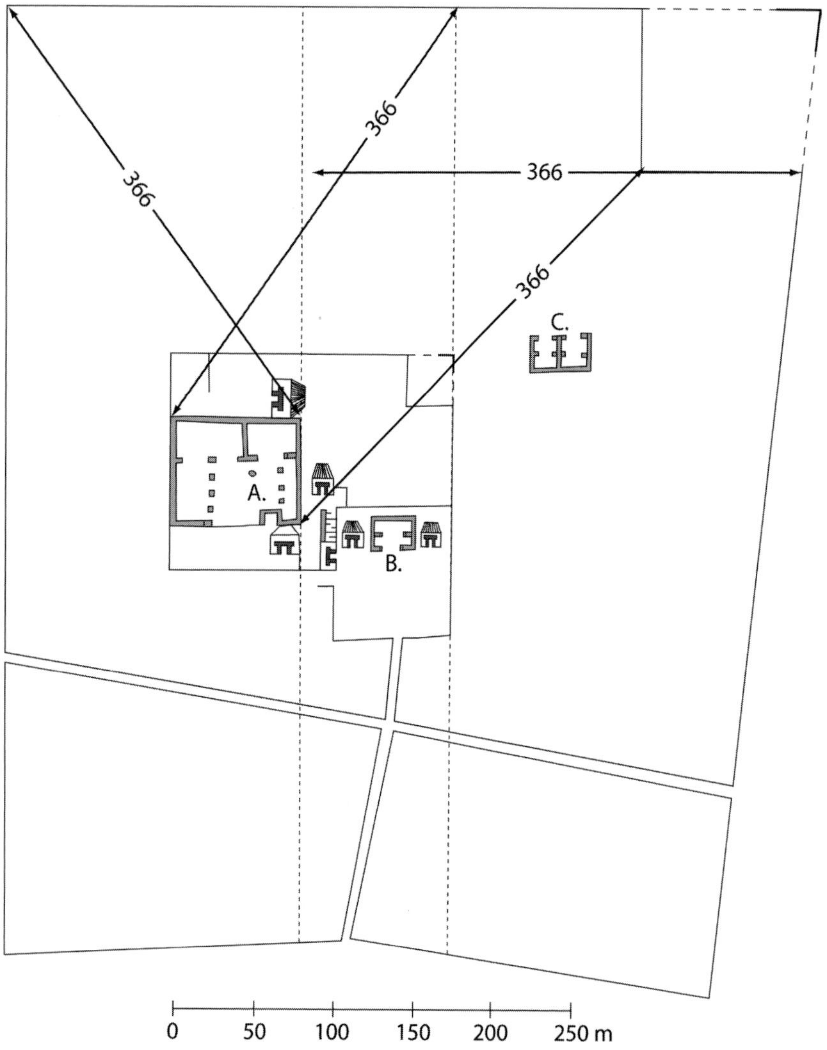

For solar counts, one must consider two different numbers, 360 and 365. Mesoamerican calendars counted 18 months of 20 days (360) with 5 evil days at the end of the year (365). Figure 12.7 illustrates the tropic solar count as 366 units instead of 365.25 because this is what the intervals indicate. The upper corners of Building A are defined from corners of the greater compound or significant points along its edges. Building A is connected to Buildings B and C by half solar counts, 183 *yollotli* (or 366 *molicpitl*). Other distance intervals define features of the right half of the central compound. This cannot be random coincidence. The placement of the palace is defined by solar counts from the compound edges, so I would not be surprised if solar symbolism and powers were associated with the palace and its occupants.

Figure 12.8 illustrates the 399-day Jupiter count. As noted, the upper edge of the greater compound is just slightly longer than a Jupiter count in *mitl* units. A Jupiter distance down from the upper edge of the compound defines the line

Figure 12.7. Tropical year counts (366) of the Oztoticpac palace in *yollotli* units.

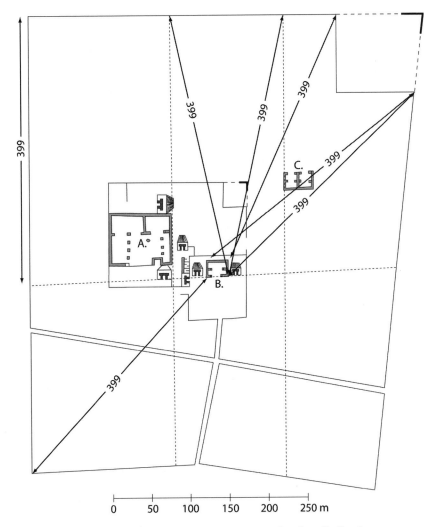

Figure 12.8. Jupiter counts (399) of the Oztoticpac palace in *yollotli* units.

Sun and then to the planets: Mercury, Jupiter, Saturn, Venus, and then back to Jupiter.

Spatial positioning of buildings provided similar associations, with solar and Saturn counts defining Building A. Venus and ritual calendar counts determined the location of Building C. I suspect the function and meaning of these buildings were signaled, at least in part, by these measured distances from the edges and corners of the compound. Documentation for the use of these buildings is not available, so the association of special counts with building function remains a tantalizing possibility that can only be checked archaeologically. A good place to start is the Sacred Precinct of Tenochtitlan.

Dimensions of Tenochtitlan's sacred precinct

Most Spanish eyewitness accounts of Aztec ceremonial architecture concern the main temple and its precinct at Tenochtitlan. The principal pyramid, known as the 'Templo Mayor', was centered in a large, rectangular precinct in the center of the city and was one of 78 reported structures. The Templo Mayor was the tallest and most impressive building. Twin staircases led up its western face to a pair of summit temples dedicated to the storm god Tlaloc (on the north) and the Aztec war god, Huitzilopochtli (south), as shown in the early representation reproduced in Figure 12.10. (Note that the upper margin of this map is east, as is probable for the Oztoticpac map.) This precinct was deliberately razed by the Spanish soon after their conquest of Mexico in 1521 (Clavijero 1976:159, note 19), so the only information we have on its buildings is from eyewitness accounts and modern archaeology.

Recent excavations at the Templo Mayor have recovered information for all but the first stage of its construction. These data are listed in Table 12.3 in meters and in Table 12.4 as *yollotli*, the measurement interval found to be so meaningful for the layout of Teotihuacan. Basal sizes for the different stages of the Templo Mayor were calculated from the map published by Eduardo Matos Moctezuma (1988:34). Outer dimensions of the Stage 7 structure are reported by Maria Luisa Franco (1990:15)

tangential to the lower edge of Building B. Remarkably, other Jupiter increments define and converge on all four corners of this same building but no other building. The dimensional data for the placement of Building B within the compound would suggest that this temple was associated with Jupiter. Alternatively, it could have been placed by *cenzontli* (400) counts.

Different counts provide major segmentation for the compound, as evident in Figure 12.9. Some of these lines are the length of the astronomical or planetary cycle indicated; others are defined by the distance from the upper edge of the compound (Mercury, Saturn, Jupiter) or from the right edge (Moon). The right edge of the greater compound is 360 *maitl* long. If this reconstruction of calendrical dimensions is correct and meaningful, movement within the greater compound mimicked movement in the heavens. Movement from right to left (south to north?) took a person from the Sun to the Moon sectors of the compound. From lower to upper margins (west to east?), one moved from Moon to the

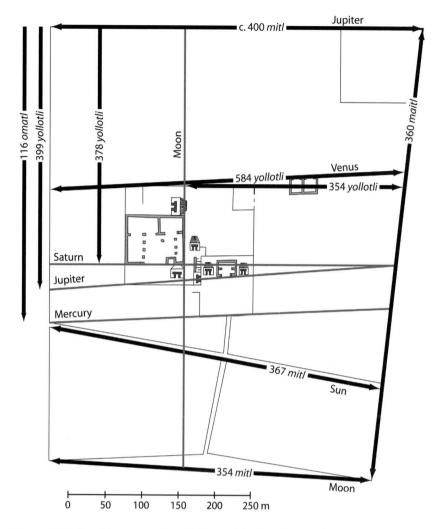

Figure 12.9. Possible astronomical divisions of the Oztoticpac palace.

as 76.6 m by 83.5 m.[3] These numbers should be considered only as approximate – pending more detailed mapping of the Sacred Precinct planned by Saburo Sugiyama and Leonardo López Luján (personal communication, 2007). Tables 12.3 and 12.4 include information on the perimeter of the base of each pyramid and its diagonal. Rather than deal with the complexities of projecting stairways, balustrades, and inset corners, I calculated the perimeter of simple rectangles represented by the maximal length and width of the base of each pyramid. Calculation of diagonals was done mathematically from these simplified rectangles.

What do the changing dimensions of the Templo Mayor through time indicate? As evident in Table 12.4, conversion of metric distances into *yollotli* units does not yield many ritual numbers. Given the imprecisions in the measurements from an archaeological map, the fractional remainders listed should not be taken seriously. One should look, instead, to see whether the reported numbers are within two to four counts of

the sorts of numbers reported for Teotihuacan. Few are, and there is no consistent pattern within the Templo Mayor sequence. This result should have been anticipated given the nature of the rebuilding program. A common Mesoamerican practice was to enlarge ceremonial structures by encasing them in bigger buildings, and this was especially true of the Templo Mayor. Each Aztec king since the founding of this pyramid added to it or rebuilt it (Matos Moctezuma 1988; Townsend 2000). The size of each expansion varied. The building changed shape through time, from a rectangle (long north-to-south), to a square, to a different rectangle (long west-to-east).

An obvious implication of the practice of rebuilding is that if original structures were built according to special counts, later expansions would have changed the counts. Sugiyama describes a clear case of this for the Pyramid of the Sun at Teotihuacan. The dimensions of the first stage of the Sun Pyramid conform to the 260 ritual count, and the later stage does not. In like manner, if the final stage of a building conforms to special numbers, its earlier and smaller stages cannot provide the same numbers unless rebuilding episodes doubled building size or changed the measurement unit, such as a shift from *yollotli* to *niquizantli* units. Not all stages of a building can be numerically significant in the same way if its size and shape change. Conservation of meaning requires some conservation of sign. Signs, symbols, and meaning can be maintained only if the building has stable points of reference unaffected by its horizontal and vertical expansion, such as central, axial points. If the numerical significances of the buildings in the Sacred Precinct were stable, this would mean they were built over marked points that were unaffected by changes in building sizes over time.

The length and width dimensions of the sequential temples listed in Table 12.4 do not follow a clear pattern. The most interesting numbers are for the perimeters of sequential buildings. These are close to the following counts: 130, 225, 250, 300, 360 or 365, and 380. The final perimeter is an unexpected number, and it is the building for which we have precise reported information. It is 100 by 91.5 *yollotli*. At first glance, only one

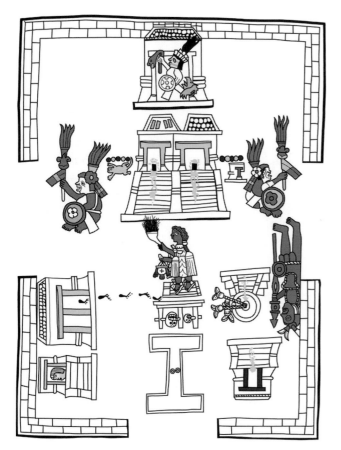

Figure 12.10. Drawing of the Sacred Precinct at Tenochtitlan showing the central position of the main pyramid and its twin temples (left to right) to Tlaloc and Huitzilopochtli (redrawn from Fray Bernardino de Sahagun's *Primeros Memoriales*, in Baird 1993:fig. 38).

of these numbers looks impressive. Multiplying both by 4, however, gives us 400 by 366 – the Aztec vigesimal number for completion (*cenzontli* = 400) and the tropical year count. These are the final stage basal dimensions reported in hand spans, or *macpalli* (1/4 *yollotli*) of 20.9 cm each, and they were surely intentional. With units so small, there would have been little room for error.

It is worth noticing that the archaeological dimensions listed for the final stage of the Templo Mayor do not accord with Spanish descriptions. The most accurate account is from the Anonymous Conqueror (for all these accounts, see Dahlgren et al. 1982). He reports the dimensions as 150 paces, or a little more, east-west, and 115–120 paces north-south. Converted to meters, this would be 104.5 m by 80.1 to 83.6 m, or 125 by 100 *yollotli* (refer to Table 12.1). It is not clear what he was measuring – the actual base of the pyramid or the base and the small altars around it.

Other descriptions (see Dahlgren et al. 1982) claim the temple was 125 varas square (104.5 m) (Tezozomoc), 360 feet square (100.3 m) (Torquemada), or 80 brazas (133.8 m) square (Ixtlilxóchitl).[4] All of these descriptions mention a dimension of nearly 100 m, so I suspect we may still be missing something archaeologically that was clear to Spanish observers.

To test the proposition that the Aztecs built calendar dimensions and special proportions into the Sacred Precinct, I rely on the most recent map of salvage operations there (Barrera Rivera 2006:fig 3). I only consider the final buildings rather than earlier stages. Figure 12.11 shows the likely location and size of the precinct walls. The surrounding precinct platform is just over 20 m wide. The roads entering the compound are described by the Anonymous Conqueror as '30 paces, or more' wide (Dahlgren et al. 1982:84), or just about 21 m. Fray Bernardino de Sahagun (Dibble and Anderson 1981:179) reports that the precinct was about 200 brazas square (334 m). Others report it as a crossbow shot across (Dahlgren et al. 1982:92). Neither description is sufficiently clear or precise for the current analysis.[5]

The data available indicate that the Sacred Precinct was smaller and more complicated than the Oztoticpac palace but shared its emphasis on calendrical and astronomical counts and proportions. Some of the special dimensions of the last stage of the Templo Mayor and Sacred Precinct are illustrated in Figure 12.11. Measurements are from building axes and edges to those of other buildings. These are only a few ritual counts among many. Ritual, calendrical, and astronomical counts are clearly present and significant. For example, the courtyard is 225 *maitl* east to west in outer dimension and is 260 *maitl* long, north to south. Just half this length, 260 *yollotli*, is the distance between the end of the central ballcourt and the eastern edge of the eastern platform. Some of the buildings have been identified and demonstrate some surprising regularities. The apex of the Sun Pyramid, for example, is precisely 365 *molicpitl* to the summit and

Table 12.3. *Dimensions of the different stages of the Templo Mayor in meters*

Stage	Length	Width	Stair width	Diagonal	Perimeter
2	37.71	16.16	32.08	41.02	107.73
3	54.16	36.93	41.04	67.10	187.56
4	59.75	45.00	56.06	74.80	209.50
5	63.94	63.29	–	89.96	254.44
6	73.34	78.02	–	107.07	302.7
7	76.6	83.5	–	113.3	320.2

Source: These dimensions were taken from a drawing of the superimposed construction phases of the Templo Mayor published by Matos Moctezuma (1988:67, fig. 34).

Table 12.4. *Dimensions of the Templo Mayor in yollotli (0.8359 m)*

Stage	Length	Width	Stair width	Diagonal	Perimeter
2	45.1	19.3	38.4	49.1	128.9
3	64.8	44.2	49.1	80.3	224.4
4	71.5	53.8	67.1	89.5	250.6
5	76.5	75.7	–	107.6	304.4
6	87.7	93.3	–	128.1	362.1
7	91.5	100.0	–	135.6	383.1

axial point of the Huitzilopochtli Pyramid – also a Sun temple. The spacing of the Pyramid of Quetzalcoatl, just north of the Sun Pyramid, is of special interest. A line bisecting the center of this pyramid connects the southwest corner of the greater compound to the point along the eastern platform defined by the golden ratio (Figure 12.11). This transect is 1,000 *molicpitl* (a.k.a. 500 *yollotli* or 250 *maitl*) long and is reminiscent of the 1,000 unit modules described by Sugiyama (1993; this volume) for Teotihuacan. The center of the pyramid divides this line at the Sacred Precinct into 416- and 584-*molicpitl* segments. The latter is the principal Venus cycle count. This is appropriate because the god Quetzalcoatl was associated with Venus as morning and evening star. The 416-*molicpitl* distance (a.k.a. 208 *yollotli*, or 104 *maitl*; 52 x 8) is clearly associated with the 260 count and the 52-year calendar round. The ballcourt is placed in the compound along the axis for the Temple of Huitzilopochtli, the Aztec war god and a Sun god. The ballcourt is placed according to ritual 260-day and Venus counts (584; 73 x 8), and this accords with the known Venus associations of the Mesoamerican ballgame. These preliminary results substantiate the pattern suspected for the Oztoticpac palace (see earlier discussion). Some buildings with special astronomical and calendrical associations appear to have been carefully placed in the compound according to the appropriate cyclical counts.

This is very clear in Figure 12.12, which shows four transects through a point on the center line and the top edge of the Templo Mayor that we can call the 'Venus' point. Lines from each of the compound's corners pass through this point and are of equal length, 584 *maitl* or brazas long (973.4 m). The transects from the eastern corners also intersect the north and south sides of the compound at a point 260 *yollotli* from the eastern side. Again, we see the association of Venus counts with 260 counts. The precision and associations could not have happened by chance.

At the bottom of the stairs on the same main axis of the Templo Mayor, just down from the Venus point, we find what could be called a 'Sun' point. As shown in Figure 12.13, numerous lines radiate out from this point and intersect edges of the compound and corners of buildings. The southern edge of the Sun Pyramid is 365 *molicpitl* units from the central axis of the Templo Mayor. Of special interest is the isoceles triangle, 365 *molicpitl* on its long sides, that connects the apex of the Sun Pyramid, the Sun point of the Templo Mayor, and the center of the major building east of the Sun Pyramid. These simple correlations evince superb precision. We can expect that once more building foundations in the northern sector of the Sacred Precinct are identified there will be many more significant correlations of building spacing with special counts.

Figure 12.14 shows ritual 260-day counts at various scales – more evidence of fractal organization in the placement of buildings. This illustration also reinforces the information from Figure 12.11 that revealed the placement of the central ballcourt was by 584 and 260 counts. Of particular interest is the fact that the center point of each end of the ballcourt is 260 *yollotli* distance from one of the western corners of the compound. Also of interest, it is clear in this illustration that the twin temples of the Templo Mayor have their own specific associations. Figure 12.13 shows general correlations to the Templo Mayor as a single entity. Figure 12.14 shows correlations to the axis of the Huitzilopochtli Temple. Other buildings in the northern sector of the Sacred Precinct are aligned to the east-west central axis of the Tlaloc Temple.

These illustrations demonstrate the promise of future, detailed examination of precise data that are only now becoming known. The final illustration shows 360-day counts at different scales (Figure 12.15). Two points are of interest here besides the obvious message that this numerical value was used to plan the placement of buildings in the Sacred Precinct. It appears clear that building foundations were sighted along transects and calculated as linear distances and radii from critical points – as seen with the Venus and Sun points at the foot and top of the stairs of the Templo Mayor. Measured points were corners and centers of buildings.

With these observations in hand, it is appropriate to state an obvious caution about the claims so far. The foregoing analyses are minimal two-dimensional views. The most impressive aspects of the Templo Mayor and the Sacred Precinct to the Spanish conquerors who described them were the height of the buildings, their superstructures, building finishes, colors, paintings, altars, incense

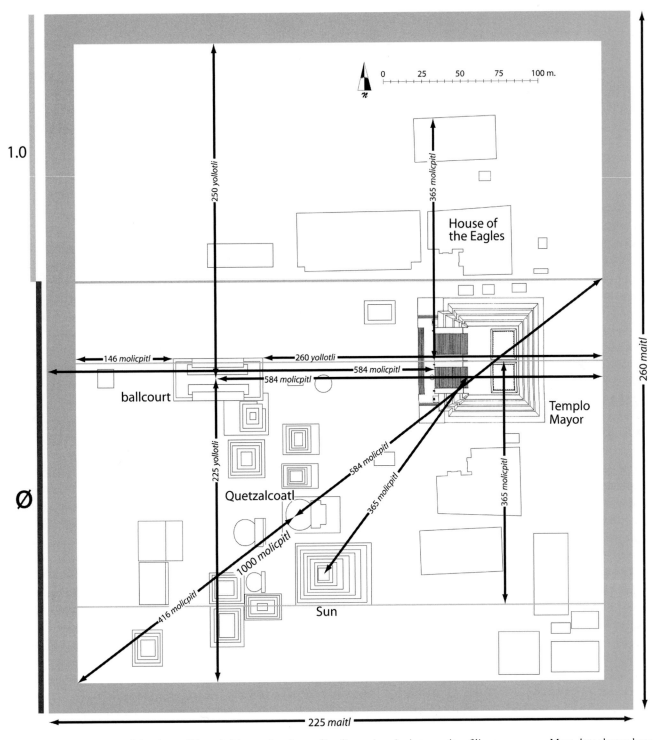

Figure 12.11. The Sacred Precinct of Tenochtitlan and various of its dimensions in Aztec units of linear measure. Most data shown here come from a recent map by José Álvaro Barrera Rivera (2006:fig. 3), with some minor adjustments from maps published by Leonardo López Luján (2006:Vol. II:fig. 18, 112, plano 1). I show a reconstruction of the Templo Mayor instead of the excavated footprint.

burners, idols, and associated blood and gore. The vertical dimensions of buildings were as important as the horizontal ones, if not more so. Building alignments to celestial phenomena and the skyline were also critical (see Aveni et al. 1988). Some buildings and views were designed to observe the celestial calendar in motion through various cycles on special days of the year. In this regard, it would be interesting to determine whether buildings designated to observe the movements of the Sun, Moon, various planets, and stars were built and placed within the compound by their related counts. For example, data show that the Temple of the Sun was located within the compound

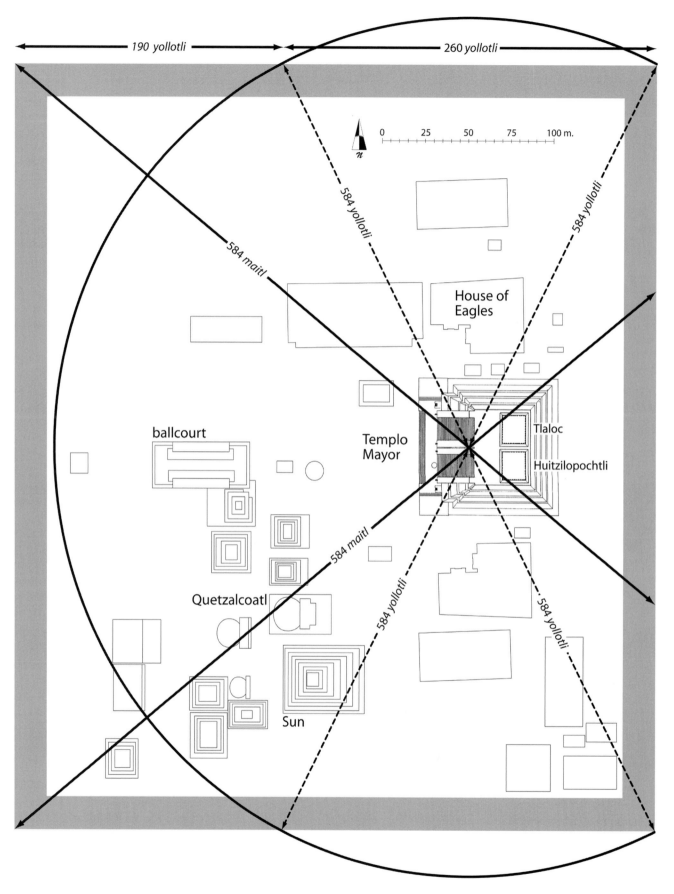

Figure 12.12. The Sacred Precinct of Tenochtitlan as organized by Venus counts (584).

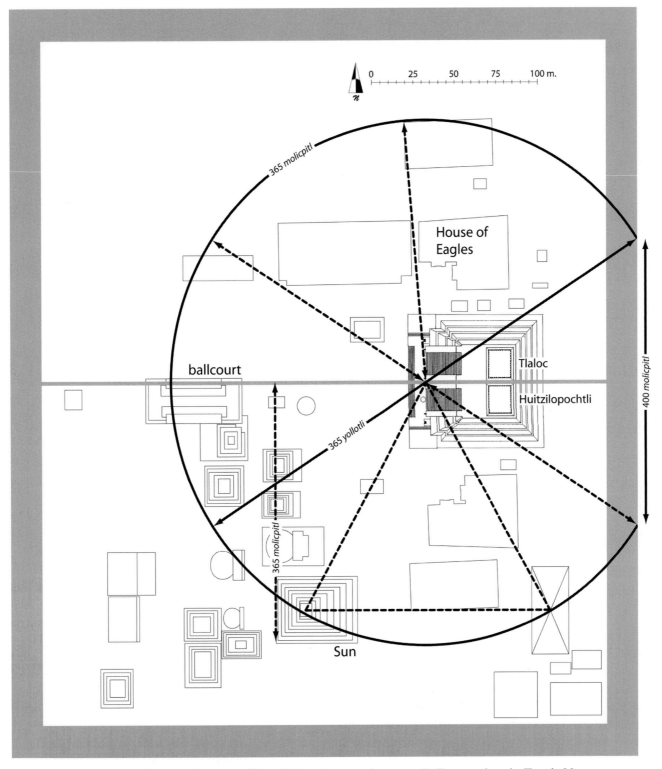

Figure 12.13. The Sacred Precinct of Tenochtitlan showing solar counts (365) centered on the Templo Mayor.

by solar counts and the Temple of Quetzalcoatl placed according to Venus counts. What about the Moon and other planets and stars? In evaluating counts, everything depends on the starting reference point and the units used. The Aztec system provides a wealth of possibilities, and judging from the rudimentary analyses of the Sacred

Precinct and the Oztoticpac palace presented here, Aztec architects took advantage of many possibilities to inscribe multiple layers of meaning into the size, form, and placement of their buildings.

To understand the Sacred Precinct and its buildings, we need eventually to visualize them realistically during

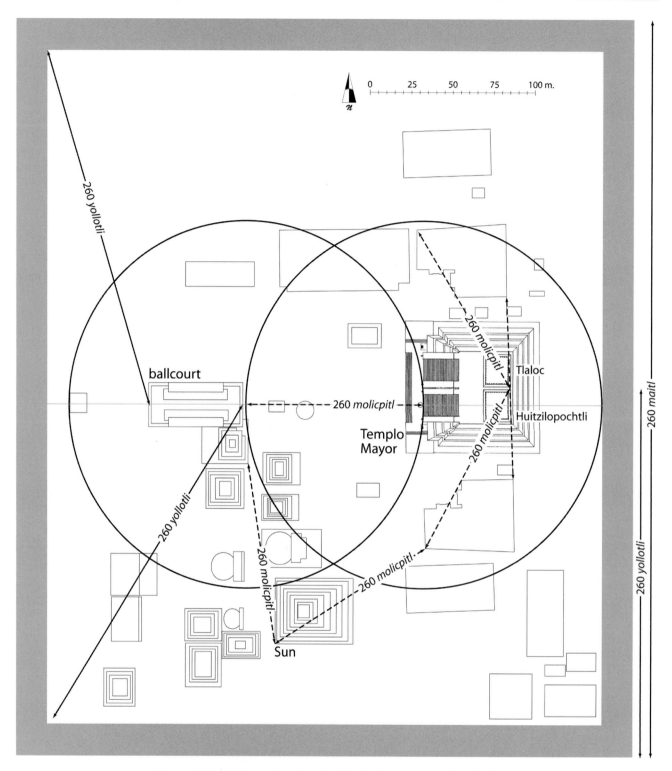

Figure 12.14. Distances based on the 260 ritual count at the Templo Mayor.

their use for significant events – with people doing things that mattered. This brings issues of spatial dimensions, astronomical time, and ritual calendars into conjunction and practical focus. Aveni and others (1988; see Aveni 2006) attempted this for the equinoctial sunrise. Spanish descriptions claim that the Sun arose between

the two temples atop the Templo Mayor on this occasion, and an early drawing corroborates this description. To understand the physical parameters of this celestial phenomenon, however, these scholars needed to know the size of the Templo Mayor (basal dimensions and height), its precise orientation, the view of the skyline

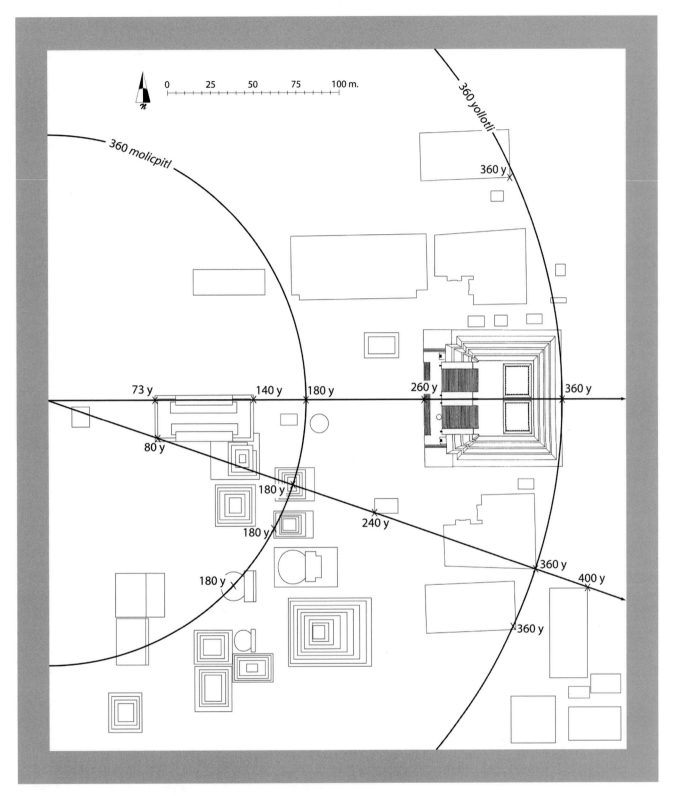

Figure 12.15. Spacing of buildings at the Templo Mayor based on 360 counts.

above the basal platform, and the appropriate viewing distance from ground level. Aveni (2001:238) calculates that "a ground-level observer would need to be about 120 meters away on axis with the Templo Mayor" to observe the Sun's rise given the building's orientation and presumed size. His analysis assumes that the Templo Mayor was 42 m tall, a hypothesis taken from Ignacio Marquina (1951). A question arising from the preceding analyses is whether or not the observation post for viewing the rising Sun was marked in a special way. If the Sun's rise on the equinox was observed between the twin temples, was that observation area a solar count away? Was it marked? If there was a small dais elevating the observer above ground level, presumably the spot could have been closer to the Templo Mayor. The proposed 120-m distance (presumably to the western toe of the Templo Mayor) would be about 145 *yollotli* or 290 *molicpitl* away. Neither number for this minimal viewing distance looks promising. If the Templo Mayor was less exalted than estimated, the viewing distance needed to see the Sun would have been less. It seems that this was indeed the case. In his eyewitness account (see Dahlgren et al. 1982), Francisco López de Gómara describes the great pyramid as 113 or 114 risers high, with each riser a "good palm" in length (20.9 cm in the Spanish system). This would make the pyramid 23.6 to 23.8 m high (28.6 *yollotli*) – less than 60 percent of Marquina's estimate. Archaeology confirms that the risers on one of the later stages of the Templo Mayor are about 20 cm high (de Teresa and Reina 1986). So the question of the equinoctial sunrise and the point from which it was viewed merits another visit – as do all questions dealing with the physical dimensions of the Sacred Precinct and their meaning.

Conclusions

My intent here has been to evaluate Aztec architecture in light of their system of mensuration and determine whether or not they constructed their public buildings and sacred space along the dimensions of celestial and/or ritual time. Analysis of a colonial map of the Oztoticpac palace and the archaeology of the Sacred Precinct demonstrates that they did so, and these findings corroborate Sugiyama's (this volume) claims for the earlier center of Teotihuacan. Aztec ethnohistoric and archaeological information about past practices exhibits a concern for proportions and asymmetrical segmentation, such as is evident at Teotihuacan – as well as ample use of ritual calendar and astronomical counts. Of course, a swarm of other distance counts are evident in the same Aztec palace compounds and precincts, so the significance of each dimension remains to be determined. I suspect that not all dimensions were created equal.

The results reported here are only a first step towards a fresh appraisal of the Templo Mayor and Aztec architecture. The demonstration that palaces and precincts were likely built to the dimensions of time provides a new starting point for understanding but does not provide much insight in and of itself. Constructed places

clearly relate to Aztec architectural and masonic practices, but their meaning and significance for other agents are matters to be investigated. What are the implications of the temporal positioning of some buildings for the ritual performances carried out in them? Whether the significance of such dimensions was for architects, masons, priests, or kings – or for other participants and observers – is an issue that needs investigation. Was conformity of architectural layouts to temporal counts something perceived and known by the populace at large? Was it generic or specific information? The foregoing exercises have attempted to decode some of the dimensions of space. Who appreciated the code and its material manifestations?

One thing that could well have been within the perception of participants is the number of steps between the stairways of various buildings, or the length of buildings and the number of steps upward, such as the 113 steps to the summit of the Templo Mayor. But paces would not yield the numerical values shown in Figures 12.6–12.15. Experiential counts would have been based on feet or paces (2.5 feet) rather than arm measures. For example, Figure 12.11 shows it was 584 *molicpitl* from the western entrance of the Sacred Precinct to the base of the Templo Mayor. This same distance would have been experienced as 350 paces or strides, quite a different count, and presumably with different meaning. Rather than representing Venus, it would be closer to a lunar year (354 days). More information is needed to work out pedestrian distances for moving around in the Sacred Precinct. Distance as experience can be perceived as different units, and these different 'experiences' could all have been valid and meaningful. My preliminary study shows the promise of evaluating Aztec sacred spaces in light of their arm measures. Future work will benefit from evaluating Aztec conceptions of space as they related to ritual performance and movement – spatial dimensions as experienced rather than as cognized or physically constructed.

The examples presented here are only a first attempt to address a significant research opportunity afforded by knowledge of Aztec mensuration and its units of linear measure. I began with an idea of the kinds of data that would be needed to test the Aztec system but with no expectations of what analyses of architecture would show. The exercises of translating meters into Aztec units surprised me at nearly every turn and forced me to surrender some preconceptions. In particular, it was unexpected that pyramids and other public buildings would not be the best units of analysis. The calendar counts that Aztecs built into some of their special places are only evident by taking a broader view that considers distances between buildings within large compounds and not the size of individual constructions or the magnitude of their periodic enlargements. These buildings and spaces must also be approached historically; one should analyze the spatial relations among contemporaneous buildings. Analyses show that the dimensions of holiness within the Sacred Precinct at Tenochtitlan conform to celestial and ritual time, and they did so from the earliest arrangement of these buildings (see Clark 2008). This is an observation to build on. Who knew about these dimensions, and what might the dimensions have meant to them? How were they meaningful? Did one need to know the secrets of their construction, or could these secrets be experienced by walking through the place? More research is needed in order to test and verify the observations made here and take them further. I hope research will move from reconstructions of the conceptual system of measurements and planned space to its possible perceptual, emotional, and behavioral effects for various agents living in their world.

ACKNOWLEDGMENTS

I appreciate the aid of Leonardo López Luján and Alfredo López Austin in answering my questions about the Templo Mayor and Aztec etymologies. Special thanks go to Trent Jensen and Neil Ransom, who prepared all of the graphics, and to Arlene Colman for her editorial help and advice. I am grateful to Richard Townsend, Anthony F. Aveni, Jesús Mora Echevarría, and José Álvaro Barrera Rivera for their helpful comments.

NOTES

1. The two maps of the Oztoticpac palace list the same dimensions, but they are not drawn by the same artist or in the same way. Howard Cline (1966:87) argues that the Oztoticpac map could not have been made later than 1544 and was probably drawn about 1540. The Humboldt Fragment VI can be dated precisely to 1546 (Cline 1968:129). The Humboldt map is more stylized than its cognate map and more obviously out of scale (as compared to Figure 12.4). Therefore, I consider the details on the earlier Oztoticpac map to be more accurate and have used it for my exploratory analyses.
2. The orientation of the map and buildings is not specific and is not known. Most native maps were oriented with east as the upper edge (as in Figure 12.10). If this is true of the Oztoticpac map, then Building C was oriented to the east and Buildings A and B opened to the west. I think this is likely the case.
3. Getting definitive dimensions for the buildings in the Sacred Precinct is exceptionally difficult because they were

originally built in a swampy place, and the buildings have subsided and moved, with the original edges of original ground level still undetermined for the earliest stages of these buildings (José Álvaro Barrera, personal communication, 2007).
4. This description by Ixtlilxóchitl is ambiguous because of the many ways the term braza was used. Braza as *maitl* appears to be excluded because it would make the building 133.8 m square, much larger than described by any other witness. If he meant the *mitl*, the dimensions would be 100.3 m and in accord with the other descriptions.
5. Sahagun states that the precinct including the Templo Mayor was "perhaps two hundred fathoms [square]" (Dibble and Anderson 1981:179). As listed in Table 12.1 and explained elsewhere (Clark 2008), early Spanish descriptions did not always distinguish clearly between various arm measures referred to as brazas or fathoms. The Aztec term listed in the Florentine Codex is *matlacpovalmatl* (ibid.), indicating that the count was 200 *maitl* units of 1.672 m rather than the longer, vertical braza of 2.09 m (*niquizantli*). The Aztec term means "10 20s" and derives from *matlactli* (10) and *poalli* (20) (Siméon 1977:259) and *maitl* (hand). Thus, Sahagun estimates the precinct to be about 334.4 m square. I presume Sahagun was describing the interior rather than the exterior dimensions of the compound, in which case, his estimates are 48 m too short for the north-south dimension (29 brazas) and precise for the east-west dimension.

REFERENCES

Aveni, A., 2001. *Skywatchers*. Austin: University of Texas Press.

Aveni, A., 2006. The Templo Mayor in sacred space, in *Arqueología e Historia del Centro de México: Homenaje a Eduardo Matos Moctezuma*, eds. L. López, D. Carrasco, and L. Cué. Mexico City: INAH, 305–315.

Aveni, A., E. E. Calnek, and H. Hartung, 1988. Myth, environment, and the orientation of the Templo Mayor of Tenochtitlan. *American Antiquity* 53:287–309.

Baird, E. T., 1993. *The Drawings of Sahagun's Primeros Memoriales: Structure and Style*. Norman: University of Oklahoma Press.

Barrera Rivera, J. Á., 2006. El Programa de Arqueología Urbana del Museo del Templo Mayor, in *Arqueología e Historia del Centro de México: Homenaje a Eduardo Matos Moctezuma*, eds. L. López, D. Carrasco, and L. Cué. Mexico City: INAH, 265–272.

Borah, W., & S.. Cook, 1958. *Price Trends of Some Basic Commodities in Central Mexico, 1531–1570*. Berkeley and Los Angeles: University of California Press.

Brinton, D. G., 1885. The lineal measures of the semi-civilized nations of Mexico and Central America. *Proceedings of the American Philosophical Society* 22: L194–L207.

Carrera Stampa, M., 1949. The evolution of weights and measures in New Spain. *Hispanic American Historical Review* 29 (1): 2–24.

Castillo F., V. M., 1972. Unidades Nahuas de medida. *Estudios de Cultura Nahuatl* **10**: 195–223.

Chavero, A., 1952. *Obras Históricas de Don Fernando de Alva Ixtlilxochitl.* Mexico City: Editorial Nacional.

Clark, J. E., 2001. Ciudades tempranas Olmecas, in *Reconstruyendo la Ciudad Maya: El Urbanismo en las Sociedades Antiguas*, eds. A. Ciudad Real, M. J. I. Ponce de León, and M. d. C. Martínez Martínez. Madrid: Sociedad Española de Estudios Mayas, 183–210.

Clark, J. E., 2004a. Mesoamerica goes public: Early ceremonial centers, leaders, and communities, in *Mesoamerican Archaeology: Theory and Practice*, eds. J. A. Hendon and R. Joyce. Oxford: Blackwell, 43–72.

Clark, J. E., 2004b. Surrounding the sacred: Geometry and design of early mound groups as meaning and function, in *Signs of Power: The Rise of Cultural Complexity in the Southeast*, eds. J. L. Gibson and P. J. Carr. Tuscaloosa: University of Alabama Press, 162–213.

Clark, J. E., 2008. Hands and hearts: How the Aztecs measured their world. *Mesoamerican Voices* III: 3–32.

Clavijero, F. J., 1976. *Historia Antigua de Mexico.* Sepan Cuantos, no. 29. Editorial Porrua, S. A., Mexico. [original 1781].

Cline, H. F., 1966. The Oztoticpac lands map of Texcoco, 1540. *Quarterly Journal of the Library of Congress* **23**: 77–115.

Cline, H. F., 1968. The Oztoticpac lands map of Texcoco, 1540: Further notes. *Actas y Memorias, Thirty-seventh International Congress of Americanists* 3: 119–138.

Dahlgren, B., E. Perez-Rocha, L. S. Diez, and P. Valle de Revueltas, 1982. *Corazon de Copil.* Mexico City: INAH.

de Teresa, C., and A. Reina, 1986. *Construcción del Templo Mayor de México Tenochtitlan.* Mexico City: Aconcagua Ediciones y Publicaciones.

Dibble, C. E., and A. J. O. Anderson, 1981. *Florentine Codex: General History of the Things of New Spain [by Fray Bernardino de Sahagun]: Book 2. The Ceremonies.* Salt Lake City: University of Utah Press.

Franco Brizuela, M. L., 1990. *Conservación del Templo Mayor de Tenochtitlan.* Mexico City: INAH.

Galván Rivera, M., 1883. *Ordenanzas de Tierras y Aguas, ó sea Formulario Geometrico-Judicial para la Designación Establecimiento, Mensura, Amojonamiento y Deslinde de las Poblaciones y todas Suertes de Tierras, Sitios, Caballerias y Criaderso de Ganados Mayores y Menores, y Mercedes de Agua.* Paris and Mexico City: Ch. Bouret.

Guillemin-Tarayre, E., 1919. Les temples de l'Anahuac: Conclusions sur l'unité de mesure chinoise introduite au mexique pour la construcion des temples. *Journal de la Société des Américanistes de Paris*, nouvelle série, **XI**: 501–512.

Hamilton, E. J., 1965. *American Treasure and the Price Revolution in Spain, 1501–1650.* New York: Octagon Books [original 1934].

Harvey, H. R., and B. J. Williams, 1980. Aztec arithmetic: Positional notation and area calculation. *Science* **210** (31): 499–505.

Islas Domínguez, A., 1999. El Templo del Sol en el centro ceremonial Mexica. In *Excavaciones el la Catedral y el Sagrario Metropolitanos: Programa de Arqueología Urbana*, ed. E. Matos Moctezuma. Mexico City: INAH, 51–61.

Ixtlilxóchitl, Fernando de Alva, 1975. *Obras Históricas.* Mexico City: UNAM and Instituto de Investigaciones Históricas.

López Arenas, G., 2003. *Rescate Arqueológico en la Catedral y el Sagrario Metropolitanos: Estudio de Ofrendas.* Colección Científica 451, Mexico City: INAH.

López Luján, L., 2006. La Casa de las Águilas: Un ejemplo de la Arquitectura Religiosa de Tenochtitlan. Fondo de Cultura Economica, Mexico City: CONACULTA, INAH.

Marquina, I., 1951. *Arquitectura Prehispánica.* Mexico City: INAH.

Martínez del Sobral, M., 2000. *Geometría Mesoamericana.* Mexico City: Fondo de Cultura Económica.

Matías Alonso, M., 1984. *Medidas Indígenas de Longitud (en Documentos de la Ciudad de México del Siglo XVI).* Cuadernos de las Casa Chata, No. 94. Mexico City: SEP Cultura.

Matías Alonso, M., 1989. La antropometía indígena en las medidas de longitud (En documentos de la ciudad de México del siglo XVI). In *Primer Coloquio de Documentos Pictográficos de Tradición Náhuatl*, ed. C. Martínez Marín. Mexico City: UNAM, 177–210.

Matos Moctezuma, E., 1988. *The Great Temple of the Aztecs: Treasures of Tenochtitlan.* London: Thames and Hudson.

Molina, Fray Alonso de, 1977. *Vocabulario en Lengua Castellana y Mexicana y Mexicana y Castellana.* Biblioteca Porrua, no. 44. Mexico City: Editorial Porrua [original 1555–1571].

Mora-Echeverría, J. I., 1984. Prácticas y conceptos prehispánicos sobre espacio y tiempo: A propósito del origen del calendario ritual Mesoamericano. *Boletín de Antropología Americana* 9: 5–46.

Orozco y Berra, M., 1880. *Historia Antigua y de las Culturas Aborigenes de Mexico.* Mexico City: Ediciones Fuente Cultural.

Petrie, W. M. F., 1877. *Inductive Metrology; or, The Recovery of Ancient Measures from the Monuments.* London: Hargrove Saunders.

Petrie, W. M. F., 1879. Metrology and geometry in ancient remains. *Journal of the Anthropological Institute of Great Britain and Ireland* **8**: 106–116.

Serrato-Combe, A., 2001. *The Aztec Templo Mayor: A Visualization.* Salt Lake City: University of Utah Press.

Siméon, R., 1977. *Diccionario de la Lengua Nahuatl o Mexicana: Redactado según los documentos impresos y manuscritos más auténticos y precedido de una introducción.* Mexico City: Siglo Veintiuno XXI [original 1885].

Sugiyama, S., 1993. Worldview materialized in Teotihuacan, Mexico. *Latin American Antiquity* **4**: 103–129.

Sugiyama, S., 2005. *Human Sacrifice, Militarism, and Rulership: Materialization of State Ideology at the Feathered*

Serpent Pyramid, Teotihuacan. Cambridge: Cambridge University Press.

Townsend, R. F., 2000. *The Aztecs.* 2nd ed. London: Thames and Hudson.

Wiercinski, A. 1980. Canon of the human body, Mexican measures of length and the Pyramid of Quetzalcoatl from Teotihuacan. *Polish Contributions in New World Archaeology, Part II* **2**: 103–123.

Williams, B. J., and H. R. Harvey, 1997. *The Códice de Santa María Asunción: Households and Lands in Sixteenth-Century Tepetlaoztoc.* Salt Lake City: University of Utah Press.

13

Establishing direction in early Egyptian burials and monumental architecture: Measurement and the spatial link with the 'other'

Kate Spence

Orientation in space is an important aspect of measurement most commonly associated with direction finding. Humans tend to divide geographical space in a horizontal plane into four primary directions or areas deriving from an embodied experience of the world: in front, behind, left and right (Tuan 1977, 34–37). As the body is mobile and positions are relative, establishing, remembering or communicating direction requires external reference. In the absence of a compass or equipment for measuring direction, reference can be made to landscape features or, over longer distances and in the absence of distinctive landscape features (for example, at sea), reference can be made to the Sun and stars, or, where they exist, prevailing winds (see also Morley, this volume).

In settled communities, patterning in orientation is sometimes found in architecture. In many regions this derives from environmental considerations: structures oriented towards or away from a prevailing wind or towards or away from the Sun, depending on the conditions of a particular area. Patterning is also frequently found in the orientation of structures toward landscape features such as the sea, a river, or a route or feature created by human intervention in the landscape. Sometimes, however, patterning in orientation may be found in contexts in which pragmatic explanations are lacking or seem unlikely. These may suggest underlying religious or cosmological considerations; examples include patterning in the orientation of tombs, the orientation of mosques toward Mecca or churches toward the east (replacing earlier orientation toward Jerusalem). Structures aligned toward astronomical events are also found; these derive from many different geographical regions and periods.

Even when they be verified to be significant, astronomical alignments can be difficult to interpret as their importance may be associated with the celestial body itself or be temporal or directional. Thus the significance may lie in creating a link with the celestial body towards which the alignment is made, reflecting the importance of an attribute or action of that celestial body: for example, structures may be oriented toward the rising Sun, using the reemerging Sun as a metaphor for reanimation after death. An alignment may be chosen because of its temporal significance (for example, towards sunrise at the summer or the winter solstice). Alternatively the alignment may be used to establish a direction important for reasons unconnected with the celestial body actually used to make the alignment: such practices are common in navigation (particularly maritime) and may be used to establish building alignments toward places too far distant to be visible.

Here I examine evidence for the orientation of early Egyptian burials and tombs. I suggest that patterning in the orientation of the body in burial relates to a widespread underlying cosmology situating the deceased in relation to a cosmos comprising both the visible world and the intangible realms lying within and beyond it. The act of orientation, however, relates closely to the practice of direction finding in the Nile Valley, which was primarily based on local river direction. Burials were thus oriented in relation to the local direction of the river Nile, which does not always flow south to north, resulting in variation in alignments of burials (and later structures such as temples), especially on bends in the river. The fact that the position and orientation of the body changed a number of times over the course of the Pharaonic Period shows that the underlying cosmology was actively considered, as was the role of the body as mediator between the tangible and intangible spheres. Finally, I consider the orientation of Old Kingdom pyramids toward the cardinal points as an extension of these themes, addressing the intentionality behind the orientation, the method of alignment, and the links between the two.

The orientation of Egyptian burials

However large or grand the tomb, the focus of the majority of Egyptian burials is a single body (although it is not unusual to find multiple burials, a tomb is usually structured for a single individual). The prominence and longevity of the practice of mummification in Egypt attest to the importance with which the body was treated after death in the historical period, and an interest in the orientation of the body can be traced well back into the prehistoric period on the basis of archaeological data. There is unfortunately no detailed and comprehensive study of the orientation of the body in Egyptian burials, although Raven (2005) deals with many of the underlying concepts. An unpublished study by Josephine Schnohr (1996) provides a useful analysis of Early Dynastic to Ptolemaic burials in the Badari region of Middle Egypt; comments on Predynastic burials are made by Debono and Mortensen 1988, 45–46) and Castillos (1982, esp. tables 3–4), while Janine Bourriau (2001) has studied changing body position from the Middle Kingdom to the early New Kingdom. From the evidence it is clear that patterning is visible both in the position of the body in burial and in the orientation of bodies within a single cemetery. In Predynastic cemeteries in the Nile Valley bodies were usually oriented with the head approximately to the south, on their left sides in a contracted position facing west, although there is some variation between cemeteries and within individual cemeteries (Castillos 1982, tables 3–4; Debono and Mortensen 1988, 45–46). In the north of Egypt burial practices were different as bodies usually lay on their right sides with heads to the south facing east (Debono and Mortensen 1988, 46). The patterning found in these burials indicates an interest in the postmortem positioning of the body in relation to landscape and a more broadly conceived understanding of setting.

The evidence suggests that local directions were usually established from the river Nile at its closest point, with the upstream direction functioning as a local 'south'. This method of direction finding through reference to the river has been common in the Nile Valley throughout Egyptian history. Although for much of its course the Nile runs approximately south to north, in some areas of Egypt (most significantly on the Qena bend) it does not, and this results in significant discrepancies between absolute directions and local perceived direction (for later temple alignments relative to the river see Badawy 1968, 183–189; Shaltout and Belmonte 2005, 279–281). Away from the Nile Valley, an alternative method of orientation must have been used: recent analysis of later building orientations in the western desert and oases suggests that solar sightings could have been used (Belmonte and Shaltout 2006).

Trends in the orientation and position of the body changed around the beginning of the historical period and, from at least the First Dynasty, elite burials in the Memphite region were placed with the head to the north (Emery 1949, 98–99 gives two First Dynasty examples). The earliest royal sarcophagi and coffins (such as those of Khufu and Khentkawes) that have been found in situ also indicate positioning with the head to the north. The provincial evidence from Badari shows relatively rapid adoption of this new orientation of the body with 45 percent of bodies buried with the head to the north (40 percent south, 15 percent east or west) during the Early Dynastic Period while by the Fourth and Fifth Dynasties 95 percent were positioned with their heads to the north (Schnohr 1996, 18, Appendix 2). Despite the change in the placement of the head, bodies continued to be placed on their left side and now faced east.

Burials also gradually became more extended over this period. This change is most probably the result of the process of mummification, which was becoming increasingly important in elite circles (Schnohr 1996, 25); the limited use of mummification beyond the elite probably explains why extended burial spread rather slowly in provincial areas of Egypt (Schnohr 1996, Appendix 1). A further change in the orientation of the body is found from the end of the New Kingdom, from which time the body was placed on its back with the head to the west. This orientation is seen in royal contexts for the first time in the burial of Ramesses III of the Twentieth Dynasty (Spence 1998, 182). A continuous interest in the orientation and position of the body can thus be traced from Predynastic burials right through the historical periods of Pharaonic Egypt and, in fact, on into the Christian and Islamic Periods. The fact that dominant trends in the orientation of the body change suggests that such practices were actively considered throughout Egyptian history and that major changes should be viewed as significant.

One of the most interesting aspects of the changes in body position and orientation is the clear importance of positioning the body with directionality in a horizontal plane. The corpse was initially positioned on its left side so that it faced in a particular direction: west in the Predynastic Period and east from the Early Dynastic Period. The practicalities of mummification and changes in coffin design increasingly led to bodies being buried flat on their backs. However, where possible, the directionality of the body was maintained by carving or painting a pair of eyes on the east (left) side of the coffin at the head end, a practice that was continued for much of Egyptian history in nonanthropomorphic coffins and sarcophagi. Occasional discoveries of undisturbed burials also show that, during the Middle Kingdom and Second Intermediate Period, mummified bodies and bodies in anthropoid coffins were sometimes propped up on their left sides within rectangular coffins (Bourriau 2001). From the New Kingdom, anthropoid coffins were increasingly decorated with images associated with symbolic orientation so that when placed upright (as they were at funerals and would be when the body was transfigured) the deceased still faced east (Spence 1998, 182; for general discussion of symbolic orientation see

Wilkinson 1994, 66–81). Those responsible for burying the dead thus took care to ensure horizontal directionality for the deceased, creating a link between the body and the region or feature they faced.

Interpreting the orientation of early burials

In Dynastic Egypt 'the west' was considered to be the abode of the dead and 'the east' the realm of the living (Kessler 1977; Raven 2005, 38): orientational patterning in burials provides strong grounds for suggesting that this idea predates the historical period. The significance of this westerly orientation would seem to be that the deceased are being 'pointed in the right direction' by the living to aid them on a postmortem journey to the west (Debono and Mortensen 1988, 46): the orientation thus provides a link between the corpse and the intangible location of the afterlife. The reason for an association between the west and the afterlife is thought to concern the setting Sun, which disappears in the west to a hidden region from which it later reemerges in the east: the solar cycle providing a potent analogy for rebirth (Debono and Mortensen 1988, 46).

The easterly orientation of dynastic burials can be interpreted more securely as a result of considerable textual and architectural evidence. The east (as the opposite of the west) was considered to be the realm of the living. As the location of sunrise it was also the place of rebirth. With the face positioned looking east, the deceased anticipated rebirth and was prepared to move towards and communicate with the living, receiving funerary prayers and the offerings considered essential for continued existence in the afterlife. The first few dynasties witnessed an increasing emphasis on a mortuary cult, the facilities for which were increasingly situated to the east of the burial itself.

The change in the orientation of the burial also highlights the role of the body as a mediator between the living and the dead and the tangible and intangible, a role that it seems to have maintained throughout Pharaonic history. The body is positioned within the burial by the living and offerings are placed in its vicinity at the time of the funeral and as part of later cult activity. Preservation of the body was essential to ensuring that the immaterial aspects of the deceased person such as his *ba* (which was able to travel to the afterlife) could return to the body to gain sustenance from these offerings. Early positioning of the body facing west may indicate that the burial of the corpse was considered to take place within the sphere of the living, with the aspiration that the immaterial

aspects of the deceased would move towards an afterlife in the west. The change to easterly orientation perhaps relates to the conception that the burial and tomb were thought to be situated in the west (a fact frequently stated in textual sources), from where the aspiration was to view or move towards the sunrise, with its promise of rebirth, and to maintain contact with the living and gain nourishment from the funerary offerings.

Although river direction seems to have been used to establish local orientation for early burials, showing the importance of the river in Egyptian thought and spatial reckoning, the river itself was not the focus of the orientation: depending on the side of the river on which the cemetery is located, burials can be oriented facing toward or away from the river at any period. However, the variation in the absolute orientation of the bodies resulting from the use of the river for alignment suggests that there was no attempt to establish precise orientation using celestial bodies, surprising given the apparent importance of solar analogy in orienting the dead. Instead it seems that the body was positioned to face abstractly conceived regions – usually 'the west' in the Predynastic Period and 'the east' in the Dynastic Period – the perceived location of which varied according to local topography and was usually determined by the course of the river.

These burial practices suggest, unsurprisingly, that the Egyptians had a well-developed cosmology from long before the Dynastic Period (this is in line with interpretations of Predynastic Egyptian culture based on artistic evidence). They suggest that concepts of direction were abstracted early on and expressed on the ground through reference to local river direction. Orientation practices appear to show that there was considered to be continuity between the physical world and the intangible regions of significance to the afterlife and that these could be linked in some way through the physical placement of the body within the burial by the living.

The orientation of Old Kingdom pyramids

Against this background of Predynastic and Early Dynastic interest in the orientation of burials, the use of the local river direction for orientation was abandoned in favour of precise orientation to the cardinal directions in the context of royal burials in the Fourth Dynasty. The evidence for this change is incontrovertible. The Third Dynasty pyramid complexes of Djoser and Sekhemkhet are oriented ca. 4° (Dorner 1981, 119) and roughly 11° (measured from plans of the site, e.g., Baines and Málek

1980, 144–145) from true north, respectively, and appear to follow topographical features, in this case ridges that run roughly parallel with the river. Thereafter, of the 10 pyramids of the Fourth and Fifth Dynasties for which we have accurate modern measurements of alignment, nine are oriented within half a degree of the cardinal directions and three are within one-sixth of a degree (10 minutes of arc). The most accurately aligned – the pyramid of Khufu – has sides that deviate from the cardinal directions by an average of less than 3 minutes of arc (1/20 degree) (see Spence 2000, 320 for measurements with references). These pyramids are constructed at five different sites, showing that alignments must have been independently established in at least the majority of cases. Given the significance of the act of alignment, which seems to have formed an important part of the foundation ceremony (for which see later discussion), orientation seems likely to have been established independently in each case. Although there are few accurate measurements of later pyramids, the evidence appears to suggest that interest in precise orientation declined in the Sixth Dynasty, as the pyramid of Teti clearly deviates significantly from the cardinal directions in published plans of Saqqara (e.g., Baines and Málek 1980, 144–145).

Orientation methods

In the absence of any contemporary textual evidence, there remains disagreement as to the most likely method of orientation used by the Egyptians. However, precise orientation to the cardinal points can only have been achieved through alignments to the Sun or stars, and there is thus no doubt at all that the alignments were celestial. The use of solar orientation methods has on occasion been proposed, most recently by Martin Isler (1989; 2001, 157–174, 181–187) and Dusan Magdolen (2000), although the majority of researchers favour stellar methods (Žaba 1953; Edwards 1993, 247–251; Dorner 1981; Spence 2000; Belmonte 2001). It is considered most unlikely that the precision and consistency of orientation seen in particular in the Fourth Dynasty pyramids could have been achieved using solar methods (Edwards 1993, 247–248; Belmonte 2001, S2). Most solar methods rely on marking two shadow positions and bisecting the angle to establish north: the size of the visible Sun renders both sightings and shadows imprecise; in addition, the necessity of bisecting angles adds additional scope for inaccuracy; experimental work by Josef Dorner shows that stellar methods can be very precise (Stadelmann 1990, 254). New Kingdom images thought

to represent the act of orientation, such as that shown on the ceiling of Senenmut, also show the use of stars (Žaba 1953, 44–55; Wilkinson 1991).

Many different stellar orientation methods have been proposed over the years. There was no star marking precisely the position of the celestial north pole at the time the pyramids of the Fourth Dynasty were constructed (the closest star was α Draconis, around 2° from the pole) so a more complex method than a simple sighting to a north star must have been used. A few methods have been put forward proposing alignment towards stars rising or setting on the east or west horizons (e.g., Haack 1984); these must be discounted because of variable horizon conditions and the difficulty of making a precise alignment toward a laterally moving star at the moment it becomes visible (Belmonte 2001, S3). Other proposed stellar methods can be divided into bisection methods and precession-dependent methods. Bisection methods involve establishing equivalent positions on the trajectory of a circumpolar or near-circumpolar star, either positions of equivalent height, as in Edwards' artificial horizon method (Edwards 1993, 247–251), or extreme easterly and westerly positions (Žába 1953, 70–72; Dorner 1981, 137–148). Suggested precession-dependent methods respond to the fact that there appears to be a correlation between time and the small errors found in most pyramid alignments of the Fourth to Fifth Dynasties. Unless this feature is coincidental, it can only be explained by the use of a precession-dependent method such as the use of two stars in simultaneous transit (Spence 2000; 2001; Belmonte 2001, S3).

The question of orientation methods remains controversial, and it is not my intention to present the subject in detail here. Instead I wish to explore the significance of the orientation, a subject that has tended to be eclipsed by the focus on method.

The direction of alignment

All plausible methods of stellar orientation involve establishing the direction of true north, either through bisecting observed positions of a circumpolar or near-circumpolar star, or through alignments directly to circumpolar stars. (Proposed solar orientation methods also involve establishing the direction of true north, although it is unlikely that they were used.) Establishing north must thus be considered the goal of the act of celestial alignment, regardless of the method used, with the ground plan of the pyramid being constructed geometrically from this northerly alignment.

The significance of northerly alignment

It is worth considering whether any significance is attached to the northerly direction of alignment or an object in the northern sky, or whether the orientation method was used simply as a means of establishing precisely the directions of the cardinal points. As no celestial bodies rise or set exactly to the north, and all regularly cross the meridian (north-south line dividing the sky and passing through the zenith) at some point, it is highly unlikely that the alignment's primary significance is temporal or associated with a specific celestial event.

The evidence of burials suggests that the Egyptians divided space into four cardinal directions from well before the historical period (see also Raven 2005, 39 for linguistic evidence) but, as discussed previously in relation to early burials, it seems that these were treated as abstractly conceived regions: there is no evidence that absolute directions were carefully established before the Fourth Dynasty. East and west seem to have been associated with the course of the Sun and were most probably linked with life and rebirth (east) and the realm of the dead (west). North and south seem in the minds of the Egyptians to have been closely linked with a geographical division of Egypt into separate areas, united during much of the historical period under a single king. Early royal regalia and iconography along with elite titles reflect this perception of Egypt as divided into northern and southern halves (Wilkinson 1992, 80–81; Kemp 2005, 69–73) but, again, these are abstractly conceived regions understood in relation to the course of the river and do not reflect any concern with absolute direction. Nor does this geographical division of Egypt give precedence to north, with south (as the source of the Nile) being seen as the focus of terrestrial orientation (Posener 1965, 69–72). Before the construction of the pyramids, the Egyptians seem to have been orienting burials in such as a way as to reflect the significance of east and west as abstract geographical regions without recourse to precise orientation or alignment toward the Sun, the course of which seems to have endowed east and west with their significance (Debono and Mortensen 1988, 46). It thus seems unlikely that the impetus for precise orientation derives directly from earlier practices.

All plausible stellar methods of orientation (bisection methods and methods involving direct sighting) involve the use of circumpolar or near-circumpolar stars. Although we have no relevant texts exactly contemporary with the earliest use of cardinal orientation, the Pyramid Texts, first inscribed in pyramids dating to around 200 years later (although many of the texts are thought to have earlier origins), make frequent reference to a group of stars known as the *ikhemu sek*, the 'indestructibles' or 'those that do not know destruction', widely accepted to be the circumpolar stars (Badawy 1964; Allen 1989, 4; Krauss 1997, 86–130). The king is repeatedly identified with these stars in the texts (Badawy 1964, 195–198; Allen 1989, 1–2). The sky goddess Nut is addressed thus: "you have set this King as an Imperishable Star who is in you" (Faulkner 1969, 142). Another, addressed to the king, reads, "O you who are high exalted among the Imperishable Stars, you shall never perish" (Faulkner 1969, 155), and the king is explicitly said to rise up to the circumpolar stars: a goddess is said to speak "to the king when he ascends to the sky among the stars, among the Imperishable Stars" (Faulkner 1969, 162). It thus seems very likely that the decision to use these stars for the purposes of aligning burial monuments is closely associated with their important role within mortuary beliefs as a model for eternal existence and the location of the king's afterlife (Žaba 1953, 20–23).

Such an interpretation is supported by an increasing emphasis on the northerly direction in the architecture of royal burials. Virtually all pyramids constructed before the middle of the Twelfth Dynasty had their entrances on the north side, and Pyramid Texts in inscribed pyramids show that this passage was viewed as an exit for the dead king to reach the sky rather than an entrance through which his body was introduced to the tomb (Allen 1993, esp. 27–28). While these entrance passages do not seem to have been intended to point toward any particular star, they all face the circumpolar region. In the pyramid of Khufu, additional small shafts run in a north-south alignment upwards from two of the internal chambers and are thought by many to be aligned toward specific stars (Badawy 1964; Trimble 1964; Edwards 1993, 284–285). The northern shafts are apparently aligned toward the circumpolar stars, specifically to α Draconis (the closest star to the pole at the time) and β Ursae Minoris (Badawy 1964, 206; Trimble 1964; Bauval and Gilbert 1995, 179–183).

The use of circumpolar stars to align the bases of pyramids may therefore have been seen as a way to link these burial structures with a region of the sky viewed as a physical location of importance to the postmortem existence of the deceased and simultaneously considered significant in providing a model for eternal existence (Žaba 1953, 20–23; Allen 1989, 1–2) However it was established, the alignment points toward the celestial pole itself, which was not marked precisely by any star at the time: the burial is thus oriented toward the invisible point in the sky around which the other stars appear to rotate, which could also be seen as governing the movement of the stars in the sky. Pyramid Text 374 tells us that "the king guides the Imperishable Stars" (Faulkner 1969, 77).

The pyramid, as an extension of the body carefully placed within it, is therefore linked through its orientation with the celestial regions that the Pyramid Texts show to be the perceived location of the afterlife of the king (Allen 1989). The orientation also overrides the local topographical considerations seen in earlier burials, with their links to terrestrial setting, in favour of universal celestial links considered appropriate to the royal context and the whole of Egypt. Interestingly, the change to the use of celestial orientation appears to coincide with the construction of the first true pyramids at the beginning of the Fourth Dynasty under King Sneferu.

From where does the interest in celestial bodies derive?

The use of the stars to orient the pyramids precisely to the cardinal points seems to have been a new development in a longstanding practice of orienting burials with care. However, it suggests a degree of knowledge about the movement of celestial bodies among the Egyptians that deserves consideration as it predates any textual sources detailing astronomical practices. By the time of the Fourth Dynasty the Egyptians had clearly gained the practical knowledge and technical expertise to use celestial bodies to establish orientation, and those celestial bodies must already have gained the symbolic significance that made such a practice desirable (see Krauss 1997 for discussion of the astronomical aspects of the Pyramid Texts, with references).

An element of early interest in and knowledge of the Sun and stars is likely to derive from practices of direction finding, particularly in areas distant from the Nile Valley (Belmonte and Shaltout 2006), which were more frequented in prehistoric periods before the desiccation of the Sahara than they were in historical times. However, the emphasis given to local or river orientation throughout the earlier periods of Egyptian history suggests that this is unlikely to account for the extent of knowledge and changes in practice seen in the pyramids. The most likely reason for increased interest in the movement of the Sun and stars in the Early Dynastic Period and the Old Kingdom lies in timekeeping. Three aspects of time measurement are of particular interest here because of their associations with early astronomical observation: quantifying the length of the year, subdividing the year, and subdividing the night.

The textual evidence for measuring time in Egypt postdates the appearance of the first pyramids, but some of the practices they represent are likely to be earlier. For the most part, textual and pictorial evidence suggests that Egypt fits within broad trends of approximate time reckoning using celestial bodies seen in ethnographic studies throughout Africa (see Warner 1996 for a useful summary). The use of heliacal risings of stars to fix the length of the year is paralleled elsewhere, and use of the Moon to mark shorter periods (months) is common (although the Egyptians abandoned the use of the Moon to measure months early in their history, the lunar association survives in the use of the crescent Moon to write the word for 'month'). The Milky Way was used to observe the passage of time at night in Africa (Warner 1996, 308–309), and the most prominent stars and constellations used by the Egyptians – Sirius, Orion, Ursa Major and the Milky Way (which are depicted on coffin lids from ca. 2100 BC) – are commonly distinguished and recognised (Warner 1996, 308–310).

Egypt stands out from the ethnographic record for Africa in a number of ways. The establishment of a 'civil' year of 365 days, further subdivided into artificial months of 30 days, each comprising 3 'decades' of 10 days (created according to a decimal counting system that must have predated the calendar) with the addition of 5 'extra' days, is unique. The division of the day and night into units (even if these are not equal) is also unusual. These developments are closely related to astronomical observation as a basis for the measurement of time (Clagett 1995 provides detailed discussion of the evidence for calendars and timekeeping).

The fact that the Egyptian civil calendar was only 365 days long resulted in the civil year's drifting in relation to the solar year by one day every four years. Recorded observations of the heliacal rise of Sirius (the dates of which can be reconstructed today) correlated with dates in the civil calendar form the basis for establishing absolute chronologies for Egypt and the Old World. However, the Sothic cycles can also be counted backwards to give a date for the origin of the civil calendar around 2781–2778 BC (Claggett 1995, 28–37), a date currently thought to fall in the Second Dynasty (ca. 2890–2686 BC). Prior to this, it is assumed that the beginning of the year was marked approximately by the annual flooding of the Nile. Neugebauer's suggestion (1942) that the length of the year was established by averaging the very variable dates of the Nile's flooding seems unlikely to be correct; counting the length of time between two heliacal risings of Sirius (the historical marker of the beginning of the year) seems a far more plausible and precise method of measurement that could be easily checked.

The date for the origin of the civil calendar shows that careful observation and recording of the heliacal rise of Sirius must date back towards the beginning of the third millennium BC in order for the practice to have been codified by 2781–2778 BC. It should also be noted that a spatial aspect is inherent in the practice of observation of heliacal risings. To catch the first appearance of the star it is necessary to know where to look. The direction could have been established in a number of ways: the observer could have oriented him- or herself in an approximate direction established in relation to the circumpolar stars as a fixed point; or the expected alignment could have been noted for a particular landscape in relation to topographical features; or physical markers could have been created to mark the alignment for future years. Interestingly, around the date of the origin of the civil calendar, the north celestial pole was marked reasonably precisely by the star α Draconis.

The year was subdivided into 36 10-day periods or 'decades' grouped into 12 months of 30 days. The so-called decanal stars are likely to have originated as stars marking by their rising the beginnings of these 10-day periods. By the time these decanal stars were shown on coffin lids dating from ca. 2100 BC they were being used as a method of marking the division of the night (Neugebauer and Parker 1960; Claggett 1995, 48–56; Leitz 1995, 58–116). Although these sources date to well after the construction of the first pyramids, the Egyptian words for 'hour-stars' and 'duty priesthoods' (the latter derived from the former) are written with hieroglyphs of stars and are attested in the Old Kingdom (Claggett 1995, 49; Hannig 2003, 347), suggesting that the practice of dividing time using the stars is much earlier than explicit sources suggest. Again, the need to observe these stars at a particular point on the horizon adds a spatial dimension to the measurement of time, whilst the observation and recording of stars are clear from the primary sources. Spatial alignments toward the Sun and stars have been suggested in the interpretation of prehistoric monuments at Nabta Playa (Applegate and Zedeño 2001; Wendorf and Malville 2001), but these monuments are without parallels and the archaeology is somewhat ambiguous, as a result of which such interpretations remain controversial.

I would therefore suggest that the interest in and knowledge of the stars seen in the orientation of pyramids derive from observation and recording of the appearance of stars as part of early attempts to divide and measure time, some of which can be shown to predate the Fourth Dynasty. The link between the measurement of space and measurement of time is also clear from early periods in the activities of the goddess Seshat, the goddess associated with the foundation ceremony, during which the orientation of buildings was established.

The goddess Seshat and the foundation ceremony

Seshat was a divinity of some importance at the beginning of the historical era in Egypt, as is clear from a record of a First Dynasty ceremony involving one of her priests inscribed on the Palermo Stone (a set of annals for Egypt's earliest kings) as well as the creation of a statue of the goddess during the same reign (Wilkinson 2000, 111–112, 118; see also Wainwright 1940, 32). After the Old Kingdom there is no evidence that a cult was maintained although Seshat herself appears in royal images and inscriptions with a limited set of roles. Foremost of these roles is that of recording the king's reign length: "her chief mission was to mark the king's life-period on the palm-stick. To cut notches, or to make marks, on a stick is the earliest of all forms of keeping a count or tally, and of itself would suggest an origin in the time before writing proper had been invented" (Wainwright 1940, 32); she is frequently depicted with a notched central rib of a palm frond. The significance of recording reign lengths is great as it was by adding up the reign lengths of successive kings that Egyptians measured time in a linear fashion throughout the historical period. Seshat seems primarily to have been a tally keeper, and at least one of her priests bears a title attesting to such a role during the Old Kingdom (Wainwright 1940, 32). During the Fifth Dynasty her symbol is found in images of the royal jubilee, she is described as "Before the House of the Books of the Royal Offspring" and she records booty brought from abroad (Wainwright 1940, 32).

Seshat's second important role was associated with the foundation ceremony for buildings (see Weinstein 1973 for discussion of the ceremony with references): she is repeatedly depicted performing the 'stretching of the cord' ritual in the company of the king. The first reference to this ritual is found on the Palermo stone, where it is said to have been conducted by a priest of Seshat (Wilkinson 2000, 111–112). A poorly preserved granite doorjamb of Khasekhemwy (Second Dynasty) from Hierakonpolis is the earliest known depiction of the ceremony (Engelbach 1934), and further examples are found from all periods of Egyptian history during which significant building works were carried out. The earliest records suggest that the ceremony was concerned with measurement of the length of sides of a structure rather than its alignment; the Palermo Stone entry reads "stretching the cord (at the) great door (of the building) 'thrones of the gods' (by) the priest of Seshat, 4 cubits, 2 palms?" (Wilkinson 2000, 111). Seshat's role in the measurement of space and time is therefore clear.

The Pyramid Texts describe Seshat as 'Lady of Builders' (Faulkner 1969, 119).

The act of aligning a building must also have been part of the foundation ceremony (see Weinstein 1973). Ptolemaic texts are explicit in linking the 'stretching of the cord' ceremony with the stars (specifically with Ursa Major) and with the measurement of time. A text from the Temple of Edfu translates as "Je prends le jalon et j'empoigne le manche du maillet; j'empoigne le cordeau avec Séchat. J'ai tourné ma vue d'après le mouvement des étoiles et j'ai fait entrer mon regard dans (l'astérisme de) *Msxtyw* (le Grande Ourse). Le dieu Indicateur du Temps était debout à côté de son *merkhet*. J'ai établi les 4 angles de ton temple" (Žaba 1953, 58). It should be noted, however, that these texts date to over two millennia after the first pyramids; earlier texts on the foundation ceremony are limited and far less explicit.

The question of whether the act of stellar observation was original to the foundation ceremony is difficult to answer and cannot be discussed at length here. As mentioned, there is no evidence that buildings were aligned using celestial bodies before the Fourth Dynasty. Seshat clearly had celestial associations from the beginning: her symbol in its early writings includes a crescent Moon and she is considered an aspect of the sky goddess Nephthys (Wainwright 1940, 30–31, 34). The crescent Moon (later used as the hieroglyph for a month) suggests association with timekeeping rather than with stellar orientation. It seems to me most likely that the practice of stellar alignment was grafted onto the foundation ceremony at the time of the Fourth Dynasty for the creation of the most significant monuments of that era: the pyramids. Had stellar alignment been important prior to this, one would expect to see evidence of this in royal burials, but there is none.

The evidence suggests that stellar aspects of the foundation ceremony were retained through the millennia, presumably as a result of their symbolic significance in linking Earth and the celestial realms. Certainly the majority of royal buildings for which the foundation ceremony was performed over the course of Egyptian history were not oriented to the cardinal points, but the Ptolemaic texts show that ceremonies conducted two millennia after the construction of the first true pyramids were still associated with stellar sightings. Despite some uncertainty about the early form of the foundation ceremony, by the time of the Fourth Dynasty, the measurement of space, time and orientation was clearly linked through the person of the goddess Seshat and her role in the foundation ceremony.

Conclusions

Interest in the orientation of the body in burial can be traced from prehistoric times through the millennia of Pharaonic power and on into the Christian and Islamic Periods in Egypt. The dominant trends in orientation change a number of times over the course of the Pharaonic Period, showing that the practice was actively considered. Orientation practices would appear to derive from direction finding, with the corpse given horizontal directionality in order to create a link between the burial place and the intangible regions of importance to the afterlife. These regions, 'the west' and later 'the east', seem from the beginning to have been abstractly conceived regions, the location of which was established according to local topographical considerations – primarily river direction.

Precise orientation to the cardinal points emerged with the practice of building true pyramids in the Fourth Dynasty. It seems to have been accomplished using a stellar method and served to link these pyramids with the circumpolar stars, which are closely identified with the afterlife of the dead king in the Pyramid Texts and served as a model for eternal existence. The practice associates these monuments with the celestial pole, the point seen to govern the movement of the stars, providing an important parallel for the universal power of the king and its anticipated continuation in the sky after death. As such it overrides the local terrestrial relevance of the topographical orientation it replaced.

I have argued that the knowledge of the movement of the stars underlying this practice is likely to derive from early timekeeping practices. Despite sparse textual evidence, it is possible to trace practices such as marking the beginning of the year and establishing its length back to well before the Fourth Dynasty. Links between the measurement of time, space and orientation are evident in the attributes and activities of the goddess Seshat and in the foundation ceremony that she performs with the king. Although most monumental buildings constructed after the pyramids were aligned using river direction or other topographical features, aspects of stellar orientation seem to have been retained as part of the foundation ceremony, allowing symbolic links with the intangible to be established for each royal structure for which it was performed.

REFERENCES

Allen, J., 1989. The Cosmology of the Pyramid Texts, in J. Allen et al. (eds.), *Religion and Philosophy in Ancient Egypt*, 1–28. New Haven: Yale Egyptological Studies.

Allen, J., 1993. Reading a Pyramid, in C. Berger, G. Clerc and N. Grimal (eds.), *Hommages à Jean Leclant*, Vol. I, 5–28. Cairo: Institut Français d'Archéologie Orientale.

Applegate, A., and N. Zedeño, 2001. Site E-92-9: A Possible Late Neolithic Solar Calendar, in F. Wendorf, R. Schild et al. (eds.), *Holocene Settlement of the Egyptian Sahara*. Vol. 1: *The Archaeology of Nabta Playa*, 463–467. New York: Kluwer Academic/Plenum.

Badawy, A., 1964. The Stellar Destiny of Pharaoh and the So-Called Air-Shafts of Cheops' Pyramid, *Mitteilungen des Instituts für Orientforschung* 10, 189–206.

Badawy, A., 1968. *A History of Egyptian Architecture: The Empire (the New Kingdom). From the Eighteenth Dynasty to the End of the Twentieth Dynasty, 1580–1085 B.C.* Berkeley and Los Angeles: University of California Press.

Baines, J., and J. Málek, 1980. *Atlas of Ancient Egypt*. Oxford: Phaidon.

Bauval, R., and A. Gilbert, 1995. *The Orion Mystery*, rev. ed. London: Mandarin.

Belmonte, J. A., 2001. On the Orientation of Old Kingdom Egyptian Pyramids, *Archaeoastronomy* 26, S1–S20.

Belmonte, J. A., and M. Shaltout, 2006. On the Orientation of Ancient Egyptian Temples: (2) New Experiments at the Oases of the Western Desert, *Journal for the History of Astronomy* 37, 173–192.

Bourriau, J., 2001. Change of Body Position in Egyptian Burials from the Mid XIIth Dynasty until the Early XVIIIth Dynasty, in H. Willems (ed.), *Social Aspects of Funerary Culture in the Egyptian Old and Middle Kingdoms*, 1–20. Leuven: Peeters.

Castillos, J. J., 1982. *A Reappraisal of the Published Evidence on Egyptian Predynastic and Early Dynastic Cemeteries*. Toronto: Benben.

Clagett, M., 1995. *Ancient Egyptian Science*. Vol. II: *Calendars, Clocks and Astronomy*. Philadelphia: American Philosophical Society.

Debono, F., and Mortensen, B., 1988. *The Predynastic Cemetery at Heliopolis: Season March–September 1950. Archäologische Veröffentlichungen*, 63. Mainz am Rhein: von Zabern.

Dorner, J., 1981. *Die Absteckung und astronomische Orientierung ägyptischer Pyramiden*. Unpublished PhD dissertation: University of Innsbruck.

Edwards, I. E. S., 1993. *The Pyramids of Egypt*. First published 1947. London: Penguin.

Emery, W. B., 1949. *Great Tombs of the First Dynasty*, I. Cairo: Government Press.

Engelbach, R., 1934. A Foundation Scene of the Second Dynasty, *Journal of Egyptian Archaeology* 20, 183–184.

Faulkner, R. O., 1969. *The Ancient Egyptian Pyramid Texts*. Oxford: Oxford University Press.

Haack, S., 1984. The Astronomical Orientation of Egyptian Pyramids, *Archaeoastronomy* 7, S119–S125.

Hannig, R., 2003. *Ägyptisches Wörterbuch I. Altes Reich und Erste Zwischenzeit*. Von Zabern: Mainz am Rhein.

Isler, M., 1989. An Ancient Method of Finding and Extending Direction, *Journal of the American Research Center in Egypt* 26, 191–206.

Isler, M., 2001. *Sticks, Stones and Shadows: Building the Egyptian Pyramids*. Norman: University of Oklahoma Press.

Kemp, B., 2005. *Ancient Egypt: Anatomy of a Civilization*, 2nd ed. London: Routledge.

Kessler, D., 1977. Himmelsrichtungen, in W. Helck & E. Otto (eds.), *Lexikon der Ägyptologie*, Vol. II, 1213–1214. Wiesbaden, Harrassowitz.

Krauss, R., 1997. *Astronomische Konzepte und Jenseitsvorstellungen in den Pyramidentexten* (Ägyptologische Abhandlungen 59). Wiesbaden, Harrassowitz.

Leitz, C., 1995. *Altägyptische Sternuhren*. Leuven: Peeters.

Magdolen, D., 2000. On the Orientation of Old-Kingdom Royal Tombs, in M. Bárta and J. Krejcí (eds.), *Abusir and Saqqara in the Year 2000*. Praha: Czech Academy of Sciences.

Neugebauer, O., 1942. The Origin of the Egyptian Calendar, *Journal of Near Eastern Studies* 1, 396–403.

Neugebauer, O., and R. Parker, 1960. *Egyptian Astronomical Texts*. Vol. I: *The Early Decans*. Providence and London: Brown University Press.

Posener, G., 1965. Sur l'orientation et l'ordre des points cardinaux chez les Egyptiens, *Nachrichten der Akademie der Wissenschaften in Göttingen*, no. 2, 69–78.

Raven, M., 2005. Egyptian Concepts on the Orientation of the Human Body, *Journal of Egyptian Archaeology* 91, 37–53.

Schnohr, J., 1996. *Variation in the Treatment of the Body in Burials of the Historic Period in Middle Egypt*. Unpublished MPhil dissertation: University of Cambridge.

Shaltout, M., and Belmonte, J. A., 2005. On the Orientation of Ancient Egyptian Temples: (1) Upper Egypt and Lower Nubia, *Journal for the History of Astronomy* 36, 273–298.

Spence, K., 1998. *Orientation in Ancient Egyptian Royal Architecture*. Unpublished PhD thesis: University of Cambridge.

Spence, K., 2000. Ancient Egyptian Chronology and the Astronomical Orientation of Pyramids, *Nature* 408, 320–324.

Spence, K., 2001. Astronomical Orientation of the Pyramids. *Nature* 412, 699–700.

Stadelmann, R., 1990. *Die Großen Pyramiden von Giza*. Graz: Akademische Druck-u. Verlangsanstalt.

Trimble, V., 1964. Astronomical Investigation Concerning the So-Called Air-Shafts of Cheops' Pyramid, *Mitteilungen des Instituts für Orientforschung* 10, 183–187.

Tuan, Y.-F., 1977. *Space and Place: The Perspective of Experience*. London: Arnold.

Wainwright, G. A., 1940. Seshat and the Pharaoh, *Journal of Egyptian Archaeology* 26, 30–40.

Warner, B., 1996. Traditional Astronomical Knowledge in Africa, in C. Walker (ed.), *Astronomy before the Telescope*, 304–317. London: British Museum Press.

Weinstein, J., 1973. *Foundation Deposits in Ancient Egypt*. Ann Arbor: University Microfilms.

Wendorf, F., and Malville, J. M., 2001. The Megalithic Alignments, in F. Wendorf, R. Schild et al. (eds.), *Holocene*

Settlement of the Egyptian Sahara. Vol. 1: *The Archaeology of Nabta Playa*, 489–502. New York: Kluwer Academic/Plenum.

Wilkinson, R., 1991. New Kingdom Astronomical Paintings and Methods of Finding and Extending Direction, *Journal of the American Research Center in Egypt* **28**, 149–154.

Wilkinson, R., 1992. *Reading Egyptian Art.* London: Thames and Hudson.

Wilkinson, R., 1994. *Symbol and Magic in Egyptian Art.* London: Thames and Hudson.

Wilkinson, T., 2000. *Royal Annals of Ancient Egypt: The Palermo Stone and Its Associated Fragments.* London and New York: Kegan Paul International.

Žába, Z., 1953. *L'Orientation astronomique dans l'ancienne Égypte, et la précession de l'axe du monde.* Prague: Academie Tchècoslovaque des Sciences.

SECTION IV

Calendar and cosmology

The theme of the relationships between terrestrial and celestial aspects of the world is elaborated further in Section IV, whose chapters are united by a principal focus on the measurement of time. The opening section of David Brown's contribution focuses on the notions of concrete and abstract number in Mesopotamia, before going on to consider in detail the measurement of time and its relationship with terrestrial and cosmological measures. Brown initially argues that the existence of 'concrete number' systems in Mesopotamia (with both quantity and quality [commodity] being represented by a single symbol, repeated the appropriate number of times) does not represent a lacuna in human cognition (an inability to conceptualise abstract number) but is instead a product of administrative practice. When this administrative mechanism changes, the use of abstract number becomes conspicuously part of the arithmetical system. However, he argues, evidence for the cognition of the concept of abstract number exists before; that is, it is a transformation in practice, rather than human cognition, that is represented by this change.

In Mesopotamia the measurement of the passage of time became linked intimately with the measure of distance, via the distance between 'rest stops' (covered at walking speed on foot march) and the duration of a day. This formed part of an idealised system of relationships among distance, time and astronomical movements, including idealised durations for days, months and years, which, Brown suggests, accorded with a concept of the ideal creation. Such astronomical phenomena, whilst cyclical, also exhibit variation within that cyclicality, and Brown argues that the natural (real) divergence from these cycles would have created a disjunction between cyclicality and predictability, boded ill, and been explained in terms of the prerogatives of associated deities. Much of the subsequent development of this

measurement system was initially in terms of astrological predictions – related to the date of birth or conception of the ruler, and subsequently others. This growth in systematic zodiacal divination was largely responsible for the wide transmission of understanding and techniques throughout the Near East and eastern Mediterranean in the subsequent centuries.

Moving our focus from the Near to the Far East, Mark Edward Lewis provides a remarkable account of the development of a calendar and its relationship with the increasingly specific prescription of ritual activities. The focus of his chapter is the origins of the calendrical system and measurement of time in China, drawing upon the divinatory inscriptions of the Shang dynasty. These are intimately tied in with religion and cosmology; the majority of Shang inscriptions are concerned with the performance of rituals, the identification of deities to whom the rituals are to be directed and the nature of sacrifices to be made. The foci of these inscriptions became increasingly specialised, until they were concerned solely with a 10-day cycle and its attendant sacrifices.

The Shang ritual calendar was thus derived initially entirely from human activity – in relation to perceived activity of spirits and ancestors – rather than from astronomical or meteorological *phenomena*. The only units of time used in these early manifestations were a day and the period of 10 days, which initially ignored cycles of the Sun and Moon. These began to be incorporated into a sexagesimal ritual cycle of six of the 10-day ritual periods, with each day attributed to a specific spirit or ancestor. Lewis discusses how periods approximating lunar cycles came to be incorporated subsequently, with a fixed number of months of varying length. These were calculated from the time of the last winter solstice, and the total ritual cycle was extended to approximately the same length as the solar year. Thus it was possible ultimately for several modes of reckoning time to be used simultaneously and cited in the inscriptions. Finally, Lewis discusses how this developed Shang system was later integrated with that of the succeeding (conquering) Zhou dynasty's own system.

Shifting the lens back to Mesoamerica, Tony Aveni discusses and analyses the remarkably precise cosmological and calendrical calculations undertaken by the Maya in the creation of their almanacs. The practice of the calculation of these cycles and mathematical sequences was motivated by deeply rooted religious concerns. Aveni discusses the relationships between cycles identified by the Maya and their terrestrial and cosmological concerns. For example, the passage of time was conceived of in terms of distance mythologically measured out with feet. Time was also conceived of both as a road/ journey and as a burden carried along that road. The cardinal count of 260 days, Aveni suggests, has its origins in a recognition of its similarity to a combination of natural phenomena, including the growth cycle of crops in Mesoamerica, the length of human gestation, and a variety of cosmological phenomena, and as a multiple of the vigesimal count on human fingers and toes. The religious concerns underlying the calculation of cycles also extended to the creation, orientation and use of the architecture. Aveni goes on to discuss how the preoccupation with cycles and time amongst the Maya seems to have formulated their worldview of their present.

Charles Stanish focuses on the relationship between the Inca measurement of time and the creation of ideological mechanisms to create social and political stability in the state. With particular reference to the archaeological evidence from the sacred Island of the Sun in Lake Titicaca, Stanish discusses how the positioning of Tikani stone marker pillars, used to mark the sunset at the solstices, illustrates that a key aspect of such marking of time was the communal experience of the appropriate ceremonial activities by a large cross section of the society. Stanish discusses how the demarcation of sacred space at the sites can be related directly to the management of complex social hierarchical relations between dominant and absorbed social groups, with particular social strata being in a position to witness directly the setting of the Sun between the pillars and others not. The observation of such communal ceremonial activities appears to have fulfilled an essential role in the delineation of social status and ideologies of the expanding Inca empire.

In the final archaeological chapter of the volume, Peter F. Biehl moves the focus to the prehistory of Europe. He discusses the relationship of Neolithic enclosures, in particular the example at Goseck, Germany, with ritual systems and cosmologies. The Goseck enclosure features pit burnings and a human burial, and Biehl goes on to discuss how a 'contextual attribute approach' – examining ideational and symbolic aspects of an artefact – can be useful in interpreting finds in these contexts. Indeed, he considers the enclosure itself in these terms and thus seeks to understand it in terms of the material manifestation of a large number of symbolic and practical decisions, decisions that form part of a set of cultural rules. He discusses various possible interpretations of the role of these enclosures and their relationships with ritual (cultic and feasting) and other activities, and their role as not just the location of such activities but part of their formation.

14

The measurement of time and distance in the heavens above Mesopotamia, with brief reference made to other ancient astral sciences

David Brown

The evidence concerning mensuration and numeration to be gleaned from clay tablets unearthed in and around Mesopotamia has much to say of profound importance for the history of human cognition, if indeed *human* cognition has a history and we are not merely tracing the results of individual endeavour. We should, for the sake of the perceived relevance of our disciplines, be prepared to state how our research might permit us to say something about 'becoming human', and I will, in particular, in the following react to the supposition of the editors of this volume who, when organizing the symposium from which these chapters are derived, wrote that

> the construction of measurement systems implies, in a certain sense, the construction of new means for recognizing and engaging the material world, in a broader sense for cognizing the world. It is in this process that both aspects of spirituality and the more specific conceptions of early religions must emerge.

I will concentrate on the evidence pertaining to the measurement of distances and times in the heavens mainly from Mesopotamian, but also briefly from Greek, Indian, Iranian, and Chinese sources, and the implications thereof for 'becoming human'. This will be preceded by some comments on the earliest evidence for numeration and measurement in Mesopotamia, matters that concerned the assembled delegates in particular, but first a note of caution must be sounded.

We Assyriologists work on the assumption that the endeavours of the 19th- and 20th-century decipherers of the variety of languages intermittently represented in cuneiform have made possible some measure of communication to us of the intentions of the texts' authors. The extent of commensurability is deeply variable, however, and Assyriology and its related disciplines are ones where the working hypotheses of one generation are all

too rapidly adopted as the orthodoxy of the next. We feel we know what the texts mean, when really all we have done is to translate according to the rules of grammar and philology and apply a model co-opted from a neighbouring discipline as to what, say, 'magic', 'divination', 'witchcraft', 'medicine', 'astronomy', or 'numeration' or 'mathematics', could possibly have entailed in ancient Iraq, anywhere between ca. 9,000 and 2,000 years ago. We sometimes take a further step, then, and use the hard-won interpretation to make suggestions as to how the ancients thought and thus, perhaps, something about human cognition. Our suggestions are then, sometimes, taken up by others with a particular interest in one aspect of cognition and repeated without sufficient regard to the robustness or fragility of the many steps that lead from an object to its interpretation.

Nevertheless, progress has been made, and in a few cases we can begin to approach what a text may mean with some sense that the interpretations are reliable. In this, the ability to place our sources in context is vitally important, for all too often they are unprovenanced and a lack of immediate context has meant that they were open to all sorts of interpretations. Producing context has been a long, slow and unspectacular process of drawing implications from other better-provenanced or understood sources, and the results take time to filter out into the wider community, though their implications are profound. So far as we are concerned here, there are two major implications: firstly, they force us to take another look at a widely accepted model of the role of tokens and early numerical tablets from southern Mesopotamia in regard to the cognition of the concept of number and the development of writing; secondly, they have made us rethink why the heavens were measured and the times of heavenly phenomena recorded by scholars writing cuneiform, as well as how astronomy was developed and why it spread from Mesopotamia.

Number and script

The interpretation of the evidence for counting and measurement in the earliest written documents from ancient Iraq is the subject of intense debate within Assyriology, a debate glossed over in Justus (2004) in an article written for linguists, for example. While it is self-evident that the notion of measure is dependent upon a prior notion of counting, it is by no means clear what concept of 'number' lies behind that counting. The measurements of objects, cattle, areas, volumes, weights, work schedules, time, and so forth, are each recorded in a different 'numerical-symbol system' in the earliest Mesopotamian texts written some 5,000 years ago. Since the 1980s, 13 different numerical-symbol systems, in which the number signs indicate both quantity and quality, have been identified in the earliest inscribed tablets by the (then) Berlin team of Nissen, Damerow and Englund. In some cases a sign used in one system is found in another, representing a different quantity and quality.[1] Through the course of the third millennium BCE the number of numerical-symbol systems recorded reduces to five. Most scholars argue that a pressure to make accounting ever more efficient in a rapidly expanding urban environment led, in some way, to this change. Does this mean, however, that an abstract concept of number emerged during this process? This was a question that exercised the delegates. Surely, argued some, ancient shepherds employed an abstract concept of number to count their sheep long before the invention of writing without having to rely on a method of one-to-one (or pair-to-one, quartet-to-one, etc.) correspondence with pebbles, say, in their pockets.

The view that numbers were indeed first 'concrete' and then abstracted out as a result of administrative necessity has been promulgated over the last three decades. That view was, in part, tied to a model concerning the evolution of script from tokens, as outlined by Schmandt-Besserat in 1992 and again in this volume. See also Damerow, Englund and Nissen 1988; Glassner 2000; Selz 2000. Bluntly put, according to this view, the tokens are 'concrete number-symbols' signifying both a quality and a quantity. The earliest 'numerical tablets', which appear towards the end of the fourth millennium BCE, are interpreted as the two-dimensional versions of these tokens, and as having paved the way for the abstraction out of number-symbols.[2] They did this, supposedly, by providing the opportunity for listing these 'concrete number-symbols' side by side and showing visually how the quality being represented could be separated from the quantity, and thus produce a new encoding, namely, 'number-symbol; commodity-symbol'. Context, however, suggests that this move from concrete number-symbols to 'number-symbol; commodity-symbol' was a local administrative change rather than a profound step in the history of human cognition:

Accepting that there was indeed a shift from the representation of quantity and quality in 'concrete number-symbols' to one in terms of a binary 'number-symbol; commodity-symbol', to what extent does the use of a number-symbol show that an abstract notion of number was understood? Equally, does the use of concrete number-symbols imply that abstract numbers were not understood? Addressing the first question, Damerow (1999) describes the transition from the arithmetic of concrete number-symbols (such as the tokens) to that

found on those tablets with number-symbols and commodity-symbols, as the change from 'proto-arithmetic' to 'symbolic arithmetic'. Symbolic arithmetic is not algebra as we might understand it, however, since we treat number today as 'pure magnitude', a notion first elaborated by Euclid in the fourth century BCE (Damerow 1999: 52). Even in the most erudite of cuneiform mathematical compositions, which date to ca. 1800 BCE, or the Old Babylonian period, abstract notions of quantity are not in evidence. Again, this is a view held amongst specialists but is not the view most widely promulgated beyond the confines of Assyriology. See Høyrup (2002), Robson (2001) and Melville (2005), *inter alia*, who stress the mechanical nature of the mathematical processes outlined in such compositions. They argue that measures were converted into a system of signs (usually and mistakenly called the 'sexagesimal system') in which calculations were performed easily, and the results then converted back. The process was analogous to our transliterating of an ancient document into a script form that can be more readily handled, or the treating of a calculation in pounds, shillings and pence by first converting to decimal. Symbolic arithmetic does not prove one way or another that number was understood in ancient Mesopotamia in the abstract way that we understand it today.

The evidence of the tokens and the earliest numerical tablets reveals that a nomenclature had been developed around 3200 BCE that *apparently* separated quantity from quality for most things being measured. The later evidence, however, shows that a particular system of number-symbols that had been used in the very earliest texts to measure countable objects, such as humans and animals, livestock products, fish, utensils and containers (Nissen, Damerow & Englund 1990: 64), became the system of choice for a wide range of mathematical problems. It happened to be the system in which the same sign represented both 1 and 60 and was best suited to dealing with complicated algebraic problems. Despite the assertions of previous generations of scholars (e.g., Neugebauer & Sachs 1945: 37), this later mathematics cannot be argued to represent more than a form of play with those symbols. What we see, then, through the course of the third millennium BCE is not the separation of quantity and quality, but the application of the arithmetic of countable objects to a wider and wider area of the measurable universe.

As to the question, Does the use of concrete number-symbols imply that abstract numbers were not understood? Cancik-Kirschbaum and Chambon (2006) argue that despite the multiplicity of number-symbol systems in the very earliest tablets, a concept of number independent of that which was being measured can be detected. They point to the systematic ordering of these 'concrete number-symbols', from those that represent the greatest number to those that represent the least (see further Cancik-Kirschbaum & Mahr 2005). Without the prior notion of numerical magnitude, such an order would not be expected, they argue. The authors also point to the polyvalency of most signs used in the earliest texts, and indeed in all subsequent logographic-syllabic cuneiform scripts, to explain why it is that one sign could signify differing amounts of differing things. English speakers have no problem understanding that the sign 'ton' can mean '100 runs' (in cricket, say) and '2,240 pounds of weight', for example. For different reasons, then, these authors also do not see that a concept of number is gradually abstracted out from 'concrete number-symbols', but that an abstract notion preexisted the earliest inscribed tablets. Such a notion must then have coexisted with the use of tokens and be older than ca. 3200 BCE.

It would appear, then, that the latest views within Assyriology simultaneously argue for the absence of any direct written evidence for abstract number in cuneiform at any period, and for the existence of indirect evidence that abstract number was understood from the earliest times. Contradictory, they may seem, until we recall that our oldest sources are administrative, official documents and the means by which they recorded data was a consequence of their need to gain official acceptance and to be free of errors. Context is everything. The use of one-to-one correspondence between a commodity item, or amount of some commodity, and a concrete number-symbol inscribed on a tablet reflects administrative practice rather than the state of human cognition. Each symbol represented an item checked in, or approved for quality, or the like, I suggest. The tokens were similar. They provide evidence for the need for good proof of transaction, not for the lack of an understanding of abstract number, and their demise is evidence for a change in administrative practice, not for a revolution in human cognition. In *The Epic of Gilgamesh*, our hero reaches Uta-napishtim exhausted and demands to know the secret of eternal life. Uta-napishtim states that he will reveal the knowledge if Gilgamesh does not sleep. The latter does and awakens seven days later denying that he did more than close his eyes. Uta-napishtim's wife, however, had baked a loaf of bread on each of those days and their state of decay convinces Gilgamesh to cease with his protests. Each loaf represented a day-count of one, but the purpose of symbolizing one-to-one correspondence was not to overcome an inability to count abstractly, but to be *convincing*. That this part of the great epic appears so odd to us today is perhaps, in part, because we are unaware of the authority then attached to the presentation of number in one-to-one correspondence form.

As to the evidence provided by the mathematical texts of a later period, the only thing of which we are reasonably sure is that they employ an efficient script form ('sexagesimal') used earlier to record countable commodities. As to the question as to the understanding of number as an abstract entity of 'pure magnitude' in Mesopotamia, the best we can say at the moment is that it remains controversial. Perhaps such an understanding existed long before 3200 BCE, or perhaps numeration was always tied to what was being counted but an advanced level of mathematical complexity was arrived at despite this.

Measurement and script

Artefactual remains in the form of weights or the dimensions of buildings, field sizes and population densities all help form the picture of how the universe was measured in Mesopotamia. We have very few measuring devices (for a possible sinking-style waterclock see Brown 2000b: Appendix), but some iconographical evidence and, most importantly, written descriptions help to fill that gap. The role of script, though, was not merely passively to record measurements and how measurements were made, for script also had a profound, direct impact on how measuring was done, just as it likely had in widening the use of one set of number-symbols, as implied earlier.

Goody (e.g., 1977) stressed the influence of writing on cognition and made use of the lexical sources from Mesopotamia to make his point that writing forced on its exponents questions as to hierarchy and placement that might otherwise not have occurred in the oral context. Much of the evidence that Goody relied on is now interpreted somewhat differently, in particular in terms of the pedagogical uses to which this lexical material was put (see, for example, Veldhuis 1997 with literature), and more nuanced treatments of the significance of the advent of script for cognition exist, particularly those that also address the information provided by studying the texts as artefacts.[3] It is suggested later (and in Brown 2000a; 2003; in press) that being able to record astral data provoked a revolution in the conception of the heavens. Still closer to Goody's model, the production of a general system of measurement (as discussed in Powell 1987–1990) with units from barleycorn to dana (a length of ca. 11 km), for example, created gaps in the 'table' that needed to be filled. This was done with units such as the UŠ with the result that these units could then become the objects of future research, with some important consequences for 'becoming human'.

The evidence provided by the compositions concerned with astral science

Turning now to those materials that deal with the division of time and space in the heavens, the hope is to account for why those materials say what they do. Although I addressed the relevant Mesopotamian compositions and artefacts in 2000b and would continue to argue the same points, for the last five years I have been working on the transmission of astral science in the period up to ca. CE 700 in the region from Rome and Greece, via Egypt, through Mesopotamia, Iran and India, to China, which has made possible a considerable extension to those first thoughts. Precisely because the ancient and modern categories are not always commensurable, I use this catchall rubric 'astral science' because the former classifications of the cuneiform material into astronomy, astrology, divination, iatromathematics (medical astrology), and so forth, do not work well. Where I refer to 'astronomy' I mean by that the prediction of astral movement, and not mere 'star-ordering'.

Early concepts – a cognitive model

In Brown 2000b (which should be consulted for evidence) it was argued that the units for celestial space and time used in the earliest cuneiform texts were derived from the magnitude of certain observable natural phenomena and a series of ratios derived from the observation of the number of lunations in a year, which were then linked by means of a constant of speed, namely walking pace. Implicit in this account was that the units derived were rationalizations of phenomena and objects that continue to make sense today. To that extent I made and would still make the assumption that this process of rationalizing the observed behaviour of the sky in terms of the familiar objects of the local environment is 'typically human', even if I would shy away from applying it universally. These propositions were also implicitly supposed to apply to the population at large, though the further development of the resultant units for performing astral science was regarded as being one to which only the scholarly class devoted itself. That class is usually understood by Assyriologists to have adhered to past norms and to have preserved earlier compositions by repeatedly copying them while learning the scribal trade. Parallels with the scholastic traditions of ancient China

and contrasts with the aims of some Greek scholars of the classical period can readily be made (see Lloyd 1996; 2002; Lloyd & Sivin 2002). We have no reason to doubt the conservative nature of cuneiform scholarship, and, as we shall see, this view helps account for the way in which celestial units of space and time came to be formulated and the way the heavens were perceived.

By the time units of celestial space and time appear in the written record with any frequency they have been fitted into a scheme of length units that had become standard by the latter third of the third millennium BCE. This scheme was permeated by that system of signs noted earlier called inexactly 'sexagesimal', or 'base 60'; 60 unites all bases from 2 to 6, as well as 10, 12, 15, 20, and 30, and was, as noted, present in the earliest tablets. It is also not without significance that the ideal month (see later discussion) has 30 days and the ideal year 360. Ease of calculation and a pseudo-coherence with the behaviour of the luminaries may both have played some part in the choice of this number-symbol system, but other factors cannot be ignored.

The overarching nature of the system likely ensured that the ratio between cubit and finger settled first on 1:30, and latterly 1:24; both ratios are maintained when these measures are taken over into astronomy. Likewise, the barleycorn's 'length' was determined as 1/180 of a cubit. The nindan (this is the Sumerian term, for which we have no established translation), comes in at 12 cubits.[4] The UŠ was 60 nindan and thus some 360 m (720 cubits) long; 30 UŠ were a dana, the Akkadian for which suggests that this distance was that between rest stops on a march.

Lengths: 6 barleycorn = 1 finger
          30 fingers = 1 cubit
          12 cubits = 1 nindan a 'standard measure?'
          60 cubits = 1 UŠ 'a sixty?'
          30 UŠ = 1 dana 'a rest stop?'

Each 24-hour period (nychthemeron) comprised 12 such rest stops, and the connection between the measurement of time and distance was thereby made. There is some evidence for the earlier measurement of time in terms of direct fractions of the day, but once the standard system had been imposed, time was almost without exception measured in units first used to measure lengths, or in units fitted into the general scheme of lengths.

Time: 1 dana represented 1/12 of a (night-day) nychthemeron, and thus 2 hours.
       1 UŠ was 1/30 of a dana, and equivalent to 4 minutes.
       1 nindan was 1/60 of an UŠ and equivalent to 4 seconds.

Even when time was measured in terms of the weight of water in a waterclock, the units used corresponded directly to the UŠ and nindan (Brown 2000b: 111 n.7).

Three points may be made at this point:

1. For well over two millennia the ratios between the nindan, UŠ, and dana did not vary, regardless of the context in which they were used, be that distances on Earth, time or distances in the heavens. The ratio between the barleycorn and finger remained constant, too, and that between the finger and cubit varied only between 1:30 and 1:24. These three units were also employed to record celestial distances, but never times.

2. This system of fixed ratios, linking the smallest to the largest unit by means of multiples of sexagesimally round numbers, was likely the product of bureaucracies servicing the needs of the temples and latterly the courts of transregional empires appearing at the end of the third millennium (Powell 1987–1990).

3. The ratios between units were sexagesimally round, but this still does not answer the question as to why 12 dana were fitted into a nychthemeron and not 10 or 15. Certainly, the change in walking pace implied for either would not have been beyond the realms of possibility. One dana measured some 10.8 km, quite achievably walked in 1/10 or 1/15 of 24 hours, rather than in 2 hours. The answer, I suspect, is that the number of dana in a nychthemeron derived from the observation of the behaviour of the Sun. There is a clearly observable parallel between the behaviour of the Sun over the course of one nychthemeron and one year. In one nychthemeron the Sun moves through ca. 360°, and in one year the rising or setting point of the luminary does the same. In one month the Sun rises 30 times (ideally) and its rising point has moved through the sky roughly the same distance that the Sun moves in one dana. In this sense, the dana mark the 'months' of the nychthemeron, and the UŠ the 'nychthemeron of the nychthemeron'. The standard system of length measures incorporates this notion, I suggest, and thereby connects the temporal length of the dana to the physical length of the barleycorn, while adhering to observable reality (a plausible walking pace, the size of a cubit and finger), to traditional norms (the nindan) and to the strictures of base 60.

The link between solar movement and time opened up the possibility for describing celestial distances in terms of motion orthogonal to the line of sight, though it was not until the seventh century BCE that we find any evidence that this was done. 360° was just mentioned, and 360 is, of course, the number of UŠ in one nychthemeron. The

UŠ is indeed the ancestral unit to the degree, though we must be very careful about our terms here, for a degree is a far more abstract concept. The UŠ was never understood to describe an angle subtended at the eye, nor, initially, 1/360 of the circumference of any circle. It was firstly a length on Earth and an interval of time lasting 1/360 of a nychthemeron. Latterly it was a length in space corresponding to that time interval, and finally in its most abstract form it was 1/360 of any 'great circle'. We will return to this later.

Idealization

Given the variety of number-symbol systems employed at the end of the fourth millennium to quantify and measure commodities, the calculating usefulness of the system we call 'sexagesimal' no doubt accounted for its increasing predominance in Mesopotamian numeration, but its attraction was also in part due to its pseudo-coherence with the behaviour of the time-marking luminaries. The observed number of months and days in a year, the closest round-number approximations to which were 12 and 360, with 360 being 12 times 30, the most common number of days in a month, are all expressed succinctly in this system. Slightly fewer than a half of all months are 29 days in length, however. It is, in my opinion, impossible that it was widely believed in Mesopotamia that a year really lasted 360 days, or months 30 days. Nevertheless, a number of compositions appear to treat the year in precisely these terms. Some of these texts also assert that the longest day is twice the length of the shortest in Mesopotamia and that the Moon is visible all night on the 15th of each month. Neither of these is true, and both are indeed wide of the mark. Why, then, do these texts make these assertions? The answer is simple, but widely ignored, namely, that the texts in question are not treating the phenomena as they are, but as they might be.

Accounting efficiency lies behind the use of a 360-day year in the economic records of the early third millennium (Englund 1988), but according to literary texts dating to the end of the millennium and thereafter, a 360-day year, with a 2:1 ratio of day length, and 12 30-day months with luni-solar opposition on the 15th was the way the universe was when first constructed (Brown 2000a: 234–237; Brown & Zólyomi 2001). On this basis it became possible to observe the real universe and compare what was seen with the ideal and interpret accordingly. Observed coherence with the ideal boded well, noncoherence ill. A 30-day month boded well; a 29-day one boded ill. There is ample evidence to support this view of early cuneiform astral science, and I have been arguing for it in print since 2000.

The standard system of measure, thus, embraced a powerful divinatory method used by royalty, for it was they to whom these omens comparing reality with the ideal were directed (Brown 2006). The system of measure for both time and celestial space cohered with a tool that was presented to the population as a way to protect the king against supernatural interference. Signs of ill fortune, such as planets and luminaries not behaving according to their ideals, were interpreted and sent to the king and formed part of the multilayered process of legitimization that his actions were felt to require (Pongratz-Leisten 1999 in Brown 2004).

Descriptions of the motions of the luminaries, and indeed of the stars and planets, in cuneiform texts might not necessarily, therefore, be approximating reality, but evoking, or elaborating on, ideality (e.g., the composition edited by Al-Rawi & George 1991–1992, previously thought to be 'early astronomical'). With care we are able to determine the intentions of these texts. Numerous explanations by ad hoc means over the years for their lack of correspondence with reality (Neugebauer 1947; Bremner 1993; Brack-Bernsen 2005) are, in my view, irrelevant. No longer on the basis of *such* texts can we talk of the accuracy to which the Mesopotamian scholars measured the year, the month, the length of daylight and so forth.

Another contribution to our understanding of the intentions lying behind the surviving cuneiform texts of astral science is the realisation that the widely held assumption that the predictability of heavenly phenomena is made apparent by the discovery of their periodicity is false. One look at the month gives the lie to this supposition, for it is clear that the Moon repeats its cycle every 29 or 30 days, but it is a matter of some complexity to know for sure whether the next month will last 29 or 30 days. Instead (Brown 2001; 2007), the observation of the cyclical behaviour of the planets proved to be astrologically very useful and did not lead to 'astronomy', as defined earlier. The very fact that the length of the month could be 29 or 30 days, for example, or that luni-solar opposition could occur on a number of days around the 14th, or that Venus rises *on average* in the same place every 8 years, but that the actual day and thus month of rising remains in doubt, and so forth, only revealed to the cuneiform scholars that the actual date of the phenomenon in question was the prerogative of the relevant sign-making god – the Moongod Sîn, the Sungod Šamaš, Ištar for Venus and so on. Each rising, setting, opposition, each so-called phase, was thereby imbued with meaning according to the ideal period of its recurrence and the character of the associated divinity.

It was for this reason that ideal values such as 360, 30, 12 and 2:1, and so forth, could remain so useful over centuries in astral context even though they were astronomically very poor.

The discovery of the periodicities of the heavenly bodies and the idealisation of those periods made the behaviour of those bodies amenable to interpretation. Such work had a well-defined place within the running of society, and the systems of measure used as part of it reflect this. Resonances with the situation in early Vedic astral science, in particular, abound.

Prediction and the nature of the sign giver

If the predictability of heavenly phenomena is not a logical consequence of the observation that they recur periodically, why does the accurate prediction of such phenomena begin around 700 BCE in Babylonia (Brown 2000a: see further now Britton 2004; Steele 2002; Brack-Bernsen & Steele 2005)? Bookwork is the answer, and script and the long-lasting clay medium the facilitators. The long-term record of the times and locations of phenomena permitted the discovery of longer periods after which the phenomena did indeed recur. Just such a long-term record from Babylon has survived, the so-called Diaries (Sachs & Hunger 1988–1996; Hunger 2001), the earliest examples of which record data in the way that celestial omina were described. It is as if a systematic record of ominous phenomena lay behind the discovery of those parameters that made astronomy possible (Swerdlow 1998: 16f – *contra* Hunger & Pingree 1999: 139–140, *pro* Brown 2000a: 93–103), a development that makes good sense given what we know of the importance of royal celestial divination. In Brown (2000a: 239–243), I proposed that scholars were deliberately placed into competition with each other for royal favour, and that one way in which they could curry just that was by anticipating ill-boding celestial configurations, that is, by predicting phenomena, or doing astronomy. I adduced what evidence there was from the correspondence of the scholars preserved in the archives at Nineveh and suggested that herein lay the motivation for astronomy.

True or not, the cuneiform record indicates that astronomy begins around 700 BCE and develops into a powerful industry with enormous ramifications for the history of science, for measurement and for 'becoming human'.

Units for recording and predicting accurately

The advent of astronomy introduced some important changes in the way in which time and celestial space were measured. Parameters for making astronomical predictions were improved by measuring the time and position of observed celestial phases, such as heliacal risings or eclipses. The predicted location and time of phases, and in due course the predicted location of an asterism at any given moment, were expressed in completely new units. The names of these units, however, and their forms continued to adhere to the norms for the units of spatial measure on Earth established millennia earlier.

Details can be found in Brown (2000b: 111f); in brief, the UŠ was sometimes used to measure observed distances between heavenly bodies from the seventh century BCE on (Brown 2000b: 112; Steele 2003: n.40), though both it and the dana were in general used for calculated longitudes, that is, distances along the ecliptic.[5] The cubit, here meaning ca. 2 to 2½° (where by degree we mean 1/360 of a great celestial circle, such as the equator, the ecliptic or the meridian), and its smaller derivatives, the finger and barleycorn, were commonly used to record observed distances, also from the seventh century BCE on.

The zodiac was an invention of seminal importance in the history of science. It marked off the ecliptic, the path of the Sun, Moon, and star planets, into 12 dana (each 30-UŠ) bands. It is remarkable that a great circle that lies obliquely to the equator should have been divided up in this way, since the UŠ and dana had long since been primarily time units when it came to the heavens, and a direct relationship exists between time and the distance moved in the sky *only* along lines parallel to the equator. The zodiac shows that the UŠ and dana had truly become units of celestial distance, abstracted out from units of time measure and put to a new use. The description, however, of the ecliptic in this way meant that a system of mensuration of high accuracy was produced from one whose roots lay in an ideal image of the universe. In the ideal universe, the Sun traveled once through the stars in 360 days made up of 12 30-day months, an approximation far too inaccurate for astronomy. With the zodiac, however, the Sun traveled precisely 360° made up of 12 30-UŠ signs (each designated either by month name, number or nearby constellation) in one sidereal year. The ancient structure of the system of mensuration was preserved, but transformed into something accurate.

In the centuries following ca. 700 BCE astronomical predictions were made in two ways. The first, and older, method derived accurate parameters from the study of records after which phenomena recurred. These parameters were then used with more recent observations to make new predictions. This astronomy was 'database-dependent' and could only systematically be applied by those working for institutions that made and kept good records of astral phenomena. From the sixth century BCE on, first for eclipses and lunar behaviour and later for the planets, however, a 'database-independent' astronomy was developed in Babylon and Uruk, which modeled the mean motion of the asterisms and their behaviour around the mean mathematically. Provided one epoch value of location at a given time was known, these schemes predicted the motion of the heavenly bodies for any time without any need to consult recorded data. This form of astronomy was eminently more transmissible than the database-dependent variety.

So far as we are able to judge, texts that recorded observed celestial locations or predicted them using database-dependent methods did so in cubits of 24 fingers each (Steele 2003: 283–284). The situation for the relationship between the cubits and fingers in the database-independent texts is less clear-cut (despite Steele 2003: 284–286), and a 1:30 ratio still seems to have held some sway. By this period in Mesopotamian history a 24-finger cubit was in use in nonastral contexts (Powell 1987–1990: 470), and this perhaps lies behind the ambiguity. Still more intriguing is that the cubit actually corresponded to ca. 2.4° according to Jones's (2004) detailed study of the observed distances between stars and planets recorded in texts such as the Diaries. The size of the finger, 24 of which compose a cubit in these texts, is accurately established as 1/12° on the basis of other texts, which deal with the calculated latitude of the Moon (Neugebauer 1975: 514). We would expect, therefore, the cubit of 24 fingers to measure 2° of celestial space. A further confusing factor is that one text states that the size of the Moon is 12 fingers (BM 41004: obv. 11 – see now Steele 2003: 285–286), which at 1° is approximately twice reality. Are the 'fingers' here 1/24°? All in all, the situation with regard to the use of cubits and fingers in the astronomical cuneiform texts is inconsistent. The units used to measure observed distances in the heavens applied the convention that 1 cubit was equal to 24 fingers, but their absolute size seems to have been highly variable. The angle subtended by a finger held up at arm's length is vastly greater than 1/12°, so it is impossible to argue that this simple expedient lay behind the use of this particular unit. Instead, it appears that the cubit (and thus the finger) was based on a numerical relationship with the UŠ (Brown 2000b: Box 6). Something along the lines of a Jacob's staff may well have been used to measure observed distances (Brack-Bernsen 2005: 243–244), though we have no iconographic, archaeological or textual evidence to back up this hypothesis, and for our purposes it is enough to note that the cubit and finger units, despite their names, had become disconnected from the physical world of real body parts.

The observed times between phases were measured in years, months, days and UŠ. The records of the times of phases, particularly eclipses, ultimately led to highly accurate values for the length of the month and year (see now Britton 2002). One discovery was that lunar eclipses separated by 235 months occur at the same place in the sky, and thus at the same time of year since the Sun is involved. A total of 235 months lasts 19 years to a high degree of accuracy, and a means had been found not only to assign an accurate value to the length of the year, but also to regulate the luni-solar calendar, which had administrative and religious uses, as well as astronomical. Much has been written about how time intervals shorter than a day were measured (e.g., Stephenson & Fatoohi 1994; Stephenson, Morrison & Steele 1997; Huber 2000), and it seems likely that a constant-head waterclock was used (Brown et al. 1999/2000) and a set of stars whose moments of culminating provided useful temporal reference points. The calculated times of phases were often expressed in a new unit, often and incorrectly referred to as a *tithi* since the Mesopotamian unit has nothing to do with the Indian one. This unit, called by the name 'day', was in reality 1/30 of the length of a month. It greatly simplified calculations, but it is also noteworthy that it echoed the number of days in an ideal month.

From ca. 700 BCE a concerted effort was made by scholars associated with the royal courts in Assyria and with the large temples in Babylonia accurately to record the times and locations of planetary phases, and to use these data to determine parameters that could then be used to predict future celestial scenarios, or to calculate the state of the heavens at a given moment, be that in the past or the future. We are able to trace the development of this astronomical endeavour and to say something about its *Sitz im Leben*. It was traditional to see the motivation as calendrical, or even as an example of study for its own sake, but recent research has pointed to its fulfilling a strong astrological need. That need was at first to provide for the king but by the fifth century BCE had diversified to provide for the individual. Assigning significance to the state of the heavens at the moment of an individual's birth or conception achieved this. The details of this change and the reasons behind it cannot be discussed in detail here (see Brown 2003; 2010; in press; Rochberg 2004), but some of its ramifications will be touched upon. Before that, it is worth noting that the use of different units for measuring observations and predictions is somewhat removed from our norms. So is the idea of providing a multiplicity of answers to the question of where or when a given phase will occur depending on whether database-dependent or -independent methods were used. The astronomical calculations remained at some level an elaborate

exegesis on the nomenclature associated with celestial divination, combined with bookwork on those records. The former is to be compared with the 'symbolic arithmetic' of the Old Babylonian mathematical texts, and the latter with the opportunity writing afforded for the abstraction out of number-symbols from concrete number-symbols. There is little sense that the new discipline of astronomy was intended to account for the nature of the universe. For such ideas we have to turn to Mesopotamia's neighbours.

The unfolding universe

It was noted that the unpredictability of cyclical phenomena provided for regular exhibitions of the judgement of the gods on current affairs. A 29-day month signified the Moongod's ire, which was interpreted as being caused by the current or potential behaviour of the king, the land or the people, and steps were taken accordingly. The advent of accurate astronomical prediction, however, might be expected to subvert the god's role. If it is known that the next month will last 29 days, based on accurate measurement of the length of the mean month, and a carefully formulated model of the variation about that mean, or on the discovery of the recurrence of critical intervals between moonrise and sunrise, say, what then of the Moongod's free will when it came to his commenting on current mundane affairs?

Despite the undeniable logic of this, in the cuneiform record from ca. 700 BCE on there is no sudden diminution in the role of the gods associated with the asterisms. In Brown (2010), I discussed what evidence there was for a change in *Weltanshauung*, and the picture is complex. There are merely hints in some texts of an overarching godhead pulling the strings; however, it is not without interest that just as developments in astronomy are occurring in Mesopotamia the so-called pre-Socratic thinkers, fragments of whose works have come down to us, are concerned with notions of prediction and with the systematic unfolding of the universe. The idea of the first mover plays into concepts of monotheism, and I speculate in that article that the invention of astronomy in Mesopotamia, itself underpinned by the construction of new measuring systems, was one of the stimuli behind the complex of changes leading in monotheistic directions in the Near East and classical world.

Scale and age of our universe

A further, and perhaps clearer, consequence of the accurate measure of celestial space and time is the opportunity astronomy afforded for putting figures to the size and age of the universe. As to the universe's size, I am unaware of any deliberations in cuneiform that stem from astronomy. Cosmological and cosmogonical compositions in cuneiform there are (see now Horowitz 1998, and for the speculations of one Middle Babylonian text on the absolute distances between stars see Brown 2000b: 111), but none connected with measurement.

With regard to the age of the universe, however, more can be said. Compositions such as *The Sumerian King List* (etcsl t.2.1.1)[6] describe the long reigns of mythical antediluvian kings. Compositions attributed to the Babylonian Berossos, who wrote a history of Babylonia in Greek in the early third century BCE, assign 432,000 years to the period before the flood. This number, however, appears as the *kaliyuga* parameter in far later Indian astronomical texts, where it is directly connected to the age of the universe. Pingree (1963: 238) argues that the *kaliyuga* value was borrowed from Mesopotamia, and although it is unlikely that it traveled directly from Babylonia to India, the role of the Greeks in that possible transmission may be important. Plato in *Timaios* 39 and *Republic* VIII 546 B-D and X 615 B describes a Great Year. The doctrine of *apokatastasis*, or eternal recurrence, is attributed to Berossos by Seneca (*Quaest. nat.*, 3.2.1), and in an early Stoic version of the eternal recurrence a cycle, a Great Year (*SVF*, 2.599),[7] lasts until the planets realign in their original position or zodiacal sign (*SVF*, 2.625). Greek and Latin astrological compositions sometimes discuss a perfect or Great Year made up of multiples of periods between recurring phases of the planets – values that were first determined in Babylonia (Neugebauer 1975: 603; n.21, 606; 618). A multiple of these periods leads back to a supposed time when all the planets were simultaneously rising, or setting, and small adjustments would lead to a date when the planets were all in conjunction, or in critical positions within the zodiac. Such a time could thus be equated with the start of the universe, as in some Stoic and Indian thought, and a similar idea also underlies the so-called horoscope of the world of Iranian inspiration (e.g., Ch. 5a of the *Bundahišn*).[8] The possibility, therefore, exists that Babylonian scholars also speculated on the age of the universe using astronomical parameters.

The debt of some Greek scholars to the achievements of the Babylonian astronomers is substantial, but before the former made use of some of the parameters of the latter (from the third century BCE on; details in Brown in press) Greek astral science had established several areas of concern that did not overlap with those of their Babylonian counterparts. One involved the scale of the universe. Hipparchus in the second century

BCE determined the distances of the Sun and Moon in terms of Earth radii by measuring lunar parallax, apparently with a dioptre, and by determining solar parallax to be less than seven seconds of arc (for details see Toomer 1976). Hippolytus in *Refutation of All Heresies* IV, 8, gives lunar distances supposedly established by Archimedes and Apollonius, and the calculations of Aristarchus of Samos of the distances of the Sun and Moon survive. All three worked during the third century BCE.[9] Measurement of celestial distances provided some Greek thinkers with data upon which to base a quantitative picture of the universe.

Shape and scale of the Earth

If an interest in taking accurate measurements of the distances of the heavenly bodies influenced the conceptions of some Babylonians as to the shape and scale of the Earth, no record of such has come down to us. By the early sixth century BCE, however, Anaximander was promulgating a view of a spherical universe at the centre of which lay a spherical Earth. This view, with some variation, became widespread, and attempts were made to give it some scale. Eratosthenes in the early third century BCE measured the altitude of the Sun at differing latitudes to determine the size of the Earth. Ptolemy in *Geography* I. 4 notes that Hipparchus determined latitude on the basis of the elevation of the pole, and then goes on to mention the usefulness of eclipse observations for determining longitude. It seems reasonable, then, to suggest that the use of eclipses for determining geographical longitude was known to Hipparchus, and this, with latitude values, paved the way for producing maps of the world, with profound consequences for relations among far-flung peoples.

Generalization, transmissibility and conclusions

The adherence of many Greek scholars to an idea of the circularity of the Earth and of the universe, and to the notion that the heavenly bodies moved in circles, provided for a rich dialogue with profound implications for the history of the astral sciences. Central to this was the belief that Earth measures (geometry) pertain in the heavens. Geometrical proof, one deriving logically from accepted premises, the *more geometrico*, was regarded as the benchmark for correct reasoning. Observations of parallax, or solar altitude, led logically to values for the scale of the Earth and universe by means of geometry, and these are substantial intellectual achievements born of measurement helping to contextualize the human in his or her environment.

Most astral science done in Greek and Latin after the fourth century BCE, however, was concerned with personal astrology, for which the locations of the heavenly bodies at specific moments need to be known. This divinatory art spread from Babylonia, but outside Babylonia the challenge of making the relevant astronomical calculations was at first only poorly met, using local methods. The achievements of the cuneiform scholars were not easy to reproduce, and it is clear that their database-dependent astronomy could not travel easily without substantial translations of their records occurring. In due course, though, database-independent methods did leave Babylonia, sounding the death knell for cuneiform in so doing (Brown 2008). The vast majority of astronomy conducted in Greek, Demotic and Latin until the third century CE was done using methods identical, or akin, to those formulated by the Babylonians (e.g., Jones 1999), and the reason for its spread throughout the entire Hellenistic world and on into Iran, India and China was the growing market for zodiacal divination. It constitutes the greatest testimony to the consequences of taking accurate measurements of astral distances and times. Most of what has survived today of Mesopotamian intellectual life has done so because of the spread of zodiacal astrology. The discovery that the heavenly bodies did not move arbitrarily and the notion that their location at a specific moment encoded valuable information on what occurred at that moment (birth, the start of a business trip, etc.) raised huge questions as to the relationship between the heavens and Earth, questions that the many religions and philosophical schools strove to answer. The solutions were multifarious, but a greater commonality of challenge existed thereafter than before, I would suggest.

Those scholars interested in geometrical astronomy strove to participate in this market. Hipparchus rose first to the challenge, making astute use of the Babylonian parameters along with his own observations using new apparatus and his substantial mathematical gifts. He probably developed spherical geometry to help meet this end (Sidoli 2004). The Babylonian parameters had been derived from observations made at the latitude of Babylonia and were designed for use there. Hipparchus's adherence to the circularity of the heavens meant that his astronomical model could, with some care and trigonometric work, be made to work at any latitude. Furthermore, Babylonian methods calculated locations relative to the stars (sidereal) and not to the vernal equinox (tropical), the gradual shift of the equinox to the stars being of no relevance to their astrology. Hipparchus noticed the discrepancy between the sidereal and tropical years and was thus able to devise an astronomical method that plotted locations relative to the equinox. In other words, by means of more careful measurement of the unit of the year, his form of astronomy could be used not only at any latitude but also at any period. His astronomy was potentially universal. In reality it was not until the second century CE that Hipparchus's achievements were fully realized in the works of Ptolemy. From that point on, though, the accurate measurement of the times and distances of the heavenly bodies from each other and the horizons was underpinning a science, and a view of the universe, that did spread throughout the world. To what extent did it show that science produced results that pertained universally? To what extent did it show that those results were for everyone? To what extent did it provide a new means of 'cognizing the world'?

Writing assisted in the elaboration of number-symbols that greatly facilitated the creation of a system of mensuration linking lengths, times and distances in space. Measurement of the times of and distances between astral phases made astronomy possible. Royal astral divination accounts for why that measurement took place and when. Astronomy, in turn, made personal zodiacal astrology possible, and its spread brought the new science to the attention of vast numbers of men and women. The new science was transformed through further measurement into one that could explain the shape, nature and age of the universe and was formulated in such a way that all humanity could make use of it. It played a significant role in our 'becoming human'.

NOTES

1. One and the same sign is used to indicate '10 livestock', '6 standard capacities of cereal', and an 'area of 18 standard units', for example. See Nissen, Damerow & Englund 1990: 176.
2. It should be noted that the stratigraphic dating of the texts concerned is extremely muddled, and it is possible that these 'numerical tablets' are not intermediate between the complex tokens and bullae, on the one hand, and tablets with number symbols and ideograms, on the other, but are simply the products of a different administrative system in Uruk, whence they come.
3. We mentioned earlier the observation as to the order of the concrete number-symbols on the earliest tablets, and what that tells us. Robson 2001: 201 reminds us that the Old Babylonian mathematical texts, for example, are artefacts as much as 'a pot sherd or a bus' and that our understanding of them depends significantly on their being treated as such.
4. The sign nindan is first attested as a unit for the daily ration of food (the sign is a picture of a bowl), and then co-opted

as the side of a standard garden plot – a plot presumably assigned to a family to fulfill its needs. It appears to have been read by the Akkadians as 'a standard'.

5. Calculated latitudes (the orthogonal distance from the ecliptic) are sometimes given in fingers, sometimes in UŠ.

6. *The Electronic Text Corpus of Sumerian Literature*, composition number, available at www-etcsl.orient.ox.ac.uk.

7. *Stoicorum veterum fragmenta*, ed. J. von Arnim (Leipzig: Teubner, 1903).

8. Completed in the ninth century CE, this composition drew on earlier Pahlavi and Avestan precursors. All relevant bibliographical information can be found at www.avesta.org.

9. Diogenes' attribution to the sixth century BC Thales of a ratio of 1:720 of the Sun's diameter to its distance (Kirk et al. 1983: 83, n.1) is clearly anachronistic.

REFERENCES

Al-Rawi, F. N. H. & A. R. George 1991 Enūma Anu Enlil XIV and Other Early Astronomical Tables. *Archiv für Orientforschung* **38/39**: 52–73.

Brack-Bernsen, L. 2005 The "Days in Excess" from MUL.APIN – On the "First Intercalation" and "Water Clock" Schemes from MUL.APIN. *Centaurus* **47**: 1–29.

Brack-Bernsen, L. & J. M. Steele 2005 Eclipse Prediction and the Length of the Saros in Babylonian Astronomy. *Centaurus* **47**: 181–206.

Bremner, R. W. 1993 The Shadow Length Table in MUL.APIN, H. D. Galter, ed., *Die Rolle der Astronomie in den Kulturen Mesopotamiens: Beiträge zum 3. Grazer Morgenländischen Symposion (23.–27. September 1991)*. Graz: Rm-Druck and Verlagsgesellschaft. Grazer Morgenländische Studien 3, 367–382.

Britton, J. P. 2002 Treatments of Annual Phenomena in Cuneiform Sources, J. Steele & A. Imhausen, eds., *Under One Sky – Astronomy and Mathematics in the Ancient Near East*. AOAT 297. Münster: Ugarit Verlag, 21–78.

Britton, J. P. 2004 An Early Observation Text for Mars: HSM 1899.2.112 (=HSM 1490), C. Burnett, J. P. Hogendijk, K. Plofker & M. Yano, eds., *Studies in the History of the Exact Sciences in Honour of David Pingree*. Leiden, Boston: Brill, 33–55.

Brown, D. R. 2000a *Mesopotamian Planetary Astronomy-Astrology*. Groningen: Styx.

Brown, D. R. 2000b The Cuneiform Conception of Celestial Space and Time. *Cambridge Archaeological Journal* **10**: 103–121.

Brown, D. R. 2001 Astronomy-Astrology in Mesopotamia. *Bibliotheca Orientalis* **58**: 41–59.

Brown, D. R. 2003 The Scientific Revolution of 700 BC, Alaisdair A. MacDonald, Michael W. Twomey and Gerrit J. Reininck, eds., *Learned Antiquity: Scholarship and Society in the Near-East, the Greco-Roman World, and the Early Medieval West*. Leuven, Paris, Dudley, Mass.: Peeters: 1–12.

Brown, D. R. 2004 Review article of Pongratz-Leisten, Beate. 1999. *Herrschaftswissen in Mesopotamien. Formen der Kommunikation zwischen Gott und König im 2. Und 1. Jahrtausend v. Chr.* [= State Archives of Assyria Studies 10.] Helsinki: State Archives of Assyria Project. *Zeitschrift für Assyriologie* **94**: 112–121.

Brown, D. R. 2006 Astral Divination in the Context of Mesopotamian Divination, Medicine, Religion, Magic, Society, and Scholarship. *East Asian Science Technology and Medicine* **25**: 26–83.

Brown, D. R. 2007 Mesopotamian Astral Science, G. Leick, ed., *The Babylonian World*. New York and London: Routledge, 460–472.

Brown, D. R. 2008 Increasingly Redundant: The Growing Obsolescence of the Cuneiform Script in Babylonia from 539 BC, J. Baines, J. Bennet & S. Houston, eds., *The Disappearance of Writing Systems: Perspectives on Literacy and Communication*. London and Oakville, Conn.: Equinox, 73–101.

Brown, D. R. 2010 Disenchanted with the Gods? The Advent of Accurate Prediction and Its Influence on Scholarly Attitudes towards the Supernatural in Ancient Mesopotamia and Ancient Greece, H. D. Baker, E. Robson, and G. Zólyomi, eds., *Your Praise Is Sweet: A Memorial Volume for Jeremy Black by Students, Colleagues, and Friends*. London: British Institute for the Study of Iraq, 11–28.

Brown, D. R. In press *The Interactions of Ancient Astral Science*. [= *Vergleichende Studien zu Antike und Orient*; X.] Bremen: Hempen.

Brown, D. R., John Fermor & Christopher Walker 1999/2000 The Water Clock in Mesopotamia. *Archiv für Orientforschnung* **46/7**: 130–148.

Brown, D. R. & G. Zólyomi 2001 "Daylight Converts to Nighttime": An Astrological-Astronomical Reference in Sumerian Literary Context. *Iraq* **63**: 149–154.

Cancik-Kirschbaum, E. & G. Chambon 2006 Maßangaben und Zahlvorstellungen in archaischen Texten, *Altorientalische Forschungen* **33**: 189–214.

Cancik-Kirschbaum, E. & B. Mahr 2005 Anordnung und ästhetisches Profil: Die Herausbildung einer universellen Kulturtechnik in der Frühgeschichte der Schrift, Birgit Schneider, ed., *Diagramme und bildtextile Ordnungen*, in Horst Bredekamp & Gabriele Werner, general eds., *Bildwelten des Wissens – Kunsthistorisches Jahrbuch für Bildkritik*. Berlin: Akademie, 97–114.

Damerow, P. 1999 The Material Culture of Calculation: A Conceptual Framework for an Historical Epistemology of the Concept of Number, Preprint 117, Max-Planck Institute for the History of Science.

Damerow, P., R. K. Englund & H.-J. Nissen 1988 Die ersten Zahldarstellungen und die Entwicklung des Zahlbegriffs. *Spectrum der Wissenschaft* **3**: 46–55.

Englund, R. K. 1988 Administrative Timekeeping in Ancient Mesopotamia. *Journal of the Economic and Social History of the Orient* **31**: 121–132.

Glassner, J.-J. 2000 *Écrire à Sumer: L'invention du cunéiforme*. Paris: Editions du Seuil.

Glassner, J.-J. 2003 *The Invention of Cuneiform, Writing in Sumer*. Baltimore: Johns Hopkins University Press.

Goody, J. 1977 *The Domestication of the Savage Mind*. Cambridge: Cambridge University Press.

Heeßel, N. 2005 "Stein, Pflanze und Holz" – ein neuer Text zur 'medizinischen Astrologie'. *Orientalia* NS **74**: 1–22.

Horowitz, W. 1998 *Mesopotamian Cosmic Geography*. Winona Lake, Ind.: Eisenbrauns.

Høyrup, J. 2002 *Lengths, Widths, Surfaces: A Portrait of Old Babylonian Algebra and Its Kin*. New York: Springer.

Huber, P. J. 2000 Babylonian Short-Time Measurements: Lunar Sixes. *Centaurus* **42**, 223–234.

Hunger, H. 2001 *Astronomical Diaries and Related Texts from Babylonia*. V: *Lunar and Planetary Texts*. Vienna: Verlag der Österreichischen Akademie der Wissenschaften.

Hunger, H. & D. Pingree 1999 *Astral Sciences in Mesopotamia*. Leiden: Brill.

Jones, A. 1999 Astronomical Papyri from Oxyrhynchus. *Memoirs of the American Philosophical Society*, vol. 233. 2 vols. in 1. Philadelphia: American Philosophical Society.

Jones, A. 2004 A Study of Babylonian Observations of Planets near Normal Stars. *Archive for History of Exact Sciences* **58**, 475–536.

Justus, C. F. 2004 On Language and the Rise of a Base for Counting. *General Linguistics* **22**: 17–43.

Kirk, G. S., J. E. Raven & M. Schofield 1983 *The Presocratic Philosophers*, 2nd ed. Cambridge: Cambridge University Press.

Lloyd, G. E. R. 1996 *Adversaries and Authorities*. Cambridge: Cambridge University Press.

Lloyd, G. E. R. 2002 *The Ambitions of Curiosity*. Cambridge: Cambridge University Press.

Lloyd, G. E. R. & N. Sivin 2002 *The Way and the Word: Science and Medicine in Early China and Greece*. New Haven, Conn.: Yale University Press.

Melville, D. J. 2005 The Area and the Side I Added: Some Old Babylonian Geometry. *Revue d'histoire des mathématiques* **11**: 7–21.

Neugebauer, O. 1947 The Water Clock in Babylonian Astronomy. Isis 36: 37–53.

Neugebauer, O. 1975 *A History of Ancient Mathematical Astronomy*. Berlin: Springer Verlag.

Neugebauer, O. & A. Sachs 1945 *Mathematic Cuneiform Texts*. New Haven, Conn.: American Oriental Society 29.

Nissen, H.-J., P. Damerow & R. K. Englund 1990 *Frühe Schrift und Techniken der Wirtschaftsverwaltung im alten Vorderen Orient*. Bad Salzdetfurth: Franzbecker

Nissen, H.-J., P. Damerow & R. K. Englund 1993 *Archaic Bookkeeping: Early Writing and Techniques of Economic Administration in the Ancient Near East*. Chicago: University of Chicago Press.

Pingree, D. 1963 Astronomy and Astrology in India and Iran. *Isis* **54**: 229–246.

Powell, M. 1987–1990 Maße und Gewichte. *Reallexikon der Assyriologie und Vorderasiatischen Archäologie* 7: 457–517.

Robson, E. 2001 Neither Sherlock Holmes nor Babylon: A Reassessment of Plimpton 322. *Historia Mathematika* **28**: 167–206.

Rochberg, F. 2004 *The Heavenly Writing – Divination, Horoscopy, and Astronomy in Mesopotamian Culture*. Cambridge: Cambridge University Press.

Sachs, A. & H. Hunger 1988–1996 *Astronomical Diaries and Related Texts from Babylonia*, 3 vols. Vienna: Verlag der Österreichischen Akademie der Wissenschaften.

Schmandt-Besserat, D. 1992 *Before Writing*, I and II. Austin: University of Texas Press.

Selz, G. 2000 Schrifterfindung als Ausformung eines reflexiven Zeichensystems. *Wiener Zeitschrift für die Kunde des Morgenlandes* **90**: 169–200.

Sidoli, N. 2004 Hipparchus and the Ancient Metrical Methods on the Sphere. *Journal for the History of Astronomy* **35**: 71–84.

Steele, J. 2002 A Simple Function for the Length of the Saros in Babylonian Astronomy, J. Steele & A. Imhausen, eds., *Under One Sky – Astronomy and Mathematics in the Ancient Near East*. AOAT 297. Münster: Ugarit Verlag, 405–420.

Steele, J. 2003 Planetary Latitude in Babylonian Mathematical Astronomy. *Journal for the History of Astronomy* **34**, 269–89

Stephenson, F. R. & L. J. Fatoohi 1994 The Babylonian Unit of Time. *Journal for the History of Astronomy* **25**, 99–110.

Stephenson, F. R., L. V. Morrison & J. Steele 1997 The Accuracy of Eclipse Times Measured by the Babylonians. *Journal for the History of Astronomy* **28**: 337–345.

Swerdlow, N. 1998 *The Babylonian Theory of the Planets*. Princeton, N.J.: Princeton University Press.

Toomer, G. 1976 Hipparchus. *Dictionary of Scientific Biography* **15**, Supplement: 207–224.

Veldhuis, N. 1997 *Elementary Education at Nippur: The List of Trees and Wooden Objects*. Ph.D. dissertation, Groningen: Rijksuniversiteit.

15

Evolution of the calendar in Shang China

Mark Edward Lewis

The calendar(s) employed by the earliest known Chinese state, the Shang (ca. 1600–1044 BC), have been tentatively reconstructed from the divinatory inscriptions carved on bovine scapulae and tortoise plastrons.[1] The calendar is woven into these inscriptions because they are all dated, and the forms and content of dating evolve over the few centuries in which the inscriptions were made (roughly 1300–1050 BC). These materials show the close interconnection of the measurement of time not only with divinations but with a broader range of ritual practice organized around the ancestral cult. They also present an interesting case in which we can observe the interplay among the calendar as a liturgical schedule, the calendar as a mode of divination, and the calendar as a measure of the cycle of lunations and solar seasons. In this chapter I will briefly sketch what the inscriptions reveal about the origins of the calendar in China and about the enduring impact of those origins on the uses of calendars and time measurement in Chinese civilization.

The earliest method of measuring and recording time in the inscriptions employs the sexagesimal cycle formed by the sequential and synchronized enumeration of a cycle of 10 graphs (later called the 'celestial trunks' [*tian gan*]: *jia, yi, bing, ding, wu, ji, geng, xin, ren, gui*) and another cycle of 12 graphs (later called the 'earthly branches' [*di zhi*]: *zi, chou, yin, mou, chen, si, wu, wei, shen, you, shu, hai*). Thus the cycle begins with *jiazi*, followed by *yichou*, and proceeds in order until it returns to *jiazi*. Since even terms match only with even ones, and odd with odd, it produces a total of 60 named units. This system was already in use from the earliest writings that we have found, so we have no secure explanation of the origins of the cycle or how it came to be linked to the enumeration of time. I will discuss certain speculative explanations in the following.

As a method of measuring time, the cycle in its earliest uses was applied solely to the counting of days as measured from one rising of the Sun to the next. There is no indication in the inscriptions of any numerical subdivision of the day, which is divided only into such empirical events as 'dawn' (*chao*, pictographically "time when the Sun appears through the trees with the Moon still visible"), 'midday meal', 'midday' (*zhong ri*), 'afternoon' (*ze*, pictographically "time when the Sun casts an oblique shadow of a person"), 'late meal', and 'evening' (*mu*, pictographically "time when the Sun disappears in the trees") (Dong 1945: ch. 1, pp. 5–7). The unit of 10 days between the recurrences of the initial graph *jia* also formed a measure of time (*jun*, the graph combines the number '10' with a spiral indicating a cycle) that would be the closest Chinese equivalent to the Western week. That the day and the *jun* were the sole units for measuring ritual time is indicated by the fact that even lengthy periods would use only these two terms. Thus one inscription on the prolonged process of opening new land describes it as lasting "five hundred days, four *jun*, and seven days". The day of the completion of the process, identified as *dingmao*, is also given (Yu 1972: 41). Months or years do not figure in the calculation, perhaps because they were variable in length and hence did not allow precise reckoning.

Certain scholars have argued that the 10-day 'week' was a subdivision of a lunar month, which would consist of 29 or 30 days (Guo 1929: 367). However, this argument is not persuasive for several reasons. First, if the Shang calendricists had been attempting to derive a subunit of a month, why would they construct it from a cycle of 60 days, rather than 30? As noted previously, the 60-day cycle existed prior to any demonstrable use of the 10-day unit, and the lunar month played no part in the cycle. Second, and more importantly, if they had been attempting to line up the 10-day unit with months, then they would have had to intercalate some embolismic unit periodically to prevent the *jun* from progressively diverging, but they did not do so. Third, the absence of months and years in the calculation of longer periods suggests that these units were not essential to the reckoning of time at the Shang court. Finally, it is perhaps noteworthy that later myths of a time when 10 Suns existed in the sky are quite plausibly references to the origin of the 10-day cycle, and there are certain graphs in Shang inscriptions that may be linked to early forms of those myths (Allan 1991: 19–56). These mythic and ritual origins of the 10-day cycle of Suns suggest no relation to the Moon.

The 'calendar' of the early Shang would thus have consisted of a simple table or 'almanac' constituted solely by the sexagesimal cycle. Interestingly, several inscribed bones consist of nothing except the cycle (*Hou* 2, 1, 5; *Qian* 3, 3, 2; *Lin* 1, 15 and 1, 15, 7 [*He ji* 24440, 21783]). These inscriptions would presumably have assisted the diviners in calculating the chronological distance between actions on the basis of their place in the cycle or figuring the cyclic 'date' on the basis of knowing the number of days elapsed.

Before discussing the later evolution of the Shang calendar, I will briefly consider theories of the origins of the 60-unit cycle that formed its basis. As mentioned, the cycle was already in place by the time of the earliest inscriptions, so we lack any conclusive evidence on its origins. The conventional Chinese approach has been to look at the later meanings of the graphs that made up the 10-unit and 12-unit cycles and attempt to thereby deduce the origins of the system. The results, however, have been thoroughly unsatisfactory, and sometimes comical. Thus, in the most extended effort of this kind, Guo Moruo (Guo 1929) argued that the first four characters of the 10-graph cycle referred to parts of fish, while the last six were types of weapons or tools. From this he argued that the cycle had been created in two stages. The first stage had been that of a fishing people so primitive that they could only count to 4. The later six were added in the Bronze Age, when metal tools had come to the fore and people had managed to count to 10. As for the cycle of 12, he appealed entirely to reconstructed phonetic values, which he thought could be identified as numbers and linked with the proto-Iranian names of major astrological mansions. The argument, however, hinges on faulty phonetic reconstructions, unproven links of early Chinese astronomy with ancient Iranian, and the considerable backdating of evidence for any link between astral phenomena and the 60-unit cycle.

The only discussion of the cyclic units that is even vaguely plausible was offered by Léon Vandermeersch (Vandermeersch 1980: 322–323). Without presenting an exhaustive treatment of all 22 graphs, he suggested that each of them could be explained as one element of a religious ritual – a weapon used to perform sacrifices, a mask worn in the performance, an object offered – and that they were in fact all the names of sacrifices. In this case the two cycles would originally have been sacrificial sequences, the performance of which constituted a recurring unit of time. In order to account for the fusion of the two cycles, he hypothesized that one had derived from the proto-Shang religion and the other from some major subject people, perhaps the semi-mythic Xia whom the Shang supplanted in later historical accounts.

While this model goes far beyond what the evidence will bear, it has the virtue of at least suggesting links between the origins of the cycle and its actual uses as seen in the Shang inscriptions. Thus while the inscriptions are conventionally treated as though their purpose were to foretell the future, in fact the vast majority of them concern the performance of sacrificial rituals. Their contents generally consist of establishing the deity or ancestor to whom sacrifices are to be offered, the category of the sacrifice, and the types and number of animals to be slain. A second category of divinations cited disasters that had already occurred, such as a disease or drought, and sought to establish which spirit was the cause of the disaster. In the earliest inscriptions these were accompanied by divinations about the sacrifices that should be made to assuage the spirits. Thus it is likely that even those divinations that dealt with the success or safety of future actions were actually part of a larger process of establishing what sacrifices were necessary to secure that success or safety (Allan 1991: 112–123). In short, it is probable that the entire divinatory process was ultimately part of a broader program of assuring performance of the proper sacrifices, so the chronological fixing of those divinations in terms of an earlier sacrificial sequence is not wholly implausible.

The links between the 10-day unit and a sacrificial sequence became even stronger and clearer over time. As numerous scholars have noted, while the earlier inscriptions deal with a whole range of topics (sacrifices, the auspiciousness of the 10-day week, military campaigns, hunting expeditions, excursions, the auspiciousness of the day or night, the weather, agriculture, sickness, childbirth, dreams, building of settlements, commands, tribute payments, divine assistance, unspecified troubles), by the period of the last few Shang rulers the range of topics had narrowed so that they dealt with nothing but the auspiciousness of the 10-day period and its now regularized sacrifices.

Another, more speculative, link of the divinatory inscriptions and their calendar to sacrificial rituals is the possibility that the practice of divination through reading cracks in bones and shells was itself an outgrowth of sacrifice. While the exposure of these parts of animal bodies to fire, and the discovery of their cracking, could have occurred in the context of cooking game, the idea that such cracks were a means of reading the will of gods and ancestors would have been more likely to occur in a context where such cooking was part of an offering to those spirits, that is, a sacrifice.

A fourth link of the 10-day cycle to sacrifice was the fact that each Shang king received a name or title, probably posthumous, that included one of the graphs from the cycle. While the means by which the particular graph was assigned to a given ancestor remain unclear (Chang 1979: 72–92), the Shang divinatory inscriptions themselves show that ancestors received their sacrifices on the days included in their names. In short, the sexagesimal cycle not only specified particular days and 10-day 'weeks', while ignoring the cycles of the Moon and the Sun, it also specified the sequence of sacrificial offerings to Shang ancestors, as well as their posthumous names. Thus whatever the merit of Vandermeersch's hypothesis that this cycle *originated* as one or two series of sacrificial offerings, it is clear that by the time of the divinatory inscriptions it had become both an enumeration of a sacrificial sequence and a calendar for the locating of human actions in time.

Given the clear links of divination to sacrificial rituals, the routine inclusion of the sexagesimal 'date' on the divinatory inscriptions merits reflection. The contents of the inscriptions vary from case to case, with the most elaborate including pronouncements by the king on the results of the divination and a recording of the fact that the king's pronouncement later proved to be true or efficacious. However, the minimal structure of an inscription consists of nothing but the date and topic. This insistence on the primordial importance of noting the date, all the more striking because locating an event in a 60-day cycle scarcely serves to situate it 'historically', suggests not only that the earliest calendar was derived from sacrificial sequences, but that the efficacy of those sacrifices was bound to the date on which they were performed. Since each day 'belonged' to a specific ancestor or spirit power, time itself was spiritually structured, and the calendar served to map out that structure. This idea of the structuring of time by spirit or cosmic powers, and the determining of the success of human actions by adherence to that structure, remained fundamental to later Chinese calendrics.

While the earliest inscriptions were dated solely in terms of the 60-day cycle, and durations counted only in terms of days and 10-day weeks, the cycles of the Moon and the solar year gradually came to play a role in the counting of time. Interestingly, as suggested by Chen Mengjia, the behavior of the Moon and Sun seems to have been assimilated to that of eclipses, sun spots, rainbows, and other astronomical or meteorological phenomena that were read as omens (Chen 1956, 223–226). The winter solstice, which to judge from graphs was discovered and marked through use of the gnomon, is noted on certain inscriptions as a significant event, but not one used for regular dating. Indeed some inscriptions treat the arrival of the solstice as a matter of divination, just as they would an eclipse (*Jia* 3550; *Ye* 3, 38, 6;

Yi 5399; *Qian* 7, 42, 2 and 4, 9, 1 [*He ji* 11652, 5652, 22046, 8884, 12808]). This suggests that it was not yet calculated and perhaps not regarded as a normatively recurring phenomenon. It is in relation to the solstice that the practice of noting Moons as a means of keeping time first appeared.

The practice of counting the number of lunar cycles after the winter solstice first appears in postscript notations on certain inscriptions. Given the relatively short horizon of the 60-day cycle, and the consequent frequency with which the identical date returned, the gradual accumulation of divination records confronted Shang calendricists with the problem of keeping a prolonged record of the actual sequence of divinations and sacrifices. For whatever reason, they did not adopt the option of numbering cycles, perhaps because they did not choose to make some arbitrary choice of an absolute beginning. Instead they began the practice of making the aforementioned postscript notations on bones or plastrons of the number of lunar cycles that had taken place since the last winter solstice. It is important to note here that the 'months' did not figure as part of the regular system of time measurement that prefaced the divination proper, because they had no fixed relation to the sexagesimal cycle. Instead they seem to have functioned as observed astronomical events, like eclipses, but ones which recurred frequently enough to distinguish any date name in the 60-day cycle from the date of the same name in a different cycle. They were perhaps added as a postscript for purposes of storage.

However, by the second phase of the Shang inscriptions (we cannot provide any absolute dates for the stages of Shang inscriptions, but simply group and order them in terms of the names of ancestors to whom sacrifices are made, the names of diviners, the structure of the divinations, and – more controversially – the calligraphy) we find evidence of a move towards treating lunar cycles as a normative phenomenon to be incorporated into the ritual calendar. First, as pointed out by Dong Zuobin, whereas the early postscript notations are not grammatically linked to the divinatory inscription and seem to pertain to the storage of the material rather than the reading of the divinatory charge, some of the second and third period inscriptions, and all of those from the fourth period, begin to add the character ancestral to the modern *zai* ('at [a place or time]') prior to the noting of the month (Dong 1945: ch. 1, p. 8). Thus a typical inscription would now read: "On the day [graph missing] *wei*, with the king divining: 'The 10-day week will be without calamity'. In [*zai*] the 10th month, with the king at Wei while on expedition against the country Yi. (*Qian* 2, 5, 1 [*He ji* 36486])". Here, as Dong argued, while the month is still not actually part of the marked divinatory 'date', it has become more explicitly integrated into the process of fixing the divination in time by means of the inscription.

However, the clearest evidence for the normalization of lunar cycles within the ritual calendar is the fact that whereas the number of months following the solstice in early inscriptions could be as high as 14, from the third phase on, the maximal number was 12 (Dong 1945: part 1, ch. 1, p. 10; Rao 1959: 1207). In order to achieve this result it was necessary to exclude certain months from the count or to count two months as one. One example of the latter case was reconstructed by Dong Zuobin from the dates provided on all the divinations on a single (reconstructed) scapula (Dong 1962: 576, reedition of a work from 1934 citing *Yicun* 399 [*He ji* 26643]). On this bone three dates over the span of 40 days are recorded as falling within the sixth month, with the seventh month not appearing until 50 days after that. Thus the two months covered at least 90 days, and since we know the sixth month was at least 40 days it is likely that it was a double month. This would be an early form of the intercalary months inserted in later calendars in China and elsewhere, except that its function was not to reconcile the solar year with the lunar cycles, but instead to fix the number of months at 12, perhaps because the number of months would thereby map neatly onto the 60-day cycle. The calculation of such uncounted embolisms may have been related to a method outlined in a later Zhou text, but that is impossible to verify.[2]

Whatever the method used for calculating such double months, their appearance is significant because they show that the Shang calendricists had become concerned about the cycles of the Moon, but not in order to reconcile them with a solar year. The latter still did not figure in any enumerations of time. Indeed neither of the two words that later came to mean 'year' – *nian* and *sui* – functioned in that sense in the inscriptions. The former simply meant 'harvest' and the latter was a term for sacrifices that marked the two identified seasons: spring and summer. Instead it seems that as months became a more regular element of measuring time, the baseline from which they were counted was marked by the solstice, and as the solstice began to be treated as a calculable and recurring phenomenon that was part of the calendrical process, the Shang calendricists became concerned with finding some regular correspondence between two recurrent but independent phenomena: the cycles of the Moon and the movement of the Sun along the ecliptic as marked by the progressive lengthening and shortening of days. It was, in short, not in order to correct a solar-lunar

calendar that the intercalary months were introduced. Instead it was the introduction of the intercalary months used to correlate lunar cycles with the 60-day cycle (or its 12-unit element) that first made the links between the Sun and the Moon an issue, and thereby created the possibility of calculating and fixing the measurements of a solar year in the ritual context.

However, as demonstrated by Dong Zuobin, the emergence of the solar year as a constitutive unit of the Shang court calendar seems to have resulted from reforms in the schedule of sacrifices under the king posthumously known as Zu Jia. As mentioned earlier, each Shang ruler was posthumously named for one of the graphs of the 10-unit cycle, which thus corresponded to one of the days in the 10-day week. As noted, the method by which the posthumous name was selected remains unclear, and no proposed explanation has yet been able to work out any meaningful pattern.[3] Whatever the significance of the posthumous names, as the generations passed and the number of kings accumulated, it became necessary to select which of several ancestors named for a particular cyclic unit would receive sacrifice on the corresponding day. At first the selection seems to have been made by divination. However, perhaps disquieted by the increasing number of ancestors who consequently might not receive sacrifice for long periods, ritualists under Zu Jia undertook a major reworking of the sacrificial calendar. Under this new calendar five major sacrifices were made to all royal ancestors, both kings and those queens who had been the mothers of kings, in a fixed order based on their cyclic names. This became a fixed, regular liturgy that no longer required divination.

I will sketch here the structure of the calendar, as worked out by Dong Zuobin in several essays and synthesized by Chen Mengjia (Chen 1956: 386–396). The calendar consisted of three cycles, each marked by the sequential presentation of a specific sacrifice or sacrifices to all royal ancestors. In the first cycle the *rong* sacrifice was presented, in the second the *yi* sacrifice, and in the third one the joint *xie ji*, and *zai* sacrifices. In each cycle the specified sacrifices were made to the same ancestors in the same order. Each of the grand cycles was followed immediately by one 10-day week devoted to certain complementary rituals, after which the next grand cycle immediately began. Thus the complete liturgical calendar consisted of three grand cycles – *rong*, *yi*, and *xie* – and three intercyclical weeks, after which the calendar began again with the *rong* cycle.

At the time of the reform under Zu Jia, the *rong* cycle and the *yi* cycle each lasted nine 'weeks', while the *xie* cycle lasted for 11 because of the greater number of sacrifices that had to be performed. With the addition of the three weeks placed between the major cycles, the liturgical calendar lasted for 32 weeks of 10 days each, for a total of 320 days. Since this new calendar was more than five times longer than the old 60-day cycle, it offered the possibility of distinguishing recurring temporal units much more effectively than simply adding postscript notations of months. Thus from the reign of Zu Jia we begin to find divinations in which the day is calendrically fixed with a reference to which sacrifice is being performed to which king, as in the following example:

> On the day *guichou*, the king divining: "This ten-day week will be without calamity." In the fourth month, on the day *jiayin* [of the week in question] prior to the sacrifice *yi* made to Shang Jia.(*Yicun* 906 [*He ji* 22669])

Since Shang Jia was the ultimate ancestor in the royal genealogy, and the first to receive sacrifice in each of the cycles, this inscription would date from the intervening ritual week prior to the beginning of the *yi* sacrificial cycle, about the first week of which it divined. The same piece includes a subsequent inscription on the same topic that dates from the next 10-day 'week', with the date identified both by month and by the name of the sacrifice made on that day to a specified ancestor. Thus the liturgical sequence now provided an extended 320-day calendar over and above the 60-day cycle and the numbering of lunar cycles.

However, since this liturgical calendar was determined by the sequence of offerings to royal ancestors, it did not remain fixed but enlarged with each royal death and the consequent entry of the deceased into the sacrificial sequence. Thus, according to Dong Zuobin, by the time of the final Shang king, Di Xin, the liturgical calendar had been extended to 37 10-day weeks, or 370 days. It is striking that it is precisely in the divinations from the last two reigns, when the sacrificial calendar had come to last one solar year (or in the final reign just more than one), that the postscript giving the date began to include not only the day in the 60-day cycle, the month, and the day in the sacrificial calendar, but also the number of times that the sacrificial calendar had been completed in the reign in question, that is, how many solar years had elapsed in the reign of that king. Thus we see inscriptions such as the following:

> On the day *guisi*, the king divining: "This ten-day week will be without calamity." The king prognosticated, "Auspicious." In the sixth month, the day *jiawu*, prior to the *rong* sacrifice to Qiang Jia. This was the third cycle of the reign.

Other inscriptions omitted any mention of the daily sacrifice, so that the day was noted simply by month and number of sacrificial cycles, which was tantamount to month and year. In the postscript notations, at least, an astronomical, lunar-solar calendar had begun to emerge from behind the liturgical one

> On the day *guiwei*, divining at Shangxie: "'The king will be without calamity in this 10-day week.' In the ninth month of the twentieth sacrificial cycle of the reign.

The same pattern of noting the date in terms of the number of months and sacrificial cycles (solar years) also appeared in the bronze inscriptions in this period.

However, it is worth noting that the enumeration of months and sacrificial cycles = years was still used only in the postscript notations, while the ritual inscriptions themselves continued to supply only the date as identified by the sexagesimal cycle of days. The number of lunar cycles since the solstice and the number of sacrificial cycles since the beginning of the reign continued to serve as 'events' that distinguished different days with the same name. This is most clearly shown by the fact that other inscriptions from the same period placed political or meteorological events in the postscript to fix a divination in time, just as they did with the number of Moons or sacrificial cycles.

> On the day *guisi*, divining: "The king will be without calamity in this ten-day week". In the second month, at Qici. It was when the king had gone there on an expedition against the state of Ren. (*Qian*, 2, 15, 3 [*He ji* 36493])

> In the ninth month. At the time of the *rong* sacrificial sequence of the sixth sacrificial sequence of the reign, when the king had gone there on an expedition against the lord of the state of Yu. (*Jia*, 3939 [*He ji* 37398])

It is clear that these political events remained accidental landmarks used solely to clarify which day of a given name was actually in question, while the liturgical calendar measured and mapped out the underlying structure of time as defined by the sacrifices and the spirits as named in the 60-day cycle. In this case the near identity of the solar year and the full sacrificial cycle probably still appeared to Shang calendricists as no more than an interesting coincidence.

However, it is possible that the identity had begun to seem normative. Through a reconstruction of the ritual calendar at the end of the Shang that differs from that of Dong Zuobin, Shima Kunio has argued that the calendricists were in fact actively manipulating the ritual sequence to make sure that it took place entirely within the length of a single solar year (Shima 1958: 115–116). Shima argues that in the reign of Di Yi, the penultimate

Shang king, the liturgical calendar should, according to the traditional practice, now have lasted 38 10-day weeks – 13 for the *xie* cycle, 11 each for the *rong* and *yi*, and 3 for the intersequential rituals. However, in order to keep the cycle within the span of a year the Shang court combined the rituals of either one or two of the intercyclic weeks with the last week of the grand cycle that preceded it. By thus compressing the sequence, they were able to prevent it from exceeding the bounds of the solar year as the number of sacrifices grew. Indeed Shima argues that they alternated the overlapping of one week – giving a cycle of 370 days – and of two – giving a cycle of 360 days. This would have resulted in a two-year sequence with an average year of exactly 365 days. In the subsequent reign of Di Xin, Shima argues that the sacrifices to Di Yi were squeezed into the schedule in such a way that they did not need to add another week to the sequence. The fortuitous overthrow of the dynasty in the reign of Di Xin would thus have saved the Shang calendricists from any further tinkering with the calendar.

While Shima's reconstructions remain disputed, the linkage of the Shang ritual calendar at the end of the dynasty to the solar year is suggested by the fact that a tradition preserved down into imperial China states that the Shang had conducted a major cycle of sacrifices, identified by the term *si*, which had lasted 'four seasons'. While the tradition of the Shang cycle is not specifically mentioned until Guo Pu's fourth-century AD commentary to the *Er ya*, the use of *si* to mean 'year' appeared in Zhou bronze inscriptions from shortly after the conquest.

In recent decades, scholarship on the mainland related to early calendars has focused on new textual discoveries, and more recently on the state-sponsored attempt to provide an absolute chronology of the early dynasties based on records of datable astronomical events and on reconstructions of the *Bamboo Annals*. The most important contributions to the study of the Shang calendar have been a series of articles by Feng Shi, which were synthesized in slightly different forms in two books published in 2001. These articles examined divinations regarding sacrifices to asterisms whose appearances marked the solstices, later myths and décor on Neolithic pottery and jades that hint at early Sun worship and the emphasis on a solar year, a reconstruction of the duration of the Shang agricultural calendar from divinations on agricultural activities, and interpretations of the names of the four Shang deities of the directions and their associated winds that Feng argues indicate that they were named for the solstices and equinoxes (Feng 2001: 129–190, 166–225). While these articles have provided new details

about the Shang agricultural calendar and Shang observations of the celestial patterns that marked the solar year, they have not led to any modification of the earlier reconstruction of the Shang calendar by Dong Zuobin and Chen Mengjia. Indeed, as Feng Shi has demonstrated, the Shang had not even integrated the solar year marked by the sequence of solstices and equinoxes with that which defined the agricultural calendar, much less made the solar year an integral part of the court ritual calendar.

The practices of the Shang, straddling the transition from a ritual calendar based on the sexagesimal cycle to a solar year (with the sexagesimal cycle continuing to be used as a means of enumerating days), still figure in early dating by the Zhou conquerors. As Léon Vandermeersch has pointed out, some of the earliest Zhou inscriptions still follow the late Shang system of recording a ritual date based on the sexagesimal cycle, and then fixing it more clearly in time with a reference to a political event and, sometimes, the number of the month. He provides the following example:

> On the day *yimao* the king ordered the Protector to go to the dwelling of Xi, marquis of Wu in the eastern region of Yin [Shang], and to award him six groups [of captured Shang population]. The Protector congratulated the marquis, who gave him the gifts offered to a guest. With the gifts the Protector made this precious offering vessel for the temple of his father Gui. This happened when the people of the four directions had all submitted in a grand sacrificial ceremony at the Zhou capital. In the second month, the third quarter of the moon.

Since later records indicate that the ceremony cited here followed immediately on the Shang conquest, this vessel dates to the very beginning of the Zhou. Notably it preserves the old Shang system of dating (Vandermeersch 1980: 356–358).

Within a few decades, however, the standard method of recording dates in Zhou bronzes (and hence clearly the officially approved method) had completed the transition to the solar-lunar calendar. The form of such inscriptions began with the particle *wei*, followed usually by the number of years of the reign of the present ruler, then invariably the number of the month, almost invariably the phase of the Moon, and finally the day, still indicated in sexagesimal cycle. It is noteworthy that the indication of the day in the sexagesimal cycle is regularly preceded with the formula "the astronomical sign *chen* was in …" where *chen* was the name of an imaginary star whose course through the sky supposedly marked out the 60-day cycle. The invention of this astronomical fiction by Zhou calendricists shows how they now understood themselves as operating in a solar-lunar, astronomical calendar into which the sexagesimal cycle with its purely ritual origins could be incorporated only by pretending that it was actually derived from some observable, sequential astral phenomenon. In this way the original position of the Shang calendricists, with their ritual calendar in which astronomical cycles appeared as outside accidents, had been completely inverted.

Conclusion(s)

This brief reconstruction offers several possible conclusions about early Chinese calendars and the measurement of time. First, we can see a clear distinction, such as that posited by Bourdieu, between the formal or intellectualist calendar of the Shang court and the conventional body of practice and oral wisdom that would have formed the calendar of the Shang peasants (Bourdieu 1977: 97–109). As an agrarian society, the Shang would clearly have operated according to a seasonal calendar of plowing, planting, weeding, and harvest that was tied to the solar cycle. The detachment of the Shang ritual calendar from the cycle of the seasons does not suggest some ignorance of the latter, but simply that the precise measurements of a structured calendar do not need to be tied to astral or meteorological phenomena. Indeed, as various scholars have noted, the rise of modern science in association with the clock and its hours, minutes, seconds, and nanoseconds has marked a progressive detachment from time as a question of astronomical phenomena or biological patterns. The Shang measurement of time was similarly abstracted from the 'events' of the sky and of nature, but in the pursuit of a different mode of ordering the world. This is an important point for the later history of Chinese calendrics, in which the annual issuing of a ritual/divinatory calendar by the court was a fundamental aspect of imperial power, while peasants practiced agriculture according to calendrical lore of natural signs provided by animals and plants. Some Western scholars have argued that the issuing of the imperial calendar was in some way essential to the agrarian economy, which was clearly no more the case in imperial China than in the Shang.

Second, it is significant that the story of the Shang calendar cannot be told as a series of increasingly accurate measurements of the solar year and attempts to link it with the cycles of the Moon in a single system (which is how the history of Chinese calendrics is conventionally written). The sequences in which the Shang calendricists structured time for the court were built on the human

world, and not that of the stars. The cycles around which time was structured, and the events in the world that those cycles guided, were both tied into a calendar of liturgical performances by which the Shang simultaneously defined the structure of their own society and maintained links with the divine forces that underpinned that structure.

Third, as is often the case with calendars, the Shang measurement and demarcation of time were tied into their practice of divination. The genealogical sequence that fixed the past, the divinatory record that fixed the future, and the calendrical cycle that ran through past, present, and future all formed a single, interlocking system. The nomenclature of time was identical with the posthumous names of the ancestors whose guidance or assistance they sought in divination, and the sequence of time was defined by the sequence of sacrifices to those ancestors. Thus, the spirits who were the presumptive interlocutors in the divinatory and sacrificial exchange were themselves temporal units, they were assigned their structuring role through divination, and the sequences of their sacrifices fixed the liturgical calendar that defined the structure of time. Furthermore, the fundamental initial act of a divinatory formula was to fix its location in time. Finally, in the last stage of the Shang the sole topic of divination, as in the examples cited, had become the auspicious or inauspicious character of the next 10-day period. Thus divination and its attendant sacrifices not only defined the sequence of days, but also fixed the unrolling of the sequence of 10-day weeks.

Fourth, the Shang calendar was intertwined with death. Several thinkers, most notably Heidegger, have argued that the distinctively human perception of time is inextricably tied to an awareness of death (Adam 1990: ch. 6). This awareness leads to a consciousness of personal finitude in relation to the seeming endlessness of the world, which in turn generates a constant projection backward and forward in time in assorted projects of transcendence. In the case of the Shang the past was structured in terms of a genealogy of ancestors. These ancestors, however, were in David Keightley's phrase "dead but not gone" (Keightley 1978), for they continued to structure the present in terms of the calendar of sacrifices that provided a fixed sequence of days that shared the ancestors' names. They also gave order and some sense of control to the future, for in the dialogue of the divinatory cracks they gave the Shang information on the sacrifices necessary to secure the successful pursuit of actions yet to come. The past, present, and future, and the entire structure of time as counted out in the sequence of the named days and their associated sacrifices, all merged in the figures of the dead, the sequence of whose posthumous titles constituted the fundamental calendar of the Shang.

NOTES

1. All studies of the Shang calendar are based on the work of Dong Zuobin, above all, his pathbreaking *Yin li pu* (1945). Other important essays are collected in Dong 1962 and Dong 1963. A very useful critical synthesis of aspects of Dong's work is Vendermeersch 1980, pp. 317–353. For the standard forms of citations of individual inscriptions, see Keightley 1978, ch. 3, note 5.

2. The method, entitled the "method of lacking breath" (*wu zhong qi fa*), is part of a theory that visualized the tropical year as an alternation of 24 "breaths" in which 12 units of roughly one half-month were described as "full breaths" (*zhong qi*) and placed in alternation with 12 units of "cut-off breath" (*jie qi*). The period from the beginning of one "cut-off breath" to the next was counted as one respiratory month. Any respiratory month that did not contain a period of "full breath" was treated as supernumerary and given the same number as the preceding month. This method is described in *Yi zhou shu*, ch. 6, pp. 613–621. The possible link was elaborated in several essays by Dong Zuobin. See particularly Dong 1963: 45–55. See also Vandermeersch 1980: 329–330.

3. The most detailed and persuasive attempt remains that of Chang 1979, which sketches and refutes various earlier proposals. However, Chang's own argument that the cyclic names represent kin groups clustered in two moieties that engaged in cross-cousin marriages still requires leaving basic points unexplained, and overlooking or denying several points of data that contradict his model.

REFERENCES

Adam, Barbara, 1990. *Time and Social Theory.* Cambridge: Polity.

Allan, Sarah, 1991. *The Shape of the Turtle: Myth, Art, and Cosmos in Early China.* Albany: State University of New York Press.

Bourdieu, Pierre, 1977. *Outline of a Theory of Practice.* Tr. Richard Nice. Cambridge: Cambridge University Press.

Chang, Kwang-chih, 1979. Lineage System of the Shang and Chou Chinese, in *Early Chinese Civilization: Anthropological Perspectives.* Cambridge, Mass.: Harvard University Press.

Chen, Mengjia, 1956. *Yinxu buci zongshu.* Beijing: Kexue.

Dong, Zuobin, 1945. *Yin li pu.* 2 Vols. Nanqi, Sichuan: Zhongyang Yanjiuyuan Lishi Yuyan Yanjiusuo.

Dong, Zuobin (ed.), 1948. *Jia. Yinxu wenzi jia bian.* Nanjing: Zhongyang Yanjiuyuan Lishi Yuyan Yanjiusuo. Reprint [Taipei]: 1977.

Dong, Zuobin (ed.), 1948–49, 1953. *Yi. Yinxu wenzi yi bian.* 3 vols. Nanjing: Zhongyang Yanjiuyuan. Lishi Yuyan Yanjiusuo, 1948–1949 (Vols. 1–2); Taipei: Zhongyang Yanjiuyuan Lishi Yuyan Yanjiusuo, 1953 (Vol. 3).

Dong, Zuobin, 1962. *Dong Zuobin xueshu lunzhu.* 2 vols. Taipei: Shijie.

Dong, Zuobin, 1963. *Pinglu wencun.* Taipei: Yiwen.

Feng, Shi, 2001. *Zhongguo tianwen kaoguxue.* Beijing: Shehui Kexue Wenxian Chubanshe.

Guo, Moruo, 1929. Shi zhigan, in *Jiagu wenzi yanjiu*, reprinted in *Moruo wenji.* Beijing: Renmin Wenxue, 1963.

Guo, Moruo & Houxuan Hu (eds.), 1982. *He ji. Jiaguwen he ji.* Beijing: Zhonghua Shuju.

Huang, Jun (ed.), 1935. *Ye. Yezhong pianyu chu ji.* Beijing: Zungu Zhai. Reprint [Taipei]: 1972.

Keightley, David, 1978. *Sources of Shang History: The Oracle-Bone Inscriptions of Bronze Age China.* Berkeley: University of California Press.

Lin, Daifu (ed.), 1921. *Lin. Guijia shougu wenzi.* N.p..

Luo, Zhenyu (ed.), 1913. *Qian. Yinxu shuqi qian bian.* N.p. Reprint [Taipei]: n.d.

Luo, Zhenyu (ed.), 1916. *Hou. Yinxu shuqi hou bian.* N.p.. Reprint [Taipei]: n.d.

Rao, Zongyi, 1959. *Yindai zhenbu renwu tongkao.* Hong Kong: Hong Kong University Press.

Shang, Chengzuo (ed.), 1933. *Yicun. Yinqi yicun.* Nanjing: Zhongyang Yanjiuyuan Lishi Yuyan Yanjiusuo. Reprint [Tokyo]: 1966.

Shima, Kunio, 1958. *Inkyo bokuji kenkyû.* Hirosaki: Chûgokugaku Kenkyûkai.

Vandermeersch, Léon, 1980. *Wangdao ou la voie royale: Recherches sur l'esprit des institutions de la Chine archaïque.* Paris: École Française d'Extrême-Orient, 1977–1980.

Yu, Xingwu, 1972. Cong jiaguwen kan Shang dai de nongtian kenzhi, in *Kaogu* 1972:4, pp. 40–41, 45.

16

The measure of time in Mesoamerica: From Teotihuacan to the Maya

Anthony F. Aveni

Thus it was recorded [by] the first sage, Melchise [dek], the first prophet, Napuc Tun, the priest, the first priest. This is a song of how the *uinal* [20-day period] came to be created before the creation of the world. Then he began to march by his own effort alone. Then said his maternal grandmother, then said his maternal aunt, then said his paternal grandmother, then said his sister-in-law: "What shall we say when we see man on the road?" These were their words as they marched along, when there was no man [as yet]. Then they arrived there in the east and began to speak. "Who has passed here? Here are footprints. Measure it off with your foot." So spoke the mistress of the world. Then he measured the footstep of our Lord, God, the Father. This was the reason it was called counting off the whole earth, *lahca* (12)Oc.[1] This was the count, after it had been created by [the day] 13 Oc, after his feet were joined evenly, after they had departed there in the east. Then he spoke its name when the day had no name, after he had marched along with his maternal grandmother, his maternal aunt, his paternal grandmother and his sister-in-law. The uinal was created, the day, as it was called, was created, heaven and earth were created, the stairway of water, the earth, rocks and trees; the things of the sea and the things of the land were created.

(Roys 1967, 116–117, author's brackets)

Time's journey, time's number

There are few cosmologies in which time does not begin with creation. The Maya, being no exception, speak of its measure in precisely this context. Ethnologists working among the Jacalteca (Popti') Maya of the highlands in the south of Yucatan have acquired evidence to back up the notion articulated in the aforequoted colonial period

document from Chumayel in northeast Yucatan, that the Maya have long conceived of the measurement of time as a pacing off of duration "in feet". They say that the basic subdivision of their year is 40 days, which they call "one foot of the year" (LaFarge and Byers 1931, 58), which they term *yoc habil*, the word *yoc*, or *oc*, meaning foot, footprint, or track in the Popti' Maya language. Often one sees the passage of time meted out in the surviving Pre-Columbian documents, or codices, in footprints (circled in Figure 16.1). This simile regarding time as the undertaking of a journey is analogous to the conception of time as a load carried on the backs of the gods of number (Figure 16.2) (or so noted more abstractly in dot [one] and bar [five]) notation) in Maya monumental inscriptions. The bundles they bear, a measure of lapsed time between the most recent creation of the world up to the event being celebrated, usually the accession or victory in battle of the ruler pictured on the other side of the carved stone or stela, are ordered in a vigesimal counting scheme that undoubtedly developed out of the prenumerate habit of counting on fingers and toes, thus: 1, 20, 360, 7,200, 144,000.[2]

Sometimes the concepts of time's road or journey and time's cargo borne along that road appear conflated. Thus Thompson (1950, 60) cites several prophecies from postconquest texts, among them: "This is the removal of

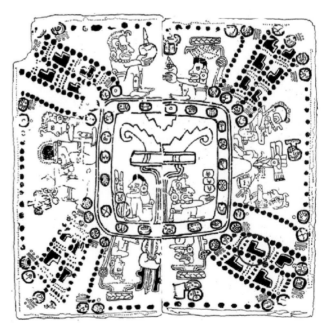

Figure 16.1. Footprints in a cosmogram from the Madrid Codex, pp. 75–76, showing time's 260-day journey via feet about the periphery of the sacred space of the gods (after J. Villacorta and C. Villacorta 1977, LXXV–LXXVI).

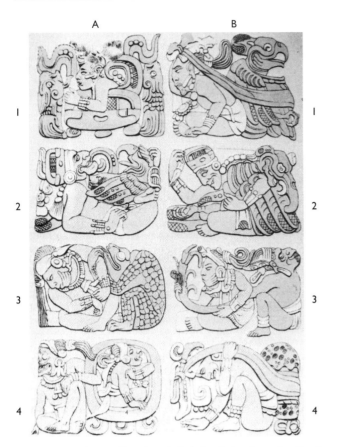

Figure 16.2. Copan (Honduras), Stela D, dating from the Classic Maya Period (eighth century AD), depicts the gods of number as full figure hieroglyphs, each carrying his own bundle of time; for example, the deity in frame B1 is 15, that in B2, five, in B3, zero (Maudslay 1889–1902 I: pl. 48).

his burden … fire is his burden … (in reference to) the fifth katun"; the burden is attached to its bearer: "On the day of the binding of the burden of Lord 5 Ahau," and so on. Writes another chronicler: "According to what [the Indians] say [these four first days] are those which take the road and bear the load of the month, changing in time" (Edmonson 1982, 113). In some of the examples cited by Edmonson time appears as an essence carried along the roadway of eternity, finally being seated or brought to rest at various stopping points: "Heaven Born Merida was the seat of the katun (3 Ahau)"; "This katun, which is 5 Muluc, the time of his taking his road" (78). In the monumental inscriptions the elaboration of dates with durations of cosmic dimension connecting them is thought to "provide calendrical and numerological charter attesting to the legitimacy of the position of the ruler and the dynasty that he founded" (Lounsbury 1978, 80).

While units of 20 and 40 are seminal in Maya time reckoning,[3] the count of 260 emerges as the ubiquitous Maya number of time. In all the inscriptions that we know of, this cycle, called the *tzolkin*, or "count of days",

runs nonstop, heedless of its position in the seasonal calendar. Much attention has been devoted to the problem of the origin of the tzolkin, which appears in the archaeological record as early as ca. 500 BC (Lounsbury 1978, 810). My own view is that 260 rose to prominence when it was realized that that number was a measure of a great range of basic human activities and diverse natural periodicities, all of which merge in the unique ecological/ celestial niches of Mesoamerica:

a. nine lunar synodic months (265.8^d)
b. the gestation period of the human female (266 to 288^d),
c. the mean interval of appearance of Venus as morning or evening star (263^d),
d. the mean agricultural growth cycle in southern Mesoamerica,
e. the interval between solar passages across the zenith in southern Mesoamerica (varies with latitude; see later discussion)
f. the eclipse half-year ($173^d.32$), being commensurate with the tzolkin in the ratio of 3 to 2, and finally
g. a body count, 13 x 20 = 260, the 20-day base being related to the number of fingers and toes, and 13 to the number of layers in heaven.

While there is no reason to believe that the 260-day cycle originated strictly as a result of the process of permuting smaller cycles to make bigger ones, it would be presumptuous to propose any one item from the preceding list of Mesoamerican life experiences as a first cause, though one might imagine (with Schultze-Jena 1950) that commensuration with the eclipse cycle occurred later, when the precise, rigid calendrical canons of the type written in the Maya Dresden Codex (see later discussion) were firmly laid in place and well practiced. Nor is there enough evidence to indicate which two, or three, of the aforementioned periodicities were first discovered by some hypothetical genius of the pre-Classic period (before AD 200) to fit together harmoniously; however, the archaeological evidence supports the argument that with the advent of the large urban center during the Classic Period, the stable, more secular 365-day solar year (*sans* leap year) was instituted as a more reliable means of disseminating the calendar to areas within the Maya sphere of influence wherein the conditions of climate might vary.

Like many subseasonal calendars, the ancient 260-day cycle once may have constituted a lunar-based kind of seasonal short count. Though we know of no other calendar in the world that employs an interval equal to 260, a structural comparison of the tzolkin with other subseasonal forms of day counting renders it not so unusual. For example, the 328-day year of the Inca (Zuidema 1982), the Trobriand calendar (Leach 1950), even the 304-day calendar of the preimperial Roman state (Aveni 1989) may share with the Maya tzolkin the property of commensurability; that is, these "years" all contain whole numbers of smaller cycles, some of which are natural rhythms, some celestially derived. Celestially based periods may emerge as unique to the locale where a given civilization developed. Moreover, they count only active time. Such subseasonal calendars contain an interval of "dead time", which, taken together with the active period, measures up to the solar yardstick. Thus, the Trobriand calendar began as a 10-lunar month count (not counting the inactive months that rounded out the seasonal year), which later expanded to 12 slightly corrupted lunar months totaling 360 days. The commencement of each month was fixed to coincide optimally with natural and human agrarian activity. In part such activity was regulated by the culmination times of certain bright stars, such phenomena being latitude dependent. Thus, the Inca calendar was expanded from 328 to 365 days, the heliacal rising of the Pleiades serving as the reset mechanism. For the Trobrianders it was the spawning of the Palolo worm. But the Mesoamerican case may be a bit peculiar, for while it seems likely that the subseasonal, agriculturally based 260-day count was the earliest calendrical period, it remains a mystery why, by classical times (ca. AD 200), it seems not to have been fixed within the seasonal 365-day cycle; that is, the first day of the next 260-day cycle immediately followed the 260th day of the previous one.

Time in the Maya Codices

Whereas the monuments celebrate dynastic achievement, the development of writing and numeration in the codices were due exclusively to religious concerns. According to one Spanish chronicler, the day keepers in charge of the painted bark divinatory texts were literally "priests of time":

> The nations of Yucatan … had a high priest whom they called *Ah Kin* (Lord of the Days).… In him was the key of their learning and it was to these matters that they dedicated themselves mostly.… They provided priests for the towns when they were needed, examining them in the sciences and ceremonies, and committed to them the duties of their office, and the good example to people and provided them with the books and sent them forth. And they employed themselves in the duties of the temples and in teaching their sciences as well as in

> writing books about them.… The sciences which were taught were the computation of the years, months and days, the festivals and ceremonies, the administration of the sacraments, the fateful days and seasons, their methods of divination and their prophecies, events and the cures for diseases, and their antiquities and how to read and write with the letters and characters, with which they wrote, and drawings which illustrate the meaning of the writings.[4](Tozzer 1941, 27–28)

The almanacs in the codices are clearly divinatory in nature, being dedicated to rites and prognostications concerning agriculture, hunting, and trapping, the renewal of deity imagery, weather, disease, medicine, completion of the year, and astronomy. The last category includes intricate ephemerides associated with eclipse prediction and the movements of Venus and Mars (cf. Aveni 2001, 169–205, for an overview). As Thompson (1972, 27) has pointed out, the major purpose of time reckoning in the codices seems to have been "to bring all celestial and human activities into relationship with the sacred almanac by multiplying the span they were interested in until that figure was a multiple of 260." By far the largest number of counting schemes coalesce around 260; for example, there are almanacs exhibiting fivefold (5 x 52) and fourfold (4 x 65) equipartitioning of the days (cf. Aveni, Morandi, and Peterson 1995, S7, for a full taxonomy). In all of these schemes the day emerges as the fundamental unit of Maya temporal currency, though a recent study suggests that in some instances almanacs may have been reckoned in units of years (Vail 2004). There is no evidence that the day ever was formally subdivided; that is, there appear in the codices no units resembling hours, minutes, seconds, and so forth, such as one finds in the Old World. Thus the degree of precision in short-term time reckoning seems to fall far short of what appears in Mesopotamia (see Brown, this volume). Moreover fractions seem to have been avoided, the Maya preferring to employ repeated addition and subtraction in place of multiplication and division to achieve their fundamental goal of arriving at larger commensurate periods (Figure 16.3).

Rather than targeting events in a time grid, such as we do on a monthly calendar page, the Maya employed what I have termed intervallic time reckoning (Aveni et al. 1995; Aveni 2004); that is, to the date (painted in red) of a given event one adds an interval (painted in black) to arrive at the next date, and so on. Thus, to judge by the numbers, the duration or movement of time between resting points is given as much attention as the date itself (Figure 16.4).[5] The date or event arrived at is frequently accompanied by a figure giving or receiving a particular offering, together with a brief hieroglyphic

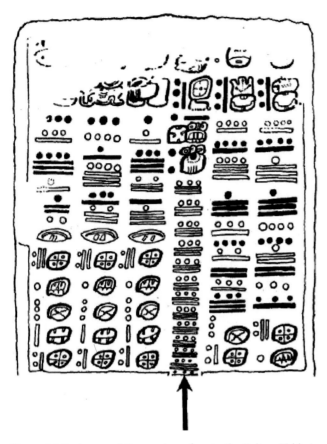

Figure 16.3. A part of the user's preface to the Eclipse Table in the Dresden Codex (pp. 51a–52a) shows a column of 13 13s hastily squeezed in. The scribe may have used them in some sort of additive scheme to facilitate computations related to the table of multiples of eclipse-related periods on the adjacent page.

text identifying the offertory apparatus, the name of the deity involved, and a resulting omen: for example, "surplus of bread and water from (goddess on the left), flowers, relatives; and surplus of bread and water from (goddess on the right); ?bad winds" (Schele and Grube 1997, 108).

The path of time in the almanacs usually runs left to right, a number of consecutive passes through the table being necessary to complete the round. For example, a 5-x-52-day almanac (such as the one sampled in Figure 16.4) would consist of five horizontal passes each totaling 52 days, placing the user at the end of the almanac in step, so that one may reenter without a break in time. But other almanacs challenge the eye to move in zigzag fashion, as dates and intervals climb and descend across a page (Figure 16.5). In some instances the scattering of black and red numbers seems almost random, causing the unexperienced reader to expend considerable effort in working out time's path (Figure 16.6).

In our examination of 303 almanacs in the Dresden and Madrid Codices, we (Aveni, Morandi, and Peterson 1996; Aveni 2004) discovered some 16 cognate (homologously constructed) almanacs that appear in both documents. These exhibit slight day shifts with respect to one another. We speculated that dates of celebratory ritual in a later cycle needed to be adjusted because the time was inauspicious, or a related astronomical event had shifted its position in the calendar. But our studies also indicate that there is good reason to believe that qualities believed to be attributed to pure number itself may have affected the assignment of tabulated intervallic entries.

Ever since Galileo levied his devastating critique of the Pythagorean view of number in his Dialog (Drake 1967, 11), science historians of ancient texts have focused mostly on materials related to the foundation of the modern scientific disciplines, largely eliminating the metaphysical aspects of ancient timekeeping and astronomy presumably without a loss of meaning. In an attack on the dean of science historians, George Sarton, who had pronounced the study of ancient astrology so much superstitious Middle East flotsam, the equally renowned Otto Neugebauer (1983, 3) was moved to remark that the foundation of our studies ought to be to seek to recover and study texts "as they are, regardless of our own tastes and prejudices."

Space does not permit a full disclosure of the nature of Maya numerology, but, in the spirit of Neugebauer, I will offer a few disclosures to illustrate the nature of both its complexity and its relevance to the concept of temporality extant in the codices (again consult Aveni et al. 1995; 1996; Aveni 2004 for details). While a number of intervallic sequences consist of equal intervals (e.g., 4 x 13 = 52, 5 x 13 = 65), others exhibit near equipartition, with a remainder tacked on at the end (e.g., 16 + 16 + 16 + 17 = 65, 9 + 9 + 9 + 9 + 9 + 7 = 52, or 7 + 7 + 7 + 5 = 26). This property also appears in the Andean khipus (see Urton, this volume). Other almanacs display intervals in a curious sinusoidal pattern (e.g., 12 + 8 + 12 + 8 + 12 = 52, or 6 + 7 + 6 + 7 + 6 + 7 + 6 + 7 = 52). Vestiges of intervallic numbers commonly employed in the almanacs, such as 13, often appear oddly fractured (e.g., 2 + 2 + 4 + 2 + 3 + 10 + 3 = 26) (add the first five intervals and then the last two to arrive at 13 + 13 = 26) or 1 + 2 + 5 + 3 + 2 + 11 + 2 = 26 (the same). In a set of almanacs in the Madrid Codex related to prognostications for deer hunting, an extraordinary iconic playfulness seems to emerge between the numbers and the animal pictured: the numbers seem to mimic deer droppings (Figure 16.6).

The almanac on pages 65a–69a of the Dresden Codex offers an extraordinary example of the devotion to pure number that went into the making of an almanac. The sequence of intervals that compose it runs as follows: 9, 5, 1, 10, 6, 2, 11, 7, 3, 12, 8, 4, 13. Note

Figure 16.4. This Maya almanac (Dresden pp. 17c–18c) concerns the burdens of particular periods of time, shown being carried by a goddess who personified the Earth. It includes *tzolkin* dates, given by the coefficient in red (white in the present copy), of the day name of the tzolkin followed by the interval required to reach the next date to the right. Each red date is accompanied by a picture, pertaining to the date. Thus, 4 Ahau + 15 = 6 (Men) + 33 = 13 (Lamat) + 4 = 4 Eb, and so on (after Villacorta and Villacorta 1977, XVII–XVIII).

Figure 16.5. An almanac (Dresden p. 9c) in which time's pathway zigzags its way down the page. A solid line is added to show the progression (after Villacorta and Villacorta 1977, IX).

Figure 16.6. An almanac in the Madrid Codex (p. 49b) related to deer hunting. Note the playful positioning of one of the intervals of three.

that every third term is one more than the previous, or (modulo 13) each term descends from its predecessor by a constant amount, namely, 4. Indeed as Lounsbury has suggested (quoted earlier): a calendrical and *numerological* charter (what we moderns might term 'number mysticism') seems to be a major part of the motive force that drives the Maya keeper of the days.

What most of us might tend to think of as the serious side of the content of the codices, namely, precise astronomy, is manifested in a number of tables that clearly exhibit precise astronomical measures and predictions. For want of space, I refer the reader to full treatments of these texts in the scholarly literature (cf., e.g., Lounsbury 1978; Aveni 2001). Here two examples will suffice. First, there is wide agreement that the Venus Table (p. 24, 46–50) of Codex Dresden was among an undetermined number of updated ephemerides used to target the heliacal risings of Venus. Accurate to one day in 500 years, the table employed a two-part correction mechanism that consisted of a) readjusting the starting date of the Venus cycle to coincide with a morning heliacal rise of that object and b) dropping either four or eight day counts from the canonic Venus synodic period (584 days)[6] at regular intervals so that the gain of the tabulated ephemeris on the true period (583.92 days) could be kept to a minimum. I have noted that such a procedure is analogous to the Gregorian reform (Aveni 1987), except that Venus at horizon is substituted for the Sun at the intersection of the celestial equator and the ecliptic. Second, Martian retrograde motion may have beguiled Maya astronomers as much as it intrigued Kepler. Recently (Bricker and Bricker 2006; Bricker,

Aveni, and Bricker 2001), a number of tables in the codices have been shown to reckon the sidereal period of Mars via a pair of long and short empirically based sidereal intervals not known to Western astronomers (the former includes the retrograde loop; the latter omits it). When arranged in indicated sequences, these average out to the familiar 687-day Martian cycle.[7]

At the same time, it is worth reiterating that whether an almanac or an astronomical ephemeris, all of the instruments in the codices are ultimately deeply grounded in religious concerns, especially the acquisition of omens. For example, the text accompanying one of the pages of the Venus Table reads: "woe to (?) the moon, woe to (?) man, its omen is 2-green-yellow [unripe and ripe maize], woe to (?) the maize god, woe to (?) food" (Vail, personal communication 24 Jul 2006).

Time and the archaeological record: The spatialization of time

One may justifiably enquire, How did the ancient Maya attain such precise knowledge in the striking absence of evidence, written or archaeological, that instruments

Figure 16.7. Scene from a Mixtec codex showing a figure situated in a temple doorway looking toward the horizon over one of a number of putative crossed-stick sighting devices. Was such a device used to align temples with celestial objects? Bodley Codex, 32 (by permission of The Bodleian Library, University of Oxford).

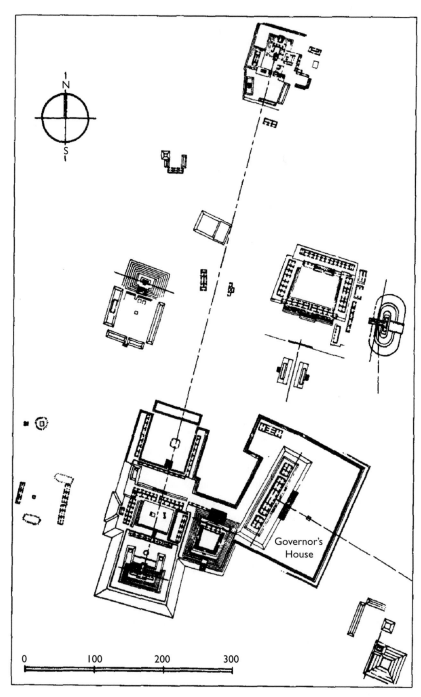

Figure 16.8. Uxmal, the Governor's House, an oddly oriented Maya temple likely arranged to summon the resurrected ancestor lord Venus/Kukulcan. Note the pronounced skew relative to the axes of the other buildings. The Venus alignment is indicated (Aveni 1997, Figure 4.12).

however, lacking further evidence one is precluded from hypothesizing precisely how it might have been used.

Like the codices, astronomically aligned buildings suggest that incorporating cosmic directions into urbanistic plans was part of a ritual process that required setting the stage for a performance in which the sky played a direct role. One must be reminded that, in stark contrast to the process of worship in Central Europe, which took place in the interior of cathedrals penetrated by divine light via stained glass windows, in the tropical climate of Yucatan communal religious rituals took place almost entirely out of doors. Mesoamerican architecture knows almost no substantial interior space. Worshippers assembled in large open plazas in front of tall temple facades, where they might anticipate the divine ruler's emerging from the inner sanctum atop the pyramid to perform a blood sacrifice demonstrating his divine kinship. To assure efficacy of a particular rite, the drama would be scheduled for a particular time when the astral deity was present in the sky. Let me cite one example to illustrate: an interurban cosmic axis that may have served to summon a sky deity.

Built (ca. AD 900) on an artificial platform, the Palace of the Governor at Uxmal in west Yucatan is skewed 20° with respect to the other structures at the site (Figure 16.8). Also unlike its companion structures it looks outward, away from the center of the site. The palace fronts a small altar overlooking an unobstructed view of the distant eastern horizon. Its central doorway aligns with the largest temple at a neighboring site called Cehtzuc. The alignment is also directed toward the southernmost standstill of Venus at horizon, a position attained by that planet every eight years (see note 6). A study of the iconography on the building reveals more than 300 Venus hieroglyphs identical to those found in the Dresden Venus Table, together with a pair of stucco masks of the rain god with the number 8 clearly sculpted over the eye sockets. Finally a zodiacal frieze above the central doorway identifies positions of the planet with respect to the Sun consistent with the

such as the quadrant, astrolabe, or even the simple *merkhet* (a sighting stick used in ancient Egypt) were employed? On the basis of imagery related to place names in the codices of southern highland Mexico I have argued that pairs of crossed sticks (Figure 16.7) may have been employed to fix horizon positions (Aveni 2001, 19–20). In at least one case, Spanish glosses note that such a device is associated with 'seeing clearly';

date of construction of the building (Bricker and Bricker 1996).

The measure of seasonal as well as Venerean time is also evident in astronomically aligned Maya architecture. The Group E assemblage at Uaxactun, located in the Petén rain forest of southern Yucatan and dated to the third century AD, consists of a pyramid accessible by stairways on all four sides, situated on the western side of an open plaza. A low range structure on the east side of the plaza accommodates three structures so placed that, observed from the pyramid, the Sun rises on the June solstice, the equinoxes, and the December solstice over their respective tops (Aveni and Hartung 1989). Similar horizon calendar complexes have been discovered at some 30 neighboring sites, many of which lie in a ruined state. Surveys at 12 of those that can be precisely measured reveal that, while the earliest Group E-type structures are orientated in a similar manner as the prototype at Uaxactun, alignments at a number of later complexes indicate that a calendar reform may have taken place. The revised calendar reckoned 20-day months based on the date(s) of passage of the Sun across the zenith, an event that takes place only in tropical latitudes. For example, we (Aveni, Dowd, and Vining 2003) found a high coincidence between alignments and dates counted 20, 40, and 60 days prior to the first solar zenith passages (about 1 May).[8] This was the time associated with the end of the dry season leading up to the commencement of planting and the rainy season, a time of great anticipation, as the rain god would need to be propitiated or paid his debt (as the chroniclers would say) for giving a bountiful harvest.

Lastly, concerning evidence related to the spatial expression of time in the archaeological record, one must mention the pecked cross petroglyphs (Figure 16.9). This ubiquitous symbol, pecked with some sort of percussive device into stucco floors as well as on rock outcrops, consists of (usually) a double circle of points or holes centered on what resembles a set of cartesian axes. Some 70 pecked crosses have been found all over Mesoamerica, including Uaxactun. The design likely emanated from Teotihuacan in the central Mexican highlands, where most forms of it have been encountered. It seems to have functioned variously as an architect's benchmark (cf. esp. Aveni, Hartung, and Kelley 1982), a calendar keeping device (Aveni 2005, 39–40), and possibly even a religious board game (Aveni 2006, 223–227).

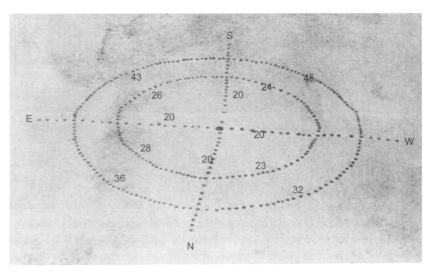

Figure 16.9. Pecked cross carved in the floor of Str. A-V, Uaxactun. Numbers indicate tallies on quadrants and axes (Aveni 2000, Figure 9.2).

The case for astronomical/architectural orientation emanates from the alignment of the precise east-west axis of Teotihuacan (15° 28′ clockwise), in the Mexican highlands, which fits a line between a pair of pecked cross petroglyphs. There are two possible astronomical connections with this alignment. First, the Sun sets along that axis on April 29 and August 12. These dates are separated by a period of 260 days, during which interval the Sun passes to the south of that alignment, and 105 days, when it passes to the north. Second, looking along the same urban axis in the east-west direction, one would have seen the Pleiades star group set about the time Teotihuacan's grid structure was set in place. The Pleiades made their first yearly appearance in the east before dawn (heliacal rise) on the first of the two dates when the sun passed overhead (May 18 in the latitude of Teotihuacan). Thus, the signal to restart the seasonal count would have consisted of the reappearance of the conspicuous Pleiades star group, an asterism frequently mentioned in the (later) Aztec chronicles as a celestial announcer of the New Fire ceremony when it crossed the zenith.[9]

But as Figures 16.9 and 16.10 will attest, there is no doubt that calendar keeping was tied to the pecked cross symbol as well. The histograms in Figure 16.10 record counts taken on various segments of, as well as totals on, 65 petroglyphs that we have examined to date (Aveni 2005). Note the coincidence in both histograms between peaks and significant Mesoamerican calendrical numbers, especially the number 20 and its multiples. Note especially the peaks rightward of 80 (86–90), rightward of 60 (68) and possibly leftward of 40 (30–34). All three, as well as the peak at 60, correspond to recognizable seasonal intervals, as we shall see. While Figure 16.10b

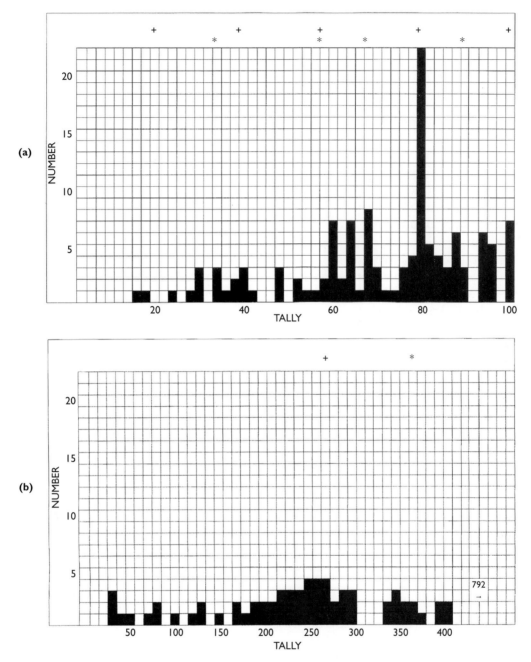

Figure 16.10. Histograms showing distribution of a) tallies on segments of pecked cross petroglyphs (+ indicates 20, * indicates basic intervals in the Teotihuacan seasonal calendar; cf. Table 16.1); and b) total tallies for all pecked cross petroglyphs in Mesoamerica (+ indicates 260, * indicates 365) (Aveni 2005, Figs. 16–17).

shows that grand totals range from just a few dozen up to nearly 800, the peaks seem to break down into two well-defined zones. First there is the "260 group", consisting of those that appear to peak around that number. Thus, a sample of 40 designs ranging between counts of 218 and 302 yielded an average of 254.1 ± 23.1 s.d. A second cluster, the "365 group", yields an average count of 365.7 ± 25.9 s.d. in the range 340–402. Recall that one of the paramount goals in the making of the codices, which date from a much later period (cf. AD 300

vs. AD 1300), is the commensuration of 260 and other numbers, among them 365. One wonders whether such practical elements related to the seasonal calendar and its relationship to the sacred count might have been in place before the advent of a full-fledged writing system.

The Uaxactun pecked cross petroglyph shown in Figure 16.9 bears a striking resemblance in fine detail to the majority of the Teotihuacan pecked designs; moreover it offers evidence of cross-cultural contact pertaining to calendrical matters. Confinement of this design and two (regrettably lost) companion figures to the early stages of the first vault phase of Str. A-V (ca. AD 278) places it early in the construction of the building. The presence of Stela 26 (which carries a long count date) in the layer atop the artifacts yields a *terminus post quem* date of AD 445.

In Table 16.1 I have charted the annual cycles and their breakdowns for both Teotihuacan and Uaxactun. Interestingly, at Teotihuacan it is exactly 60 (or 3 x 20) days from the March equinox to the first solar zenith passage, as well as from the second zenith passage to the September equinox. But what is not so well known is that the east-west axial alignment of Teotihuacan, marked by the pair of pecked crosses, is orientated so that the Pyramid of the Sun faces the sunset 2 x 20, or 40 days – one "foot of the year" – after the vernal equinox, and 20 days before first solar zenith passage (the intervals are reversed when the Sun returns toward the south). Of all the manifold hypotheses that discuss the orientation problem at Teotihuacan (see Millon 1992, 383–388, and Aveni 2001, 226–235 for a summary and assessment of them), this is both the least discussed and, in my view, one of the most sensible and least contrived. There is an extensive body of literature exploring the idea that 20-day solar periods were figured into horizon observational astronomy across Mesoamerica (cf. Aveni, Calnek, and Hartung 1988 and references therein).

Further consulting the table, note that at Uaxactun the interval between the equinox and the first solar passage across the zenith is reduced to 51 days. Also the interval between solar zenith passages, which includes the June solstice, and which amounts to 67 days at Teotihuacan, is equal to 85 days at Uaxactun; that is, the Sun spends 298 days south of the zenith at noon and 67 days north of it at Teotihuacan, while a similar bifurcation of the seasonal year at Uaxactun yields the intervals 280 and 85 days. The last number is close to the universal quarter-year interval mentioned earlier. Finally, intervals between the dates when the Sun passes the zenith can be divided into 33 + 34 = 67 days north of it at Teotihuacan and 43 + 42 = 85 days at Uaxactun. All of these periods and subperiods would be the very numbers one might anticipate finding in artifacts used to tally observable solar time.

Now compare the natural intervals in Table 16.1 with the count and arrangement of elements that make up the Uaxactun pecked cross petroglyph in Figure 16.9. Note first the large number of carefully placed elements that make up the whole design (338), and the insistence of 20 on each axis; and second, the asymmetry of the distribution of points, particularly on the outer circle: there are 88 (43 + 45) on the southern (top) half as opposed to 68 (36 + 32), or 20 fewer, on the northern (bottom) half. If we compare the observable solar year intervals indicated with the breakdown of elements on various parts of the design, we also discover that the way the counts are grouped supports the hypothesis that the petroglyph functioned as a year tally device. First, the sum of the inner SE plus SW quadrants (26 + 24), as well as that of the inner NW plus NE quadrants (23 + 28), is close to the observed equinox-solar zenith interval at Uaxactun (51 days). Second, the sum of the SE plus SW outer quadrants (43 + 45) equals the observed interval between the autumn equinox and December solstice, as well as that between the December solstice and spring equinox (89–90 days). Finally, the intervals in the NW plus NE outer circle quadrants (32 + 36) add up to the interval between zenith passages, not at Uaxactun, but instead at Teotihuacan (60 days).

If the point-by-point count on artifacts conceived as tally markers were used in practice to tabulate real solar time, that is, time as actually marked out by the course of the Sun in the local environment, then one might expect to find slight asymmetries and inequalities due to modification by nonastronomical calendrical considerations. At two locales as widely separated as Uaxactun and Teotihuacan, discernible differences in naturally-based calendars ought to be apparent, indeed to a degree even predictable.

Whether in all instances the existence of these calendrical elements implies that the pecked cross petroglyphs were specifically intended as instruments for counting

Table 16.1. *Seasonal intervals at Teotihuacan and Uaxactun*

Time counted from	To	At Teotihuacan	At Uaxactun
First solar zenith passage*	June solstice (21.5 Jun)	33.5d	42.5d
June solstice	Second solar zenith passage	33.5d	42.5d
Second solar zenith passage	September equinox (23.0 Sep)	59.5d	51d
Autumn equinox	December solstice (21.5 Dec)	89.5d	89.5d
December solstice	Vernal equinox (20.5 Mar)	89.0d	89.0d
Vernal equinox	First solar zenith passage	60.0d	51.0d
	Length of rainy season	(120d–140d)	(180d)

* May 19 for Teotihuacan, May 10 for Uaxactun.

days, perhaps via the movement of one or more pebbles about the circuit, or that the correct counts need only have exhibited a symbolic presence (as, for example, in the number of stars on a U.S. flag), we cannot say. The directional properties and calendrical symbolism present in the accompanying carved designs, being consistent with those found in Teotihuacan protowriting, support the notion that the entire assembly was put to some sort of ritual use. One can well imagine the site as a place for calendrical divination of the type we see much later in the codices. There specific offerings are shown being made to particular agrarian deities (rain, maize, sky, etc.) on carefully chosen dates that suited both the sacred 260- and seasonal 365-day cycles. Performing the count of the days and assessing them for good or bad luck in a tabular format could well have been part of the sort of process one still finds in contemporary Mesoamerican divinatory practices.

Discussion

To judge from the legacy carved in stone, writ in bark paper, and standing in ancient architecture, few cultures of the world have exhibited so absorbing an interest in time as the Maya. Two aspects of Maya timekeeping and astronomy trouble us in particular. First, regarding the acquisition of precise knowledge, we are scarcely able to reconcile what we read in the calendar with the near absence of any sort of sophisticated technology. Our second difficulty lies in the recognition that religion provides the motivation that underpins calendrical invention and innovation both in texts (such as the Dresden Venus Table) and in architecture (such as the Venus alignment at Uxmal). To judge by the evidence, theirs was clearly a "science of time" enveloped in astrological prognostication.

What can we make of our studies of Maya time in relation to problems and questions on this vast subject confronted by Western scholars: Is time a translucent principle? What is the essence of time relative to those who live in it? How is the past related to the future? How do chronology, history, and narrative interact in this exotic view of temporality as a journey outlined by footprints?

The monumental inscriptions clearly exhibit a strong past-directed quality. The present seems to be an aggregate of happenings that have gone before, a configuration of particular combinations and sets of prior phenomena and events. Maya time emerges not as an abstract concept but as an entity that directly affects the lives of individuals. The rulers portrayed on the Maya stelae place themselves at seminal points in time by enhancing the record through date manipulation,[10] as well as through reference to cosmic phenomena; thus they enable themselves to have accomplished great acts on the anniversaries of their mythical ancestors. The long-term cycles they contemplated were among the large number of lived temporal rounds intended to give structure to Maya history.

The cosmology that framed the Maya calendar was participatory, a far cry from its role in contemporary Western thought. The participatory role of the Maya worshipper is reflected in particular in the content of the codices. The business of laying out the calendar that prescribes Maya ritual behavior must have been very complex. A multitude of offerings needed to be made to the gods in the proper locations and at designated times when the gods of number dropped their loads, and the periods between ritual events surely were not arbitrary.

But did the events related to the measure of time in the codices determine the intervals, or did the intervals decide the events? Or was it both ways? We cannot yet answer that question, though there are cross-cultural analogies to guide us. For example, in the Christian calendar the occurrence of the vernal equinox, coupled with that of the full Moon that follows it, fixes precisely when the Easter holiday shall take place: it must be the first Sunday after the first full Moon after the spring equinox. In this case the interval is determined by two events and it can vary between 1 and 37 days after March 20 in our modern calendar. On the contrary, Lent is always 40 days long regardless of when Ash Wednesday falls, the latter being fixed by back calculation from the Paschal date; therefore, the interval fixes the date. In the Andean world there are examples of rites celebrated one week later than scheduled simply because people are not ready as they have not finished tending their crops (Urton 1986).

The Maya ritual calendar is equally complex. On the one hand, 4-x-65-day almanacs seem to be a clear reflection of the Mesoamerican habit of the directional quadripartition of time. The 5-x-52-day almanacs incorporate the fifth (up) direction. On the other hand, some almanacs (e.g., Dresden pp. 65a–69a) may reflect the intrusion of celestial events that follow periods of their own into purely numerologically based periods contrived in the almanacs. There seems to have been no such concept as a pure law of astronomy versus a pure law of divination in the Maya mentality. The history of matter and the history of people are inextricably intermingled. As a result calendrical dictates conspired together to convolute the time structure of the almanacs. In a number of instances the semantic values of numbers and day names appear to have been elements involved in the corruption or perturbation of intervallic sequences, resulting in arrays that look complex and unfamiliar to us, but may have made perfect sense to Maya timekeepers.

Above all, the arbiters of time who wrote the ancient books that follow the journey of the "feet of the year" were not just "playing with numbers", as oft portrayed by modern scholars. In devising their divinatory schedule they were following numerological and temporal rules still largely unknown to us and, consequently, much more difficult for us to appreciate than the universal astronomical cycles that seem to pop out at us from the Venus, Mars, and Eclipse Tables thanks to our own familiarity with them. Little wonder we are scarcely able to scratch the surface of meaning in the Maya almanacs.

In his wide-ranging discussion of Maya calendrics, Lounsbury (1978, 804) spoke of two different motives in the Maya use of number. The better-known preoccupation of court arithmetician and astronomer lay in using large numbers as a way of tying the lives of the rulers to their mythic ancestors of the past – the gods who created the world – and to anniversaries of creation events in the future, when the rulers themselves would become gods. But there is another type of numerology that involves smaller numbers, more like the kind we have dealt with in the codices, that covers brief intervals and time spans. The latter, Lounsbury opines, is far more interesting, for here we discern numbers being chosen largely because of the nature of what they are – the very same kinds of choices the Pythagoreans made and Galileo derided as purely fanciful. But while we may elevate Galileo to heroic status for helping to erect the foundations of modern science (an enterprise in which number plays a purely descriptive role in relation to physical reality), we also can cite him for his lack of appreciation of a once equally valid and complex worldview in which number, like word in the Old Testament, was believed to possess a power all its own.

ACKNOWLEDGEMENT

I gratefully acknowledge the comments by Gabrielle Vail and John Justeson on an earlier draft.

NOTES

1. The position in the count of 260 days (see later), consisting of a coefficient (1–13) placed alongside a day name (1 of 20).
2. These units are named, respectively, *kin* (Sun, day, time); *uinal* (month); *haab* (year or stone), also called a *tun; katun* (score of tun); and *baktun* (score of score of tun). Numbers in excess of 1 million calendar years have also been recorded

in Maya documents. Exclusively related to a time count, as opposed to trade count, the substitution of 18 for 20 to complete the second place (18 x 20 = 360) was probably devised in order to approximate the length of the year.

3. The 40-day count discussed previously was probably so chosen because it advances by 1 the coefficient (modulo 13) of the day name (modulo 20) in the 260-day count. Thus in the earlier example: 12 Oc + 40 days = 13 Oc.
4. Parts of only four such documents survive; the remainder, to hear the Spanish chroniclers boast of the conflagrations they set to destroy them (Tozzer 1941, 77), must have numbered in the thousands.
5. The same is true in the monumental inscriptions wherein one adds a "distance number" to a stated event to arrive at the next event.
6. This number is commensurate with the seasonal year in the almost perfect ratio of 5 to 8.
7. There is, however, no evidence to suggest that the Maya exhibited any interest in the heliocentric model of the solar system, or for that matter any notions involving planetary orbits, a purely Greek geometrical concept.
8. The date varies by one or two days in the relevant area because of its dependence upon latitude.
9. The New Fire ceremony was celebrated upon the completion of the 52-year cycle, which commensurates the seasonal year and the 260-day cycle; thus 52 x 365^d = 73 x 260^d.
10. See the discussion in Lounsbury 1978, 804–808. One such number, a long count, turns out to be not only a whole multiple of Venus and Mars synodic periods, but also of a cluster of prime numbers multiplied together. It clearly attests to the incorporation of both real time cycles and numerology in the temporal equation.

REFERENCES

Aveni, A. 1987 Some parallels in the development of Maya and Roman calendars. *Interciencia* **12**, 108–115.

Aveni, A. 1989 *Empires of Time: Calendars, Clocks and Cultures.* New York, Basic.

Aveni, A. 1997 *Stairways to the Stars.* New York, Wiley.

Aveni, A. 2000 Out of Teotihuacan, origins of the celestial canon in Mesoamerica. In *Mesoamerica's Classic Heritage, from Teotihuacan to Aztecs*, ed. D. Carrasco, L. Jones, S. Sessions. Boulder, CO, University Press of Colorado, 253–268.

Aveni, A. 2001 *Skywatchers: A Revised and Updated Version of Skywatchers of Ancient Mexico.* Austin, University of Texas Press.

Aveni, A. 2004 Intervallic structure and cognate almanacs in the Madrid and Dresden Codices. In *The Madrid Codex: New Approaches to Understanding an Ancient Maya Manuscript*, ed. G. Vail and A. Aveni. Boulder, University Press of Colorado, 147–170.

Aveni, A. 2005 Observations on the pecked cross designs and other figures carved on the south platform of the

Pyramid of the Sun. *Journal for the History of Astronomy* **36**, 31–47.

Aveni, A. 2006 *Uncommon Sense: Understanding Nature's Truths across Time and Culture*. Boulder, University Press of Colorado.

Aveni, A., E. Calnek, and H. Hartung 1988 Myth, environment, and the orientation of the Templo Mayor of Tenochtitlan. *American Antiquity* **53**, 287–309.

Aveni, A., A. Dowd, and B. Vining 2003 Maya calendar reform? Evidence from orientations of specialized architectural assemblages. *Latin American Antiquity* **14**(2), 159–178.

Aveni, A. and H. Hartung 1989 Uaxactun, Guatemala, Group E and similar assemblages: An archaeoastronomical reconsideration. In *World Archaeoastronomy*, ed. A. Aveni. Cambridge, Cambridge University Press, 441–460.

Aveni, A., H. Hartung, and J. C. Kelley 1982 Alta Vista Chalchihuites: Astronomical implications of a Mesoamerican ceremonial outpost at the Tropic of Cancer. *American Antiquity* **47**, 316–335.

Aveni, A., S. Morandi, and P. Peterson 1995 The Maya number of time, Part I. *Archaeoastronomy* no. 20 (Supplement to *Journal for the History of Astronomy* 26), S1–28.

Aveni, A., S. Morandi, and P. Peterson 1996 The Maya number of time, Part II. *Archaeoastronomy* no. 21 (Supplement to *Journal for the History of Astronomy* 27), S1–32.

Bricker, H., A. Aveni, and V. Bricker 2001 Ancient Maya documents concerning the movement of Mars. *Proceedings of the National Academy of Sciences* **98**, 2107–2110.

Bricker, H. and V. Bricker 1996 Astronomical references in the throne inscription of the Palace of the Governor at Uxmal. *Cambridge Archaeological Journal* **6**(2), 191–229.

Bricker, H. and V. Bricker 2006 Astronomical references in the water tables on pages 69–74 of the Dresden Codex. In *Painted Books and Indigenous Knowledge in Mesoamerica: Manuscript Studies in Honor of Mary Elizabeth Smith*, ed. E. Boone. New Orleans, Middle American Research Institute Pub. 69, 213–229.

Codex Bodley. Bodleian Library, Oxford, Mex. d.l. (HMAI Census no. 31).

Drake, S. 1967 *Galileo: Dialog Concerning the Two Chief World Systems*. Salt Lake City, University of Utah Press.

Edmonson, M. 1982 *The Ancient Future of the Itza: The Book of Chilan Balam of Tizimin*. Austin, University of Texas Press.

LaFarge, O. II and D. Byers 1931 The year bearers people. *Middle American Research Series* Publ. No. 3.

Leach, E. R. 1950 Primitive calendars. *Oceania* **20**, 245–262.

Lounsbury, F. 1978 Maya numeration, computation and calendrical astronomy. In *Dictionary of Scientific Biography* 15, suppl 1, ed. C. C. Gillispie. New York, Scribners, 759–818.

Maudslay, A. P. 1889–1902 *Archaeology, Biologia Centrali-Americana*, 6 vols. London, Porter.

Millon, R. 1992 Teotihuacan studies: From 1950 to 1990 and beyond. In *Art, Ideology and the City of Teotihuacan*, ed. J. Berlo. Washington, DC, Dumbarton Oaks Research Library and Collection, 339–429.

Neugebauer, O. 1983 *Astronomy and History, Selected Essays*. New York, Springer-Verlag.

Roys, R. 1967 *The Book of Chilam Balam of Chumayel*, 2nd ed. Norman, University of Oklahoma Press.

Schele, L. and N. Grube 1997 *Notebook for the XXIst Maya Hieroglyphic Workshop, March 8–9, 1997*. Austin, University of Texas Department of Art and Art History, College of Fine Arts and Institute of Latin American Studies.

Schultze-Jena, L. 1950 *Wahrsagerei, Himmelskunde und kalender der alten Azteken: Quellewerke zur Alten Geschichte Americas 4*. Stuttgart, W. Kohlammer.

Thompson, J. E. S. 1950 *Maya Hieroglyphic Writing: An Introduction*. Washington, DC, Carnegie Institution of Washington Pub. 589.

Thompson, J. E. S. 1972 *A Commentary on the Dresden Codex, a Maya Hieroglyphic Book*. Philadelphia, American Philosophical Society, Memoirs, No. 93.

Tozzer, A. 1941 Landa's Relación de las cosas de Yucatán (1566). *Peabody Museum Papers, Harvard University* 18, Cambridge, MA, Peabody Museum, Harvard.

Urton, G. 1986 Calendrical cycles and their projections in Pacariqtambo, Peru. *Journal of Latin American Lore* **12**: 45–64.

Vail, G. 2004 A reinterpretation of *Tzolkin* in almanacs in the Madrid Codex. In *The Madrid Codex: New Approaches to Understanding an Ancient Maya Manuscript*, ed. G. Vail and A. Aveni. Boulder, University Press of Colorado, 215–252.

Villacorta, J. and C. Villacorta 1977 *Codices Mayas*. Guatemala City: Reproducidos y Desarrolados, Tipografia.

Zuidema, R. T. 1982 The role of the Pleiades and of the Southern Cross and Alpha and Beta Centauri in the calendar of the Incas. In *Ethnoastronomy and Archaeoastronomy in the American Tropics*, ed. A. Aveni and G. Urton. *Annals of the New York Academy of Sciences* **385**, 203–229.

17

Measuring time, sacred space, and social place in the Inca Empire

Charles Stanish

The Inca Empire of Andean South America emerged in the 15th century AD as one of the great political triumphs of world history. In a short 100 or so years, the Inca developed in the central Andean highlands out of a multitude of competing polities in the post–Middle Horizon period (Figure 17.1). The Middle Horizon, circa AD 500–1100, represented the apogee of the three first-generation states of the Andes – first Moche in the first centuries AD up to around AD 700, then Wari and Tiwanaku (Figure 17.2). The latter two states developed almost in tandem circa AD 500–1000 extending their reach over most of the Andean highlands, from northern Peru to north central Chile.

The collapse of the Wari and Tiwanaku states created a volatile political context throughout the region. In the north coast, several polities developed out of the remains of the Moche state, ultimately culminating in the first empire of Chimor in the beginning of the second millennium AD. Moche defined statecraft as it was practiced in the pre–European contact Andes, beginning at the end of the first millennium BCE and continuing into the middle of the first millennium AD. Moche culture most likely directly influenced Wari and Chimu and indirectly influenced Tiwanaku as these two cultures developed their models of statecraft in the immediate post-Moche periods.

The Quechua-speaking Inca peoples were one of a number of smaller polities that developed in this general

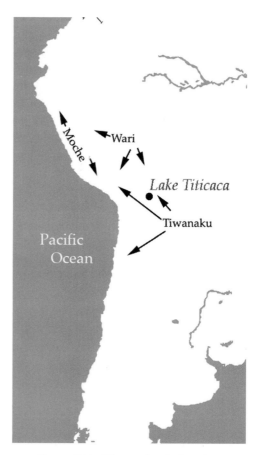

Figure 17.1. South America.

Figure 17.2. Western South America.

cultural context of the post–Middle Horizon period. This time, known by scholars as the Late Intermediate Period, was referred to by Inca intellectuals as a "time of war" or "time of warriors". It was a period of conflict, environmental change, demographic growth, and intense competition among various polities. The Incas emerged victorious in the central area of the Andean highlands and quickly expanded over western South America. At its height, the Inca Empire covered an area of over 1 million square kilometres and covered a vast array of ecological zones, from the dense tropical forest to the driest desert in the world, known as the Atacama, in present-day northern Chile.

Successful strategies of empire building must go beyond simple military force. As is well known in the comparative literature, imperial governments create great ideologies of power that serve the interests of the state. The Inca were no different. There is a vast literature on the ideological mechanisms employed by the Inca state that need not be restated in any depth here.[1] Inca intellectuals developed creation myths that incorporated the peoples from the three great language groups of the empire, Mochic, Quechua, and Aymara. The three most important pilgrimage destinations in the empire corresponded to these languages – Pachacamac on the coast, Pacarictambo in Cuzco, and the Island of the Sun in Collasuyu. The Inca brilliantly linked their royal dynasties to some kind of ancestral tie in these three areas. I argue here that measuring time, sacred space, and social place was intimately linked with these pilgrimage destinations. In turn, these destinations were nested within ideologies of power that were given expression in these seemingly contradictory creation stories.[2]

In this chapter, I will focus on one kind of ideological mechanism. This is the creation of a pilgrimage destination on the Island of the Sun in Lake Titicaca, in what is now Bolivia. The northern end of the island was converted into sacred space linked intimately to the measurement of solar events. Specifically, I will examine how the seemingly simple measurement of the June and December solstices was vastly more complex than is immediately apparent. By using pairs of towers to mark a period of time, as opposed to a single tower or other point on the landscape to mark a single moment, the Inca were incorporating generations of Andean statecraft practices. The solar towers marked the solstices indeed, but they also served to demarcate sacred space and social place. The use of paired towers provided a means to define a large area of sacred space and, more subtly, to demarcate varying degrees of sacredness in the sanctuary area. Likewise, participation in the solstice events served to mark and reinforce social and political status in the

empire. It was not just proximity to the elite in these ceremonies that was important. As we will see with the Island of the Sun data, the Inca had to deal with the reality of nested hierarchies in their fast-growing empire. Nested hierarchies are those conquered or absorbed complex polities with their own social classes that must be incorporated into an expanding empire (Stanish 2000). Such hierarchies create potential political tensions in expanding states. Indigenous lesser nobilities, in particular, can be very unstable. For the political class of rapidly expanding empires, it is necessary to balance the needs of pacifying conquered elites with not alienating indigenous ones in the imperial hierarchy.

By replicating the principles of the sacred viewing platform of the Inca capital Cuzco near the Sacred Rock on the Island of the Sun immediately outside the sanctuary area, the Inca were able to accommodate non-Inca elites in their ceremonies. The replication itself played off the rich traditions of duality in Andean statecraft. They were able to accord status to these local elites while not threatening their own lesser nobles, a sophisticated political balancing act indeed. Inca measurement of time, in this case the June and December solstices, was not simply the counting of sunsets or marking a period of time for ceremonies. The Inca created a highly charged ceremonial landscape where the complexities of social status, political strategies, religion, and imperial stresses all were played out during these elaborate solstice ceremonies.

Sun worship in the Inca state

Worship of the Sun was one of the most important, perhaps the most important, component of official Inca religion. Marking the summer and winter solstice was of particular significance. We have good documentary evidence on the nature of Inca Sun worship. Most notably, the chronicles of Bernabé Cobo, Juan de Betanzos, Guaman Poma, and Garcilaso de la Vega tell us much about the marking of solar time in the Inca capital in Cuzco by the use of stone towers on the hills above the city.

One of the earliest accounts of the solar pillars is by the chronicler Juan de Betanzos in 1557. His fascinating observation of how the great Inca emperor Inca Yupanque created the solar markers is central to understanding the nature of Inca timekeeping and deserves a lengthy quote:

> So that, as time passed they [the lords of the empire] would not lose count of these months [that the Inca

Yupanque created] and the times for sowing and celebrating the fiestas that he had already told them about, he had made those *pacha unan chac*, which means "clocks".... He made the clocks in the following way. Each morning and every afternoon of every month of the year he looked at the sun, watching for the times for sowing and harvesting. Also when the sun went down, he watched the moon when it was new, full, and waning. He had the clocks made of cut stone placed on top of the highest hills at the place where the sun rose and where it went down.... Since he could tell the line along which the sun moved as it was setting straight ahead from that place where he stood, he had four marble stone pyramids made on the highest part of the hills. The middle ones were smaller than the ones on the sides. The pyramids [pillars] were two *estados* high, square and set about one *braza* apart.... As the sun rose, if one stayed where Inca Yupanque stood to look and calculate, the sun comes straight up and goes straight between the pillars, and it did the same when it went down to the place where it sets. (Juan de Betanzos 1996 [1557]:68)

The chronicler Bernabé Cobo provides additional information that supports Betanzos's account. He authored an exhaustive list of the *huacas* or sacred places in the Cuzco region (in Rowe 1980). Cobo, a Jesuit intellectual and one of the first modern naturalists, completed his *Historia del Nuevo Mundo* in 1653 (in Cobo 1979; 1990 [1653]), more than a century after the Spanish conquest of the Inca Empire. As John Rowe (1980:4) mentions in his translation and commentary on this document, the list is not complete and the original source or sources are unknown. It is also likely that Cobo edited the list for internal consistency. Nevertheless, the huaca list is an extremely important source of information on Inca solar observations.

Consistent with Betanzos, Cobo describes stone markers on hills several times in his text. The first example is "The ninth guaca [huaca] was a hill named Quiangalla which is on the Yucay road. On it were two markers or pillars which they regard as indication that, when the sun reached there, it was the beginning of the summer" (in Rowe 1980:25). Another is "The seventh was called Sucanca. It was a hill.... On it there were two markers as an indication that when the sun arrived there, they had to begin to plant the maize. The sacrifice which was made there was directed to the Sun, asking him to arrive there at the time which would be appropriate for planting" (in Rowe 1980:27). And finally, a third example: "The third [guaca of a particular ceque or ritual line], chinchincalla, is a large hill where there were two markers; when the sun reached them, it was time to plant" (in Rowe 1980:59).

These early texts note that there were between 4 and 16 towers in the Cuzco region that could be seen up to 15 kilometres away.[3] They were about three times the height of a person and were so durable that they were observed relatively intact more than 100 years after the Spanish conquest. The pillars were inevitably built on hills, ensuring that they could be seen from a considerable distance. As Dearborn, Seddon, and Bauer (1998:244) note, the chronicles differ in regard to the distance between the pillars. Betanzos refers to four pillars about one metre apart while an anonymous document (the Anonymous Chronicler) circa 1570 refers to several pillars about 50 paces apart spread over 200 paces. Nevertheless, most documentary evidence on the towers indicates that pairs of stone markers fixed the setting and/or rising of the Sun. These towers were located on hills, were built of very durable cut stone, and were visible from substantial distances because of their height and size.[4]

Why pairs of pillars?

The brief discussion earlier immediately begs a critical question: Why were there *pairs* of pillars to mark some of the solstices? Marking a solstice from a fixed point on the landscape, for instance, from the plaza in Cuzco to the markers on Picchu, does not require two pillars. It only requires one marker. In fact, it would have been considerably more precise to have one pillar mark a sunset or sunrise if one was making precise date observations.

Tom Zuidema (1981:338–340) discusses the Anonymous Chronicler's mention of two pillars and concludes that they served to define an "Incaic period of either 29.5 or 27.5 days". The towers therefore are seen as marking off a block of time in the Inca calendar. Dearborn, Seddon, and Bauer (1998:244) offer a broader suggestion related to this question. They note that the wide separation of markers would not permit a precise date determination. On the other hand, it would have allowed a much larger group of people to gather and see a sunset from a fixed location. In the case of Cuzco, "the pillars were used in large ritual gatherings during which group participation was considered *more* important than precise date determination" (Dearborn, Seddon, and Bauer 1998:244).

I agree with Dearborn, Seddon, and Bauer on this particular point – that the use of paired markers indicates that a group of people, and not just a few individuals, were part of the solstice ceremony. However, I believe that evidence from the Island of the Sun, presented later, indicates that the solstice marking ceremonies were designed to impart much more information than is apparent from the chroniclers' descriptions. I argue that the paired markers were in fact intended to mark both a precise date for certain individuals, as well as a longer period of festivities. Even more important is that the entire architecture of the built landscape associated with the solstice ceremony not only marked a precise time and a ceremonial period, but delineated a "cline" of sacred space as well as marking the differential social status of individuals in Inca society. The construction of these pillars, huacas, temples, ceques, and roads goes well beyond simple time observations and formed a complex system of social marking, political power projection, religious observation, and other social practices central to the ideological underpinnings of empire. Determining time was important, but it was secondary to a whole host of practices underlying these great solstice events in the imperial calendar of the Inca state.

The Island of the Sun

The Island of the Sun and the Island of the Moon are located in the far south of Lake Titicaca (Figures 17.3 and 17.4). Together with the towns of Copacabana and Yunguyu, they constituted a vast sacred area and pilgrimage destination in the Inca Empire (Figure 17.5). The Inca scholar Brian Bauer and I conducted work on the Islands of the Sun and Moon for three seasons between 1994 and 1996. This work has been amply documented in a number of publications (Bauer and Stanish 2001; Seddon 1998; 2005; Stanish and Bauer 2004; and others) and will not be extensively restated here. In short, we confirmed earlier scientific research (e.g., Bandelier 1910; Julien 1993; Hyslop 1990; Ponce S. et al. 1992; Reinhard 1992) and the chroniclers' accounts of a huge Inca use of both islands. The Island of the Sun in particular was converted into a major pilgrimage destination. At least two roads, one near the lake and a second on the hill above, reached the northern tip of the island, known as the Titikala or Sacred Rock (Figures 17.6–17.9).[5] The Titikala is a modest red sandstone outcrop (Figures 17.10–17.11) that was considered to be the origin place of the Sun and Moon and the location where the founding couple of the Inca dynasty miraculously emerged, according to some of the creation myths described in the classic chronicles.

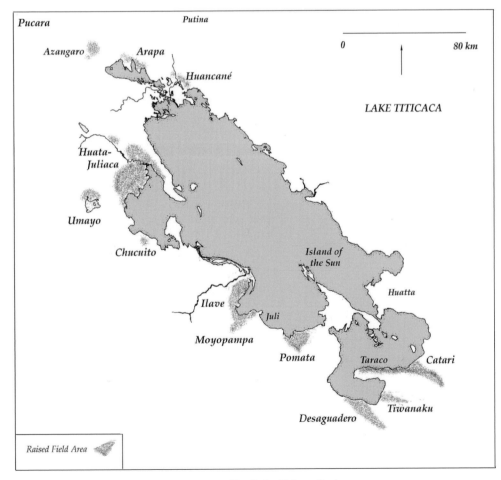

Figure 17.3. The Lake Titicaca Basin.

Figure 17.4. Aerial view of the Island of the Sun (courtesy of Johan Reinhard).

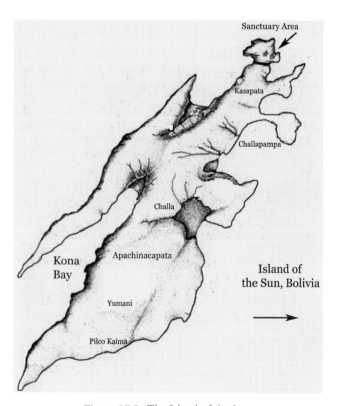

Figure 17.5. The Island of the Sun.

The chroniclers described how a wall, known as La Raya de los Incas, located at the first gate or entrance to the sacred area, marked off the entire Titikala area. We discovered this wall foundation. The wall cut the neck of the island in an almost perfect north-south path (Figure 17.12). A paved road can be seen passing through this wall at the top, where the first gate was most likely located. Other sites were found adjacent to or near this wall. We also confirmed the location of the building called Mama Ojila at the base of the walkway to the Sacred Rock. The

central wall of the Mama Ojila in fact lines up precisely with two islands in the lake (Figure 17.13). A niche was carved out of the natural hill to provide a sight-line for this view. The closest island was completely terraced with very fine walls. On top of the island was a trapezoidal plaza. We could not visit the other island, but it clearly is lined up with the Mama Ojila.

Excavations in front of the Sacred Rock confirmed use of the area by the Inca, including underground canals to drain liquid offerings at the rock (Bauer et al. 2004). There were also remains of Inca buildings around and near the rock, all of which generally conformed to the historical descriptions by chroniclers such as Cieza de León, Bernabé Cobo, Ramos Gavilán, and Garcilaso de la Vega. Survey of the entire island discovered numerous Inca sites. Most of these were small hamlets. Others included the historically documented sites such as Pilco Kaima, Kasapata, and the Chincana. Still other newly discovered sites included small ceremonial platforms on the hilltops where offerings were left. In short, the Inca use of the Island of the Sun as a great ceremonial destination for empire-wide pilgrimages was confirmed by our archaeological research.

We also discovered two solstice markers on a hill called Tikani, located a short distance above the Sacred Rock (Seddon and Bauer 2004).[6] These markers are about 600 hundred metres to the northwest of the sacred area (the sacred area is large and imprecisely defined so a specific distance cannot be provided), as seen in Figure 17.11. As first noted by David Dearborn and published in Dearborn, Seddon, and Bauer (1998), the towers mark the winter or June solstice precisely if one stands in the centre of the plaza in the Sacred Rock area. This plaza was demarcated on the northwest by an original wall, to the northeast by the Sacred Rock, and to the southeast by a rise in the landscape. It is not possible to locate the exact sacred area to the southwest, but the topography does not allow much space beyond a few hundred metres in this direction (Figure 17.14).

The towers are very similar to those described in the chronicles for Cuzco. They are made of stone and are filled with a solid rubble core. The two towers are 32 metres apart. Excavations supervised by Matt Seddon and reported on in Dearborn, Seddon, and Bauer (1998) convincingly demonstrate that these were in fact towers and not burial chambers or other kinds of structures.

Figure 17.6. The upper Inca road on the Island of the Sun.

Figure 17.7. View of the sacred area on the Island of the Sun, distance view from the southeast.

Subsequent analysis of the Island of the Sun data using virtual reality modelling indicates that the summer solstice (December) sunset, from the same spot in the temple area that one views the June solstice, falls between the two hills on the nearby island of Chuyu. This island is located to the southwest of the Sacred Rock area (Figure 17.7). A quick survey of the island did not discover any pottery on the surface, but an intensive search for small structures like the Tikani towers has yet to be conducted. While this observation has not been precisely ground confirmed, it is evident that the December solstice was at least framed by the natural hills on this island, while the Tikani towers framed the June solstice.

Our research also discovered one and only one site that directly abutted the wall (La Raya de los Incas) that separates the sacred area from the rest of the island. This unnamed site, called by its registry number 019, is a platform located directly outside the Sacred Rock area (Figure 17.15). It would have been a slightly elevated area on the low rise between the road and first gate to the sanctuary and the high ground above. The fact that the

Figure 17.8. View of the sacred area on the Island of the Sun, closeup view from the southeast.

Figure 17.9. The sacred area from the Tikani ridge.

fact, similar (about 30 metres) to the width of the plaza in the Sacred Rock area and the distance between the two towers. Site 019, sitting just outside the sacred area, appears to be the second and only other 'special' spot where the solstice can be seen.

Marking time

The solstice markers on the Island of the Sun functioned almost precisely like those described for Cuzco by several independent chroniclers. They marked a period of a few days during the winter solstice (June) from the front of the Sacred Rock. There is a special spot in the sacred area, quite near the Sacred Rock, where the Sun sets precisely between the two towers. The December or summer solstice is framed by the hills of Chuyu island from this spot as well. From this precise location in the Sacred Rock area, the exact date of the June solstice is marked directly in the centre of the two towers. As just mentioned, there is a special spot on the site of 019 where the solstice can be seen to set exactly in the middle of the two towers.

However, there is only one line from which one can see the Sun set precisely in the middle of the two towers on this day. That line, of course, goes through the two special spots near the Sacred Rock and on the platform of 019. The rest of that sight line would have been either obscured by buildings or restricted from walking. A substantial proportion of that line between the Sacred Rock and site 019, for instance, is a rocky area that some chronicles state was covered with 'gardens'. There is, in fact, evidence of springs near Mama Ojila that may have watered these hills. Between the temple area and Tikani towers, there is some rocky terrain and some low ground. There are no sites or any kind of archaeological remains in this area. In sum, we have no archaeological evidence, either to the northwest or to the southeast, of any other platform or building that was on this sight line.

To repeat, the exact date of the solstice as marked by the Tikani towers can be seen only from two archaeologically

site was not on the higher area, nor adjacent to the road, led Dearborn to check the orientation of the platform vis-à-vis the Sacred Rock and the solstice towers. As they explain in their article, Dearborn, Seddon, and Bauer (1998:255–256) recognized that a person standing in the middle of this platform would also have a view of the June solstice between the two towers on the Tikani ridge (Figure 17.16). The width of the platform is, in significant spots on the Island of the Sun. The two towers would also mark about one day before and one day after the precise solstice day from these two spots (Brian Bauer, personal communication 2006). In other words, from these two special places, the Inca could mark *both* a three-day period in which the Sun set between the two towers and the precise day of the solstice. In effect, the Tikani towers served to define both a multi-day ceremonial period and a precise moment when the Sun fell exactly between the two towers.

From the two special places, one can define the sacred time of the winter solstice ceremony; it is that which begins with the first sunset through the towers, peaks at the middle sunset, and ends with the last sunset to the other side. The people who were seated or stood in these special places used the towers to define the sacred days. Those days can be precisely fixed, and the precise moment in the middle of that time can be exactly marked.

Marking sacred space

As Dearborn, Seddon, and Bauer note, because the Tikani ridge towers are so close to the Sacred Rock area, the exact spot at which the Sun disappears during the solstice "changes visibly as one moves about the plaza" (1998: 252). This is an extremely important observation. If we view the towers from another perspective, not as markers of time but as markers of space, we can see why a pair is necessary and how a pair of towers could be used to define sacred space in a place like the Titikala sanctuary.

As one moves about the Sacred Rock area in any direction even slightly off the sight line that marks the solstice between the special places and the centre of the towers, one has less time to view the setting of the Sun during the 'official' solstice. The special spots where the solstice Sun sets directly in middle of the two towers, of course, determine the 'official' time. Dead set in the middle of the plaza on that special spot, or on 019 in its corresponding special spot, one sees the full three sunsets pass through the towers. These precise spots determine the definition of sacred time. Move a bit to the left

Figure 17.10. The Titikala or Sacred Rock, northeast side.

Figure 17.11. The Titikala or Sacred Rock, southeast side.

or right of that line and one has less sunset-viewing time. At some point off this line, one cannot see even one day of a sunset during the sacred time as determined by the view of the towers from the special spots.

It is clear how easy it is to mark sacred space at the precise moment of the solstice sunset. At that moment (which lasts for a number of minutes) anybody in the entire area who can see a sunset through the towers *is* in the sacred area. If the Sun at that moment is blocked by one of the towers, then you are *not* in the sacred area. Moreover, one can see how a cline of sacred space can be constructed. At the first sunset through the towers from the special spots, there will be a well-defined area from which one can view the sunset. During the precise

Figure 17.12. La Raya de los Incas. This wall separates the sacred area from the rest of the island.

Figure 17.13. Sight line in the structure known as the Mama Ojila. Note that the wall lines up with a carved niche in the hill slope with two islands to the north.

Figure 17.14. The sight line of the winter (June) solstice from the Titikala to the Tikani towers.

Figure 17.15. A view from the Mama Ojila to the road that descends from the La Raya de los Incas and site 019.

moment of the solstice, there will be a slightly different though overlapping area for the sacred space. The same effect would be seen for the third sunset. In other words, the people in the special spots will be able to define degrees of sacredness depending upon the position of the setting Sun. Any spot on the entire landscape of the sacred area can be defined relative to its position to the special spot in the middle. Sacred space is easily defined and understood by all those participating in the ceremonies.

Marking social place

It is hypothesized that proximity to the special spots defines the degree to which a place in the sanctuary is sacred. Likewise, proximity to the people in the sacred spots corresponds to a person's social status. Like virtually all empires in antiquity, the Inca had a caste structure that defined a person's place in that society. As the pilgrims participated in the solstice ceremonies, they would be located to greater or lesser degrees near the special spots where the Inca nobility were located. The location of a person in the ceremony at the time of the solstice would be directly correlated to his or her social status. Their entire experience of the solstices would be impacted by where people stood during the sunsets. The closeness of your position to the highest-ranking person occupying the special spot would determine the degree of status that you had at that moment. Your status would be created by your proximity to other people and then ideologically reinforced by the amount of time you witnessed the solstice passing through the towers.

It is not, however, a simple correlation of status and distance from the Sacred Rock. We have seen that the site of 019 also afforded an unrestricted view of the solstice between the two towers. The site location of 019 precisely replicates the experience of someone in the sacred area itself, at least in terms of how he or she would witness

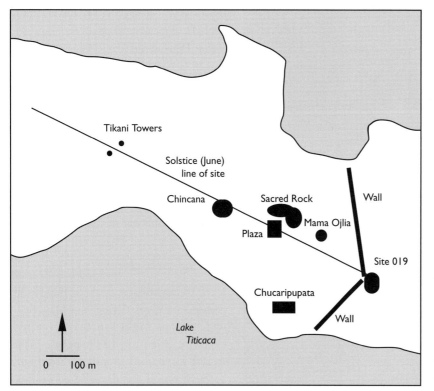

Figure 17.16. Schematic view of the sight line and other features in the sanctuary area.

spot to view the solstice through the Tikani towers was just uphill from the Intipuncu gate, as determined by the archaeological remains.

It can be argued that the people in the special spot at 019 actually had substantial status, perhaps even more, from their perspective, than those in the least sacred areas of the Sacred Rock sanctuary. In essence, the Inca used the widespread Andean concept of duality to its full expression. It created two roads to the Sacred Rock and created two viewing areas for the June solstice. The high road led directly to the Sacred Rock; the lower road led past 019 and then onto the Sacred Rock area. We cannot be certain exactly who used the 019 platform to view the solstice. What is clear, however, is that the status of the two areas was very complex. There was a hierarchy within the viewing area at 019, and this hierarchy was nested within the larger one in the sacred area itself.

the sunsets during the solstice ceremonies. This represents a classic instance of an empire dealing with nested social and political hierarchies (Stanish 2000). One of the most fundamental problems facing a rapidly expanding empire is the question of local elites and their place in the imperial social and political structure. The cooperation or at least acquiescence of these elites is essential to running an empire. But the political class that runs the empire cannot afford to accord local elites too much status, risking alienating their own lesser nobility and other socially subordinate groups.

Dearborn, Seddon, and Bauer (1998:256–257) argue quite convincingly that site 019 was built for people who were not permitted access to the actual Sacred Rock area. Cobo (1990[1653]:96) writes that "they [common pilgrims] did not get close to the crag [Sacred Rock]; they were only allowed to view it from the gateway called Intipuncu [appropriately translated as 'Gate of the Sun'], and there they handed over their offerings to the attendants who resided there". The Intipuncu was almost certainly the first gate in the wall leading to the Sacred Rock area (Figure 17.15). The Intipuncu was therefore located only a few dozen metres from site 019, an archaeological datum strongly corroborating the historical documents. Cobo's reference to the pilgrims' having to hand their offerings to the guards at Intipuncu is particularly instructive in this regard. The "special"

Conclusion

The contribution by Gary Urton in this volume emphasizes the fact that we have to go beyond a superficial interpretation of many features of Inca life. The chroniclers saw the quipu as a simple accounting device, used to keep track of goods and people. Deeper analysis reveals a much more complex system. This is not surprising. The early chroniclers brought to bear their own cultural views and biases. They wrote what they saw but did not engage in serious analysis of most features of Andean life. One could even argue that there were strong motivations to keep the conquered peoples as 'primitive' as possible, a bias that most certainly can be seen in many of the 16th- and 17th-century documents.

The solar markers are similar in this regard. Superficially, they mark the sunsets of the year. Some of them mark the solstices; others marked the calendar of ceremonies and socially and politically significat acts. However, as with the quipu, a deeper analysis of the solstice towers reveals a more complex understanding and use of these features by the indigenous Andean peoples.

Archaeology contributes to this deeper understanding. The interpretation offered here is a combination of empirical facts and informed suppositions. Empirically, we know beyond doubt that the Island of the Sun sanctuary was one of the three most important in the empire.

The Inca invested a huge amount of labour and material resources to build and maintain this shrine. A temple was built near the Sacred Rock. Fine roads were constructed, demarcation walls built, support facilities built, and towers constructed. The use of the Tikani towers as solstice markers is effectively a fact, as demonstrated by Dearborn, Seddon, and Bauer (1998). The Sacred Rock area and adjoining islands were places of intense sacrifice, as written in the historical accounts and confirmed by archaeology. Sight lines were utilized by the Inca on the Island of the Sun, as confirmed by the construction of the Mama Ojila walls. The site of 019 was built in a manner to allow the solstice sunsets to be viewed virtually identically to the way in which they could be seen in the Sacred Rock area. Virtual reality reconstructions indicate that the summer solstice fell between the two hills on a nearby island.

On the basis of these data, we can infer that the Island of the Sun area hosted a solstice ceremony that was substantially more complex than suggested by the historical documents. The Inca did not just arrive to count the solstice days. The entire landscape was altered to create a monument where time, sacred space, and social space were defined and negotiated in ways that we are just beginning to understand fully.

ACKNOWLEDGMENTS

I thank Professor Colin Renfrew and Dr. Iain Morley for the invitation to participate in the Measuring the World and Beyond symposium. I also thank Brian Bauer and Joyce Marcus for critical comments and help with this chapter. The research on the Island of the Sun was funded by the National Science Foundation, the Wenner-Gren Foundation, the Heinz Foundation, The Field Museum, and anonymous private donors. Mr. Charles Steinmetz and GTE/Verizon supported the virtual reconstruction at the Virtual Reality Laboratory at the University of California, Los Angeles.

NOTES

1. Gary Urton (this volume) refers to the theoretical work of M. Foucault: "From this perspective, accounting systems are understood to be devised and manipulated by political elites with an eye to the maintenance of the status quo." Indeed, even accounting systems can be viewed as part of the ideological repertoire to reinforce social and political boundaries and statuses.

2. The various creation stories appear to be contradictory. Indeed, they do contradict each other in certain details. However, by going beyond a literal and superficial analysis, we can see a clear and rational logic at work in promoting these religious traditions (Stanish 1997).

3. The Andean scholars Anthony Aveni (1981), Brian Bauer and David Dearborn (1995), and Dearborn, Seddon, and Bauer (1998) provide excellent summaries of these solar markers and/or interpretations of their use.

4. Other astronomical phenomena, including solstices, were marked by features other than paired towers. In this essay I am concerned only with paired towers.

5. The word "Titikala" has an ambiguous etymology. In an earlier publication (Stanish 2003), I suggest that the word is a corruption of "Thaksi Kala". In the 1612 dictionary of Ludovico Bertonio, this word means "piedra fundamental" or "fundamental rock" evoking clear theological themes. The name of the Sacred Rock or Titikala lent its name to the island, which in turn was adopted as the name of the lake by common usage. In contrast, Professor Rodolfo Cerrón-Palomino informs me (pers. comm. 2009) that the word "titi", which translates as "mountain cat", most likely was part of the original name. The "rock of the mountain cat" would be consistent with the central place that felines had in Inca and earlier cultures. Data that support Professor Cerrón-Palomino's theory come from an entry in Bertonio's dictionary: the word "titi" has several meanings one of which is: "the daughters of the said officials [those that were charged with obtaining felines] and the sons called Copa that later inherited these offices for obtaining the said cats" (Bertonio 1984 [1612]:bk 2:353). Copacabana is the name of the town near the Island of the Sun that was part of the regional ritual complex.

6. The towers were first discovered on survey by the author as listed as burial towers or chulpas. After the survey Dearborn and Bauer noted that the towers were in the general direction of the winter solstice. Subsequent archaeoastronomical work and excavations by Dearborn, Seddon, and Bauer (1998) definitely demonstrated that these were indeed solid, rubble-filled towers and not burials.

REFERENCES

Aveni, A. F. 1981. Horizon Astronomy in Incaic Cuzco. In *Archaeoastronomy in the Americas*, edited by R. A. Williamson. Ballena Press, Los Altos, pp. 305–318.

Bandelier, A. 1910. *The Islands of Titicaca and Koati*. Hispanic Society of America, New York.

Bauer, B. S. and D. Dearborn 1995. *Astronomy and Empire in the Ancient Andes*. University of Texas Press, Austin.

Bauer, B., M. Futrell, L. Cipolla, R. A. Covey, and J. Terry 2004. Excavations at Inca Sites on the Island of the Sun. In *Archaeological Research on the Islands of the Sun and Moon, Lake Titicaca Bolivia: Final Results from the Proyecto Tiksi Kjarka*, edited by C. Stanish and B. Bauer. Cotsen Institute of Archaeology Press, Los Angeles, 43–82.

Bauer, B. S. and C. Stanish 2001. *Ritual and Pilgrimage in the Ancient Andes: The Islands of the Sun and Moon*. University of Texas Press, Austin.

Bertonio, L. 1984 [1612]. *Vocabulario de la lengua Aymará*. Juli. Facsimile edition, La Paz.

Betanzos, J. de 1996 [1557]. *Narrative of the Incas*, translated and edited by Roland Hamilton and Dana Buchanan. University of Texas Press, Austin.

Cieza de León, P. de 1553. *Crónica de la conquista del Perú*. Editorial Nueva España, S.A., Mexico D.F.

Cobo, B. 1979 [1653]. *History of the Inca Empire*, translated by R. Hamilton. University of Texas Press, Austin.

Cobo, B. 1990 [1653]. *Inca Religion and Customs*. University of Texas Press, Austin.

Dearborn, D. S. P., M. T. Seddon, and B. S. Bauer. 1998. The Sanctuary of Titicaca: Where the Sun Returns to Earth. *Latin American Antiquity* 9, 240–258.

Garcilaso de la Vega 1961. *The Royal Commentaries of the Inca*. Discus Books, New York.

Guaman Poma de Ayala, F. 1980. *El primer nueva crónica y buen gobierno*. Siglo Veintiuno, Mexico.

Hyslop, J. 1990. *Inka Settlement Planning*. University of Texas Press, Austin.

Julien, C. 1993. Finding a Fit: Archaeology and Ethnohistory of the Incas. In *Provincial Inca*, edited by M. Malpass. University of Iowa Press, Iowa City, 177–233.

Ponce Sanginés, C., J. Reinhard, M. Portugal, E. Pareja, and L. Tiílla 1992. *Exploraciones arqueológicas subacuáticas en el Lago Titikaka*. Editorial La Palabra Producciones, La Paz.

Ramos Gavilan, A. 1988 [1621]. *Historia del santuario de Nuestra Señora de Copacabana*, edited by I. Prado Pastor. Gráfico P. L. Villanueva S.A., Lima.

Reinhard, J. 1992. Investigaciones arqueológicas subacuáticas en el lago Titikaka. In *Exploraciones arqueológicas subacuáticas en el Lago Titikaka*, edited by P. Sanginés, J. Reinhard, M. Portugal, E. Pareja, and L. Ticlla. Editorial La Palabra Producciones, La Paz, 421–530.

Rowe, J. H. 1980. An Account of the Shrines of Ancient Cuzco. *Ñawpa Pacha* 17, 1–80.

Seddon, M. T. 1998. *Ritual, Power, and the Development of a Complex Society: The Island of the Sun and the Tiwanaku State*. Ph.D Dissertation, Department of Anthropology, University of Chicago, Chicago.

Seddon, M. T. 2005. The Tiwanaku Period Occupation on the Island of the Sun. In *Advances in Titicaca Basin Archaeology-I*, edited by C. Stanish, A. Cohen, and A. Aldenderfer. Cotsen Institute of Archaeology Press, Los Angeles, 135–142.

Seddon, M. and B. Bauer. 2004. Excavations at Tikani. In *Archaeological Research on the Islands of the Sun and Moon, Lake Titicaca Bolivia: Final Results from the Proyecto Tiksi Kjarka*, edited by C. Stanish and B. Bauer. Cotsen Institute of Archaeology Press, Los Angeles, 83–92.

Stanish, C. 1997. Nonmarket Imperialism in a Prehispanic Context: The Inca Occupation of the Titicaca Basin. *Latin American Antiquity* 8, 1–18

Stanish, C. 2000. Negotiating Rank in an Imperial State: Lake Titicaca Basin Elite under Inca and Spanish Control. In *Hierarchies in Action: Cui Bono?* edited by M. Diehl. Southern Illinois University Center for Archaeological Investigations, Occasional Paper no. 27. Carbondale, 317–339.

Stanish, C. 2003. *Ancient Titicaca: The Evolution of Complex Society in Southern Peru and Northern Bolivia*. University of California Press, Berkeley.

Stanish, C. and B. S. Bauer 2004. *Archaeological Research on the Islands of the Sun and Moon, Lake Titicaca Bolivia: Final Results from the Proyecto Tiksi Kjarka*. Cotsen Institute of Archaeology Press, Los Angeles.

Stanish, C., A. B. Cohen, and M. S. Aldenderfer 2005. *Advances in Titicaca Basin Archaeology-I*. Cotsen Institute of Archaeology Press, Los Angeles.

Zuidema, R. T. 1981. Inca Observations of the Solar and Lunar Passages through Zenith and Anti-zenith at Cuzco. In *Archaeoastronomy in the Americas*, edited by R. A. Williamson. Ballena Press, Los Altos, 319–342.

18

Measuring time in the European Neolithic? The function and meaning of Central European circular enclosures

Peter F. Biehl

In this chapter I will focus on the archaeology of Neolithic circular enclosures in order to understand better their potential for further analysis regarding early measurement of space and time. In particular I will focus on the Neolithic circular enclosure in Goseck and not only introduce the site, but also present fresh data that may help shift our understanding of the meanings and functions of the phenomenon of the Middle Neolithic enclosures in Europe. These enclosures are especially interesting because they emerged and were used over a period of approximately two centuries (ca. 4900–4700 BC) and then just as abruptly disappeared. I will also discuss evidence for the astronomical function of the Goseck enclosure. This evidence is mainly based on

Wolfhard Schlosser's work on the Goseck material, and I am grateful to him for letting me use and present his astronomical results in my analysis of the Goseck excavation data. Furthermore, I will discuss how this evidence could be operationalized to address questions of an early measuring system as well as of cosmology, cult and ritual, and the complex roles of these regarding identity, memory and experience for these early agriculturalists in Europe.

Neolithic enclosures in Europe

Neolithic enclosures have been known in Europe for over 100 years and have fascinated archaeologists and the public alike.[1] The image of monumental architecture made of stone, wood or earth constructed some 7,000 years ago was so powerful that it has long incited archaeologists to search for the origin of this European phenomenon and to investigate its spread and function.

There has been extensive research over the last 20 years on Neolithic enclosures (Petrasch 1990; Trnka 1991; Andersen 1997; Darvill & Thomas 2001; Bertemes, Biehl & Meller in press), and the overall spread of enclosed sites can now be seen "as ranging across most of the lower-lying plains and river systems from the Black Sea in the east to Portugal in the west, and from Sicily in the south to Scotland in the north" (Darvill & Thomas 2001, p. 7). Niels Andersen has catalogued some 800 enclosed Neolithic sites within this area (Figure 18.1), all

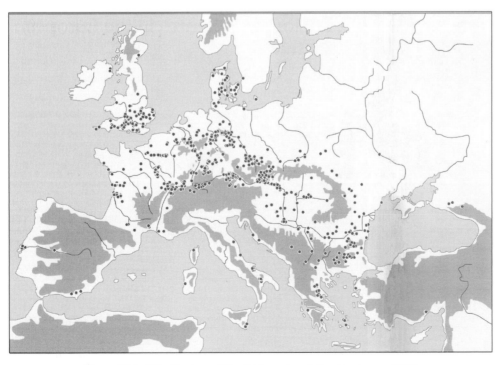

Figure 18.1. Distribution of Neolithic enclosed sites (Andersen 1997).

dating from the sixth to the third millennium BC, and points out that they are just a fraction of known Neolithic enclosures (Andersen 1997). This is due to the fact that large swaths of Europe sat behind the Iron Curtain for decades, and we still do not have a proper idea of how Neolithic enclosures were distributed in many nations from the former Eastern Bloc; until 1989, political and military factors made it virtually impossible to carry out sustained aerial surveys in these regions.

But more importantly, if we have a closer look at Andersen's catalogue and distribution map (Andersen 1997, pp. 134–135, fig. 178) we realize that only a few of the enclosed sites dotting this landscape have been uncovered or excavated fully. This fragmented state of research might be one reason why the functions of the sites have been debated for decades. Clearly, knowing only little about each site provides dangerously wide parameters for interpretation.

Today, wading through all the possible theories, we can see three major trends in the way Neolithic enclosures are perceived in the archaeological record: first, it is clear now that Neolithic enclosures were an extremely widespread phenomenon across Europe. Second, their variation in form and context is so evident that one has no problem agreeing with Timothy Darvill and Julian Thomas that "the idea that all Neolithic enclosures had a similar role or function within the societies that created and used them is as laughable as the idea that some kind of universal classification can be applied to all sites" (Darvill & Thomas 2001, p. 13). And finally, the map of Neolithic enclosures remains a map of the distribution of the application of techniques such as aerial and geophysical survey techniques (Darvill & Thomas 2001).

Still, regardless of their exact numbers, clearly these enclosures were abundant. But how should we go about understanding them? I believe it is too difficult to approach such a large class of archaeological monuments with sweeping spatial and chronological frameworks. Instead, I argue that it is much more promising to start working at a more basic, individual level: that is, to look at one site first and analyse and contextualise it within the landscape in which its meaning and function were embedded and the region to which it belonged culture-historically.[2]

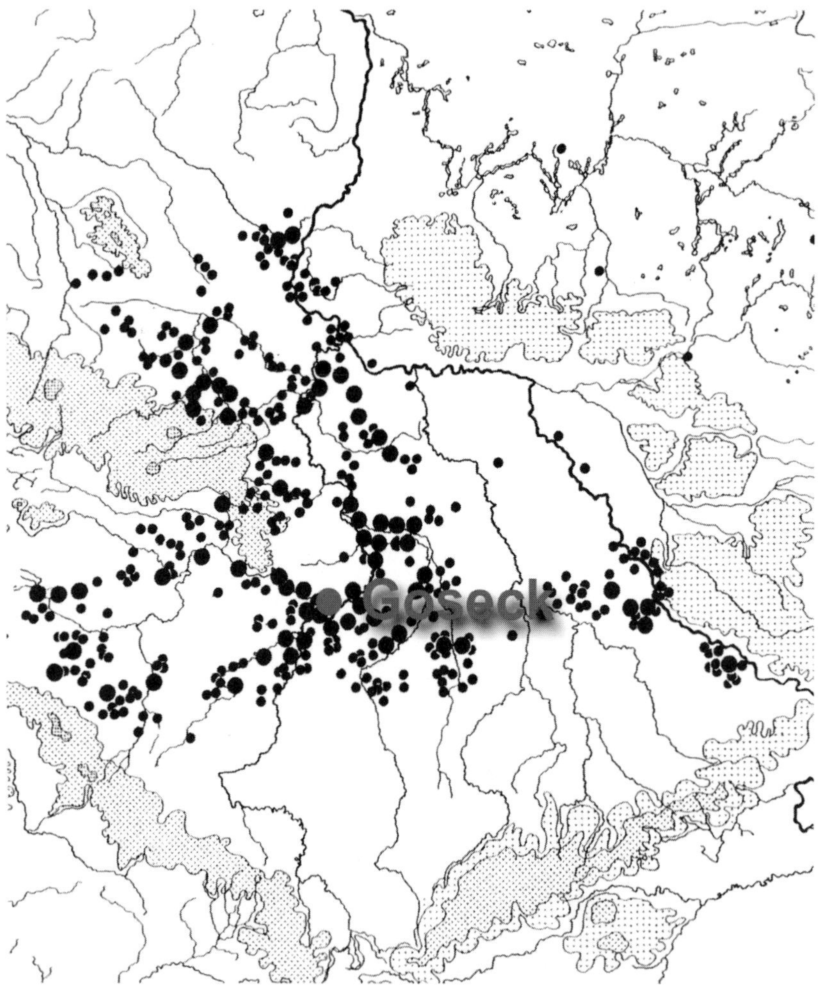

The best way to explain this contextual approach to cult places is to discuss it with a specific case study. I will, therefore, focus on the so-called *Kreisgrabenanlagen* – circular ditched enclosures – of the Central European Middle Neolithic of the first half of the fifth millennium BC, and specifically on the site of Goseck.[3]

The C-14 dates and the analysis of its material culture show that the site can be dated to the so-called Middle Neolithic *Stichbandkeramik* or culture with *stroke-ornamented pottery* (ca. 4900–4600 BC) (Figure 18.2). To date we know of approximately 120 circular enclosures (Neubauer & Trnka 2005a) belonging to a culture complex of Theiß-Herály-Csöszhalom, Lengyel, Stichbandkeramik, Oberlauterbach, Rössen and Großgartach in a circumscribed area reaching from Slovakia and Hungary in the east to Bavaria in the south and Hesse and Brandenburg in the west and north (Figure 18.3).[4]

Goseck serves well to introduce the Middle Neolithic variant of enclosed

Figure 18.2. Distribution of the Middle Neolithic stroke-ornamented pottery culture (*Stichbandkeramik*) in Central Europe.

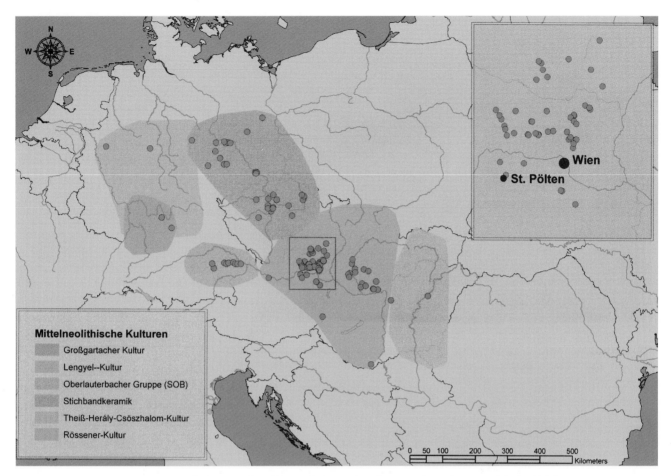

Figure 18.3. Distribution of Middle Neolithic enclosed sites in Central Europe (Trnka 2005).

sites in Central Europe since it was built and used during the few centuries in which this type of enclosure suddenly emerged and then abruptly disappeared again. Like most enclosures of this time period,[5] it is situated on a slightly sloped loess-covered terrace in an open unwooded landscape and close to a spring and a river (Figure 18.4). From 2002 to 2005 we fully excavated the enclosure, and in 2006 it was reconstructed on its original location (Figure 18.5).[6]

The enclosure consisted of a circular ditch over 70 meters in diameter, furnished with three entrances with out-turned terminals and with traces of two wooden palisade rings inside it, each with a narrow in-turned entrance that exactly lined up with the ditch entrances (Figure 18.6). The ditch in Goseck was some 3 m wide, and its V-shaped section likely reached over 3 m in depth and narrows at its base to 30 cm wide. It had an earth bank in front of the ditch, which we could document in the profile and the filling of the ditch. The V-shaped ditch silted up quickly by natural erosion of the loess and was cleaned out and recut several times. The upper part of the profile of the ditch shows a darker and more homogeneous layer, and the buildup of humus indicates

that the ditch was open and unused over a longer period. We still do not know just how long this period was, but it may have been as long as the construction – that is, the wooden parts – endured. There is no evidence that they were renewed.[7] It is important to note that we have found no evidence of contemporaneous structures inside the enclosure. Some contemporary pits close to the eastern and western entrances of the enclosure (both inside and outside) may have been connected with ritual practices and depositions, which I will discuss later (Figure 18.7). Two larger pits at the western entrance to the enclosure have calcined walls and floors, which indicate that fires were burnt there. These pits had a thick layer of ash containing pieces of charcoal and shards of stroke-ornamented pottery. We can assume that these pits were also used for some sort of activity, possibly of a ritual nature. Interestingly, items such as pottery and stone tools were deposited only in the entrance area in the south. The same is true for animal bones, most of which are from cattle.

Also of particular interest was a special type of a burial found in the inner southeast area of the enclosure. Here, parts of an adult skeleton were deposited together

Figure 18.4. Aerial photograph of the Goseck enclosure after removing the topsoil (photo by Ralj Schwarz, Landesamt für Denkmalpflege und Archäologie Sachsen-Anhalt, Halle/Saale).

Figure 18.5. Reconstructed enclosure in Goseck at its original location (photo by Ralj Schwarz, Landesamt für Denkmalpflege und Archäologie Sachsen-Anhalt, Halle/Saale).

or body parts are known for example from Friebritz in Lower Austria and Ippesheim in Hesse (Neubauer & Trnka 2005b; Neugebauer-Maresch 2005; Schier 2005b).

Having introduced the site,[9] I want to discuss what sort of meaning and function this type of enclosed place might have had, why such places were built and enclosed the way they were and how we can approach these questions methodologically.

The method of contextual attribute analysis

The key element on which my thesis is based is the concept of 'context'.[10] The problem is that "we are all aware of the difficult issues surrounding contexts and that easy-to-read contexts are more of a rarity than a norm" (Conkey & Tringham 1998, p. 28). This is especially true for the Neolithic circular enclosures with their multiphased ditches and wooden palisades, which cannot be conceived of as so-called closed finds[11] such as burials, depositions or burnt-down buildings, and so on. Does this mean that we cannot study these Neolithic monuments contextually because we have only artefacts which to use Hodder's definition are 'out of context'? I believe we can. Elsewhere, I have demonstrated that we can use artefacts without any secure context and include them in our analyses (Biehl 2003; 2006). I have named the method I use 'contextual attribute analysis'[12] and have suggested that we conceive of an artefact as a 'closed find' unto itself, that is, that we consider

with two flint arrowheads and clots of ochre.[8] This discovery is not only fascinating in terms of the question of ritual actions that might have taken place inside the enclosure, but also because of its potential to help date the enclosure and clarify its relative chronology: The burial has been cut by the outer palisade, and it looks very much as if the skeleton was knowingly deposited there before or in the course of the construction of the wooden palisades. Similar depositions of human bodies

each object a contextual structure replete with meaningful attributes. When we look at the artefact, we must see it as the result of a system of making. That is, we must assume that it did not come about at random, but that somehow it was thought about and considered useful within a set structure (Biehl 2003; 2006).[13] This has complementarity to a *chaîne opératoire* approach but differs significantly in that the technological choices and the nature and role of technical activities are not the principal focus; instead my approach focuses more on the ideational and symbolic considerations than the material aspects. When all of the attributes have been analyzed and compared, we can begin to understand the significance of an artefact and eventually gain insight into its hidden symbolism and the communication system embedded in it.

I believe that we can use contextual attribute analysis in the same way for places and monuments such as Neolithic circular enclosures. We should begin to view

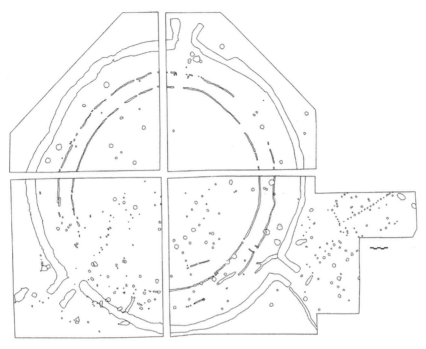

Figure 18.6. Goseck excavation plan.

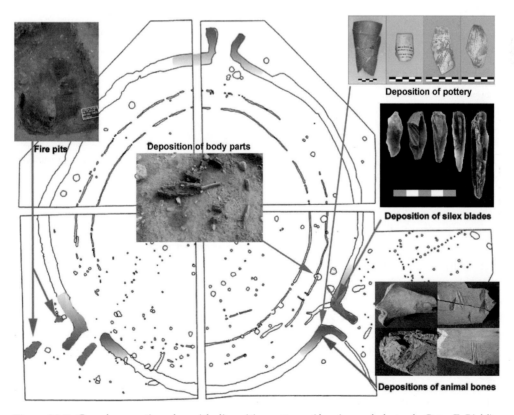

Figure 18.7. Goseck excavation plan with disposition patterns (drawing and photos by Peter F. Biehl).

each enclosure as a context in itself. In other words, an enclosure should be analyzed as a contextual structure of meaningful attributes, or a 'structural context' of both the artefact and the place.

With this as our theoretical and methodological framework, we can begin to recognise the system under which such a monument was created by conceptualising and then contextualising all discernible and chronological contemporaneous attributes of its structure. Though this procedure does not allow us to view the monument as a physical end product, we can study it as the material reflection – or the 'coming into form/being' – of a vast variety of individual and collective decisions that were both practical and symbolic. These decisions underscore and may help us read and reconstruct the cultural rules to which the builders of the enclosure had to conform. In order to study these attributes and begin to see patterns in them, we must first separate all discernible attributes into the smallest of categories. That means chronological and geographical, material and symbolic, and functional.

Once we accept the idea that such a system may have existed within a prehistoric community, we must then decipher what roles the individual and the group played, how the system was transmitted and what meanings such enclosed spaces embedded in the system can carry.

Enclosing space – meanings and functions of enclosed cult places

The contextual approach applied to the Goseck enclosure not only moves us away from thinking about a place as a static end product, it also emphasizes the *multi-scalar nature* of place and illuminates the broader context of power relations and social structures within which place is both product and producer (Figure 18.8). The contextual approach helps us to recognize that the enclosed place is constructed and reconstructed continuously through reiterative practices. It is not only the product of human practice and experience; it is also the arena through which they emerge.

The question remains: What sort of practices occurred inside and outside these mysterious places, and how can we grasp them archaeologically? And why were these places built and enclosed the way they were?

To begin with, I discount defense and fortification (see also Trnka 1991 and Neubauer 2007), though it is interesting to note that this was one of the earliest interpretations of this monumental architecture (Wagner 1928). Had these been major factors, one could expect more of these kinds of sites in Europe and throughout

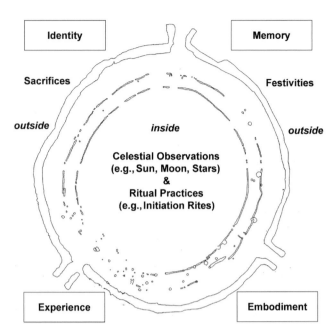

Figure 18.8. Diagram of the multi-scalar approach to cult places.

the Neolithic. One would also expect traces of violence and destruction along with corresponding artefacts. In Goseck, the earth bank *in front* of the ditch also clearly speaks against such an interpretation.

Use as a corral or kraal can also be excluded (see also Neubauer 2007, pp. 224–225): it took too much human labour to build and maintain these enclosures for the construction for such a mundane task to have been worthwhile. Also the fact that there was no phosphate in the ground, which would be deposited through animal dung, clearly speaks against such a function. Moreover, in Goseck the entrances through the palisades are way too narrow to have been designed for cattle or other animals to pass through.

Some scholars interpret these places as centres or 'central places' of sociopolitical preeminence (Neubauer 2007, pp. 225–228; Petrasch 1990 and in press; Stäuble 2007, p. 175; see also Bertemes, Biehl & Meller in press),[14] where labour could be mobilized for impressive collective undertakings, but the most intriguing interpretation – and the one I most closely adhere to – is that these enclosures functioned as cult places (Biehl 2007).

This kind of interpretation has vast and endlessly exciting possibilities and seems to me the most logical and all-encompassing explanation, that sites not only be linked with ritual actions but also with means of consecrating place, of honoring ancestors, as the symbolic representation of communal cohesion and of marking time. The defined ways in which people must have approached, entered and experienced such monuments could be seen as a metaphor for the regularities of the comings and goings of their own lives, both from year to year and from generation to generation: this could have been achieved through reinforced attachment to specific places, chosen times for communal gathering and ritual and predetermined ways of seeing and experiencing ordered space.

One important part of these ceremonies and rituals was most likely feasting. This can be seen at Goseck in the ordered depositions of animal bones (with cut marks and signs of extraction of the marrow), of stone tools (for slaughtering the animals), pottery (for food and drink) and fire pits (for cooking the meat and food) (Figure 18.7) (Biehl, Marciniak, Mooney & Whitlow forthcoming). Another important part of the rituals was human sacrifices and the disposition of the body or parts of the body at meaningful places inside the enclosure. The fact that we only find single bodies or at most two bodies, as at Friebritz, highlights the importance of the people deposited and/or the ritual involved. And finally, we have to take other rituals such as rites of passage/initiation rites into account (see also Bertemes & Northe 2007, pp. 164–165; Neubauer 2007, pp. 228–229; Stäuble 2007, p. 180; Biehl 2007, p. 180). This becomes clear when we think of the enclosed places as frontiers, between inside/outside, culture/nature, domesticated/wild, sacred/profane, and so forth (Becker et al. 2005, p. 43; Bertemes & Northe 2007, pp. 162–163; Stäuble 2007, pp. 179–180 and fig. 4, and in press). The architecture of the ditched circular enclosures supports such an interpretation: the entrances, for example, are often constricted, and people would have been forced to enter in single file or double file, causing them to enter the enclosed place in procession. Alex Gibson highlights that this was "perhaps an essential part of the ritual, by severely restricting access to the enclosures and necessitating controlled and ordered entry" (Gibson in press). For him this suggests that "at least some were closed monuments. If such is the case, they must have been closed, both physically and visually, to certain members of the community at certain times. Perhaps the ceremonies were even based on cults with several degrees of initiation" (ibid.). In Goseck the entrances through the ditch are exactly aligned with the narrow entrances through the palisades. This construction restricts the physical as well as the visual access to the enclosure, which is especially important regarding the practices inside and outside the Goseck enclosure. And we should also think about the visual and acoustic effects created by wooden palisades of ca. 2.50-m height. Even when we are standing in the enclosure today our experience of light, colour and sound as well as the general feeling of insularity are important, as well as its being protected from views from outside.

Astronomical functions of enclosures

External views are also crucial for the understanding of the Middle Neolithic circular enclosures and may have been very focused, for example, on specific solar, lunar or stellar events. Archaeoastronomers have insisted on the astonishingly precise stellar orientations of numerous megalithic sites (e.g., Ruggles & Whittle 1981; Schlosser & Cierny 1996; Ruggles 1998; see also Aveni, this volume; Clark, this volume; Saburo, this volume). They have also managed to formulate (or reformulate) together with archaeologists complex calendrical functions for stone circles. As early as 1972 Olaf Höckmann had pointed out that the Neolithic enclosures might have been built following astronomical orientations (Höckmann 1971/1972). But it is only since the beginning of the 1990s that archaeoastronomy has become an important part of the interpretation of the Central European Middle Neolithic circular enclosures (e.g., Becker 1989, 1996; Becker & Fassbinder 2005; Gervautz & Neubauer 2005; Kastowski, Löcker, Neubauer & Zotti 2005; Schier 2005a; Schmidt-Kaler 2005; Zotti 2005a & b; Neubauer 2007, especially pp. 214–227). Indeed, although they seem simple on the outside, these monuments may have served complex and highly advanced cyclical roles. It was especially Helmuth Becker in his extensive work on the enclosure in Meisternthal who promoted the astronomical interpretations of these monuments (Figure 18.9) (Becker 1989; 1996; Becker & Fassbinder 2005). This is, naturally, a subject of great debate. Though there is much of importance in the work of the archaeoastronomers, it is important to recall that proving sites *could have been* used in this way does not mean they *were* used this way.[15]

Nevertheless, there is a growing body of evidence to suggest that solar observation was practised at these sites. The number of cardinal orientations encountered is too many to be coincidental. For instance, at Goseck, Wolfhard Schlosser was able to demonstrate that the circular enclosure was constructed in an almost perfect circle (Figures 18.10 and 18.11) and might have served as a solar observatory (Bertemes et al. 2004, p. 141; Bertemes & Schlosser 2004; Schlosser 2006/2007a and in press): the orientations of the southern entrances of the ditch and the palisades form an exact bearing from which to observe the winter solstice (Figures 18.12 and 18.13). Holes in the northern part of the palisades are also exactly aligned with the summer solstice (Figure 18.14). These measurements are too exact to be unintentional. He points out that the most important part of his analysis is the inclusion of the measurements of the horizon in Goseck (Figure 18.15) (Schlosser

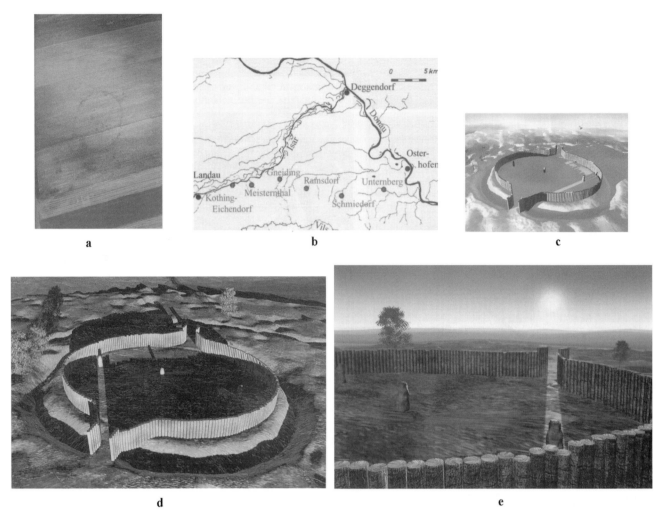

Figure 18.9. The Middle Neolithic enclosure in Meisternthal, Bavaria, Germany: a) geophysics, b) map with other enclosures, c) winter solstice, d) summer solstice, e) midsummer sunrise (Becker & Fassbinder 2005).

2006/2007a, p. 282; Schlosser 2006/2007b, p. 286 and in press).[16] In contrast to colleagues in the Austrian research team (Neubauer 2007, pp. 217–222), Schlosser rejects the inclusion of stellar or lunar observations in his analysis[17] and argues that because of the abundance of possibilities, as well as the 'short-lived' existence of stellar constellations, such an approach is too speculative (Bertemes & Schlosser 2004, p. 51). There are two other problems with the astronomical interpretation of the Goseck enclosure that have to be considered regarding early measuring systems: first, the identification of important dates in the year of early agriculturalists such as the winter or summer solstice can only be approximate, at best within a range of one week, that is, about two or three days before and after the actual event (Figure 18.15); second, to date the meaning and function of the northern entry gate are still unclear. Schlosser argues that this gate did not have any astronomical orientation (Figure 18.11) (Schlosser 2006/2007a, p. 284 and in press; Bertemes & Schlosser

2004, p. 51). One could argue that this gate was used as the actual entry gate to the enclosure, as indicated in the reconstruction drawing by Karul Schauer, but other interpretations are equally possible. As can be seen in current work in Ippesheim (Schier 2005a, 2005b) and Austrian and Slovakian enclosures (Neubauer 2007, p. 218), prominent landmarks such as mountains, knolls or valley cuttings, as well as markers that cannot be seen or traced today such as trees, special plant cover or architectural features made from wood, could have been significant points for the orientations of entry gates such as the northern gate of the Goseck enclosure. There is an additional argument that supports the thesis that this gate had a different function from the two southern gates. The palaeobotanical and archaeozoological analyses have shown that the structured deposition of animal bones and grain in ritual practices can mainly be found in the southern gates (Biehl et al. forthcoming). It is true that these gates are aligned on a bearing from which to observe the winter solstice – the middle

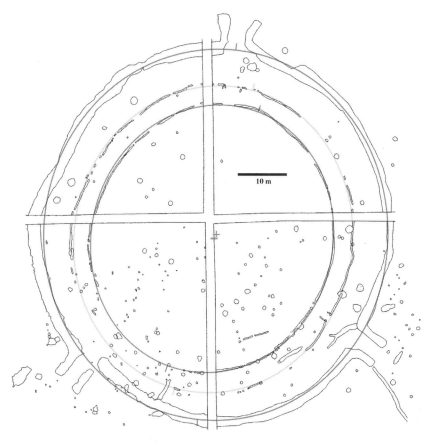

Figure 18.10. The construction of the Goseck circular enclosure using perfect circles for comparison (Schlosser in press).

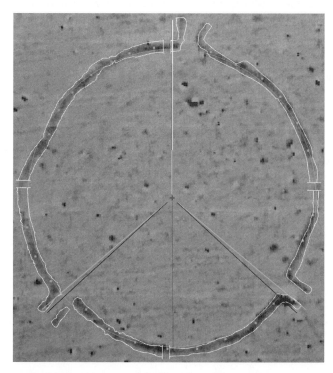

Figure 18.11. Diagram of the Goseck enclosure indicating astronomical features, including excavated features, magnetic north, astronomic meridian, ditch and optimal circle equalization, and sunrise and sunset at the winter solstice (Bertemes & Schlosser 2004, p. 49, and Schlosser in press).

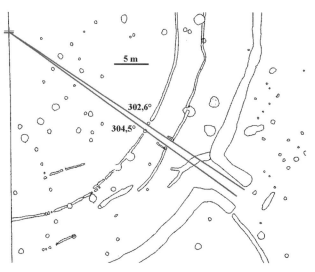

Figure 18.12. Bearing at the southeast entrance gate during the sunrise on the winter solstice (ca. 4900 BC) (Bertemes et al. 2004, fig. 8, and Schlosser in press).

of winter, when few plants are green and all the world seems cold and dead – but of critical importance to the early agriculturalists here must surely be that the agricultural cycle will continue: that the seeds in the ground will grow to provide the next year's harvest. Making such ritual offerings as animal bones and grain at this time of year could serve to "situate social reproduction in the timeless and unchanging cycle" of agriculture (Williams 2003, p. 223), as has been illustrated in various contexts across prehistoric Europe since the advent

of farming (Bradley 2005). However, this is only one theory in a multitude of potential explanations.

Summary

To conclude, I firmly believe that these enclosures were used as places for ritual practice. The evidence seems to me to be overwhelming in terms of both material culture and interpretive possibility. It is true that the functions and practices performed in or with these enclosed places are difficult to determine, but when we examine the Middle Neolithic enclosures across Europe, we find a fundamental similarity: they enclose an empty space. I want to stress the multi-scalar nature of enclosed places and the broader context of social structures and religious belief systems within which place is not only the product of ritual practices – such as astronomical observations and feasting – and experience, but also the arena through which they emerge.

It seems that monocausal interpretations need to be replaced by a more complex concept of ritual including multicausal and multi-scalar interpretations, as I have demonstrated with the Goseck case study. I would also argue that the people who built and used the Goseck enclosure might have conceived it as a 'sacred place', and the defined ways in which people must have approached, entered and experienced such monuments could be seen as a metaphor for the regularities of the comings and goings of the winter and summer solstices; their own lives, both from year to year and from generation to generation, reinforced through communal gathering and ritual; and predetermined ways of seeing and experiencing ordered space.

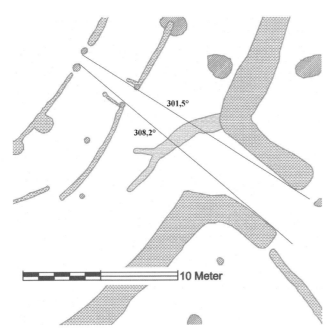

Figure 18.13. Bearing at the southeast entrance with azimuth angles; entries in the palisades are directly connected with the entrances in the circular enclosure (Schlosser in press; see also Schlosser 2006/2007, fig. 2).

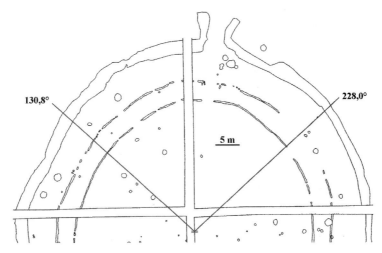

Figure 18.14. Sunrise and sunset during the summer solstice (ca. 4900 BC) (Schlosser in press; see also Schlosser 2006/2007, fig. 2).

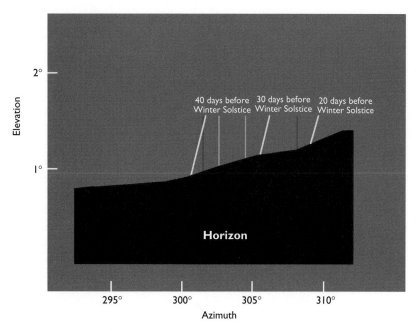

Figure 18.15. Timeline of the winter solstice (40–20 days before) in relation to the profile of the horizon in Goseck (elevation – azimut) (Schlosser in press).

Figure 18.16. Closeup of the southeast entrance of the reconstructed enclosure in Goseck at its original location (from outside and inside) (drawing and photos by Peter F. Biehl).

NOTES

1. The first Neolithic enclosure was discovered in Krpy in Bohemia towards the end of the 19th century (Woldřich 1886). See also J. Petrasch for an extensive overview of the history of research of Neolithic enclosure (Petrasch in press).

2. The same approach is taken by Niels Andersen in his seminal publication of the Sarup enclosures (Andersen 1997).

3. The enclosure in Goseck (Saxony-Anhalt/Germany) was fully excavated between 2002 and 2005. The excavation

was codirected by François Bertemes and me and carried out within the framework of an apprentice field school by students mainly from the Institute of Prehistoric Archaeology at the Martin-Luther-University, Halle-Wittenberg. It was funded by the State of Saxony-Anhalt, the Heritage Management Service and several sponsors. A publication of the Goseck enclosure is forthcoming as a monograph (Biehl forthcoming). For preliminary excavation reports, see Bertemes, Biehl, Northe & Schröder 2004, Bertemes & Biehl 2005, Becker, Bertemes, Biehl & Schier 2005,

Bertemes & Northe 2006/2007, Bertemes & Northe 2007, Biehl in press, Biehl forthcoming.

4. Whilst there have always been attempts to compare the Middle Neolithic circular enclosures with the British *henge* monuments (as early as Behrens 1981), it seems that it is widely accepted now that "British and European circles, so different in time, space and morphology, cannot be regarded as related in any way other than the medium of their construction and their role in defining space" (Gibson 2005, p. 81). See also Trnka 1991, pp. 298–299, Neubauer 2007, p. 224.

5. One of the exceptions is the circular enclosure of Immendorf/Austria, which was built on a high plateau, which is different not only with regard to its location but also to its form, dimensions and astronomical orientations (Neubauer 2007, p. 222).

6. As were so many discoveries in countries of the former Eastern Bloc, the site was first discovered in 1991 as intensive aerial photography that was prohibited until 1989 was done. After its discovery it was analysed and documented with a geophysical survey, which took place in 1995; see Bertemes et al. 2004, pp. 137–139.

7. Results of a small number of C-14 dates (done by the University of Poznan) indicate a date of 4900–4800 cal BC for the construction and use of the enclosure. Only an extensive set of C-14 dates from stratified contexts will provide a better understanding of the relative chronology of the monument.

8. Body parts together with arrowheads have also been found in the burials at Friebritz 1 (Neugebauer-Maresch 2005, Neubauer 2007, pp. 230–233). Neubauer also points to the finds at the enclosure Ruzindol-Borova in Southwest Slovakia, where at least 18 bodies were found in the ditch of the enclosure, showing clear indications of violence. He further argues that since we do not know very much about cemeteries in the Austrian Middle Neolithic (Neubauer 2007), it is difficult to identify these "special burials" as the typical burial rites of this period. But it is important to note that death and fragmentation of the body played an important role in the meaning and function of these enclosed places. In the Lengyel distribution area, which certainly shows a noticeable concentration of Middle Neolithic circular enclosures and has been interpreted as the region where this phenomenon originated (Trnka 1991), the fragmentation of pottery and figurines (see also Biehl 2006) seems to play an important role (Neubauer 2007; see also Neugebauer-Maresch 2005, Ruttkay 2005, Podborsky 1988). Though fragmentation of the human body and pottery can also be proven for the western distribution area of the enclosures, finds of figurines are so far unknown. This might not have a particular importance for the interpretation of the enclosures, because the area of the stroke-ornamented pottery does in general – in contrast to the area of the Lengyel Culture – produce anthropomorphic figurines (Hansen 2007, pp. 303–309).

9. In addition to the Middle Neolithic features there are four other interesting discoveries, which I would like to mention briefly because they are important for the overall argument in this article: Outside the enclosure, we found a grave of a 1- to 2-year-old child with two pots of the Linear Pottery Culture (ca. 5200 BC). Some pits – chronologically about 2,000 years younger than the enclosure – close to but outside the eastern entrance of the enclosure – had calcined walls and floors, indicating fires. Interestingly, they seem to have been thoroughly cleaned out after usage so that there are no remains of the fire nor any artifacts, although, even more interestingly, the pits contained human bones, which were evidently deposited into them after their cleaning. Furthermore, there are two small ditches leading towards the enclosure. Both ditches have been excavated and were ca. 30–50 cm wide and 20–40 cm deep and belong to a later period (Bertemes & Northe 2007). And finally, outside the enclosure, we also surveyed and partly excavated a longhouse most likely from the Early Bronze Age (ca. 1600 BC). All these features show that this place was occupied long before and long after the enclosure was built and used.

10. The 'rediscovery' and appraisal of context in this sense are due to Ian Hodder's seminal work on so-called contextual archaeology (Hodder 1987). But my conception of context differs in a couple of points from Hodder's definition. I agree with his definition of the context of an archaeological attribute as "the totality of the relevant environment, where 'relevant' refers to a significant relationship to the object – that is, a relationship necessary for discerning the object's meaning" (Hodder 1991, p. 143; see also Hodder 1982a, pp. 23, 27, 211; 1985, p. 14; 1987, p. 4; 1991, pp. 121–155; 1999); and also that a context is always 'situation specific'. But I disagree with his somehow relativistic statement that context also depends on and varies with the dimensions of variation in similarities and differences being considered, and with the questions being asked. This consequently leads him to the conclusion that "in many areas contextual archaeology can hardly begin until more data have been collected" (Hodder 1991, p. 146). Elsewhere (Biehl 1999, 2003, 2006) I have argued against Hodder's assertions that, firstly, "an object out of context is not readable", and, secondly, that "in prehistoric archaeology, the further one goes back in time, so that the survival rates diminish, the more difficult it becomes to ground hypotheses in data" (Hodder 1991, p. 46), and have suggested the concept of a 'structural context' of an artefact. This gives us the tools to include 'artefacts out of context' – which overwhelmingly form the archaeological record – in our analyses. For critical approaches to 'context' in archaeology see also Papaconstantinou 2006.

11. The notion of the 'closed find' has been developed from Oscar Montelius's notion and definition of a 'secure find' as "the sum of objects which has been found under such conditions that it can be assumed that they were deposited at the same time" (Montelius 1903; see also Eggers 1986,

pp. 91–105; Trigger 1989, p. 157). Although Montelius focused on chronological questions, the epistemological potential of his conception of material context provides the groundwork to make inferences between material culture and the socioeconomic and ideological-religious contexts of the societies that left it behind.

12. For a detailed definition of this new conception of *context* and its application in the *contextual attribute analysis,* see Biehl 2003.

13. The underlying concept of such a system of regularities is based on Pierre Bourdieu's concept of *habitus* and practice theory. In this case, it refers to commonsense attitudes and dispositions and the routines of the everyday social and/or ritual practices in making and decorating pots in a way that is possible and appropriate. The relative freedom in individual creativity – e.g., in aesthetically adding some decorative elements to the central design motif, which is fixed in its placement and meaning (Biehl 1996) – can only be understood within the framework of social structure and human agency.

14. The teamwork of various groups required for the construction of the ditches (Bertemes & Biehl 2005, p. 36) and the ca. 2,000 wooden posts needed for the construction of the opaque palisades exemplify the effort invested and strongly support this interpretation (see also Petrasch 1990, pp. 498–500).

15. For a detailed summary of the criticism and further references, see Trnka 1991, pp. 316–317. See also Stäuble 2007, p. 176 and in press.

16. The importance of this point is also stressed by Neubauer and his team (most recently, Neubauer 2007, pp. 216–218). He makes a further interesting point that the palisades create an artificial horizon line, which most likely helped to facilitate the observation of not only the Sun but also stars (Neubauer 2007, p. 219).

17. Though he indicates that the wide-stretching Hyades could be associated with the southeastern entry gate of the Goseck enclosure (Bertemes & Schlosser 2004, p. 51 and fig. 5).

REFERENCES

Andersen, N. H. 1997. *The Sarup Enclosures: The Funnel Beaker Culture of the Sarup Site Including Two Causewayed Camps Compared to the Contemporary Settlements in the Area and Other European Countries.* Moesgaard: Aarhus University Press (Jutland Archaeological Society Publications XXXIII:1).

Becker, H. 1989. Die Kreisgrabenanlage auf den Aschelbachäckern bei Meisternthal, ein Kalenderbau aus der mittleren Jungsteinzeit? *Das Archäologische Jahr in Bayern* 1989: 27–35.

Becker, H. 1996. Kultplätze, Sonnentempel und Kalenderbauten aus dem 5. Jahrtausend v. Chr. Die mittelneolithischen Kreisanlagen in Niederbayern. In: Becker, H. (ed.) *Archäologische Prospektion: Luftbildarchäologie und Geophysik.* München: Arbeitshefte Bayerisches Landesamt für Denkmalpflege 59: 101–122.

Becker, H., Bertemes, F., Biehl, P. F. and Schier, W. 2005. Zwischen Himmel und Erde. *Archäologie in Deutschland,* 6: 40–43.

Becker, H., and Fassbinder, J. W. E. 2005. Der Sonne entgegen. *Archäologie in Deutschland,* 21: 28–31.

Behrens, H. 1981. The First "Woodhenge" in Middle Europe. *Antiquity* 55: 172–178.

Bertemes, F., and Biehl, P. F. 2005. Goseck: Archäologie geht online. *Archäologie in Deutschland* 6: 36–38.

Bertemes, F., Biehl, P. F. and Meller, H. (eds.) in press. *Neolithische Kreisgrabenanlagen in Europa/Neolithic Circular Enclosures in Europe.* Halle/Saale: Veröffentlichungen des Landesamtes für Denkmalpflege und Archäologie Sachsen-Anhalt – Landesmuseum für Vorgeschichte.

Bertemes, F. and Northe, A. 2006/2007. Neolithisches Heiligtum in prähistorischer Kulturlandschaft – die Abschlussuntersuchungen in der Kreisgrabenanlage von Goseck und weitere Grabungen in deren Umgebung. *Archäologie in Sachsen-Anhalt* 4.2: 269–281.

Bertemes, F. and Northe, A. 2007. Der Kreisgraben von Goseck – Ein Beitrag zum Verständnis früher monumentaler Kultbauten Mitteleuropas. In: Schmotz, K. (ed.) *Vorträge des 25. Niederbayerischen Archäologentages.* Rahden: Verlag Marie Leidorf: 169–184.

Bertemes, F., Biehl, P. F., Northe, A. and Schröder, O. 2004. Die neolithische Kreisgrabenanlage von Goseck, Ldkr. Weißenfels. *Archäologie in Sachsen-Anhalt* 2: 137–145.

Bertemes, F. and Schlosser, W. 2004. Der Kreisgraben von Goseck und seine astronomischen Bezüge. In: Meller, H. (ed.) *Der geschmiedete Himmel: Die weite Welt im Herzen Europas vor 3600 Jahren.* Halle: Landesamt für Denkmalpflege und Archäologie in Sachsen-Anhalt/ Landesmuseum für Vorgeschichte: 48–51.

Biehl, P. F. 1996. Symbolic Communication Systems: Symbols on Anthropomorphic Figurines in Neolithic and Chalcolithic Southeast Europe. *Journal of European Archaeology* 4, 153–176.

Biehl, P. F. 1999. Analogy and Context: A Re-Construction of the Missing Link. In: Owen, L. and Porr, M. (eds.) *Ethno-Analogy and the Reconstruction of Prehistoric Artefact Use and Production.* Tübingen: MoVince Verlag (Urgeschichtliche Materialhefte 14), 13–26.

Biehl, P. F. 2003. *Studien zum Symbolgut der Kupferzeit und des Neolithikums in Südosteuropa.* Bonn: Habelt Verlag (Saarbrücker Beiträge zur Altertumskunde, Bd. 64).

Biehl, P. F. 2006. Figurines in Action: Methods and Theories in Figurine Research. In: Layton, R., Shennan, S. and Stone, P. (eds.) *A Future for Archaeology – the Past as the Present.* London: UCL Press: 199–215.

Biehl, P. F. 2007. Enclosing Places: A Contextual Approach to Cult and Religion in Neolithic Central Europe. In: Malone, C. (ed.) *Cult in Context: Comparative Approaches to Prehistoric and Ethnographic Religious Practices.* Oxford: Oxbow: 173–182.

Biehl, P. F. in press. Multifunktionalität und soziale Praxis. Überlegungen zur Bedeutung der Stichbandkeramischen

Kreisgrabenanlage von Goseck. In: Bertemes, F., Biehl, P. F. and Meller, H. (eds.) *Neolithische Kreisgrabenanlagen in Europa/Neolithic Circular Enclosures in Europe.* Halle/Saale: Veröffentlichungen des Landesamtes für Denkmalpflege und Archäologie Sachsen-Anhalt – Landesmuseum für Vorgeschichte.

Biehl, P. F. forthcoming. *Untersuchungen zur Chronologie, Funktion und Bedeutung Neolithischer Kreisgrabenanlagen in Mitteleuropa.* Halle: Veröffentlichungen des Landesmuseum für Vorgeschichte Halle.

Biehl, P. F., Marciniak, A., Mooney, D. and Whitlow, R. forthcoming. Feasting in Middle Neolithic Circular Enclosures: Contextual Archaeological, Palaeobotanical and Archaeozoological Analysis of the Goseck Enclosure.

Bradley, R. 2005. *Ritual and Domestic Life in Prehistoric Europe.* London: Routledge.

Conkey, M. and Tringham, R. 1998. Rethinking Figurines: A Critical Analysis of Archaeology, Feminism and Popular Culture. In: C. Morris and C. Goodison (eds.) *Ancient Goddesses: The Myths and the Evidence.* London: British Museum Press.

Darvill, T. and Thomas, J. (eds.) 2001. *Neolithic Enclosures in Atlantic Northwest Europe.* Neolithic Studies Group Seminar Papers 6. Oxford: Oxbow Books.

Eggers, H. J. 1986. *Einführung in die Vorgeschichte* [1959]. Third edition. München: Piper.

Gervautz, M. and Neubauer, W. 2005. Sonne, Mond und Sterne. In: Daim, F. and Neubauer, W. (eds.) *Zeitreise Heldenberg: Geheimnisvolle Kreisgräben* (Katalog zur Niederösterreichischen Landesausstellung 2005). Horn-Wien: Verlag Berger: 73–74.

Gibson, A. 2005. *Stonehenge and Timber Circles.* Stroud: Tempus.

Gibson, A. in press. Palisade Enclosures and Timber Circles in Britain and Ireland. In: Bertemes, F., Biehl, P. F. and Meller, H. (eds.) *Neolithische Kreisgrabenanlagen in Europa/Neolithic Circular Enclosures in Europe.* Halle/Saale: Veröffentlichungen des Landesamtes für Denkmalpflege und Archäologie Sachsen-Anhalt – Landesmuseum für Vorgeschichte.

Hansen, S. 2007. *Bilder vom Menschen der Steinzeit: Untersuchungen zur anthropomorphen Plastik der Jungsteinzeit und Kupferzeit in Südosteuropa.* Mainz: Philipp von Zabern (Archäologie in Eurasien 20).

Höckmann, O. 1971/1972. Andeutungen zu Religion und Kultus in der bandkeramischen Kultur. *Alba Regia* **12**: 187–209.

Höckmann, O. 1975. Wehranlagen der jüngeren Steinzeit: Ausgrabungen in Deutschland. *Monographien des RGZM Mainz* **1.3**: 278–296.

Hodder, I. 1982a. *The Present Past: An Introduction to Anthropology for Archaeologists.* London: Batsford.

Hodder, I. 1982b. *Symbols in Action: Ethnoarchaeological Studies of Material Culture.* Cambridge: Cambridge University Press.

Hodder, I. 1985. Postprocessual Archaeology. In: Schiffer, M. B. (ed.) *Advances in Archaeological Method and Theory.* New York: Academic Press: Vol. 8, 1–26.

Hodder, I. 1987. The Contextual Analysis of Symbolic Meanings. In: Hodder, I. (ed.) *The Archaeology of Contextual Meanings.* Cambridge: Cambridge University Press (New Directions in Archaeology): 1–10

Hodder, I. 1991. *Reading the Past: Current Approaches to Interpretation in Archaeology,* 2nd ed. Cambridge: Cambridge University Press.

Hodder, I. 1999. *The Archaeological Process: An Introduction.* Oxford/Malden: Blackwell.

Kastowski, K., Löcker, K., Neubauer, W. and Zotti, G. 2005. Drehscheibe des Sternenhimmels? Die Kreisgrabenanlage Immendorf. In: Daim, F. and Neubauer, W. (eds.) *Zeitreise Heldenberg: Geheimnisvolle Kreisgräben* (Katalog zur Niederösterreichischen Landesausstellung 2005). Horn-Wien: Verlag Berger: 80–82.

Montelius, O. 1903. *Die älteren Kulturperioden im Orient und in Europa,* I. Stockholm.

Nemejcova-Pavukova, V. 1997a. Kreisgrabenanlage der Lengyel-Kultur in Ruzindol-Borova. *Studia Archaeologica et Mediaevalia* **3**.

Neubauer, W. 2007. Monumente der Steinzeit zwischen Himmel und Erde – Interdisziplinäre Kreisgrabenforschung in Österreich. In: Schmotz, K. (ed.) *Vorträge des 25. Niederbayerischen Archäologentages.* Rahden: Verlag Marie Leidorf: 185–242.

Neubauer, W. and Trnka, G. 2005a. Rätselhafte Monumente der Steinzeit. In: Daim, F. and Neubauer, W. (eds.) *Zeitreise Heldenberg: Geheimnisvolle Kreisgräben* (Katalog zur Niederösterreichischen Landesausstellung 2005). Horn-Wien: Verlag Berger: 3–9.

Neubauer, W. and Trnka, G. 2005b. Totenbrauchtum. In: Daim, F. and Neubauer, W. (eds.) *Zeitreise Heldenberg: Geheimnisvolle Kreisgräben* (Katalog zur Niederösterreichischen Landesausstellung 2005). Horn-Wien: Verlag Berger: 223–224.

Neugebauer-Maresch, C. 2005. Tod im Kreisgraben. In: Daim, F. and Neubauer, W. (eds.) *Zeitreise Heldenberg: Geheimnisvolle Kreisgräben* (Katalog zur Niederösterreichischen Landesausstellung 2005). Horn-Wien: Verlag Berger: 224–227.

Papaconstantinou, D. (ed.) 2006. *Deconstructing Context: A Critical Approach to Archaeological Practice.* Oxford: Oxbow.

Petrasch, J. 1990. Mittelneolithische Kreisgrabenanlagen in Mitteleuropa. *Bericht Römisch Germanische Kommission* **71**: 407–564.

Petrasch, J. in press. Die mittelneolithischen Kreisgrabenanlagen in Zentraleuropa: Forschungsstand und Interpretationstheorien zu Funktion und Bedeutung. In: Bertemes, F., Biehl, P. F. and Meller, H. (eds.) *Neolithische Kreisgrabenanlagen in Europa/Neolithic Circular Enclosures in Europe*. Halle/Saale: Veröffentlichungen des Landesamtes für Denkmalpflege und Archäologie Sachsen-Anhalt – Landesmuseum für Vorgeschichte.

Podborsky, V. 1988. Tesetice-Kyjovice 4. Rondel osady lidu s moravskou malovanou keramikou. Opera Universitatis Purkynianae Brunensis, Facultas Philosophica. Brno.

Ruggles, C. 1998. Ritual Astronomy in the Neolithic and Bronze Age British Isles: Patterns of Continuity and Change. In: Gibson, A. and Simpson, D. (eds.) *Prehistoric Ritual and Religion: Essays in Honour of Aubrey Burl*. Stroud: Alan Sutton: 203–208.

Ruggles, C. and Whittle, A. (eds.) 1981. *Astronomy and Society in Britain during the Period 4000–1500 BC*. Oxford: British Archaeological Reports 88.

Ruttkay, E. 2005. Innovation vom Balkan: Menschengestaltige Figuralplastik in Kreisgrabenanlagen. In: Daim, F. and Neubauer, W. (eds.) *Zeitreise Heldenberg:. Geheimnisvolle Kreisgräben* (Katalog zur Niederösterreichischen Landesausstellung 2005). Horn-Wien: Verlag Berger: 194–202.

Schier, W. 2005a. Kalenderbau und Ritualkomplex. *Archäologie in Deutschland* **6**: 32–35.

Schier, W. 2005b. Kopfüber ins Jenseits: Ein Menschenopfer in der Kreisgrabenanlage von Ippesheim? In: Daim, F. and Neubauer, W. (eds.) *Zeitreise Heldenberg: Geheimnisvolle Kreisgräben* (Katalog zur Niederösterreichischen Landesausstellung 2005). Horn-Wien: Verlag Berger: 234–238.

Schlosser, W. 2004. Geometrisch-astronomische Analyse der Kreisgrabenanlage von Goseck, Ldk. Weißenfels. *Archäologie in Sachsen-Anhalt* **2**: 145–150.

Schlosser, W. 2004. Die Himmelsscheibe von Nebra – Astronomische Untersuchungen. In: Meller, H. (ed.) *Der geschmiedete Himmel: Die weite Welt im Herzen Europas vor 3600 Jahren*. Halle: Landesamt für Denkmalpflege und Archäologie in Sachsen-Anhalt/Landesmuseum für Vorgeschichte: 44–47.

Schlosser, W. 2006/2007a. Lichtblicke – geometrisch-astronomische Analyse der Kreisgrabenanlage von Goseck, Ldkr. Weißenfels. *Archäologie in Sachsen-Anhalt* **4.2**: 282–284.

Schlosser, W. 2006/2007b. Alles nur Zufall? Ein statistischer Test zur Überprüfung vorgeschichtlicher Denkmäler. *Archäologie in Sachsen-Anhalt* **4.2**: 285–288.

Schlosser, W. in press. Astronomische Untersuchungen der Kreisgrabenanlage von Goseck. In: Bertemes, F., Biehl, P. F. and Meller, H. (eds.) *Neolithische Kreisgrabenanlagen in Europa/Neolithic Circular Enclosures in Europe*. Halle/Saale: Veröffentlichungen des Landesamtes für Denkmalpflege und Archäologie Sachsen-Anhalt – Landesmuseum für Vorgeschichte.

Schlosser, W. and Cierny, J. 1996. *Sterne und Steine: Eine praktische Astronomie der Vorzeit*. Darmstadt: Wissschaftliche Buchgesellschaft.

Schmidt-Kaler, T. 2005. Die Neolithische Kalender-Revolution. *Archäologie in Deutschland* **6**, 2005: 31.

Schmotz, K. 2007. Die mittelneolithischen Kreisgrabenanlagen Niederbayerns – Anmerkungen zum Gang der Forschung. In: Schmotz, K. (ed.) *Vorträge des 25. Niederbayerischen Archäologentages*. Rahden: Verlag Marie Leidorf: 71–106.

Stäuble, H. 2007. Mittelneolithische Kreisgrabenanlagen im Wandel der Zeit. In: Schmotz, K. (ed.) *Vorträge des 25. Niederbayerischen Archäologentages*. Rahden: Verlag Marie Leidorf: 169–184.

Stäuble, H. in press. Stichbandkeramische Kreisgrabenanlagen in Sachsen: Neues zu einem alten Thema? In: Bertemes, F., Biehl, P. F. and Meller, H. (eds.) *Neolithische Kreisgrabenanlagen in Europa/Neolithic Circular Enclosures in Europe*. Halle/Saale: Veröffentlichungen des Landesamtes für Denkmalpflege und Archäologie Sachsen-Anhalt – Landesmuseum für Vorgeschichte.

Trigger, B. G. 1989. *A History of Archaeological Thought*. Cambridge: Cambridge University Press.

Trnka, G. 1991. *Studien zu mittelneolithischen Kreisgrabenanlagen*. Wien: Mitteilungen der Prähistorischen Kommission der Österreichischen Akademie der Wissenschaften 26.

Trnka, G. 2005. Kreise und Kulturen – Kreisgräben in Mitteleuropa. In: Daim, F. & Neubauer, W. (eds.) *Zeitreise Heldenberg: Geheimnisvolle Kreisgräben* (Katalog zur Niederösterreichischen Landesausstellung 2005). Horn-Wein: Verlag Berger: 10–19.

Wagner, F. 1928. Prehistoric Fortifications in Bavaria. *Antiquity* **2**: 43–55.

Williams, M. 2003. Growing Metaphors: The Agricultural Cycle as a Metaphor in the Later Prehistoric Period of Britain and North-Western Europe. *Journal of Social Archaeology* **3**: 223–55.

Woldřich, J. N. 1886. Beiträge zur Urgeschichte Böhmens (III. Teil) f, Reste der neolitischen Ansiedlung bei Řepín. *MAGW* **16**: 72–96.

Zotti, G. 2005a. Kalenderbauten? Zur astronomischen Ausrichtung der Kreisgrabenanlagen in Niederösterreich. In: Daim, F. and Neubauer, W. (eds.) *Zeitreise Heldenberg: Geheimnisvolle Kreisgräben* (Katalog zur Niederösterreichischen Landesausstellung 2005). Horn-Wien: Verlag Berger: 75–80.

Zotti, G. 2005b Kalender der Steinzeit. *Archäologie in Deutschland* **6**: 27.

SECTION V

The spirituality of measure

The concluding section of the book takes a specific look at theological conceptions of the relationships among the measurable finite, the immeasurable infinite, cosmology and worldview. These chapters represent reactions to the evidence and questions asked of it in the preceding sections and present additional perspectives on the relationships between measurement and our attempts to engage with the material world and elements beyond it.

LeRon Shults, from a background in theology and philosophy, focuses his commentary in particular on human engagement with the 'beyond' element of the title of the conference, 'Measuring the World and Beyond'. With the ability to measure and quantify the world arises an awareness of the immeasurability of certain phenomena. Shults draws out the theme of 'control' as being central to many of the chapters within the volume and, in particular, how this often leads to attempts to control the uncontrollable – for example, the uncontrollability of time and the degeneration of our corporeal form and material goods. He says that the questioning of such issues as what lies at the ends of our personal time – birth and death – lies at the roots of spirituality. If spirituality can be considered to be (at least partly) the process of making meaning of the experience of finite temporality, then as archaeologists we can hope to identify attempts to engage in this process. But as well as the uncontrollability of the finite, the necessity of engagement with concepts of 'the infinite' must also form a key component of spirituality, and this requires the negotiation of the relationship between quantitative measurement and qualitative experience of the immeasurable.

This reorganisation of the relationships of mind, body and things – with symbolism and the engagement with material (and immaterial) objects – is something that we can hope will manifest itself in certain ways archaeologically. As Shults puts it, "For scientists, the question would be how to recognize evidence of the human thematization of the intensive infinite in the archaeological record. For theologians, the question would be how the evolution of the cognitive capacity for mensuration of space contributed to or shaped the idea of divine infinity".

Also speaking from a theological perspective, Jeremy Begbie closes the volume by discussing the ways in which we can enquire about religious motivations underlying human action, especially past human action. To this end he explores the application of a concept of 'worldview', making the point that religious motivations form part of a complex package of attitudes and behaviours; these manifest themselves in a variety of ways that may or may not include explicitly articulated convictions (to use his phrase). A 'worldview' of a culture or individual is more than cosmology (in the sense of an explicit set of beliefs), but encompasses the entire process of apprehending and cognising the world. Begbie elucidates how this manifests itself in five key questions, and how these are addressed in the context of the measuring systems explored in the chapters throughout the volume. He goes on to elaborate the nature of the questions that must necessarily rebound from such explorations, such as the relationships between the material and the religious, and the very nature of the question of the 'roots of spirituality'.

Comprehending heaven, earth and time in ancient societies

The notion of 'becoming human' (Renfrew, 2007; Renfrew and Morley, 2009), in long time depth, implies a number of different and essentially independent trajectories of cultural development in different parts of the world – building upon, and perhaps diverging from, common foundations, following our dispersal from Africa – in which human societies, living in very different ecological circumstances, developed social, technological and physical solutions to the problems they faced. Whilst the particular problems and their solutions were specific to particular circumstances and cultures, they were nevertheless ultimately motivated by key human requirements, and the repertoires of solutions that emerged have collectively come to constitute ingredients of what it is to be human. In the case of quantification, each society had to construct its own solution to the problems of counting when material exigency made that desirable. Indications of what may be counting activities appear in the archaeological record during the Upper Palaeolithic period, and many of the activities undertaken then must have involved some forms of quantification; direct indications of measure appear somewhat later, and in relation to a variety of activities – in commerce, in planning and design, and in ritual practice. The construction of these more formal measurement systems underlies or at least accompanies the development of science and of technology and took different forms when and where the earliest recording and writing systems were developed. But the implications of, and motivations behind, measurement activities extend beyond the more obvious 'economic' quantifications. The reckoning of the passage of time could have great importance for human societies before quantification of the properties of objects became important. Indeed, it is difficult to conceive of distance practically without a conception of time (see Brown, Aveni, Morley, this volume).

Many aspects of spiritual belief systems are motivated by a requirement to explain aspects of the world, to understand events and the relationships between events. Measurement activities constitute analytical systems through which patterns of structure and action in the world, terrestrial and celestial, can be identified, and with that identification arises a need for explanation – of agency behind the patterns and causal relationships that emerge. Thus, as well as having the potential to provide some explanation for such phenomena, and cosmological frameworks for doing so, measurement activities have the potential to generate awareness of yet more aspects of the world requiring explanation.

What all of the contributions to this book have in common is that they illustrate that the construction of measurement systems constitutes, to a significant degree, the construction of new means for recognising and engaging with the material world, in a broader sense, for cognising the world. It is in this process that structures for addressing key concerns of cosmological belief systems emerge, for articulating relationships among the human form, human action and the world, as well as the generation of new concerns and understandings of relationships between events in the terrestrial world and beyond it.

REFERENCES

Renfrew, C., 2007. *Prehistory: Making of the Human Mind*. London, Weidenfeld and Nicholson.

Renfrew C. and I. Morley, 2009. *Becoming Human: Innovations in Prehistoric Material and Spiritual Culture*. Cambridge, Cambridge University Press.

19

The roots of spirituality and the limits of human mensuration

F. LeRon Shults

'Measuring the World and Beyond' was the official title of the conference that led to this book. In my response to the papers that became the chapters of this book and the discussion, I would like to focus on the phrase 'and Beyond' as a point of entry into the broader issue explored by this particular symposium and the project as a whole – the roots of spirituality. The archaeological insights gathered from data analysis around the globe shed new light on the extent to which the construction of modes of measurement in early cultures functioned as a new means of recognizing and engaging with the material world. How is this related to that which we experience as 'beyond' the world, 'beyond' measurement?

From a philosophical and theological point of view, it is not simply the emergence of the capacity for mensuration that makes early human cultures interesting but also, and even especially, the growing self-awareness among human beings of their lack of capacity in this regard. That is, the human construction of measurement may be a manifestation both of an evolutionary and an adaptive skill for controlling the environment and of an awakening to the recognition of the limits of adaptation mechanisms for manipulating the cosmos. Alongside the discovery of the susceptibility of the world to measurement arose the discovery of the concept of the immeasurable, which invites questions about spirituality and religious awareness.

I would like to focus on three concepts that came to mind as I read the chapters and listened to the discussion. These are space, time and matter, all of which are considered explicitly in various contributions to the symposium. Today we know that these three dimensions are intertwined within fields of energy. None of the chapters deal with this latter aspect of the measurable physical cosmos, simply because none of the early societies measured energy explicitly. This may have been due in part to the fact that notions of energy, movement and 'spirit' were often connected in ancient religious worldviews. Although space, time and matter are inextricably related, I will distinguish between them and treat them in order for the sake of analysis.

In each case, measurement has to do with *control*. Biehl illustrates this in his analysis of Neolithic circular enclosures; the enclosure of space in early cultures may be linked to the desire to carry out consistent observations. Biehl notes that "this immediately implies an element of control – or desire for control" and points to the broader context of power relations and social structures in which these 'places' are constructed. Similarly, Morley observes the connection between religiously oriented mensuration and the desire to control the cosmos: "belief in the ability to influence the natural world through ritual behaviour diminishes this sense of powerlessness and the corresponding potential for frustrated inactivity or, at worst, debilitating depression".

Contemporary human cultures are in the same situation vis-à-vis the 'Beyond'. Our techniques for measurement have improved, but we are still faced with our incapacity to control our world, and we still respond to the idea of a wholly uncontrollable presence 'beyond' the world with a mixture of fear and desire. During the conference, a conversation arose about developing ways to increase public interest in these themes. It seems to me that demonstrating the link between contemporary forms of spirituality and the roots of spirituality in the existentially threatening experience of lack of control we share with our ancestors might grab the attention of the public. Space stretches out indefinitely, time moves ever forward, and our embodiment and material goods slowly degenerate, as we lose our energy to live. The roots of spirituality may well be found in the soil of the human response to the inability to control space, time and matter through measurement. It is precisely in confrontation with the idea of the immeasurable, discovered through reflection on the process of mensuration, that religiously charged phenomena such as anxiety and hope emerge.

First, let us take the question of the measurement of space, an issue explicitly treated by several contributors. For example, Spence shows how Egyptian architecture related to the burial of kings was connected to the stellar 'control point' of the universe. Stanish demonstrates the link between sacred space and social place among the Inca. Human measurement of space is related to the need for useful architectural construction but is also inextricably tied to the desire to feel in control of one's place in the cosmos. In relation to finite space, the immeasurable is often called the infinite. A full treatment of this issue would require that we trace two different concepts of the infinite in the history of philosophy: one is mathematical (dealing with the indefinite or endless) while the other is metaphysical (dealing with the perfect or absolute). The measurement of space engages the former and is concerned with extension and quantitative issues. The metaphysical concept of the infinite has to do with what medieval philosophers called "a measure of a different greatness", which is concerned with the intensity of experience and qualitative issues.

Linking archaeological interest in quantitative measurement and theological or philosophical interest in qualitative experience of the immeasurable would require a more detailed analysis of the differences between these notions of infinity. The point here is simply that such analysis might help us clarify the relation between measurement and the roots of spirituality. For scientists, the question would be how to recognize evidence of the human thematization of the intensive infinite in the archaeological record. For theologians, the question would be how the evolution of the cognitive capacity for mensuration of space contributed to or shaped the idea of divine infinity.

Several of the chapters also explicitly treat the second theme: the measurement of time in early cultures. For example, Justeson explores the experience of time among ancient Meso-Americans in relation to the creation of calendars based on astronomical observation. Attention to the celestial spheres is perhaps the most common way to measure time, but Lewis illustrates the use of seasonal calendars (not necessarily tied to meteorological phenomena) in the agrarian society of the Shang. It is important to remember that the measurement of time and measurement of space are typically connected; Aveni appropriately writes of the "spatialization of time" in early cultures. Farr explores the way in which boat journeys could become a metaphor for an individual life (or the beginning and end of time) and their relation to the creation of concepts of time in some Neolithic cultures and suggests that belief systems in the central Mediterranean may have emerged as a means of ordering knowledge of the world.

As noted, several chapters document the relation between the measurement of time and the desire for *control*. Brown argues that writing assisted in the elaboration of number-symbols and this facilitated the creation of mensuration systems. He points in particular to the importance of royal astral divination as an attempt at prediction, which is a form of control. In his analysis of Shang China, Lewis notes the connection between the experience of time and the interpretation of death. For the Shang, the structuring of time in relation to sacrifices to ancestors "brought order and some sense

of control to the future … the past, present and future, and the entire structure of time … merged in the figures of the dead".

In relation to time the immeasurable is the 'eternal'. How might this help us understand the roots of spirituality? Several chapters deal with what we might call the endogenous (internal, physiological) and the exogenous (external, environmental) dimensions of the interpretation of time. For example, Malafouris explores the neuroscience of mensuration (endogenous) and Morley suggests that the experience of cycles of natural phenomena (exogenous) contributed to the emergence of new possibilities for thinking about time. Theologically we would want also to engage what I would call the epiphanic dimension of temporal experience. By this I mean the experience of an Other, the appearance of a reality that disrupts time, or evokes a new intense awareness of the limits of one's temporality. This could be manifest in the experience of shamanism, for example, or other similar forms of spirituality.

The thematization of Eternity emerges alongside the recognition of the limits of temporality, of the inability of human mensuration to halt or control the flow of time. This limitation is most intense at the extremes, in birth and in death. But what is 'beyond' these limits? Religions give a variety of answers, such as 'the spirit world of the ancestors', but the deeper point is that it is precisely this questioning that is at the roots of spirituality. Are there instances of religious responses to the experience of the limitations of time that are not characterized by attempts to control and manipulate temporality, but that interpret and receive it as gift from that which is 'beyond'? If we think of spirituality broadly as a way of making meaning in relation to the experience of limited temporality, then archaeologists might be able to search for evidence in early cultures of the thematization of such experiences and interpretations.

Finally, I point briefly to the question of the measurement of matter, which comes under consideration in several of the chapters that deal in particular with weights and weighing. Here too control, or more specifically the lack of and the desire for control, is a central theme. For example, Michailidou notes that in the Late Bronze Age, Aegean metrology was ascribed to the god Thoth but at the same time functioned as a means of power for bureaucratic hierarchical societies. Sugiyama shows how quantification is often deeply rooted in creation myths; in the case of the cosmogram at Teotihuacan, this plays itself out in the measurement and placement of the bodies of sacrificial victims. For Justeson the measurement of material objects is linked to the use of fingers to manage numbers, a process that provides "grounding metaphors" (numbers are like collections of objects) and provides the capacity for increased mental control of sets of objects. Schmandt-Besserat makes a similar connection between the use of material objects that are easy to manipulate and the facilitation of counting; material tokens make it possible to manipulate numerosity more effectively.

How can we connect the materiality to the roots of spirituality? I believe that the concept of symbolicity may function as a mediator. The chapter by Malafouris is particularly helpful for clarifying this interdisciplinary possibility. He suggests that material engagement with tokens contributed to the emergence of the concept of number (as symbol) in the mind of *Homo sapiens*. This provides a link between what he calls brains, bodies and things, and between what I have called the endogenous and exogenous dimensions of human experience. Malafouris argues that material engagement led to a "culturally and practice-effected *reorganization*" in the neural connectivity of intraparietal areas, which enabled the emergence of new mental capacities.

We might take this hint and develop it further in light of the sciences of emergent complexity and claim that 'spirituality' is an autopoetic function of new properties that emerge as the material relations between brain-body-things are self-organized in a more complex way. On this model, we could speak of spirituality as a qualification of materiality, as an organized and organizing complex of embodied social relations out of which emerge new capacities for self-awareness, self transcendence and the use of symbolism.

Several chapters observe that cultural symbols have power. From a philosophical-theological point of view, we can also say that the inability or impotence of symbols is also relevant for understanding the roots of spirituality. Religious practices emerge out of and are most existentially relevant in the context of facing that which is beyond our control. What we call the (metaphysical) infinite and the eternal are beyond the control of our symbolic species, yet our interpreted experience of this 'beyond' is always mediated through symbols.

No less than in early cultures, today we are tempted to take 'our' culture's material engagement and symbolic construction as absolute, total, final – which then authorizes our attempt to control the other violently, to protect the material goods we have accumulated. It seems to me archaeology can make an important contribution to our understanding of spirituality insofar as it can illuminate the role of material engagement in the emergence and formulation of religious symbols that mediate and interpret the experience of an immeasurable, infinite, eternal, uncontrollable presence that evokes both fear and hope – an experience that we share with the earliest of our ancestors.

Worldview, measurement and 'the roots of spirituality'

Jeremy S. Begbie

It is sometimes said that in interdisciplinary conversation, "iron sharpens iron". When those trained in different intellectual pursuits meet for serious discussion, the result is often a sharpening of insight with respect to their own particular field, as well as a clearer perception of another. I was asked as a professional theologian to engage with the material in these chapters (and to take part in the symposium that led to them) with an eye to the Templeton Foundation's enquiry into 'the roots of spirituality' – the origins of religious belief and practice. The following is offered in the hope that, just as I gained an enormous amount from being plunged into the world of archaeology, those at work in that world might find it useful to consider their findings from the perspective of someone at work in the world of religion and 'spirituality'.

It is far beyond the scope of a single chapter even to outline the various connections between religion and the material in these fascinating contributions. What I attempt here is something much more modest: to highlight some of the basic issues implied in any enquiry into the 'religious' or 'spiritual' dimensions of human behaviour, not least when the attempt is made to trace the links between archaeological data and religious activity. Especially illuminating in this respect, I am going to suggest, is the concept of 'worldview'. I shall argue that to enquire about religious actions and motivations entails very much more than examining explicitly articulated convictions (if there be any). It involves taking account of a whole complex of phenomena with which religious or 'spiritual' matters are bound up, phenomena that together express or embody a 'worldview'. I shall then go on to show that taking worldview seriously means that profound questions inevitably rebound upon the enquirer, questions about the methodological assumptions governing any scientific enquiry, and indeed, about

the viability or otherwise of religious truth claims. As so often happens in the academy, the questioner becomes questioned.

Worldview

Most of the chapters here deal, either explicitly or implicitly, with 'cosmology' – in the sense of a coherent view or account of the universe considered as a totality. Cosmologies, so understood, offer a kind of 'map' of the spatiotemporal order, complete – very often – with a cosmogony (an account of the world's origins). In common use today, of course, cosmology is often understood fairly narrowly as 'physical cosmology': where the universe is treated solely from the perspective of the natural sciences, especially physics. But cosmologies may incorporate into their thinking a god-figure or gods, and/or other metaphysical realities that are believed to lie behind, impinge upon or influence the physical world in various ways. All the cosmologies cited in this collection are of this latter 'theological' or 'metaphysical' sort.

A worldview, however, is something much broader and deeper than this, though incorporating or entailing a cosmology.[1] We are speaking of something precognitive, pretheoretical. As such, a worldview is not fundamentally an object of intellectual reflection (though it may become such, especially when challenged or flouted), but is rather that *through which* a society or an individual thinks about, knows, interacts with and interprets the world he or she inhabits. We are not aware of a worldview as we exercise it: it is not that *of* which we are aware, but that *through* which we become aware of, and engage with, the world.

Worldviews can be viewed under four features: characteristic *stories*, a set of *questions and answers*, fundamental *symbols*, and habitual *praxis*. It is worth considering each in turn.

Built in to many, if not most, worldviews are *stories* or narratives, and, very often, one large ('controlling') narrative or 'myth' that provides some form of overarching reference for human life (Naugle 2002, 297–303). It would seem that human beings are 'hardwired' to situate themselves in relation to beginnings and ends (and to find some kind of continuity between them), not only with respect to their own lives, but to the lives of the communities of which they are part, and, indeed, to the cosmos as a whole.[2] As David Naugle puts it, "the development of the human mind and consciousness is a function of the weightiness of stories and their plots, their characters, their denouements, and their overall explanation of things" (Naugle 2002, 297). Alasdair MacIntyre even goes as far as claiming that "there is no way to give us an understanding of any society, including our own, except through the stock of stories which constitute its initial dramatic resources. Mythology, in its original sense, is at the heart of things" (MacIntyre 1984, 216). In this context, human actions can be construed as 'enacted narratives', as ways in which humans inhabit a narrative, whether small- or large-scale: if our government takes action to reduce carbon emissions to offset global warming, it is 'acting out' a narrative of ecological crisis that includes possible disaster in the future. Thus, stories do not merely bear information but embody and reinforce (perhaps modify) a worldview: they are 'lived in', indwelt. Further, stories should not be regarded as poor substitutes for something more basic (such as concepts, theories, commands, or statements about 'bare facts'). Although they are capable of limited elucidation in nonnarrative terms, their full meaning and significance are inseparable from their form. Their full semantic power can only be experienced when they are taken seriously *as* stories. The story of a particular white race who believed they had the right to rule South Africa during the apartheid regime was just that: a *story* stretching back generations, told and retold repeatedly; therein lay a large part of its power to captivate and hold millions.

Stories that express a worldview will, among other things, provide answers to the basic *questions* that shape human existence. Five may be singled out as of critical importance:

i. Who are we? The question of identity.
ii. Where are we? The question of our physical or spatial environment.
iii. What time is it? The question of our temporal situatedness: where are we in the story now (our own story and the story of the world as a whole)?
iv. What is wrong? The question arising from a sense that the world is not as it should be.
v. What is the solution? The question about how the world's predicament is to be resolved.

A worldview's stories and the answers to its basic questions are expressed in cultural *symbols*, whether artefacts (e.g., artworks, buildings) or events (e.g., festivals, rituals). The Twin Towers of the World Trade Center symbolized North American pride and wealth for many (including the terrorists who destroyed them); a Protestant march in Belfast provides a potent visible reminder of the identity of a cultural group. Symbols like this are often revealed as such when they are challenged and provoke fear or outrage – as when a Protestant march is forbidden by the police. Further, symbols frequently function as social and/or cultural boundary markers: those who observe

the regular rituals of a university fraternity, for example, are 'insiders' – the rituals are part of what distinguishes them from nonmembers.

The fourth element of a worldview is *praxis*, a way of being-in-the-world. The answer to the fifth question in particular – what is the solution? – will normally entail action, doing something that contributes to solving the problem. The most telling actions with regard to worldview are habitual, ones undertaken unreflectively. For example, an instinctive tendency to treat financial considerations as the most important factor in taking any decision may very well betray a worldview in which identity (whether individual or social) is shaped and determined by the acquisition of wealth.

Worldviews, it ought to be added, receive their most regular and repeated airing in the form of *beliefs and aims*. Modern British society, for example, could be understood as holding a worldview of sorts, which is articulated in fairly basic beliefs about economic growth and prosperity, equal opportunity, and so forth, and in aims concerning domestic and foreign policy. Beliefs and aims may change without altering a worldview in any fundamental way: someone might decide to change his or her view of the morality of the invasion of Iraq, for instance, without a change in worldview.

Matters, of course, are hugely more complex than we have space to discuss here. Worldviews change and adapt; different worldviews can coexist and overlap; different social groups within a culture can hold different worldviews; and so on. But our sketch will nonetheless suffice as we go on to ask: what of the relation between worldview and religion?

Religion and Worldview

In most of the societies relevant to the studies in this volume, a religious or quasi-religious dimension appears to have been present (although there is clearly an enormous variation in type). We cannot enter here the massive and immensely complex debate surrounding the parameters of the word 'religion', let alone 'spirituality' (for clarification of terms and issues at stake, see, e.g., Bowker 1997; Bregman 2004; Harrison 1990; Lash 1996; Segal 2006; Shults & Sandage 2006). However, this much at least can be said. As far as the *origins* of what are widely regarded as religious belief and behaviour are concerned, although sociobiologists may have been guilty of making extreme and unfounded claims about religion (for a good discussion of the follies of reductionist approaches to religion, see Bowker 1995), in at least one respect they are almost certainly correct: religions are "early, and, for millennia, successful *protective systems* tied to the potentialities of the brain and body, and to the necessity of survival" (Bowker 1997, xvii, my italics). According to 'biogenetic structuralism', humans appear to be biogenetically prepared for certain behaviours normally called religious, a preparedness geared towards survival and replication in the world. (This in itself does not constitute the claim that religion is entirely a human construction, nor that humans are predetermined to use their preparedness for religion in any particular way; the point is merely about preparedness, nothing more.) Protective systems provide a safe 'space', so to speak, for humans to explore their own nature and society, as well as the physical world in which they live, and this leads very naturally into the realm of the specifically religious. 'Somatic' or bodily exploration (the most basic form) leads in some cases to 'inversive systems' of religion (religions that proceed through inward exploration – towards enlightenment, peace, and so forth, as in Jainism, Buddhism), and in other cases to 'extroversive systems' (religions that explore the meaning and value of what has been discovered outside the body, and of relationships with various 'others', including a god or gods, as in Judaism, Islam) (Bowker 1997, xvii). As far as the religious phenomena described in this book's chapters are concerned, it is generally the latter form that is most evident and on which we shall concentrate in what follows.

With regard to the material examined in this collection, then, we can ask: How might the religious dimensions of various worldviews, and the ways in which they relate to the practices of measurement, be highlighted through considering the constituent elements of a worldview we have just spoken about?

There is now a substantial body of literature on the place of *stories* in religious faith, the ways in which narratives frequently articulate the story of the world, or human history in relation to a god or gods, who (very often) are believed to have created and regularly interact with the world (see, for example, Day 1993; Ricoeur 1984, 1985, 1988; Ricoeur 1995; Yamane 2000). As we might expect, there are numerous allusions to the 'storied' character of religion in the chapters in this collection, and to the way in which narratives (including 'controlling' narratives) are not so much examined as indwelt by a people or culture, providing frames of reference by means of which the world is negotiated. To cite just two examples – the development of the measurement of celestial space and time in ancient Mesopotamia appears to have played a key role in speculations about the gods in relation to the order of the universe (Brown, this volume); the Maya court arithmeticians and astronomers used large numbers as a means through which rulers could be linked to the gods who created the world,

as well as to the anniversaries of creation events in the future (Aveni, this volume).

The five *questions* shaping human existence are alluded to many times in these chapters, with measurement often playing an integral part in negotiating them. So, for example, the question "Who are we?", the question of identity – often addressed and answered with reference to a god or gods – lies behind much of the data explored here. In many of the chapters it is evident that the practices of measurement are being employed to form a culture's identity, its sense of significance and standing in the world – whether, for example, in ancient Egypt through the alignment of pyramids (Spence, this volume), or at Teotihuacan through the dimensions and relative location of its edifices (Clark, this volume).

Measurement is seen to play a much more direct role in addressing the second question – "Where are we?" Indeed, mensuration appears to be one of the prime ways in which humans situate themselves effectively in relation to their material environment; humans learn the formative importance of space and place (Biehl, this volume), they learn to navigate the sea with respect to distance (Farr, this volume) and to position themselves with respect to the sun and stars (Spence, Brown, this volume), and so forth. Common here is the notion that some patterns of interaction with the material world are *intended* for humans by divine intelligence or intelligences beyond them, indeed, that the material world is in some sense ordered with such patterns in mind. So, for instance, Kate Spence argues that the celestial alignment of the pyramids is inextricably linked to religious and mortuary beliefs; Peter F. Biehl contends that the carefully measured and oriented Neolithic enclosures unearthed at Goseck, linking the practitioners to solar and lunar events, functioned as 'cult places'.

As far as the third question – "What time is it?" – is concerned, these chapters provide numerous examples of measurement being used to position groups and societies religiously in relation to days, months, years and so forth, and, indeed, to longer time scales extending beyond human death (as evinced, for example, in Chinese calendrical systems (Lewis, this volume). Measurement also plays a role in engaging the religious dimensions of the questions "What is wrong?" and "What is the solution?" This is strikingly highlighted in David Brown's essay on Mesopotamian measurement, especially when read in relation to Iain Morley's chapter. Morley proposes that the origins of at least some spiritual belief and behaviour may lie in the perceived regularity of events, specifically in recurring sequences of happenings, and in the tendency to attribute a cause-effect relation to temporally close events. He suggests that this gives rise to ritualized behaviour that is thought to influence certain outcomes, as well as the attribution of 'spiritual' or 'supernatural' character to celestial bodies. While this may be so in some cases, David Brown finds that more critical to conceptions of supernatural agencies, in certain Mesopotamian texts at any rate, is the *discrepancy* between the ideal and the real – an ideal length of, say, a month, and the real or actual length it turns out to be. This was perceived as having religious significance in that the actual date of the occurrence of the phenomenon was a matter for the gods. The 'out of sync' occurrences were thus interpreted as omens, signs of ill fortune: "Observed coherence with the ideal boded well, noncoherence ill" (Brown, this volume). In this case, the anomaly is more religiously significant than the regularity. In other words, measurement is being used, within a religious context, as a way of addressing the question "What is wrong?" As for 'solutions' to the perceived problems, these were multifarious in ancient culture, as is evident from these chapters, and again, measurement can play its part: meticulously measured rituals, carefully timed sacrifices, and so forth.

The *symbols* appropriate to a religious worldview can be artefacts or events. In these chapters, examples abound of measurement incorporated into the religiously symbolic: to take only two at random – the solar towers demarcating sacred space and social place in Inca culture (Stanish, this volume), the sacrificial rituals at Teotihuacan relating to a Mesoamerican cosmogram (Sugiyama, this volume). And as far as *praxis* is concerned – ways of life appropriate to the worldview – the stories, symbols and practices related to measurement we have already mentioned appear to be intertwined with patterns of daily living connected with the religious dimensions of worldview. In these chapters, we might point to divination as one such way of life (Brown, Lewis), or the way in which life patterns in Shang China seem to have been pervaded by an intense awareness of the presence of ancestors (Lewis).

It will be seen, therefore, that to enquire about religion or spirituality in relation to ancient measuring practices is to enquire about very much more than articulated specific beliefs (if there are such). It is to enquire about the pretheoretical grids through which the material world is recognized, engaged and cognised, to be alert to the ways in which stories, symbols and praxis interweave to express or embody an engagement with the fundamental questions that shape human existence. It is to enquire, in other words, about worldview, and we have seen that what we have called the 'elements' of a worldview can be of substantial help in throwing into relief the shape of the religious life of a people or culture.

When the questioning rebounds

For the purposes of this chapter and this symposium, even though we have acknowledged that worldviews are not properly objects of reflection but lenses or filters through which we apprehend and interact with the world, we have nevertheless had to treat them as objects, as entities that can be studied and scrutinized. This is quite proper in a chapter of this sort. And yet it would perhaps be unwise to leave matters there, at the level of a (supposedly) 'pure' description of phenomena, in such a way that we – the archaeologists (or any other enquirers) – are left essentially undisturbed and unchanged. For if we allow them to do so, foreign worldviews have the capacity to disconcert us, and, it might well be argued, very often to our benefit.

As many will testify, interrogating worldviews is a process that frequently rebounds upon the enquirer. This can happen on two fronts: with regard to a worldview in general, and with regard to a religious worldview in particular. To take the first: it is very appealing to imagine that although we are examining a worldview or worldviews, we ourselves, insofar as we adopt the methods and norms associated with contemporary natural science, are free of any worldview. The scientist, it might be presumed, operates according to methods that can at least approximate to and perhaps even attain a description of 'the way things really are', unencumbered by the biases and distortions of pretheoretical schemes, presuppositions, cultural agendas, power interests, and so forth. It is an illusion that dies hard. But illusion it is. The epistemology variously termed 'objectivism' or 'naïve realism' has quite properly come under considerable fire in the last 200 years or so (not least from natural scientists who have reflected on such matters). The quest for the Holy Grail of the neutral, detached perspective, the 'view from nowhere,' is highly questionable, for we are all immersed in space and time, societies and cultures, and thus shaped by the limits, assumptions, concerns, political arrangements, ideological drives, and so forth, of our contexts. This is not to say that there can be no knowledge and no truth claims, that there can be no access to a reality beyond ourselves on which we can confidently rely. But it is to say that we never achieve the absolute certainty of a knowledge without human (and thus potentially distorting) presuppositions, a 'god's-eye view' that yields indubitable and pure 'bare facts' (for extensive discussions of these matters see, for example, Bernstein 1991; Lopez 2001; McGrath 2001; Polanyi 1964; Sayer 2000). (Indeed, contemporary archaeological and anthropological theory, as evidenced in various forms in the chapters in this volume, makes clear endeavours to avoid falling into the trap of assuming that we can achieve such a view.) To put this in terms of the previous discussion: all enquiry after truth proceeds according to a worldview or worldviews. No enquirer is free of the stories, questions, symbols and praxis that express worldviews. Indeed, the very pretence that we can escape worldviews altogether is *itself* the product of a very particular (post-Enlightenment, Western) worldview, fuelled by a (mis)conception of the way successful natural science operates.

What does this entail for those investigating ancient measuring practices? When the Western academic analyses mensuration in, say, ancient Maya culture, he or she is required to bear in mind that this is not a case of someone *without* a worldview meeting a culture *with* a worldview, but of an encounter between two worldviews. And in this case it is manifestly clear that the worldviews are radically different: the Maya's interpretation of reality diverges dramatically from that typical of, and predominant in, Western academic life. Just because of these acute differences, in the process of interrogating this worldview, it is quite possible (even likely) that the enquirer's worldview, or aspects of it, will be challenged. The same could be said of all the cultures dealt with in these chapters. In the discussions at the symposium from which these chapters are derived, I could not help being struck by the lack of any patronizing posture to ancient cultures (as in: "but of course we know so much better now"); indeed, there was more than a hint that the ancient wisdom being studied was precisely that: *wisdom*, which, at least in some respects, might contest our own and to our benefit.

This takes us to the second front on which questions may rebound, of more direct concern: the religious dimension of worldviews. Arguably, the most striking difference between most of the worldviews opened up by this collection and that of the contemporary Western academic climate concerns religion. And it is just here that enquirers today might find themselves most uncomfortable. European and North American university culture, while by no means always hostile to religion, is nonetheless marked by a general agreement that religious matters should not be allowed to shape or determine any aspect of serious academic enquiry (especially enquiry into religion, we should note). Among other things, it is believed that this will import an unacceptable bias in a process that should pursue scrupulous 'objectivity', a process exemplified (it is thought) by the natural sciences. This is of a piece with a more widespread (and fairly recent) cultural assumption that science is objective, public, sharable, publicly verifiable and equally available to anyone, whereas religion is private, subjective and a matter of

private conviction, to do with 'inner' experience alone, and just because it is subject to considerable individual differences, cannot be allowed to influence or adjudicate in matters of public truth and interest. This assumption, of course, is part of a worldview. We may well so take it for granted that we think it hardly worth questioning – but as we have seen, that is just how a worldview functions.

Until, that is, it is challenged by close encounter with a contrasting worldview – such as might happen in the case of these chapters. Potentially, I would suggest, such an encounter can destabilize some of our most cherished assumptions about religion. Of course, there can be no question of a wholesale return to this or that ancient worldview; an idealizing nostalgia for supposedly 'primitive' culture is fashionable in many quarters today, but much of it is overdependent upon Western guilt about the imperialistic smothering of indigenous peoples, and much of it conveniently ignores the darker sides of the cultures that are held up as exemplary. (This is another trap studiously avoided in these chapters.) But I am suggesting that archaeological findings such as we have here can nevertheless throw some awkward questions about religion back at us from prehistory.

For example, why need we assume that religion *essentially* concerns the private sphere, the zone of individual experience? As far as I am able to tell, for all the ancient peoples represented in these chapters, such a conception would have been exceedingly odd. And it will seem no less odd today to any orthodox adherent of Islam or Judaism, or indeed to any Christian who takes his or her foundational texts with any seriousness.[3] The Scriptures of the Christian tradition, so often assumed to centre on 'my soul and my God', in fact narrate the story of the entire cosmos, in which the human race is given special responsibilities, and for which a future has been promised through the Creator's direct involvement with the material world in Jesus Christ – in this scenario, any divorce between private faith and the material world, belief and politics, nonphysical and physical, is nonsensical. (This is not of course to deny that there are some religious traditions that do bear resemblance to the popular conceptions of a privatized and internalized faith, and that Christians, among others, have often veered towards such notions.)

A further question is prompted: why need we assume that religion is *predominantly* about 'the spiritual' – where 'spiritual' is construed as the nonmaterial, set in stark contrast, and sometimes even strongly opposed to, the material? To survey the different conceptions of the relation of material and nonmaterial in these archaeological chapters would take us far beyond what is possible here, but it is abundantly clear from those that do engage religious matters that the beliefs and practices concerned have as much to do with the bodily negotiation of this world ('material engagement') as with extramaterial or extraworldly reality. An assumption that all religions, whether ancient or contemporary, are concerned with (or originate from) a deep desire to evade or escape materiality, and with this, that they advocate a denigration of materiality (including the human body), would be woefully wide of the mark. (In the New Testament, it is worth noting, when the apostle Paul speaks of human destiny in terms of possessing a 'spiritual body' beyond death, he does not mean a nonmaterial body, but a body animated by God's Spirit.) The widely held belief that religions originate out of the desire for 'pie in the sky' – in order to obtain rewards or avoid punishment in 'another world' – has in fact very little to support it. As we have indicated, there is much more to suggest they have arisen in the course of this-life, bodily exploration, in the business of finding a 'participatory' cosmology (Aveni, this volume), a worldview in which the material order can be inhabited as our home. Lambros Malafouris's chapter (this volume) chimes in with this strikingly. In contrast to the dichotomous scenario that has dogged modernity – the internal mind set against the utterly distinct external material world, disembodied thinking divorced from embodied activity – in his chapter on number competency, Malafouris advocates a view of 'material engagement' that would seek to understand the emergence of numerocity through the inseparable intertwining of cognition and culture, mind and materiality. This is an example of method properly following subject matter: if we refuse to impose dualistic habits of mind in the study of early measuring culture, we are far more likely to elicit the dynamics of practices that by their very nature arose through somatic activity. We suggest that this can be extended to the study of the religious dimensions of measuring practices: if we resist the tendency to presume the fundamental thrust of all religion is *away* from materiality, we will be much less likely to misinterpret such dimensions.[4]

Considerations such as these press us in turn to raise deeper questions about the methodological assumptions made in enquiries about religious beliefs and practices. We might be pressed, for example, to question the cogency of 'methodological naturalism' – the view that if any study of the world is to qualify as 'scientific', it cannot make reference to God's creative activity (or any sort of divine activity). A number of years ago, the philosopher Alvin Plantinga, now at the University of Notre Dame, mounted a famous and powerful case against the supposition that science is by its very nature religiously

neutral, arguing that the standard arguments for methodological naturalism suffer from grave shortcomings, not least the highly dubious bifurcation of 'public' science and 'private' religion.[5] We might well be pressed even further still: to question the validity of a worldview that presupposes a priori that all religious experience and phenomena are *entirely* the product of the human evolutionary process, a worldview, in other words, that has jumped from methodological naturalism to 'ontological' or 'metaphysical' naturalism (excluding even the possibility of, say, the existence of a god or divine activity) and that then (very strangely) fosters the assumption that this will make no difference to the way religion is studied.[6] The issues multiply and cannot be pursued at length here. But my suggestion is that if the trajectories these chapters generate are given appropriate space, such questions will be hard to avoid. To bring matters to a head: when the question "What are the roots of spirituality?" is raised, it might be worth pondering what an odd question it is. If they were philosophically inclined, the majority of humans in history would be asking something like "What are the roots of the worldview that makes you ask that question?"

NOTES

1. The concept of worldview has been the object of much discussion recently and has a distinguished intellectual history, especially in Germany (as *Weltanschauung*), where it has played a central role in theoretical reflection upon culture. For a very fine survey of the concept in modern thinking and writing since Immanuel Kant's first use of *Weltanschauung* in 1790, see Sire 2004, esp. chs. 3–8. In this article I follow (with some adjustments) the account of worldview developed by N. T. Wright in Wright 1992, 122–126 and 1996, 100–101, 137–144. Wright himself is heavily indebted to Middleton & Walsh 1995.

2. The philosopher Alasdair MacIntyre has perhaps done more than any other contemporary philosopher to recover a sense of the narrative structuring of human existence, shared communally. MacIntyre 1984, 204–225. Recent decades have seen a growing interest in narrative across a wide range of disciplines, including history, law, philosophy, anthropology, theology, sociology, psychology, literary studies and politics. Interdisciplinary collections include Hinchman & Hinchman 1997; Mitchell 1981. For an introduction to the role of narrative in history, literature, psychology and social science research, see Polkinghorne 1988.

3. As I write this, the United Kingdom is in the midst of a storm of controversy about whether or not the adherents of religious groups should be allowed to wear overt symbols of their faith (veils, crosses, etc.). If it were not deeply ingrained in the British consciousness that religion is fundamentally a 'private' matter, there would not be nearly

so much puzzlement as to why a Muslim woman should want to wear a veil in public; the relegation of religion to what consenting adults do in private is entirely foreign to an Islamic worldview, and, for that matter, to Judaism or Christianity, properly conceived.

4. Significantly, the kind of engagement between humans and the material world sketched in Malafouris's chapter (this volume) is one that has received considerable attention in much contemporary Christian theology, eager as it is to resist dualist habits of thought and recover a sense of human embodiedness and embeddedness in the material order. See, e.g., the volume edited by the psychologist Malcolm Jeeves (Jeeves 2002); also Gunton 1998 (ch. 9).

5. See his article, 'Methodological Naturalism', at <http://www.arn.org/docs/odesign/od181/methnat181.htm>and http://www.arn.org/docs/odesign/od182/methnat182.htm.

6. Metaphysical naturalists will, of course, treat all claims to religious experience, all purported claims about a god or gods, as entirely the product of human invention. At the time of writing, Richard Dawkins, probably the most vociferous metaphysical naturalist currently writing, is enjoying best-seller status, through his fiercely antireligious book *The God Delusion* (Dawkins 2006). His case is purportedly made on the basis of scientific evidence, yet, as many have pointed out, none of the data he cites leads inexorably to the conclusions he draws. His surprising and somewhat embarrassing lack of knowledge of the religion(s) he speaks about only weakens his case further (see McGrath 2005).

REFERENCES

Bernstein, R. J., 1991. *Beyond Objectivism and Relativism: Science, Hermeneutics, and Praxis.* Philadelphia: University of Pennsylvania Press.

Bowker, J., 1995. *Is God a Virus? Genes, Culture and Religion.* London: SPCK.

Bowker, J., 1997. Religion, in *The Oxford Dictionary of World Religions*, ed. J. Bowker. Oxford: Oxford University Press, xv–xxiv.

Bregman, L., 2004. Defining spirituality: Multiple uses and murky meanings of an incredibly popular term. *Journal of Pastoral Care and Counseling* **58**, 157–68.

Dawkins, R., 2006. *The God Delusion.* New York: Bantam.

Day, J. M., 1993. Speaking of belief: Language, performance, and narrative in the psychology of religion. *International Journal for the Psychology of Religion* **3**, 213–29.

Gunton, C. E., 1998. *The Triune Creator: A Historical and Systematic Study.* Edinburgh: Edinburgh University Press.

Harrison, P., 1990. *'Religion' and the Religions in the English Enlightenment.* Cambridge: Cambridge University Press.

Hinchman, L. P. & S. K. Hinchman (eds.), 1997. *Memory, Identity, Community: The Idea of Narrative in the Human Sciences.* Albany: SUNY Press.

Jeeves, M. (ed.), 2002. *From Cells to Souls and Beyond.* Grand Rapids, MI: Eerdmans.

Lash, N., 1996. *The Beginning and the End of 'Religion'.* Cambridge: Cambridge University Press.

Lopez, J., 2001. *After Postmodernism: An Introduction to Critical Realism.* London: Athlone Press.

MacIntyre, A. C., 1984. *After Virtue: A Study in Moral Theory.* Notre Dame, IN: University of Notre Dame Press.

McGrath, A. E., 2001. *A Scientific Theology. Vol. 2: Reality.* Edinburgh: T & T Clark.

McGrath, A. E., 2005. *Dawkins' God: Genes, Memes, and the Meaning of Life.* Oxford: Blackwell.

Middleton, J. R. & B. J. Walsh, 1995. *Truth Is Stranger Than It Used to Be: Biblical Faith in a Postmodern Age.* Downers Grove, IL: InterVarsity Press.

Mitchell, W. J. T., 1981. *On Narrative.* Chicago: University of Chicago Press.

Naugle, D. K., 2002. *Worldview: The History of a Concept.* Grand Rapids, MI: Eerdmans.

Polanyi, M., 1964. *Personal Knowledge: Towards a Post-critical Philosophy.* New York: Harper & Row.

Polkinghorne, D., 1988. *Narrative Knowing and the Human Sciences.* Albany: State University of New York Press.

Ricoeur, P., 1984, 1985, 1988. *Time and Narrative.* Chicago: University of Chicago Press, 3 vols.

Ricoeur, P., 1995. *Figuring the Sacred: Religion, Narrative, and Imagination.* Minneapolis: Fortress Press.

Sayer, R. A., 2000. *Realism and Social Science.* Thousand Oaks, CA: Sage.

Segal, R. A. (ed.), 2006. *The Blackwell Companion to the Study of Religion.* Oxford: Blackwell.

Shults, F. L. & S. J. Sandage, 2006. *Transforming Spirituality: Integrating Theology and Psychology.* Grand Rapids, MI: Baker.

Sire, J. W., 2004. *Naming the Elephant: Worldview as a Concept.* Downers Grove, IL: InterVarsity Press.

Wright, N. T., 1992. *The New Testament and the People of God.* London: SPCK.

Wright, N. T., 1996. *Jesus and the Victory of God.* London: SPCK.

Yamane, D., 2000. Narrative and religious experience. *Sociology of Religion* **61**, 171–89.

Index

Abrus precatorius, 116
accounting, 5, 27, 31, 32, 33, 57, 58, 59, 60, 62, 65, 66, 73, 74–75, 184, 187
  census, 58, 66
  hierarchy, 65, 66
  khipu, 60, 62, 65, 66, 226
Acosta, J. de, 55
Adam, B., 201
addition, 43, 55, 205
administration
  city-state, 27, 32
  Inca, 58, 59, 65–66
  Near East, 29
  palatial, 82
Adriatic Sea, 20, 21–22, 24
Aegean
  balance weights, 88–98
  jars, 76
  weights, 72, 73
Afghanistan, 106
afterlife, 172, 174, 175, 177
agate, 111, 116
Aghia Irini (Kea), 93
Aghia Photia (Crete), 72
agriculture, 3, 5, 27, 132, 196, 201, 205
  calendar, 200
  Goseck, 238
  Indus, 107
Akkadian, 90
  measure, 186
  tablet, 32
  textiles, 78
Akkermans, M.M.G., 100
Akrotiri (Thera), 74, 77–79
Alberti, M.E., 72, 73, 75, 81, 82, 98
Algaze, G., 31
Allahdino, 117
Allan, S., 195, 196
Allen, J., 174, 175
almanacs, 206, 213
  Maya, 205
  Shang, 195
Almaráz, R., 133
alpacas, 56, 60
Alram-Stern, E., 100
Al-Rawi, F.N.H., 188
alum, 75

Amazonian tribes, 37
amazonite, 111
Ammerman, A.J., 19
Anatolia
  balance weights, 88–98
  mina, 74
Anaximander, 191
anchor stone, 80
Andean
  duality, 226
  highlands, 216, 217
  languages, 56
  peoples, 226
  rites, 213
  statecraft, 217
Andersen, N.H., 229, 230
Anderson, A.J.O., 159
Andres, M., 41
angular gyrus, 40
animals
  behaviour, 1
  domesticated, 28
  Goseck, 235, 236
  migration, 12
  offering, 31
  recording, 60, 74
  totemic, 117
Anonymous Chronicler, 218
Anonymous Conqueror, 159
Anoubis, god, 80
Antell, S.E., 35
Antheraea sp., 112
anthropomorphisation, 16, 17, 115, 171
Apollonius, 191
Applegate, A., 176
approximation, 6, 35, 38
Aravantinos, V., 73, 74, 82, 98
archaeo-astronomy, 235
Archi, A., 90
Archimedes, 191
architecture, 1, 3, 7
  Aztec, 150–67
  Egyptian, 170
  Harappan, 117
  Indus, 106, 107, 108, 109, 110, 113–14, 125–28

Maya, orientation of, 210–13
  Mehrgarh, 107
  Mesoamerican, 133, 209
  Minoan, 93
  Teotihuacan, 134
Arica (Chile), 60
Aristarchus of Samos, 191
arithmetic, 35
  symbolic, 184, 190
  thinking, 37
Arnaud, D., 89
Aruz, J., 95, 101
Ascalone, E., 94, 95
Ascher, M., 54, 55, 66
Ascher, R., 55, 66
Ash Wednesday, 213
Asia Minor, 75, 78
Assur, 32, 78, 79
Assyria(n), 190
  lexicon, 77
  texts, 82
  trade, 78
Assyriology, 183, 184, 185
astral science, 186, 192
  Greek, 191
astrology, 181, 186, 192, 206
  Mesoamerica, 132
astronomy, 1, 183, 186, 188, 190, 192, 208, 212
  alignments, 170
  and enclosures, 235–38
  Maya, 213
  Mesoamerican, 156
Atacama (Chile), 217
Australia, 23
Austria, 232, 236
autism, 37
Aveni, A., 146, 153, 156, 161, 164, 182, 205, 206, 208, 210, 212, 248, 252, 255
Aymara, 64
  language group, 217
Aztecs, 132, 133, 139
  calendars, 132
  chronicles, 210
  measurement, 131, 150–51
  palaces, 151–57

Babylon, 32, 81, 188, 189
Babylonia, 79, 188, 190, 191, 192
    astronomers, 191
Bachhuber, C., 76
Bactro-Margiana, 107
Badari, 171
Badawy, A., 171, 174
Baines, J., 172, 173
baktuns, 47, 48, 132
balance weights. *See* weights, balance
balances, 71, 72–73, 76, 79, 81, 116
Balkans, 21
ballcourts, 160
Baluchistan, 106, 107, 112
Bamboo Annals, 200
Banat (Serbia), 98
Bandelier, A., 219
Barber, E.W., 15
Barber, P.T., 15
barley, 27, 30, 74, 77, 79, 107, 116
Barrera Rivera, J.Á., 159
barter, 9, 77
    Indus, 111
Bass, B., 21
Bass, G.F., 73, 81
Batek, 16
Batres, L., 130, 138
Bauer, B., 218, 219, 220, 222, 223, 226,
    227
Bauval, R., 174
Bavaria, 230
beads, 95, 107
    agate, 116
    Indus, 110, 111–12
Beale, T.W., 32
Becker, H., 235
Bednarik, R., 7
beer, 74, 79
beliefs, 1, 3, 4, 7, 14, 17, 25, 114, 174, 251,
    252, 253, 255
Belmonte, J.A., 171, 173, 175
Beltran de Santa Rosa, 51
Bennett, E.L., 73
Bernstein, R.J., 253
Berossos, 191
Bertemes, F., 229, 234, 235, 236
Betanzos, J. de, 217, 218
Biehl, P.F., 229, 232, 234, 235, 236, 247,
    252
Biro, D., 35
Black Sea, 229
Blue, L., 20
board games, 210
boats
    construction, 19, 20
    log, 20, 24
    Neolithic, 21
body parts and measurement, 56, 71, 118,
    133, 150
bone
    balance beams, 100
    seals, 114
    tools, Indus, 111
bones
    animal, 231, 235, 236, 238
    and divination, 196
    inscribed, 196, 198

notched, 38
    as symbols, 153
Books of Chilam Balam, 49
Bora wind, 25
Borah, W., 151
Bordjoš (Serbia), 98
Botocudo, language, 43
Boulotis, C., 78, 79, 80
Bourdieu, P., 22, 201
Bourriau, J., 171
Bowker, J., 251, 252
bowls, 32
Boyer, P., 16, 17
Bracciano, Lake, 20
Brack-Bernsen, L., 188, 189
Bradley, R., 238
brain, 6, 38, 40, 41, 252
    calculation, 36
    and language, 41
    lesions, 37
    systems, 36, 37
Brandenburg (Germany), 230
Brannon, E.M., 35
bread, 28, 32, 75
Bregman, L., 251
Bremner, R.W., 188
Brezine, C.J., 54, 62, 65
Bricker, H., 208, 210
Bricker, V., 208, 210
bricks
    fired, 109, 118–19
    Indus, 108, 110, 113–14, 117–18
    Mehrgarh, 107
    Mohenjo-Daro, 126
Brinton, D., 150, 151
Britton, J.P., 188, 190
Brogan, T.M., 72, 80
bronze, 99, 200
    balance pans, 116
    door, 77
    inscriptions, 200
    pans, 79, 80
    rod, 117
    working, 75
Bronze Age, 19, 196
    Aegean, 81
    tokens, 28
    weighing, 88–101
Broodbank, C., 19, 24
Brown, C.H., 13
Brown, D.R., 185, 186, 187, 188, 189, 190,
    191, 192, 248, 252
Buddhism, 252
bureaucracy, Mesopotamia, 29
Burgos, 151
burials, 81, 232
    Egyptian, 170–72, 247
    extended, 171
    Goseck, 231, 232
Burkitt, R., 51, 52
Butterworth, B., 27, 35, 37, 39, 41
Byers, D., 203

Cabrera, C., 131, 133, 134, 135
Cabrera, R., 130, 140
Cajamarca, 61
Calabria, M., 36

calculation, 23, 24, 36, 37, 38, 83, 90, 92,
    98, 158, 182, 184, 186, 190, 191, 192,
    195, 198, 213
calendars, 6, 19, 47, 144, 146
    Chinese, 195–202
    Christian, 213
    Egyptian, 175
    Far Eastern, 181
    Inca, 218
    Mayan, 182, 204, 210, 213
    Mesoamerican, 47, 132, 135, 153, 154,
        156
    solar, 132
    stones, 128
calendrical numbers, 210
calendricists, 199, 201
Calnek, E., 212
camelid fibers, 55
canals, 220
Canas Indians, 62
Cancik-Kirschbaum, E., 184, 185
canoes, 24
caravans, 75, 78, 83
cardinal directions, 13, 108, 114, 173, 174,
    235
    alignment to, 173–75
cardinality. *See* numerocity
Cari, M., 62
carnelian, 95, 111
Caroline Islands, 24
Carrera Stampa, M., 151
carts
    bullock, 108
    terracotta, 107, 108
Caskey, M.E., 73
Caso, A., 132, 133
Castagnino Berlinghieri, E.F., 19
caste structure, 225
Castillian system, 150
Castillo, F.V.M., 133, 145, 150, 151
Castillos, J.J., 171
Catholic Church, 49
cattle, 95, 107, 183
    bones, inscription on, 195, 197
    Goseck, 231
cause-and-effect relationships, 15, 17
Cauvin, J., 27
Cehtzuc (Yucatan), 209
celestial cycles, 15, 16, 22–23. *See also* lunar
    cycles; solar cycles; *and under names of
    individual planets*
cemeteries, 94
    Predynastic, 171
censuses, 58, 62
    khipu, 56
Center for Maritime Archaeology (Roskilde),
    20
centuries, 132
ceques, 219
ceremonies
    foundation, 176–77
    Goseck, 235
Cerro Gordo, 146
Cerrón-Palomino, R., 64
Chadwick, J., 74, 75
chaîne opératoire, 232
Chambon, G., 184

Chancay, 61
Chang, K., 197
Chanhu-daro, 116, 117
chariots, 74, 75
Chavero, A., 151
Chen, M., 197, 198, 200
Cherry, J., 93
chert, 111
    weights, 107, 109, 110, 116
Chiapa de Corzo, 48
Chile, 60, 216, 217
Chimu, 216
China, 110, 181, 186, 192
    calendars, 195–202
Chincana, 220
Chogha Mish, 31
Christian, 254
    calendar, 213
    Period, 171
chronology
    absolute, 175
    Indus, 107–10
Chucuito, 62
Chumayel, 203
Chupachu, 59
Chuyu, 221, 222
Cierny, J., 235
Cieza de León, P., 58, 64, 220
Cilicia, 90
citadel
    Mohenjo-Daro, 125
Citadel
    Teotihuacan, 141–42, 143, 144, 146
cities, 2, 27
    Indus, 106, 109, 117, 119–20, 125–28
    layout, 135–38
Clagett, M., 175, 176
Clark, A., 40
Clark, J., 133, 145, 150, 154, 167, 252
Clavijero, F.J., 151, 157
clay
    balls, 29, 30
    tokens, 39
Cline, H.F., 153
clock, 201. See also waterclocks
Closs, M.P., 132
clothing, 28, 77, 79. See also textiles
Coba, 51
Cobo, B., 58, 61, 217, 218, 220, 226
Codex Chimalpopoca, 133
Codex Fejérváry Mayer, 132
codices, 203, 206, 208, 211, 213
    Maya, 205–08
Coe, M.D., 132, 145
coffins
    design, 171
    Egyptian, 171
    lids, 175, 176
Coggins, C., 145
cognition
    history of, 183
    numerical, 6, 35, 44–46
    origins of, 1–2
    spatial, 6
    and tokens, 32–33
Cohen, L., 36
coinage, 77

Collasuyu, 217
commodities, 8–10
    accounting of, 74–75
condiments, 75
Conkey, M., 232
Conklin, W.J., 55, 66
constellations, 16, 114, 127, 132, 146, 175,
    189, 236
contextual attribute analysis, 232–34
control, concept of, 247
Cook, S.F., 151
Cooper, J.S., 27
Cooper, L., 100
Copacabana, 219
copper, 77, 80, 82, 83
    balance pans, 116
    blade, 112
cosmogony, 250
cosmograms, Teotihuacan, 145–47
cosmology, 1, 3, 250
    archaeology of, 4
    Egyptian, 170, 172
    Indus, 106, 107
    Maya, 203–14
count(s)
    long, 48, 49, 143, 146
    of days. See tzolkin
counters, 55. See also tokens
counting, 5, 27, 39
    finger, 45
    Iraq, 183
    Mesopotamia, 31
    routine, 37
    schemes, Maya, 205
    and tokens, 28–29
    vigesimal, 45, 47, 50, 51, 52, 153, 156,
        182, 203
    visual, 38
Courtois, J.C., 74, 82
Cowgill, G.L., 130
cowry shells, 24
creation myths, 217, 219
Crete, 72, 73, 75, 76, 77, 78, 79, 80, 98
    hieroglyphs, 73
    weights, 81
Croatia, 24
Cucarzi, M., 126
cult places, 234–35
cuneiform, 27, 31, 183, 185, 186, 188, 190,
    191, 192
currency, 7, 77
currents, 21, 22, 24
Cusi, M., 62
Cuzco, 61, 64, 217, 218, 220, 222
Cyclades, 73, 98
cycles, 12, 13–17. See also celestial cycles;
        lunar cycles; solar cycles; and under
        names of individual planets
    concept of, 7
Cyprus, 76
    jars, 76
    merchants, 81
Czichon, R.M., 90

D'Altroy, T., 57
D'Errico, Francesco, 7
Dahlgren, B., 159, 166

dairy products, 31, 32
Dales, G., 119, 125, 126
Dalmatian islands, 21, 24
Daly, P., 13
Damerow, P., 184
Darius, king, 32
Darvill, T., 229, 230
Darwin, C., 1
Davaras, C., 72
Davis, H., 35
Day, J.M., 252
Day, P.M., 76
days, 135, 138, 143, 144, 153, 154, 161,
        175, 182, 187, 190, 198, 208
    of ancestors, 197
    counting, 47, 195, 196, 213
    duration, 14
    Maya, 205
    signs, 132
De Fidio, P., 74
dead reckoning, 23
Dearborn, D.S.P., 218, 220, 222, 223, 226,
        227
death, 201
Debono, F., 171, 172, 174
decimal system
    administration, 58–60
    khipu, 55
deer hunting, 206
Dehaene, S., 36, 38, 40, 44
Deir el-Medina (Egypt), 72
Demakopoulou, K., 98
developmental dyscalculia, 36
Dholavira, 109, 110
Di Xin, king, 199, 200
Di Yi, king, 199, 200
Diakonoff, I.M., 28
Diaries, 188, 189
Dibble, C.E., 159
dictionaries
    Assyrian, 77
    colonial, 56
Diéz de San Miguel, G., 62
Dilmun, 83
Dimopoulou, N., 80
displacement, 21
distance, 56
    calculating, 11
    concept of, 5, 7
    numbers, 47
    in seafaring, 22
    and time, 181
Divari-Valakou, N., 98
divination, 186, 188, 190, 192, 195, 196,
        197, 199, 200, 201, 213, 253
division, 8, 55, 205
Djoser, 172
Dong, Z., 197, 198, 199, 200
Dorner, J., 172, 173
Doumas, C., 77, 79, 80
Dow, J.W., 146
Dowd, A., 210
Draco, constellation, 127
Draconis, 173, 174, 176
drains, 118
Dresden Codex, 204, 206, 208, 209, 213
Drewitt, R.B., 133

Drucker, R.D., 133, 146
dualism, 56

Earle, T., 57
Early Formative period, 133
earth, extent of, 191
Easter, 213
Ebla, 90, 95
eclipses, 144, 189, 197, 214
    cycles, 132, 139, 141
    prediction, 205
ecology, 11, 16
economy, 31–32
    complex, 1
    subsistence, 150
Edfu, 177
Edmonson, M., 204
Edwards, I.E.S., 173, 174
Eger, E., 36
eggs, 79
Egypt, 73, 76, 95, 110, 186
    burials, orientation of, 170–72
    cubit, 71, 126
    iconography, 80
    Old Kingdom tomb, 71
    records of weights, 73
    trade, 77
Elam, 31
    early writing, 30
elephants
    on seal, 115
    tusks, 75
elites
    Inca, 226
Emery, W.B., 171
empire building, 217
enclosures, Neolithic, 229–38
Engelbach, R., 176
Englund, R.K., 31, 32, 184, 187
Enkomi (Cyprus), 76
envelopes, token, 29–30, 39
Epic of Gilgamesh, 185
equinoxes, 14, 200, 210, 212, 213
Eratosthenes, 191
Etak, 23, 24
eternity, 249
    concept of, 248
ethnography, and seafaring, 23–24
Euclid, 184
Europe, 6, 182
    Neolithic, 229–38
    weighing systems, 88
Evans, A.J., 73, 74
Evans-Pritchard, E.E., 4
Evening Inanna, festival, 32
exchange, 9, 75. *See also* barter; trade
    down the line, 20

farming, 2, 238. *See also* agriculture
Farr, R.H., 19, 20, 22, 248, 252
Fassbinder, J.W.E., 235
Fatoohi, L.J., 190
Fauconnier, G., 40
Faulkner, R.O., 71, 80, 174, 175, 177
feasting, 235, 238
Feathered Serpent Pyramid, 130, 132, 133,
    135, 141–42, 144, 146

Feigenson, L., 38
Feng, S., 200
Ferioli, P., 31
Fertile Crescent, tokens, 27
fertility, 16
Fiandra, E., 29, 31
Fieller, N.R.J., 93, 100
figs, 74, 79
figurines, 126
    Indus, 109, 115
Finney, B.R., 23
fire pits, 235
fish, 31, 75, 79, 196
Flam, L., 108
floods, 126, 191
    Indus, 125
    Nile, 175
Flores island, 23
flour, 74, 79
Foot of Nippur, 126
foraging, 8, 13, 16, 107
Forenbaher, S., 21
fortification, 125, 234
Fowler, C.S., 13, 16–17
fractions, 10, 15, 55, 73, 98, 134, 144, 151,
    153, 154, 186, 205
Franco Brizuela, M.L., 157
Frangipane, M., 31
Frankfort, H., 4
Freidel, D., 132
frescoes. *See* wall paintings
Friebritz (Austria), 232, 235
Fugazzola Delpino, M.A., 20
funerary contexts
    Aegean, 81
funerary prayers, 172

Galileo, 206, 214
Gallistel, C.R., 37
Galván Rivera, M., 151
Gamble, C., 9
Gamio, M., 130
Ganweriwala, 109
Garavan, H., 40
Garcilaso de la Vega, E., 55, 56, 58, 59, 60
Gáva-Belegiš, 98
Gelinodya, cape, 81
Gell, A., 22
Gelman, R., 35, 37, 39
gemstones, 75
Gentile, L., 55
geometric symbols, 114
geometry, 191
George, A.R., 188
Germanic languages, 11
Germany, 98, 182
Gervautz, M., 235
Gibson, A., 235
Gibson, W., 16
gift(s), 77
    exchange, 82
    reciprocal giving, 9
    royal, 82, 83
Gilbert, A., 174
Gilgamesh, 185
Girsu, 31
    tablets, 31

Gladwin, T., 24
Glassner, J.-J., 184
Gleitman, H., 15
goats, 107
    hair, 75
goddesses, 174, 176, 177, 206
Godin Tepe, 30
gods, 132, 133, 157, 160, 188, 203, 209,
    210, 213, 214, 250, 252, 253
    and the universe, 190
gold, 74, 76, 95
    mines, 80
Goldman, H., 90, 92
Gómara, F.L. de, 166
Gondelsheim, 98
González Holguín, D. de, 56
Goody, J., 185
Gordon, P., 37
Goseck, 182, 229, 230–32
Graf, W., 126
graffiti, 80
grain, 79, 95
    Goseck, 236
    offering, 31
granary, 125
granite, 116
grave goods, 81
graves, 98
Greece, 71, 76, 186
    scholars, 186, 191
Greenberg, J.H., 43, 44, 45, 46
Gregorian reform, 208
Großgartach, 230
Grube, N., 206
Guaman Poma de Ayala, F., 64, 217
Guana, language, 43
Gui, 200
Guillemin-Tarayre, E., 151
Gujarat, 106
Gulf Sokean, 48
Guo, M., 195, 196
Guo, P., 200
Guthrie, S., 16

Haack, S., 173
Habuba Kabira, 29, 31
haematite, 80, 89, 90, 92, 94, 100
Hallstatt, 98
Hamilton, E.J., 151
hammerstones, 115
Hannig, R., 176
Harappa
    measurement systems, 106–20
    weights, 94, 100
harbours, 73, 82, 126
Harding, A.F., 101
Harrison, P., 251
Hartung, H., 210, 212
Harvey, H.R., 150, 151, 152
Hatag, 23, 24
Hatti, 89
Heidegger, E., 201
Helmand, 107
Helms, M.W., 19
Hemmy, A.S., 115, 116, 126
Herodotus, 75, 76
Hesnard, A., 19

Hierakonpolis, 176
hierarchies, nested, 217
hieroglyphs
    Crete, 73
    Egyptian, 176
    Mayan, 48, 50
    Venus, 209
Hinde, R., 16
Hindu iconography, 114
Hipparchus, 191, 192
Hippolytus, 191
Höckmann, O., 235
Hodder, I., 232
Homer, 82
Homo erectus, 23
honey, 28
Horowitz, W., 191
Horton, R., 4
houses
    Aztec, 150, 151
    Mohenjo-Daro, 127
Høyrup, J., 33, 184
huacas, 218, 219
Huanca, 62
Hubbard, E.M., 36, 40
Huber, P.J., 190
Huitzilopochtli, god, 157, 160
Hunger, H., 188
hunter-gatherers, 5, 12, 13
    subsistence, 7
hunting, 8, 12
    deer, 206
Hurford, J.R., 43
Hutchins, E., 38
Huy, viceroy, 80
Hyslop, J., 219

iconography
    Egyptian, 80, 174
    figurative, 2
    Hindu, 114
    Near East, 76
idealization, 187–88
ideology
    Indus, 106, 110, 114
Ifrah, G., 37, 39
Inca, 5, 216–27
    calendar, 205
    record keeping, 54–66
    time measurement, 182
    year, 205
Inca Yupanque, emperor, 217
India, 94, 95, 100, 106, 186, 191, 192
Indus
    architectural measurement, 125–28
    culture, 94, 106
    valley, 95
infinite, concept of, 248, 249
inscriptions
    Linear A, 72, 80
    Maya, 203, 213
    Shang, 181, 195, 197, 199
    Zhou, 200
insularity, 19
Intipuncu, 226
intraparietal sulcus, 36, 40
Ippesheim, 232, 236

Iran, 27, 29, 186, 192
    astronomy, 196
    bowls, 32
    tablets, 30
Iraq, 27, 29, 183
    tablets, 30
Iriki, A., 40
Iron Age, 88
Irwin, G., 23
Isaacs, E.B., 36
Islam, 252, 254
Islamic Period, 171
Island of the Moon, 219
Island of the Sun, 217, 218, 219–22, 226
Isler, M., 173
Israel, 27
Italy, 21, 22
    obsidian, 20
ivory, 74, 75
Ixtlilxóchitl, F. de A., 150, 153, 159

Jacalteca Maya, 203
Jacob's staff, 189
jades, 200
Jainism, 252
James, T.G.H., 76, 77
Jansen, M., 107, 118, 126, 127
Japan, 23
Jarrige, J.-F., 107
jasper, 111
Jebel Aruda, 31, 32
Jerusalem, 170
jewellery, 31, 76, 81, 95, 101
    Indus, 109
Joannés, F., 81
Johnstone, P., 19
Jones, A., 189, 192
Jordan, 27, 29
Juchtas (Crete), 77
Judaism, 252, 254
Julien, C., 58, 59, 219
Jupiter, 154, 156, 157
Justeson, J., 45, 49, 132, 248
Justus, C., 31, 32, 33
Justus, G.F., 183

Ka-irer, 71
Kaiser, T., 21
Kakridis, I.T., 72
Kalibangan, 118
Kaminaljuyu, stela, 47
Karkemish, 89
Karlsruhe, 98
Karnava, A., 73
Kasapata, 220
Kastowski, K., 235
Kastri (Syros), 93
Katsa-Tomara, L., 79
katuns, 47, 49, 132
Kaufman, T.S., 45, 49
Kea, 93
Keating, D.P., 35
Keightley, D., 201
Kelley, J.C., 210
Kelly, A.M.C., 40
Kemp, B.J., 72, 76, 174
Kenamun, tomb of, 76

Kendall, D.G., 92
Kendall Formula, 92, 100
Kenoyer, J.M., 107, 108, 109, 110, 111, 112,
    114, 115, 119, 120, 125
Kepler, J., 208
Kessler, D., 172
Khasekhemwy, 176
Khentkawes, 171
khipus, 5, 47, 54–55, 57–66, 206, 226
Khufu, 171, 173, 174
Kilian-Dirlmeier, I., 94
Killen, J., 80
kilns, 113
Kingsborough, Lord, 151
Kirch, P.V., 23
Kisch, B., 71
Kiviharju, J., 66
klasmatograms, 73, 79
Knossos (Crete), 75, 76, 80
Kopcke, G., 72
Kot Diji, 108, 109, 111, 114, 115
Krauss, R., 174, 175
Kubler, G., 132
Kullasuyu, 62
Kültepe, 79
Kusura, 88
Kutch, 106

La Marmotta, 20
La Mojarra, stela, 47
La Raya de los Incas, 220, 221
La Venta, 154
Laborel, J., 19
labour
    service, 58
    tax, 6
LaFarge II, O., 203
Lakoff, G., 45
Lakshmi, goddess, 114
Lal, B.B., 118
Lambeck, K., 19
Landauer, T.K., 36
Lang, M., 92
language, 1, 6, 38, 43
    Andean, 56
    Maya, 203
    Mesoamerican, 45, 50
    and number, 37–38
    universals, 44–46
lapis lazuli, 95, 111
Lash, N., 251
Lassen, H., 74
lateral intraparietal, 40
Lauer, J.P., 71
Law, R.W., 112
Leach, E.R., 205
lead weights, 73, 77, 79, 80, 81, 98
league, 12, 56
Lechtman, H., 118
Lee, K.M., 36
Lee, V.R., 55, 56, 57
Lefkas, 94
Leitz, C., 176
Lemnos, 89
length, 10, 11
Lengyel, 230
Lent, 213

León-Portilla, M., 132
Lerna, 90
Levant, 73
    standard, 82
Levine, T.Y., 58
Levy, L.M., 36
Lévy-Bruhl, L., 4, 16
Lewis, M., 248, 252
Lima, 65
limestone weights, 108, 115
Lindsten, E., 89
Linear A, 77, 78, 79, 80
Linear B, 73, 74, 75, 76, 77, 78, 79, 80,
    82, 83
Lipari, 19, 20, 21
Lipton, J.S., 35
Liverani, M., 31
llamas, 56, 60
Lloyd, G.E.R., 186
Locke, L.L., 54, 55
Löcker, K., 235
locusts, 79
looms, 111
    weights, 77, 79, 100
López, A., 133, 141, 146
Lopez, J., 253
López, L., 130, 140, 146
López Luján, L., 158
Lothal, 116, 117
Lounsbury, F., 49, 204, 208, 214
Lowe Museum of Art (Miami), 61
Loza, C.B., 62
lunar
    count, 154, 156
    cycles, 12, 13, 15, 16, 22, 132, 181, 188,
        195, 197, 198, 199
    months, 205
Lurin Valley, 65

Maat, goddess, 71
maceheads, 92
MacIntyre, A., 250
Mackay, E.J.H., 116, 117, 125, 126
Madrid Codex, 206
Magdolen, D., 173
Mahr, B., 185
Mainkar, V.B., 116, 117
maize, 56, 60
Malafouris, L., 38, 39, 40, 248, 249, 255
Malaysia, 16
Málek, J., 172, 173
Malmstrom, V.H., 146
Malta, 20
Malville, J.M., 176
Mama Ojlia, 220, 222, 227
maps, 13, 24
    Aztec, 152, 153
    colonial, 166
    mental, 22
    Mesoamerican, 132
    Oztoticpac, 154, 155
    Teotihuacan, 133
marble, 100
    weight, 80
Marciniak, A., 235
Mari, 81, 95
    archives, 82

army, 81
    tablet, 83
Marinatos, E.S., 79
marine navigation. *See* navigation
Marquina, I., 165, 166
Mars, 154, 205, 208, 214
Marshack, A., 7
Marshall, J.H., 115, 116, 117
Marshall, S.J., 125, 126
Marshall Islands, 24
Martínez del Sobral, M., 154
masks, 209
material engagement, 1, 39, 249, 255
materiality, 249, 255
mathematics, 11, 23, 38, 47, 66, 92, 184
Matías Alonso, M., 151
Matos Moctezuma, E., 130, 139, 157, 158
Matsuzawa, T., 35
Maula, E., 128
Maya, 47, 48, 132, 143
    almanacs, 182
    calendars, 3, 132
    cosmology, 203–14
    Lowland, 45
McGrail, S., 20
McGrath, A.E., 253
Meadow, R.H., 107, 108, 110, 115
measurement
    absolute, 10, 72
    definition, 54
    and early symbolic relationships, 2–4
    equipment, 72–74
    Harappa, 116
    linear, 117–18, 126
    linear, Aztec, 150–51
    proportional relative, 11, 15
    standard, 32
    types, 7–15
Mecca, 170
medicines, 117
Mediterranean, 5, 19, 22, 24, 79, 181
    weighing systems, 88
Medović, P., 98
Mehrgarh (Pakistan), 107
Meller, H., 229, 234
Melville, D.J., 184
Memphis (Egypt), 76, 171
menstrual cycles, 16
merchants, 79, 81, 82
Mercury, 154, 157
Mesoamerica
    calendars, 3, 6, 153, 154, 156
    languages, 45
    notation, 47
    ritual, 49
    society, 130
    worldview, 131, 132–33
Mesopotamia, 73, 79, 81, 89, 106, 110, 186,
    191, 205
    astronomy, 190
    number systems, 181
    texts, 184
    time and distance, 181
    writing, 27–31
Messina, Strait of, 22
metal(s), 28, 56, 75, 76, 77, 82, 95, 101, 117
    technology, 81

tools, 196
    vessels, 107
    weights, 99
metallurgy, 101
    Mehrgarh, 107
metaphor, 24
    collection, 45–46
    and number, 44–45
metric system, 74, 83, 133, 150
metrograms, 73
metrology, 72, 88, 151
Metz, 98
Mexican National Institute of Anthropology
    and History, 130
Mexico, 150, 157, 209
Miccaotli phase, 141, 142
Michailidou, A., 71, 72, 73, 74, 75, 77, 79,
    80, 81, 248
Michalowski, P., 31, 33
Michel, C., 79, 81, 83
Micronesia, 23
Midea, 98
Mije-Sokean languages, 48
Milano, L., 90
Milky Way, 175
Miller, M.E., 132
Millon, R., 130, 134, 135, 137, 138, 141,
    145, 146, 212
mina, 72, 74, 79, 82, 89
Minoan
    architecture, 93
    bureaucrats, 74
    economy, 77
    unit of weight, 73
    weighing system, 98
    weights, 72
mnemonics, 13, 24
Moche, 216, 217
Mochlos (Crete), 72, 80
Mohenjo-daro (Mohenjo-Daro) (Pakistan),
    106, 108, 109, 110, 116, 117, 125–28
money. *See* currency
monotheism, 190
Monte Arci, 19
months, 47, 132, 188, 190
moon, 157, 177, 187, 189. *See also* lunar
Moon Plaza, 136, 138, 144
Moon Pyramid, 130, 131, 133, 134, 138,
    139–41, 144, 146
Mooney, D., 235
Mora-Echeverría, J.I., 154
Morandi, S., 205, 206
Morelos, N., 130
Morhange, C., 19
Morley, I., 2, 245, 247, 248, 252
Morrison, L.V., 190
Mortensen, B., 171, 172, 174
Moyer, R.S., 36
Muduruku, 37, 38
Mughal, M.R., 107, 108
mules, 75
multiplication, 43, 55, 205
mummification, 170, 171
Mundurukú, 37
Múnera B., L.C., 141
mung bean, 116
Mureybet, 27

Murra, J.V., 58, 60
Murray, W.M., 21
Murúa, F.M. de, 58, 60, 64
Museum für Völkerkunde (Berlin), 57
mustard, 116
Mycenaean
    archives, 80
    balances, 72
    bureaucrats, 74
    graves, 98
    Palace period, 98, 99
    people, 82, 83
    tablets, 82
mythology, 250
    creation, 217, 219
    Mesoamerica, 132

Nabta Playa, 176
Nagar, 95
Nahua, 133
Nakassis, D., 82
narratives, 24, 251, 252
Nasir, H., 116
nature and time, 13–15
Naugle, D.K., 250
navigation, 5, 11–13, 170
Near East, 5, 6, 27, 82
    mina, 74
    prehistoric economy, 31
    records of weights, 73
    weighing systems, 88
necklaces, 112
Neolithic
    Europe, 229–38
    Mehrgarh, 107
    pottery, 200
    seafaring. See seafaring, Neolithic
Nephthys, goddess, 177
Neubauer, W., 230, 232, 234, 235, 236
Neugebauer, O., 175, 176, 184, 188, 189,
        191, 206
Neugebauer-Maresch, C., 232
neuroscience, 6, 35–36
New Fire ceremony, 210
New Guinea, 23
New Testament, 255
Nezahuacóyotl, king, 150, 151, 152, 153
Nidri (Lefkas), 94
Nieder, A., 35, 36
Nile, 20, 170, 171, 174, 175
Ninara, L.M., 62
Nineveh, 188
Nippur, 126
Nissen, H.-J., 30, 184
nobility, 64
North Star, 127
Northe, A., 235
notation, 6, 47–49
Nubia, 80
number(s), 30, 36, 185
    abstract, 5, 6, 31, 181, 184, 185
    Aegean, 74
    compound, 151
    concept of, 183
    concrete, 181, 184
    Mayan, 50, 205, 206
    Mesopotamian, 27, 187

Pythagorean, 206
    representation of, 5
    and script, 183–85
    signs, 54, 184, 192
    and space, 36–37
    words, 6, 28, 35, 37, 38, 43–44
numeracy, 6, 14
numerical-distance effect, 36
numerocity, 31, 35, 37, 255
    and archaeology, 38–41
    neuroscience of, 35–36
Nuñez, R., 45
Nut, goddess, 174

Oates, J., 90
Oberlauterbach, 230
objectivism, 253, 254
observation, systematic, 1
obsidian, 5, 19, 22
    Liparian, 21
Oceania, 23
ochre, 232
offerings, 32, 172, 205, 213
oil, 28, 31, 33, 74, 75, 76, 79, 94
Old Babylonian, 184
    mathematics, 190
Old Testament, 52, 214
olives, 79
Olivier, J.-P., 72, 80
Olmecs, 47, 48
    monuments, 49
omens, 208
oral traditions, 24
order, Indus, 106, 107
orientation, 107
    building, 114, 127, 130
    celestial, 127, 128
    city walls, 119
    methods, 173
    in seafaring, 22
    street, 127
Orion, 175
Orkney Isles, 22
Orozco y Berra, M., 151
ostrakon, 79
ostrich eggs, 79
oxen, 79
Oztoticpac, 153, 154, 159, 160, 166
Özyar, A., 90

Pacarictambo, 217
Pachacamac, 61, 217
Pacific, 5, 23
Pakistan, 95, 106
Palace of the Governor (Uxmal), 209
palaces, 73
    Aegean, 80–81
    Aztec, 150, 151–57
Palagruža, 21, 24
Palaima, T.G., 75, 76
Palamedes, 72
Palermo Stone, 176
Palmarola, 19
Palolo worm, 205
Palyvou, K., 71
Pantelleria, 19, 20
papyrella, 24

papyrus, 71
parallax, 191
Pare, C., 72, 75, 76, 81, 82, 98
parietal lobe, 37
Parise, N.F., 73, 74, 89
Parker, R., 176
Pärssinen, M., 58, 60, 66
Patlachique phase, 140
Pereyra, H., 55
Pérez, J.R., 138
perfume, 28, 75, 117
Peroni, R., 100
Persian Empire, 32
Peru, 5, 59, 61, 65, 216
Pérusse, R., 35
Pesenti, M., 37
Pestac, stela, 50
pestles, 88, 89, 93, 115
Petén, rain forest, 210
Peterson, P., 205, 206
Petrasch, J., 229, 234
Petrie, W.M.F., 99, 151, 153
petroglyphs, 143, 210, 211, 212
Petruso, C., 89
Petruso, K.M., 72, 73, 74, 80, 82, 92, 93,
        98, 99
Peyronel, L., 94, 95
Philippines, 23
Phoenicia, 76
Pica, P., 37
Picchu, 218
pigments, 94, 95
Pilco Kaima, 220
pilgrimage destinations, 217, 219
pillars, 217–19
pilotage skills, 23
Pingree, D., 188, 191
Pirahã, 37
Pirazzoli, P.A., 19
Pizarro, H., 61
Pizzaro, F., 61
planets, 156. See also under names of
        individual planets
    movements, 16
Plantinga, A., 255
Plato, 191
Platt, T., 55
Pleiades, 114, 132, 146, 205, 210
poetry, 24
Polanyi, M., 253
Poldrack, R.A., 40
Poliochni (Lemnos), 89, 90, 100
Polo de Ondegardo, J., 55
Pomata, 62
Ponce Sangunés, C., 219
Pongratz-Leisten, B., 188
ponikijo, 75
Popti' Maya. See Jacalteca Maya
Poros (Crete), 80
ports, 73, 82, 126
Portugal, 229
Posener, G., 174
Possehl, G.L., 107, 116
pottery
    Goseck, 231, 235
    impressed wares, 21
    Indus, 107, 108, 109, 110, 114

pottery (*cont.*)
  Mehrgarh, 107
  Neolithic, 200
  standard capacity, 32
  standardized, 79
  wheel, 94
Powell, M., 72, 185, 189
Pozarenco, J. de, 51
pre-Columbian
  documents, 203
  languages, 50
prediction, 1, 181, 186, 208, 248
  of celestial bodies, 188–90
  eclipse, 205
Predynastic burials, 171
Price, T.D., 21
priests, 51
Princely Inanna, festival, 32
Proyecto Arqueológico de Teotihuacan, 130,
  134
psychostasia, 71
Ptolemy, 191, 192
  texts, 177
Pulak, C., 73, 74, 75, 76, 81, 82, 83, 91, 98
pulses, 74, 79
Puluwat Atoll, 24
Puruchuco, 62, 65, 66
Pyramid of the Sun, 212
Pyramid Texts, 174, 175, 177
pyramids
  Egyptian, 173
  orientation of, 174
  Teotihuacan, 130
Pythagoreans, 206, 214

Q'eqchi', 51, 52
Qena, 171
Qici, 199
quality, measurement of, 60
quantification, 7, 19, 88
  archaeology of, 4
  attributive, 9, 10
  fundamental, 9
  Teotihuacan, 130
quantity, 35
  conceptualisation of, 5
quartzite, 115
Quechua, 56, 64, 216
Quetzalcoatl, god, 160, 163
Quiangalla, 218
Quilter, J., 55, 62

Radicati di Primeglio, C., 55, 61
radiocarbon dates
  Goseck, 230
  Harappa, 109
  Teotihuacan, 130
Rahmstorf, L., 73, 88, 89, 90, 92, 93, 94,
  95, 99, 100, 101
Raikes, R., 126
rainbows, 197
Rakhigarhi, 109
Ramesses III, 171
Ramos Gavilán, A., 220
Rao, S.R., 116, 198
Ratnagar, S., 81, 94
Rattray, E.C., 130

Raval, M.H., 116
Raven, M., 171, 172, 174
Ravi Phase, 110–11, 113
rebirth, 172
record keeping
  Babylon, 188
  Inca, 54–66
  Mesopotamia, 27
Reina, A., 166
Reinhard, J., 219
religion, 2, 17, 248, 254
  Inca, 217–18
  Mesoamerica, 133
  proto-Shang, 196
  and worldview, 251–53
Ren, 199
Renfrew, C., 2, 3, 20, 93, 94, 245
Renger, J., 79
resources, 8–10
rhesus monkeys, 35
Rhind Mathematical Papyrus, 76
Richemont-Pépinville, 98
Ricoeur, P., 252
Rimac Valley, 65
ritual(s), 24, 235
  Andean, 213
  Goseck, 235
  Maya, 213
  Neolithic, 238
  speech, 49
  systems, 7
  Teotihuacan, 133
  Yucatan, 209
roads, Inca, 56, 219
Roaf, M., 83
Robins, G., 76
Robson, E., 184
Rochberg, F., 190
rock art, 16
Rodriguez, I., 130, 141
Rogers, E.M., 100
Rogers, H., 27
Rohri, hills, 116
Rojdi, 116
Roman calendar, 205
Romance languages, 11
Rome, 186
Rosengarten, Y., 31
Rössen, 230
Rossetti, Y., 36
Rostworowski de Kiez Canseco, M., 56
Rottländer, R.C.A., 126
Rowe, J.H., 218
Ruggles, C., 235
rulers, Teotihuacan, 147
Rutter, J.B., 76

Sacconi, A., 77
Sachs, A., 184, 188
Sacred Precinct (Tenochtitlan), 157–66
Sacred Rock, 219, 220, 221, 222, 223,
  225–26, 227
sacred space, 182, 217, 219, 220, 223–25
sacrifices, 133, 145, 146, 196–97, 198, 199,
  200, 201, 209, 235
safflower, 75

saffron, 75, 79
Sahagún, F.B., 132, 139, 159
Sahara, desert, 175
Sahul, 23
sailing, 20
  canoes, 24
Salazar, O., 130
Salomon, F., 60, 61, 66
Salonen, A., 77
Šamaš, god, 188
San Juan, river, 138
sanctuaries, 73
Sandage, S.J., 251
sandals, 79
Sanhueza Tohá, C., 56
Sapotekos, 45
Saqqara, 173
Saraswati-Ghaggar-Hakra, river, 106
Sarcina, A., 127
sarcophagi, 171
Sardinia, 19
Sarpaki, A., 75
Sarton, G., 206
Saturn, 154, 157
Sayer, R.A., 253
scales. *See* balances
Schauer, K., 236
Schele, L., 132, 206
Schier, W., 232, 235, 236
Schlosser, W., 229, 235
Schmandt-Besserat, D., 27, 39, 40, 184, 249
Schmidt-Kaler, T., 235
Schnohr, J., 171
Schultze-Jena, L., 204
Schwartz, G.M., 100
Scotland, 229
scribe, 80, 82
script. *See also* writing
  Indus, 108, 117
  and measurement, 185–86
  and number, 183–85
sculptures, 2, 109
sea levels, 19, 21
seafaring, Neolithic, 19–25
sealings, 79, 108
seals, 94, 95, 107
  button, 114–15
  Indus, 108, 109
seascapes, 22
  dynamic, 24–25
seasonality, 22
seasons, 14, 15
seaworthiness, measuring, 20
Seddon, M., 218, 219, 220, 222, 223, 226,
  227
sedentism, 3
sedimentation, 21
seeds, 116
Segal, R.A., 251
Séjourné, L., 133
Sekhemkhet, 172
self-awareness, 249
self-transcendence, 249
Selz, G., 184
Sempat Assadourian, C., 60
Seneca, 191
Senenmut, 173

seniority, 8
Serbia, 98
Seshat, goddess, 176–77
settlement(s), 73
    Aegean, 79–80
    Harappan, 120
    Indus, 109, 114, 117
    Indus valley, 107
    Mohenjo-Daro, 127
    Mycenaen, 98
    patterns, 108, 110
Shackley, M.S., 19
Shaffer, J.G., 107
Shaltout, M., 171, 175
shamanism, 248
Shang, 181, 195, 197
    almanacs, 195
    calendars, 196
    calendricists, 195, 197
    inscriptions, 195, 196
    rulers, 196
sharing, 8
sheep, 78, 79, 80, 107
shekels, 74, 89, 93
shell(s), 107
    and divination, 196
    plaque, 117
    representation of, 50
Sherratt, A., 73, 77
Sherratt, S., 73, 77
Shima, K., 199
ships, 75, 76, 81–82
shipwrecks, 19, 73, 74, 76, 81, 91
shoes, 79
Shults, F.L., 251
Shute, C., 76
Sicily, 20, 22, 229
    obsidian, 20
Sidoli, N., 192
Sieger, 80
silk, 80, 112
silver, 74, 77, 93, 95
Sin, god, 188
Sindh, 116
Sirius, 175
Sirocco wind, 25
Sivin, N., 186
Skeates, R., 21
Slotta, R., 75
Slovak Republic, 230, 236
Sneferu, king, 175
Soke, 51
solar
    calendars, 132
    count, 153, 154, 156, 157, 166
    cycles, 132, 144, 172, 187, 195, 201, 212
    markers, 226. See also stone pillars
    orientation methods, 173
    time, 217
    towers, 217
    year, 13, 182, 197, 198, 199, 200, 204
Soles, J.S., 72
solstices, 182, 200, 210, 217, 218, 220, 226, 235, 236
    ceremonies, 225
song, 24
space

concept of, 11
    enclosure of, 247
    management, Teotihuacan, 131
    measurement of, 247–48
    and number, 36
Spanish
    chronicles, 56, 66
    conquest, 52, 133, 157, 218
    documents, 61
    measurement, 150
    priests, 51
spatial cognition. See cognition, spatial
Spatial Numeric Association Response Code
        Effect, 36
spatio-visual problems, 40
speciation phase, 3
speed, relative, 24
Speiser, E.A., 90
Spelke, E., 35, 38
Spence, K., 171, 173, 247, 252
spices, 76
spindle whorls, 110
spinning, 110, 111
spirituality, 247, 248, 249
    roots of, 2
spondylus, 56, 88, 100
stability, 20
Stadelmann, R., 173
stamp seals, 107, 108
Stampe, R., 43
standardization, 99, 101
    Aegean, 76
    Harappan, 110
    Indus, 106, 110, 117
    khipu, 62–65
    pottery, 79
Stanish, C., 217, 219, 226, 247, 253
stars
    compass, 23
    courses, 22, 24
    imperishable, 174, 175
    knowledge of, 175–76
    orientation by, 114, 127, 173, 174, 235
state
    formation, 27, 29, 130
    labour, 58
statecraft, Andean, 217
Stäuble, H., 234, 235
steatite, 111
    microbeads, 112
    seals, 114
Steele, J., 188, 189, 190
Steinfurth, 98, 99
stelae, 47, 48, 49, 50, 213
Steno (Lefkas), 94
Stephenson, F.R., 190
Stichbandkeramik culture, 230
sticks, crossed, 209
Stieglitz, R.R., 81
stirrup-jars, 76
stone
    anchor, 80
    beads, 111–12
    marker pillars, 182
    pillars, 217–19
    ring, 128
    sculptures, 109

tools, Goseck, 231, 235
    value, 95
    weights, 72, 106, 115–17
    working, 107
Stonehenge, 3
storehouses, 57, 60, 61
    Akrotiri, 79
stories. See narratives
strings
    knotted, 38. See also khipus
subitizing capacities, 6
subsistence
    pattern, 13
    societies, 14
subtraction, 55, 205
Sucanca, 218
Sugiyama, S., 130, 131, 133, 134, 135, 138, 140, 144, 146, 150, 153, 158, 160, 166, 248, 253
Sumerian, measure, 72, 186
Sumerian King List, 191
sun. See also solar
    spots, 197
    worship, 200, 217–18
Sun Pyramid (Teotihuacan), 130, 132, 134, 138–39, 143, 144, 146, 158, 159, 160
survival value, 9
Susa, 31
swastika, 114
Swerdlow, N., 188
symbolic thought, emergence of, 2
symbolicity, concept of, 249
symbolism, 249, 253
    and power, 249
    Teotihuacan, 147
Syria, 27, 29, 31, 83
    balance weights, 88–98
    bowls, 32
    desert, 76
    merchants, 81
    mina, 79
    tokens, 27
Syro-Canaanite jars, 76
Syro-Mesopotamia, 95
Syros, 93
Szarzynska, K., 32

tablets, 39, 186
    Knossos, 75
    Kültepe, 79
    Linear A, 73, 78
    Linear B, 74, 76, 78, 82, 83
    Mari, 82, 83
    Mesopotamia, 30
    Mycenaean, 82
    numerical, 183, 184
Takalik Abaj, stela, 48, 49
tallying, 37
Tarsus, 88, 90, 92, 93
taxation, 31, 117
Tecpatan Soke, 51
tectonic activity, 3, 21
Tell Beydar, 90
Tell Brak (Syria), 90, 95
Tell Munbaqa, 90
Tell Sweyhat, 90

temples, 219
    Babylonia, 190
    Inca, 227
    Yucatan, 209
Templeton Foundation, 2
Templo Mayor (Tenochtitlan), 157–58,
    166
Tenochtitlan, 150, 152
Teotihuacan, 130–47, 150, 153, 154, 155,
    158, 210, 211, 212
Teotihuacan Mapping Project, 130
Teotihuacan Measurement Unit, 131,
    133–38, 145
Tepe Gawra, 90
Teresa, C. de, 166
Terrace, H.S., 35
terracotta
    balance pans, 116
    beads, 111–12
Teti, 173
Texcoco, 150, 151, 152, 153
textiles, 28, 31, 56, 75, 78, 80, 100, 111
Tezozomoc, 159
Theaetetus, 71
Thebes (Greece), 75, 82, 98
Theiß-Herály-Csöszhalom, 230
Thera, 77–79
Thomas, J., 229, 230
Thompson, J.E.S., 203, 205
Thoth, god, 72, 80
Thuban, star, 127
Thuraeu-Dangin, F., 72
tides, 22, 24
Tikal, stela, 49
Tikani, 182, 220, 221, 222, 223, 226
time, 11, 13–17
    archaeological record, 208–13
    concept of, 7
    counts, 47
    and distance, 181
    elapsed, 22–23
    interpretations of, 248
    -keeping, 213, 217, 222–23
    Maya codices, 205–08
    measurement of, 3, 175, 217, 248
    Mesoamerica, 182
    sacred, 150
tin, 75, 83, 95
Tiryns, 88, 89, 90, 99
Titicaca, Lake, 62, 182, 217, 219
Titikala, 219, 220
Tiwanaku, 216
Tlaloc, god, 157
    Temple, 160
Tlamimilolpa phase, 144
Tobriner, S., 146
tokens, 27–29, 39, 40, 79, 183, 184, 185
tombs, 73, 80, 81
    robbers, 71
tools, 31, 231, 235
Toomer, G., 191
Torquemada, 159
Torres Islanders, 37
tortoise plastrons, 195, 197
Townsend, R.F., 158
Tozzer, A., 205
trade, 9, 32, 101

Aegean, 74
Assyrian, 78
Indus, 109, 111
    obsidian, 19
transportation, 75
Trantalidou, K., 75
Tremitis, 21
tribute, 58, 59, 60
Trimble, V., 174
Tringham, R., 232
Trnka, G., 229, 230, 232, 234
Trobriand calendar, 205
Trojan war, 72
Troy, 88, 89, 90, 93, 100
Tuan, Y.-F., 170
Tupicocha, 61
tupu, 56
Turkey, 27, 29
Turnbull, D., 23
Turner, M., 40
Turner, N.J., 13, 16–17
Tylor, E.B., 17
Tzachili, I., 77, 78, 79
Tzacualli phase, 138
Tzalas, H., 21, 24
tzolkin, 132, 204, 205

Uaxactun, 210, 211, 212
Ugarit, 73, 81, 82, 83, 89
Uluburun, 81, 82, 98
    shipwreck, 74, 75, 76, 91
underwater archaeology, 19
unicorn, 117
universe, extent of, 190–91
University of Miami, 61
Ur, 83
urbanism, 130
    Indus, 107
Ursa Major, 175, 177
Ursae Minoris, 174
Urton, G., 54, 55, 57, 58, 61, 62, 65,
    226
Uruk, 30, 31, 32, 189
Ushijima, I., 20
Uta-napishtim, 185
Uxmal, 209, 213

Vail, G., 205, 208
value, 9, 60
    monetary, 13
    relative, 11
Vandenabeele, F., 72
Vandermeersch, L., 196, 197, 200
vases, 76
Vats, M.S., 117
vectors, 24
Vedic astral science, 188
Veenhof, K.R., 78
Vega, G. de la, 217, 220
Veldhuis, N., 185
ventral intraparietal, 40
Venus, 132, 135, 157, 188, 205, 208, 209,
    213, 214
    count, 153, 154, 160
    counts, 160
    cycles, 132, 141, 144, 146, 160, 208

Vercoutter, J., 80, 81
Vidale, M., 126
Vining, B., 210
volume, 74, 75, 183

Wagner, F., 234
Wainwright, G.A., 176, 177
Walberg, G., 98
wall paintings
    Aegean, 76
    Akrotiri, 79
    Thera, 77
walls
    Harappan, 119–20
    Incan, 220, 221
    Indus, 109
Wanzke, H., 127
Wari, 216
Warner, B., 175
warriors, 60
waterclocks, 185, 187, 190
wax, 75, 77
weapons, 196
    counting of, 74
weaving, 77, 110
Wei, 197
weighing
    activities, 75–77
    Bronze Age, 88–101
weight, 2–3, 13, 20
    Aegean Bronze Age, 71–83
    boat, 21
    evolution of, 32
    metrology, 101
weights, 7, 19, 45, 183, 185
    Akrotiri, 77
    balance, 72, 74, 75, 76, 79, 81, 82,
        88–98
    chert, 109, 110
    Indus, 107
    loom. *See* looms, weights
    pebble, 98
    standardization, 32
    stone, 106, 115–17
    written records, 73
Weingarten, J., 79
Weinstein, J., 176, 177
wells, 119, 126
    Indus, 107
Wendorf, F., 176
Werner, P., 90
wheat, 74, 75, 107, 116
Wheeler, R.E.M., 106
Wheeler, Sir M., 125, 126, 127
whitewash, 77
Whitlow, R., 235
Whitten, D.G.A., 19
Whittle, A., 235
Whorfian thesis, 37
Wiener, M., 76
Wiercinski, A., 152
Wilkinson, R., 172, 173, 174
Wilkinson, T., 176
Williams, B.J., 150, 151, 152
Williams, M., 238
Williams-Thorpe, O., 19
Wilson, D.E., 93

winds, 23, 24
    prehistoric, 21
wine, 74, 76, 79
winter solstice, 197
wood, 75, 79
wool, 32, 75, 77, 78, 79, 80, 112
workshops, 27, 32
    Akrotiri, 77
worldview
    concept of, 250–51
    interrogating, 253–54
    and religion, 251–53
writing, 1, 2, 5, 23, 183, 185, 192
    and counting, 31
    Indus, 107, 108, 110
    Maya, 205
    pictographic, 27
    proto-, 213
    Zapotec, 47
Wu, 200
Wynn, K., 35

Xauxa, 60, 61

Xeste 3 (Akrotiri), 80
Xi, 200
Xia, 196
Xolalpan phase, 138
Xu, F., 35

Yalçin, U., 75
Yamane, D., 252
yarn, 75
year, 132, 190
    divisions of, 15
    Egyptian, 175
    Maya subdivision of, 203
Yi, 197
Yin, 200
Younger, J.G., 79
Yschma, 65
Yu, 199
Yu, X., 195
Yucatan, 203, 210
    rituals, 209
Yucatec, 47, 49, 52
Yucay, 218

Yunguyu, 219
yupanas, 55

Žába, Z., 173, 174, 177
Zaccagnini, C., 74, 82
Zapotec, writing, 47
Zebian, S., 37
Zedeño, N., 176
zero, 44
    concept of, 6, 47–52
Zhou, 182
    inscriptions, 200
    text, 198
Zimansky, P., 31
Zimri-Lim, king, 83
zodiac, 189, 191, 192, 209
Zólyomi, G., 187
Zorzi, M., 36
Zotti, G., 235
Zu Jia, king, 198
Zubrow, E., 13
Zuidema, R.T., 205
Zuidema, T., 218